# Lecture Notes in Computer Scie

*Commenced Publication in 1973*
Founding and Former Series Editors:
Gerhard Goos, Juris Hartmanis, and Jan van Leeuwen

Angelos D. Keromytis (Ed.)

# Financial Cryptography and Data Security

16th International Conference, FC 2012
Kralendijk, Bonaire, February 27-March 2, 2012
Revised Selected Papers

 Springer

Volume Editor

Angelos D. Keromytis
Columbia University
Department of Computer Science
1214 Amsterdam Avenue
New York, NY 10027-7003, USA
E-mail: angelos@cs.columbia.edu

ISSN 0302-9743                           e-ISSN 1611-3349
ISBN 978-3-642-32945-6                   e-ISBN 978-3-642-32946-3
DOI 10.1007/978-3-642-32946-3

Springer Heidelberg Dordrecht London New York

Library of Congress Control Number: 2012945011

CR Subject Classification (1998): E.3, K.6.5, K.4.4, J.1

LNCS Sublibrary: SL 4 – Security and Cryptology

*Typesetting:* Camera-ready by author, data conversion by Scientific Publishing Services, Chennai, India

Printed on acid-free paper

Springer is part of Springer Science+Business Media (www.springer.com)

# Preface

This volume contains the proceedings of the 16th International Conference on Financial Cryptography and Data Security (FC), held at the Divi Flamingo Beach Resort, Bonaire, February 27-March 1, 2012.

FC is a well-established international forum for research, advanced development, education, exploration, and debate regarding information assurance in the context of finance and commerce. The conference covers all aspects of securing transactions and systems.

This year we assembled a diverse program featuring 29 paper and a panel on "Laws Against Adopting PETs (Privacy Enhancing Technologies)." The conference was opened by Scott M. Zoldi, Vice President for Analytic Science at FICO, with a keynote address on "Analytic Techniques for Combating Financial Fraud."

The program was put together through a standard peer-review process by a technical Program Committee selected by the Program Chair. This year we received 88 submissions from authors and institutions representing 26 countries. All submissions received at least three reviews from the 32 members of the Program Committee or from the 31 outside experts. A further online discussion phase that lasted more than 2 weeks led to the selection of 29 papers (representing an overall acceptance rate of 33%).

This conference was made possible through the dedicated work of our General Chair, Rafael Hirschfeld, from Unipay Technologies, The Netherlands. Ray also acted as our (tireless) Local Arrangements Chair. The Program Chair would like to thank especially the Program Committee members and external reviewers for contributing their time and expertise to the selection of papers for the program and for providing feedback to improve all submissions. Finally, the members of the International Financial Cryptography Association (IFCA) board should be acknowledged for keeping the FC conference going through the years. This year's conference was made more affordable thanks to the generosity of our sponsors.

March 2012                                                    Angelos D. Keromytis

# Organization

## Program Committee

| | |
|---|---|
| Mikhail Atallah | Purdue University, USA |
| Konstantin Beznosov | UBC, Canada |
| Mike Bond | |
| Jan Camenisch | IBM Research, Zurich Research Laboratory, Switzerland |
| Sonia Chiasson | Carleton University, Canada |
| Nicolas Christin | Carnegie Mellon University, USA |
| David Mandell Freeman | Stanford University, USA |
| Virgil Gligor | CMU, USA |
| Dieter Gollmann | Hamburg University of Technology, Germany |
| J. Alex Halderman | University of Michigan, USA |
| John Ioannidis | |
| Sotiris Ioannidis | FORTH-ICS, Greece |
| Stanislaw Jarecki | University of California, Irviné, USA |
| Somesh Jha | University of Wisconsin, USA |
| Jonathan Katz | University of Maryland, USA |
| Angelos Keromytis | Columbia University, USA |
| Engin Kirda | Institut Eurecom, France |
| Tadayoshi Kohno | University of Washington, USA |
| Wenke Lee | Georgia Institute of Technology, USA |
| Corrado Leita | Symantec Research |
| Arjen Lenstra | |
| Ninghui Li | Purdue University, USA |
| Helger Lipmaa | Cybernetica AS and Tallinn University, Estonia |
| Tal Malkin | Columbia University, USA |
| Patrick Mcdaniel | Pennsylvania State University, USA |
| Catherine Meadows | NRL |
| David Molnar | Microsoft Research |
| Fabian Monrose | The University of North Carolina at Chapel Hill, USA |
| Anil Somayaji | Carleton University, Canada |
| Jessica Staddon | Google |
| Angelos Stavrou | George Mason University, USA |
| Carmela Troncoso | IBBT-K.U.Leuven, ESAT/COSIC, Belgium |
| Lenore Zuck | University of Illinois in Chicago, USA |

## Additional Reviewers

Balasch, Josep
Barrera, David
Bos, Joppe
Boshmaf, Yazan
Brakerski, Zvika
Camp, Jean
Fan, Junfeng
Fredrikson, Matt
Henginer, Nadia
Hinrichs, Tim
Hiremagalore, Sharath
Jeske, Tobias
Jia, Quan
Koshy, Diana
Krell, Fernando

Lee, Adam J.
Meiklejohn, Sarah
Muslukhov, Ildar
Naehrig, Michael
Osvik, Dag Arne
Qardaji, Wahbeh
Raghunathan, Ananth
Raykova, Mariana
Rial, Alfredo
Seymer, Paul
Sun, San-Tsai
Uhsadel, Leif
Venkatakrishnan, Venkat
Wang, Zhaohui
Wei, Lei

# Table of Contents

# Social Authentication: Harder Than It Looks

Hyoungshick Kim, John Tang, and Ross Anderson

Computer Laboratory,
University of Cambridge, UK
{hk331,jkt27,rja14}@cam.ac.uk

**Abstract.** A number of web service firms have started to authenticate users via their social knowledge, such as whether they can identify friends from photos. We investigate attacks on such schemes. First, attackers often know a lot about their targets; most people seek to keep sensitive information private from others in their social circle. Against close enemies, social authentication is much less effective. We formally quantify the potential risk of these threats. Second, when photos are used, there is a growing vulnerability to face-recognition algorithms, which are improving all the time. Network analysis can identify hard challenge questions, or tell a social network operator which users could safely use social authentication; but it could make a big difference if photos weren't shared with friends of friends by default. This poses a dilemma for operators: will they tighten their privacy default settings, or will the improvement in security cost too much revenue?

## 1 Introduction

Facebook[1] recently launched a new user authentication method called "social authentication" which tests the user's personal social knowledge [15]. This idea is neither unique nor novel [18] but Facebook's implementation is its first large-scale deployment. A user is presented with a series of photos of their friends and asked to select their name of a highlighted face from a multiple-choice list (see Figure 1). The current system is used to authenticate user login attempts from abroad.

Facebook has invited security experts to find flaws in the current system before a wider roll-out. If it were deployed for regular authorization and login systems and attacks were to be found subsequently, this could have wide repercussions for the many online merchants and websites which use Facebook to identify their customers, using the Facebook Connect OAuth 2.0 API[2]. We therefore set out to find the best attacks we could on social authentication, and this paper presents our results.

Social authentication is based on the intuition that the user can recognize her friends while a stranger cannot. At first glance, this seems rather promising. However, we argue here that it is not easy to achieve both security and usability:

---

[1] http://www.facebook.com/

[2] http://developers.facebook.com/docs/authentication

A.D. Keromytis (Ed.): FC 2012, LNCS 7397, pp. 1–15, 2012.

**Fig. 1.** Social authentication on Facebook. Facebook typically asks the user to name people in three photos.

(1) the user's personal social knowledge is generally shared with people in her social circle; (2) photo-based social authentication methods are increasingly vulnerable to automatic attacks as face recognition and social tagging technologies develop; and (3) we face the same problems as in previous "personal knowledge questions".

In the rest of this article, we will analyse the risk of guessing attacks, then propose several schemes to mitigate them. In community-based challenge selection we use social topology; if a user's friends divide into several disjoint communities, we can select challenge sets that should not be known to any individual friend. We can also reduce the risk of impersonation attacks leveraging the mutual friends between the target user and the adversary; we demonstrate this empirically on realistic data.

## 2   Why Is It Difficult to Provide Secure Social Authentication?

We analyse three security issues in the photo-based social authentication used in Facebook.

### 2.1   Friend Information Is Not Private Enough

Social authentication may be effective against pure strangers. However, the people against whom we frequently require privacy protection are precisely those in our own social circle. For example, if a married man is having an affair, some random person in another country is not likely to be interested; the people who are interested are his friends and his wife's. In short, users may share a lot of their friends with their adversaries. This is nothing new; 2,400 years ago, Sun-Tzu said 'Keep your friends close, and your enemies closer'. So a proper assessment of the protective power of social authentication in real social networks must be made using real data.

Formally, we view social connections between users in Facebook as an undirected graph $G = (U, E)$, where the set of nodes $U$ represents the users and the set of edges $E$ represents "friend" relationships. For any user $u \in U$, we use $f_u$ to denote the set of $u$'s friends. If each challenge image is selected by the method $\mathcal{M}$, we define the advantage of an adversary $a$ who tries to impersonate the target user $u$ as:

$$\mathbf{Adv}_{\mathcal{M},a}(u, k, \rho) \geq \prod_{i=1}^{\min\{k, |f_u|\}} \Pr\left[c_i \in f_a^{(i)} : c_i \xleftarrow{\mathcal{M}} f_u^{(i)}\right] \cdot \rho \qquad (1)$$

where $f_x^{(i)} = f_x - \{c_1, \cdots, c_{i-1}\}$ and $k$ is the number of challenges (such that all $k$ challenges need to be answered correctly) and $\rho$ is the adversary $a$'s *average* success rate to recognize a person in a challenge image $c_i$ when $c_i \in f_a$. It seems reasonable to introduce $\rho$ less than 1 since it may sometimes be difficult to recognize friends if tricky images are selected. For simplification, however, we use $\rho$ as a system parameter.

For any $u, k$ and $\rho$, we define the impersonation attack advantage of $\mathcal{M}$ via

$$\mathbf{Adv}_{\mathcal{M}}(u, k, \rho) \geq \max_{a \in A_u} \{\mathbf{Adv}_{\mathcal{M},a}(u, k, \rho)\} \qquad (2)$$

where the maximum is over all potential adversaries $a \in A_u$ and $A_u$ is the set of users who share mutual friends with $u$.

In other words, at least one potential adversary $a$ can impersonate the user $u$ with probability at least $\mathbf{Adv}_{\mathcal{M}}(u, k, \rho)$ when $k$ challenge images are provided by the selection method $\mathcal{M}$. If we assume that $k$ challenge images of different friends are randomly selected, the advantage of the impersonation attack in Equation (2) can be computed as follows:

$$\mathbf{Adv}_{\mathcal{R}}(u, k, \rho) \geq \max_{a \in A_u} \left\{ \prod_{i=1}^{\min\{k, |f_u|\}} \frac{|f_{ua}| - (i - 1)}{|f_u| - (i - 1)} \cdot \rho \right\} \qquad (3)$$

where $f_{ua}$ is the intersection of $f_u$ and $\{f_a \cup a\}$ and $\mathcal{R}$ denotes the random selection method.

For example, in Figure 2, since $|f_u| = 5$ and $|f_{ua}| = 2$, we get the probability that $a$ chooses the answer correctly for a challenge image about $u$ is at least $(2/5) \cdot \rho$ when $k = 1$. The probability decreases to $(1/10) \cdot \rho$ when $k = 2$.

One might think that authentication might be made arbitrarily secure since increasing $k$ will lead to an exponential decrease in the adversary success probability. We decided, however, to use real datasets to explore what value of $k$ might give a good balance between usability and security. With an ideal $\rho$ value

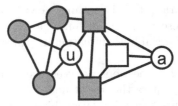

**Fig. 2.** An example graph with $u$ and $a$. Nodes represent users and links represent *friend* relationships. The nodes $u$ and $a$ have five ($f_u$, grey) and three ($f_a$, square) friends, respectively. They commonly share two friends ($f_{ua}$, grey-square).

($\rho = 0.99$), we compute the $\mathbf{Adv}_{\mathcal{R}}(u, k, \rho)$ value for each user $u$ by varying $k$ from 1 to 5 on the real Facebook network crawled from both university and regional sub-networks. These sub-networks are summarised in Table 1.

**Table 1.** Summary of datasets used. $\langle d \rangle$ and $n_{cc}$ represent the "average number of friends" and the "number of connected components", respectively. The sub-networks of universities are highly connected compared to those of regions.

| Network | Type | $|U|$ | $|E|$ | $\langle d \rangle$ | $n_{cc}$ |
|---|---|---|---|---|---|
| **Columbia** | University | 15,441 | 620,075 | 80.32 | 16 |
| **Harvard** | University | 18,273 | 1,061,722 | 116.21 | 22 |
| **Stanford** | University | 15,043 | 944,846 | 125.62 | 18 |
| **Yale** | University | 10,456 | 634,529 | 121.37 | 4 |
| **Monterey Bay** | Region | 26,701 | 251,249 | 18.82 | 1 |
| **Russia** | Region | 116,987 | 429,589 | 7.34 | 3 |
| **Santa Barbara (SB)** | Region | 43,539 | 632,158 | 29.04 | 1 |

We display the histograms to show the distributions of the $\mathbf{Adv}_{\mathcal{R}}(u, k, \rho)$ values for all the users in each sub-network. The experimental results are shown in Figure 3.

In order to identify the high-advantage attackers, we calculate the Pearson correlation coefficients between $\mathbf{Adv}_{\mathcal{R}}(u, k, \rho)$ and some representative network centrality that are widely used for measuring the relative importance of nodes in network: degree (**Deg**), closeness (**Clo**), betweenness (**Bet**) and clustering coefficient (**CC**) centrality (see 'Appendix: Network centrality'). The scatter plots in Figure 4 showing the correlation between the adversary's advantage and network centrality visually when $\rho = 0.99$ and $k = 3$. For degree, closeness and betweenness centrality, we can see a negative correlation between the adversary's advantage and nodes' centrality values, although this trend appears to be rather weak for betweenness. In particular, the correlation coefficients for the university datasets are much higher than those for the region datasets. For example, the correlation coefficients between the adversary's advantage and closeness central- ity of -0.485 and -0.584 are obtained for each scatter plot graph of the university

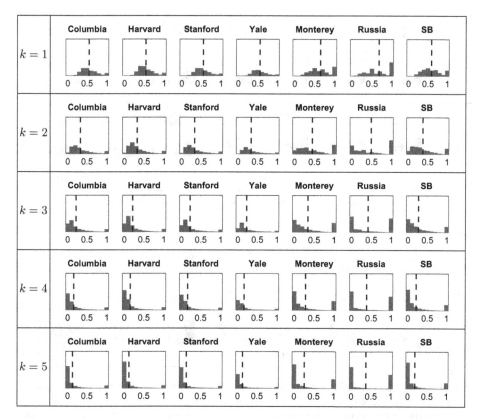

**Fig. 3.** The histograms of $\mathbf{Adv}_{\mathcal{R}}(u, k, \rho)$ when $\rho = 0.99$ for the users in the seven sub-networks of Facebook in Table 1. The black dotted lines represent the mean of $\mathbf{Adv}_{\mathcal{R}}(u, k, \rho)$ values over the all users in a sub-network.

sub-networks, respectively, while those ranged from -0.00439 to -0.0425 for the region sub-networks. These results indicate that social authentication should not be offered to people with low centrality values.

Another key observation is the correlation between the adversary's advantages and nodes' clustering coefficients. We can see there is a clear correlation (ranged from 0.307 to 0.633) between them although the results are somewhat inconsistent in the cases of 'Monterey Bay' and 'Santa Barbara'. That is, users with high clustering coefficients will become more vulnerable than those with low clustering coefficients. It is natural; the clustering coefficient quantifies how well a node's friends are connected to each other — we should conclude that social authentication is not recommended for users with high clustering coefficients.

## 2.2   Automatic Face Recognition

Social authentication is an extension of image-recognition CAPTCHAs. So we should consider its vulnerability to machine learning attacks; Golle [9] showed

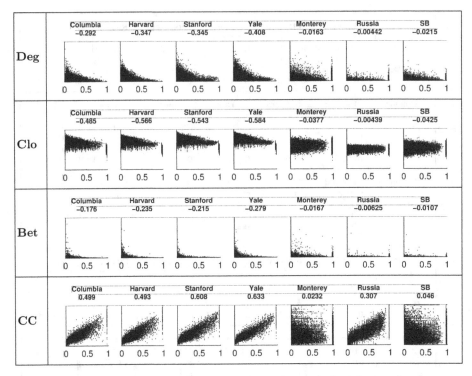

**Fig. 4.** Scatter plot graphs showing the correlation between the adversary's advantage ($X$-axis) and network centrality ($Y$-axis) over nodes when $\rho = 0.99$ and $k = 3$. We also calculate the Pearson correlation coefficient for each scatter plot. These graphs indicate that there exists a negative correlation between the adversary's advantage and network centrality while there exists a positive correlation between the adversary's advantage and clustering coefficient.

that Microsoft's image-recognition CAPTCHA (Asirra) can be broken using machine learning by an adversary who can collect and label a reasonable sample set. So automatic image recognition will be a significant threat to photo-based social authentication. Although face recognition is not a completely solved problem, face recognition algorithms do well under certain conditions. For example, current algorithms are about as good as human judgements about facial identity for "mug shot" images with frontal pose, no facial expression, and fixed illumination [8].

Recent evaluation of face recognition techniques with the real photo images in Facebook [4] showed that the best performing algorithms can achieve about 65% accuracy using 60,000 facial images of 500 users. This shows that the gap between the legitimate user and a mechanised attack may not be as large as one might think.

As with CAPTCHAs, if adversaries use ever-better face recognition programs, the designers could use various tricks to make image recognition – e.g. by noise or distortion – but such images are also hard for legitimate users to identify. The usability costs could be nontrivial. For example, if we reduce $\rho$ to 0.9, then even for $k = 3$ we get an unacceptable user success rate of $(0.9)^3 \approx 0.73$.

To make matters worse, face recognition attacks could be easily extended to large-scale automated attacks by combining the photo collection and recognition processes. As Facebook provides APIs to get images with Facebook ID easily from photo albums, an adversary might automatically collect a lot of high-quality images from the target's friends since many casual users expose their photos in public [2,13]. Although some users do have privacy concerns about sharing their photos, many casual users often struggle with privacy management [14]. Social networks make it difficult for users to manage privacy; it is in their commercial interests for most users to stick with the (rather open) default settings. Therefore an adversary attempting to circumvent social authentication could simply login to Facebook with her own account, access the photos of the victim's friends via the openly available *public search listings* [6,11]. Acquisti et al. [1] demonstrated the technical feasibility of this automatic attack. Using a database of images taken from Facebook profiles, their face recognition software correctly identified about one third of the subjects in their experiment.

### 2.3 Statistical Guessing Attacks

Finally, we revisit statistical guessing attacks which have been studied in the context of personal knowledge questions [10,7]. In particular, Bonneau et al. [7] showed that many personal knowledge questions related to names are highly vulnerable to trawling attacks. The same issues arise in social authentication when the names of a user's friends are sought. The probability distribution of names is not uniform but follows Zipf's law, and the target's language and culture can give broad hints. Even a subject's racial appearance can increase the guessing probability. Since there is a significant correlation between name and race (or gender), the subject's appearance may help an attacker guess his or her name.

## 3 Toward More Secure Social Authentication

Having identified security problems of photo-based social authentication in Section 2, we now consider what can be done to improve matters.

### 3.1 Community-Based Friend Selection

In Section 2.1, we observe that there exists a potential adversary $a$ who can impersonate the target user $u$ with a high probability if the number of challenges $k$ is small. This is because $a$ shares many mutual friends with the user. In this case, random selection of challenge images may be ineffective.

We propose instead "community-based challenge selection"; our intuition is that a user's friends often fall into several social groups (e.g. family, high school friends, college classmates, and work colleagues) with few, if any, common members. So if we select challenges from different groups, this may cut the attack success probability significantly. We describe this process in detail. For a user $u$, the $k$ challenges are selected as follows:

1. Extract the subgraph $H$ induced on the user $u$'s friends' nodes $f_u$ from the social graph $G$.
2. Find the set of community structures $S = \{\eta_1, \cdots \eta_l\}$ in $H$ where $\eta_i$ represents the $i$th community structure in $H$ and $l = |S|$.
3. For $i$th challenge generation for $1 \leq i \leq k$, choose randomly $c$ and remove it from $\eta_{(i \text{ MOD } l)}$ where $\eta_l = \eta_0$. After removing $c$ from $\eta_{(i \text{ MOD } l)}$, if $\eta_{(i \text{ MOD } l)}$ is empty, remove it from $S$ and decrease the indices of the following community structures $\{\eta_m : (i \text{ MOD } l) < m \leq l\}$ and the total number of community structures $l$ by 1.

For example, we extract the subgraph $H$ induced on $f_u$ in Figure 5(a) and then find two community structures of $H$ by applying a community detection algorithm. Although a specific heuristic method [5] is used here for community detection, we expect that any community detection algorithm can be used for this purpose. In this example, unlike the results of the random selection in Section 2.1, $v$ cannot impersonate $u$ since we choose a challenge from the community structure $\eta_1$ in Figure 5(b) when $k = 1$.

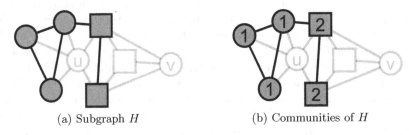

(a) Subgraph $H$            (b) Communities of $H$

**Fig. 5.** An example of how the community structures are detected. **(a)** The subgraph $H$ is induced on the user $u$'s friends' nodes $f_u$ ($f_u$, grey). **(b)** Two community structures $S = \{\eta_1, \eta_2\}$ are detected in $H$.

Formally, if we select $k$ challenge images using community-based challenge selection, the advantage of the impersonation attack $A$, $\mathbf{Adv}_A(u, k, \rho)$, can be computed as follows:

$$\mathbf{Adv}_C(u, k, \rho) \geq \max_{\substack{v \in U \\ u \neq v}} \left\{ \prod_{i=1}^{\min\{k, |f_u|\}} \frac{|\eta_{(i \text{ MOD } l)}(v)|}{|\eta_{(i \text{ MOD } l)}|} \cdot \rho \right\} \tag{4}$$

where $\eta_i(v)$ is the intersection of $\eta_i$ and $\{f_v \cup v\}$ and $C$ denotes the community-based challenge selection method.

To validate the effectiveness of this selection method, we compute the mean values of $\mathbf{Adv}_C(u, k, \rho)$ on the preceding datasets in Section 2.1 and compare those of $\mathbf{Adv}_R(u, k, \rho)$ with random selection. The experimental results (for $\rho = 0.99$)

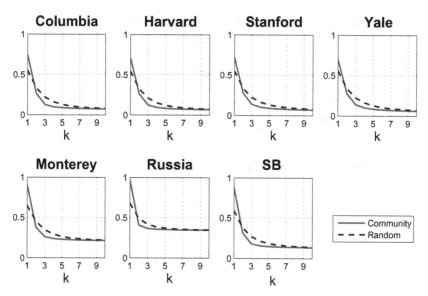

**Fig. 6.** Comparison of the mean values of adversary advantage between community-based challenge selection (red solid line) and the random challenge selection (black dashed line)

are shown in Figure 6 which shows almost the same slope patterns for all the datasets. Community-based selection (**C**, red solid line) performed significantly better than random selection (**R**, black dashed line) from $k = 2$ to 5. But if we use a single challenge image (i.e. $k = 1$), it does worse! Since the first challenge is selected from the first community $\eta_i$ only, the attack success probability of anyone in that community $\eta_i$ is increased. The gap between community-based and random challenge selection is largest for $k = 3$ or 4, and the mean values of the adversary's advantage tend to converge slowly. In fact, community-based challenge selection is comparable at $k = 3$ to random selection at $k = 10$.

We hypothesised that setting $k$ to the "number of community structures" would enable community-based selection to get a good tradeoff between security and usability. In order to test this, we analysed the average number of community structures for each user's friends. The results are shown in Table 2 where friends can be divided into about three or four communities on average except in the Santa Barbara sub-network.

We verified this hypothesis by calculating the average number of community structures for each user's friends and found that indeed friends can be divided into about three or four communities on average; the exception being Santa Barbara sub-network which had 5 communities.

We now discuss how adversary advantage may change with the friend recognition success rate $\rho$ (see Figure 7). To demonstrate this we fix $k = 3$. As $\rho$ decreases from 0.99 to 0.84, the advantage values of both selection methods also slightly decrease. However, the change of $\rho$ does not significantly affect the advantage values

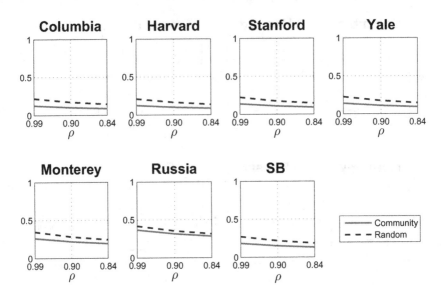

**Fig. 7.** The adversary advantage between the *community-based challenge selection* (red solid line) and the *random challenge selection* (black dashed line) by varying $\rho$ from 0.99 to 0.84 when $k = 3$

**Table 2.** The average number of communities for each user's friends

| Columbia | Harvard | Stanford | Yale | Monterey | Russia | Santa |
|----------|---------|----------|------|----------|--------|-------|
| 3.779 | 3.371 | 3.227 | 2.812 | 3.690 | 3.099 | 4.980 |

compared to the change of $k$ or the challenge selection methods. These values were derived from user success rates for existing image-based CAPTCHAs [12].

In all our experiments, the average number of communities is always a small number (less than 5). Since we use campus or region networks, the number of communities might be small compared to real friendship patterns in Facebook, which could include structures of high school friends, college classmates, work colleges and so on. Recently, some social networking services such as Google+[3] and Facebook have started to encourage users to divide their friends into explicit community groups; community-based challenge selection should be even more useful in such situations.

## 3.2    Exclusion of Well-Known or Easily-Recognizable Friends

In order to mitigate the threat via automatic face recognition program discussed in Section 2.2, some might suggest that we should educate users about these attacks, but that has been found in many applications to not work very well; "blame and train" is not the way to fix usability problems.

---

[3] https://plus.google.com/

One approach may be to exclude users who make all their photos visible to everyone or "friends of friends" – an option in Facebook. This will prevent collection of the training data needed for automatic face recognition tools. There may be technical options too. As face-recognition software tools improve, they can be incorporated into the challenge generation system – by rejecting candidate challenge images whose subjects they can identify.

However, we should be cautious in using a long blacklist of photos; such a policy may shrink the space of challenge photos to the point that an adversary can just guess the answer to a given challenge.

### 3.3    Weighted Random Sampling

In order to reduce the risk of the statistical guessing attacks discussed in Section 2.3, and which leverage the probability distribution of people's names, we suggest using weighted random sampling instead of uniform random sampling.

Under uniform sampling, a name $n$ is selected with the probability $f(n)$ where $f$ is the probability density function for a set of names of people $\mathcal{P}$. Alternatively, in weighted random sampling, $n$ is selected with the following probability:

$$w(n) = \frac{f(n)^{-1}}{\sum_{p \in \mathcal{P}} f(p)^{-1}} \tag{5}$$

Intuitively, in this case, friends with infrequent names will be selected with higher probability compared to friends with popular names when a challenge image is chosen. In a global view, the estimated probability density function of the users' names in challenge images might tend to be the uniform distribution if the number of users with popular names is much greater than that with unpopular name. So selecting popular names as challenge answers won't help the attacker any.

However, if an adversary can crawl all names of a victim's friends successfully, weighted random sampling is worse than uniform random sample unlike our expectation; an attacker can choose a name from the crawled names in proportion to the above probability since the challenge image is chosen with the probability. Thus in practice a more complicated weighted random sampling technique should be considered based on real statistics of privacy settings. As part of the future work, we plan to design more advanced weighted sampling methods.

## 4    Related Work

Our work focuses on the security and usability of photo-based social authentication methods. Social authentication was introduced under the belief that adversaries halfway across the world might know a user's password, but they don't know who the user's friends are.

Yardi et al. [18] proposed a photo-based authentication framework and discussed some security issues including Denial of Service (DoS) attacks: an adversary can spam the system with photos with wrong tagging information so legitimate users cannot pass the authentication test. They also mentioned attacks by a network outlier belonging to the same group as the target. We extended this attack formally and experimentally measured the level of threat.

In social networks, photo privacy may become even more problematic as social networking websites such as Facebook have become the primary method of sharing photos between people [17]. Ahern et al. [3] examined users' decisions when posting photos to Flickr[4] with mobile camera phones, finding that many users were concerned with protecting their personal images and keeping them out of public view. Most social networking websites already provide mechanisms for fine-grained photo sharing control, but user surveys [2,13] have shown that over 80% of social network users do not change their privacy settings at all from the default. This implies that photo-based social authentication is very vulnerable in practice to face recognition tools.

## 5   Conclusion

Facebook recently launched an interesting authentication method [15], and is currently waiting for feedback from the security community before pushing it out to a wider range of authentication and login services including, potentially, third-party merchants who utilise the Facebook Connect API.

This article provides that feedback. We found that the current social authentication scheme is susceptible to impersonation both by insiders and by face-recognition tools, and a naive approach to selecting friends isn't effective against either attack. It is hard to identify the social knowledge that a user holds privately since social knowledge is inherently shared with others. A critical observation is that many likely attackers are 'insiders' in that the people who most want to intrude on your privacy are likely to be in your circle of friends.

We set out to formally quantify the difficulty of guessing the social information of your friends (and your friends' friends) through the analysis of real social network structures and analysed how this can interact with technical attacks such as automatic face recognition and statistical guessing.

We proposed several ways to mitigate the threats we found. Community-based challenge selection can significantly reduce the insider threat; when a user's friends are divided into well-separated communities, we can select one or more recognition subjects from each. We can also avoid subjects with common names or who are known in multiple communities. But perhaps the most powerful way to improve social authentication will be to exclude subjects who make their photos visible to friends of friends. At present, that's most users, as 80% of users never change the privacy defaults – presumably there was some marketing advantage to Facebook in having relaxed privacy defaults, in that making the photos of friends' friends visible helped draw in new users, increasing the network effects; so a change to a default of sharing photos only with friends could give a real security improvement.

---

[4] http://www.flickr.com/

In analysing the adversary's advantage, we assumed some fixed constants (e.g. the adversary's average success rate to recognize a person in a challenge image) rather than actual testing results through user studies on Facebook. So our analysis is still rather limited. To verify this point in a practical environment, we plan to conduct a user study to evaluate the effectiveness of the attack and mitigation techniques.

**Acknowledgements.** We thank Ben Y. Zhao and Joseph Bonneau for their Facebook datasets.

## Appendix: Network Centrality

Formally, we use the standard definition [16] of the *degree, closeness* and *betweenness* centrality values of a node $u$.

**Degree centrality** simply measures the number of direct connections to other nodes. This is calculated for a node $u$ as the ratio of the number of edges of node $u$ to the total number of all other nodes in the network. Degree centrality can be simply computed but does not take into account the topological positions of nodes and the weights of edges.

**Closeness centrality** expands the definition of degree centrality by measuring how close a node is to all the other nodes. That is, this metric can be used to quantify in practical terms how quickly a node can communicate with all other nodes in a network. This is calculated for a node $u$ as the average shortest path length to all other nodes in the network:

$$\mathbf{Clo}(u) = \frac{1}{|V| - 1} \sum_{v \neq u \in V} \text{dist}(u, v) \tag{6}$$

where $\text{dist}(u, v)$ is the length of the shortest path from node $u$ to node $v$. In an undirected graph, $dist(u, v)$ is the number of hops in the shortest path from node $u$ to node $v$.

**Betweenness centrality** measures the paths that pass through a node and can be considered as the proportional flow of data through each node. Nodes that are often on the shortest-path between other nodes are deemed highly central because they control the flow of information in the network. This centrality is calculated for a node $u$ as the proportional number of shortest paths between all node pairs in the network that pass through $u$:

$$\mathbf{Bet}(u) = \frac{1}{(|V| - 1) \cdot (|V| - 2)} \sum_{s \neq u, t \neq u \in V} \frac{\sigma_{s,t}(u)}{\sigma_{s,t}} \tag{7}$$

where $\sigma_{s,t}$ is the total number of shortest paths from source node $s$ to destination node $t$, and $\sigma_{s,t}(u)$ is the number of shortest paths from source node $s$ to destination node $t$ which actually pass through node $u$. For normalization, it is divided by the number of all pairs of $s$ and $t$.

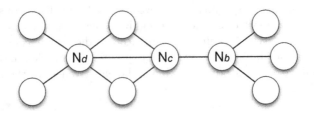

**Fig. 8.** The characteristics of network centrality. In this network, $N_d$ has higher *degree* centrality than $N_c$ since $N_d$ has five neighbours while $N_c$ has higher *closeness* centrality than $N_d$. We note that $N_d$ is located at the periphery of the network compared to $N_c$. Interestingly, $N_b$ has the highest *betweenness* centrality. We can see that $N_b$ plays a 'bridge' role for the rightmost nodes.

In Figure 8, for example, the nodes $N_d$, $N_c$, and $N_b$ illustrate the characteristics of these network centrality metrics. These nodes have the highest *degree*, *closeness* and *betweenness* centrality, respectively.

**Clustering coefficients** measures the probability of neighbours of a node to be neighbours to each other as well. This is calculated for a node $u$ as the fraction of permitted edges between the neighbours of $u$ to the number of edges that could possibly exist between these neighbours:

$$\mathbf{CC}(u) = \frac{2 \cdot \Delta}{(\kappa_u)(\kappa_u - 1)} \tag{8}$$

where $\Delta$ is the number of the edges between the neighbours of node $u$ and $\kappa_u$ is the number of the neighbours of node $u$ (i.e. the degree of node $u$).

# References

1. Acquisti, A., Gross, R., Stutzman, F.: Faces of facebook: Privacy in the age of augmented reality (2011),
   http://www.heinz.cmu.edu/~acquisti/face-recognition-study-FAQ/
2. Acquisti, A., Gross, R.: Imagined Communities: Awareness, Information Sharing, and Privacy on the Facebook. In: Danezis, G., Golle, P. (eds.) PET 2006. LNCS, vol. 4258, pp. 36–58. Springer, Heidelberg (2006)
3. Ahern, S., Eckles, D., Good, N.S., King, S., Naaman, M., Nair, R.: Over-exposed?: privacy patterns and considerations in online and mobile photo sharing. In: CHI 2007: Proceedings of the SIGCHI Conference on Human Factors in Computing Systems, pp. 357–366. ACM, New York (2007)
4. Becker, B.C., Ortiz, E.G.: Evaluation of face recognition techniques for application to facebook. In: IEEE International Conference on Automatic Face and Gesture Recognition, pp. 1–6 (2008)
5. Blondel, V.D., Guillaume, J.L., Lambiotte, R., Lefebvre, E.: Unfolding communities in large complex networks: Combining defensive and offensive label propagation for core extraction. Physical Review E 83(3), 036103 (2011)

6. Bonneau, J., Anderson, J., Anderson, R., Stajano, F.: Eight friends are enough: social graph approximation via public listings. In: Proceedings of the Second ACM EuroSys Workshop on Social Network Systems, SNS 2009, pp. 13–18. ACM, New York (2009)

7. Bonneau, J., Just, M., Matthews, G.: What's in a Name? Evaluating Statistical Attacks on Personal Knowledge Questions. In: Sion, R. (ed.) FC 2010. LNCS, vol. 6052, pp. 98–113. Springer, Heidelberg (2010)

8. Daugman, J.: The importance of being random: statistical principles of iris recognition. Pattern Recognition 36(2), 279–291 (2003)

9. Golle, P.: Machine learning attacks against the Asirra CAPTCHA. In: CCS 2008: Proceedings of the 15th ACM Conference on Computer and Communications Security, pp. 535–542. ACM, New York (2008)

10. Just, M.: On the design of challenge question systems. IEEE Security and Privacy 2, 32–39 (2004)

11. Kim, H., Bonneau, J.: Privacy-enhanced public view for social graphs. In: SWSM 2009: Proceeding of the 2nd ACM Workshop on Social Web Search and Mining, pp. 41–48. ACM, New York (2009)

12. Kluever, K.A., Zanibbi, R.: Balancing usability and security in a video CAPTCHA. In: SOUPS 2009: Proceedings of the 5th Symposium on Usable Privacy and Security, pp. 1–11. ACM, New York (2009)

13. Krishnamurthy, B., Wills, C.E.: Characterizing privacy in online social networks. In: WOSP 2008: Proceedings of the First Workshop on Online Social Networks, pp. 37–42. ACM, New York (2008)

14. Lipford, H.R., Besmer, A., Watson, J.: Understanding privacy settings in facebook with an audience view. In: Proceedings of the 1st Conference on Usability, Psychology, and Security, pp. 2:1–2:8. USENIX, Berkeley (2008)

15. Rice, A.: A Continued Commitment to Security (January 2011),
    `http://blog.facebook.com/blog.php?post=486790652130`

16. Wasserman, S., Faust, K.: Social Network Analysis: Methods and Applications. Cambridge University Press (1994)

17. Willinger, W., Rejaie, R., Torkjazi, M., Valafar, M., Maggioni, M.: Research on online social networks: time to face the real challenges. SIGMETRICS Performance Evaluation Review 37, 49–54 (2010)

18. Yardi, S., Feamster, N., Bruckman, A.: Photo-based authentication using social networks. In: WOSP 2008: Proceedings of the First Workshop on Online Social Networks, pp. 55–60. ACM, New York (2008)

# The MVP Web-Based
# Authentication Framework
## (Short Paper)

Sonia Chiasson, Chris Deschamps, Elizabeth Stobert,
Max Hlywa, Bruna Freitas Machado, Alain Forget,
Nicholas Wright, Gerry Chan, and Robert Biddle

Carleton University, Ottawa, Canada
chiasson@scs.carleton.ca

**Abstract.** MVP is a framework allowing websites to use diverse knowledge-based authentication schemes. One application is its use in conducting ecologically valid user studies of authentication under the same experimental conditions. We introduce MVP and its key characteristics, discuss several authentication schemes, and offer lessons learned from running 9 hybrid (lab/online) and 3 MTurk user studies over the last year.

**Keywords:** Authentication, usable security, graphical passwords, MTurk.

## 1 Introduction

Despite the ubiquity of password systems, knowledge-based authentication remains an important and active research area. Many current systems have low security, and even then users often devise insecure coping strategies in order to compensate for memorability and usability problems. Alternatives such as biometrics or tokens raise other issues such as privacy and loss. Various graphical password schemes have received considerable attention in response. A systematic review of the literature on graphical passwords [8] shows no consistency in the usability and security evaluation of different schemes. The situation is similar for text passwords, making fair comparison between schemes nearly impossible.

We present MVP (Multiple Versatile Passwords), a framework for using diverse knowledge-based authentication schemes on websites. In particular, it allows user studies of authentication in the same context. These can be deployed in the field where ecological validity is improved by the use of real websites with real content, making authentication a secondary task. MVP is not a single-sign-on system; it serves as a platform for different types of authentication and therefore facilitates research in this area. Another testing framework for authentication was described briefly in a workshop paper by Beautement and Sasse [7]. It asked users to log in to claim credits as part of an online bartering game.

A.D. Keromytis (Ed.): FC 2012, LNCS 7397, pp. 16–24, 2012.
© International Financial Cryptography Association 2012

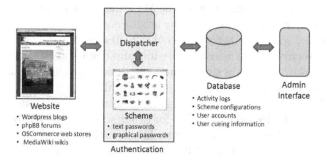

**Fig. 1.** Diagram of the MVP framework

We have implemented several authentication schemes within MVP and so far have conducted 12 user studies with the system. We have also used it as a classroom platform for students to gain experience in running user studies. Amongst the schemes, we offer an implementation of Draw-A-Secret (DAS) [14], a recall-based graphical password scheme that to our knowledge has only been tested as a paper prototype. Our implementations of the cued-recall schemes PassPoints [16] and Persuasive Cued Click-Points [10] are the first in the literature to include fully functional systems using discretization, hashing, and image selection. The MVP implementations of recognition-based schemes such as Face (similar to the commercial Passfaces system) are the first to be implemented at password-level security strength rather than PIN-level security.

## 2   MVP System Features

MVP has the following system characteristics:

***Web-Based Usage:*** MVP is web-based (e.g., as a Wordpress plug-in) and functions with most popular browser and operating system configurations, therefore allowing participants to access the sites from any computer. The only modifications necessary are to server-side software, and these are minor. No modifications are needed on users' computers.

***Easy Addition of New Schemes:*** Figure 1 presents MVP's design. The website's password field is replaced by a button that invokes the MVP dispatcher and opens a new window with the appropriate authentication scheme. The dispatcher returns a password string based on the user input that is evaluated by the website as it would normally evaluate any entered text password. In this way, the websites remain responsible for authentication, while MVP controls which password scheme is displayed and its configuration.

MVP is designed for interchangeable use of different password schemes. The schemes are modular components that administrators can add and remove like server plug-ins. Password systems can be written in any web language. Currently, the password systems are written in either Java or JavaScript. The password schemes use PHP to communicate with the MVP dispatcher. A mySQL database stores administrative data to support the schemes.

MVP allows for easy parameterization of schemes so they may be used at different levels of security. User accounts are initially defined by an administrator, who selects the authentication scheme and the desired parameters for the website. A user may be assigned different schemes for different sites. Tools facilitate the process of defining multiple accounts. By default, a simple plain-text password system is used. However, modules for other schemes can easily be written and added to MVP. Currently, password schemes include PassPoints [16], Cued Click-Points [9], Persuasive Cued Click-Points [10], Draw-a-Secret [14], GrID-sure [3], PassTiles [15]; and recognition-based schemes using face, object, house, and word images. As well, MVP supports various text password systems.

***Ecological Validity:*** MVP is especially designed to allow passwords to be deployed and accessed by users in their regular environments over longer periods of time. The system allows authentication to become a secondary task, by supporting primary tasks on real websites that require users to log in as part of the process. This allows the collection of more realistic usage data. MVP exists as a Wordpress plugin for blogs. We have also modified instances of other popular open-source systems, including phpBB forums, OSCommerce online stores, and the MediaWiki platform. Figure 2 provides a screenshot of the login interface for a Wordpress blog using PCCP as an authentication scheme, while Figure 3 shows the DAS, Face, and Word Recognition login interfaces.

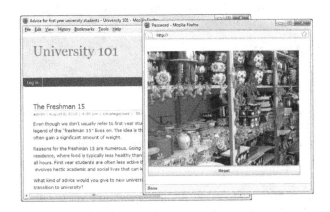

**Fig. 2.** A blog using PCCP for authentication

***Instrumentation for Analysis:*** Since user behaviour can significantly impact security, we collect and analyze data representing user choices and behaviour for susceptibility to security threats as well as for evaluating usability. MVP is instrumented to record all user interactions, including keyboard and mouse entries, timestamps, and details of the user's computing environment. Logging is done asynchronously with the server, allowing detailed data to be collected without creating delays affecting user experience. Data is stored in a mySQL database.

Different authentication schemes can be tested under identical conditions while recording the same performance measures. We use LimeSurvey [4] running on our servers in conjunction with MVP to administer study questionnaires.

***Password Reset without Admin Intervention:*** Forgotten passwords are to be expected, especially in long-term studies or studies requiring users to remember multiple passwords. MVP allows users to reset forgotten passwords without intervention from a system administrator. The real-time password reset mechanism minimizes disruption to users, encourage completion of assigned tasks, and supports the ecological validity of the system. MVP records details about password resets to allow later analysis of this user behaviour.

Password resets are triggered by clicking the "forgot password" link on the given website. When a user resets their password, they are emailed a URL that directs them to the website, where they are prompted to choose a new password with their assigned authentication scheme. In some cases, it can be desirable to discourage users from resetting their password each time they want to log in. MVP allows password resets to be delayed by any period of time (typically 5 minutes, and the user is warned about the delay). This time delay is intended to subtly discourages users from relying on password resets as a login mechanism.

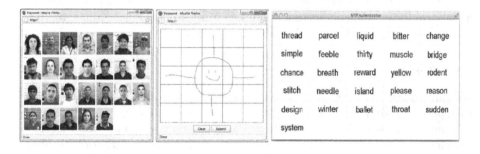

**Fig. 3.** The Face, DAS, and Word Recognition login interfaces

***Training:*** MVP provides an interface for users to practice using new schemes and receive immediate feedback about whether they are entering passwords correctly. MVP also supports audio/video tutorials, interactive demo systems, and static text/image help pages. Some schemes (e.g., PassTiles) include the option of practicing passwords directly within the password creation interface where users can show/hide their password and practice it until it is memorized.

***Administration Tools:*** MVP includes several study administration tools. A notification system automates the process of emailing participants at specific intervals prompting them to complete at-home tasks. A log query system allows experimenters to retrieve information in real-time from the database about the activities of specific users. While experiments are in-progress, the query system is especially useful to monitor whether users are completing tasks and to troubleshoot any problems from users. A modified version of the MRBS [5] scheduling software allows in-person participants to sign-up for study sessions.

*Crowdsourcing Functionality:* Online crowdsourcing websites (such as Amazon's Mechanical Turk [1] — MTurk) are increasingly used as a source of participants for usable security studies, and MVP includes tools to help conduct studies using such systems. Crowdsourcing studies differ from traditional studies in the volume of system traffic, the pace of the study, and the methods of communication and payment. An MVP validation protocol verifies that the correct tasks have been completed, and users must validate their work to receive payment for that session. MVP tracks user identifiers from the crowdsourcing site (e.g., MTurk worker ID) and email addresses to reduce the possibility that a user participates multiple times in the same study or in closely related studies. The system also ensures that users cannot join partway through a multi-task study without having completed earlier steps.

## 3    MVP Deployment for User Studies

MVP has been deployed for 12 user studies over the last year (see Table 1). To situate the "Lessons Learned" from Section 4, we briefly describe their methodology and overall results. MVP was also used in a university course to give students a platform for learning about user studies. Seventy students in 8 groups ran user studies with approximately 200 participants overall.

### 3.1    Hybrid Studies

We ran several hybrid studies of authentication systems. Participants initially took part in a lab session where they received training on how to use the websites and authentication schemes, and created accounts on two to four websites. The accounts were for various Wordpress blogs (e.g., a dream vacation photo blog, and a daily opinion poll site), and a phpBB forum to discuss the best locations for various activities. The websites were fully populated with real content to engage users realistically. In each case, participants' main tasks were to comment on a specific blog post or forum thread, tasks requiring them to log in. In the week following the initial session, participants received email asking them to complete further tasks from any web-enabled computer.

*1. PCCP:* Persuasive Cued Click-Points (PCCP) [11] is a cued-recall click-based graphical password system where passwords consist of one user-selected click-point per image on a sequence of images. The study's results support and confirm earlier lab-based studies of the usability and security of PCCP.

*2. Recognition - image type, 3. Recognition - in-depth:* Face [6,12] is a recognition-based scheme where users must identify their assigned images of faces from among decoys. It was suggested that the human proficiency for recognizing faces would help with remembering such passwords [6]. We implemented Face and two variations where the type of image was modified to either everyday objects or houses [13]. A second study conducted an in-depth comparison of face

**Table 1.** Summary of MVP user studies. The number of sessions includes the total number of in-lab sessions and at-home tasks.

| Study Name | Number of Sessions | Number of Users | Accounts Per User | Pswd Space | Pswd Selection | Study Type |
|---|---|---|---|---|---|---|
| 1.  PCCP | 4 | 24 | 3 | $2^{43}$ | Chosen | Hybrid |
| 2.  Recognition - image type | 5 | 60 | 3 | $2^{28}$ | Assigned | Hybrid |
| 3.  Recognition - in-depth | 5 | 20 | 4 | $2^{28}$ | Assigned | Hybrid |
| 4.  DAS | 4 | 26 | 3 | $2^{58}$ | Chosen | Hybrid |
| 5.  PassTiles - user-choice | 4 | 33 | 2 | $2^{21}$ | Chosen | Hybrid |
| 6.  PassTiles - memory type | 5 | 81 | 3 | $2^{21}$ | Assigned | Hybrid |
| 7.  Text | 4 | 21 | 3 | $2^{36}$ | Chosen | Hybrid |
| 8.  Text - memory type | 4 | 36 | 3 | $2^{36}$ | Assigned | Hybrid |
| 9.  Text - interference | 4 | 20 | 3 | $2^{36}$ | Assigned | Hybrid |
| 10. PassTiles - MTurk | 4 | 77 | 3 | $2^{21}$ | Assigned | MTurk |
| 11. PassTiles - MTurk 2 | 4 | 92 | 3 | $2^{28}$ | Assigned | MTurk |
| 12. PCCP - MTurk Training | 4 | 30 | 3 | $2^{28}$ | Chosen | MTurk |

and object images. In our configuration, 6 panels of 26 images were shown in sequence, each panel containing one of the user's 6 images. Results showed that objects were as easy or easier to remember than faces while houses was most difficult. No evidence was found to support higher performance for face images.

*4. DAS:* Draw-A-Secret (DAS) [14] is a recall-based scheme where users sketch on a grid using a mouse. Our system used a 5 × 5 grid. Results showed that users often misunderstood the scheme (e.g., users drew their figure within one grid square, not realizing that this was equivalent to one dot in a square). Users also tended to draw simple figures that would be easily guessed, and often re-used passwords across different accounts.

*5. PassTiles - background type, 6. PassTiles - memory type:* PassTiles passwords consist of a set of squares (tiles) on a grid [15]. The scheme was implemented with a blank background or an image behind the grid, or with individual objects in each tile. The systems used an 8 × 6 grid and a password consisted of 5 tiles. The first study allowed users to choose their own passwords while the second provided assigned passwords. Results showed that offering users the opportunity to combine memory retrieval methods (e.g., having an image or objects as a cue) may increase memorability of graphical passwords.

*7. Text:* Text passwords with a minimum length of 6, including at least one digit and one letter, were also tested. Results showed that although users could quickly log in ($\approx$ 6 seconds), the majority re-used passwords across accounts.

*8. Text - memory type, 9. Text - interference:* These studies [17] tested different types of text passwords: 6 randomly assigned characters, 4 randomly assigned common words, and a recognition-based system where the "images" were words ("Word Recognition", Figure 3). Results showed only minor differences in memorability, but slower login times for the recognition scheme.

## 3.2  Mechanical Turk Studies

MVP also enables fully online user studies with no in-person component. We have completed two MTurk studies and a third study is in progress.

**10. PassTiles - MTurk:**  Study 6 of PassTiles was replicated using participants from MTurk. Instructions were provided entirely through webpages and email. Results supported those found using the hybrid study.

**11. PassTiles - MTurk 2:**  A second MTurk study of PassTiles used an $8 \times 10$ grid and 6 tiles. Results were similar to the earlier studies, indicating that the larger theoretical password space did not negatively affect usability.

**12: PCCP - MTurk Training:**  We are currently investigating different delivery methods for training in online studies. Three instruction sets have been compiled for the PCCP authentication system: a static text/image webpage, an interactive demo webpage, and a video tutorial.

## 4  Discussion and Lessons Learned

Based on web server log information about their browsers, participants used MVP on a variety of computers and platforms without problem. The participation rate was high during the at-home tasks. Several participants mentioned enjoying the websites and inquired whether they would be available beyond the study, providing evidence that participants engaged with the web content as their primary task. When users forgot their passwords, they reset them from home without intervention from an administrator.

In this section, we outline a number of lessons learned while running studies using MVP. This list is not comprehensive, but we hope that these findings may assist other experimenters in designing and conducting similar studies.

**Force Logoffs:** One problem with using real websites for experimental purposes is that they may not be configured appropriately for password studies. The Wordpress blogs were pre-configured to allow users to remain logged in. We enforced server-side logoffs, so that users would need to log in with each visit.

**Ethics:** In running user studies of any kind (whether lab, hybrid or online), not only it is important to obtain permission from the appropriate research ethics board, but also to give consideration to key issues such as privacy. In our online studies, email address and crowdsourcing identifier were the only identifying information collected about each participant, and this was never displayed publicly. Consent forms were completed online and included only the participant's email address as a "signature". All data collected in the study (including questionnaire data) was collected and stored on our servers, allowing us to have complete control of the data and ensuring that it is accessed only by authorized researchers. We are considering an email aliasing system to further anonymize data while still helpind to detect users trying to participate more than once.

**Practicing:** In an early MVP study, we noticed a few participants with several logins immediately preceding a required study task. It appeared that before returning to the lab, participants were practicing entering their passwords! When running studies, and considering ecological validity, it is important to consider that participants may be putting in a different effort (whether greater or less) than they would in a real life scenario.

***Avoiding the Task at Hand:*** We have occasionally noticed that participants will develop coping strategies that avoid performing the correct task. In one study of text passwords, we noticed that instead of remembering their passwords, participants were resetting their passwords at every login because it was quicker and easier. In another study (of PassTiles), participants seemed to be coping with the study tasks by writing all of their passwords down. It is important to consider how participants may be circumventing your tasks, and either prevent them from doing so, or collect sufficient information to be aware of these coping strategies. Such behaviours may in fact reflect real-life behaviour and may offer important insight into the real usage of authentication systems.

***Global Researchers, Global Audience:*** To our initial surprise, we could not post tasks on MTurk as non-US citizens. We instead use Crowdflower [2] as a intermediary that can post tasks to several crowdsourcing systems, including MTurk. We also had minor issues with international participants who were running older computer systems and had slow or unreliable internet connections. Having a robust system that is compatible with a wide variety of environments is critical. The system should also be able to withstand significant web traffic when running MTurk studies and be robust enough to withstand users trying to cheat and circumvent the system in a variety of ways.

## 5  Conclusions

MVP is a web-based authentication framework which we used for conducting more ecologically valid user studies of authentication schemes. It uses instances of real web-based applications that have been modified to require login using configurable, interchangeable authentication schemes. Now that MVP has been tested with these shorter studies, we are preparing larger, longer-term (several months) comparison studies of various authentication schemes.

## References

1. Amazon Mechanical Turk, https://www.mturk.com
2. Crowdflower, http://crowdflower.com/
3. GrIDsure corporate website, http://www.gridsure.com
4. LimeSurvey: The open source survey application, http://www.limesurvey.org
5. MRBS, http://mrbs.sourceforge.net/
6. Passfaces Corporation, http://www.passfaces.com/
7. Beautement, A., Sasse, A.M.: Gathering realistic authentication performance data through field trials. In: SOUPS USER Workshop (2010)
8. Biddle, R., Chiasson, S., van Oorschot, P.C.: Graphical Passwords: Learning from the First Twelve Years. ACM Computing Surveys 44(4) (in Press)

9. Chiasson, S., Biddle, R., van Oorschot, P.C.: A second look at the usability of click-based graphical passwords. In: ACM SOUPS (July 2007)
10. Chiasson, S., Forget, A., Biddle, R., van Oorschot, P.C.: Influencing users towards better passwords: Persuasive Cued Click-Points. In: BCS-HCI (2008)
11. Chiasson, S., Stobert, E., Forget, A., Biddle, R., van Oorschot, P.C.: Persuasive Cued Click-Points: Design, implementation, and evaluation of a knowledge-based authentication mechanism. IEEE Transactions on Dependable and Secure Computing, TDSC (in press, 2012)
12. Davis, D., Monrose, F., Reiter, M.: On user choice in graphical password schemes. In: USENIX Security Symposium (2004)
13. Hlywa, M., Biddle, R., Patrick, A.: Facing the facts about image type in recognition-based graphical passwords. In: ACSAC (2011)
14. Jermyn, I., Mayer, A., Monrose, F., Reiter, M., Rubin, A.: The design and analysis of graphical passwords. In: USENIX Security Symposium (1999)
15. Stobert, E.: Memorability of Assigned Random Graphical Passwords. Master's thesis, Department of Psychology, Carleton University (August 2011)
16. Wiedenbeck, S., Waters, J., Birget, J., Brodskiy, A., Memon, N.: Authentication using graphical passwords: Effects of tolerance and image choice. In: SOUPS (2005)
17. Wright, N.: Do you see your password? Applying recognition to textual passwords. Master's thesis, Department of Psychology, Carleton University (August 2011)

# A Birthday Present Every Eleven Wallets?
# The Security of Customer-Chosen Banking PINs

Joseph Bonneau, Sören Preibusch, and Ross Anderson

Computer Laboratory
University of Cambridge
{jcb82,sdp36,rja14}@cl.cam.ac.uk

**Abstract.** We provide the first published estimates of the difficulty of
guessing a human-chosen 4-digit PIN. We begin with two large sets of
4-digit sequences chosen outside banking for online passwords and smartphone unlock-codes. We use a regression model to identify a small number of dominant factors influencing user choice. Using this model and
a survey of over 1,100 banking customers, we estimate the distribution
of banking PINs as well as the frequency of security-relevant behaviour
such as sharing and reusing PINs. We find that guessing PINs based on
the victims' birthday, which nearly all users carry documentation of, will
enable a competent thief to gain use of an ATM card once for every 11–
18 stolen wallets, depending on whether banks prohibit weak PINs such
as 1234. The lesson for cardholders is to never use one's date of birth as
a PIN. The lesson for card-issuing banks is to implement a denied PIN
list, which several large banks still fail to do. However, blacklists cannot
effectively mitigate guessing given a known birth date, suggesting banks
should move away from customer-chosen banking PINs in the long term.

## 1 Introduction

Personal Identification Numbers, or PINs, authenticate trillions of pounds in
payment card transactions annually and are entrenched by billions of pounds
worth of infrastructure and decades of customer experience. In addition to their
banking role, 4-digit PINs have proliferated in a variety of other security applications where the lack of a full keypad prevents the use of textual passwords
such as electronic door locks, smartphone unlock codes and voice mail access
codes. In this work, we provide the first extensive investigation of the security
implications of human selection and management of PINs.

### 1.1 History of PINs

We refer the reader to [4] for a good overview of the history of banking cards and
ATMs; we summarise the development of PINs for security here. The historical
record suggests that PINs trace their origins to automated dispensing and control
systems at petrol filling stations. In the context of banking, PINs first appeared
in separate British cash machines deployed in 1967, with 6-digit PINs in the

A.D. Keromytis (Ed.): FC 2012, LNCS 7397, pp. 25–40, 2012.

Barclays-De La Rue system rolled out in June and 4-digit PINs in the National-Chubb system in September. According to John Shepherd-Barron, leader of the De La Rue engineering team, after his wife was unable to remember six random digits he reduced the length to four.

Early cash machines were stand-alone, offline machines which could only exchange cash for punched cards (which were kept by the machine). The primary use case was to cease branch operations on Saturdays and still allow customers to retrieve cash. Interestingly, cash machines deployed contemporaneously in Japan and Sweden in 1967 used no PINs and absorbed losses from lost or stolen cards. As late as 1977, Spain's La Caixa issued cards without PINs.

PINs were initially bank-assigned by necessity as they were hard-coded onto cards using steganographic schemes such as dots of carbon-14. Soon a variety of schemes for storing a cryptographic transformation of the PIN developed.[1] The IBM 3624 ATM controller introduced an influential scheme for deriving PINs in 1977 [5]. PIN verification consisted of a DES encryption of the user's account number, converting the first 4 hexadecimal digits of the result into decimal using a lookup table, adding a 4-digit PIN offset modulo $10^4$, and comparing to the entered PIN. Changing the PIN offset stored on the card enabled the user to choose their own PIN. Banks began allowing customer-chosen PINs in the 1980s as a marketing tactic, though it required substantial infrastructure changes.

The development of Visa and MasterCard and the interconnection of ATM networks globally in the 1990s cemented the use of PINs for payment card authentication in both the 1993 ISO 9564 standard [3] and 1995 EMV standard [1]. Today, most cards use the Visa PVV scheme, which stores a DES-based MAC of the account number and PIN called the pin-verification value (PVV) which can be re-computed to check if a trial PIN is correct.

The EMV standard further led to PINs taking on the role of authorising payments at merchant tills, with the card's chip verifying the customer's PIN internally.[2] Technically, this use of PINs uses a different mechanism than that for ATM authentication, though in all practical deployments the two PINs are the same and may only be changed at an ATM. With the advent of EMV, PINs must be entered more often and into a plethora of vendor terminals, increasing the risk of compromise.

Chip cards have also enabled the deployment of hand-held Chip Authentication Program (CAP) readers since 2008 for verifying Internet transactions [10]. CAP readers allow muggers to verify a PIN demanded from a victim during an attack; they can also be used to guess offline the PIN on a found or stolen card.

## 1.2 Standards and Practices in PIN Selection

Published standards on PIN security provide very brief treatment of human factors. The EMV standard [1] requires support for PINs of 4–12 digits, in line

---

[1] James Goodfellow patented a cryptographic PIN derivation scheme in 1966 [12]. Amongst others, he has been called be the inventor of PINs and ATMs.

[2] EMV was deployed in the UK from 2003 under the branding "Chip and PIN." It is now deployed in most of Europe, though notably not in the United States.

with earlier Visa standards, but makes no mention of PIN selection. Separately, Visa maintains *Issuer PIN Security Guidelines* with several recommendations for users, specifically that they never write down their PIN or use it for any other purpose. The document is neutral between issuer-assigned PINs or customer-chosen PINs, providing one sentence about PIN selection [2]: "Select a PIN that cannot be easily guessed (i.e., do not use birth date, partial account numbers, sequential numbers like 1234, or repeated values such as 1111)."

ISO 9564 [3] covers PIN security and is largely similar to Visa's guidelines, mostly focusing on PIN transmission and storage. It adds a recommendation against "historically significant dates," and PINs chosen as words on the keypad. Neither standard mentions using a "denied PIN list" to blacklist weak PINs, as is recommended in standards for text passwords [8].

As a result of the vague standards, PIN requirements vary significantly but the minimal 4-digit length predominates. PIN length appears integrated into cultural norms: there is rarely variation within competitive regions, while in some locales most card issuers require PINs longer than 4 digits.[3] Similarly, most banks allow user-chosen PINs, with a few regional exceptions such as Germany.

Because denied PIN lists aren't publicly advertised, we evaluated several banking cards by requesting the PIN 1234.[4] In the UK, this was denied by Barclays, HSBC and NatWest but allowed by Lloyds TSB and The Co-op Bank. In the USA, this was denied by Citibank and allowed by Bank of America, HSBC and Wells Fargo. We only identified card-specific denied PIN lists; we found no ATM implementing local restrictions. At one bank we tested, Chase in the USA, self-service PIN changes are not possible and changes must be made in-person. Banks's policies may vary with time or location (note the inconsistency of HSBC between the USA and UK), but denied PIN lists are clearly not universal.

### 1.3   Academic Research

Research on authentication systems involving human-chosen secrets consistently finds that people favour a small number of popular (and predictable) choices. Strong bias has been analysed for textual passwords starting with Morris and Thompson in 1979 [15] and confirmed in many studies since [19]. Similar bias been identified in responses to personal knowledge questions [6] and in graphical password schemes [20]. Despite their wide deployment, there exists no academic research about human selection of PINs.

The best-known research on PINs, such as Murdoch et al.'s "no-PIN attack" [16], has identified technical flaws in the handling and verification of PINs but not addressed PIN guessing. Kuhn identified in 1997 that the use of unbalanced decimalisation tables introduced a bias into the distribution of PIN offsets which could be exploited by an attacker to improve PIN guessing [13]. Bond and

---

[3] For example, banks in Switzerland assign 6–8 digit PINs, and banks in Italy typically use 5-digit PINs. Canadian banks use a mix of 4-digit and 6-digit PINs.

[4] We assume any reasonable denied PIN list would include 1234 and allowing this PIN indicates no restrictions exist.

Zieliński developed further decimalisation-based attacks in 2003 [5]. Both attacks can be improved with knowledge of human tendencies in PIN selection.

## 2   Quantifying Resistance to Guessing

We consider abstractly the probability distribution[5] of PINs $\mathcal{X}$ over the set $\{0000, \ldots, 9999\}$. We consider each PIN $x_i$ to have probability $p_i$, with $p_1 \geq p_2 \geq \cdots \geq p_N$. Several works have formally treated the mathematics of guessing an unknown value $X \xleftarrow{R} \mathcal{X}$ [14,9,7,17]. We use the notation and terminology from [6] throughout this paper.

A traditional measure of guessing difficulty is Shannon entropy:

$$H_1 = -\sum_{i=1}^{N} (p_i \cdot \log_2 p_i) \tag{1}$$

However, this is mathematically unsuited to measuring guessing difficulty[6] [14,9] and recently been confirmed experimentally to be a poor measure of cracking difficulty for human-chosen passwords [21]. A more sound measure is *guesswork*:

$$G = \sum_{i=1}^{N} (p_i \cdot i) \tag{2}$$

$G$ represents the expected number of sequential guesses to determine $X$ if an attacker proceeds in optimal order [14]. Both $G$ and $H_1$ are influenced by rare events significantly enough to make them misleading for security analysis. A preferable alternative is *marginal guesswork* $\mu_\alpha$, which measures the expected number of guesses required to succeed with probability $\alpha$:

$$\mu_\alpha = \min \left\{ j \in [1, N] \middle| \sum_{i=1}^{j} p_i \geq \alpha \right\} \tag{3}$$

In particular, $\mu_{0.5}$, representing the number of attempts needed to have a $1/2$ chance of guessing correctly, has been suggested as a general alternative to $G$, as it is less influenced by low-probability events [17]. In the case of PINs, attackers are almost always externally limited in the number of guesses they can try. In this case, the best metric is the *marginal success rate* $\lambda_\beta$, the probability that an attacker can correctly guess $X$ given $\beta$ attempts:

$$\lambda_\beta = \sum_{i=1}^{\beta} (p_i) \tag{4}$$

Locking a payment card after 3 incorrect guesses is standard practice. However, different counters are used for ATM requests and payment requests, meaning a thief with a CAP reader and access to an ATM can typically make 6 guesses.

---

[5] The distribution may vary between different populations, or with knowledge of auxiliary information (such as a card holder's birthday).

[6] Shannon entropy represents the average number of bits needed to encode a variable $X \xleftarrow{R} \mathcal{X}$. It measures the expected number of yes/no queries an attacker must make about the membership of $X$ in subsets $\mathcal{X}' \subset \mathcal{X}$, which is fundamentally different from guessing individual values.

**Table 1.** Guessing metrics for 4-digit sequences in RockYou passwords and iPhone unlock codes. Values are also shown for the regression-model approximation for each distribution and for a uniform distribution of 4-digit PINs.

| distribution | $H_1$ | $\tilde{G}$ | $\tilde{\mu}_{0.5}$ | $\lambda_3$ | $\lambda_6$ |
|---|---|---|---|---|---|
| RockYou 4-digit sequences | 10.74 | 11.50 | 9.11 | 8.04% | 12.29% |
| RockYou regression model | 11.01 | 11.79 | 9.39 | 5.06% | 7.24% |
| iPhone unlock codes | 11.42 | 11.83 | 10.37 | 9.23% | 12.39% |
| iPhone regression model | 11.70 | 12.06 | 10.73 | 9.21% | 11.74% |
| random 4-digit PIN | 13.29 | 13.29 | 13.29 | 0.03% | 0.06% |

Thus, we are primarily concerned with estimating $\lambda_3$ and $\lambda_6$, though other values are of interest if a user has reused a PIN for multiple cards.

The metrics are not directly comparable, as $H_1$ is in units of bits, $G$ and $\mu_\alpha$ in units of guesses, and $\lambda_\beta$ is a probability. It can be helpful to convert all of the metrics into bits by taking the base-2 logarithm of a uniform distribution which would have the same value of the metric, as demonstrated in [6]:

$$\tilde{G} = \log_2\left(2 \cdot G(\mathcal{X}) - 1\right); \quad \tilde{\lambda}_\beta = \log_2\left(\frac{\beta}{\lambda_\beta(\mathcal{X})}\right); \quad \tilde{\mu}_\alpha = \log_2\left(\frac{\mu_\alpha(\mathcal{X})}{\lambda_{\mu_\alpha}}\right) \quad (5)$$

For example, a distribution with $\mu_{0.5} = 128$ would be equivalent by this metric to an 8-bit random variable, denoted as $\tilde{\mu}_{0.5} = 8$. We may use units of *dits* (also called hartleys or bans) by taking base-10 logarithms instead of base-2. This represents the number of random decimal digits providing equivalent security.

## 3    Human Choice of Other 4-Digit Sequences

To the best of the authors' knowledge, no dataset of real banking PINs has ever been made public. However, public datasets have recently become available for two other sources of human-chosen secret 4-digit sequences.

**RockYou.** The leak of 32 million textual passwords from the social gaming website RockYou in 2009 has proved invaluable for password research [21]. We extracted all consecutive sequences of exactly 4 digits from the RockYou passwords. There were 1,778,095 such sequences; all possible 4-digit sequences occurred. 1234 was the most common with 66,193 occurrences (3.7%), while 8439 was the least common with 10 occurrences (0.0006%).

Though these sequences occurred as part of longer strings, a manual inspection of 100 random passwords which include a 4-digit sequence identified only 3 with an obvious connection between the digits and the text (feb1687, classof2007 and 2003chevy), suggesting that digits and text are often semantically independent. Users also show a particular affinity for 4-digit sequences, using them more significantly more often than 3-digit sequences (1,599,959) or 5-digit sequences (497,791).

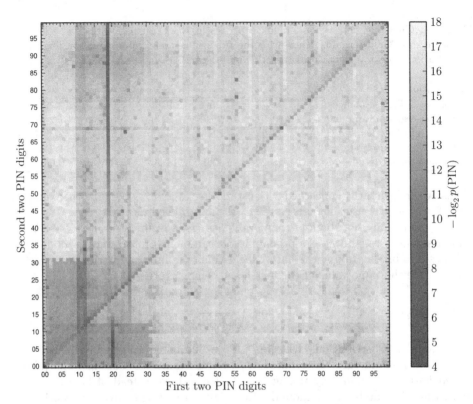

**Fig. 1.** The distribution of 4-digit sequences within RockYou passwords. Each cell shows the frequency of an individual sequence, a proxy for PIN popularity.

**iPhone.** Our second dataset was published (in aggregate form) in June 2011 by Daniel Amitay, an iPhone developer who deployed a screen locking mechanism which requires entering a 4-digit sequence to unlock. This dataset was much smaller, with 204,508 PINs. It doesn't support reliable estimates of low-frequency PINs, as 46 possible PINs weren't observed at all. 1234 was again the most common, representing 4.3% of all PINs. The screen unlock codes were entered using a square number pad very similar to standard PIN-entry pads. Geometric patterns, such as PINs consisting of digits which are adjacent on the keypad, were far more common than in the RockYou sequences.

Plotting the RockYou distribution in a 2-dimensional grid (Figure 1) highlights some basic factors influencing popularity. The most prominent features are the stripe of recent years and the range of calendar dates in MMDD and DDMM format, which trace the variation in lengths of each month. Many other features, such as a diagonal line of PINs with the same first and last two digits, and a horizontal line of PINs ending in 69, can be clearly seen.

To quantitatively measure important factors in PIN selection, we performed linear regression on each distribution with a number of human-relevant functions of each PIN as regressors. The datasets were well suited to this analysis, with nearly 10,000 samples of the response variable (the frequencies of each PIN). The

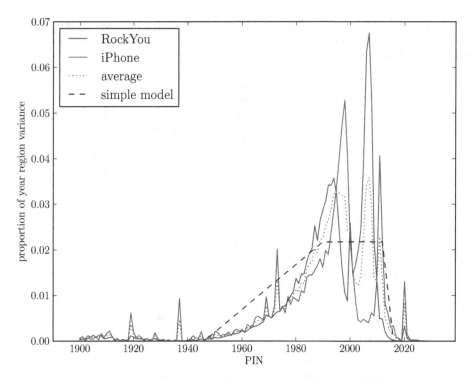

**Fig. 2.** Probability of 4-digit years from 1900–2025 in the RockYou dataset. Some outliers demonstrate confounding factors: **1937** and **1973** represent the four-corners of a numeric keypad, **1919** and **2020** are repeated pairs of digits, and **1969** demonstrates users' affinity for the number 69.

assumption of a linear model simply means that the population can be divided into distinct groups of users employing different PIN selection strategies, such as choosing specific date formats or geometric patterns.

Our process for identifying relevant input functions was iterative: we began with none, producing a model in which each PIN is equally likely, and progressively added functions which could explain the PINs which were the most poorly fit. We stopped at the point when we could no longer identify intuitive functions which increased the fit of the model as measured by the adjusted coefficient of determination $\bar{R}^2$, which avoids bias in favour of extra input functions.

We were cautious to avoid over-fitting the training datasets, particularly for PINs which represent recent years, shown in Figure 2. The popularity of recent years has peaks between the current year and the year 1990, this range probably represents recent events like graduations or marriages (or perhaps registration). There is steady decline for older years, likely due to the drop-off in frequency of birthdays and events which are still memorable. Due to the large fluctuations for recent years in both datasets, and a possibly younger demographic for both datasets compared to the general population, we used a biased model for the popularity of different years in PIN selection: constant popularity for all years

**Table 2.** Results of linear regression. The percentage of the variance explained by each input function is shown for the RockYou and iPhone datasets. The final column shows estimates for the prevalence of each category from our user survey.

| factor | example | RockYou | iPhone | surveyed |
|--------|---------|---------|--------|----------|
| | | date | | |
| DDMM | 2311 | 5.26 | 1.38 | 3.07 |
| DMYY | 3876 | 9.26 | 6.46 | 5.54 |
| MMDD | 1123 | 10.00 | 9.35 | 3.66 |
| MMYY | 0683 | 0.67 | 0.20 | 0.94 |
| YYYY | 1984 | 33.39 | 7.12 | 4.95 |
| *total* | | 58.57 | 24.51 | 22.76 |
| | | keypad | | |
| adjacent | 6351 | 1.52 | 4.99 | — |
| box | 1425 | 0.01 | 0.58 | — |
| corners | 9713 | 0.19 | 1.06 | — |
| cross | 8246 | 0.17 | 0.88 | — |
| diagonal swipe | 1590 | 0.10 | 1.36 | — |
| horizontal swipe | 5987 | 0.34 | 1.42 | — |
| spelled word | 5683 | 0.70 | 8.39 | — |
| vertical swipe | 8520 | 0.06 | 4.28 | — |
| *total* | | 3.09 | 22.97 | 8.96 |
| | | numeric | | |
| ending in 69 | 6869 | 0.35 | 0.57 | — |
| digits 0-3 only | 2000 | 3.49 | 2.72 | — |
| digits 0-6 only | 5155 | 4.66 | 5.96 | — |
| repeated pair | 2525 | 2.31 | 4.11 | — |
| repeated quad | 6666 | 0.40 | 6.67 | — |
| sequential down | 3210 | 0.13 | 0.29 | — |
| sequential up | 4567 | 3.83 | 4.52 | — |
| *total* | | 15.16 | 24.85 | 4.60 |
| random selection | 3271 | 23.17 | 27.67 | 63.68 |

in the past 20 years, and linear drop-offs for years from 20–65 years in the past, and for 5 years into the future. This model, plotted in Figure 2, was used for PINs representing 4-digit years directly as well as DMYY and MMYY PINs.

After fixing the year model, we removed the range of years from the regression model to avoid skewing the model's estimation of other parameters to correct for the intentionally weakened model of the year distribution. We similarly added single-element input functions for 1234, 0000, 1111, and 2580 to avoid omitted-variable bias caused by these significant outliers.

The complete results of our final model with 25 input functions are shown in Table 2. All of the input functions were binary, except for years, calendar dates (in which Feb. 29th was discounted), and words spelled on a keypad.[7] All of

---

[7] We used the distribution of four-letter passwords in the RockYou dataset to approximate words used in spelled-out PINs. 'love' was the most common 4-letter password by a large margin, and its corresponding PIN 5683 was a significant outlier.

the input functions we chose contributed positively to the probability of a PIN being selected, making it plausible to interpret the weight assigned to each input function as the proportion of the population choosing a PIN by each method. The intercept term fits this interpretation naturally as the proportion of users choosing a random PIN. This simple model was able to fit both distributions quite accurately: the coefficient of determination $\bar{R}^2$ was 0.79 for the RockYou dataset and 0.93 for the iPhone dataset. Under the conventional interpretation, this means the model explained 79% and 93% of the variation in PIN selection.

Support for our model also comes from its accurate approximation of the source data's guessing statistics seen in Table 1. The model consistently provides an over-approximation by about 0.2–0.3 bits ($< 0.1$ dit) indicating that the inaccuracy is mainly due to missing some additional sources of skew in the PIN distribution. This is acceptable for our purposes, as it will enable us to estimate an upper bound on the guessing difficulty of the banking PINs.

## 4    Surveying Banking PIN Choices

The low frequency of many PINs in the RockYou dataset means a survey of hundreds of thousands of users would be needed to observe all PINs. Additionally, ensuring that users feel comfortable disclosing their PIN in a research survey is difficult. We addressed both problems by asking users only if their PINs fall into the generic classes captured by our regression model.

We deployed our survey online using the Amazon Mechanical Turk platform, a crowd-sourcing marketplace for short tasks. The study was advertised to US-based 'workers' as a "Short research survey about banking security" intended to take five minutes. We deliberately displayed the University of Cambridge as the responsible body to create a trust effect. To reduce the risk of re-identification, no demographic or contact information was collected. The design was approved by the responsible ethics committee at the University of Cambridge.

The survey was piloted on 20 respondents and then administered to 1,351 respondents. 1,337 responses were kept after discarding inconsistent ones.[8] Respondents were rewarded between US $0.10–0.44 including bonuses for complete submission and thoughtful feedback. Repeated participation was prohibited.

### 4.1    PIN Usage Characteristics

The 1,177 respondents with a numeric banking PIN were asked a series of questions about their PIN usage. A summary of the question phrasing and responses is provided in Appendix A. A surprising number (about 19%) of users rarely or never use their PIN, relying on cash or cheques and in-person interaction with bank tellers. Several participants reported in feedback that they distrust ATM security to the point that they don't even know their own PINs. Many

---

[8] It is common practice on Mechancial Turk tasks to include carefully-worded "test questions" to eliminate respondents who have not diligently read the instructions.

others stated that they prefer signature verification to typing in their PIN. However, 41% of participants indicated that PINs were their primary authentication method for in-store payments, with another 16% using PINs or signatures equally often. Of these users, nearly all (93%) used their PINs on at least a weekly basis.

Over half of users (53%) reported sharing their PIN with another person, though this was almost exclusively a spouse, partner, or family member. This is consistent with a 2007 study which found that about half of online banking users share their passwords with a family member [18]. Of the 40% of users with more than one payment card, over a third (34%) reported using the same PIN for all cards. This rate is lower than that for online passwords, where the average password is reused across six different sites [11]. The rate of forgotten PINs was high, at 16%, although this is again broadly consistent with estimates for online passwords, where about 5% of users forget their passwords every 3 months at large websites [11]. Finally, over a third (34%) of users re-purpose their banking PIN in another authentication system. Of these, the most common were voicemail codes (21%) and Internet passwords (15%).

## 4.2  PIN Selection Strategies

We invited the 1,108 respondents with a PIN of exactly 4 digits to identify their PIN selection method. This was the most sensitive part of the survey, and users were able to not provide this information without penalty, removing a further 27% of respondents and leaving us with 805 responses from which to estimate PIN strength. We presented users with detailed descriptions and examples for each of the selection strategies identified in our regression model. Users were also able to provide free-form feedback on how they chose their PIN. The aggregated results of our survey are shown alongside our regression model in Table 2.

The largest difference between our survey results and the regression models was a huge increase in the number of random and pseudo-random PINs: almost 64% of respondents in our survey, compared to 23% and 27% estimated for our example data sets. Of these users, 63% reported that they either used the PIN initially assigned by their bank or a PIN assigned by a previous bank.[9] Another 21% reported the use of random digits from another number assigned to them, usually either a phone number or an ID number from the government, an employer, or a university (about 30% for each source).[10]

Of users with non-random PINs, dates were by far the largest category, representing about 23% of users (comparable to the iPhone data and about half the rate of the RockYou data). The choice of date formats was similar to the other datasets with the exception of 4-digit years, which were less common in our survey. We also asked users about the significance of the dates in their PINs: 29%

---

[9] We explored the possibility that some of our participants kept their initial PIN simply because they rarely or never used their card, but the rate was statistically indistinguishable for users using their PIN at least once per week.

[10] While reusing identification numbers and phone numbers in PINs may open a user to targeted attacks, they should appear random to a guessing attacker.

**Table 3.** Guessing metrics for banking PINs, using the model computed from our survey and regression results on the iPhone dataset

| guessing scenario | $H_1$ | $\tilde{G}$ | $\tilde{\mu}_{0.5}$ | $\lambda_3$ | $\lambda_6$ |
|---|---|---|---|---|---|
| baseline | 12.90 | 12.83 | 12.56 | 1.44% | 1.94% |
| with blacklist | 13.13 | 12.95 | 12.79 | 0.12% | 0.24% |
| known birth date | 12.57 | 12.80 | 12.49 | 5.52% | 8.23% |
| blacklist, known birth date | 12.85 | 12.92 | 12.75 | 5.11% | 5.63% |
| random 4-digit PIN | 13.29 | 13.29 | 13.29 | 0.03% | 0.06% |

used their own birth date, 26% the birth date of a partner or family member, and 25% an important life event like an anniversary or graduation.

Finally, about 9% of users chose a pattern on the keypad, and 5% a numeric pattern such as repeated or sequential digits. Our sample size was insufficient to provide an accurate breakdown of users within these categories.

## 5   Approximating Banking PIN Strength

Using our survey data and regression model we estimated the distribution of banking PINs for our survey population. This was straightforward for random PINs and PINs based on dates. Within the other two categories we used the sub-distribution from the iPhone dataset due to lack of sufficient sample size.

Statistics for our best estimation are show in Table 3. By any of the aggregate metrics $\tilde{\mu}_{0.5}$, $\tilde{G}$, or $H_1$, the strength is actually quite good—between 12.6 and 12.9 bits (3.8–3.9 dits), close to the maximum possible. In other words, if an attacker can try many PINs for a targeted card, the introduction of human choice does not significantly reduce security compared to randomly-assigned PINs.

Banking PINs appear considerably more vulnerable against marginal guessing attacks. As noted in Table 3, an attacker with 3 guesses will have a $\lambda_3 = 1.4\%$ chance of success and an attacker with 6 guesses a $\lambda_6 = 1.9\%$ chance of success, equivalent to $\tilde{\lambda}_6 = 8.3$ bits of security (2.5 dits). This is significantly better than the estimates based on the RockYou or iPhone distributions (Table 1), for which $\lambda_6 > 10\%$. The optimal guessing order is 1234 followed by 1990–1986.

### 5.1   Known Birth Date Guessing

Given the large number of users who base their PIN on their birth date (nearly 7% in total, or 29% of those using some type of date), we evaluated the success of an attacker who can leverage a known birth date, for example if a card is stolen in a wallet along with an identification card. The exact effects vary slightly with the actual birth date: if variants of the date also correspond to common PINs such as 1212, the attacker's success rate will be higher. We calculated guessing probabilities for all dates from 1960–1990 and report results for the median date of June 3, 1983. In this scenario, the attacker's optimal strategy shifts to guessing, in order, 1983, 6383, 0306, 0603, 1234, and 0683. As seen in Table 3, the attacker benefits considerably from this knowledge: $\lambda_6$ increases to 8.2%, providing only $\tilde{\lambda}_6 = 6.2$ bits (1.9 dits) of security.

**Table 4.** Probability of a successful attack given multiple cards from one user. The final column is an expected value given the observed rate of card ownership.

| guessing scenario | number of stolen cards | | | | exp. |
|---|---|---|---|---|---|
| | 1 | 2 | 3 | 4 | |
| baseline | 1.9% | 2.9% | 3.9% | 4.9% | 2.5% |
| with blacklist | 0.2% | 0.5% | 0.7% | 0.9% | 0.4% |
| known birth date | 8.2% | 9.7% | 10.3% | 10.9% | 8.9% |
| blacklist, known birth date | 5.6% | 6.0% | 6.2% | 6.4% | 5.8% |
| random 4-digit PIN | 0.1% | 0.1% | 0.2% | 0.2% | 0.1% |

### 5.2  Effectiveness of Blacklisting

Assuming that users with a blacklisted PIN will be re-distributed randomly according to the rest of the distribution (as assumed in [21]), the effects of blacklisting the top 100 PINs are substantial—$\lambda_6$ drops to 0.2%.[11] This is equivalent to $\tilde{\lambda}_6 = 11.6$ bits (3.9 dits) of security, indicating that a very small blacklist may eliminate most insecurity due to human choice. Unfortunately, as seen in Table 3 and Table 4, blacklisting is much less effective against known birth date attacks, only reducing $\lambda_6$ to 5.1% ($\tilde{\lambda}_6 = 6.9$ bits/2.1 dits). With a reasonable blacklist, it is only possible to block the YYYY format, leaving an attacker to try DDMM, MMDD, and so on; preventing this would require user-specific blacklists.

### 5.3  Expected Value of a Stolen Wallet

We calculate the guessing probability of a thief with multiple stolen cards, for example from an entire wallet or purse, in Table 4. Though most of our surveyed users own only one card with a PIN, on expectation stealing a wallet instead of a single card raises a thief's guessing chances by over a third. Our survey results suggest that virtually all payment card users (99%) carry documentation of their birth date alongside their card.[12] Thus, we conclude that a competent thief will gain use of a payment card once every 11–18 stolen wallets, depending on the proportion of banks using a denied PIN list.

## 6  Concluding Remarks

The widespread security role assigned to 4-digit PINs is a historical accident which has received surprisingly little scrutiny. While complete analysis is impossible without access to a huge list of real banking PINs, it appears that user choice of banking PINs is not as bad as with other secrets like passwords. User management of PINs is also comparatively good, with lower rates of reuse and

---

[11] The optimal blacklist suggested by our model is given in Appendix B.
[12] The prevalence of carrying ID may vary by locale. In 24 US states carrying ID is legally required. In the UK, carrying ID is not required and fewer citizens carry it.

sharing and many users reporting serious thought about PIN security. However, the skew introduced by user choice may make manual guessing by thieves worthwhile—a lost or stolen wallet will be vulnerable up to 8.9% of the time in the absence of denied PIN lists, with birthday-based guessing the most effective strategy. Blacklisting appears effective only if a thief doesn't know the user's date of birth (or users stop using this to choose their PIN). We advise users not to use PINs based on a date of birth, and those banks which do not currently employ blacklists to immediately do so. Still, preventing birthday-based guessing requires a move away from customer-chosen PINs entirely.

# References

1. EMV Integrated Circuit Card Standard for Payment Systems version 4.2. EMVco (2008)
2. Issuer PIN Security Guidelines. Technical report, VISA (November 2010)
3. ISO 9564:2011 Financial services – Personal Identification Number (PIN) management and security. International Organisation for Standardisation (2011)
4. Bátiz-Lazo, B., Reid, R.J.: The Development of Cash-Dispensing Technology in the UK. IEEE Annals of the History of Computing 33, 32–45 (2011)
5. Bond, M., Zieliński, P.: Decimalisation table attacks for PIN cracking. Technical Report UCAM-CL-TR-560, University of Cambridge (January 2003)
6. Bonneau, J., Just, M., Matthews, G.: What's in a Name? Evaluating Statistical Attacks against Personal Knowledge Questions. In: Sion, R. (ed.) FC 2010. LNCS, vol. 6052, pp. 98–113. Springer, Heidelberg (2010)
7. Boztas, S.: Entropies, Guessing, and Cryptography. Technical Report 6, Department of Mathematics, Royal Melbourne Institute of Technology (1999)
8. Burr, W.E., Dodson, D.F., Polk, W.T.: Electronic Authentication Guideline. NIST Special Publication 800-63 (April 2006)
9. Cachin, C.: Entropy measures and unconditional security in cryptography. PhD thesis, ETH Zürich (1997)
10. Drimer, S., Murdoch, S.J., Anderson, R.: Optimised to Fail: Card Readers for Online Banking. In: Dingledine, R., Golle, P. (eds.) FC 2009. LNCS, vol. 5628, pp. 184–200. Springer, Heidelberg (2009)
11. Florêncio, D., Herley, C.: A large-scale study of web password habits. In: WWW 2007: Proceedings of the 16th International Conference on World Wide Web, pp. 657–666. ACM, New York (2007)
12. Ivan, A., Goodfellow, J.: Improvements in or relating to Customer-Operated Dispensing Systems. UK Patent #GB1197183 (1966)
13. Kuhn, M.: Probability Theory for Pickpockets—ec-PIN Guessing. Technical report, Purdue University (1997)
14. Massey, J.L.: Guessing and Entropy. In: Proceedings of the 1994 IEEE International Symposium on Information Theory, p. 204 (1994)
15. Morris, R., Thompson, K.: Password security: a case history. Commun. ACM 22(11), 594–597 (1979)
16. Murdoch, S.J., Drimer, S., Anderson, R., Bond, M.: Chip and PIN is Broken. In: IEEE Symposium on Security and Privacy, pp. 433–446 (2010)
17. Pliam, J.O.: On the Incomparability of Entropy and Marginal Guesswork in Brute-Force Attacks. In: Roy, B., Okamoto, E. (eds.) INDOCRYPT 2000. LNCS, vol. 1977, pp. 67–79. Springer, Heidelberg (2000)

18. Singh, S., Cabraal, A., Demosthenous, C., Astbrink, G., Furlong, M.: Password
    Sharing: Implications for Security Design Based on Social Practice. In: CHI 2007:
    Proceedings of the SIGCHI Conference on Human factors in Computing Systems,
    pp. 895–904. ACM, New York (2007)
19. Spafford, E.: Observations on Reusable Password Choices. In: Proceedings of the
    3rd USENIX Security Workshop (1992)
20. van Oorschot, P.C., Thorpe, J.: On Predictive Models and User-Drawn Graphical
    Passwords. ACM Trans. Inf. Syst. Secur. 10(4), 1–33 (2008)
21. Weir, M., Aggarwal, S., Collins, M., Stern, H.: Testing metrics for password creation
    policies by attacking large sets of revealed passwords. In: Proceedings of the 17th
    ACM Conference on Computer and Communications Security, CCS 2010, pp. 162–
    175. ACM, New York (2010)

# A   Survey Presentation and Results

The following is a summary of questions about user PIN management. The
complete survey, including questions about PIN selection, is available online at:
`http://preibusch.de/publications/pin_survey/`.

*Do you regularly use a PIN number with your payment cards?*($N = 1337$)

| yes, a 4-digit PIN | yes, a PIN of 5+ digits | no |
|---|---|---|
| 1108 (82.9%) | 69 (5.2%) | 160 (12.0%) |

*When making purchases in a shop, how do you typically pay?*($N = 1177$)

| | |
|---|---|
| I use my payment card and key in my PIN | 477 (40.5%) |
| I use my payment card and sign a receipt | 357 (30.3%) |
| I use my payment card with my PIN or my signature equally often | 184 (15.6%) |
| I normally use cash or cheque payments and rarely use payment cards | 159 (13.5%) |

*Overall, how often do you type your PIN when making a purchase in a shop? And
how often do you type your PIN at an ATM/cash machine?*($N = 1177$)

| | shop | | ATM | |
|---|---|---|---|---|
| Multiple times per day | 81 | (6.9%) | 14 | (1.2%) |
| About once per day | 117 | (9.9%) | 19 | (1.6%) |
| Several times a week | 342 | (29.1%) | 118 | (10.0%) |
| About once per week | 241 | (20.5%) | 384 | (32.6%) |
| About once per month | 113 | (9.6%) | 418 | (35.5%) |
| Rarely or never | 283 | (24.0%) | 224 | (19.0%) |

*How many payment cards with a PIN do you use?*($N = 1177$)

| 1 | 2 | 3 | 4 | 5 | 6 |
|---|---|---|---|---|---|
| 708 (60.2%) | 344 (29.2%) | 89 (7.6%) | 23 (2.0%) | 11 (0.9%) | 2 (0.2%) |

Median: 1, Mean: 1.5

*If you have more than one payment card which requires a PIN, do you use the same PIN for several cards?* $(N = 469)$

| yes | no |
|---|---|
| 161 (34.3%) | 308 (65.7%) |

*Have you ever changed the PIN associated with a payment card?* $(N = 1177)$

| Never | Yes, when I initially received the card | Yes, I change periodically |
|---|---|---|
| 591 (50.2%) | 376 (31.9%) | 210 (17.8%) |

*Have you ever forgotten your PIN and had to have your financial institution remind you or reset your card?* $(N = 1177)$

| yes | no |
|---|---|
| 186 (15.8%) | 991 (84.2%) |

*Have you ever shared your PIN with another person so that they could borrow your payment card?* $(N = 1177)$

| | | |
|---|---|---|
| spouse or significant other | 475 | (40.4%) |
| child, parent, sibling, or other family member | 204 | (17.3%) |
| friend or acquaintance | 40 | (3.4%) |
| secretary or personal assistant | 1 | (0.1%) |
| **any** | **621** | **(52.8%)** |

*Have you ever used a PIN from a payment card for something other than making a payment or retrieving money?* $(N = 1177)$

| | | |
|---|---|---|
| password for an Internet account | 180 | (15.3%) |
| password for my computer | 94 | (8.0%) |
| code for my voicemail | 242 | (20.6%) |
| to unlock the screen for mobile phone | 104 | (8.8%) |
| to unlock my SIM card | 29 | (2.5%) |
| entry code for a building | 74 | (6.3%) |
| **any** | **399** | **(33.9%)** |

*Do you carry any of the following in your wallet or purse?* $(N = 415)$[13]

| | | |
|---|---|---|
| driver's license | 377 | (90.8%) |
| passport or government ID card | 68 | (16.4%) |
| social security or other insurance card | 155 | (37.3%) |
| school or employer ID listing date of birth | 23 | (5.5%) |
| other document listing date of birth | 78 | (18.7%) |
| **any item with date of birth** | **411** | **(99.0%)** |

# B   Suggested Blacklist

According to our computed model, the following blacklist of 100 PINs is optimal:
0000, 0101–0103, 0110, 0111, 0123, 0202, 0303, 0404, 0505, 0606, 0707, 0808, 0909, 1010, 1101–1103, 1110–1112, 1123, 1201–1203, 1210–1212, 1234, 1956–2015, 2222, 2229, 2580, 3333, 4444, 5252, 5683, 6666, 7465, 7667.

---

[13] This question was sent to a random subset of respondents after the main survey.

# C   Acknowledgements

We thank Mike Bond, Andrew Lewis, Saar Drimer, Steven Murdoch, and Richard Clayton for helpful discussions about PIN security, Bernardo Bátiz-Lazo for comments about ATM history, Alastair Beresford for assistance with survey design, and Daniel Amitay for sharing data. We also thank Andra Adams, Jon Anderson, Alexandra Bowe, Omar Choudary, William Swan Helvestine, Markus Kuhn, Niraj Lal, Will Moreland, Frank Stajano, Paul van Oorschot and Robert Watson for help identifying banking practices around the world. Joseph Bonneau was supported by the Gates Cambridge Trust during this research.

# The Postmodern Ponzi Scheme: Empirical Analysis of High-Yield Investment Programs

Tyler Moore[1], Jie Han[2], and Richard Clayton[3]

[1] Computer Science Department, Wellesley College, USA
`tmoore@cs.wellesley.edu`
[2] Computer Science Department, Wellesley College, USA
`jhan@wellesley.edu`
[3] Computer Laboratory, University of Cambridge, UK
`richard.clayton@cl.cam.ac.uk`

**Abstract.** A High Yield Investment Program (HYIP) is an online Ponzi scheme, a financial fraud that pays outrageous levels of interest using money from new investors. We call this fraud 'postmodern' in that sophisticated investors understand the fraud, but hope to profit by joining early. These investors support 'aggregators' – reputation websites that track the status of HYIPs. We examine 9 months of aggregator data and show that there is no evidence of collusion between different aggregators. We use their data to measure the time until HYIPs collapse, finding – perhaps unsurprisingly – that longer lifetimes are associated with lower interest payments and longer mandatory investment terms. We look at the role of digital currencies in supporting HYIPs, finding that a handful of systems dominate. Finally, we estimate that this type of criminality is turning over at least $6 million/month and set out ways in which it might be disrupted.

## 1 Introduction

A High Yield Investment Program (HYIP) is an online version of a financial scam in which investors are promised extremely high rates of return on their investments. Payments are made to existing investors from the funds deposited by newcomers, continuing until insufficient funds remain and the scheme collapses. Similar schemes have operated in the offline world for 150 years or more and are often called *Ponzi schemes* after a famous swindler in 1920's Boston.

Despite being illegal to operate in most jurisdictions, there are a considerable number of active HYIP websites at any given time. We call them 'postmodern' Ponzi schemes because we believe that many of the investors are well aware of the fraudulent nature of the sites, but are of the opinion that by investing at an early stage – and withdrawing their money before the scheme's collapse – they will be able to make a profit at the expense of less savvy investors.

An extensive online ecosystem has developed in support of HYIPs, involving discussion websites, digital currencies, and third-party 'aggregator' websites that track HYIP performance. These aggregators list dozens of active HYIPs, tracking

A.D. Keromytis (Ed.): FC 2012, LNCS 7397, pp. 41–56, 2012.

**Fig. 1.** Screenshot of HYIP `macrotrade.com` and the corresponding entry on the aggregator `hyip.com`

core features such as interest rates, minimum investment terms and funding options. They operate forums in which individuals can report their experiences; but more significantly, the aggregators appear to make their own investments in some of the HYIPs and report on when interest payments cease. As an illustrative example, Figure 1 shows a screenshot of the HYIP `macrotrade.com`, along with its entry on the aggregator website `hyip.com`.

We have spent many months collecting data from HYIP websites and aggregators to measure the extent of HYIP activity, so that we can improve our understanding of this particular type of online criminality.

In Section 2 we explain our data collection and measurement methodology. In Section 3 we discuss our evidence as to whether the aggregator sites are making truthful[1] reports. In Section 4 we examine HYIP lifetimes and investigate the extent to which it is possible to predict their collapse. In Section 5 we discuss the role of 'digital currencies' in this ecosystem and then in Section 6 we estimate the scale of this particular type of online criminality and discuss various ways that it might be discouraged, if not entirely stamped out. In Section 7 we survey related work and finally in Section 8 we summarize what we have learned so far and consider what further work might reveal.

---

[1] We avoid the word 'honest' because this is not an appropriate word to use in conjunction with criminal activity.

# 2    Data Collection Methodology

We term the websites that provide reputation services for HYIP programs 'aggregators'. Given that HYIPs are confidence games that keep growing so long as new investors can be recruited, these ratings are potentially very powerful indicators of HYIP success or failure. From a Google search for "HYIP" issued in November 2010, we identified 9 aggregator websites to monitor (myhyip.com, maxhyip.com, iehyip.com, hyipranks.com, hyipmonitor.com, hyipinvestment.com, hyip.com, hothyips.com, and everyhyip.com).

Between November 17, 2010 and August 21, 2011 we made daily visits to each aggregator website (with the exception of four days in November and December 2010 due to a bug in our crawler). We parsed the pages we fetched to extract the key characteristics of the HYIPs they listed: interest rate, investment term(s), user and aggregator ratings, along with payment status (i.e., paying, not paying). The names aggregators use for each of these fields varied slightly, so we manually unified the terminology and stored each observation in a database. A total of 141 014 observations were made.

All the aggregator websites provide links to the HYIPs, though some of these links pass via an interstitial page. From January 2011 onwards, we determined the URL of each of the HYIPs and captured the WHOIS record for each HYIP domain. Our automated system also visited each HYIP website, and stored the source files linked to or loaded from the home page. These daily visits to the HYIP websites were made over Tor[2]; its anonymity properties help ensure that the website would not be able to identify us or trivially connect our visits.

## 2.1    Measuring HYIP Activity

We have used the collected data to derive several key measurements, whose calculation we now describe.

*Linking HYIP records across aggregators.* Unfortunately, it can be difficult to determine when two aggregators are reporting on the same HYIP. We use the website address of the HYIP as a canonical identifier, but when we failed to ascertain this (e.g., the HYIP website was shut down before we followed the link), we have compared the names that the aggregator gave to HYIPs – stripping out whitespace and punctuation and doing a caseless match.

The 9 aggregators listed 1 576 distinct HYIPs – of these, 211 did not resolve to a website and could not be identified as an HYIP which had ever been resolved. 595 HYIPs appeared on more than one aggregator website, while the other 981 appeared only once. It is likely that some of the 981 unique HYIPs are duplicates that we failed to link up; however, we treat them as distinct in our study.

*Measuring HYIP lifetimes.* One key measure of HYIP performance is how long after initial creation the scheme collapses. Identifying when a website is ready for

---

[2] http://www.torproject.org/

business is impracticable, so we deem the HYIP lifetime to be the elapsed time between the HYIP's first appearance as reported by an aggregator site (which we believe will be contemporaneous with the first accounts being created) and its eventual disappearance from that aggregator (invariably because the HYIP has collapsed and is no longer paying).

*Normalizing profit rates, investment terms, and expected payouts.* There is enormous variation in the interest rates promised by HYIPs, from the outrageous 440% in 10 minutes offered by `top-capital.com` to the comparatively modest 1–2% per day offered by `macrotrade.com`. Many HYIPs offer a menu of investment choices that vary by investment level and term, just as a legitimate bank does for their certificates of deposit (CDs).

For this paper, we start by normalizing the published interest rates and investment terms to a daily rate. We then compute an expected payout value that is standardized across HYIPs. To arrive at the expected payout, we had to infer a model of how investments grow over time. Subtly different phrasing must be interpreted differently, as indicated in the following table:

| Phrase | Interest Rate | Investment Term | Expected Payout |
|---|---|---|---|
| $x\%$ for $y$ days | $x\%$ | $y$ | $x \times y \times$ principal |
| $x\%$ in $y$ days | $\frac{x}{y}\%$ | $y$ | $x\times$ principal |
| $x\%$ after $y$ days | $\frac{x}{y}\%$ | $y$ | $x\times$ principal |
| $x\%$ daily | $x\%$ | - | - |

In every case we do *not* compound daily on the current value, but compound on the original principal. In other words, we do not assume that any of the interest that is paid out will be reinvested. We take this approach because it is consistent with the returns on investment (ROI) reported by the vast majority of aggregators. Additionally, if HYIP investors are indeed 'postmodern' and know to take profits as rapidly as possible, then their strategy will be to be put in their maximum investment at the earliest possible time and never add to it.

## 3  Can the Reports of HYIP Aggregators Be Trusted?

Given that all HYIPs are fraudulent, it is natural to ask whether the reports from aggregators should be trusted. While ascertaining ground truth is impossible, we have devised a number of measurements to assess the relative accuracy of data reported on HYIPs.

In particular, 595 of the 1 576 HYIPs (38%) are tracked by at least two aggregators and so we can compare the reports about the same HYIP across different aggregators. If there is rough consensus then, either the aggregation sites are in a universal conspiracy, or they are independently assessing the HYIPs in a truthful manner.

## 3.1 Reporting of HYIP Attributes

We determined what the aggregators reported to be the maximum and minimum investment levels allowed by the HYIP, the referral rates offered to affiliates for signing up new investors, and the withdrawal method offered (automatic, manual, or instant). When we collate this information and look for similarity we get these results:

| | Investment | | Referral Rate | | Withdrawal |
| | max | min | high | low | type |
|---|---|---|---|---|---|
| Perfect Agreement | 0.40 | 0.87 | 0.44 | 0.43 | - |
| Diversity Index | 0.72 | 0.94 | 0.77 | 0.75 | 0.88 |

The first row of this table reports the fraction of HYIPs where all aggregator reports are in perfect agreement. As can be seen, for 40% of HYIPs, the maximum allowed investment values are in agreement, while 87% of the time the minimum investment value is reported to be the same by different aggregators.

Of course these attributes are all matters of fact, which the aggregator will have obtained from the HYIP websites (or perhaps from the filling in of a form). However, the aggregators are imperfect and errors are being made. If there was collusion between aggregators and HYIPs then we would have expected to see perfect agreement – either from better channels of communication, or from a consistent set of mistakes being made.

By contrast, when we consider the amount of money that the aggregators report that they have in invested into particular HYIPs, we see very little agreement at all:

| | Aggregator Investment |
|---|---|
| Perfect Agreement | 0.10 |
| Diversity Index | 0.51 |

Any investment at all allows the aggregators to assess whether the HYIP is paying, and we have just noted there is reasonable agreement about what the minimum value might be. Therefore, we presume that the amounts being invested reflect the initial opinion of the aggregator about the prospects for the HYIP. If there was some kind of universal conspiracy then we would expect to see consistency here, but the aggregators invest the same amount of money into HYIPs in only 10% of cases.

Naturally, even when there isn't unanimous agreement across aggregators, it could still be the case that almost all of aggregators report the same values. Consequently, the two tables also report Simpson's diversity index [1] for each attribute. This measures the similarity of a sample population and it is computed as the sum of the squares of all the probabilities for each attribute value, with a 0 score showing complete diversity and complete uniformity giving a score of 1. Once again, using this measure, we see a high, but imperfect, agreement on matters of fact, but continuing diversity in the investment amount.

## 3.2   Reporting of HYIP Lifetimes

We now consider the elapsed time between when HYIPs are reported to be created – or at least when the aggregator learns of their existence – and when the HYIPs collapse and the aggregator is no longer prepared to track them.

Figure 2 (left) plots the Cumulative Distribution Function (CDF) of the standard deviations of the reported starting and ending times of HYIPs across aggregators. For around 80% of HYIPs, the standard deviation is very small, at most a few days. However, for the remaining 20% of HYIPs, there is substantial disagreement between aggregators. Furthermore, that disagreement is greater for the last observed time for an HYIP than for the starting time, as indicated by the slightly lower blue dashed line than solid red line in the graph. This is not surprising, given that deciding when to drop an HYIP from results is more of a judgement call for an aggregator than deciding whether to report its existence.

The green dotted line plots the standard deviations for an alternative measure of HYIP collapse. Aggregators keep track of their own investments in HYIPs, reporting each day the cumulative return on investment (ROI). Often, the ROI will 'flat-line' – suddenly stop changing – a few days before the aggregator stops tracking the program, because the HYIP is no longer paying out. Hence, we can view the time when the ROI stops changing as an alternative indicator of collapse. As the graph indicates, there is even more variation here – some aggregators stop receiving payments before others. Again, this is not surprising, since HYIPs may not stop all payments at once.

Aggregators generally agree on lifetime, but when there are differences they can be large, so for lifetime value we use the median of the aggregator reports. By using the median (rather than computing the mean), we are better protected against a highly divergent aggregator polluting the overall measure.

Overall, our analysis of aggregator reports is that there is no evidence of collusion, but that their measurements are generally consistent, and that our further analysis based on the median of aggregator values will be robust.

## 4   The Collapse of HYIP Programs

An HYIP scheme collapses when it can no longer make the interest payments that it has promised. While it may not have completely run out of money, a rational HYIP operator will eventually conclude that paying the next round of interest payments (or refunding someone's capital) is less lucrative than shutting the scheme down and absconding. These calculations are slightly different in cyberspace than for real world Ponzi schemes because there will be no bankruptcy and no liquidators checking to see if any value can be salvaged from the ruins.

### 4.1   How Long Do HYIPs Survive?

One subtlety in measuring HYIP lifetimes is that some schemes remained viable at the end of our study, making it impossible to observe when these schemes

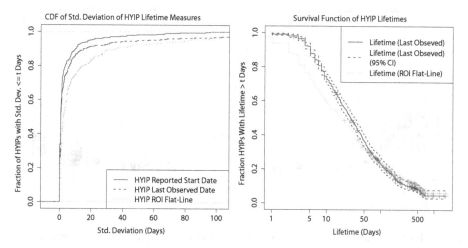

**Fig. 2.** CDF of the standard deviations of HYIP lifetimes (left); the graph indicates that aggregators assess similar lifetimes for around 80% of HYIPs. Survival function of HYIP lifetime (right); the graph shows that most HYIPs collapse within a few weeks, but that a small fraction can remain open for several years.

ultimately collapsed. This can be solved using survival analysis: the 187 (12% of the 1 576 total) HYIPs that were still operational at the end of our investigation are said to be 'right-censored'.

A survival function $S(t)$ measures the probability that an HYIP's lifetime is greater than time $t$. This is similar to a complementary cumulative distribution function, except that the censored data points must be taken into account and the probabilities estimated. We use the standard Kaplan-Meier estimator [2] to calculate a survival function for HYIP lifetimes.

Figure 2 (right), has a logarithmic x-axis and plots the observed survival function for HYIPs (using the median observed lifetimes across all aggregators). The solid blue line indicates the survival function computed using the HYIP's last observed time, while the green dotted line plots the survival function using the ROI flat-line method described in the previous section. For very short-lived HYIPs (i.e., less than one week), the lifetime measured using the ROI flat-line method is considerably shorter. However, for longer-lived schemes, the lifetimes are nearly indistinguishable, so we ignore the ROI flat-line method for subsequent analysis, and just use the median of the lifetime values.

The survival function data shows us that the while the median lifetime of HYIPs is just 28 days, one in four will last more than three months, and one in ten for more than ten months. That is, although many HYIPs collapse almost immediately, a substantial minority persist for a very long time.

## 4.2  What Factors Affect HYIP Time-to-Collapse?

Given such regular turnover and wide variation in lifetimes, it is natural to wonder what might prolong or trigger collapse.

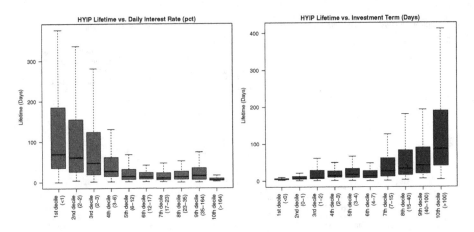

**Fig. 3.** HYIP lifetimes: HYIPs with lower daily interest rates tend to last longer before collapsing (left); HYIPs with longer mandatory investment periods tend to survive longer (right)

Figure 3 examines how the generosity of the HYIP investment terms affects the observed lifetimes. On the left, box plots for HYIP lifetimes are given that span different profit rates. When an HYIP offers a less generous profit rate (less than a few percent daily), there is a greater chance that the HYIP will survive for longer. Once the profit rates become more outlandish (such as the half of HYIPs offering more than 10% daily returns), HYIP lifetimes are more consistently short. We conclude that the offering of higher rates of return does not bring in sufficient investment to offset the cost of servicing existing commitments.

Another factor is the minimum investment period required by the HYIP. Figure 3 (right) plots HYIP lifetimes sorted by investment term. As expected, HYIPs that require longer investment terms tend to be more stable. However, we note that there is still substantial variation in lifetime even for less generous interest rates and longer investment terms. Evidently, some HYIPs cannot attract enough investment to sustain even these more modest programs.

### 4.3   Can Users or Aggregators Predict Collapse?

Several aggregators rate HYIP 'quality', often on a scale of zero to five stars. The rating can vary considerably over time, ostensibly according to the risk level associated with the scheme. Some aggregators also compile user ratings, typically collected in the form of positive (and sometimes negative) votes. We now examine how the crowd's rating compares to that of the curator's.

We focus on the four aggregators that report both user and aggregator ratings on a finite scale. Some aggregators simply tally the total number of user votes, while others report the absolute difference between positive and negative votes. We exclude these reports from our analysis to ease comparisons. The ratings we study are based on a score of zero to five, zero to ten, or out of 100; we normalize all ratings to a percentage.

While the ratings have been collected throughout an HYIP's lifespan, we have decided to take a closer look at the rating given 7 days prior to each HYIP's collapse. A low rating issued at this point would indicate to prospective investors that the bottom will soon fall out (if it has not already). The results are given in the following table.

| Aggregator | # HYIPs | User Rating | | | Aggregator Rating | | |
|---|---|---|---|---|---|---|---|
| | | Avg. | ≤50% | ≥80% | Avg. | ≤50% | ≥80% |
| everyhyip.com | 46 | 87% | 13% | 85% | 20% | 83% | 9% |
| hyip.com | 265 | 52% | 45% | 47% | 8% | 94% | 3% |
| hyipranks.com | 107 | 96% | 4% | 96% | 35% | 89% | 7% |
| hothyips.com | 292 | 50% | 48% | 46% | 32% | 92% | 0.3% |
| Average | - | 60% | 38% | 57% | 22% | 92% | 3% |

Overall, user ratings are consistently much more positive than aggregator ratings. Consider the ratings for hyipranks.com: the average user rating one week prior to collapse is 96%. Across all HYIPs, 96% were awarded a user score of 80% or higher, but only 4% had a score below 50%. By contrast, the average assessment directly issued by hyipranks.com is only 35%. Moreover, 89% of HYIPs are given a low score, compared to just 7% that receive a score over 80%.

Why do we see such divergence in ratings? Those who have already invested in an HYIP have a very strong incentive to attract new investors. Consequently, they are highly motivated to vote early and often in support of their investment. The aggregators, on the other hand, fully expect HYIPs to collapse and must provide more accurate assessments in order to gain the trust of visitors. Viewed in this way, it is not surprising that the crowd will not accurately predict collapse.

## 5    The Role of Digital Currencies

Digital currencies are an essential component of a functioning HYIP ecosystem. They allow investors to convert local hard currency into a multi-national form that is suitable for transfers to and from the HYIP. Occasionally an HYIP will directly accept wire transfers or credit card payments. However, this is unusual because if the HYIP operator works within the traditional financial system, then they risk being identified when the fraud collapses, and they will be less sure that they will be able to hang on to any profits.

We found that 22 currencies were accepted for use at the HYIPs we tracked. Most of these were only offered by a handful of HYIPs (including 14 HYIPs that took PayPal, 7 Moneybookers and 1 Western Union). We list the six most common currencies below and note that the most common, by far, were Liberty Reserve and Perfect Money, accepted by 83% and 70% of HYIPs, respectively. Both currencies are based in Central America.

| Currency | HYIPs # | % | Country | % HYIP Backlinks |
|---|---|---|---|---|
| Liberty Reserve | 1 309 | 83% | Costa Rica | 33% |
| Perfect Money | 1 095 | 70% | Panama | 72% |
| AlertPay | 397 | 25% | Canada | 10% |
| SolidTrustPay | 51 | 3.2% | Canada | 60% |
| Pecunix | 21 | 1.3% | Panama | 81% |
| GlobalDigitalPay | 20 | 1.3% | Hong Kong | 71% |

Digital currencies are riskier than traditional currencies for both the investor and the HYIP operator. When the time comes to cash in and convert back to hard currency, the exchange rate may have changed significantly, or there may be no liquidity – if many of the customers of a digital currency simultaneously ask to cash in their holdings, then the currency's operators may not be able to pay up (e.g., the HYIP-associated StrictPay currency appears to have collapsed in this way [3]).

The digital currencies that HYIPs accept have terms and conditions that forbid their use with HYIPs. This creates the additional risk that assets could be frozen or confiscated for violating the rules. Furthermore, any digital currency that facilitates widespread criminality runs the risk of being shut down by law enforcement, as happened to e-gold [4].

Liberty Reserve has a warning on its website advising against investing in HYIPs, noting that payments are 'non-revocable' and that they cannot be held liable for fraudulent activities by its users. Such admonishments raise the question: how much of these currencies' profits come from HYIP activity?

We attempt to shed light on this by examining the backlinks from other websites into the currency websites. We used Yahoo Site Explorer[3] to gather 1 000 backlinks for each of the most common currencies and calculated what proportion of the incoming links came from HYIP-related websites. The results are listed in the right-most column of the table.

72% of the backlinks to Perfect Money are from HYIP-related websites, as are 33% of the backlinks to LibertyReserve. This leads us to conclude that a substantial proportion of the revenue to these currencies comes from HYIPs. Note that for AlertPay, the third-most popular currency, only 10% of the incoming links are from HYIPs. Indeed, many of AlertPay's other incoming links are from legitimate businesses, such as the web-hosting company prodhosting.net, which uses AlertPay to process payments. AlertPay is based in Canada, and that may mean that they are more easily pressured by first world regulators, than the currencies based in Panama and Costa Rica.

## 6    Policy Options for Disrupting the HYIP Ecosystem

One of the first questions to ask when considering policy interventions into online scams is how prevalent the scam is. If only a few people are affected, then the

---

[3] http://siteexplorer.search.yahoo.com

criminality may not be worth pursuing, especially when – as in this case – many of the investors are aware that the sites are fundamentally fraudulent.

It is difficult to directly measure how many people and how much money are invested in HYIPs. However, we can use some publicly available proxies to derive an order-of-magnitude estimate of HYIP impact.

As part of its Adwords program, Google offers a Keyword Tool that returns similar search phrases to those given as input.[4] We entered the phrases "hyip" and "high yield investment program", and were returned 100 closely related phrases. Google also offers a related service called Traffic Estimator that estimates for any phrase the number of global monthly searches. We plugged all 102 HYIP-related phrases into the tool to arrive at an estimate of 441 000 monthly searches for these terms on Google.

We can use this value to create a rough estimate of the monthly investment levels to HYIPs using the following formula:

$$\frac{\$\ \text{HYIP invest}}{\text{month}} = \frac{\#\ \text{Google mo. searches}}{\text{Google market share}} \times \%\ \text{invest} \times \text{invest amount}$$

Google's global market share in search is known to be 64.4% but the other terms in this equation are much harder to estimate. We do not have reliable data on the fraction of users who learn about HYIPs that ultimately invest, or how much money they put in. A plausible, conservative, guess is that at least 1% of people who search for HYIPs go on to invest in an HYIP.

Researchers investigating spam-advertised pharmaceuticals found that 0.5% of site visitors added items to their shopping carts [5], while in an earlier study they found an approximately 8% conversion rate for non-pharmaceutical goods [6]. Leontiadis et al. estimated that between 0.3% and 3% of people looking for drugs via web search ultimately purchased the goods from illicit retailers [7]. While the investment rate for HYIPs could undoubtedly differ from that for pharmaceuticals, these data points do suggest that a 1% conversion rate for HYIPs is plausible.

From observation of the statistical information that some sites provide, we will guess that the average investment is $1 000. Plugging these numbers into the above formula we estimate that HYIPs attract at least $6 million per month in revenue.

Given that around 600 000 people search for HYIPs each month, we conclude that HYIPs are indeed a substantial scam worthy of policymakers' attention. So what should be done? We now consider a range of interventions and assess their likely impact.

*Option 1: Engage Law Enforcement.* Given that HYIPs are illegal in nearly all jurisdictions, it is logical to seek the support of law enforcement. In the US, the Commodity Futures Exchange Commission (CFTC) has been given the power to enforce violations of the Commodities Exchange Act of 1936. The CFTC regularly uncovers Ponzi schemes whose perpetrators and victims are based in

---

[4] https://adwords.google.com/select/TrafficEstimatorSandbox

the US. International cooperation is possible: the CFTC recently arrested Jeffrey Lowrance and extradited him from Peru for allegedly running a Ponzi scheme that solicited investors via the Internet [8]. Consequently, engaging the CFTC could lead to successful criminal prosecution.

However, the usual warnings about prosecuting online crime [9] apply: collecting evidence across international borders is difficult, slow and expensive; the perpetrators may be located in countries unwilling to cooperate. Google's data shows that that 85% of HYIP-related searches are made from outside the US, so victims will be spread across the globe, necessitating an international response.

Policy interventions that apply pressure to key intermediaries have historically been one of the most successful ways to address illicit activity online. For example, the US Unlawful Internet Enforcement Act of 2006 has largely eliminated online gambling by US residents by requiring payment processors to block credit-card payments to offshore gambling sites. The Digital Millenium Copyright Act of 1998 created a notice-and-takedown regime whereby online service providers receive immunity for complying with take-down requests issued by copyright holders. So we now turn to considering potential intermediaries that might be enlisted to disrupt the HYIP ecosystem.

*Option 2: Target Digital Currencies.* The digital currencies that HYIPs rely on for customer accounts are a logical target. As shown in Section 5, a handful of currencies facilitate most HYIP transactions. The biggest offenders (Liberty Reserve and Perfect Money) are undoubtedly aware of their role in funding HYIPs, so bringing it to their attention is unlikely to make any difference. The banking regulators in their claimed home countries (Costa Rica and Panama) might be persuaded to cooperate with an outside crackdown. However, even if they stopped processing HYIP payments, it is likely that alternative currencies would come to the fore.

*Option 3: Squeeze Credit-Card Payments.* Another option is to block the funding of digital currencies by credit cards. At present, a credit card can be used to fund the most popular digital currencies, including Liberty Reserve and Perfect Money. Although this is an obvious opportunity to apply pressure, it might prove difficult to identify all the intermediaries that can supply the currency, and ultimately the traffic would shift to wire transfers instead.

*Option 4: Undermine Aggregators.* A more promising approach is to disrupt the aggregators, since they are essential for establishing trust in HYIP transactions.

For example, one could target the registrars that have registered the domains in use. Persistent websites are essential for establishing the reputation of the aggregators, so they are more likely to be adversely affected by a domain name seizure than, say, malware-distributing sites. Many aggregators are currently served by North American companies (e.g., `hyip.com` and `hyipranks.com` are registered through GoDaddy, `maxhyip.com` is on Tucows, and `hyip.com` is for sale by American domain-parking firm Sedo). However, this is likely to require new legislation, since the aggregators are merely describing and linking to the

HYIP sites. It could be some time before such legislation was in place in the USA, let alone in all the jurisdictions to which the sites could move.

Alternatively, the aggregators' income stream could be disrupted. Four of the nine aggregators we studied – hyip.com, iehyip.com, hyipranks.com and hyipinvestment.com – are members of the Google Display Network. Google, and the other advertising networks, might choose not to work with sites that knowingly link to fraudulent sites. Whether stopping this source of income would cause all the sites to close cannot be known for certain, but it is relatively straightforward, and arguably in the best interests of the advertising networks to cease their financial association with criminality comparison sites.

*Option 5: Target most the successful HYIPs.* A final option is to attempt to expedite the demise of HYIP websites. While this might appear a hopelessly difficult task given that we have observed around 1 600 HYIPs in just nine months of data collection, targeting the small number of long-lived HYIPs could be effective. A long-lived HYIP is bound to be continuing to attract many victims, since new recruits are needed to prolong the life of the scam. Consequently, efforts to disrupt these programs are very likely to reap substantial rewards.

Over one third (49) of the 141 HYIPs that have been online for more than six months are registered via eNom, a US-based registrar. 26 are registered through Indian-based Directi, along with another 14 on US-based GoDaddy. Consequently, making registrars aware of the criminal behavior being facilitated by these websites could trigger a short-term disruption.

On balance, while each of the discussed options may help, we expect that options 4 and 5 are likely to be most helpful for disrupting the current HYIP ecosystem. We also believe that action by law enforcement (option 1) could do a lot of good in the longer term.

# 7   Related Work

During the past decade, online criminality has proliferated [9]. In response, a number of measurement studies have quantified various frauds and recommended suitable interventions . Of particular relevance are studies that examine user susceptibility to various scams, such as fake antivirus [10,11] and extortionate social-engineering scams [12]. Stajano and Wilson identify seven principles common to offline scams that often translate into online scams [13]. At least five of these principles apply to HYIP investment: the herd principle (false safety in numbers), the dishonesty principle (victim's own illegal behavior held against him), deception principle (things are not what they seem), need and greed principle (desperation increases vulnerability), and the time principle (time pressures increase bad choices). Consequently, while we believe that many HYIP investors are likely to be aware of the fraudulent nature of their investment, they are nonetheless being masterfully deceived by con artists. Furthermore, it is entirely plausible that some victims fully believe in the legitimacy of their investment.

The use and abuse of digital currencies has been examined since the inception of the Financial Cryptography conference. Optimists pointed to the potential to enhance revenue [14] or freedom through anonymity [15]. However, even in these early days, others fretted about the potential for abuse of digital cash, such as money laundering [16]. More recently, Anderson identified non-revocability as the key feature of digital payments that appeals most to online criminals [17]. Indeed, the non-revocability of payments issued in the currencies underpinning the HYIP ecosystem is essential for its successful operation.

The security and reliability of crowdsourcing in information security applications has been investigated by Moore and Clayton [18] (phishing) and Chia and Knapskog [19] (web security). These papers discuss the distinct challenges of crowdsourcing applications when participants may be motivated to lie, as we have found for users promoting flagging HYIPs.

A final area of relevant work is in the examination of interventions to combat online crime. In an expansive study of goods advertised by email spam, Levchenko et al. [20] found substantial concentration in the registrars used by spam-advertised websites. They also found that only 3 banks processed the bulk of payments. We report similar levels of concentration in the HYIP ecosystem. Clayton described how shutting down hosting providers that facilitate spam transmission can have a disruptive short term effect [21]. Finally, Liu et al. [22] examine the prospects of enlisting registrars to suspend 'known bad' domains, concluding that the criminals are more adept at shifting to new domains faster than the offending domains can be suspended. While this may be true for domains used in email spam, we are more optimistic for registrar-level intervention in combating HYIPs due to the persistence of successful schemes.

## 8   Conclusions and Future Work

We have presented the first detailed analysis of HYIPs – fraudulent online Ponzi schemes. We have provided some baseline measurements by leveraging data from the aggregator sites that exist to help investors pick where to place their money. We have shown that the aggregators are basically truthful, and used their data to show that HYIPs last longer with lower interest rates delays before payments are made. We have also shown that the aggregators are better than 'the crowd' in warning of HYIP collapse, which we believe is directly related to the crowd actively wishing to hype the prospects of the HYIP they are invested in.

Nontheless, this paper has only scraped the surface in measuring and understanding HYIPs, and there is much more data to collect and process. It is already clear to us that many of the sites are related to each other as criminals create new instances to replace HYIPs that have collapsed. We have been unable, so far, to use WHOIS data to identify serial offenders but we expect to make headway when we consider the structure and content of the websites.

We are particularly interested in the subset of HYIPs that provide a running commentary on the number of accounts opened, and the sums of money being invested, withdrawn and paid out as interest. We hope to use these to build a better model of HYIP collapse, and provide better estimates of the sums of money passing through these criminal enterprises.

As we extend our analysis and measurement of harm, we intend to ensure that this paper's other key contribution – a detailed analysis of how this criminality might be disrupted – may be of even greater relevance to policy makers.

# References

1. Simpson, E.H.: Measurement of diversity. Nature 163, 688 (1949)
2. Kaplan, E., Meier, P.: Nonparametric estimation from incomplete observations. Journal of the American Statistical Association 53, 457–481 (1958)
3. Lorenzini, M.: Strictpay scam: Thoughts before strictpay shutdown. HYIP News (June 2010), http://www.hyipnews.com/news/17190/
STRICTPAY-SCAM-THOUGHTS-BEFORE-STRICTPAY-SHUTDOWN/
4. Zetter, K.: Bullion and bandits: The improbable rise and fall of e-gold. Wired (June 2009), http://www.wired.com/threatlevel/2009/06/e-gold/
5. Kanich, C., Weaver, N., McCoy, D., Halvorson, T., Kreibich, C., Levchenko, K., Paxson, V., Voelker, G.M., Savage, S.: Show me the money: Characterizing spam-advertised revenue. In: Proceedings of USENIX Security 2011, San Francisco, CA (August 2011)
6. Kanich, C., Kreibich, C., Levchenko, K., Enright, B., Voelker, G., Paxson, V., Savage, S.: Spamalytics: An empirical analysis of spam marketing conversion. In: Conference on Computer and Communications Security (CCS), Alexandria, VA (October 2008)
7. Leontiadis, N., Moore, T., Christin, N.: Measuring and analyzing search-redirection attacks in the illicit online prescription drug trade. In: Proceedings of USENIX Security 2011, San Francisco, CA (August 2011)
8. Commission, C.F.E.: Press Release PR6074-11: CFTC charges Jeffery A. Lowrance and his company, First Capital Savings and Loan, with operating a million dollar foreign currency Ponzi scheme (July 2011),
http://www.cftc.gov/PressRoom/PressReleases/pr6074-11.html
9. Moore, T., Clayton, R., Anderson, R.: The economics of online crime. Journal of Economic Perspectives 23(3), 3–20 (2009)
10. Cova, M., Leita, C., Thonnard, O., Keromytis, A.D., Dacier, M.: An Analysis of Rogue AV Campaigns. In: Jha, S., Sommer, R., Kreibich, C. (eds.) RAID 2010. LNCS, vol. 6307, pp. 442–463. Springer, Heidelberg (2010)
11. Stone-Gross, B., Abman, R., Kemmerer, R.A., Kruegel, C., Steigerwald, D.G., Vigna, G.: The underground economy of fake antivirus software. In: 10th Workshop on the Economics of Information Security, Fairfax, VA (June 2011)
12. Christin, N., Yanagihara, S., Kamataki, K.: Dissecting one click frauds. In: ACM Conference on Computer and Communications Security (CCS), Chicago, IL, pp. 15–26 (October 2010)
13. Stajano, F., Wilson, P.: Understanding scam victims: seven principles for systems. security. Commun. ACM 54, 70–75 (2011)
14. Birch, D.G.W., McEvoy, N.A.: Electronic Cash - Technology will Denationalise Money. In: Hirschfeld, R. (ed.) FC 1997. LNCS, vol. 1318, pp. 95–108. Springer, Heidelberg (1997)
15. Chaum, D.: Achieving electronic privacy. Scientific American, 96–101 (August 1992)
16. Wayner, P.C.: Money Laundering: Past, Present and Future. In: Hirschfeld, R. (ed.) FC 1997. LNCS, vol. 1318, pp. 301–306. Springer, Heidelberg (1997)

17. Anderson, R.: Closing the phishing hole: Fraud, risk and nonbanks. In: Federal Reserve Bank of Kansas City – Payment System Research Conferences (2007)

18. Moore, T., Clayton, R.: Evaluating the Wisdom of Crowds in Assessing Phishing Websites. In: Tsudik, G. (ed.) FC 2008. LNCS, vol. 5143, pp. 16–30. Springer, Heidelberg (2008)

19. Chia, P.H., Knapskog, S.J.: Re-evaluating the Wisdom of Crowds in Assessing Web Security. In: Danezis, G. (ed.) FC 2011. LNCS, vol. 7035, pp. 299–314. Springer, Heidelberg (2012)

20. Levchenko, K., Chachra, N., Enright, B., Felegyhazi, M., Grier, C., Halvorson, T., Kanich, C., Kreibich, C., Liu, H., McCoy, D., Pitsillidis, A., Weaver, N., Paxson, V., Voelker, G., Savage, S.: Click trajectories: End-to-end analysis of the spam value chain. In: IEEE Symposium on Security and Privacy, Oakland, CA, pp. 431–446 (May 2011)

21. Clayton, R.: How much did shutting down McColo help? In: Sixth Conference on Email and Antispam, CEAS (July 2009)

22. Liu, H., Levchenko, K., Felegyhazi, M., Kreibich, C., Maier, G., Voelker, G.M., Savage, S.: On the effects of registrar-level intervention. In: USENIX Workshop on Large-scale Exploits and Emergent Threats (LEET), Boston, MA (March 2011)

# Deploying Secure Multi-Party Computation for Financial Data Analysis

## (Short Paper)*

Dan Bogdanov[1,2], Riivo Talviste[1,2,3], and Jan Willemson[1,3]

[1] Cybernetica, Akadeemia tee 21, 12618 Tallinn, Estonia
{dan,riivo,janwil}@cyber.ee
[2] University of Tartu, Institute of Computer Science, Liivi 2, 50409 Tartu, Estonia
[3] STACC, Akadeemia tee 15A, Tallinn 12618, Estonia

**Abstract.** We show how to collect and analyze financial data for a consortium of ICT companies using secret sharing and secure multi-party computation (MPC). This is the first time where the actual MPC computation on real data was done over the internet with computing nodes spread geographically apart. We describe the technical solution and present user feedback revealing that MPC techniques give sufficient assurance for data donors to submit their sensitive information.

**Keywords:** financial data analysis, secure multi-party computation.

## 1 Introduction

Financial metrics are collected from companies to analyze the economic situation of an industrial sector. Since this data is largely confidential, the process can not be carried out just by sending the data from one company to another. We claim that the use of secure multi-party computation (MPC) distributes the role of a trusted third party among many parties so that none of them has to be trusted unconditionally. The greatest added value for the companies is that no single data value can be seen by a single outside party after it leaves the user's computer.

In this paper we describe a secure system for collecting and analyzing financial data in an industrial consortium. The system was deployed for ITL—an Estonian non-governmental non-profit organization with the primary goal of promoting co-operation between companies engaging in the field of information and communication technology. The data collection and analysis system was built using the SHAREMIND secure computation framework [7].

Some of the details of this work have been omitted because of space limitations. The extended version of this paper that covers all these details can be found in the IACR ePrint Archive [8].

MPC has been studied for almost thirty years and recently, many MPC projects have started reaching practical results [9,10,1,7,13,15,4,11]. However, to the best

---

* This research was supported by the ERDF through EXCS and STACC; the ESF Doctoral Studies and Internationalisation Programme DoRa; the target funded theme SF0012708s06 and the Estonian Science Foundation, grant No. 8124.

A.D. Keromytis (Ed.): FC 2012, LNCS 7397, pp. 57–64, 2012.

of our knowledge, this is the first time where the actual secure multi-party function evaluation was done over a wide area network (the internet) using real data.

In 2004, J. Feigenbaum et al. implemented a privacy-preserving version of the Taulbee Survey[1] using MPC [11]. Their implementation used secret sharing at the data source and two parties evaluating a Yao circuit over a wide area network. However, their implementation was never used with real data [12].

MPC was first used in a large-scale practical application in Denmark in 2008 when a secure double auction system allowed Danish sugar beet farmers to trade contracts for their production on a nation-wide market [9]. The Danish system used three secure computation servers. In the farmers' computers, each share of private data was encrypted with a public key of one of the computation servers. The encrypted shares were sent to a central database for storing. In the data analysis phase, each computation node downloaded their corresponding shares from the central database and decrypted them. The actual MPC process was performed in a local area network set up between the three computation nodes.

## 2   Sharemind

SHAREMIND [7] is a distributed virtual machine that uses secure multi-party computation to securely process data. SHAREMIND is based on the secret sharing primitive introduced by Blakley [6] and Shamir [16]. In secret sharing, a secret value $s$ is split into a number of shares $s_1$, $s_2$, ..., $s_n$ that are distributed among the parties. Depending on the type of scheme used, the original value can be reconstructed only if the shares belonging to some predefined sets of parties are known. SHAREMIND uses the additive secret sharing scheme in the ring $\mathbb{Z}_{2^{32}}$ as this allows it to support the efficient 32-bit integer data type.

SHAREMIND uses three *data miners* to hold the shares of secret values. Secret sharing of private data is performed at the source and each share is sent to a different miner over a secure channel. The miners are connected by secure channels and run MPC protocols to evaluate secure operations on the data. The SHAREMIND protocols are secure in the *honest-but-curious* model with no more than one corrupted party. The honest-but-curious model means that security is preserved when a malicious miner attempts to use the values it sees to deduce the secret input values of all the parties without deviating from the protocol.

To set up a SHAREMIND application we first have to find three independent parties who will host the miner servers. In a distributed data collection and analysis scenario, it is possible to select the parties from the organizations involved in the process. Second, we have to implement privacy-preserving data analysis algorithms using a special high-level programming language called SECREC [14]. In the third step, we use the SHAREMIND controller library to build end-user applications that are used for collecting data, starting the analysis process and generating the reports.

---

[1] Computing Research Association, Taulbee Survey,
  http://www.cra.org/statistics

# 3    The Application Scenario

In Estonia, the Ministry of Economic Affairs and Communications publishes an economic report every year, combined from all of the annual reports of Estonian companies. However, while this report is accurate and gives a detailed overview of the country's economic situation, it is only compiled once a year and by the time it is published, the data is already more than half a year old.

Since ICT is a rapidly evolving economic sector, ITL members would like to get more up-to-date information about the sector to make better business decisions. ITL decided to collect basic financial data from its members twice a year and publish them as anonymized benchmarking results for its members. As the collected data does not have to be audited, the data collection periods can be shorter, which means that the published benchmarking results will be up-to-date.

During our interviews, ITL representatives described a solution they had imagined. They would collect the following financial indicators:

- total return, number of employees, percentage of export, added value — semi-annually;
- all of the above plus labour costs, training costs and profit — annually.

After each collection period, the values would be anonymized (i.e. the company identifiers removed) and each indicator would be sorted independently to reduce the risk of identifying some companies by just looking at a set of financial indicators. For example, combining total return, number of employees and profit, it could be easy to identify some ICT companies. However, when sorting by each indicator independently, a company that is the first when sorted by one indicator might not be the first when sorted by another indicator.

Sorting the collected data by each indicator separately gives us a slightly stronger privacy guarantee than just stripping away the identifying information. However, all of the collected data is still accessible by the ITL board, which consists of the leaders of competing ICT companies. This means that ITL members must trust the ITL board not to misuse or leak the collected information. Consequently, ITL member companies might be reluctant to participate and give away their sensitive economic information, as it can be seen by their competitors. ITL members are required to trust the board with their data and this is quite a significant assumption.

## 3.1    Reducing Trust Requirements

We proposed to use the SHAREMIND framework to collect and analyze the financial data to address the shortcomings of the initial solution. By using secret sharing at the source and distributing the sensitive values among the three SHAREMIND data miners we make sure that no single party has access to the original values. Hence, we also have a lower risk of insider attacks and unintentional disclosures (e.g. data leak via backup). Most importantly, the use of MPC reduces the trust that ITL members need to have in any single party.

After data has been collected from all of the members, the data miners engage in secure MPC protocols and sort all the collected economic indicators. The sorted indicators are then published as a spreadsheet and made accessible to the board members of ITL. The board can then calculate aggregate values and/or charts and give this edited report to the members. The data flow and visibility to different parties for this solution is shown on Figure 1.

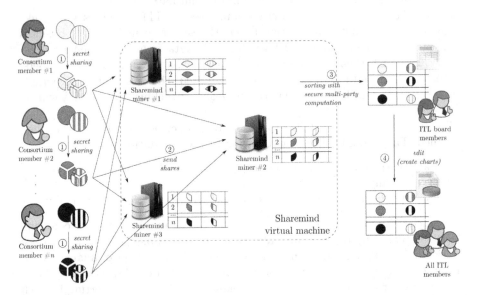

**Fig. 1.** Data flow and visibility in the improved solution using the SHAREMIND framework

## 4   The ITL Secure Data Aggregation System

### 4.1   Deployment

In the real-life deployment, the SHAREMIND miners are hosted by three Estonian companies and ITL members—Cybernetica, Microlink and Zone Media. Choosing the miner hosts among the consortium members fulfills the following requirements set for the data miners: *a*) they are motivated to host the miners, as this project would also be beneficial for themselves; *b*) they are independent and will not collude with each other as they are also inserting their own data into the system and want to keep it private; *c*) ITL members act in the field of information technology, thus they have the necessary infrastructure and competence to host a SHAREMIND server.

As the miner hosts provided their servers with no cost, they wished to reduce the effort needed to maintain the servers. Thus, all of the three miner hosts were set up by a single administrator who also regularly executes the computations. Ideally, each host should be maintained by its respective owner and this should be a rule in all future deployments of the technology. We consider it an important challenge to reduce the administrative attention required for managing a SHAREMIND miner to a minimum as this makes miner host selection easier and makes the technology easier to deploy in practice.

## 4.2 Securing Web-Based Data Collection

ITL requested that the online data submission form should be integrated into their web-based member area. This way, the representatives of ITL members can access everything related to ITL from one familiar environment. It also allows us to reuse the authentication mechanisms of the ITL web page.

We have developed a JavaScript library that can be used to turn a basic HTML form into an input source for secure MPC applications with minimal effort. This library [17] performs secret sharing on the user-entered data and distributes the shares among the three miner hosts using HTTPS connections.

*Security.* The representatives of an ITL member company can log in to the ITL member area over an HTTPS connection using either their credentials (username and password) or more securely, using the Estonian ID-card or Mobile-ID.

We use access tokens to make sure that only representatives of ITL member companies are able to send shares to the miners. A random access token is generated by the ITL web server and sent together with the form each time the financial data submission form is requested by one of the logged-in users. The JavaScript library used in the submission form sends this token together with the corresponding shares and other submission data to each miner. Before saving the received shares into the database, the miner contacts the ITL web server and confirms that this token was really generated for the current submission form, the current company and has never been used for any submission before. The latter means that access tokens also act as nonces to rule out any replay attacks.

All the communication between a miner and the ITL web server is done over the HTTPS protocol and a unique, previously agreed and pre-configured passphrase is used to identify each miner to the ITL web server. If a miner receives a positive reply from the ITL web server, it saves the received shares to its local database and notifies the submission form. If the latter receives these notifications from all three miners, it marks this submission form as "submitted" in the ITL web server. This also invalidates the used nonce.

## 4.3 Maintaining Confidentiality During Data Analysis

After the data collection period has ended, the secure MPC protocols can be started. Each SHAREMIND miner has a copy of a SECREC script that loads shares from the miner's database and uses a secure MPC implementation of an oblivious Batcher's odd-even merge sorting network [3] to sort the underlying private data vector. All of the collected financial indicator vectors are sorted separately in that manner and the results are published on the ITL web page member area for the ITL board members as an Excel spreadsheet. After reviewing the results, the board forwards this report to all other ITL members.

**Table 1.** The secure analyses performed on the collected financial data

| Analysis operation | Required MPC primitives |
|---|---|
| Sorting each financial indicator vector. | Oblivious sorting algorithm using a sorting network. Requires multiplication, addition and comparison. |
| Privacy-preserving filtering to keep only the data values that were really submitted by the end user. | Casting boolean to integer, vector multiplication. |
| Calculating a new composite indicator, *added value per employee.* | Division of secret shared values. |
| Time series for each financial indicator over all of the three forms. | Sorting the columns in a secret shared matrix by the values in one of the rows. |

*Security.* SHAREMIND uses the RakNet library[2] for its network layer. The RakNet library provides secure connections between the data miners using efficient 256-bit elliptic curve key agreement and the ChaCha stream cipher [5]. While the latter choice is not standard, the best known attacks against ChaCha are still infeasible in practice [2]. This technique is used to encrypt all the communication between the SHAREMIND miners as well as between the miners and the controller applications (e.g. analysis applications).

## 5    Secure Financial Statistics in Practice

The described solution was deployed in the beginning of 2011 and has been already used to collect financial data for several periods. After each data collection period, the system used secure MPC protocols to sort each financial indicator vector and published the results as a spreadsheet for the ITL board.

In addition to this, the ITL board requested a few extra reports. A list of the analyses performed on the collected financial data, together with the required computational routines, are listed in Table 1. The implementation was relatively effortless as we were able to create new algorithms in SECREC and deploy them at the miners. This justifies the use of a general-purpose secure MPC framework.

We conducted a survey among ITL members in the second data collection period, asking about the motivation and privacy issues of the participants. While the number of responders is not large enough to draw statistically significant conclusions, they still cover the most important players in the Estonian ICT market. As seen in Figure 2a, most of the participants feel that collecting and analyzing the sector's financial indicators is beneficial for themselves. We can also see that most of the participants are concerned about their privacy as they familiarized themselves with the security measures taken to protect the privacy of the collected data (Figure 2d) and about half of the participants submitted their data only because they felt that the system is secure in that matter (Figure 2c).

---

[2] RakNet – Multiplayer game network engine, http://www.jenkinssoftware.com

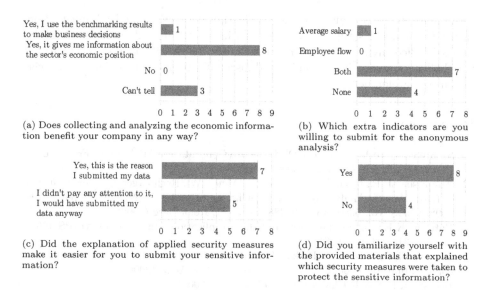

**Fig. 2.** Results from the feedback questionnaire

The fact that most of the participants are willing to submit even more indicators (see Figure 2b) shows once more that ITL members are pleased with the security measures employed in this system to protect the participants' privacy.

# 6   Conclusions and Future Work

We have described a solution for securely collecting and analyzing financial data in a consortium of ICT companies. Companies are usually reluctant to disclose their sensitive financial indicators, as it is difficult for them to trust the parties who have access to their data for the purpose of analyzing it. The use of secure MPC means that the companies do not have to trust any one party unconditionally and their sensitive data stays private throughout the analysis process.

The system was implemented and deployed in the beginning of 2011 and is in continuous use. To the best of our knowledge, this is the first practical secure MPC application where the computation nodes are in separate geographic locations and the actual MPC protocol is run on real data over the internet.

A survey conducted together with one of the collection periods shows that ICT companies are indeed concerned about the privacy of their sensitive data and using secure MPC technology gives them enough confidence to actually participate in the collective sector analysis process. Moreover, thanks to the increased security and privacy measures, many companies are also willing to submit some extra indicators during the data collection process in the future.

Based on the experience of the ITL financial statistics application we conclude that MPC-based applications can be successfully deployed for real-life problems. Performance of the available implementations is no more a bottleneck, but more effort needs to be put into making application deployment and administration easier. Our current setup works over open internet, but still assumes relatively well controlled environment for the miner hosts. The next logical step is to study the challenges arising from cloud-based installations, and this remains a subject for future developments.

# References

1. SecureSCM. Technical report D9.1: Secure Computation Models and Frameworks (July 2008), http://www.securescm.org
2. Aumasson, J.-P., Fischer, S., Khazaei, S., Meier, W., Rechberger, C.: New Features of Latin Dances: Analysis of Salsa, ChaCha, and Rumba. In: Nyberg, K. (ed.) FSE 2008. LNCS, vol. 5086, pp. 470–488. Springer, Heidelberg (2008)
3. Batcher, K.E.: Sorting networks and their applications. In: Proc. of AFIPS 1968, pp. 307–314. ACM (1968)
4. Ben-David, A., Nisan, N., Pinkas, B.: FairplayMP: a system for secure multi-party computation. In: Proc. of CCS 2008, pp. 257–266. ACM (2008)
5. Bernstein, D.J.: ChaCha, a variant of Salsa20 (2008), http://cr.yp.to/chacha.html
6. Blakley, G.R.: Safeguarding cryptographic keys. In: Proc. of AFIPS 1979, pp. 313–317. AFIPS Press (1979)
7. Bogdanov, D., Laur, S., Willemson, J.: Sharemind: A Framework for Fast Privacy-Preserving Computations. In: Jajodia, S., Lopez, J. (eds.) ESORICS 2008. LNCS, vol. 5283, pp. 192–206. Springer, Heidelberg (2008)
8. Bogdanov, D., Talviste, R., Willemson, J.: Deploying secure multi-party computation for financial data analysis. Cryptology ePrint Archive, Report 2011/662 (2011)
9. Bogetoft, P., Christensen, D.L., Damgård, I., Geisler, M., Jakobsen, T., Krøigaard, M., Nielsen, J.D., Nielsen, J.B., Nielsen, K., Pagter, J., Schwartzbach, M., Toft, T.: Secure Multiparty Computation Goes Live. In: Dingledine, R., Golle, P. (eds.) FC 2009. LNCS, vol. 5628, pp. 325–343. Springer, Heidelberg (2009)
10. Burkhart, M., Strasser, M., Many, D., Dimitropoulos, X.: SEPIA: Privacy-Preserving Aggregation of Multi-Domain Network Events and Statistics. In: Proc. of USENIX Security Symposium 2010, pp. 223–239 (2010)
11. Feigenbaum, J., Pinkas, B., Ryger, R., Saint-Jean, F.: Secure computation of surveys. In: EU Workshop on Secure Multiparty Protocols (2004)
12. Feigenbaum, J., Pinkas, B., Ryger, R., Saint-Jean, F.: Some requirements for adoption of privacy-preserving data mining. PORTIA Project White Paper (2005)
13. Henecka, W., Kögl, S., Sadeghi, A.-R., Schneider, T., Wehrenberg, I.: TASTY: tool for automating secure two-party computations. In: Proc. of CCS 2010, pp. 451–462. ACM (2010)
14. Jagomägis, R.: SecreC: a privacy-aware programming language with applications in data mining. Master's thesis, Inst. of Comp. Sci., Tartu University (2010)
15. Malka, L., Katz, J.: VMCrypt - modular software architecture for scalable secure computation. Cryptology ePrint Archive, Report 2010/584 (2010)
16. Shamir, A.: How to share a secret. Commun. ACM 22, 612–613 (1979)
17. Talviste, R.: Deploying secure multiparty computation for joint data analysis — a case study. Master's thesis, Inst. of Comp. Sci., Tartu University (2011)

# Cryptographic Rule-Based Trading
## (Short Paper)

Christopher Thorpe and Steven R. Willis

General Cryptography
{cat,swillis}@generalcryptography.com

**Abstract.** We present an interesting new protocol where participants in a securities exchange may submit cryptographically encrypted rules directly to an
exchange rather than orders to buy and sell. We define this in two parts: a secure,
partially trusted computer that runs the exchange and proves its actions correct,
and a set of participants who define the rules and submit them to the exchange.
At each "tick" of the exchange, market prices are taken from the national market system, all submitted rules are evaluated, with any resulting trades executed
at market prices. Cryptography reduces information leakage, masks participants'
intent, and provides for verification. A cryptographic audit trail proves that all
transactions executed by the exchange are according to a set of published exchange rules and the encrypted trading rules.

## 1 Introduction

In [19,18] Thorpe and Parkes introduced cryptographic exchanges for individual securities and baskets of securities, motivated by increasing transparency without the un-
favorable price impact and possible exploitation of information associated with full
disclosure. The cryptographic securities exchanges they describe require market participants to submit specific intended trades to a marketplace. Our protocol is designed to
enable a marketplace in which participants send firm commitments to rules that trigger
trades rather than the trades themselves.

Our work is motivated by growing demand for algorithmic trading, including in the
context of alternative trading systems (ATSs) and electronic clearing networks (ECNs)
for block trading. Many of these systems, known as "dark pools", keep trade information secret, and instead introduce counterparties interested in trading with one another. They typically trade large positions that would result in significant price impact
if traded on a primary securities exchange like the NASDAQ or New York Stock Exchange. Some of these systems also offer participants the ability to indicate interest in a
transaction for a defined quantity of one particular security. This limitation implies that
orders are nonbinding, which means that sometimes trades don't work out and parties
feel like they disclosed information unnecessarily.

Disclosure typically has a cost; academic and applied finance accepts that foreknowl-
edge of an large trade can be exploited for financial gain [11,9]. On the other hand,
binding orders at a fixed price result in the *free trading option* problem: a limit order
grants other market participants an option to buy or sell securities at that price, for free.

A.D. Keromytis (Ed.): FC 2012, LNCS 7397, pp. 65–72, 2012.

We illustrate the problem with an example: Say Alice places an order in a dark pool to buy 100,000 shares of XYZ Corp. at $9.00. The stock is currently trading at $10.00. Then Alice goes away for lunch and returns to discover that XYZ's CFO resigned due to accounting irregularities and the stock immediately dropped 25% to $8.00 with trading volume at several times the 90-day average. Since she was literally out to lunch and unable to cancel her buy order, Alice's order would have been immediately filled as the price dropped, as her free trading option was exercised by someone in the market. (She loses $100,000.) Harris' *Trading & Exchanges* [8] offers a detailed description of the free trading option.

Our exchange allows Alice to submit a rule-based trade rather than a simple limit order, still in the context of a dark pool where her intentions can remain secret from other market participants. The exchange executes (or does not execute) every order based on its rules, and proves that every action was based on the committed rules, rather than requiring that participants simply trust its activities. This, in the context of hardware and network security, can reduce the risk of unauthorized disclosure or trading.

These are not theoretical risks: the SEC has already settled with a major dark pool operator and two of its executives after alleging it was facilitating client trades using a subsidiary without disclosing that conflict, and leaking information to internal staff [3].

### 1.1  Properties of Our Exchange

We describe a small example language with which various rules may be expressed and represented in an encrypted form that does not reveal unnecessary information about the rules.

Such an exchange where the rules are submitted secretly but uses no cryptography has the following positive (+) and negative (−) characteristics:

+ Rules can avoid the free trading option problem.
+ Network latency between the participants and the exchange is no longer as valuable, because it is only relevant when the rules change. In fact, the exchange could require that a participant's rules can only change when the exchange is not operating.
− Everyone must trust that the exchange is operating fairly.
− Participants may be unwilling to reveal their rules, which prevents transparency or external verification.

By adding cryptography, we obtain the following characteristics:

+ The exchange can issue a trustworthy audit trail based on all market participants' encrypted algorithms.
+ The audit trail does not have to reveal anything except the encrypted algorithms and the trades they took.
+ The only trust is that the exchange is secure, and information is not leaking. The audit trail ensures correct outcomes.
+ Cryptography adds complexity and time in fast-moving markets. We separate real-time decisionmaking from asynchronous correctness proofs so that the exchange may run the rules as efficiently as possible, while still proving its activities correct after the fact.

There are clearly dangers in such a system, though these exist already in modern algorithmic trading. For example, algorithmic trading is likely to have led to a "flash crash" where computers programmed to exit in panic sold significant holdings all at once [20,10]. Algorithms could create circular trading patterns that simply trade with each other absent other information entering the market. Other risks include the security of the computer operating the exchange and its cryptographic keys, the particular implementation of the underlying cryptographic scheme, and other standard security risks associated with an applied cryptographic system.

Finally, although a collection of algorithms can lead to unintended consequences, a model in which the exchange hosts the algorithms may actually help to alleviate market risk.[1] Armed with the suite of algorithms defining how its participants behave, the exchange could run tests on the entire market to identify areas of instability without revealing any particular participant's algorithms. The ability to simulate a cohort of trading agents in various market conditions could eventually lead to better risk management for participating institutions and improve overall market stability.

In fact, U.S. senators who regulated and investigated financial markets have argued for the necessity of better audit trails and protections against future flash crashes [10]. Practical technologies may offer important solutions to these very real problems.

## 1.2  Preliminaries

For convenience and brevity, we assume a set of primitive operations for provably correct secure computation based on homomorphic cryptography as set forth in various sources, e.g. [18]. Most important is the ability to prove that a ciphertext is the encryption of the result of a polynomial function over multiple encrypted values and/or constants known to a verifier (and whose corresponding plaintexts are neither known nor learned.)

In addition, these systems permit proving inequalities: which of two ciphertexts represents a larger value; and equality: that two ciphertexts represent the same value; without revealing any further information about the ciphertexts. Interval proofs (see, for example, [2,12,15]) make this possible.

If a homomorphic cryptosystem used for the computations is homomorphic only in addition, such as the system described by Paillier [14] and elaborated by Damgård in [5] and Parkes et al. in [15], then additional preparation is required to prove results of computations employing both additions and multiplications. Rabin et al.'s scheme [16] based on splitting values into hashes of random pairs also enjoys the provably correct secrecy on addition and multiplication necessary to perform these computations. Gentry's "fully homomorphic" scheme [6,7] and related systems [21,4] do not require the prover to prove multiplications correct, simplifying the verification operations. Although they have been implemented and tested, in practice they seem to be less efficient than Paillier's scheme.

Finally, we observe that in high-frequency implementations the ability to pre- and post-process the bulk of the cryptography is critical. For example, in Paillier

---

[1] Szydlo [17] introduced the idea of homomorphic cryptography for risk analysis, though his work is limited only to an individual portfolio and not market risk.

cryptography, the most expensive operation in an encryption is a modular exponentiation of a random help value, which may be precomputed provided the result is kept secure. In practice, a market participant might prepare a large number of these precomputed values to enable rapid submission of information into a rapidly changing market. Traders are now using field-programmable gate arrays to reduce execution time [13], and some have even considered creating application-specific integrated circuits encoding the most valuable trading algorithms. Simple rules could be encoded in these hardware or firmware structures, allowing hardware to make decisions at lightning speed with software proving the results correct.

That said, our or similar protocols could be implemented on a platform such as secure multi-party computation (see e.g. Bogetoft et al. [1]) that offers stronger security guarantees. In our view, provable correctness with a partially trusted exchange is an important, intentional tradeoff of perfect security versus business pragmatics.

In this short paper, we refer the reader to this previous work for further detail on the various cryptosystems.

## 2    The Protocol

We describe an example protocol with sample rules to illustrate our idea. Our objective is not to define the only way to implement such an exchange, but to show how market designers may design an exchange in our framework.

### 2.1    The Rules

A rule is an optional trigger and an action. The trigger is a set of conditions in the marketplace, such as a price target, a difference in price movement versus that of another asset, or a trading volume target. It is inherently conditional: take an action if the conditions are true. A rule with no trigger takes place at each tick.

A trigger may also be a combination of other triggers via (else) or logical operator (and, or, xor).

The action is a trade, which we represent by a set of quantities for each security in the universe served by the market. For example, in an exchange specializing in the S&P 500 stocks, the action would consist of 500 encrypted positive or negative integers to represent how many shares to buy or sell, respectively, with each integer corresponding to a security. Some rules might have a null action (all zeroes) so that a participant can always submit the same number of rules to hide trading interest.

Some trades include a price vector which includes the least attractive prices at which the associated quantities may be traded. We also use the term "order" to refer to a trade caused by an action.

In our example, observers can also learn something about the structure of the rules by the way they are evaluated, but can't learn to which securities the rules apply. All rules are applied to vectors of securities. For example, in our universe of 500 securities, VECTOR might be a vector of 500 encryptions of prices, volume, etc. which are mostly zeroes in order to mask the relevant securities.

There may be situations in which only one of two or more rules may be triggered. Thus, the exchange also needs a policy to break ties. A rigorous treatment of tiebreaking is beyond the scope of the short paper format, but because arbitrary computations can be proven correct, many tiebreaking functions are possible; some of these include random precedence, global welfare maximization, or precedence by submission time.

An `alert` is a "panic button" in which a rule may indicate that the computer has encountered an unexpected market situation and seeks human intervention or guidance.

For our example, we define a simple language in which each rule may be built. We propose a simple language to illustrate what this might look like. Each executed action results in an `id`, e.g. a confirmation number so that an order may be canceled later. Some orders are easily encoded, e.g. stop loss orders, which are a trigger to sell when the market prices drop below the stop loss. It would be straightforward to extend to more complex orders, e.g. "fill or kill" that required immediate and complete execution.

```
RULE:      ACTION
RULE:      if TRIGGER ACTION
RULE:      if TRIGGER ACTION else RULE
ACTION:    ACTION, ACTION            -- an action may be a sequence
ACTION:    trade VECTOR              -- market order: shares
ACTION:    trade VECTOR at VECTOR    -- limit order:  shares at prices
ACTION:    cancel ACTION_ID
ACTION:    alert
TRIGGER:   (TRIGGER)
TRIGGER:   TRIGGER and|or|xor TRIGGER
TRIGGER:   now between BEFORE and AFTER    -- date/time comparison
TRIGGER:   prices > VECTOR
TRIGGER:   volume > VECTOR
VECTOR:    [AMOUNT, AMOUNT, ... AMOUNT]    -- one for each security
AMOUNT:    +|- (${dollar amount}|{integer} shares)
SYMBOL:    { universe of securities }
ACTION:ID: { id of previously executed action }
```

So, for example, one rule might be "At each round, I'd like to buy 1,000 shares of security #2 for up to $50 per share if volume is less than 10,000 shares, or up to $45 per share if volume is less than 20,000 shares."[2]

```
if ( volume < [NA, 10000, ...] and prices <= [NA, 50, ...] )
   or ( volume < [NA, 20000, ...] and prices <= [NA, 45, ...] )
trade [0, +1000, ...]
```

A market maker might guarantee certain securities can be traded at all points in time at some cost with simple price-bounded rules.

For her part, Alice, to avoid losing her lunch upon returning to the office, might have submitted an order like the following:

```
if ( price <= [NA, 9.00, ...] and volume < [NA, 20000000, ...] )
   id = trade [0, +100000, ...] at [NA, 9.00, ...]
if ( volume > [NA, 20000000, ...] )
   cancel id
```

---

[2] A participant may wish to trade a smaller number of shares in several trades over time to obtain an average price.

Alice places a conditional order to buy 100,000 shares if the price drops to $9.00 per share and volume is within 2x of normal. However, she also places an order to cancel her limit order if it is triggered and volume later exceeds normal trading volume. Alice can keep her orders secret but retain protection against the free trading option of a limit order.

In practice, NA values will be implemented by an extremely large (functionally infinite) positive integer for upper bounds, and an extremely large negative integer for lower bounds, so that those elements of each vector are always matched. Care should be taken if encoding these values in a finite field commonly used by homomorphic encryption schemes to ensure that the interval proofs remain valid.

## 2.2  Exchange Process

For simplicity, we have designed the process to occur at discrete time intervals rather than as a stream of orders as is common in many electronic trading systems.

The exchange is able to decrypt the trading rules in the setup phase, and the verification takes place after the fact. All live trading is conducted in real time by the exchange; the cryptographic proofs serve to keep everyone honest.

The discrete ticks driving the exchange forward might occur at the arrival of each new quotation, every second, every hour, or at other designated times of day. At each tick, the exchange establishes a "market price" for the securities from existing quotations for the security. In synchronous models with longer discrete times between ticks, the exchange would obtain market prices from a fair source, for example, equities traded on the New York Stock Exchange and NASDAQ might trade at the midpoint of the national best bid and offer (NBBO). This technique is used by existing dark pools.

The exchange conducts the following steps:

**Setup.** *The exchange accepts encrypted rules from all participants* before evaluating the rules at each tick. The exchange and the participants also publish their encrypted rules. These are used to validate the audit trail.

The following steps are repeated for each tick:

**Step 0.** (Optional.) *The exchange withdraws any rules at participants' requests.*

**Step 1.** *The exchange evaluates all the rules* based on the time and date of the tick, and the market prices at the time of the exchange.

**Step 2.** *The market clears at exchange prices* according to the submitted trading rules and exchange policies. In this step, the market first evaluates every trigger, then generates a list of trades to execute. In the event of incompatible trades, ties are broken according to published rules (possibly including randomness).

**Step 3 (offline).** *The exchange publishes a proof* proving why the accepted trades are consistent with policies and the trading rules. For example, to prove

( volume < [NA, 10000, ...] and prices <= [NA, 50, ...] )

the proof would use the participant's encryptions of [NA, 10000, ...], [NA, 50, ...] and issue pairwise proofs for the current trading volume and price of each security. Proofs of any broken ties are also issued.

In this case, the exchange would prove that (a) the volume of security 0 is less than NA (a huge integer) and the volume of security 1 is less than 10,000; and (a) the price of security 0 is less than NA (a huge integer) and the price of security 1 is less than $50. This adds the (encrypted) trade vector [0, 1000, ...] to the list of executed trades for that participant. Because the trade vectors can be encrypted, an aggregate trade vector across all trades can be printed. This can further mask a trading algorithm while still providing transparency and auditability.

**Step 4 (offline).** *The exchange publishes a record* ("prints the ticker") of the accepted trades in accordance with regulation and notifies the participants whose rules generated trades. The exchange issues a proof that the encrypted trade vectors of all executed trades sum to the zero vector [0, 0, ... 0] (assuming no public offerings!).

**Afterward,** *anyone can verify the proof* using the encrypted trading rules.

# 3   Conclusions

When compared to existing dark pools, our protocol offers a few material advantages. First, it permits participants to see that their trades are being executed according to the rules without favoring particular parties (e.g. clients with other business.) Second, it protects them from having to monitor exchange movements in real time on their own. Third, it enables the exchange to examine systemic risks or even simulate various scenarios on the market in a fundamentally new way.

There are rich implications for risk management. Participants are able to judge for themselves what "bad news" looks like based on market information ahead of time and have those rules within the exchange before a big event. That also means that participants don't have to worry about whether their connection to the exchange will be up or whether they can get trade execution during a crisis moment.

On the other hand, it is not known whether market participants will be willing to share trading rules with a third party, even if it is a locked down computer system. This information may be simply too sensitive for some. Based on the evidence that some institutions share meaningful information with ECN's like LiquidNet and Pipeline, we believe that an exchange that offers better liquidity, lower price, or reduced disclosure may be interesting.

It may also be challenging to craft a set of rules that offer sufficient expressiveness while still working within our provably correct framework. Nonetheless, we view this novel approach as an interesting continuation of past research in applications of cryptography in exchanges of assets.

Future work on this topic might include a richer set of trading rules, a prototype implementation of an exchange with performance analysis, and additional discussion with market participants about what features they would like to see.

# References

1. Bogetoft, P., Damgård, I., Jakobsen, T., Nielsen, K., Pagter, J., Toft, T.: A Practical Implementation of Secure Auctions Based on Multiparty Integer Computation. In: Di Crescenzo, G., Rubin, A. (eds.) FC 2006. LNCS, vol. 4107, pp. 142–147. Springer, Heidelberg (2006)
2. Boudot, F.: Efficient Proofs that a Committed Number Lies in an Interval. In: Preneel, B. (ed.) EUROCRYPT 2000. LNCS, vol. 1807, pp. 431–444. Springer, Heidelberg (2000)

3. Bunge, J.: 'dark pool' settlement shines light on potential abuses. The Wall Street Journal (October 25, 2011)
4. Coron, J.-S., Mandal, A., Naccache, D., Tibouchi, M.: Fully Homomorphic Encryption over the Integers with Shorter Public Keys. In: Rogaway, P. (ed.) CRYPTO 2011. LNCS, vol. 6841, pp. 487–504. Springer, Heidelberg (2011)
5. Damgård, I., Jurik, M.: A Generalisation, a Simplification and Some Applications of Paillier's Probabilistic Public-key System. In: Kim, K. (ed.) PKC 2001. LNCS, vol. 1992, pp. 119–136. Springer, Heidelberg (2001)
6. Gentry, C.: Fully homomorphic encryption using ideal lattices. In: STOC, pp. 169–178 (2009)
7. Gentry, C., Halevi, S.: Implementing Gentry's Fully-Homomorphic Encryption Scheme. In: Paterson, K.G. (ed.) EUROCRYPT 2011. LNCS, vol. 6632, pp. 129–148. Springer, Heidelberg (2011)
8. Harris, L.: Trading and Exchanges. Oxford University Press (2003)
9. Johnson, J., Tabb, L.: Groping in the dark: Navigating crossing networks and other dark pools of liquidity (January 31, 2007)
10. Kaufman, E.E., Levin, C.M.: Preventing the next flash crash. The New York Times (May 5, 2011)
11. Keim, D.B., Madhavan, A.: The upstairs market for large-block transactions: Analysis and measurement of price effects. Review of Finacial Studies 9, 1–36 (1996)
12. Kiayias, A., Yung, M.: Efficient Cryptographic Protocols Realizing E-Markets with Price Discrimination. In: Di Crescenzo, G., Rubin, A. (eds.) FC 2006. LNCS, vol. 4107, pp. 311–325. Springer, Heidelberg (2006)
13. Madhavapeddy, A., Singh, S.: Reconfigurable data processing for clouds. In: Proc. IEEE 19th Annual International Symposium on Field-Programmable Custom Computing Machines (FCCM), May 1-3 (2011)
14. Paillier, P.: Public-Key Cryptosystems Based on Composite Degree Residuosity Classes. In: Stern, J. (ed.) EUROCRYPT 1999. LNCS, vol. 1592, pp. 223–239. Springer, Heidelberg (1999)
15. Parkes, D.C., Rabin, M.O., Shieber, S.M., Thorpe, C.A.: Practical secrecy-preserving, verifiably correct and trustworthy auctions. In: Electronic Commerce Research and Applications (2008) (to appear)
16. Rabin, M.O., Servedio, R.A., Thorpe, C.: Highly efficient secrecy-preserving proofs of correctness of computations and applications. In: Proc. IEEE Symposium on Logic in Computer Science (2007)
17. Szydlo, M.: Risk Assurance for Hedge Funds Using Zero Knowledge Proofs. In: Patrick, A.S., Yung, M. (eds.) FC 2005. LNCS, vol. 3570, pp. 156–171. Springer, Heidelberg (2005)
18. Thorpe, C., Parkes, D.C.: Cryptographic Combinatorial Securities Exchanges. In: Dingledine, R., Golle, P. (eds.) FC 2009. LNCS, vol. 5628, pp. 285–304. Springer, Heidelberg (2009)
19. Thorpe, C., Parkes, D.C.: Cryptographic Securities Exchanges. In: Dietrich, S., Dhamija, R. (eds.) FC 2007 and USEC 2007. LNCS, vol. 4886, pp. 163–178. Springer, Heidelberg (2007)
20. U.S. CFTC and U.S. SEC. Findings Regarding the Market Events of May 6, 2010 (September 30, 2010)
21. van Dijk, M., Gentry, C., Halevi, S., Vaikuntanathan, V.: Fully homomorphic encryption over the integers. Cryptology ePrint Archive, Report 2009/616 (2009)

# Efficient Private Proximity Testing
# with GSM Location Sketches

Zi Lin, Denis Foo Kune, and Nicholas Hopper

Computer Science & Engineering, University of Minnesota,
Minneapolis, MN 55455
{lin,foo,hopper}@cs.umn.edu

**Abstract.** A protocol for private proximity testing allows two mobile users communicating through an untrusted third party to test whether they are in close physical proximity without revealing any additional information about their locations. At NDSS 2011, Narayanan and others introduced the use of unpredictable sets of "location tags" to secure these schemes against attacks based on guessing another user's location. Due to the need to perform privacy-preserving threshold set intersection, their scheme was not very efficient. We provably reduce threshold set intersection on location tags to equality testing using a de-duplication technique known as shingling. Due to the simplicity of private equality testing, our resulting scheme for location tag-based private proximity testing is several orders of magnitude more efficient than previous solutions. We also explore GSM cellular networks as a new source of location tags, and demonstrate empirically that our proposed location tag scheme has strong unpredictability and reproducibility.

## 1 Introduction

The ability to test for physical proximity to one's friends, co-workers, family, or acquaintances can be useful in a variety of settings. For example, proximity testing has been found to facilitate in-person collaboration and thus increase work productivity [17]. It also has potential for building social networks, since sharing proximity frequently over time indicates common activities and interests, an important factor in friendship [25]. Narayanan et al. [22] list a variety of further scenarios in which it might be useful.

Although RF-based Inter-personal awareness devices (IPAD) were developed in 1991 [17], proximity awareness did not gain much attention until the proliferation of smartphones and online social networking sites. Equipped with GPS receivers and/or base station triangulation, most smartphones are able to pinpoint their geographic coordinates. As a result, several social networking services have been built to use these features. These location-based services ask phone users to submit their presence in a given venue ("check-in") so that friends can interact based on the location proximity. While these services offer many benefits, they also carry significant risks: users must trust the service providers and their friends to handle this location data properly. Unfortunately, it is well-established that indiscriminate handling of location information can lead to a variety of undesirable outcomes, including threats to the physical safety and well-being

A.D. Keromytis (Ed.): FC 2012, LNCS 7397, pp. 73–88, 2012.

of users. As a result, a variety of "privacy-preserving" proximity tests have been proposed, allowing users to compare their locations so that nothing about their locations is revealed if they are not nearby.

Perhaps the most efficient such construction is due to Narayanan et al. [22] who also point out that most previous approaches suffer a common vulnerability; a malicious user can substitute a different location from her own in an attempt to learn or confirm the location of other users. To cope with this problem, Narayanan et al. introduce the concept of location tags. A location tag is a collection of characteristic features derived from the unique combination of time and location. In other words, an ephemeral key that can only be obtained at a given time and a given location. Proximity testing through location tags eliminates the threat of an online attacker who wants to learn the location of the other remote party by actively lying about her own location. Friends recording location tags will be able to test whether they are proximate by measuring the similarity of their tags privately. If they are close enough, i.e. the simiarlity is above a preset threshold, they will be notified, otherwise they learn nothing. However, private threshold set intersection is an expensive primitive that mobile phones may not be capable of executing in a timely fashion.

We address the similarity test in a novel way. We observe that since location tags are sets of high-entropy elements, they are either essentially disjoint or essentially identical. Thus an efficient test that has high probability of accepting near-identical sets and high probability of rejecting near-disjoint sets is sufficient. We adopt de-duplication techniques to reduce "nearly identical" testing to simple equality testing. We also seek to compute location tags from sources other than WiFi, which has a limited coverage and leaves blind voids between different access points.

The main contributions of this work are the following:

1. We reduce location tag based proximity testing to efficient private equality testing, using the shingling de-duplication technique. Via shingling, we generate a concise sketch for each set of location tags. Location proximity should lead to two nearly-identical sets of location tags. Nearly identical sets should yield the same sketch with high probability. Therefore, we are able to test proximity through equality. Private equality testing is more efficient than private threshold set intersection, and requires less tuning.
2. We explore the cellular network as a source of location tags. Compared to WiFi, cellular networks have much better coverage and are much more reliable. In particular, we are able to take the content from the broadcast "paging" channel of GSM cellular networks. Two phones listening to the same channel at the same time period should hear almost identical content. This source of location tags has not been proposed or investigated in the literature previously. We evaluate these location tags by building a prototype that records actual readings from cellular networks.

We organize the paper as follows: We briefly reviewed related literature in section 2. And A high-level description of our system is given in section 3. We elaborate how we capture location tags in the cellular infrastructure and explain in detail how we integrate shingling with location tag requirements in sections 4 and 5. Experiments and results are reported in section 6, followed by discussion in section 7. Our conclusions appear in section 8.

## 2 Related Work

**Proximity Awareness Devices.** Wireless RF-based devices that detect physical proximity, called Inter-Personal Awareness Devices (IPAD), were introduced by Holmquist et al. in 1991 [17]. A prototype, Hummingbird, [17] was developed: wearable devices that hummed when two of them were close enough, e.g. within 100 meters. The hummingbird provided continuous updates while complementing the usage of phones, pagers and computers since it did not require infrastructure support.

**Location Privacy.** Atallah and Du studied secure multi-party geometry computations [6]. Although computationally expensive, these protocols allowed honest users to learn whether they are closer than a mutually agreed threshold. But a malicious user could have lied about his/her location in order to learn the other party's rough location. Based on their work, Zhong, Goldberg and Hengartner introduced three protocols for private proximity detection [27] that can either reveal the liar or cost him an exceptional amount of work.

Location privacy by anonymization has been studied extensively. Beresford and Stajano introduced the concept of "mix zones" [7] and Gruteser and Grunwald [14] introduced "cloaking" for k-anonymization. Hundreds of papers have since been published for location anonymization. However, anonymization by quantization or mixing may not provide the desired privacy for a variety of reasons [24]; in one example, the obfuscated location becomes more accurate when well populated.

Location tags, initially studied by Qiu et al. in [11,23] as time-invariant location characteristics, were extended by Narayanan et al. to be a nonce associated with a unique location and time combination [22]. With proper location tags, location proximity can be reduced to measuring similarity between two sets of tags. Narayanan et al. suggested deriving tags from surrounding environment including WiFi traffic and Access Point identifiers, GSM signals, audio and even atmospheric gas composition.

**Private Set Operations and Private Equality Testing (PET).** In multi-party protocols for Private set operations, each participant has a set of elements as input and the parties wish to compute some operation on the sets while revealing nothing about the inputs beyond the result. Freedman et al. studied a private set intersection (PSI) protocol based on homomorphic encryption [13]. Kissner and Song presented a general protocol for multi-party set operations [21]. Protocols focusing on different aspects of private set intersection have been abundant [10, 15, 16, 19, 20]. When both participants have a singleton set, PSI reduces to private equality testing (PET).

A seminal work by Fagin, Naor and Winkler presented multiple PET protocols [12]. Inspired by PSI protocols, Narayanan et al. [22] described two efficient PET protocols, which we describe in the next section. In contrast to these works, we study how to reduce set *similarity* measurements – operations on non-singleton sets – to PET.

# 3   System Overview

In this section we first give a brief high-level overview of our approach. Details of the new building blocks are discussed in sections 4 and 5. The overall architecture is shown in Figure 1. It has three major ingredients, the first two of which are new in this work:

1. GSM paging channel dumping: mobile phones record all messages received on a special broadcast channel used by all phones in range of the same cellular tower, or in the same location area.
2. Location sketch generation by shingling: phones use the shingling document de-duplication technique to produce a short string (a *sketch*) that represents the set of broadcast messages received, such that if two sets are similar, then they will have the same sketch with high probability; if they are not similar, then with high probability the sketches will be different.
3. Private equality testing: Given a location sketch, phones can test for proximity using a private equality test on their sketches.

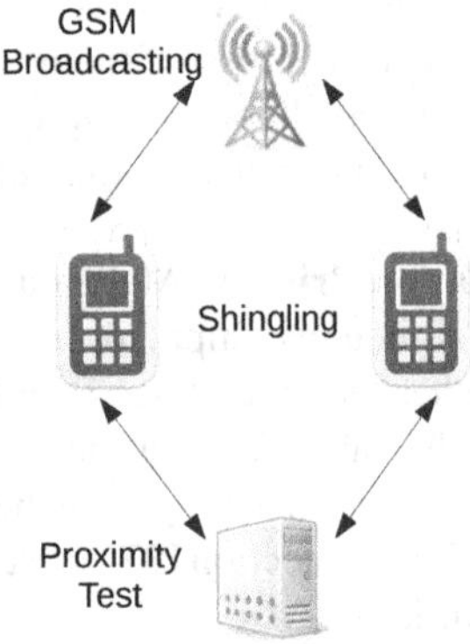

## 3.1   GSM Location Tags

The previous work on location tags used wireless broadcast messages over IEEE 802.11 networks [22], but with a range limited to the access points belonging to a given WLAN. To provide wider coverage, we use the GSM network with base stations broadcasting at much higher power and covering a much wider area. Particularly, we use the set of messages received on the GSM paging channel as elements of a location tag set. When the cellular network initiates contact with a mobile station (phone), it issues a paging request on the broadcast paging channel of all base stations within a specific local calling area (of size at most $100km^2$) referred to as a Location Area Code (LAC). The mobile station then answers back and is assigned radio resources specific to a particular base transceiver station (BTS) with an immediate assignment message, with a range of at most $1km^2$. Each mobile station is assigned a Temporary Mobile Subscriber Identity (TMSI) or a unique International Mobile Subscriber Identity (IMSI). In our measurements, we observed that paging requests are mostly issued using TMSIs (90% of the total paging requests

**Fig. 1.** The overall architecture of location tag system

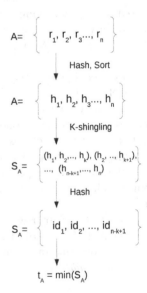

**Fig. 2.** The shingling process

captured). Since the TMSIs are local to a given LAC and one mobile phone only belongs to one LAC at a time, a mobile phone will get a new random TMSI once it travels from one LAC to another. As a consequence, two phones on the same LAC will likely observe the same set of TMSIs on paging requests. On the contrary, two phones on different LACs will likely see disjoint sets of TMSIs. This makes the set of TMSIs seen on the paging channel a good candidate for location tags. In addition, the Immediate Assignment traffic is specific to each base tower within an LAC and can be combined with the TMSIs of paging requests to produce finer-grained location tags.

## 3.2   Location Sketches

To measure the similarity between two sets of location tags, we adopt a mechanism called "Shingling" from the area of text mining/fingerprinting, which originally was used to detect (almost-)identical documents. The intuition is that we derive a sketch from a document such that the similarity between sketches will be high with a high probability when two documents are close to identical. Rather than viewing documents as ordered lists, we consider sets by simply reducing each document to a canonical sorted collection of elements. In this paper, the shingling process is shown in Figure 2.

We define the following concepts adopted from document shingling:

**Definition 1.** *k-shingle: a k-tuple which consists of k consecutive elements of a set D, which is presented as a list of sorted elements. We define the k-shingling of a set D to be the set of all unique k-shingles of D, $S_D = \{s_1, s_2, \ldots, s_n\}$*

For example, the 3-shingling of set { step, on, no, pets, } is the set {(no, on, pets), (on, pets, step) }.[1] It is not hard to see that nearly identical sets will generate nearly identical shingling. Furthermore, each unique shingle can be indexed by a numerical unique id (UID). By shingling we convert a set $D$ into $S_D$, a set of uids. We reduce similarity testing on sets to similarity testing on shinglings.

The "resemblance" between sets $A$ and $B$ is defined by $r(A, B) = \frac{|S_A \cap S_B|}{|S_A \cup S_B|}$ Note that the resemblance definition is different than classical Jaccard index [18] of $A$ and $B$, which is $J(A, B) = \frac{|A \cap B|}{|A \cup B|}$. It is, however, the Jaccard index on shingling sets $S_A$ and $S_B$. With a random permutation $\pi: \{0, 1\}^n \to \{0, 1\}^n$, it is not hard to see that

$$\Pr[min\{\pi(S_A)\} = min\{\pi(S_B)\}] = r(A, B) ,$$

allowing us to reduce the similarity test to an equality test.

UID generation and random permutation together can be accomplished by using cryptographic hash functions $h: \{0, 1\}^* \to \{0, 1\}^n$ (In [9], Rabin fingerprinting is applied). We can therefore save the permutation step, since $min\{\pi(S_A)\}$ and $min\{S_A\}$ will have the same distribution.

**Theorem 1.** *When Jaccard index between A and B is approximately 1, $min\{S_A\}$ and $min\{S_B\}$ are identical with high probability.*

---

[1] Note that we sort the set to get the sequence (no, on, pets, step).

*Proof.* With the union bound, $\Pr[min\{S_A\} = min\{S_B\}] = r(A, B) = \frac{|S_A \cap S_B|}{|S_A \cup S_B|} \geq 1 - k(1 - J(A, B)) \approx 1$

Now we define $min\{S_A\}$ as the sketch of $S_A$, denoted as $t_A$ in Figure 2. If users $A$ and $B$ have similar sets of location tags, then with high probability $t_A = t_B$, and if their location tag sets are distinct, then with all but negligible probability, $t_A \neq t_B$. Thus similarity testing can be achieved by equality testing on sketches.

## 3.3   Private Equality Test

To test proximity, we test equality of sketches. Surely being aware of privacy issues, users doesn't want to reveal their sketches nor will they trust a third-party to carry out the operation for them. Fortunately it is possible for multiple parties to test equality privately. For example, we can utilize any of the existing solutions to Yao's millionaire problem [26]. Private equality tests (PET) have been extensively studied in the literature.

In [22], Narayanan et al. discussed two protocols for PET, that are particularly well-suited to the mobile phone with online social network setting:

- **Synchronous PET.** Based on additive homomorphic ElGamal encryption, Alice sends an encryption $E(a)$ of her input $a$ to Bob. In turn Bob derives $E(s(a - b))$ from $E(a)$, with random $s$ and his input $b$ only. If $a = b$, Alice will decrypt 0 from $E(s(a-b))$. Otherwise Alice gets a non-zero random number after decryption. The protocol requires both parties to be online.
- **Asynchronous PET with Oblivious Server.** Closely related to multi-party secret-sharing, this protocol assumes no party is colluding with any other. It allows tag submission and actual tag equality testing to happen at different times. This protocol enjoys better efficiency over the synchronous one at the cost of the additional security assumption of a non-colluding server. Essentially, the protocol assumes Alice and Bob share two keys $k_1, k_2 \in_R \mathbb{Z}_p$ and Bob and the server share a key $r \in_R \mathbb{Z}_p$. Bob first sends the server $m_b = r(b + k_1) + k_2$. Later, when Alice wants to test equality, she sends the server $m_a = a + k_1$, and the server responds with $m_s = r \cdot m_a - m_b = r(b - a) - k_2$. Alice computes $m_s + k_2$, which will be 0 if $a = b$ and a random element of $\mathbb{Z}_p$ otherwise.[2]

Originally in [22] PET protocols were used to test whether Alice and Bob were within the same location on a map divided into overlapping hexagonal grids, assuming Alice and Bob are honest. Location tags (if unpredictable and reproducible) would enhance the security because neither Alice nor Bob could gain anything by lying about their location. However, since wireless nodes in close proximity will generally see similar but not identical traffic (due to noise and physical location relative to the base station), Alice and Bob were forced to use a much more expensive threshold private set intersection protocol to determine if their location tags are similar.

The advantage of PET over private set intersection protocols is efficiency. When the sets under consideration are as large as several hundreds (or thousands) of elements,

---

[2] [22] includes additional information to pseudorandomly generate and rotate the single-use shared keys $r, k_1, k_2$.

which is the case with location tags, PET outperforms PSI by several orders of magnitude. With location sketches, we achieve the "best of both worlds," allowing the use of a simple PET with unpredictable location sketches.

## 4    Cellular Networks

The use of cellular phones is already pervasive with 5 billion users worldwide in 2010 [2]. A side effect of the protocols currently in use is that base stations are constantly broadcasting the unique or pseudorandom identifiers of mobile stations they are trying to contact. In this work, we focus on the GSM network with over 3.5 billion worldwide subscribers in 2009 [1], but the techniques are applicable to other cellular networks with broadcast paging channels similar to GSM. Since the paging traffic depends on the mobile stations (phones) being served in a geographic area, the paging channel will be different for phones in different LACs, but similar in the same LAC. Since an LAC can cover areas of up to $100km^2$, it is useful to have another test to determine proximity with higher granularity. The Immediate Assignment message traffic is specific to a BTS since it is an allocation of radio resources from that tower. Devices camped on different towers will observe different Immediate Assignment message traffic. In an urban environment, we have observed that the typical range of a BTS is around $1km^2$. We use those broadcast messages at the LAC and base station level to increase the area covered by location tags.

### 4.1    Infrastructure Overview

For the purposes of this work, we can view a typical cellular network as being composed of a number of towers (BTS) belonging to an LAC and connected to a core network. That central network contains a location register (HLR) that keeps track of each mobile station's last known location. The cellular network is then connected to the regular phone Public Switched Telephone Network (PSTN) system [5].

Most of the messages between a BTS and a mobile station including voice and data transmissions, are done with frequencies and codes unique to that BTS-mobile station

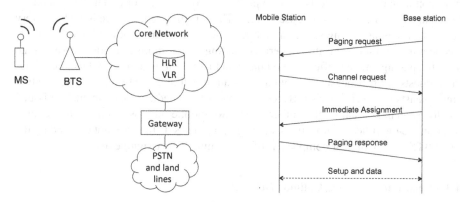

**Fig. 3.** Overview of a cellular network connected to the PSTN

**Fig. 4.** Sequence diagram for the air interface between the MS and the BTS

pair [4]. However, there are dedicated broadcast channels that all mobile stations have to listen to. In particular, the broadcast paging channel downlink is used to notify a mobile station that it needs to contact the BTS [4]. Mobile stations tune or camp on a particular frequency for their service providers and are able to hear all the pages being issued in the LAC as well as Immediate Assignment messages allocating radio resources for a particular BTS. Each paging request message contains the unique identifier of the intended destination. The set of identifiers are unique per geographic region due to the set of mobile stations in that region. Similarly, the Immediate Assignment traffic, especially the time at which those messages are broadcasted is unique by BTS as observed by mobile stations camped on those base stations.

## 4.2  Incoming Call Protocol

The logical flow for the radio interface in a GSM network during an incoming call works as follows [4]. The BTS attempts to find the mobile station over the broadcast paging channel downlink by issuing a paging request with the mobile station's identifier [4], which should be the TMSI, but can also be the IMSI. Upon receiving the paging request and matching the identifier, the mobile station will contact the BTS over the random access channel uplink which is separate from the downlink channel. The BTS will then indicate the frequency and code for the mobile station with an immediate assignment message, possibly over the same paging channel downlink. The mobile station then responds with a paging reply over another random access uplink. The rest of the protocol allows the mobile station and the BTS to negotiate the security level and other setup parameters, before data (text or voice) can be transmitted. The initial protocol proceeds as shown in Figure 4.

## 4.3  Paging Request Messages

The paging channel carries different messages including System Information, Immediate Assignment and Paging Requests. The paging requests can be of 3 types. By far the most common paging requests are of type 1 that allow a single or two mobile identities to be paged per message [4] (clause 9.1.22). Those paging requests are issued for every call or text message being sent to a mobile station within range of the BTS. Due to its frequent use and unique traffic pattern depending on the mobile stations served in the area, the paging channel offers a good medium that is unique in time and location. Paging requests are broadcast to every mobile station within a location area. The location area consists of several nearby BTSes. In contrast, immediate assignments are issued locally by an individual BTS. In other words, two mobile stations belonging to the same location area will hear almost the same paging requests. If they are not covered by the same BTS, they will hear completely different immediate assignments.

## 4.4  Location Tag Using Cellular Networks

In our evaluation in section 6, we observe that the traffic on the paging channel is a perfect candidate for LAC-level proximity testing: devices in the same LAC see very similar sets of TMSIs while devices in different (neighboring) LACs see disjoint sets. Similarly, devices camped on the same BTS hear the same Immediate Assignment traffic, but devices camped on different BTSes do not. We thus built our location tag algorithm to compare the conditions monitored by two different mobile stations.

We note that it is possible for an attacker to use high-powered directional antennae to eavesdrop on IA and PCCH traffic over longer distances. Clear lines of sight to the towers will likely be required. However, this does not guarantee that the victim's phone will be camped on that same tower, forcing the attacker to record all possible towers in the area. Moreover, interference from nearby towers using the same frequency is possible, reducing the ability to effectively eavesdrop on the target tower. In any case, this enforces that the attacker must have a device that is in physical proximity to the victim.

## 5   Location Sketch Privacy

Generally speaking, location sketch privacy is indeed location tag privacy. As Narayanan et al. point out, location tags should meet two key requirements as follows:

- **Reproducibility.** Two measurements taken in the same place and same time produces two almost-identical tags $t_1$ and $t_2$.
- **Unpredictability.** Without presence at a certain location and time, a malicious party should not be able to produce the tag for that location and time. Note we require location tags to be varying with time otherwise an adversary can pre-compute all location tags and a brute-force attack can reveal the victim's location trajectory.

The cellular mobile network broadcasts paging request messages through its base stations to alert the target mobile phone in the case of an incoming phone calls or text messages. In addition, each tower broadcasts the allocation messages to mobile stations requesting radio resources. Thus, two phones within the same location area should hear near-identical paging requests. If those phones are listening on the same tower, they will also hear near-identical immediate assignment message traffic. Heuristically, like the WiFi channel in [22], the GSM paging channel is a rich source of location tags.

Narayanan et al. reduce the similarity test to the private threshold set intersection (PTSI) problem [22]. In PTSI, Alice and Bob will execute a protocol that returns '1' (as success) when the set $A$ and $B$ have an intersection $C$ of size $> t'$, and returns '0' (as failure) when $C$ is of size $< t$. Note that we require $t' > t$. When $|C| \in [t, t']$, we expect the probability of success to gradually decrease from 100% to 0%. Here we apply shingling technique to accomplish the similarity test.

### 5.1   Shingling and Unpredictability

In the seminal work by Broder et al. [9], the shingling technique was introduced to give a binary answer on whether two documents (as web page content) are nearly identical. Decomposing a document into a set of $k$-shingles is called $k$-shingling. Since we are interested in comparing two sets of paging requests, the order of the requests makes no difference. In one time epoch, we first hash each recorded paging request to a numerical ID, sort them and then apply shingling to them.

One issue on unpredictability is the entropy of location tags. Among paging requests, we use TMSIs which are 32-bit IDs locally randomly assigned to a mobile phone. These IDs display some redundancy but still retain 24 bits of entropy. Thus with $k$-shingles, the location sketch presumably has $24k$-bits of entropy. With large enough $k$, the adversary cannot brute-force test the tag and the proximity before the victim moves to the next location. However, with larger $k$, reproducibility is decreased. With the same level of differences between two tag sets, a larger $k$ will create more unique shingles and decrease the resemblance between shinglings. A proper choice of $k$ will thus be needed to balance the tradeoff.

As described above, shingling the paging channel provides a certain level of time sensitivity because intuitively it's rare for a $k$-shingle to appear twice at different time epochs. However, exceptions do occur; some subscribers receive frequent calls or text messages and may produce many paging requests for the same TMSI over time. To cope with such issues, we append timestamps to each paging request so that the same paging request at different times will be tagged with a different UID. Because different phones will record paging requests in slightly different times, we restrict the timestamps to 10-second granularity to strike a balance between unpredictability and reproducibility.

## 5.2   Shingling and False Positive

A false positive of location promixity happens when two phones, located at two different LACs, derive the same location sketch. Two types of cases may have led to false positives: a hash collision by two different shingle, or sharing the same shingle which produces the location sketch. Notice those cases are necessary, rather than sufficient, conditions of false positives.

We are assured that either condition will not happen in practice, neither does false positive. With random inputs, we can compute the probability of collisions with birthday attack. With $m$ $k$-shingle and SHA-1 funciton, the probability of having one hash collision is roughly $p = m^2 \cdot 2^{-161}$. In practical the collision probability should be very small. Meanwhile, the probability of producing a duplicate $k$-shingle across LACs is also low. Without timestamp, the probability of having one duplicate $k$-shingle is $2^{-24k}$. It is such a rare event, let alone the case in which this $k$-shingle eventually yields the location sketch for both LACs. The timestamps make duplicate shingles even less probable. In conclusion, it is essentially impossible to yield false positive with TMSI shingling.

## 5.3   Reproducibility Boosting

Reproducibility only captures the desired outcome when two measurements are nearly the same but it doesn't define how two measurements differ when they are taken at different times. With shingling, the probability of testing positive for proximity is $p$ when the fraction $p$ of two shinglings are common elements. Also, when two measurements share a fraction $f$ of common readings, with $f \approx 1$, the fraction of shingles in common is at least $1 - k(1 - f)$ in the worst case, by the union bound. For instance, even when two phones see 90% common values, they would produce the same 3-shingle sketch at least 70% of the time. This reduction in accuracy is undesirable, since it would require two mobile devices to be closely synchronized in time and view of the network.

However, we can quickly boost the probability by repeating the protocol multiple times. After $m$ repetitions, the probability of getting at least one positive increases to $1 - k^m(1-f)^m$. The boosting effect is shown in Figure 5. Such boosting only requires a small value of $m$ to significantly weaken the required synchronization between phones. Therefore, we modify our protocol so that users compute $m$ sketches for each epoch (partitioned evenly into $m$ sub-epochs) and execute $m$ individual PETs. If there is at least one positive, they conclude they are co-located.

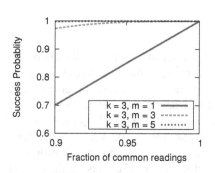

**Fig. 5.** The boosting effect on $m$ executions with $k$-shingling

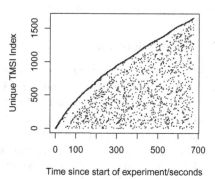

**Fig. 6.** TMSI requests recorded in an 11-minute period

## 6 Evaluation

### 6.1 Experiment Data Collection

To test our design, we used modified Motorola C118 cell phones connected to laptops and logging the paging channel traffic at varying distances. On our system, we ran the open source baseband project OsmocomBB [3]. We used the custom firmware from that project to reflash the phone, thereby acting as the layer 1 of the GSM communication stack. Using a serial link, the phone relays each message heard to a laptop running the upper layer 2 and 3 of the GSM stack. By default, upon startup, this system would scan all available frequencies, and select the one with the strongest signal. We configured our two cell phone-laptop systems to listen on the same GSM mobile network operator, but let the phone choose the appropriate frequencies based on the RSSI level. Once the system was started and selected the appropriate frequencies, it would start to listen on the broadcast paging channel (PCCH). A normal phone would ignore all paging requests and immediate assignment messages that were not intended for it. In our case, we made a small modification to the layer 3 of the system to log all those messages heard on the PCCH.

For our experiments, we selected the largest GSM cellular network service provider in our area and we listened to the paging channel in several geographic locations. We had two devices listening simultaneously at different distances apart, namely 1m, 100m and 7km. For the experiment involving the largest distance apart, we observed that the devices were reporting cells with a different Location Area Code (LAC) for the chosen operator. Devices located close together report the same LAC and if very close, they choose the same frequency. The paging request logs were recovered from the laptops and filtered for the TMSIs. Figure 6 shows a plot of unique TMSI we heard over a period of 700 seconds. A unique TMSI heard multiple times will appear as multiple dots horizontally on the plot. We have three datasets: Room (1m), Campus(100m) and and Far-away (7km). Each of them consists of two traffic logs from two systems. Each log keeps a 10-minute record of the paging channel traffic, including the paging requests and immediate assignment messages.

## 6.2   Shingling Experiment

At the shingling stage we experiment with multiple set of parameters. We choose the epoch time to be 1 minute long and use SHA-1 as the hash function. The shingling parameter $k$ is chosen to be 3, 4 and 5. To study the reproducibility, we observe how the clock offset between two mobile phones affects the resemblance. For each trial, we take a measurement of phone 1 at a random time $t1$ and one of phone 2 starting at $t1 + \delta$ as input to our system. We repeat the trial until all possible $t1$ values are exhausted. and record the empirical probability of proximity detection success, at offset $\delta$. With different $\delta$, we plot the probability of success versus the clock offset. The plots for the Campus dataset and Room dataset with different values of $k$ are shown in Figure 7. The plots for the Room dataset display a very similar behavior and the plot for the Far-away dataset is uninteresting as expected; the probability is always zero no matter what the offset is.

As Figure 7 confirms, larger $k$ values tend to decrease reproducibility because larger $k$ values are more sensitive to the set difference. Additionally, each phone observes approximately 4 paging requests per second. As a result, reproducibility quickly drops as the clock offset increases. It quantitatively matches with the analysis in Section 5. We choose $k = 3$ as it produces the best reproducibility while keeping the entropy at an acceptable level (72 bits).

For reproducibility boosting, we use $m = 5$. Here the epoch time is 5 minutes and we divide it into 5 sub-epochs, each 1 minute long. Recall that with boosting, proximity detection returns true when at least one PET returns true. As a result, we again plot the probability of success versus the clock offset on both dataset Room and dataset Campus in Figure 8. With much better success rate, we only need to loosely synchronize all phones. As the distance between two phones increases, the success rate is more sensitive to the clock offset.

## 6.3   Fine Proximity Test

Proximity testing based only on paging requests is limited to determining whether two phones are located in the same location area (LAC), which can be as large as $100 \, km^2$. On the other hand, each base station covers a relatively contant area with a radius between 100m and 1000m, allowing us to determine proximity more precisely. As a proof of concept, we utilize IA messages as location tags. We choose $k = 3$ and $m = 5$, and repeat the shingling experiments. The result is shown in Figure 9. It is clear that with tower-specific location tags we can achieve finer-grained proximity testing. However,

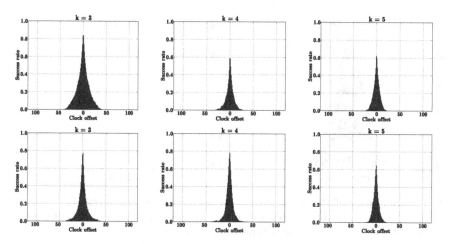

**Fig. 7.** First row is the plots on dataset Room, and the second row is those on dataset Campus. We omit the plots on dataset Far-away because they are simply blank ones. As $k$ increases, resemblances drops faster and faster as the offset drifts from zero. Also even when the offset is smaller than 1 second, the resemblance is no more than 85% for either dataset.

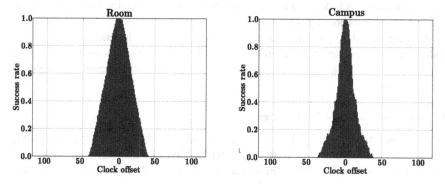

**Fig. 8.** With boosting parameter $m = 5$, shingling parameter $k = 3$ and 5-minute epoch time, the probability of success is almost 1 within 3-second offset for both datasets

we want to point out that the unpredictability of IA messages is not as strong, because of non-random channel assignment and some other issues. We will discuss this further in Section 7.

# 7 Discussion

## 7.1 Shingling with PTSI

Broder et al. in [8, 9] use shingling and threshold set intersection together to identify nearly identical documents. For each document, the smallest $k$ elements are chosen. If two documents have resemblance $p$, the (lower-bound) probability that they share $t$ common top-$k$ elements can be calculated. With proper choices of $(k, t)$ the probability

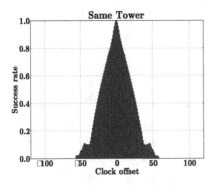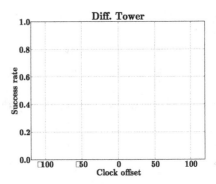

**Fig. 9.** The figure on the left shows two phones in the same room have large probability of testing positive for proximity while two phones in the same campus under different base stations will not be considered to be close at all, as shown by the figure on the right

function acts very similar to a high-pass filter, i.e. only highly resemble documents should have an intersection of size $> t$ with a high probability. In practice $k$ is usually as small as 6, and $t$ is as small as 2. In this way, it is possible to only keep the $k$ shingle for each document as a sketch and execute a private set intersection protocol to figure out if two documents are near-identical.

With the same idea, shingling can be adopted to improve the efficiency of private threshold set intersection on location tag proximity. Now we shrink each location tag set to a $k$-element sketch set so the communication and computation cost can be greatly improved as well.

### 7.2  Unpredictability of IA Messages

We have shown that proximity granularity can be controlled by different types of paging content. Specifically we have also shown that we can consider messages that are local to individual base stations, such like Immediate Assignment (IA) messages, to be used as location tags for finer granularity. We also note that utilizing IA messages as location tags has several issues. Unlike paging requests, IA messages has limited randomness. Base stations assign channels in a somewhat predictable way. Each available channel has a distinct set of parameters allowing passive attackers to enumerate the possible channels. When there is little traffic we will frequently see same IA messages due to the fact that same channel is reused. A preliminary computation shows the channel choices sent by the BTS on a university campus have entropy ranging from 8 bits to 16 bits. We will continue to investigate the security of IA messages and other resources for tags.

### 7.3  Practical Considerations

The system we used for our measurement used a modified GSM layer 3 that passively observes broadcast paging requests on the PCCH. Commercially available GSM phones also hear the same traffic, but their implementation of the layer 3 simply drops any paging request that is not intended for that particular device. For our system to work, we only need a modification in the layer 3 implementation to add the ability to record paging requests on the PCCH traffic for short periods of time. While small, this change will probably require an update of the baseband firmware on the phones in order to support our protocol. We note that there are no changes required at layers 1 and 2 of the GSM protocol stack.

Baseband firmware updates have been deployed on iPhone and Android smartphones as bug fixes are rolled out. Indeed, a number of baseband updates from Apple were intended to limit the ability to jailbreak the iPhones. With this update infrastructure in place, it would be possible to package support for our protocol in one such baseband firmware update. However, baseband updates for feature phones are far less common, making a migration of the baseband firmware to support our protocol less likely.

## 8   Conclusion

Location proximity testing has become an important social networking application. Meanwhile, concern over location privacy has also been growing. To address these concerns, Narayanan et al. [22] recently proposed Private proximity testing by location tags. We build on their work by successfully capturing location tags based on the GSM cellular network, which covers a larger area with greater reliability. Moreover, we describe a novel use of de-duplication shingling to test location tag similarity by private equality testing, a simple and efficient cryptographic primitive. We have developed prototypes that demonstrate the effectiveness of our approach. We thus describe the first privacy-preserving proximity system that builds on cellular network location tags. The use of shingling to reduce threshold set intersection to equality testing may be of interest to other private set operation protocols and is an open question for future research.

## References

1. Gsm world – market data summary (2009), http://www.gsmworld.com/newsroom/market-data/market_data_summary.html
2. United nations international telecommunication union sees 5 billion mobile subscriptions globally in 2010 (2010), http://www.itu.int/net/pressoffice/press_releases/2010/06.aspx
3. The osmocombb project – open source gsm baseband software implementation (2011), http://bb.osmocom.org/
4. 3GPP. Mobile radio interface layer 3 specification. TS 04.08, 3rd Generation Partnership Project (3GPP) (January 2004)
5. 3GPP. Network architecture. TS 23.002, 3rd Generation Partnership Project (3GPP) (March 2011)
6. Atallah, M.J., Du, W.: Secure Multi-party Computational Geometry. In: Dehne, F., Sack, J.-R., Tamassia, R. (eds.) WADS 2001. LNCS, vol. 2125, pp. 165–179. Springer, Heidelberg (2001)
7. Beresford, A.R., Stajano, F.: Location privacy in pervasive computing, Piscataway, NJ, USA, vol. 2, pp. 46–55. IEEE Educational Activities Department (January 2003)
8. Broder, A.: Identifying and Filtering Near-Duplicate Documents. In: Giancarlo, R., Sankoff, D. (eds.) CPM 2000. LNCS, vol. 1848, pp. 1–10. Springer, Heidelberg (2000)

9. Broder, A.Z., Glassman, S.C., Manasse, M.S., Zweig, G.: Syntactic clustering of the web. Computer Networks and ISDN Systems 29(8-13), 1157–1166 (1997); Papers from the Sixth International World Wide Web Conference

10. De Cristofaro, E., Tsudik, G.: Practical Private Set Intersection Protocols with Linear Complexity. In: Sion, R. (ed.) FC 2010. LNCS, vol. 6052, pp. 143–159. Springer, Heidelberg (2010)

11. Di Qiu, D., Lo, S., Enge, P.: Robust location tag generation from noisy location data for security applications. The Institute of Navigation International Technical Meeting (2009)

12. Fagin, R., Naor, M., Winkler, P.: Comparing information without leaking it. Commun. ACM, 77–85 (1996)

13. Freedman, M.J., Nissim, K., Pinkas, B.: Efficient Private Matching and Set Intersection. In: Cachin, C., Camenisch, J.L. (eds.) EUROCRYPT 2004. LNCS, vol. 3027, pp. 1–19. Springer, Heidelberg (2004)

14. Gruteser, M., Grunwald, D.: Anonymous usage of location-based services through spatial and temporal cloaking. In: Proceedings of the 1st International Conference on Mobile Systems, Applications and Services, MobiSys 2003, pp. 31–42. ACM, New York (2003)

15. Hazay, C., Lindell, Y.: Efficient Protocols for Set Intersection and Pattern Matching with Security Against Malicious and Covert Adversaries. In: Canetti, R. (ed.) TCC 2008. LNCS, vol. 4948, pp. 155–175. Springer, Heidelberg (2008)

16. Hazay, C., Nissim, K.: Efficient Set Operations in the Presence of Malicious Adversaries. In: Nguyen, P.Q., Pointcheval, D. (eds.) PKC 2010. LNCS, vol. 6056, pp. 312–331. Springer, Heidelberg (2010)

17. Holmquist, L.E., Falk, J., Wigstrm, J.: Supporting group collaboration with interpersonal awareness devices. Personal and Ubiquitous Computing 3 (1991)

18. Jaccard, P.: Étude comparative de la distribution florale dans une portion des Alpes et des Jura. Bulletin del la Société Vaudoise des Sciences Naturelles 37, 547–579 (1901)

19. Jarecki, S., Liu, X.: Efficient Oblivious Pseudorandom Function with Applications to Adaptive OT and Secure Computation of Set Intersection. In: Reingold, O. (ed.) TCC 2009. LNCS, vol. 5444, pp. 577–594. Springer, Heidelberg (2009)

20. Jarecki, S., Liu, X.: Fast Secure Computation of Set Intersection. In: Garay, J.A., De Prisco, R. (eds.) SCN 2010. LNCS, vol. 6280, pp. 418–435. Springer, Heidelberg (2010)

21. Kissner, L., Song, D.: Privacy-Preserving Set Operations. In: Shoup, V. (ed.) CRYPTO 2005. LNCS, vol. 3621, pp. 241–257. Springer, Heidelberg (2005)

22. Narayanan, A., Thiagarajan, N., Lakhani, M., Hamburg, M., Boneh, D.: Location privacy via private proximity testing. In: Network and Distributed System Security Symposium. Internet Society (February 2011)

23. Qiu, D., Lo, S., Enge, P., Boneh, D., Peterson, B.: Geoencryption using loran. The Institute of Navigation International Technical Meeting (2007)

24. Shokri, R., Troncoso, C., Diaz, C., Freudiger, J., Hubaux, J.-P.: Unraveling an old cloak: k-anonymity for location privacy. In: Proceedings of the 9th Annual ACM Workshop on Privacy in the Electronic Society, WPES 2010, pp. 115–118. ACM, New York (2010)

25. Terry, M., Mynatt, E.D., Ryall, K., Leigh, D.: Social net: using patterns of physical proximity over time to infer shared interests. In: CHI 2002 Extended Abstracts on Human Factors in Computing Systems, CHI EA 2002, pp. 816–817. ACM, New York (2002)

26. Yao, A.C.: Protocols for secure computations. In: Proceedings of the 23rd Annual Symposium on Foundations of Computer Science, SFCS 1982, pp. 160–164. IEEE Computer Society, Washington, DC (1982)

27. Zhong, G., Goldberg, I., Hengartner, U.: Louis, Lester and Pierre: Three Protocols for Location Privacy. In: Borisov, N., Golle, P. (eds.) PET 2007. LNCS, vol. 4776, pp. 62–76. Springer, Heidelberg (2007)

# Metrics for Measuring ISP Badness: The Case of Spam
## (Short Paper)

Benjamin Johnson[1], John Chuang[2], Jens Grossklags[3], and Nicolas Christin[4]

[1] Department of Mathematics, University of California, Berkeley
[2] School of Information, University of California, Berkeley
[3] College of Information Sciences and Technology, The Pennsylvania State University
[4] Information Networking Institute and Cylab, Carnegie Mellon University

**Abstract.** We consider the problem of ISP targeting for spam prevention through disconnection. Any such endeavor has to rely on adequate metrics that consider both the badness of an ISP as well as the risk of collateral damage. We propose a set of metrics that combines the two. Specifically, the metrics compare each ISP's "spamcount" with its "disconnectability". We offer a concrete methodological approach to compute these metrics, and then illustrate the methodology using datasets involving spam statistics and autonomous system relationships. This analysis represents the first step in a broader program to assess the viability of economic countermeasures to spam and other types of malicious activity on the Internet.

## 1 Introduction and Related Work

Recent studies have shown that a large percentage of all spam on the Internet is attributable to sources from a small percentage of the Internet's autonomous systems [3, 8, 24]. Thus in considering the spam-prevention problem, it makes sense to concentrate attention on those few systems who contribute to the problem the most. Evidence suggests that targeting an especially bad player can be effective. For example, the November 2008 takedown of McColo [6, 9] resulted in a significant decline in the global volume of spam (by estimates as much as 70%) [19].[1]

In this work, we address the targetability question by defining metrics to determine when an autonomous system is doing substantially more harm than good. These metrics can then be used not just for assessing the feasibility of targeting an ISP, but also for recognizing which ISP's may be susceptible to economic incentive structures designed to elicit implementation of outbound preventative mechanisms. The set of metrics we propose are based on ratios between "badness" measures which quantify the ill effects an autonomous system (AS) poses to the rest of the network, and "disconnectability" measures that quantify the collateral damage that would result from the AS's disconnection from the Internet graph.

### 1.1 Spam Measurement Studies and Mitigation

There is a diverse and growing literature on the measurement of spam and other network threats. Ramachandran and Feamster showed that network level properties can reveal

---

[1] There are also bad registrars but that is a different story [18].

A.D. Keromytis (Ed.): FC 2012, LNCS 7397, pp. 89–97, 2012.

decisive cues in the fight against spam [24]. Other contributions are the development of behavior-driven or signature-driven spam classification systems which are desirable given the transient nature of spam origins [12, 14, 25, 27, 33].

A number of studies have investigated the problem of botnet identification [11, 23, 34]. Ehrlich *et al.* proceed with a two-step methodology. First, they identify individual botnet nodes. Second, they continue their investigation to determine the command-and-control infrastructure of the botnet. In related projects, research groups have worked on building infrastructures to identify rogue networks [15, 28].

Finally, a growing number of research studies is concerned with the better understanding of spam economics, by studying large-scale spam campaigns [1, 4, 16], and by tracing click trajectories to better understand the spam value chain [20].

### 1.2  Economics of Service Provisioning and Security

Several reports have explored the economic incentives of Internet Service Providers to invest in security measures [3, 32]. A key observation is that ISPs respond differently to emerging threats leading to varying degrees of botnet infestations in their user population [3]. Some ISPs may act vigorously, while others appear to be slacking [5]. Finally, a residual group aims to derive a profit from providing a safe harbor for undesirable activities [8].

ISPs are in an excellent position to address security problems [2]. However, it is an open debate whether or to what degree liability can be assigned to them for insufficient or even detrimental behaviors [21].

But even from the perspective of well-motivated ISPs it is not obvious how to address security threats in a cost-efficient manner [26]. ISPs can incentivise users to higher security vigilance, but there are tradeoffs. Some incentive schemes target higher individual security effort levels [29], while others focus more on group-level security outcomes [13].

Another approach is to reduce the autonomy of individual users by installing security client software that monitors and controls network access. However, the majority of consumer-oriented ISPs shy away from direct technical intervention involving access to the users' home resources. Some argue this to be a government's role [7]. We are only aware of one US consumer ISP experimentally testing a similar approach [22]. However, several ISPs utilize redirection and quarantine techniques to encourage users to engage in clean-up efforts [17].

The rest of the paper is organized as follows. In Section 2, we define several metrics for use in ranking autonomous systems according to their miscreant behavior and discuss their key properties. In Section 3, we briefly describe our methodology for computing the proposed metrics on real data. Section 4 contains examples and illustrations pertaining to the ASes responsible for the most spam volume in our dataset. We discuss plans for future work and conclude in Section 5.

## 2  Proposed Metrics

In this section, we introduce metrics to formally quantify the *badness* and *disconnectability* of autonomous systems, along with the *cost-benefit tradeoff* that can be used as part of a formal basis for decisions involving AS targeting.

With respect to a given set of connectivity relations between autonomous systems, we define the following associated set of ASes. The *exclusive customer cone* of an autonomous system $X$ is the set of autonomous systems that would become disconnected from the network if $X$ were completely disconnected from the rest of the network. Note that every AS is a member of its own exclusive customer cone. The exclusive customer cone of $X$ is a subset of the *customer cone* of $X$, which was defined by Dimitropoulos *et al.* as the set of customers of $X$ together with those customers' customers, and so forth [10]. By way of contrast, the exclusive customer cone does not include those customers and subcustomers of $X$ with a connection to at least one additional provider that can move traffic to the core of the network while avoiding $X$. The customer cone is a reasonable measure of the importance of $X$, but the exclusive customer cone has a more direct bearing on the question of whether to target $X$.

We next define a set of three metrics related to the exclusive customer cone. The *exclusive customer cone size* of $X$ is the number of ASes in the exclusive customer cone of $X$. The *exclusive customer cone prefix size* of $X$ is the number of distinct /24 prefixes assigned to ASes in the exclusive customer cone of $X$. The *exclusive customer cone address size* of $X$ is the number of IP addresses assigned to ASes in the exclusive customer cone of $X$.

With respect to a given set of data attributing spam to IP addresses, we define the following two metrics. The *spamcount* of an autonomous system $X$ is the number of spam messages attributable to IP addresses directly assigned to $X$. The *spamipcount* of $X$ is the number of distinct IP addresses directly assigned to $X$ that are responsible for sending at least one spam message. We can obviously extend these definitions to negative attributes other than spam. For example, we could analogously define the *badness* of $X$ and the *ipbadness* of $X$ relative to any data set that associates a measure of badness to certain IP addresses.

Lastly with respect to both a badness measure on IP addresses and a set of connectivity relations among autonomous systems, we define a set of ratio metrics comparing the two. For example, the *spamipcount to exclusive customer cone prefix size ratio* of an autonomous system $X$ is the ratio of the spamipcount of $X$ to the exclusive customer cone prefix size of $X$.

## 3    Methodology

In this section, we briefly describe a methodological approach to computing these metrics on real data.

The metrics require three types of data for autonomous systems: a notion of badness for each AS; a measure of size for each AS; and the AS customer/peer relationship structure. The current state of the art in relationship structure is publicly available via the Cooperative Association for Internet Data Analysis (CAIDA) [31]. CAIDA also publishes size measures for autonomous systems.

Measures of badness come in many forms, and good datasets are more difficult to obtain. We carried out an illustration of our methodology using a data source consisting of about 3.4 million spam email messages collected by Ramachandran and Feamster at Georgia Tech over a period of about 17 months starting in July 2008. The methodology of that data collection was previously used and is described in an earlier publication [24]. We processed these emails to obtain a best guess source IP for each email; and then used the bulk Whois query tools provided by Team Cymru [30] to associate IP addresses obtained from the spam dataset with their associated autonomous system numbers.

## 4   Examples and Observations

The purpose of this section is to exemplify our methodological approach through illustration.

### 4.1   Exclusive Customer Cone Properties

Figure 1 in the appendix offers visualizations of the exclusive customer cones for two of the five most spammy ASes in our dataset: 4134 and 4837. The edges reflect provider-to-customer relationships. The diameter of each node increases linearly with the node's spamcount, and the color of the node moves from green to red as the spamipcount to exclusive customer cone prefix size ratio increases.

### 4.2   Aggregated Spam Characteristics

Figure 2 in the appendix shows the distributions of spamcount and spamipcount across the top 300 most spam-facilitating ASes in our dataset, as well as the cumulative distribution of these same badness measures over our entire dataset. The graphs confirm that most of the spam in our dataset is generated by IP addresses from a small percentage of autonomous systems, consistent with many other measurement studies involving spam [11, 23–25, 34]. This feature offers justification for our focus on only a few of the worst offenders. The graphs also give a sense of the relationship between spamcount and spamipcount, showing that both measures follow similar distributions and are strongly correlated.

### 4.3   Targeting ASes with High Spamcount

Table 1 below gives the computed value of several metrics for each of the top five highest-ranked ASes by spamcount.

The spam ip to exclusive customer cone prefix size ratio is given in the table's last column. As mentioned previously, this is our preferred metric for quantifying targetability. We see from the table that one particular autonomous system, ASN 45899, VPNT Corp, has a high score under this metric. It is a stub AS, with no customer ASes; it has a high badness score using both spamcount and spamipcount – in fact the spamcount is more than double that of any other AS in our entire dataset; and it does not have any counterbalancing large number of IP addresses or /24 prefixes in its exclusive customer cone.

The next few autonomous systems on the list have more exclusive customers and are generally much higher up in the internet tier hierarchy. The ratio metrics applied to these ASes is not nearly so high, by several orders of magnitude; and it would be more difficult to justify a targeting strategy for any of the next four ASes based on this metric.

**Table 1.** ASes with the highest spamcount in our dataset

| ASN | Organization Name | Spam Count | Percent of Spam | Spam IP Count | Customer Cone Prefix Size | Exclusive Cust Cone Prefix Size | Spam IP to Prefix Size Ratio |
|-----|-------------------|------------|-----------------|---------------|---------------------------|--------------------------------|------------------------------|
| 45899 | VNPT Corp | 132918 | 7.9% | 30222 | 12 | 12 | 2518 |
| 4766 | Korea Telecom | 54237 | 3.2% | 6833 | 203306 | 2537 | 2.7 |
| 4134 | Chinanet Backbone | 44482 | 2.7% | 10360 | 66172 | 1361 | 7.6 |
| 7738 | Telecomunicacoes da Bahia S.A. | 39570 | 2.4% | 7904 | 111324 | 518 | 15.3 |
| 4837 | China169 Backbone | 36617 | 2.2% | 8269 | 6438 | 1664 | 5.0 |

Due to current limitations of our data on the badness side, our true proscription towards actually targeting VPNT Corp is perhaps not very strong. The intent of this paper is not to make targeting proscriptions, but rather to introduce and illustrate a useful methodology. We have shown that well-motivated targetability metrics can be computed and applied to real ASes, using plausible data, with interesting and highly variable results. As our badness measurements become better quantified with higher quality data, proscriptive targeting arguments can be supported on this basis.

### 4.4   Discussion

What are the relative advantages of the different metrics? Our view is that it depends on the application and the quality of the datasets involved. The metrics invoking badness only at the IP level are more robust in the sense that they are less likely to change quickly over time, (since, for example, it may be easier to send additional spam messages from the same compromised IP address, then to compromise an additional IP address), and are also more applicable to the problem of diagnosing the source of badness. On the other hand, metrics equating badness with direct aggregate features such as raw spam volume are in better correspondence with the negative effects imposed on the rest of the network. In a similar fashion, metrics involving the *exclusive customer cone size* and *exclusive customer cone prefix size*, are more robust in the sense that they are less likely to change significantly if connectivity relations change by not too much. Further, if the data being used is accurate and not likely to change, then metrics involving the exclusive customer cone address size most directly correspond to the aggregate benefit to the network that would be lost if an autonomous system were targeted.

We want to emphasize that each of these metrics, based on exclusive customer cones, is a conservative metric, in the sense that the metric will generally paint an ISP as "less targetable" than it would be painted if more edges were included. This feature is important, as the connectivity data we use is approximate and is known to err on the side of omitting edges from the graph [10]. A practitioner might worry that targeting a particular AS might cause more collateral damage than expected. This would likely be the case if we used a metric based on customer cone. In such circumstance, an ISP who might otherwise be subject to targeting would have an incentive to simply add more customer edges to lower their disconnectability measure. But because we are using the exclusive customer cone, such a strategy would not be effective. Moreover, the customers of a bad AS would have the ability to adopt an alternative provider, resulting in a simultaneous decrease in target risk for the customer, and an increase in the disconnectability of the bad provider. The idea is that by publishing a metric, we create an incentive structure that tends to isolate the bad guys from the good guys. As miscreant behavior of an AS increases, the good guys have more and more of an incentive to line up an alternate provider, to avoid becoming collateral damage.

## 5   Conclusions and Future Work

Today's spam problem involves many players with competing interests; and any solution requires numerous tradeoffs. In our study of this problem, we have focused our attention on the players we see as having the most power to resolve the problem, namely the ISPs. This approach has lead us to an investigation of metrics applicable to ISP targeting through disconnection. Policy makers must consider a wide variety of technical, policy, and incentive-relevant challenges to realizing ISP disconnections in practice. Our contribution to this effort has involved demonstrating the tractability of developing an objective framework for addressing the problem.

Our goal is to continue advancing research on the prevention of Internet-related misbehavior through the publication of metrics that can affect an ISP's reputation. We consider our program as parallel to more direct technological approaches for combatting spam, such as botnet targeting and spam filtering. By developing an objective framework for considering ISP targeting through disconnection, we advance the tools available to economic researchers for use in the modeling of the Internet ecosystem, and help to foster a better understanding of the problem from crucial perspectives.

## References

1. Anderson, D., Fleizach, C., Savage, S., Voelker, G.: Spamscatter: Characterizing internet scam hosting infrastructure. In: Proceedings of 16th USENIX Security Symposium, Boston, MA, pp. 135–148 (August 2007)
2. Anderson, R.: Why information security is hard - an economic perspective. In: Proceedings of the 17th Annual Computer Security Applications Conference (ACSAC 2001), New Orleans, LA (December 2001)
3. Asghari, H.: Botnet mitigation and the role of ISPs: A quantitative study into the role and incentives of internet service providers in combating botnet propagation and activity, Master Thesis, Delft University of Technology (January 2010)
4. Böhme, R., Holz, T.: The effect of stock spam on financial markets. In: Proceedings of the Fifth Annual Workshop on Economics and Information Security, WEIS 2006, Cambridge, UK (June 2006)
5. Clayton, R.: Using early results from the 'spamHINTS' project to estimate an ISP Abuse Team's task. In: Proceedings of the Conference on E-Mail and Anti-Spam (CEAS), Mountain View, CA (July 2006)

6. Clayton, R.: How much did shutting down McColo help? In: Proceedings of the Conference on E-Mail and Anti-Spam (CEAS), Mountain View, CA (July 2009)
7. Clayton, R.: Might governments clean-up malware? In: Proceedings of the Ninth Annual Workshop on Economics and Information Security, WEIS 2010, Cambridge, MA (May 2010)
8. Danchev, D.: Bad, bad, cybercrime-friendly ISPs (March 4, 2009),
   `http://blogs.zdnet.com/security/?p=2764`
9. DiBenedetto, S., Massey, D., Papadopoulos, C., Walsh, P.: Analyzing the aftermath of the McColo shutdown. In: Proceedings of the Ninth Annual International Symposium on Applications and the Internet (SAINT), Seattle, WA, pp. 157–160 (July 2009)
10. Dimitropoulos, X., Krioukov, D., Fomenkov, M., Huffaker, B., Hyun, Y., Claffy, K., Riley, G.: AS relationships: Inference and validation. ACM Computer Communication Review 37(1), 29–40 (2007)
11. Ehrlich, W., Karasaridis, A., Liu, D., Hoeflin, D.: Detection of spam hosts and spam bots using network flow traffic modeling. In: Proceedings of the 3rd USENIX Workshop on Large-scale Exploits and Emergent Threats (LEET), San Jose, CA (April 2010)
12. Esquivel, H., Mori, T., Akella, A.: Router-level spam filtering using TCP fingerprints: Architecture and measurement-based evaluation. In: Proceedings of the Conference on E-Mail and Anti-Spam (CEAS), Mountain View, CA (July 2009)
13. Grossklags, J., Radosavac, S., Cárdenas, A.A., Chuang, J.: Nudge: Intermediaries' Role in Interdependent Network Security. In: Acquisti, A., Smith, S.W., Sadeghi, A.-R. (eds.) TRUST 2010. LNCS, vol. 6101, pp. 323–336. Springer, Heidelberg (2010)
14. Hao, S., Syed, N.A., Feamster, N., Gray, A.G., Krasser, S.: Detecting spammers with SNARE: Spatio-temporal network-level automatic reputation engine. In: USENIX Security Symposium, pp. 101–118. USENIX Association (2009)
15. Kalafut, A., Shue, C., Gupta, M.: Malicious hubs: Detecting abnormally malicious autonomous systems. In: Proceedings of the 29th IEEE International Conference on Computer Communications (INFOCOM), San Diego, CA, pp. 326–330 (March 2010)
16. Kanich, C., Kreibich, C., Levchenko, K., Enright, B., Voelker, G., Paxson, V., Savage, S.: Spamalytics: An empirical analysis of spam marketing conversion. In: Proceedings of the Conference on Computer and Communications Security (CCS), Alexandria, VA, pp. 3–14 (October 2008)
17. Kirk, J.: ISPs report success in fighting malware-infected PCs (June 2009),
   `http://www.pcworld.com/businesscenter/article/166444/`
   `isps_report_success_in_fighting_malwareinfected_pcs.html`
18. KnujOn. Registrar Report (February 2009), `http://knujon.com/registrars/`
   `#feb09RegistrarReport`
19. Krebs, B.: Takedowns: The shuns and stuns that take the fight to the enemy. McAfee Security Journal 6, 5–8 (2010)
20. Levchenko, K., Chachra, N., Enright, B., Felegyhazi, M., Grier, C., Halvorson, T., Kanich, C., Kreibich, C., Liu, H., McCoy, D., Pitsillidis, A., Weaver, N., Paxson, V., Voelker, G.M., Savage, S.: Click Trajectories: End-to-End Analysis of the Spam Value Chain. In: Proceedings of 32nd Annual Symposium on Security and Privacy (May 2011)
21. Lichtman, D., Posner, E.: Holding Internet Service Providers accountable. Supreme Court Economic Review 14, 221–259 (2006)
22. Mills, E.: Comcast pop-ups alert customers to PC infections. CNet (October 2009),
   `http://news.cnet.com/8301-27080_3-10370996-245.html`
23. Mori, T., Esquivel, H., Akella, A., Shimoda, A., Goto, S.: Understanding large-scale spamming botnets from internet edge sites. In: Proceedings of the Conference on E-Mail and Anti-Spam (CEAS), Redmond, WA (July 2010)

24. Ramachandran, A., Feamster, N.: Understanding the network-level behavior of spammers. In: Proceedings of the ACM Conference on Applications, Technologies, Architectures, and Protocols for Computer Communications (SIGCOMM 2006), Pisa, Italy, pp. 291–302 (September 2006)
25. Ramachandran, A., Feamster, N., Vempala, S.: Filtering spam with behavioral blacklisting. In: Proceedings of the ACM Conference on Computer and Communications Security (CCS 2007), Alexandria, VA, pp. 342–351 (October 2007)
26. Rowe, B., Reeves, D., Gallaher, M.: The role of Internet Service Providers in cyber security (June 2009); Available from the Institute for Homeland Security Solutions
27. Shin, Y., Gupta, M., Myers, S.: The Nuts and Bolts of a Forum Spam Automator. In: Proceedings of the 4th USENIX Workshop on Large-Scale Exploits and Emergent Threats, LEET (March 2011)
28. Stone-Gross, B., Kruegel, C., Almeroth, K., Moser, A., Kirda, E.: FIRE: FInding Rogue nEtworks. In: Proceedings of the 25th Annual Computer Security Applications Conference (ACSAC), Honolulu, HI, pp. 231–240 (December 2009)
29. Takahashi, Y., Ishibashi, K.: Incentive Mechanism for Prompting ISPs to Implement Outbound Filtering of Unwanted Traffic. In: NetGCOOP 2011: International Conference on Network Games, Control and Optimization, Paris, France (October 2011)
30. Team Cymru Research NFP. IP to ASN mapping, http://www.team-cymru.org/Services/ip-to-asn.html
31. The Cooperative Association for Internet Data Analysis. The CAIDA AS relationships dataset, http://www.caida.org/data/active/as-relationships/
32. van Eeten, M., Bauer, J. M.: Economics of malware: Security decisions, incentives and externalities. STI Working Paper (May 2008)
33. Venkataraman, S., Sen, S., Spatscheck, O., Haffner, P., Song, D.: Exploiting network structure for proactive spam mitigation. In: Proceedings of 16th USENIX Security Symposium, pp.11:1–11:18. USENIX Association, Berkeley (2007)
34. Zhao, Y., Xie, Y., Yu, F., Ke, Q., Yu, Y., Chen, Y., Gillum, E.: BotGraph: Large scale spamming botnet detection. In: Proceedings of the 6th USENIX Symposium on Networked Systems Design and Implementation (NSDI), Boston, MA, pp. 321–334 (April 2009)

# A    Appendix

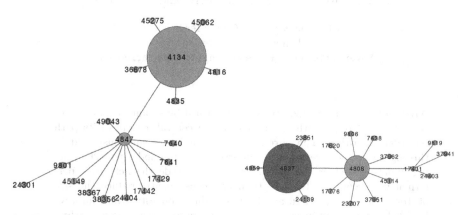

(a). The exclusive customer cone of ASN 4134    (b). The exclusive customer cone of ASN 4837

**Fig. 1.** The size of each node relates linearly to its spamcount. The color of each node relates to the ratio of its spamipcount to its individual prefix size.

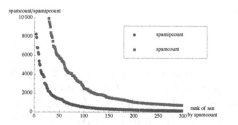

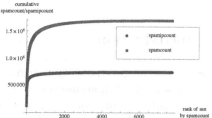

(a.) This graph shows the raw number of spam messages (spamcount) sent by the ASN with the given rank, and the raw number of distinct IP addresses (spamipcount) sending at least one spam message from the ASN with the given rank.

(b.) This graph shows the cumulative number of spam messages (spamcount) sent by all ISPs below the given rank, and number of distinct IP addresses sending at least one spam message (spamipcount) from an ASN below the given rank.

**Fig. 2.** The ASNs in order by spamcount

# Congestion-Aware Path Selection for Tor*

Tao Wang, Kevin Bauer, Clara Forero, and Ian Goldberg

Cheriton School of Computer Science
University of Waterloo
{t55wang,k4bauer,ciforero,iang}@cs.uwaterloo.ca

**Abstract.** Tor, an anonymity network formed by volunteer nodes, uses the estimated bandwidth of the nodes as a central feature of its path selection algorithm. The current load on nodes is not considered in this algorithm, however, and we observe that some nodes persist in being under-utilized or congested. This can degrade the network's performance, discourage Tor adoption, and consequently reduce the size of Tor's anonymity set. In an effort to reduce congestion and improve load balancing, we propose a congestion-aware path selection algorithm. Using latency as an indicator of congestion, clients use opportunistic and lightweight active measurements to evaluate the congestion state of nodes, and reject nodes that appear congested. Through experiments conducted on the live Tor network, we verify our hypothesis that clients can infer congestion using latency and show that congestion-aware path selection can improve performance.

## 1 Introduction

Tor is an anonymity network that preserves clients' online privacy [6]. Today, it serves hundreds of thousands of clients on a daily basis [13]. Despite its popularity, Tor suffers from a variety of performance problems that result in high and variable delays for clients [7]. These delays are a strong disincentive to use Tor, reducing the size of the network's user base and ultimately harming Tor users' anonymity [5]. One reason why Tor is slow is due to the challenges of balancing its dynamic traffic load over the network's available bandwidth. In this work, we propose a new approach to load balancing that can reduce congestion, improve performance, and consequently encourage wider Tor adoption.

**Path Selection in Tor.** The current path selection algorithm selects nodes based on the bandwidth of the nodes (adjusted by the current distribution of bandwidth in the network among entry guards, exits and other nodes), giving a higher probability of being chosen to nodes with higher bandwidth. It also takes into account a number of constraints designed to promote network diversity. However, peer-to-peer file sharing users, while discouraged from using Tor, may still do so and consume a significant portion of the available bandwidth [15]. Even though the number of such users is likely small, when these bulk downloaders

---

* An extended version of this paper is available [22].

A.D. Keromytis (Ed.): FC 2012, LNCS 7397, pp. 98–113, 2012.

use nodes with insufficient bandwidth, they may affect the performance of other clients using the nodes by introducing high delays due to congestion.

**Latency as a Congestion Signal.** Congestion occurs at the node level either when a node reaches its bandwidth rate limit configured in Tor, or when a node's connection to the Internet is congested. When a node is congested, outgoing cells must wait in the node's output queue. We find that this *node latency* is sometimes significantly larger than the *link latency*, which is dominated by the propagation delay between two nodes. Delays that do not originate from propagation effects have been found to be quite common [3]; they have also been found to be large [18]. From measurements and analysis of the live Tor network, we find that Tor's token bucket rate limiting implementation often contributes to congestion delays of up to one second per node. These delays are detrimental to interactive web browsing users, who are the most common type of Tor user [15].

**Congestion-Aware Path Selection.** To reduce congestion and improve Tor's load balancing, we introduce *node latency* as a new metric to be used when selecting nodes to form a circuit. Our approach uses a combination of lightweight active and opportunistic methods to obtain this information. Clients measure the overall latency of their circuits and use an inference technique to extract the component latencies due to congestion for each individual node along the circuit. Live experiments indicate that a typical client's circuit latency can be reduced by up to 40% if congestion information is taken into account during path selection. We also argue that the security and anonymity implications of our scheme are minimal.

**Contributions.** This paper contributes the following:

1. We identify latency as a measure of node congestion and characterize how congestion varies across different types of nodes. We describe ways to observe and isolate this node congestion from other sources of delay (such as propagation delay) with lightweight tests.
2. We design and evaluate a latency inference technique that attributes congestion-related latencies to constituent nodes along a measured circuit.
3. We extend Tor's path selection algorithm to avoid congested relays. Our approach has low overhead, can be incrementally deployed, needs no additional infrastructure, and our live evaluation shows that it improves performance.

## 2   Tor Background

Tor is the third-generation onion routing design providing source and destination anonymity for TCP traffic. A client wanting to connect to an Internet destination through Tor first contacts a *directory server* to obtain the list of Tor nodes. Next, the client constructs a *circuit* of three *Tor routers* (or nodes) and forwards traffic through the circuit to a desired Internet destination using a layered encryption scheme based on onion routing [10]. To balance the traffic load across the routers' bandwidth, clients select routers in proportion to their bandwidth capacities.

To mitigate the predecessor attack [23], the first router on the circuit (called an "entry guard") is selected among nodes with high stability and bandwidth. Clients choose precisely three entry guards to use for all circuits and new entry guards are selected every 30 to 60 days. The last router (called an "exit router") is chosen to allow delivery of the client's traffic to the destination. All data is transmitted through Tor in fixed-size 512-byte units called *cells*. More details about Tor's design can be found in its design document [6] and its protocol specification [4].

## 3   Related Work

Tor requires a good path selection algorithm to effectively distribute its traffic load across its nodes. Currently, Tor uses an algorithm that chooses routers in proportion to their bandwidth capacities. Different criteria have been proposed as possible factors in the path selection algorithm, such as autonomous system awareness [8] and application awareness [20]. In this paper, we describe a modification to Tor's existing path selection algorithm to incorporate congestion information, which improves load balancing.

Using latency as a path selection criterion has been investigated by Sherr et al. [19]. In their paper, a case is made for link-based path selection, which uses link-based properties (e.g., latency, jitter, loss). Panchenko and Renner [17] propose using round-trip time as a link-based measure to choose paths. They give a technique to obtain round-trip time and roughly analyze the increase in performance by using this criterion. In this paper, however, we look into considering latency as a *node-based* property instead of a link-based property. Link-based latency includes propagation delay, so only using link-based latency as a measure may bias path selection against circuits with nodes that are geographically far apart or on diverse networks.

Latency in Tor has also been considered from other perspectives. Hopper et al. [12] looked into how network latency can be used to deanonymize clients. Evans et al. [9] investigate using long paths to congest routers, thus revealing the identities of those connected to the router due to the change in round-trip time. Since our congestion-informed path selection approach allows clients to detect congested routers, our proposal may be a defense against such attacks; we do not, however, focus on defense mechanisms in this paper, but rather on improving Tor's performance.

Lastly, in contrast to proposals that seek to reduce congestion by redesigning Tor's congestion control mechanisms [1, 18], our work is focused solely on identifying and avoiding congested routers.

## 4   Latency Measurement and Congestion Inference

We next present a technique for inferring node-level congestion using circuit measurements. In this section, we describe our latency model and our approach to measuring latency, and present a technique for identifying congestion-related delays.

### 4.1  Latency Model

We next define a latency model for nodes. Our latency measurements on the Tor network suggest that latency measurements on a node can be cleanly divided into a *non-congested component* and *congestion time*. When a node is not congested, the latency can be attributed to

**Table 1.** Node-based latency model

| | |
|---|---|
| $t_{min}$ | the minimum round-trip time |
| $t_c$ | the congestion time |
| $t$ | the round-trip time |
| $\gamma$ | a smoothing constant |

propagation delays, which are nearly constant. Non-congested measurements can therefore be defined as measurements that are very close to the minimum of all measurements on the same node. For many nodes, this accounts for most of the data. When a node is congested, an amount of congestion time is added to the round-trip time before it can reach the client. This amount of time is frequently much larger than the non-congested measurements.

In Table 1 we define terms with respect to a node. $t_{min}$ is the minimum round-trip time for all measurements of round-trip time $t$ of a node. It is a constant, assuming all measurements are done from the same client; the chief component of $t_{min}$ is the propagation delay. We define the congestion time $t_c = t - t_{min}$. By removing $t_{min}$ from the round-trip time, we isolate the congestion time. $\gamma$ is a small smoothing constant added to the measurements to allow for quick reactions to transient congestion, as detailed further in Section 4.4. Thus, the actual congestion time is $t_c = t - t_{min} + \gamma$.

### 4.2  Measuring the Latency

We next discuss how circuit-level latency is measured by the client. This measurement should fulfill the following criteria:

1. It should be lightweight. There should be little burden on the network even if all of Tor's estimated 300,000 clients use this scheme simultaneously.
2. It should be indistinguishable from non-measurement traffic. Otherwise, it may be possible for malicious routers to influence the measurements.
3. It should exclude the destination server's latency. We want the measurement to consider only the delays within the Tor network, as delays at the destination server may be experienced regardless of whether Tor is used.

To satisfy these criteria, measurements of a circuit can be done in two ways: we can *actively* probe the circuit, or we can perform measurements *opportunistically* so as not to create a burden on Tor.

**Active Probing.**  One way to measure the round-trip time is to tell the exit node to connect to *localhost*, which the exit node will refuse to. This scheme, used by Panchenko et al. [17], works by forcing the exit node to return an error message to the client, so the client obtains the round-trip time to the exit node. However, a potential disadvantage is that a malicious exit node can identify the measurement probes and attempt to influence the results.

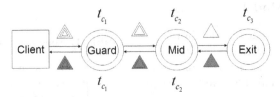

**Fig. 1.** A breakdown of congestion in testing. The test packet (colorless triangle) is sent to the exit node and a response packet (colored triangle) is returned without going through any destination server.

In our experiments, we use a technique that is conceptually similar: we use circuit build cells to measure the circuit latency. To extend the circuit to the final exit router, the client sends a circuit EXTEND cell through the entry guard and the middle router. The middle router sends a CREATE cell to the exit router, which after performing public-key cryptography replies with a CREATED cell back through the circuit to the client. The time spent performing public-key cryptography can be considered a small constant, which will later be factored out of the latency measurement.

**Opportunistic Probing.** If only active probing is used, our scheme might add too much measurement traffic into the Tor network, particularly if all clients were to perform such measurements frequently. Thus, we also use an opportunistic approach that leverages Tor's end-to-end control cells as the measurement apparatus. The stream-level and circuit-level SENDME cells are sent end-to-end in response to every 50 and 100 DATA cells, respectively. In addition, BEGIN and CONNECTED cells are sent whenever a new exit TCP stream is established, which for web browsing clients can happen several times per web page visited. As long as the client is using the circuit, we can obtain a number of measurements without any additional burden on the Tor network.

Note that if we want the exit node to immediately send a message back without spending time contacting a server, then the measurement is slightly skewed towards the first two nodes. To be precise, the message has to travel through each link among the client and the nodes twice, and it has to wait in the queue (if any) of the first two nodes twice, but it only needs to wait in the queue of the exit node once (see Figure 1).

**Overhead.** The opportunistic measurements have no overhead, as they leverage existing end-to-end control cells. However, it might be desirable to augment the opportunistic measurements with additional active measurements, at some communication cost. We can obtain one congestion time entry for each member of a circuit by sending just one cell (512 bytes). Suppose the client actively probes each circuit it builds 5 times over 10 minutes. This will add an average of 5 B/s of traffic to each node. If 300,000 users use this scheme together, they will add a total of 4.5 MB/s of traffic to Tor. This is currently around 0.5% of the total bandwidth offered by all Tor nodes, so our scheme will only add a small load to the Tor network. As will be seen in Section 4.4, a small number of measurements can be effective in detecting and avoiding congested circuits; the other measurements needed can be done opportunistically.

## 4.3   Isolating Circuit Congestion

When we obtain a measurement on the circuit, we want to highlight the congestion times $t_{c_1}$, $t_{c_2}$, $t_{c_3}$ for each node along the circuit. First, it is necessary to separate the circuit's propagation delay from the delay due to congestion. We next describe this process.

For one round-trip of the entire circuit, the time $T$ can be dissected this way:

$$T = T_{min} + (T_c - \gamma)$$
$$T_c = 2t_{c_1} + 2t_{c_2} + t_{c_3}$$

where $T_{min}$ is an estimate of the circuit's end-to-end propagation delay and $T_c$ is the circuit's delay due to congestion ($\gamma$ is a small constant described in Section 4.4). The difference between $T_{min}$ and $T_c$ is that $T_{min}$ should be constant for the same circuit, while $T_c$ varies depending on the extent of the circuit's congestion. In addition, $T_c$ only includes the last node once as in our tests, as our probes do not exit through the final node. In our tests, we find that the congestion term $T_c$ is sometimes zero, but it is often non-zero.

For each measurement of $T$ in this circuit, we save it in a list $\{T_1, T_2, ..., T_k\}$, and after all measurements of the circuit are done, we take the lowest measurement, and let this be $T_{min}$. Note that the number of measurements taken per circuit should be large to ensure that $T_{min}$ converges to the circuit's actual end-to-end propagation delay.[1] Through experimental analysis, we find that $T_{min}$ can be correctly determined within an error of 0.05 s with 80% probability by using only five measurements—in the case that $T_{min}$ is not correctly identified, the circuit being considered is likely to be heavily congested.

The $i^{th}$ measurement of congestion time ($0 \leq i < k$) is given by:

$$T_{c_i} = T_i - T_{min} + \gamma$$

In Figure 1, we summarize how a single end-to-end circuit round-trip time measurement is conducted and where the congestion occurs.

## 4.4   Attributing Circuit Congestion to Nodes

Now that we have isolated the delay due to congestion from the circuit's total delay, we need to attribute the congestion delay to the circuit's constituent nodes. Each client maintains a congestion list of all known relays paired with a number $L$ of congestion times for each relay. This list is updated as new measurements are taken. Consider a three-hop circuit. Suppose the estimated congestion times

---

[1] $T_{min}$ can also be intelligently estimated using other methods. For instance, the King method [11] can be used to approximate the pairwise network latency between any two Tor nodes without probing either of the routers directly.

of nodes $r_1, r_2, r_3$ in this circuit are respectively $t_{c_1}, t_{c_2}, t_{c_3}$. The entry guard is $r_1$, the middle router is $r_2$, and the exit router is $r_3$. Next, suppose the round-trip time taken for some cell to return across this circuit is $T$; then the total circuit's congestion time is $T_c = T - T_{min} + \gamma$. For $r_1$ and $r_2$, we assign the following congestion time:

$$t_{c_i} \leftarrow T_c \cdot \frac{2t_{c_i}}{2t_{c_1} + 2t_{c_2} + t_{c_3}}$$

Here $i = 1$ for node $r_1$ and $i = 2$ for node $r_2$. For $r_3$, we assign the following congestion time:

$$t_{c_3} \leftarrow T_c \cdot \frac{t_{c_3}}{2t_{c_1} + 2t_{c_2} + t_{c_3}}$$

**Details.** A technical issue emerges when a node becomes congested after a long period of being non-congested. In this scenario, the estimated congestion time would be very close to zero and the algorithm would not respond fast enough to assign a high congestion time to this node. This is where the term $\gamma$ comes into play. By ensuring that the minimum estimated congestion time is at least $\gamma$, we can guarantee that even nodes without a history of congestion will not be immune to blame when congestion occurs in a circuit with such a node. We empirically find $\gamma = 0.02\,\mathrm{s}$ to be a good value; this is not large enough to cover the differential between congested and non-congested nodes, yet it ensures that convergence will not take too long.

When a new estimated congestion time has been assigned to a node, the node's mean estimated congestion time should be updated. We maintain a list of congestion time measurements for each node, $L$; when this amount of data has been recorded, we push out old data whenever new data comes in. If $L$ is chosen to be large, then the client's preference for a node will not change as quickly, and vice versa.[2]

## 5   Techniques for Mitigating Congestion

Congestion can be either short term (e.g., a file sharer decides to use a certain node for their activities) or long term (e.g., a node's bandwidth is consistently overestimated or its flags and exit policy are too attractive). For short-term congestion, we want to provide an instant response to switch to other circuits. For long-term congestion, we propose a path selection algorithm that takes congestion time into account.

### 5.1   Instant Response

We provide two ways in which clients can perform instant on-the-spot responses to high congestion times in a circuit.

**Choosing the Best Pre-built Circuits.** Tor automatically attempts to maintain several pre-built circuits so that circuit construction time will not affect the

---

[2] Alternatively, an exponentially weighted moving average (EWMA) of congestion delay would reduce the space necessary to store historical congestion data.

user's experience. Two circuits are built that are capable of exiting to each port used in the past hour (a circuit can count for multiple ports). Only one of those circuits is chosen as the next circuit when the user's circuit times out or breaks. A reasonable scheme, therefore, is to test all of those circuits before choosing which to use. As stated above, those tests can be done quickly and with minimal overhead using active probing. We suggest that five active probing measurements per pre-built circuit is sufficient to choose the best, as we observe in our experiments (in Section 6). Since the circuits are pre-built, these measurements will not cause the client any further delay.

**Switching to another Circuit.** While using the circuit, a client may continue to measure the circuit and obtain congestion times. This can be done with no overhead to the Tor network by opportunistically leveraging Tor's stream-level and circuit-level SENDME cells, or the stream BEGIN and CONNECTED cell pairs (as described in Section 4.2). This gives us the round-trip time $T$, from which we can follow the procedure given in Section 4.3 to isolate the nodes' congestion time. If the estimated congestion time is large, the client should stop using this circuit and choose another circuit instead.

**Comparison.** Tor currently takes into account the circuit build time adaptively and drops circuits that take too long to build [2]. This approach, however, cannot identify circuits that may become congested after they are constructed, and the client will not learn to avoid attempting to build circuits over nodes that are consistently congested. Furthermore, propagation delays are included in the circuit building time, which is undesirable. Our two schemes improve upon Tor's circuit building timeout mechanism.

## 5.2    Path Selection

In addition to an instant response, we also want a long-term response where clients can selectively *avoid* certain nodes if they often receive poor service from these nodes. This can be helpful when there are nodes with poorly estimated bandwidth, when bulk downloaders customize their clients to use only specific relays, or when there are other unexpected load balancing issues that have not been resolved. Our congestion-aware path selection works as follows.

Each client will keep a list of all routers, each of which will be recorded with a list of their measured congestion times. The list of measured values is of size $L$; when new data comes in, old data is pushed out.

**Node Selection.** Our scheme is designed to be built atop the current path selection algorithm in this way: when we wish to extend a circuit by one node, we pick a few nodes from the list according to the original scheme (e.g., 10 nodes), and then choose one of them in negative correlation to their estimated congestion times. Estimated congestion times should be obtained by leveraging both the active and opportunistic measurements done for the instant response schemes. Suppose that node $r$'s estimated congestion time is $t_{c_r}$. We define a base constant $\alpha > 0$, and use it to obtain the probability of selecting the node $r$ for a circuit:

$$P(C_r) \propto \frac{1}{\alpha + t_{c_r}}$$

where $C_r$ is the event of node $r$ being chosen. $\alpha$ is a constant that prevents very low congestion nodes from dominating the path selection algorithm.

The effect of this scheme on the user's experience and the Tor network itself depends in part on the choice of the constant $\alpha$. A smaller $\alpha$ will impact the load balancing more as nodes with less estimated congestion become more likely to be chosen.

**Advantages.** Our approach is simple and efficient. Furthermore, this scheme requires no further infrastructure to support, and it is incrementally deployable in the sense that any client who chooses to use this scheme can immediately do so. The long term path selection scheme adds no further overhead on the network over the instant response scheme, as it can share the few measurements used to support the instant response scheme.

## 6    Experiments

We designed a number of experiments that aim to validate our assertions about latency and congestion in Tor. For all experiments, we use the Tor control protocol to instrument Tor. We use the final pair of circuit construction cells to measure the round-trip time of a circuit (as described in Section 4.2). In the remainder of this section, we present experiments and results that show that congestion is a property of Tor nodes, explore the relationship between a node's consensus bandwidth and its estimated congestion, and evaluate the performance improvements offered by our congestion-aware router selection proposal.

### 6.1    Node Congestion

We first seek to demonstrate that congestion is a property of Tor routers. For 72 hours in August 2011, we collected round-trip time data for all Tor routers that can be used on a circuit by measuring the time to construct one-hop circuits. For each node, we subtracted the node's minimum measurement (e.g., the propagation delay) to isolate the congestion delays $t_c$.

Figure 2(a) shows the distribution of congestion delays for entry guards, exits, guard/exits, and middle-only nodes. The median congestion delay is minimal (3–5 ms) across all node types; however, the tails of the distributions tell a different story. For the most congested ten percent of the measurements, nodes marked as both guard and exit experience congestion delays greater than 866 ms, and guard-only nodes have at least 836 ms of congestion delay. Exit-only and middle-only nodes tend to be the least congested. Guard nodes may be the most congested because the stability and bandwidth criteria for the guard flag is too high. Relaxing the requirements for the guard flag would enable some middle-only nodes to become guards, reducing congestion among guards.

Figure 2(b) shows congestion delays over the duration of our measurements for all routers (top) and for three representative high-bandwidth (10 MiB/s)

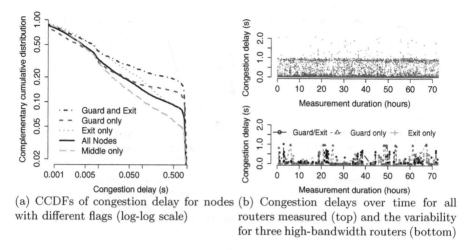

(a) CCDFs of congestion delay for nodes with different flags (log-log scale)

(b) Congestion delays over time for all routers measured (top) and the variability for three high-bandwidth routers (bottom)

**Fig. 2.** Analysis of congestion delays

routers (bottom). We note that these delays tend to be low. However, there exists noticeable variability regardless of a node's flags or bandwidth, and many of the delays are close to one second (Figure 2(a) also illustrates these one second delays where the CCDF lines become vertical). These one second delays are the result of Tor's token bucket rate limiting with a once-per-second token refilling policy (see the extended version of this manuscript [22] for more details).[3] These one-second delays indicate that nodes are being asked to forward more traffic than they are configured to handle, resulting in congestion. Thus, we conclude that congestion is a property of the Tor router itself, motivating the need for clients to consider congestion when selecting nodes for a circuit.

To investigate the possible relationship between a node's bandwidth and its congestion, we analyze the nodes' consensus bandwidth as reported by Tor's directory servers. We observe no correlation between a node's bandwidth and congestion (the Pearson's r value between log of the bandwidth and the congestion time is $-0.00842$).[4] This implies that considering only a node's bandwidth during path selection may not be sufficient to achieve optimal load balancing.

## 6.2   Performance Improvements of Our Schemes

We next present experiments that seek to quantify clients' latency improvements when using our scheme. Experiments are performed on both the instant response and long-term path selection components.

---

[3] Increasing the frequency with which the tokens are refilled may reduce or eliminate these one second delays. This design change is currently being discussed [21].

[4] Dhungel et al. report no significant correlation between bandwidth and *overall* delay [3].

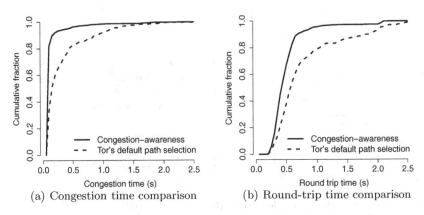

(a) Congestion time comparison        (b) Round-trip time comparison

**Fig. 3.** Improvements in congestion time and round-trip time for instant response

In these experiments, an unmodified Tor client used the current path selection algorithm in Tor. At the same time, a modified client uses the instant response components of our scheme (from Section 5.1) to determine which circuit it should use. The original client builds 225 circuits and measures each one precisely 30 times to obtain round-trip times. The modified client determines which circuits it should use based on the same data.

**Choosing the Best Pre-built Circuits.** We first tested how much of an improvement we would see if the client simply tested each circuit five times when building them preemptively and chose the one with the lowest congestion. For simplicity we assumed that the client always had three circuits to choose from. The original client tested each of its circuits 30 times, and took the mean of the congestion times as its experience with the circuit. The modified client chose the best among every three circuits to use by only looking at the first five measurements; after choosing the best out of three, all 30 measurements of that circuit are revealed to the modified client and it is taken as its experience of the circuit. Without the scheme, the mean circuit congestion time was about 0.276 s. With the scheme, it was about 0.119 s. We find that this large improvement was because most circuits were non-congested, except a minority where the congestion time was very high. Those circuits also clearly exhibited congestion in the first five measurements. This experiment demonstrates that just a few measurements are needed to effectively identify congested circuits.

**Switching to Another Circuit.** We next tested how much of an improvement we would get if the client switches to a better circuit when the current one becomes too congested. This time both the original client and the modified client can see all measurements. The modified client dropped a circuit if the last five measurements had a mean of more than 0.5 s of congestion; 73 of the 225 circuits were eventually dropped. This sufficed to improve the mean congestion experienced from 0.276 s to 0.137 s.

Finally, we combined the two instant response schemes. 75 of the 225 circuits were chosen using the first scheme, and later 11 of the 75 circuits chosen were eventually dropped using the second scheme. We achieved a mean congestion time of 0.077 s, compared to the original 0.276 s. The total round-trip time was reduced from a mean of 0.737 s to 0.448 s. Figure 3(a) shows the distribution of congestion times for the client when it used our improvements compared to the original selection scheme, and Figure 3(b) shows the distribution of round-trip time for the same comparison. Note that such a reduction in congestion delays would result in a faster time-to-first-byte for interactive clients (e.g., web browsing clients), which positively affects the users' perceived quality of service [16].

**Overhead.** One may worry that these schemes will add too much overhead because they drop existing circuits and build new ones. With the first scheme we are not dropping any circuits. With the second scheme, in our experiment we found that we would need to build about 26% more circuits, which is a relatively modest increase.[5]

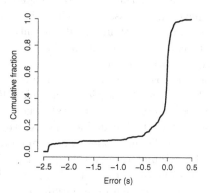

**Fig. 4.** Distribution of errors when learning individual node congestion over a large number of trials

**Long-Term Path Selection.** We evaluate the long-term path selection algorithm as follows. We ran a client that builds many circuits over the entire Tor network using the original path selection scheme. In total 13,458 circuits were built, for which the round-trip time was obtained 5 times each. One-third of the circuit build times were used as testing data; the rest were used in training the client to learn the estimated congestion times for each relay. By using the long-term path selection scheme, we observed a decrease in the mean congestion time for this experiment from 0.41 s to 0.37 s over the testing data. The improvement is not as large as in the instant response schemes, because the long-term path selection scheme tackles more persistent factors which adversely affect node performance rather than short-term bursts of congestion.

The long-term path selection scheme offers an improvement nonetheless because it is capable of deducing the congestion time of individual nodes while only measuring the congestion times of random circuits, allowing it to choose uncongested nodes. We performed a total of 379 trials where we compared deduced congestion (by building three-hop circuits) to directly measured congestion (by building one-hop circuits). Figure 4 shows the distribution of errors. We found that nearly 90% of the errors

---

[5] Circuit building cells are much rarer than data transfer cells; further, the Tor Project is working to decrease the computation required for circuit building by a factor of four [14].

were within -0.5 s to 0.5 s, and 65% of the errors were within -0.1 s to 0.1 s. The scheme very rarely overestimated node congestion, but sometimes underestimated it, as shown by the large number of negative errors. The mean error was therefore -0.2 s. This may be because high congestion is somewhat random in nature, so the scheme is less accurate in predicting the extent of a node's congestion while only given a previous record.

## 7    Anonymity and Security Implications

We consider if our schemes may be open to attacks which cause a loss of anonymity for the client. To be specific, we consider sender anonymity, which is achieved if a message and its origin cannot be traced. It is known that sender anonymity is lost in Tor if the entry guard and the exit node in a circuit are both compromised. The possibility of such depends on the attacker's control of the network. We therefore focus on the possibility of an attacker increasing their control of the network through our schemes.

We consider a particular attack called the *smearing attack*. The attacker first uses all of his available bandwidth to deploy malicious nodes. These malicious nodes attempt to give the appearance of congestion by artificially delaying cells. If a client measures a circuit containing both innocuous and malicious nodes, the innocuous nodes will be "smeared" with high estimated congestion times. The clients are then less likely to choose these nodes under the long-term path selection scheme. After a certain amount of time, these malicious nodes will be estimated to have a very high congestion as well, so the smearing becomes less effective. Once a malicious node becomes rarely selected, it is taken down, and a new one is created in order to maintain the attack. This attack is continued until all innocuous nodes can no longer be smeared further (this is bounded by the amount of bandwidth available to the attacker). After all nodes are maximally smeared, the attacker can stop the attack and enjoy a larger control of the network for a while, as his nodes will now seem more attractive.[6]

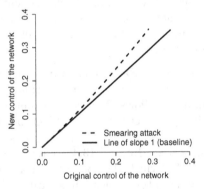

**Fig. 5.** An estimate of the how much control an attacker can gain through the smearing attack. We chose $t_{max} = 5000$ ms, $t_c = 500$ ms, $L = 20$, $C = 30$.

A parameter of the attack is $C$, which indicates for how long each malicious node will attempt to smear other nodes before being replaced. If $C = 5$, for

---

[6] Note that nodes are less likely to be chosen if they do not have the "stable" and "fast" flags. The stable flag is a barrier for malicious nodes, as it requires the node to demonstrate high stability before they can be effective. We neglect this barrier in the following analysis, giving more power to the attacker.

example, the attacker will attempt to keep each malicious node up for as long as it takes to smear other nodes five times for each client measuring the nodes, then take it down and replace it with another node. We take $t_c$ as the mean performance of the nodes (including the malicious node) and $t_{max}$ as the maximum time the client performing the latency measurement will wait for before timing out. The estimation is done by running a simulation with the simplifying assumption that all nodes can be selected in all positions.

Figure 5 shows how much bandwidth the malicious nodes must possess in order to affect the measurements of the congestion time of the non-malicious nodes. The attacker can indeed smear other nodes and gain an advantage by coming up with fresh, non-smeared nodes. We also note that the advantage gained is temporary; when the adversary stops performing the attack and uses all their bandwidth to acquire control of the network, clients will start measuring the other nodes' non-smeared congestion times as well, so their estimated congestion times will slowly return to their non-smeared levels.

Information leakage could also cause anonymity loss. The list of latencies stored on a user's computer may compromise anonymity if divulged. If the list of latencies for all users is known to an attacker, he can perform an attack by only controlling the exit node, and using the lists to probabilistically guess who is connecting by checking the frequency of connections; this will give him some amount of information. Our scheme, however, gives no reason to directly divulge the list of latencies at any point. Furthermore, this list is updated based on client behavior and measurements, which the attacker cannot easily observe or manipulate without controlling a substantial portion of the network.

While we recognize that our scheme introduces a small risk due to the smearing attack, we believe that reducing congestion would result in increased resilience to attacks that utilize congestion to identify the set of routers used by a client [9]. Due to space constraints, a full investigation is future work.

## 8    Conclusion and Future Work

Many different metrics for path selection in Tor have been proposed, some of which consider the use of latency. However, previous work treats latency as a property of a link and focuses on the delays that occur primarily due to propagation. We assume a different approach: we identify the importance of latency as an indicator of a node's congestion. To reduce congestion, improve load balancing and, ultimately, improve clients' quality of service, we propose an improved path selection algorithm based on inferred congestion information that biases path selection toward non-congested nodes. We also propose ways for clients to respond to short-term, transient congestion that improve on Tor's adaptive circuit building timeout mechanism.

Our experiments show that a single client can expect to experience up to a 40% decrease in delay when considering congestion during node selection. As future work, we plan to investigate the potential benefits and other effects when this scheme is deployed at scale through whole-network experiments.

**Acknowledgements.** This work was funded in part by NSERC, MITACS, and The Tor Project. We also thank Jean-Charles Grégoire, Angèle Hamel, Ryan Henry, Femi Olumofin, and Rob Smits for their valuable suggestions.

# References

1. AlSabah, M., Bauer, K., Goldberg, I., Grunwald, D., McCoy, D., Savage, S., Voelker, G.M.: DefenestraTor: Throwing Out Windows in Tor. In: Fischer-Hübner, S., Hopper, N. (eds.) PETS 2011. LNCS, vol. 6794, pp. 134–154. Springer, Heidelberg (2011)
2. Chen, F., Perry, M.: Improving Tor path selection (July 2008), https://gitweb.torproject.org/torspec.git/blob_plain/HEAD:/proposals/151-path-selection-improvements.txt
3. Dhungel, P., Steiner, M., Rimac, I., Hilt, V., Ross, K.W.: Waiting for anonymity: Understanding delays in the Tor overlay. In: Peer-to-Peer Computing, pp. 1–4. IEEE (2010)
4. Dingledine, R., Mathewson, N.: Tor Protocol Specification, https://gitweb.torproject.org/tor.git/blob_plain/HEAD:/doc/spec/tor-spec.txt (accessed August 2011)
5. Dingledine, R., Mathewson, N.: Anonymity loves company: Usability and the network effect. In: WEIS (June 2006)
6. Dingledine, R., Mathewson, N., Syverson, P.: Tor: The second-generation onion router. In: USENIX Security (2004)
7. Dingledine, R., Murdoch, S.: Performance improvements on Tor or, why Tor is slow and what we're going to do about it (March 2009), http://www.torproject.org/press/presskit/2009-03-11-performance.pdf
8. Edman, M., Syverson, P.F.: AS-awareness in Tor path selection. In: Proceedings of CCS, pp. 380–389 (2009)
9. Evans, N., Dingledine, R., Grothoff, C.: A practical congestion attack on Tor using long paths. In: Proceedings of the 18th USENIX Security Symposium (August 2009)
10. Goldschlag, D.M., Reed, M.G., Syverson, P.F.: Hiding routing information. In: Anderson, R. (ed.) IH 1996. LNCS, vol. 1174, pp. 137–150. Springer, Heidelberg (1996)
11. Gummadi, K.P., Saroiu, S., Gribble, S.D.: King: Estimating latency between arbitrary Internet end hosts. SIGCOMM Comput. Commun. Rev. 32(3) (2002)
12. Hopper, N., Vasserman, E.Y., Chan-Tin, E.: How much anonymity does network latency leak. In: CCS (2007)
13. Loesing, K.: Measuring the Tor network: Evaluation of client requests to the directories. Tor Project Technical Report (2009)
14. Mathewson, N.: New paper by Goldberg, Stebila, and Ostaoglu with proposed circuit handshake, https://lists.torproject.org/pipermail/tor-dev/2011-May/002641.html (accessed June 2011)
15. McCoy, D., Bauer, K., Grunwald, D., Kohno, T., Sicker, D.C.: Shining Light in Dark Places: Understanding the Tor Network. In: Borisov, N., Goldberg, I. (eds.) PETS 2008. LNCS, vol. 5134, pp. 63–76. Springer, Heidelberg (2008)
16. Nah, F.F.-H.: A study on tolerable waiting time: How long are web users willing to wait? Behaviour Information Technology 23(3), 153–163 (2004)

17. Panchenko, A., Renner, J.: Path selection metrics for performance-improved onion routing. In: Proceedings of the 2009 Ninth Annual International Symposium on Applications and the Internet, pp. 114–120. IEEE Computer Society, Washington, DC (2009)
18. Reardon, J., Goldberg, I.: Improving Tor using a TCP-over-DTLS tunnel. In: USENIX Security (2009)
19. Sherr, M., Blaze, M., Loo, B.T.: Scalable Link-Based Relay Selection for Anonymous Routing. In: Goldberg, I., Atallah, M.J. (eds.) PETS 2009. LNCS, vol. 5672, pp. 73–93. Springer, Heidelberg (2009)
20. Sherr, M., Mao, A., Marczak, W.R., Zhou, W., Loo, B.T., Blaze, M.: A3: An Extensible Platform for Application-Aware Anonymity. In: 17th Annual Network and Distributed System Security Symposium (NDSS) (February 2010)
21. Tschorsch, F., Scheuermann, B.: Proposal 182: Credit bucket, https://gitweb.torproject.org/torspec.git/blob_plain/HEAD:/proposals/182-creditbucket.txt (accessed August 2011)
22. Wang, T., Bauer, K., Forero, C., Goldberg, I.: Congestion-aware path selection for Tor. Technical Report CACR 2011-20 (December 2011), http://www.cacr.math.uwaterloo.ca/techreports/2011/cacr2011-20.pdf
23. Wright, M.K., Adler, M., Levine, B.N., Shields, C.: The predecessor attack: An analysis of a threat to anonymous communications systems. ACM Trans. Inf. Syst. Secur. 7(4), 489–522 (2004)

# Attacking the Washington,
# D.C. Internet Voting System

Scott Wolchok, Eric Wustrow, Dawn Isabel, and J. Alex Halderman

The University of Michigan, Ann Arbor
{swolchok,ewust,dki,jhalderm}@umich.edu

**Abstract.** In 2010, Washington, D.C. developed an Internet voting pilot project that was intended to allow overseas absentee voters to cast their ballots using a website. Prior to deploying the system in the general election, the District held a unique public trial: a mock election during which anyone was invited to test the system or attempt to compromise its security. This paper describes our experience participating in this trial. Within 48 hours of the system going live, we had gained near-complete control of the election server. We successfully changed every vote and revealed almost every secret ballot. Election officials did not detect our intrusion for nearly two business days—and might have remained unaware for far longer had we not deliberately left a prominent clue. This case study—the first (to our knowledge) to analyze the security of a government Internet voting system from the perspective of an attacker in a realistic pre-election deployment—attempts to illuminate the practical challenges of securing online voting as practiced today by a growing number of jurisdictions.

**Keywords:** Internet voting, e-voting, penetration testing, case studies.

## 1   Introduction

Conducting elections for public office over the Internet raises grave security risks. A web-based voting system needs to maintain both the integrity of the election result and the secrecy of voters' choices, it must remain available and uncompromised on an open network, and it has to serve voters connecting from untrusted clients. Many security researchers have cataloged threats to Internet voting (e.g. [11,15]), even as others have proposed systems and protocols that may be steps to solutions someday (e.g. [6,12]); meanwhile, a growing number of states and countries have been charging ahead with systems to collect votes online. Estonia [1] and Switzerland [2] have already adopted online voting for national elections. As of 2010, 19 U.S. states employed some form of Internet voting [5], and at least 12 more were reportedly considering adopting it [4].

Among the jurisdictions considering Internet voting, one of the most enthusiastic proponents was the District of Columbia. In 2010, the Washington, D.C. Board of Elections and Ethics (BOEE) embarked on a Federally-funded pilot project that sought to allow overseas voters registered in the District to vote

A.D. Keromytis (Ed.): FC 2012, LNCS 7397, pp. 114–128, 2012.
© International Financial Cryptography Association 2012

over the web starting with the November 2010 general election [16]. Though the D.C. system, officially known as the "D.C. Digital Vote-by-Mail Service," was technologically similar to parallel efforts in other states, BOEE officials adopted a unique and laudable level of transparency. The system was developed as an open source project, in partnership with the nonprofit Open Source Digital Voting (OSDV) Foundation [3]. Most significantly, prior to collecting real votes with the system, the District chose to operate a mock election and allow members of the public to test its functionality and security.

We participated in this test, which ran for four days in September and October 2010. Our objective was to approach the system as real attackers would: starting from publicly available information, we looked for weaknesses that would allow us to seize control, unmask secret ballots, and alter the outcome of the mock election. Our simulated attack succeeded at each of these goals and prompted the D.C. BOEE to discontinue its plans to deploy digital ballot return in the November election.

In this paper, we provide a case study of the security of an Internet voting system that, absent our participation, might have been deployed in real elections. Though some prior investigations have analyzed the security of proposed Internet voting systems by reviewing their designs or source code, this is the first instance of which we are aware where researchers have been permitted to attempt attacks on such a system in a realistic deployment intended for use in a general election.

We hope our experiences with the D.C. system will aid future research on secure Internet voting. In particular, we address several little-understood practical aspects of the problem, including the exploitability of implementation errors in carefully developed systems and the ability of election officials to detect, respond, and recover from attacks. Our successful penetration supports the widely held view among security researchers that web-based electronic voting faces high risks of vulnerability, and it cautions against the position of many vendors and election officials who claim that the technology can readily be made safe. The remainder of this paper is organized as follows: Section 2 introduces the architecture and user interface of the Digital Vote-By-Mail System. In Section 3, we describe how we found and exploited vulnerabilities in the web application software to compromise the mock election. Section 4 describes further vulnerabilities that we found and exploited in low-level network components. Section 5 discusses implications of our case study for other Internet voting systems and future public trials. We survey related work in Section 6 and conclude in Section 7.

## 2   Background: The D.C. Digital Vote-By-Mail System

*Architecture.* The Digital Vote-by-Mail (DVBM) system is built around an open-source web application[1] developed in partnership with the D.C. BOEE by the OSDV Foundation's TrustTheVote project[2]. The software uses the popular Ruby on Rails framework and is hosted on top of the Apache web server and the

---

[1] http://github.com/trustthevote/DCdigitalVBM/
[2] http://trustthevote.org

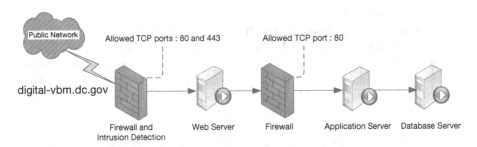

**Fig. 1. Network architecture** — The front-end web server receives HTTPS requests from users and reverse-proxies them to the application server, which hosts the DVBM election software and stores both blank and completed ballots. A MySQL database server stores voter credentials and tracks voted ballots. Multiple firewalls reduce the attack surface and complicate attacks by disallowing outbound TCP connections. The intrusion detection system in front of the web server proved ineffective, as it was unable to decrypt the HTTPS connections that carried our exploit. (Adapted from http://www.dcboee.us/DVM/Visio-BOEE.pdf.)

MySQL relational database. Global election state (such as registered voters' names, addresses, hashed credentials, and precinct-ballot mappings, as well as which voters have voted) is stored in the MySQL database. Voted ballots are encrypted and stored in the filesystem. User session state, including the user ID and whether the ballot being cast is digital or physical, is stored in an encrypted session cookie on the user's browser.

Electronic ballots are served as PDF files which voters fill out using a PDF reader and upload back to the server. To safeguard ballot secrecy, the server encrypts completed ballots with a public key whose corresponding private key is held offline by voting officials. Encrypted ballots are stored on the server until after the election, when officials transfer them to a non-networked computer (the "crypto workstation"), decrypt them using the private key, and print them for counting alongside mail-in absentee ballots.

Figure 1 shows the network architecture deployed for the mock election. HTTPS web requests are interpreted by the web server over TCP port 443. The web server then performs the HTTP request on the user's behalf to the application server, which runs the DVBM application software. The web server, application server, and a MySQL database server all run Linux. Firewalls prevent outbound connections from the web and application servers. Since the web server and application server run on separate machines, a compromise of the application server will not by itself allow an attacker to steal the HTTPS private key.

*Voter experience.* The DVBM system was intended to be available to all military and overseas voters registered in the District. Months prior to the election, each eligible voter received a letter by postal mail containing credentials for the system. These credentials contained the voter ID number, registered name, residence ZIP code, and a 16-character hexadecimal personal identification number

(PIN). The letters instructed voters to visit the D.C. Internet voting system website, which guided them through the voting process.

Upon arrival, the voter selects between a digital or postal ballot return. Next, the voter is presented with an overview of the voting process. The voter then logs in with the credentials provided in the mail, and confirms his or her identity. Next, the voter is presented with a blank ballot in PDF format. In the postal return option, the voter simply prints out the ballot, marks it, and mails it to the provided address. For the digital return, the voter marks the ballot electronically using a PDF reader, and saves the ballot to his or her computer. The voter then uploads the marked ballot to the D.C. Internet voting system, which reports that the vote has been recorded by displaying a "Thank You" page. If voters try to log in a second time to cast another ballot, they are redirected to the final Thank You page, disallowing them from voting again.

# 3   Attacking the Web Application

In this section, we describe vulnerabilities we discovered and exploited in the DVBM server application. Our search for vulnerabilities was primarily conducted by manual inspection of the web application's source code, guided by a focus on the application's attack surface. In particular, we concentrated on voter login, ballot upload and handling, database communication, and other network activity. The fact that the application was open source expedited our search, but motivated attackers could have found vulnerabilities without the source code using alternative methods. For example, one might attack voter login fields, ballot contents, ballot filenames, or session cookies, by either fuzzing or more direct code injection attacks such as embedding snippets of SQL, shell commands, and popular scripting languages with detectable side effects.

## 3.1   Shell-Injection Vulnerability

After a few hours of examination, we found a shell injection vulnerability that eventually allowed us to compromise the web application server. The vulnerability was located in the code for encrypting voted ballots uploaded by users. The server stores uploaded ballots in a temporary location on disk, and the DVBM application executes the **gpg** command to encrypt the file, using the following code:

```
run("gpg", "−−trust−model always −o
    \"#{File.expand_path(dst.path)}\" −e −r
    \"#{@recipient}\" \"#{File.expand_path(src.path)}\"")
```

The **run** method invoked by this code concatenates its first and second arguments, collapses multiple whitespace characters into single characters, and then executes the command string using Ruby's backtick operator, which passes the provided command to the shell. The Paperclip[3] Rails plugin, which the application uses to handle file uploads, preserves the extension of the uploaded

---
[3] https://github.com/thoughtbot/paperclip

ballot file, and no filtering is performed on this extension, so the result of File.expand_path(src.path) is attacker controlled. Unfortunately, in the Bash shell used on the server, double quotes do not prevent the evaluation of shell metacharacters, and so a ballot named foo.$(cmd) will result in the execution of cmd with the privileges of the web application.

The current release of the Paperclip plugin at the time of our analysis (late September 2010) was version 2.3.3. It appears that a similar vulnerability in Paperclip's built-in run method was fixed on April 30, 2010[4]. The first release containing the patch was version 2.3.2, which was tagged in the Paperclip Git repository on June 8, 2010. The degree of similarity between the DVBM application's custom run method and the Paperclip run method suggests that the DVBM application's implementation is a custom "stripped-down" version of Paperclip's, contrary to the D.C. BOEE's assertion that "a new version of [Paperclip] that had not been fully tested had been released and included in the deployed software" and "did not perform filename checks as expected." [14] Indeed, if DVBM had used the Paperclip run method together with an up-to-date version of the Paperclip library, this specific vulnerability would not have been included in the software. The resulting attack serves as a reminder that a small, seemingly minor engineering mistake in practically any layer of the software stack can result in total system compromise.

When we tested the shell injection vulnerability on the mock election server, we discovered that outbound network traffic from the test system was filtered, rendering traditional shellcode and exfiltration attempts (e.g., nc umich.edu 1234 < /tmp/ballot.pdf) ineffective. However, we were able to exfiltrate data by writing output to the images directory on the compromised server, where it could be retrieved with any HTTP client. To expedite crafting our shell commands, we developed an exploit compiler and a shell-like interface that, on each command, creates a maliciously named ballot file, submits the ballot to the victim server, and retrieves the output from its chosen URL under /images.

Interestingly, although the DVBM system included an intrusion detection system (IDS) device, it was deployed in front of the web server and was not configured to intercept and monitor the contents of the encrypted HTTPS connections that carried our attack. Although configuring the IDS with the necessary TLS certificates would no doubt have been labor intensive, failure to do so resulted in a large "blind spot" for the D.C. system administrators.

### 3.2   Attack Payloads

We exploited the shell injection vulnerability to carry out several attacks that illustrate the devastating effects attackers could have during a real election if they gained a similar level of access:

*Stealing secrets.* We retrieved several cryptographic secrets from the application server, including the public key used for encrypting ballots. Despite the use of

---

[4] The patch in question is available at https://github.com/thoughtbot/paperclip/commit/724cc7. It modifies run to properly quote its arguments using single quotes.

the term "public key," this key should actually be kept secret, since it allows attackers to substitute arbitrary ballots in place of actual cast ballots should they gain access to the storage device. We also gained access to the database by finding credentials in the bash history file (`mysql -h 10.1.143.75 -udvbm -pP@ssw0rd`).

*Changing past and future votes.*   We used the stolen public key to replace all of the encrypted ballot files on the server at the time of our intrusion with a forged ballot of our choosing. In addition, we modified the ballot-processing function to append any subsequently voted ballots to a `.tar` file in the publicly accessible `images` directory (where we could later retrieve them) and replace the originals with our forged ballot. Recovery from this attack is difficult; there is little hope for protecting future ballots from this level of compromise, since the code that processes the ballots is itself suspect. Using backups to ensure that compromises are not able to affect ballots cast prior to the compromise may conflict with ballot secrecy in the event that the backup itself is compromised.

*Revealing past and future votes.*   One of the main goals of a voting system is to protect ballot secrecy, which means not only preventing an attacker of the system from determining how a voter voted, but also preventing a voter from willingly revealing their cast ballot to a third party, even if they are coerced or incentivized to do so. While any absentee system that allows voters to vote where they choose allows a voter to reveal his or her vote voluntarily, our attack on the D.C. system allowed us to violate ballot secrecy and determine how nearly all voters voted.

Our modifications to the ballot processing function allowed us to learn the contents of ballots cast following our intrusion. Revealing ballots cast prior to our intrusion was more difficult, because the system was designed to store these ballots in encrypted form, and we did not have the private key needed to decipher them. However, we found that the Paperclip Rails plugin used to handle file uploads stored each ballot file in the `/tmp` directory before it was encrypted. The web application did not remove these unencrypted files, allowing us to recover them. While these ballots do not explicitly specify the voter's ID, they do indicate the precinct and time of voting, and we were able to associate them with voters by using login events and ballot filenames recorded in the server application logs. Thus, we could violate the secret ballot for past and future voters.

*Discovering that real voter credentials were exposed.*   In addition to decrypted ballots, we noticed that the `/tmp` directory also contained uploaded files that were not PDF ballots but other kinds of files apparently used to exercise error handling code during testing. To our surprise, one of these files was a 937 page PDF document that contained the instruction letters sent to each of the registered voters, which included the real voters' credentials for using the system. These credentials would have allowed us (or anyone else who penetrated the insecure server) to cast votes as these citizens in the real D.C. election that was to begin only days after the test period. Since the system requires that these credentials be delivered via postal mail, it would be infeasible for officials to send updated ones to the voters in time for the election.

*Hiding our tracks.*   We were able to hide the evidence of our intrusion with moderate success. We downloaded the DVBM application logs, altered them to remove entries corresponding to our malicious ballot uploads, and, as our final actions, overwrote the application log with our sanitized version and removed our uploaded files from the /tmp and images directories.

*Our calling card.*   To make our control over the voting system more tangible to nontechnical users, we left a "calling card" on the final screen of the digital voting workflow: we uploaded a recording of "The Victors" (the University of Michigan fight song) and modified the confirmation page to play this recording after several seconds had elapsed. We hoped that this would serve as a clear demonstration that the site had been compromised, while remaining discreet enough to allow the D.C. BOEE system administrators a chance to exercise their intrusion detection and response procedures.

### 3.3   Other Vulnerabilities and Potential Attacks

Our intention in participating in the trial was to play the role of a real attacker. Therefore, once we had found vulnerabilities that allowed us to compromise the system, our attention shifted to understanding and exploiting these problems. However, along the way we did uncover several additional vulnerabilities in the DVBM web application that were not necessary for our attack. Two key system deployment tasks were not completed. First, the set of test voter credentials was not regenerated and was identical to those included in the public DVBM Git repository. While the test voter credentials were fictitious, their disclosure constituted a security problem because public testers were asked to contact the D.C. BOEE for credentials, implying that the number of credentials available to each test group was to be limited.

Similarly, the encryption key used for session cookies was unchanged from the default key published in the repository. Disclosure of the key exacerbated a second vulnerability: rather than using the Rails-provided random session_id to associate browser sessions with voter credentials, the DVBM developers used the rid value, which corresponds to the automatically incremented primary key of the registration table in the system's MySQL database. This means every integer less than or equal to the number of registered voters is guaranteed to correspond to some voter. Combining this with the known encryption key results in a *session forgery* vulnerability. An attacker can construct a valid cookie for some voter simply by choosing an arbitrary valid rid value. This vulnerability could have been used to submit a ballot for every voter.

Our attack was expedited because the DVBM application user had permission to write the code of the web application. Without this permission, we would have had to find and exploit a local privilege escalation vulnerability in order to make malicious changes to the application. However, as we were able to carry out our attacks as the web application user, we did not need to find or use such an exploit.

We also identified other attack strategies that we ultimately did not need to pursue. For instance, the "crypto workstation" (see Section 2) used for decrypting and tabulating ballots is not directly connected to the Internet, but attackers may be able to compromise it by exploiting vulnerabilities in PDF processing software. PDF readers are notoriously subject to security vulnerabilities; indeed, the Crypto Workstation's lack of Internet connectivity may reduce its security by delaying the application of automated updates in the time leading up to the count. If the Crypto Workstation is compromised, attackers would likely be able to rewrite ballots. Furthermore, the web application allowed uploaded PDF ballots to contain multiple pages. If the printing is done in an automated fashion without restricting printouts to a single page, an attacker could vote multiple ballots.

# 4 Attacking the Network Infrastructure

In addition to the web application server, we were also able to compromise network infrastructure on the pilot network. This attack was independent from our web application compromise, yet it still had serious ramifications for the real election and showed a second potential path into the system.

Prior to the start of the mock election, the D.C. BOEE released a pilot network design diagram that showed specific server models, the network configuration connecting these servers to the Internet, and a CIDR network block (8.15.195.0/26). Using Nmap, we discovered five of the possible 64 addresses in this address block to be responsive. By using Nmap's OS fingerprinting feature and manually following up with a web browser, we were able to discover a Cisco router (8.15.195.1), a Cisco VPN gateway (8.15.195.4), two networked webcams (8.15.195.11 and 8.15.195.12), and a Digi Passport 8 terminal server[5] (8.15.195.8).

## 4.1 Infiltrating the Terminal Server

The Digi Passport 8 terminal server provides an HTTP-based administrative interface. We were able to gain access using the default root password (dbps) obtained from an online copy of the user manual. We found that the terminal server was connected to four enterprise-class Cisco switches (which we surmised corresponded to the switches shown on the network diagram provided by the BOEE) and provided access to the switches' serial console configuration interfaces via telnet.

We hid our presence in the terminal server using a custom JavaScript rootkit, which we installed over an SSH session (the same account names and passwords used in the web interface were accepted for SSH). The rootkit concealed an additional account with administrator privileges, "dev," which we planned to use in case our attack was discovered and the passwords changed. We also used our SSH

---

[5] A *terminal server* is a device that attaches to other pieces of equipment and allows administrators to remotely log in and configure them.

access to download the terminal server's `/etc/shadow` and `/etc/passwd` files for cracking using the "John the Ripper" password cracker[6]. After about 3.5 hours using the cracker's default settings, we recovered the secondary administrator password `cisco123` from a salted MD5 hash.

*Evidence of other Attackers.* When we inspected the terminal server's logs, we noticed that several other attackers were attempting to guess the SSH login passwords. Such attacks are widespread on the Internet, and we believe the ones we observed were not intentionally directed against the D.C. voting system. However, they provide a reminder of the hostile environment in which Internet voting applications must operate.

The first SSH attack we observed came from an IP address located in Iran (80.191.180.102), belonging to Persian Gulf University. We realized that one of the default logins to the terminal server (user: `admin`, password: `admin`) would likely be guessed by the attacker in a short period of time, and therefore decided to protect the device from further compromise that might interfere with the voting system test. We used iptables to block the offending IP addresses and changed the admin password to something much more difficult to guess. We later blocked similar attacks from IP addresses in New Jersey, India, and China.

## 4.2   Routers and Switches

After we compromised the terminal server, we found several devices connected to its serial ports. Initially, there were four Cisco switches: a pair of Nexus 5010s and a pair of Nexus 7010s. Connecting to these serial ports through the terminal server presented us with the switches' login prompts, but previously found and default passwords were unsuccessful.

The terminal server provided built-in support for keystroke logging of serial console sessions and forwarding of logged keystrokes to a remote syslog server, which we enabled and configured to forward to one of our machines. This allowed us to observe in real time as system administrators logged in and configured the switches, and to capture the switches' administrative password, `!@#123abc`.

Later in the trial, four additional devices were attached to the terminal server, including a pair of Cisco ASR 9010 routers and a pair of Cisco 7606-series routers. We were again able to observe login sessions and capture passwords. At the end of the public trial, we changed the passwords on the routers and switches—effectively locking the administrators out of their own network—before alerting BOEE officials and giving them the new password.

D.C. officials later told us that the routers and switches we had infiltrated were not intended to be part of the voting system trial and were simply colocated with the DVBM servers at the District's off-site testing facility. They were, however, destined to be deployed in the core D.C. network, over which real election traffic would flow. With the access we had, we could have modified the devices' firmware to install back doors that would have given us persistent

---

[6] http://www.openwall.com/john/

access, then later programmed them to redirect Internet voting connections to a malicious server.

## 4.3  Network Webcams

We found a pair of webcams on the DVBM network—both publicly accessible without any password—that showed views of the server room that housed the pilot. One camera pointed at the entrance to the room, and we were able to observe several people enter and leave, including a security guard, several officials, and IT staff installing new hardware. The second camera was directed at a rack of servers.

These webcams may have been intended to increase security by allowing remote surveillance of the server room, but in practice, since they were unsecured, they had the potential to leak information that would be extremely useful to attackers. Malicious intruders viewing the cameras could learn which server architectures were deployed, identify individuals with access to the facility in order to mount social engineering attacks, and learn the pattern of security patrols in the server room. We used them to gauge whether the network administrators had discovered our attacks—when they did, their body language became noticeably more agitated.

# 5  Discussion

## 5.1  Attack Detection and Recovery

After we completed our attack—including our musical calling card on the "Thank You" page—there was a delay of approximately 36 hours before election officials responded and took down the pilot servers for analysis. The attack was apparently brought to officials' attention by an email on a mailing list they monitored that curiously asked, "does anyone know what tune they play for successful voters?" Shortly after another mailing list participant recognized the music as "The Victors," officials abruptly suspended the public examination period, halting the tests five days sooner than scheduled, citing "usability issues."

Following the trial, we discussed the attack with D.C. officials. They explained that they found our modifications to the application code by comparing the disk image of the server to a previous snapshot, although this required several days of analysis. They confirmed that they were unable to see our attacks in their intrusion detection system logs, that they were unable to detect our presence in the network equipment until after the trial, and that they did not discover the attack until they noticed our intentional calling card. We believe that attack detection and recovery remain significant challenges for any Internet voting system.

## 5.2  Adversarial Testing and Mechanics of the D.C. Trial

The D.C. BOEE should be commended for running a public test of their system. Their trial was a step in the right direction toward transparency in voting technology and one of the first of its kind. Nonetheless, we reiterate that adversarial testing of Internet voting applications is not necessary to show that they are likely to be weak. The architectural flaws inherent in Internet voting systems in general and the potential disastrous implications of a single vulnerability were known and expected by researchers prior to the D.C. trial [11]. We hope not to have to repeat this case study in order to highlight these limitations once again.

The key drawback to adversarial testing is that a lack of problems found in testing *does not* imply a lack of problems in the system, despite popular perception to the contrary. It is likely that testers will have more limited resources and weaker incentives than real attackers—or they may simply be less lucky. A scarcity of testers also seems to have been an issue during the D.C. trial. During our compromise of the DVBM server, we were able to view the web access logs, which revealed only a handful of attack probes from other testers, and these were limited to simple failed SQL and XSS injection attempts.

One reason for the lack of participation may have been ambiguity over the legal protections provided to testers by the BOEE. Another possible reason is that the test began on short notice—the final start date was announced only three days in advance. If such a trial must be repeated, we hope that the schedule will be set well in advance, and that legal protections for participants will be strongly in place. In addition to the short notice, the scheduled conclusion of the test was only three days before the system was planned to be opened for use by real voters. Had the test outcome been less dramatic, election officials would have had insufficient time to thoroughly evaluate testers' findings.

Despite these problems, one of the strongest logistical aspects of the D.C. trial was that access to the code—and to some extent, the architecture—was available to the testers. While some observers have suggested that this gave us an unrealistic advantage while attacking the system, there are several reasons why such transparency makes for a more realistic test. Above and beyond the potential security benefits of open source code (pressure to produce better code, feedback from community, etc.), in practice it is difficult to prevent a motivated attacker from gaining access to source code. The code could have been leaked by the authors through an explicit sale by dishonest insiders, as a result of coercion, or through a compromised developer workstation. Since highly plausible attacks such as these are outside the scope of a research evaluation, it is not only fair but realistic to provide the code to the testers.

### 5.3   Why Internet Voting Is Hard

Practical Internet voting designs tend to suffer from a number of fundamental difficulties, from engineering practice to inherent architectural flaws. We feel it is important to point them out again given the continued development of Internet voting systems.

*Engineering practice.*   Both the DVBM system and the earlier prototype Internet voting system SERVE [11] were built primarily on commercial-off-the-shelf (COTS) software (which, despite the use of the term "commercial," includes most everyday open-source software). Unfortunately, the primary security paradigm for COTS developers is still "penetrate and patch." While this approach is suitable for the economic and risk environment of typical home and business users, it is not appropriate for voting applications due to the severe consequences of failure.

*Inherited DRE threats.* Relatively simple Internet voting systems like D.C.'s DVBM strongly resemble direct recording electronic (DRE) voting machines, in that there is no independent method for auditing cast ballots. If the voting system software is corrupt, recovery is likely to be impossible, and even detection can be extremely difficult. DRE voting is highly susceptible to insider attacks as well as external compromise through security vulnerabilities. In previous work [7,8,10,13,17], the closed, proprietary nature of DREs has been held as an additional threat to security, since there is no guarantee that even the *intended* code is honest and correct. In contrast, the DVBM system was open source, but the public would have had no guarantee that the deployed voting system was actually running the published code.

*Tensions between ballot secrecy and integrity.* One of the fundamental reasons that voting systems are hard to develop is that two fundamental goals of a secret ballot election—ballot secrecy and ballot integrity—are in tension. Indeed, the D.C. system attempted to protect integrity through the use of logs, backups and intrusion detection, yet these systems can help an intruder compromise ballot secrecy. Other security mechanisms put in place to protect ballot secrecy, such as encrypting completed ballots and avoiding incremental backups make detecting and responding to compromise much more difficult.

*Architectural brittleness in web applications.* The main vulnerability we exploited resulted from a tiny oversight in a single line of code and could have been prevented by using single quotes instead of double quotes. Mistakes like this are all too common. They are also extremely hard to eradicate, not because of their complexity, but because of the multitude of potential places they can exist. If any one place is overlooked, an attacker may be able to leverage it to gain control of the entire system. In this sense, existing web application frameworks tend to be *brittle*. As our case study shows, the wrong choice of which type of quote to use—or countless other seemingly trivial errors—can result in an attacker controlling the outcome of an election.

*Internet-based threats.* Internet voting exposes what might otherwise be a small, local race of little global significance to attackers from around the globe, who may act for a wide range of reasons varying from politics to financial gain to sheer malice. In addition to compromising the central voting server as we did, attackers can launch denial-of-service attacks aimed at disrupting the election, they can redirect voters to fake voting sites, and they can conduct widespread attacks on voters' client machines [9]. These threats correspond to some of the most difficult unsolved problems in Internet security and are unlikely to be overcome soon.

*Comparison to online banking.* While Internet-based financial applications, such as online banking, share some of the threats faced by Internet voting, there is a fundamental difference in ability to deal with compromises after they have occurred. In the case of online banking, transaction records, statements, and multiple logs allow customers to detect specific fraudulent transactions and in many cases allow the bank to reverse them. Internet voting systems cannot keep such fine-grained transaction logs without violating ballot secrecy for voters. Even with these protections in place, banks suffer a significant amount of online fraud but write it off as part of the cost of doing business; fraudulent election results cannot be so easily excused.

## 6    Related Work

Although this is, to the best of our knowledge, the first public penetration test of an Internet voting system scheduled for use in a general election, we are not the first to caution against the adoption of Internet voting.

The most closely related work is the 2004 security analysis of the Secure Electronic Registration and Voting Experiment (SERVE) by Jefferson et al. [11]. Like the D.C. DVBM project, SERVE was an Internet voting "pilot" that was slated for use in an actual election by absentee overseas voters. Jefferson et al. reviewed the system design and pointed out many architectural and conceptual weaknesses that apply to remote Internet voting systems in general, though they did not have an opportunity to conduct a penetration test of a pilot system. On the basis of these weaknesses, Jefferson et al. recommended "shutting down the development of SERVE immediately and not attempting anything like it in the future until both the Internet and the world's home computer infrastructure have been fundamentally redesigned." We emphatically reaffirm that recommendation. Despite incremental advances in computer security in the last eight years, the fundamental architectural flaws Jefferson et al. identified remain largely the same to this day.

More recently, Esteghari and Desmedt [9] developed an attack on the Helios 2.0 [6] open-audit Internet voting system. Their attack exploits an architectural weakness in home computer infrastructure by installing a "browser rootkit" or "man-in-the-browser attack" that detects the ballot web page and modifies votes. Esteghari and Desmedt note that Helios 3.0 is capable of posting audit information to an external web server *before* ballot submission, which can, in theory, be checked using a second trusted computer to detect the action of the rootkit, but it is not clear that such a second computer will be available or a sufficiently large number of nontechnical voters will take advantage of this audit mechanism.

## 7    Conclusions

Our experience with the D.C. pilot system demonstrates one of the key dangers in many Internet voting designs: one small mistake in the configuration or implementation of the central voting servers or their surrounding network infrastructure can easily undermine the legitimacy of the entire election. We expect that other fielded Internet voting systems will fall prey to such problems, especially if they are developed using standard practices for mass-produced software and websites. Even if the central servers were somehow eliminated or made impervious to external attack, Internet voting is likely to be susceptible to numerous classes of threats, including sabotage from insiders and malware placed on client machines. The twin problems of building secure software affordably and preventing home computers from falling prey to malware attacks would both have to be solved before systems like D.C.'s could be seriously considered. Although new end-to-end verifiable cryptographic voting schemes have the potential to reduce the trust placed in servers and clients, these proposals are significantly more advanced than systems like D.C.'s and may prove even more difficult for developers and election officials to implement correctly. Securing Internet voting in practice will require significant fundamental advances in computer security, and we urge Internet voting proponents to reconsider deployment until and unless major breakthroughs are achieved.

**Acknowledgments.** We are grateful to the many people who helped make this work possible, including Jeremy Epstein, Susannah Goodman, Nadia Heninger, David Jefferson, Bryan Sivak, Pamela Smith, David Robinson, and especially Joseph Lorenzo Hall. We thank the anonymous reviewers for their constructive feedback and Konstantin Beznosov for shepherding this paper to publication. The authors also wish to thank Rokey Suleman and Paul Stenbjorn of the D.C. BOEE for having the courage to allow the public to test its voting system.

# References

1. Internet voting in Estonia. Vabariigi Valimiskomisjon (February 2007), http://www.vvk.ee/public/dok/Internet_Voting_in_Estonia.pdf
2. Uncovering the veil on Geneva's Internet voting solution. Republique Et Canton De Geneve (February 2009), http://www.geneve.ch/evoting/english/doc/Flash_IT_vote_electronique_SIDP_final_english.pdf
3. District of Columbia's Board of Elections and Ethics adopts open source digital voting foundation technology to support ballot delivery. OSDV Press Release (June 2010), http://osdv.org/wp-content/uploads/2010/06/osdv-press-release-final-62210.pdf
4. Internet voting, still in beta. The New York Times editorial (January 2010), http://www.nytimes.com/2010/01/28/opinion/28thu4.html
5. Internet voting. Verified Voting (May 2011), http://www.verifiedvoting.org/article.php?list=type&type=27
6. Adida, B.: Helios: Web-based open-audit voting. In: Proc. 17th USENIX Security Symposium (July 2008)
7. Appel, A.W., Ginsburg, M., Hursti, H., Kernighan, B.W., Richards, C.D., Tan, G., Venetis, P.: The New Jersey voting-machine lawsuit and the AVC Advantage DRE voting machine. In: Proc. 2009 Electronic Voting Technology Workshop/Workshop on Trustworthy Elections (EVT/WOTE) (August 2009)
8. Butler, K., Enck, W., Hursti, H., McLaughlin, S., Traynor, P., McDaniel, P.: Systemic issues in the Hart InterCivic and Premier voting systems: Reflections on project EVEREST. In: Proc. 2008 Electronic Voting Technology Workshop/Workshop on Trustworthy Elections (EVT/WOTE) (July 2008)

 9. Esteghari, S., Desmedt, Y.: Exploiting the client vulnerabilities in Internet e-voting systems: Hacking Helios 2.0 as an example. In: Proc. 2010 Electronic Voting Technology Workship/Workshop on Trustworthy Elections (EVT/WOTE) (August 2010)
10. Feldman, A.J., Halderman, J.A., Felten, E.W.: Security analysis of the Diebold AccuVote-TS voting machine. In: Proc. 2007 Electronic Voting Technology Workshop/Workshop on Trustworthy Elections (EVT/WOTE) (August 2007)
11. Jefferson, D., Rubin, A.D., Simons, B., Wagner, D.: A security analysis of the secure electronic registration and voting experiment (SERVE) (January 2004), http://servesecurityreport.org/paper.pdf
12. Kiayias, A., Korman, M., Walluck, D.: An Internet voting system supporting user privacy. In: 22nd Annual Computer Security Applications Conference
13. Kohno, T., Stubblefield, A., Rubin, A.D., Wallach, D.S.: Analysis of an electronic voting system. In: IEEE Symposium on Security and Privacy, pp. 27–40 (May 2004)
14. Rokey, W., Suleman, I., McGhie, K.W., Togo, D., West, J., Lowery, C.: Making reform a reality: An after-action report on implementation of the Omnibus Election Reform Act. DCBOEE (February 2011), http://www.dcboee.org/popup.asp?url=/pdf_files/nr_687.pdf
15. Rubin, A.: Security considerations for remote electronic voting over the Internet, http://avirubin.com/e-voting.security.html
16. Stenbjorn, P.: An overview and design rationale memo. DCBOEE (September 2010), http://www.dcboee.us/dvm/DCdVBM-DesignRationale-v3.pdf
17. Wolchok, S., Wustrow, E., Halderman, J.A., Prasad, H.K., Kankipati, A., Sakhamuri, S.K., Yagati, V., Gonggrijp, R.: Security analysis of India's electronic voting machines. In: Proc. 17th ACM Conference on Computer and Communications Security (CCS) (October 2010)

# Security Audits Revisited

Rainer Böhme

Department of Information Systems, University of Münster, Germany
`rainer.boehme@uni-muenster.de`

**Abstract.** Security audits with subsequent certification appear to be the
tool of choice to cure failures in providing the right level of security between different interacting parties, e. g., between an outsourcing provider
and its clients. Our game-theoretic analysis scrutinizes this view and identifies conditions under which security audits are most effective, and when
they are not. We find that basic audits are hardly ever useful, and in general, the thoroughness of security audits needs to be carefully tailored to
the situation. Technical, managerial, and policy implications for voluntary, mandatory, unilateral, and bilateral security audits are discussed.
The analysis is based on a model of interdependent security which takes
as parameters the efficiency of security investment in reducing individual
risk, the degree of interdependence as a measure of interconnectedness,
and the thoroughness of the security audit.

## 1   Introduction

Information technology has spurred innovation and productivity gains [8], but
the flip side is the emergence of cyber risk. A characteristic feature that distin-
guishes this "new" kind of risk from traditional risks is the sensitivity to interdependence between decisions of individual actors [16]. Therefore, a profound
understanding of the particularities of cyber risk is essential to guide the design
of secure systems as well as supporting organizational measures. Security audits
belong to the set of organizational tools to manage and regulate risk-taking in
the internet society. This paper sets out to rigorously analyze why and under
which conditions security audits can be most effective.

### 1.1   Interdependent Cyber Risk

In the context of cyber risk, *interdependence* means that the success of risk mitigation does not only depend on the actions of the potentially affected party, but
also on actions of others. In economics jargon, interdependence can be described
as an instance where security investment generates *externalities*.

Examples for interdependent security risks exist on various levels of abstraction. For example, modern software engineering relies on the composition of
reusable components. Since the security of a system can be compromised by a
single vulnerability, the overall security of a system does not only depend on
the effort of the first-tier developer, but also on the effort of the developers of

A.D. Keromytis (Ed.): FC 2012, LNCS 7397, pp. 129–147, 2012.

components, libraries, development tools, and the transitive closure thereof (i. e., libraries used by components, development tools used to build libraries, etc.). Also service-oriented architectures provide a wide range of examples for interdependence. In supply chains and other kinds of outsourcing relations, including all types of cloud computing, the confidentiality, availability, and oftentimes also the integrity of business-relevant data depends on the security level of all involved parties. As a final example, take the internet as a whole. Botnets are the backbone for a range of threat scenarios. Their existence and growth is only possible because not all nodes connected to the network make sufficient efforts to secure their systems. So the insecurity of a victim partly depends on the inaptitude of others—that is a clear case of interdependence.

The issues arising from interdependent security, notably free-riding and lack of incentives to invest in security, are not always reflected in the literature discussing the potentials of interconnection for the sake of sharing information, services, and other resources. If not fully ignored, these issues are often described as open yet solvable (e. g., [3]). Or the problem is deferred informally to security audits and certification (e. g., [23,18]). These organizational measures would ensure high enough security standards. Such claims motivate us to take a closer look at security audits and interdependence to see if the hopes are realistic.

## 1.2  Security Audits

Generally, it is hard to directly measure the security level of products, systems, services, or organizations [14]. This has mainly two reasons: first, the difficulty of specifying all security requirements—the bug versus feature problem. And secondly, threats neither occur deterministically nor is their occurrence observable in realtime. Hence the conclusion a system be secure because no attacks were observed in the past is obviously invalid. One might just have been lucky that no attacks occurred, or the consequences of successful attacks—for instance loss of confidentiality—will only be observable at a later point in time. These difficulties impede measuring the security level of one's *own* systems. It is easy to see that the problems aggravate for systems owned by *others*, as it is the case in the context of interdependence. Therefore, security almost always has the properties of a credence good [2].

As direct measurement is hard, one can resort to examine all security-relevant attributes of an object to *estimate* its latent security level. This involves considerable effort, because these examinations are not fully automatizable and they require special knowledge and experience of the examiner. Moreover, the effort will often grow disproportionately to the complexity of the object under investigation because more and more dependencies need to be checked. We refer the reader to the literature (e. g., [28]) for an overview of different types of security assessments and their process models. According to this literature, semi-standardized examinations can at least help to identify weaknesses against specific known threats, and to fix the weaknesses thereafter.

Our notion of *security audit* in this paper goes beyond a mere examination. It also includes certification by the examiner who is trusted by third parties. This way, the result of an examination is verifiable and can serve as a credible signal to other market participants. *Pure security examinations without certification are not subject of this paper* because they cannot contribute to solve the problems arising from interdependent cyber risk.

In practice, security audits with subsequent certification are very common and cause substantial costs to the industry. Examples include the Common Criteria (where audits may last up to one year and cost up to a million dollars) and their predecessors Orange Book (U.S.) and ITSEC (Europe). These standards were designed for public procurement. Other security audits are laid down in industry standards, such as PCI DSS for payment systems or ISO 17799, respectively ISO 27001. In addition, there exists a market for a variety of quality seals issued by for-profit and non-profit organizations alike. Examples include VeriSign, TrustE, or the European data protection seal EuroPriSe.

### 1.3  Economics of Security Audits

Economic theory suggests two channels through which security audits can generate positive utility:

1. **Overcoming information asymmetries.** From the fact that security is a credence good follows a lemon market problem [2]. The demand side lacks information about the quality of goods. In the simplest case, this quality information can be thought of a binary attribute: secure versus insecure. It can be shown that the equilibrium price for goods of unknown quality drops to the price of insecure goods. As a result, no market exists for secure products. Security audits can help to signal quality and fix this market failure.
2. **Solving coordination problems.** If credible signals are available, additional strategies emerge in the game-theoretic models of interdependent security. The players not only decide about their own security investment, but also whether or not to signal information about their own security level. This can generate new welfare-maximizing equilibria or stabilize existing ones. Security audits are the means to generate credible signals in practice.

Understanding both channels is certainly relevant. However, only the second channel is directly linked to interdependent security. Therefore, we concentrate our attention in this paper on the solution of the coordination problem and refer the reader to the relevant literature [1,21,2] on the role of audits in fixing information asymmetries (cf. Sect. 4 for comments on that literature).

Note that in practice, security audits are commissioned also—if not primarily—because of legal or contractual obligations. Another reason can be liability dumping: a CIO might find it easier to repudiate responsibility after a successful attack by referring to regular security audits, no matter how sound they actually are. Both motivations can generate individual utility. In the following, we will not directly deal with these motivations. The focus of our analysis is economic in nature, that means, in the long run, uninformative audits will not help the CIO in the above example. With regard to mandatory audits, we start one step ahead. The very objective of our analysis is to scrutinize the economic justification of existing or future legal and contractual obligations *because of* their potential to prevent market failures.

## 1.4  Research Question and Relevance

Now we can formulate the research question: *Under which conditions do security audits (defined in Sect. 1.2) generate positive utility by solving the coordination problems (see Sect. 1.3), which would otherwise hinder the reduction of interdependent cyber risks?*

The response to this question is relevant for security managers who decide whether commissioning security audits is profitable[1] given:

a. the *security productivity*, a property of the organization and its business,
b. the *thoroughness* of the security audit, and
c. the *degree of interdependence*, a property of the organization's environment.

Our contribution in this paper is a new analytical model to answer this research question. The model can also be employed for decision support whenever a change in one of the conditions (a–c) is anticipated. The latter mainly concerns decisions to increase interconnectivity, for instance by supporting more interfaces or integrating new services. Each affects the degree of interdependence.

Solving the coordination problem not only increases individual utility, but also leads to improvements in social welfare. Therefore, our model and its analysis is equally relevant for regulators. For example, regulations requesting mandatory audits should be designed such that audits are only required when it is economical. Moreover, the model can help to formulate high-level requirements for security audits such that audits have a welfare-maximizing effect.

Everything that has been said for the regulator can be applied to market situations in which one market participant defines the standards for an industrial sector. This can be an industrial organization (such as in the case of PCI), or a blue chip company orchestrating its supply chain.

## 1.5  Roadmap

The next section presents our model, which is designed parsimoniously without omitting properties necessary for the interpretation. The model is solved and all pure strategy equilibria identified. Section 3 analyzes the equilibria with regard to the utility generated by security audits. We will explain under which condition security audits are helpful, and when they are not needed to solve the coordination problem. Section 4 discusses relations to prior art, both in terms of the subject area and the analytical methodology. A critical discussion and our outlook precede the final conclusion (Sect. 5).

---

[1] We are agnostic about defining a price for the security audit. Hence "profitable" should be read in the sense of strictly positive utility.

# 2   Model

The analytical model consists of three components: a formalization of the security audit process, a model of security investment, and a model of interdependent security. Each component includes exactly one free parameter, that is one for each of the three properties (a–c) described informally in Section 1.4. To the extent possible, we combine established modeling conventions. However, the resulting model as a whole is novel and specific to the analysis of security audits.

## 2.1   Stylized Audit Process

To capture security audits in an economic model, it is essential to reduce them to their most relevant features. In particular, at our level of abstraction, it does not matter *how* a security audit is conducted technically and organizationally. The only relevant outcome is its result.

For this we assume that every examinable object $X$ has a latent—i.e., not directly observable—attribute $s_X \in \mathbb{R}^+$ describing its security level. Objects $X$ of interests can include products, systems, services, or entire organizations. The probability of loss due to security incidents decreases monotonically with increasing security level $s_X$.

Now we can model a security audit as function which takes object $X$ as input, compares its security level $s_X$ to an internal threshold $t$, and returns one bit,

$$\mathsf{SecAudit}(X) = \begin{cases} 1 \text{ if } s_X \geq t \\ 0 \text{ otherwise.} \end{cases} \tag{1}$$

The result of the audit shall be verifiable by third parties. In practice this can be ensured by issuing a (paper) certificate or by having the auditor sign the result cryptographically. In any case, the result is just a snapshot in time and has to be annotated with a time stamp if state changes of $X$ are of interest. Our analysis in this paper is limited to one-shot games with fixed states.

The assumption of a threshold $t$ can be justified with the common practice to conduct security audits along semi-standardized checklists where the thoroughness of the audit has to be defined beforehand. It is certainly conceivable to consider a family of functions $\mathsf{SecAudit}_t$ from which the appropriate function is selected depending on the situation. A real-world example for this are the seven Evaluation Assurance Levels (EAL) specified in the Common Criteria. However, it most cases the number of different thresholds will be small and countable. So we cannot assume that $t$ can be chosen from a continuous interval.

Note that we simplify the audit problem to a single summative measure of security level. In practice, different aspects (e. g., protection goals, security targets in the Common Criteria terminology, etc.) or components of a system can have different levels of security. This view is compatible with our approach if one considers each system as a bundle of objects $X$ and a given security audit as a collection of functions, one for each property of the bundle.

Our abstraction ignores that practical audits may cause side effects. Audits impose costs, which typically depend on $X$ and $t$. There is also a risk of hidden information leakage as the auditor and its staff may get to know sensitive information about $X$. In a dynamic setting, there might be a non-negligible lag between the time when the audit decision is taken and the time when the output is available. All these side effects are not considered in this paper. Therefore, our simplifications may let security audits appear more useful in our analysis than they actually are in practice. Conversely, we err on the side of caution in cases where security audits turn out useless in our analysis. The reader is advised to keep this bias in mind when interpreting our results.

## 2.2   Security Investment

Consider for now a single firm[2] making security investments to reduce the probability of incurring a loss of unit size $l = 1$ due to security incidents. We adopt the functional relationship between security investment $s$ and the probability of loss $p(s)$ from the well-known Gordon–Loeb model of security investment [11],

$$p(s) = \beta^{-s}. \tag{2}$$

This function reflects a decreasing marginal utility of security investment, a property that has been confirmed empirically [17], by practitioners [11], and can be justified theoretically [7]. Parameter $\beta \geq e^2$ represents the firm-specific *security productivity*. The range of $s$ is limited to the interval $[0, 1]$. This is so because risk-neutral firms prefer $s = 0$ over all alternatives $s > l = 1$. To keep the number of parameters manageable, we fix the parameter for vulnerability in [11] at $v = 1$: without security investment, every realized threat causes a loss.

Our model shares another simplification with most analytical models of information security investment. It does not distinguish between security investment and security level. This implies the assumption that all security investment is effective. By contrast, practitioners often observe the situation of security over-investment (from a cost perspective) still leading to a suboptimal security level [6]. Hence caution is needed when transferring conclusions on security over-investment or under-investment from analytical models to the real world.

The firm's expected cost can be expressed as sum of the security investment and the expected loss,

$$c(s) = s + p(s) = s + \beta^{-s}. \tag{3}$$

This model is good enough to find optimal levels of security investment for a single firm. However, without interdependence, this is not of interest here.

---

[2] For consistency and didactic reasons, we use the term "firm" to refer to a single rational decision maker. This does not limit the generality of the model. Firm stands as placeholder for any entity conceivable in a given context, e.g., "organization", "defender", "nation state", "player", or "user".

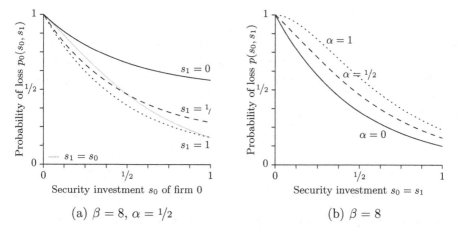

**Fig. 1.** Interdependent security: firm 0's probability of loss partly depends on firm 1's security investment (left); the probability of loss increases with the degree of interdependence $\alpha$ even if both firms invest equally (right)

### 2.3   Modeling Interdependence

The simplest possible case to model interdependence is to assume two symmetric a priori homogeneous firms who act as players in a game. Security investments $s_0$ and $s_1$ are the only choice variables. Symmetry implies that both firms share the same security productivity $\beta$. This can be justified by generalizing Carr's argument [9] to security technology. Security technology has become a "commodity" which is rarely a factor of strategic differentiation between firms.

Consider the following function for the probability of loss $p_i$ of firm $i \in \{0, 1\}$,

$$p_i(s_i, s_{1-i}) = 1 - (1 - \beta^{-s_i})(1 - \alpha \beta^{-s_{1-i}}). \tag{4}$$

This reflects the intuition that a firm evades a loss only if neither it falls victim to a security breach, nor a breach at an interconnected firm is propagated. Parameter $\alpha \in [0, 1]$ is the *degree of interdependence*, a property of the environment of both firms. For $\alpha = 0$ (no interdependence), Eq. (4) reduces to Eq. (2).

Figure 1a illustrates the effect of interdependence described informally in the introduction. We set $\alpha = 1/2$ for moderate interdependence. The black curves show that the probability of loss of firm 0, for every choice of its own security investment $s_0 > 0$, also depends on the choice of $s_1$ by firm 1. By contrast, the gray intersecting curve shows the probability of loss if both firms make equal security investments. This setting prevails in Figure 1b. Here we show curves for different settings of the degree of interdependence $\alpha$. Observe that the probability of loss grows with the degree of interdependence for every fixed security investment $s_0 = s_1 > 0$.

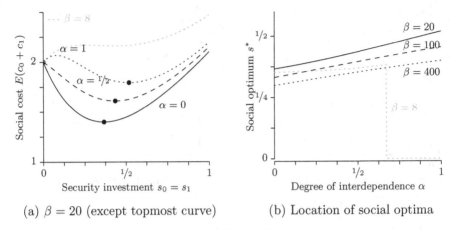

(a) $\beta = 20$ (except topmost curve)     (b) Location of social optima

**Fig. 2.** Security investment $s^*$ minimizes the expected "social" cost of both firms

### 2.4   Social Optima

A social optimum is reached if the sum of the expected costs of both firms is minimal, thus

$$s^* = \arg\min_s 2 \cdot c(s, s) \tag{5}$$

$$= \arg\min_s s + 1 - (1 - \beta^{-s})(1 - \alpha\beta^{-s}). \tag{6}$$

We may substitute $s_i$ by $s$ due to symmetry. Figure 2a shows the objective function and their minima for selected parameters. Their location can be obtained analytically from the first-order condition of Eq. (6). We get

$$s^* = -\log\left(\frac{(1+\alpha) - \sqrt{(1+\alpha)^2 - 8\alpha\log^{-1}(\beta)}}{4\alpha}\right)\log^{-1}(\beta) \tag{7}$$

for $\alpha > 0$, and

$$s^* = \log(\log(\beta))\log^{-1}(\beta) \quad \text{for the special case } \alpha = 0. \tag{8}$$

For high degrees of interdependence and low security productivity, the social optima reside at the lower end of the value range of $s$. The gray dotted curves in Figs. 2a and 2b visualize this case (for $\beta = 8$). We will discuss the implications of this special case on security audits below in Sect. 3.4.

Figure 2b shows the location of social optima as a function of $\alpha$ for selected values of $\beta$. Observe that the socially optimal security investment does not react

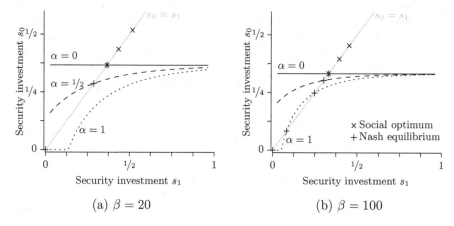

**Fig. 3.** Best response of firm 0 given security investment of firm 1; all fixed points of this function are pure strategy Nash equilibria

monotonously to changes in the security productivity $\beta$. Apart from the above-described discontinuity, increasing degree of interdependence $\alpha$ shifts the social optimum towards higher levels of security investment $s$. Frankly speaking, this means that an increasingly interconnected society ceteris paribus has to spend more and more on security to maintain a welfare-maximizing[3] level. This follows directly from the relation depicted in Figure 1b.

## 2.5  Nash Equilibria

Knowing the location of social optima does not imply that they are reached in practice. This will only happen if all players have incentives to raise their security investment to the level of $s^*$. The analysis of incentives—which obviously depend on the actions of the respective other firm—requires a game-theoretic perspective and the search for Nash equilibria.

Only pure strategies are regarded in this paper. Firm $i$'s best response $s^+$ given $s_{1-i}$ is the solution to the following optimization problem:

$$s^+(s_{1-i}) = \arg\min_s s + p(s, s_{1-i}) \tag{9}$$

$$= \arg\min_s s + 1 - \left(1 - \beta^{-s}\right)\left(1 - \alpha\beta^{-s_{1-i}}\right) \tag{10}$$

$$\text{s.t.} \quad s \geq 0.$$

After finding roots of the first-order condition and rearranging, we obtain:

$$s^+(s_{1-i}) = \sup\left\{\frac{\log\left(\log(\beta)\right) + \log\left(1 - \alpha\beta^{-s_{1-i}}\right)}{\log(\beta)}, 0\right\}. \tag{11}$$

---

[3] Welfare is defined as the reciprocal of social cost.

Figure 3 shows the best response as function of $s_1$ for three different degrees of interdependence ($\alpha \in \{0, 1/2, 1\}$) and two values of security productivity ($\beta \in \{20, 100\}$). Nash equilibria, defined as fixed points of the best response function, are located on the intersections with the main diagonal. For comparison, we also plot the social optima as given by Eq. (7).

Depending on the parameters, there exist up to three Nash equilibria at

$$\tilde{s}_{1,2} = \log \left( \frac{\log(\beta) \pm \sqrt{\log^2(\beta) - 4\alpha\log(\beta)}}{2} \right) \log^{-1}(\beta) \qquad (12)$$

(if both expression and discriminant are positive) and

$$\tilde{s}_3 = 0 \quad \text{for} \quad \alpha > 1 - \log^{-1}(\beta). \qquad (13)$$

The parameters in Figure 3 are chosen such that every case of interest is represented with at least one curve. We will discuss all cases jointly with the interpretation in Section 3. The formal conditions for the various equilibrium situations are summarized in Appendix A.1.

## 3    Analysis

For all strictly positive values of $\alpha > 0$, the Nash equilibria are located below the social optimum. This replicates a known result: security as a public good is under-provided in the marketplace [27,16]. The reasons are lack of incentives, more specifically a coordination problem [24]. If firm $i$ knew for sure that firm $1 - i$ cooperates and invests $s_{1-i} = s^*$, then it would be easier to decide for the socially optimal level of security investment as well. In practice, however, firm $i$ can hardly observe the level of $s_{1-i}$.

Security audits can fix this problem. They allow a firm to signal the own security level to its peers in a verifiable way. This can convince others of the willingness to cooperate and stimulate further cooperative responses. Now we have to distinguish between the case of coordination between multiple equilibria, and the case of coordination at non-equilibrium points. The former helps to avoid bad outcomes, the latter in needed to actually reach the social optimum.

**Coordination between Multiple Equilibria.** If multiple Nash equilibria exist, the initial conditions determine which equilibrium is chosen. So the coordination problem is to nudge the game into the equilibrium with the lowest social cost. To do this, it is sufficient if one firm unilaterally signals a security level in the basin of attraction of the best possible equilibrium. Then the other firms' rational selfish reaction is to choose a security level within that basin and the trajectory of strategic anticipation converges to the desired equilibrium solution. Therefore, in this case, it is sufficient to have *unilateral* security audits which may even be *voluntary* (if the audit costs are not prohibitive).

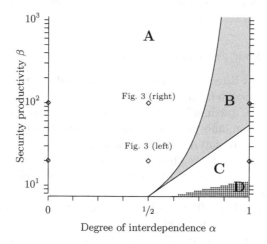

**Fig. 4.** Case distinction in $(\alpha, \beta)$-parameter space

**Coordination at Non-equilibrium Points.** The social optimum is not an attractor in general. Therefore, to reach it, *bilateral* security audits and additional incentives are needed. These incentives could come in the form of *mandatory* security audits and sanctions in case a claimed security level is not met. Sanctions can be enforced by regulation or be inherently embedded in the mechanism. For example, a tit-for-tat strategy of a multi-period prisoner's dilemma entails sanctions by other players [4]. A prerequisite for this strategy is the unambiguous observability of security levels in past rounds. Hence security audits are also essential in this setup.

Now we will analyze the equilibrium situations and discuss implications on the usefulness of security audits depending on their thoroughness $t$. For this it is useful to regard Figure 4, which identifies four equilibrium situations as regions in the $(\alpha, \beta)$-parameter space. Six diamond marks indicate the points in parameter space for which curves are displayed in Figure 3.

## 3.1   Region A: Only Thorough Audits Useful

In region A, there exists exactly one Nash equilibrium (see dashed curves in Fig. 3). The best response $s^{+}_i$ on security investments $s_{1-i} < \tilde{s}_1$ below the Nash equilibrium of Eq. (12) is always larger than $s_{1-i}$. Therefore, firms always have incentives to invest at least $\tilde{s}_1$. Security audits with thoroughness $t < \tilde{s}_1$ below that level do not improve the situation and hence are ineffective. Thorough audits with $\tilde{s}_1 > t \geq s^*$ can improve the security level and social welfare. Since this involves a coordination at non-equilibrium points, such audits must be bilateral. To specify this, it holds that unilateral audits with thoroughness above the social optimum for $\alpha = 0$—this is the only point ($*$ in Fig. 3) where the Nash equilibrium and social optimum concur—can never be more effective than unilateral security audits at this level. This is so because this value bounds the best response function from above.

## 3.2    Region B: Basic Audits Get Leverage

In region B, there exist three Nash equilibria (see dotted curve in Fig. 3b). In one of them, both firms abstain from security investments ($s_0 = s_1 = 0$). In this case, security audits can be maximally effective in solving the coordination problem between the multiple equilibria. To achieve this, the thoroughness $t$ must be just above $\tilde{s}_2$. Then a unilateral audit is enough to move both firms into the best possible equilibrium. More thorough audits in the range $\tilde{s}_2 < t \leq \tilde{s}_1$ do not improve the situation further. In other words, a basic audit just above $\tilde{s}_2$ is leveraged to maximum outcome.

Even the best possible equilibrium is below the social optimum. To approach the optimum further, more thorough audits $t > \tilde{s}_1$ are needed. Everything said for thorough audits above in Sect. 3.1 also applies here. In particular, thorough audits must be bilateral. Superficial audits $t < \tilde{s}_2$ are moderately useful. The situation corresponds to the case discussed in the next section.

## 3.3    Region C: All Audits Moderately Useful

In region C, there exists exactly one Nash equilibrium in which both firms abstain from security investment (see dotted curve in Fig. 3). The distance between this equilibrium and the social optimum reaches a maximum. This case is not a coordination game in the strict sense [24]. Therefore, the effectiveness of all audits is much more limited than in region B (Sect. 3.2). Even though audits may contribute to higher security levels, more specifically, exactly at the level of the thoroughness $t$, if both firms perform bilateral audits. Unilateral audits are less effective in general and completely ineffective within the range where the dotted curve in Figure 3 is flat at level 0. Like in regions A and B, unilateral audits above the social optimum for $\alpha = 0$ are strictly dominated by unilateral audits of thoroughness equal to this level.

## 3.4    Region D: All Audits Useless

In region D, there exists exactly one Nash equilibrium in which both firms abstain from security investment. This concurs with the corner solution of the social optimum (compare the penultimate paragraph of Sect. 2.4 and see the dotted gray curve in Fig. 2a). This means all security investment is prohibitively expensive compared to the protection it promises. In other words, the firm's business is indefensible. Of course, firms would not decide to conduct audits voluntarily (attesting the absence of security investment). Manadatory audits of thoroughness $t > 0$ coupled with sanctions would induce security over-investment and destroy social welfare. The only resorts are to improve security productivity by technological innovation or to reduce the degree of interdependence. Both measures would move the situation back to region C.

## 3.5   Left Edge: No Audits

Figures 4 hides the fact that the left edge ($\alpha = 0$) does not belong to region A. This edge rather represents the special case of independent firms who optimize on their own. There exists exactly one Nash equilibrium which concurs with the social optimum (see solid line in Fig. 3). No firm would conduct security audits voluntarily. Mandatory audits (with sanctions in case of failure) do not result in relevant signals if $t \leq s^* = \tilde{s}$. They are even counter-productive if $t > s^* = \tilde{s}$.

In summary, the most salient new result of this analysis is that even in this stylized model, the usefulness of security audits and the required thoroughness highly depends on the situation. We deem this an important insight for the design of audit standards and policies, which in practice are applied in contexts with many more potentially influential factors.

# 4   Related Work

We are not aware of any prior work addressing this specific or closely related research questions. The same holds for the combination of elements used in our analytical model. Consequently, we structure the discussion of related work broadly into two categories: works which address similar questions, and works that use similar methods for different research questions.

Anderson [2] belongs to the first category. He notes perverse incentives for suppliers of security certifications. This leads vendors who seek certification to shop for the auditor who has the laxest reading of a standard. Baye and Morgan [5] study certificates as an indicator of quality in electronic commerce. They propose an analytical model of strategic price setting in a market where certified and uncertified products compete. They find support for their model using empirical data. In another empirical study, Edelman [10] argues that less trustworthy market participants have more incentives to seek certification (and obtain it). He could show that this adverse selection inverts the intended function of TrustE seals as indicators of quality. The appearance of the seal on a representatively drawn website actually *increases* the posterior probability that the site is shady. This is largely driven by the fact that TrustE certification is voluntary, leading to self-selection. Rice [21], by contrast, recommends mandatory certification of software and services. His proposal is clearly inspired by similar efforts in the area of food and traffic safety. A similar proposal is brought forward by Parameswaran and Whinston [20], yet with a tighter focus on network intermediaries, such as Internet Service Providers. Telang and Yang [26] empirically compare the number of vulnerabilities in software products with and without Common Criteria certification. They find that certified software fixes more old vulnerabilities, but also contains more new vulnerabilities so that the net effect is neutral. All this literature has in common that audits and certification are regarded as tools to overcome information asymmetries. Interdependent security is not reflected. Since our work exclusively deals with solutions to the coordination problem in the presence of interdependence, it complements this strand of literature.

Modeling interdependent risks has quite some tradition in the field of security economics. Varian [27] as well as Kunreuther and Heal [16] belong to the second category of related work. Both teams promoted the view of information security as a public good, suggested formal models, and thus coined the notion of interdependent security. Our model is closer to Kunreuther and Heal. Varian's approach is richer if more than two firms interact. He adopts three types of aggregation functions from the economics literature of public goods [13]: weakest link, total effort, and best shot. Grossklags et al. [12] take up this idea and extend it in a series of works. The key difference to our model is the assumption of two kinds of security investments, one that generates externalities and another one that does not. Most models of interdependence are designed with the intention to find ways to internalize the externalities. This has led to literature for different contexts, including for instance cyber-insurance [19,15] or security outsourcing with [29] and without [22] risk transfer. The availability of security audits is sometimes assumed (e. g., in [25]), but their effectiveness is never scrutinized.

## 5    Discussion

Few analytical models with three parameters can quantitatively predict outcomes in reality. Nevertheless, the interaction of security productivity, degree of interdependence, and thoroughness of security audits in our model allows to draw new conclusions. These conclusions can be transferred to practical situations at least qualitatively using the insights about the underlying mechanics.

### 5.1    Technical Implications

Region A covers more than half of the parameter space, including all settings with low or moderate degree of interdependence ($\alpha < 1/2$). Even if the parameters are not exactly measurable in practice, the conclusions for region A can serve as rules of thumb. A relevant insight is that security audits and certifications at very low security levels are often ineffective. This stands in stark contrast to a plethora of (largely commercial) security seals that certify the "lowest common denominator". Engineers who develop audit standards and supporting tools should rather focus on the possibility to extract verifiable information about high and highest security levels.

Another result of our analysis is that the effectiveness of security audits is very sensitive to the situation. A practical conclusion is that security standards and audit procedures should best be designed in a modular manner to allow tailored examinations. At this point we can only speculate if, say, the seven Evaluation Assurance Levels laid down in the Common Criteria are sufficient, or whether a more granular choice of audit thoroughness is needed. Tailored audits may also require technical prerequisites which need to be considered in the design of the system to be audited. Last but not least, if auditability matters, then technical measures which imply changes to the parameters $\alpha$ and $\beta$ (e. g., change of architecture, security technology, or interconnectivity) should be evaluated with regard to the availability of appropriate audit procedures.

## 5.2   Managerial and Regulatory Implications

Interdependent security risks exhibit a special and non-trivial mechanic. This mechanic prevents that individually rational risk management decisions also lead to socially optimal outcomes. A first important step is to explain this mechanic to managers and regulators. This way, they can adapt their decisions and refrain from blindly commissioning or requesting security audits. Our analysis has shown that security audits with bad fit to the situation are often inefficient or useless. For example, voluntary (i. e., unilateral) security audits certifying a very basic level of security ($s > 0$) are unnecessary in the large majority of cases. By contrast, audits can be very effective if they require relatively little thoroughness—and thus presumably little cost—to stabilize an equilibrium at a substantially higher level of security. This is the case in region B (see Sect. 3.2). Another insight is that very thorough security audits, which attest highest security levels, should only be conducted bilaterally in mutual agreement between partners. This is the only way to effectively prevent free-riding.

Regulators should analyze carefully in which situations they require mandatory security audits of what thoroughness. Most importantly, mandatory audits seem unnecessary in situations where the firms have own incentives to conduct security audits. It goes without saying that security audits should not be required when they are useless. To prevent this, it might be reasonable to replace general audit requirements with more specific sets of rules that consider factors of the firm and its environment. If these criteria are transparent, market participants can choose, say, whether they reduce the degree of interdependence *or* be subject to more thorough security audits.

A challenge remains with the definition and measurement of practical indicators to guide decision support. Neither the degree of interdependence nor the security productivity is observable on the scales that appear in the model. Since this task requires comparable and partly sensitive data of many market participants, we see this task in the responsibility of the government.

## 5.3   Conclusion

We have presented a novel analytical model to study the effectiveness of security audits as tools to incentivize the provision of security by private actors at a socially optimal level. The model takes parameters for the efficiency of security investment in risk reduction (security productivity), the exposure to risk from other peers in a network (degree of interdependence), and the thoroughness of the security audit. The solution of this model reveals that security audits must be tailored to the very situation in order to avoid that they are ineffective. Moreover, "lightweight" security audits certifying a minimum level of security are not socially beneficial in the large majority of cases. Our results call for the revision of policies that require mandatory and undifferentiated security audits.

# References

1. Anderson, R., Böhme, R., Clayton, R., Moore, T.: Security Economics and the Internal Market. Study commissioned by ENISA (2008)
2. Anderson, R.J.: Why information security is hard – An economic perspective (2001)
3. Armbrust, M., et al.: Above the clouds: A Berkeley view of cloud computing. Technical Report EECS-2009-28, University of California, Berkeley (2009)
4. Axelrod, R.: The Evolution of Cooperation. Basic Books, New York (1984)
5. Baye, M.R., Morgan, J.: Red queen pricing effects in e-retail markets. Working Paper (2003)
6. Böhme, R.: Security Metrics and Security Investment Models. In: Echizen, I., Kunihiro, N., Sasaki, R. (eds.) IWSEC 2010. LNCS, vol. 6434, pp. 10–24. Springer, Heidelberg (2010)
7. Böhme, R., Moore, T.W.: The iterated weakest link: A model of adaptive security investment. In: Workshop on the Economics of Information Security (WEIS). University College London, UK (2009)
8. Brynjolfsson, E., Hitt, L.: Computing productivity: Firm-level evidence. The Review of Economics and Statistics 85(4), 793–808 (2003)
9. Carr, N.G.: IT doesn't matter. Harvard Business Review 81(5), 41–49 (2003)
10. Edelman, B.: Adverse selection in online "trust" certifications. In: Workshop on the Economics of Information Security (WEIS). University of Cambridge, UK (2006)
11. Gordon, L.A., Loeb, M.P.: The economics of information security investment. ACM Trans. on Information and System Security 5(4), 438–457 (2002)
12. Grossklags, J., Christin, N., Chuang, J.: Secure or insure? A game-theoretic analysis of information security games. In: Proc. of the Int'l Conference on World Wide Web (WWW), pp. 209–218. ACM Press, Beijing (2008)
13. Hirshleifer, J.: From weakest-link to best-shot: The voluntary provision of public goods. Public Choice 41, 371–386 (1983)
14. Jacquith, A.: Security Metrics: Replacing Fear, Uncertainty, and Doubt. Addison-Wesley (2007)
15. Johnson, B., Böhme, R., Grossklags, J.: Security Games with Market Insurance. In: Baras, J.S., Katz, J., Altman, E. (eds.) GameSec 2011. LNCS, vol. 7037, pp. 117–130. Springer, Heidelberg (2011)
16. Kunreuther, H., Heal, G.: Interdependent security. Journal of Risk and Uncertainty 26(2-3), 231–249 (2003)
17. Liu, W., Tanaka, H., Matsuura, K.: An empirical analysis of security investment in countermeasures based on an enterprise survey in Japan. In: Workshop on the Economics of Information Security (WEIS). University of Cambridge, UK (2006)
18. Molnár, D., Schechter, S.: Self hosting vs. cloud hosting: Accounting for the security impact of hosting in the cloud. In: Workshop on the Economics of Information Security (WEIS). Harvard University, Cambridge (2010)
19. Ogut, H., Menon, N., Raghunathan, S.: Cyber insurance and it security investment: Impact of interdependent risk. In: Workshop on the Economics of Information Security (WEIS). Harvard University, Cambridge (2005)
20. Parameswaran, M., Whinston, A.B.: Incentive mechanisms for internet security. In: Rao, H.R., Upadhyaya, S. (eds.) Handbooks in Information Systems, Emerald, vol. 4, pp. 101–138 (2009)
21. Rice, D.: Geekonomics – The Real Cost of Insecure Software. Addison-Wesley, New York (2007)

22. Rowe, B.R.: Will outsourcing IT security lead to a higher social level of security? In: Workshop on the Economics of Information Security (WEIS). Carnegie Mellon University, Pittsburgh (2007)
23. Sackmann, S., Strüker, J., Accorsi, R.: Personalization in privacy-aware highly dynamic systems. Communications of the ACM 49(9), 32–38 (2006)
24. Schelling, T.: The Strategy of Conflict. Oxford University Press, Oxford (1965)
25. Shetty, N., Schwartz, G., Felegyhazi, M., Walrand, J.: Competitive cyber-insurance and internet security. In: Workshop on Economics of Information Security (WEIS). University College London, UK (2009)
26. Telang, R., Yang, Y.: Do security certifications work? Evidence from Common Criteria certification. In: IEEE International Conference on Technologies for Homeland Security (2011)
27. Varian, H.R.: System reliability and free riding. In: Workshop on the Economics of Information Security (WEIS). University of California, Berkeley (2002)
28. Winkler, S., Proschinger, C.: Collaborative penetration testing. In: Business Services: Konzepte, Technologien, Anwendungen (9. Internationale Tagung Wirtschaftsinformatik), vol. 1, pp. 793–802 (2009)
29. Zhao, X., Xue, L., Whinston, A.B.: Managing interdependent information security risks: A study of cyberinsurance, managed security service and risk pooling. In: Proceedings of ICIS (2009)

# A    Proof Sketches

## A.1    Formal Conditions of Equilibria

**Border between Region A and B**

Idea: Take fixed point from Eq. (12) and set it to zero,

$$\alpha = 1 - \log^{-1}(\beta).$$

**Border between Region B and C**

Idea: Take determinant of Eq. (12) and set it to zero,

$$\beta = e^{4\alpha}.$$

**Border between Region C and D**

Idea: Set $c(s^*) = c(0)$ (from Eqs. (3) and (7)),

$$s^* - \left(1 - \beta^{-s^*}\right)\left(1 - \alpha\beta^{-s^*}\right) = 0.$$

## A.2    Social Optima

Start with Eq. (6):

$$s^* = \arg\min_s s + 1 - (1 - \beta^{-s})(1 - \alpha\beta^{-s})$$

Root of first-order condition of $s$:

$$1 = \log(\beta)\left(1 - \alpha\beta^{-s^*}\right)\beta^{-s^*} + \alpha\log(\beta)\left(1 - \beta^{-s^*}\right)\beta^{-s^*}$$
$$1 = \log(\beta)\beta^{-s^*} + \alpha\log(\beta)\beta^{-s^*} - 2\alpha\log(\beta)\beta^{-2s^*}$$
$$1 = (1 + \alpha)\log(\beta)\beta^{-s^*} - 2\alpha\log(\beta)\beta^{-2s^*}$$

**Case 1:** $\alpha = 0$

$$1 = \log(\beta)\beta^{-s^*}$$
$$s^* = \log(\log(\beta))\log^{-1}(\beta)$$

This expression corresponds to Eq. (8).

**Case 2:** $\alpha > 0$. We obtain the root by substituting $u = \beta^{-s^*}$, solving the quadratic equation, and subsequent resubstitution:

$$s^* = -\log\left(\frac{(1 + \alpha) - \sqrt{(1 + \alpha)^2 - 8\alpha\log^{-1}(\beta)}}{4\alpha}\right)\log^{-1}(\beta)$$

This expression corresponds to Eq. (7).

### A.3    Best Response

Start with Eq. (10):

$$s^+(s_{1-i}) = \arg\min_s s + 1 - \left(1 - \beta^{-s}\right)\left(1 - \alpha\beta^{-s_{1-i}}\right)$$
$$\text{s.t.}\quad s \geq 0$$

Root of first-order condition of $s$:

$$0 = 1 - \log(\beta)\beta^{-s^+}\left(1 - \alpha\beta^{-s_{1-i}}\right)$$
$$1 = \log(\beta)\beta^{-s^+}\left(1 - \alpha\beta^{-s_{1-i}}\right)$$
$$\beta^{s^+} = \log(\beta)\left(1 - \alpha\beta^{-s_{1-i}}\right)$$
$$s^+\log(\beta) = \log(\log(\beta)) + \log\left(1 - \alpha\beta^{-s_{1-i}}\right)$$

Rearrangement subject to constraints:

$$s^+ = \sup\left\{\frac{\log(\log(\beta)) + \log\left(1 - \alpha\beta^{-s_{1-i}}\right)}{\log(\beta)}, 0\right\}$$

This expression corresponds to Eq. (11).

## A.4  Nash Equilibria

Fixed points of the best response $\tilde{s} = s^+(\tilde{s})$ without considering constraints:

$$\tilde{s} = \frac{\log\left(\log(\beta)\right) + \log\left(1 - \alpha\beta^{-\tilde{s}}\right)}{\log(\beta)}$$

$$\tilde{s}\log(\beta) = \log\left(\log(\beta)\right) + \log\left(1 - \alpha\beta^{-\tilde{s}}\right)$$

$$\log(\beta^{\tilde{s}}) = \log\left(\log(\beta)\right) + \log\left(1 - \alpha\beta^{-\tilde{s}}\right)$$

$$\log(\beta^{\tilde{s}}) = \log\left(\log(\beta)\left(1 - \alpha\beta^{-\tilde{s}}\right)\right)$$

$$\log(\beta^{\tilde{s}}) = \log\left(\log(\beta) - \alpha\beta^{-\tilde{s}}\log(\beta)\right)$$

$$\beta^{\tilde{s}} = \log(\beta) - \alpha\beta^{-\tilde{s}}\log(\beta)$$

$$\beta^{\tilde{s}} - \log(\beta) = -\alpha\beta^{-\tilde{s}}\log(\beta)$$

$$\beta^{2\tilde{s}} - \log(\beta)\beta^{\tilde{s}} = -\alpha\log(\beta)$$

$$\beta^{2\tilde{s}} - \log(\beta)\beta^{\tilde{s}} + \alpha\log(\beta) = 0$$

We obtain the root by substituting $u = \beta^{\tilde{s}}$, solving the quadratic equation, and subsequent resubstitution:

$$\tilde{s}_{1,2} = \log\left(\frac{\log(\beta) \pm \sqrt{\log^2(\beta) - 4\alpha\log(\beta)}}{2}\right)\log^{-1}(\beta)$$

This expression corresponds to Eq. (12).

Fixed points are Nash equilibria if they fulfill the constraint $\tilde{s} > 0$. Because of the constraint in Eq (10), there exists another corner equilibrium at $\tilde{s}_3 = 0$ if $s^+(0) = 0$:

$$0 \geq \frac{\log\left(\log(\beta)\right) + \log\left(1 - \alpha\right)}{\log(\beta)}$$

$$1 \geq \log(\beta)\left(1 - \alpha\right)$$

$$\alpha \geq 1 - \log^{-1}(\beta)$$

This expression corresponds to Eq. (13).

# Efficient, Compromise Resilient and Append-Only Cryptographic Schemes for Secure Audit Logging

Attila A. Yavuz[1], Peng Ning[1],
and Michael K. Reiter[2]

[1] Department of Computer Science,
North Carolina State University
Raleigh, NC 27695-8206
{aayavuz,pning}@ncsu.edu
[2] Department of Computer Science
University of North Carolina, Chapel Hill
Chapel Hill, NC
reiter@cs.unc.edu

**Abstract.** Due to the forensic value of audit logs, it is vital to provide *compromise resiliency* and *append-only* properties in a logging system to prevent active attackers. Unfortunately, existing symmetric secure logging schemes are not publicly verifiable and cannot address applications that require public auditing (e.g., public financial auditing), besides being vulnerable to certain attacks and dependent on continuous trusted server support. Moreover, Public Key Cryptography (PKC)-based secure logging schemes require Expensive Operations (ExpOps) that are costly for both loggers and verifiers, and thus are impractical for computation-intensive environments.

In this paper, we propose a new class of secure audit logging scheme called *Log Forward-secure and Append-only Signature (LogFAS)*. LogFAS achieves the most desirable properties of both symmetric and PKC-based schemes. LogFAS can produce publicly verifiable forward-secure and append-only signatures without requiring any online trusted server support or time factor. Most notably, LogFAS is the only PKC-based secure audit logging scheme that achieves the high verifier computational and storage efficiency. That is, LogFAS can verify $L$ log entries with always a small-constant number of ExpOps regardless of the value of $L$. Moreover, each verifier stores only a small and constant-size public key regardless of the number of log entries to be verified or the number of loggers in the system. In addition, a LogFAS variation allows fine-grained verification of any subset of log entries and fast detection of corrupted log entries. All these properties make LogFAS an ideal scheme for secure audit logging in computation-intensive applications.

**Keywords:** Secure audit logging, applied cryptography, forward security, signature aggregation.

## 1 Introduction

Audit logs have been used to track important events such as user activities and program execution in modern computer systems, providing invaluable information about

A.D. Keromytis (Ed.): FC 2012, LNCS 7397, pp. 148–163, 2012.

the state of the systems (e.g., intrusions, crashes). Due to their forensic value, audit logs are an attractive target for attackers. Indeed, an experienced attacker may erase the traces of her malicious activities from the logs, or modify the log entries to implicate other users after compromising the system. Therefore, ensuring the integrity, authenticity and accountability of audit logs in the presence of attackers is critical for any modern computer system [9, 20, 25, 29].

There are straightforward techniques to protect audit logs from active adversaries: (i) Using a tamper resistant hardware on each logging machine to prevent the adversary from modifying audit logs and (ii) transmitting each log entry as soon as it is generated to a remote trusted server. Unfortunately, these approaches have significant limitations as identified in [9, 19–21]: First, it is impractical to assume both the presence and the "bug-freeness" of a tamper resistant hardware on all types of platforms (e.g., wireless sensors [18], commercial off-the-shelf systems [7]) [17, 20]. Second, it is difficult to guarantee timely communication between each logging machine and the remote trusted server in the presence of active adversaries [11, 19, 29].

**Limitations of Previous Cryptographic Log Protection Techniques:** Cryptograp-hic mechanisms can protect the integrity of audit logs without relying on such techniques. In these settings, the log verifiers might not be available to verify the log entries once they are generated. Hence, a logger may have to accumulate log entries for a period of time. If the adversary takes full control of the logging machine in this duration, no cryptographic mechanism can prevent her from modifying the post-attack log entries. However, the integrity of log entries accumulated before the attack should be protected (i.e., *forward-security* property) [1, 7, 9, 12, 17, 19, 20, 29]. Furthermore, this protection should not only guarantee the integrity of individual log entries but also the integrity of the log stream as a whole. That is, no selective deletion or truncation of log entries should be possible (i.e., *append-only (aggregate)* property [17, 18, 20]). Forward-secure and aggregate signatures (e.g., [17, 18, 20, 29, 30]) achieve forward-security and append-only properties simultaneously.

Pioneering forward-secure audit logging schemes [6, 7, 25] rely on symmetric primitives such as Message Authentication Code (MAC) to achieve computationally efficient integrity protection. However, the symmetric nature of these schemes does not allow public verifiability. This property is necessary for applications such as financial auditing applications where financial books of publicly held companies need to be verified by the current and potential future share holders [12, 20]. Furthermore, symmetric schemes require online remote trusted server support, which entails costly maintenance and attracts potential attacks besides being a potential single-point of failures. Finally, these schemes are shown to be vulnerable against the truncation and delayed detection attacks [19, 20] (no append-only property).

To mitigate the above problems, several PKC-based secure audit logging schemes have been proposed (e.g., [12, 17, 18, 20, 29]). These schemes are publicly verifiable and do not require an online TTP support. However, they are costly for loggers (except for BAF [29]) and extremely costly for the log verifiers. Second, to verify a particular log entry, all these schemes [17–19, 29] force log verifiers to verify the entire set of log

**Table 1.** Comparison of LogFAS schemes and their counterparts for performance, applicability, availability and security parameters

| Criteria | | LogFAS | FssAgg/iFssAgg AR \| BM \| BLS | | | BAF | Logcrypt | SYM [7, 25] |
|---|---|---|---|---|---|---|---|---|
| Computational | | | PKC-based | | | | | |
| On-line | Sig&Upd (per item) | $ExpOp$ | $ExpOp$ | | | $H$ | $ExpOp$ | $H$ |
| | Ver, (L items) | $ExpOp + O(L \cdot H)$ | $O(L \cdot (ExpOp + H))$ | | | | | $O(L \cdot H)$ |
| | Subset ver ($l' < L$) | $ExpOp + O(l' \cdot H)$ | $O(2l'(ExpOp + H))$ | | Not immutable | | | $O(l' \cdot H)$ |
| | Efficient Search | Available | Not Available | | | | | - |
| Key Generation (Offline) | | | $O(L \cdot ExpOp)$ | | | | | $O(L \cdot H)$ |
| Storage | Verifier | $|K|$ | $O(S \cdot |K|)$ | | | $O(L \cdot S)|K|$ | | $O(S \cdot |K|)$ |
| | Signer | $O(L \cdot (|D| + |K|))$ | $O(L \cdot |D|) + |K|$ | | | $O(L \cdot |K|)$ | | $O(L \cdot |K|)$ |
| Communication | | | $O(L \cdot |D|)$ | | | | | |
| Public Verifiability | | Y | Y | | | | | N |
| Offline Server | | Y | Y | | | | | N |
| Immediate Verification | | Y | Y | | | | | N |
| Immediate Detection | | Y | Y | | | | | N |
| Truncation Resilience | | Y | Y | | | N | | N |

LogFAS is the only PKC-based secure audit logging scheme that can verify $O(L)$ items with a small-constant number of ExpOps; all other similar schemes require $O(L)$ ExpOps. Similarly, LogFAS is the only one achieving constant number of public key storage (with respect to both number of data items and log entries to be verified) on the verifier side, while all other schemes incur either linear or quadratic storage overhead ($S, |D|, |K|$ denote the number of signers in the system, the approximate bit lengths of a log entry and the bit length of a keying material, respectively). At the same time, LogFAS is the only scheme that enables truncation-free subset verification and sub-linear search simultaneously.

entries, which entails a linear number of Expensive Operations (ExpOps)[1], and failure of this verification does not give any information about which log entry(ies) is (are) responsible for the failure.

**Our Contribution:** In this paper, we propose a new secure audit logging scheme, which we call *Log Forward-secure and Append-only Signature (LogFAS)*. We first develop a main LogFAS scheme, and then extend it to provide additional capabilities. The desirable properties of LogFAS are outlined below. The first three properties show the efficiency of LogFAS compared with their PKC-based counterparts, while the other three properties demonstrate the applicability, availability and security advantages over their symmetric counterparts. Table 1 summarizes the above properties and compares LogFAS with its counterparts.

1. *Efficient Log Verification with $O(1)$ ExpOp*: All existing PKC-based secure audit logging schemes (e.g., [12, 17–20, 29, 30]) require $O(L \cdot (ExpOp + H))$ to verify $L$ log entries, which make them costly. LogFAS is the first PKC-based secure audit logging scheme that achieves signature verification with only a small-constant number of ExpOps (and $O(L)$ hash operations). That is, LogFAS can verify $L$ log entries with only a small-constant number of ExpOps regardless of the value of $L$. Therefore, it is much more efficient than all of its PKC-based counterparts, and is also comparably efficient with symmetric schemes (e.g., [7, 18, 25]) at the verifier side.

---

[1] For brevity, we denote an expensive cryptographic operation such as modular exponentiation or pairing as an ExpOp.

2. *Efficient Fine-grained Verification and Change Detection*:    LogFAS    allows
   fine-grained verification with advantages over iFssAgg [20], the only previous solution for fine-grained verification:
   (i) Unlike iFssAgg schemes [20], LogFAS prevents the truncation attack[2] in the
   presence of individual signatures without doubling the verification cost.
   (ii) LogFAS can verify any selected subset with $l' < L$ log entries with a small-
   constant number of ExpOps, while iFssAgg schemes require $O(2l')$ExpOps.
   (iii) LogFAS can identify the corrupted log entries with a *sub-linear* number of ExpOps when most log entries are intact. In contrast, iFssAgg schemes always require
   a linear number of ExpOps.
3. *Verifier Storage Efficiency with $O(1)$ Overhead*: Each verifier in LogFAS only stores
   one public key independent of the number of loggers or the number of log entries
   to be verified. Therefore, it is the most verifier-storage-efficient scheme among all
   existing PKC-based alternatives. This enables verifiers to handle a large number of
   log entries and/or loggers simultaneously without facing any storage problem.
4. *Public Verification*: Unlike the symmetric schemes (e.g., [7, 18, 25]), LogFAS can
   produce publicly verifiable signatures, and therefore it can protect applications requiring public auditing (e.g., e-voting, financial books) [12, 20].
5. *Independence of Online Trusted Server*: LogFAS schemes do not require online
   trusted server support to enable log verification. Therefore, LogFAS schemes achieve
   high availability, and are more reliable than the previous schemes that require such
   support (e.g., [7, 25, 30]).
6. *High Security*: We prove LogFAS to be forward-secure existentially unforgeable
   against adaptive chosen-message attacks in Random Oracle Model (ROM) [4]. Furthermore, unlike some previous symmetric schemes [7, 25], LogFAS schemes are
   also secure against both truncation and delayed detection attacks.

## 2   Preliminaries

**Notation.** $||$ denotes the concatenation operation. $|x|$ denotes the bit length of variable
$x$. $x \xleftarrow{\$} S$ denotes that variable $x$ is randomly and uniformly selected from set $S$. For
any integer $l$, $(x_0, \ldots, x_l) \xleftarrow{\$} S$ means $(x_0 \xleftarrow{\$} S, \ldots, x_l \xleftarrow{\$} S)$. We denote by $\{0,1\}^*$
the set of binary strings of any finite length. $H$ is an ideal cryptographic hash function,
which is defined as $H : \{0,1\}^* \to \{0,1\}^{|H|}$; $|H|$ denotes the output bit length of $H$.
$\mathcal{A}^{\mathcal{O}_0, \ldots, \mathcal{O}_i}(\cdot)$ denotes algorithm $\mathcal{A}$ is provided with oracles $\mathcal{O}_0, \ldots, \mathcal{O}_i$. For example,
$\mathcal{A}^{Scheme.Sig_{sk}}(\cdot)$ denotes that algorithm $\mathcal{A}$ is provided with a *signing oracle* of signature
scheme *Scheme* under private key $sk$.

**Definition 1.** *A signature scheme SGN is a tuple of three algorithms $(Kg, Sig, Ver)$
defined as follows:*

---

[2] The truncation attack is a special type of deletion attack, in which the adversary deletes a continuous subset of tail-end log entries. This attack can be prevented via "all-or-nothing" property [18]: The adversary either should remain previously accumulated data intact, or should
not use them at all (she cannot selectively delete/modify any subset of this data [20]). LogFAS
is proven to be secure against the truncation attack in Section 5.

- $(sk, PK) \leftarrow SGN.Kg(1^\kappa)$: *Key generation algorithm takes the security parameter $1^\kappa$ as the input. It returns a private/public key pair $(sk, PK)$ as the output.*
- $\sigma \leftarrow SGN.Sig(sk, D)$: *The signature generation algorithm takes $sk$ and a data item $D$ as the input. It returns a signature $\sigma$ as the output (also denoted as $\sigma \leftarrow SGN.Sig_{sk}(D)$).*
- $c \leftarrow SGN.Ver(PK, D, \sigma)$: *The signature verification algorithm takes $PK$, $D$ and $\sigma$ as the input. It outputs a bit $c$, with $c = 1$ meaning* valid *and $c = 0$ meaning* invalid.

**Definition 2.** *Existential Unforgeability under Chosen Message Attack (EU-CMA) experiment for SGN is as follows:*

Experiment $Expt_{SGN}^{EU\text{-}CMA}(\mathcal{A})$

$(sk, PK) \leftarrow SGN.Kg(1^\kappa)$, $(D^*, \sigma^*) \leftarrow \mathcal{A}^{SGN.Sig_{sk}(\cdot)}(PK)$,

*If $SGN.Ver(PK, D^*, \sigma^*) = 1$ and $D^*$ was not queried, return 1, else, return 0.*

EU-CMA-advantage *of $\mathcal{A}$ is $Adv_{SGN}^{EU\text{-}CMA}(\mathcal{A}) = Pr[Expt_{SGN}^{EU\text{-}CMA}(\mathcal{A}) = 1]$.*
EU-CMA-advantage *of $SGN$ is $Adv_{SGN}^{EU\text{-}CMA}(t, L, \mu) = \max_{\mathcal{A}}\{Adv_{SGN}^{EU\text{-}CMA}(\mathcal{A})\}$, where the maximum is over all $\mathcal{A}$ having time complexity $t$, making at most $L$ oracle queries, and the sum of lengths of these queries being at most $\mu$ bits.*

LogFAS is built on the Schnorr signature scheme [26]. It also uses an Incremental Hash function $\mathcal{IH}$ [3] and a generic signature scheme $SGN$ (e.g., Schnorr) as building blocks. Both Schnorr and $\mathcal{IH}$ require that $H : \{0, 1\}^* \to \mathbb{Z}_q^*$ is a random oracle.

**Definition 3.** *The Schnorr signature scheme is a tuple of three algorithms $(Kg, Sig, Ver)$ behaving as follows:*

- $(y, \langle p, q, \alpha, Y \rangle) \leftarrow Schnorr.Kg(1^\kappa)$: *Key generation algorithm takes $1^\kappa$ as the input. It generates large primes $q$ and $p > q$ such that $q|(p - 1)$, and then generates a generator $\alpha$ of the subgroup $G$ of order $q$ in $\mathbb{Z}_p^*$. It also generates $(y \xleftarrow{\$} \mathbb{Z}_q^*, Y \leftarrow \alpha^y \bmod p)$, and returns private/public keys $(y, \langle p, q, \alpha, Y \rangle)$ as the output.*
- $(s, R, e) \leftarrow Schnorr.Sig(y, D)$: *Signature generation algorithm takes private key $y$ and a data item $D$ as the input. It returns a signature triplet $(s, R, e)$ as follows:*

  $R \leftarrow \alpha^r \bmod p$, $e \leftarrow H(D||R)$, $s \leftarrow (r - e \cdot y) \bmod q$, *where $r \xleftarrow{\$} \mathbb{Z}_q^*$.*
- $c \leftarrow Schnorr.Ver(\langle p, q, \alpha, Y \rangle, D, \langle s, R, e \rangle)$: *Signature verification algorithm takes public key $\langle p, q, \alpha, Y \rangle$, data item $D$ and signature $\langle s, R, e \rangle$ as the input. It returns a bit $c$, with $c = 1$ meaning* valid *if $R = Y^e \alpha^s \bmod p$, and with $c = 0$ otherwise.*

**Definition 4.** *Given a large random integer $q$ and integer $L$, incremental hash function family $\mathcal{IH}$ is defined as follows: Given a random key $z = (z_0, \ldots, z_{L-1})$, where $(z_0, \ldots, z_{L-1}) \xleftarrow{\$} \mathbb{Z}_q^*$ and hash function $H$, the associated incremental hash function $\mathcal{IH}_z^{q,L}$ takes an arbitrary data item set $D_0, \ldots, D_{L-1}$ as the input. It returns an integer $T \in Z_q$ as the output,*

Algorithm $\mathcal{IH}_z^{q,L}(D_0, \ldots, D_{L-1})$
  $T \leftarrow \sum_{j=0}^{L-1} H(D_j)z_j \bmod q$, *return $T$.*

Target Collision Resistance (TCR) [5] of $\mathcal{IH}$ relies on the intractability of *Weighted Sum of Subset (WSS) problem* [3, 13] assuming that $H$ is a random oracle.

**Definition 5.** *Given* $\mathcal{IH}_z^{q,L}$, *let* $\mathcal{A}_0$ *be an algorithm that returns a set of target messages, and* $\mathcal{A}_1$ *be an algorithm that returns a bit. Consider the following experiment:*
*Experiment* $Expt_{\mathcal{IH}_z^{q,L}}^{TCR}(\mathcal{A} = (\mathcal{A}_0, \mathcal{A}_1))$
$(D_0, \ldots, D_{L-1}) \leftarrow \mathcal{A}_0(L)$, $z = (z_0, \ldots, z_{L-1}) \overset{\$}{\leftarrow} \mathbb{Z}_q^*$,
$T \leftarrow \mathcal{IH}_z^{q,L}(D_0, \ldots, D_{L-1}), (D_0^*, \ldots, D_{L-1}^*) \leftarrow \mathcal{A}_1(D_0, \ldots, D_{L-1}, T, \mathcal{IH}_z^{q,L})$
*If* $T = \mathcal{IH}_z^{q,L}(D_0^*, \ldots, D_{L-1}^*) \wedge \exists j \in \{0, \ldots, L-1\} : D_j^* \neq D_j$, *return* 1, *else,*
*return* 0.

TCR-advantage *of* $\mathcal{A}$ *is* $Adv_{\mathcal{IH}_z^{q,L}}^{TCR}(\mathcal{A}) = Pr[Expt_{\mathcal{IH}_z^{q,L}}^{TCR}(\mathcal{A}) = 1]$.
TCR-advantage *of* $\mathcal{IH}_z^{q,L}$ *is* $Adv_{\mathcal{IH}_z^{q,L}}^{TCR}(t) = \max_{\mathcal{A}}\{Adv_{\mathcal{IH}_z^{q,L}}^{TCR}(\mathcal{A})\}$, *where the maximum is over all* $\mathcal{A}$ *having time complexity t.*

## 3   Syntax and Models

LogFAS is a Forward-secure and Append-only Signature (FSA) scheme, which combines *key-evolve* (e.g., [2, 15]) and *signature aggregation* (e.g., [8]) techniques. Specifically, LogFAS is built on the Schnorr signature scheme [23, 26], and it integrates forward-security and signature aggregation strategies in a novel and efficient way. That is, different from previous approaches (e.g., [17–20, 25, 29, 30]), LogFAS introduces verification with a constant number of ExpOps, selective subset verification and sublinear search properties via incremental hashing [3] and masked tokens in addition to the above strategies.

Before giving more details, we briefly discuss the *append-only* signatures. A forward-secure and aggregate signature scheme is an *append-only* signature scheme if no message can be re-ordered or selectively deleted from a given stream of messages, while new messages can be appended to the stream [18, 20]. In Section 5, we prove that LogFAS is an append-only signature scheme.

**Definition 6.** *A FSA is comprised of a tuple of three algorithms* $(Kg, FASig, FAVer)$
*behaving as follows:*
- $(sk, PK) \leftarrow FSA.Kg(1^\kappa, L)$: *The key generation algorithm takes the security parameter* $1^\kappa$ *and the maximum number of key updates* $L$ *as the input. It returns a private/public key pair* $(sk, PK)$ *as the output.*
- $(sk_{j+1}, \sigma_{0,j}) \leftarrow FSA.FASig(sk_j, D_j, \sigma_{0,j-1})$: *The forward-secure and append-only signing algorithm takes the current private key* $sk_j$, *a new message* $D_j$ *to be signed and the append-only signature* $\sigma_{0,j-1}$ *on the previously signed messages* $(D_0, \ldots, D_{j-1})$ *as the input. It computes an append-only signature* $\sigma_{0,j}$ *on* $(D_0, \ldots, D_j)$, *evolves (updates)* $sk_j$ *to* $sk_{j+1}$, *and returns* $(sk_{j+1}, \sigma_{0,j})$ *as the output.*
- $c \leftarrow FSA.FAVer(PK, \langle D_0, \ldots, D_j \rangle, \sigma_{0,j})$: *The forward-secure and append-only verification algorithm takes* $PK$, $\langle D_0, \ldots, D_j \rangle$ *and their corresponding* $\sigma_{0,j}$ *as the input. It returns a bit c, with* $c = 1$ *meaning valid, and* $c = 0$ *otherwise.*

In LogFAS, private key $sk$ is a vector, whose elements are comprised of specially constructed Schnorr private keys and a set of tokens. These tokens later become the part of append-only signature $\sigma$ accordingly. The public key $PK$ is a system-wide public key that is shared by all verifiers, and is comprised of two long-term public keys. Details are given in Section 4.

### 3.1  System Model

LogFAS system model is comprised of a *Key Generation Center (KGC)* and multiple signers (i.e., logging machines that could be compromised) and verifiers. As in forward-secure stream integrity model (e.g., [7, 17, 18]), signers honestly execute the scheme until they are compromised by the adversary. Verifiers may be *untrusted*.

The KGC executes *LogFAS.Kg* once offline before the deployment, and distributes a distinct private key/token set (auxiliary signature) to each signer, and two long-term public keys to all verifiers. After the deployment, a signer computes the forward-secure and append-only signature of log entries with *LogFAS.FASig*, and verifiers can verify the signature of any signer with *LogFAS.FAVer* via two public keys without communicating with KGC (constant storage overhead at the verifier side).

In LogFAS, the same logger computes the append-only signature of her own log entries. Note that this form of signature computation is ideal for the envisioned secure audit logging applications, since each logger is only responsible for her own log entries.

### 3.2  Security Model

A FSA scheme is proven to be *ForWard-secure Existentially Unforgeable against Chosen Message Attack (FWEU-CMA)* based on the experiment defined in Definition 7. In this experiment, $\mathcal{A}$ is provided with two types of oracles that she can query up to $L$ messages in total as follows:

$\mathcal{A}$ is first provided with a *batch signing oracle* $FASig_{sk}(\cdot)$. For each batch query $j$, $\mathcal{A}$ queries $FASig_{sk}(\cdot)$ on a set of message $\vec{D}_j$ of her choice once. $FASig_{sk}(\cdot)$ returns a forward-secure and append-only signature $\sigma_{0,j}$ under $sk$ by aggregating $\sigma_j$ (i.e., the current append-only signature) on $\vec{D}_j$ with the previous signature $\sigma_{0,j-1}$ on $\vec{D}_0, \ldots, \vec{D}_{j-1}$ that $\mathcal{A}$ queried. Assume that $\mathcal{A}$ makes $i$ batch queries (with $0 \leq l \leq L$ individual messages) as described the above until she decides to "break-in".

$\mathcal{A}$ then queries the *Break-in* oracle, which returns the remaining $L - l$ private keys to $\mathcal{A}$ (if $l = L$ *Break-in* rejects the query).

**Definition 7.** FWEU-CMA experiment *is defined as follows:*
*Experiment* $Expt_{FSA}^{FWEU\text{-}CMA}(\mathcal{A})$

$\quad (sk, PK) \leftarrow FSA.Kg(1^\kappa, L), (\vec{D}^*, \sigma^*) \leftarrow \mathcal{A}^{FASig_{sk}(\cdot), Break\text{-}in}(PK),$

$\quad$ *If* $FSA.FAVer(PK, \vec{D}^*, \sigma^*) = 1 \wedge \forall I \subseteq \{0, \ldots, l\}, \vec{D}^* \neq \|_{k \in I} \vec{D}_k,$ *return* 1, *else,*
*return* 0.
FWEU-CMA-advantage of $\mathcal{A}$ is $Adv_{FSA}^{FWEU\text{-}CMA}(\mathcal{A}) = Pr[Expt_{FSA}^{FWEU\text{-}CMA}(\mathcal{A}) = 1].$

FWEU-CMA-advantage     of     *FSA*     is     $Adv_{FSA}^{FWEU\text{-}CMA}(t, L, \mu) = \max_{\mathcal{A}}$
$\{Adv_{FSA}^{FWEU\text{-}CMA}(\mathcal{A})\}$, *where the maximum is over all $\mathcal{A}$ having time complexity $t$, making at most $L$ oracle queries, and the sum of lengths of these queries being at most $\mu$ bits.*

The above experiment does not implement a random oracle for $\mathcal{A}$ explicitly. However, we still assume the *Random Oracle Model (ROM)* [4], since Schnorr signature scheme [26] on which LogFAS is built requires the ROM. Note that this experiment also captures the *truncation attacks*:

*(i)* The winning condition of $\mathcal{A}$ subsumes the truncation attack in addition to data modification. That is, $\mathcal{A}$ wins the experiment when she either modifies a data item or keeps data items intact but outputs a valid signature on a subset of a given batch query (i.e., she splits an append-only signature without knowing its individual signatures).

*(ii)* LogFAS uses a standard signature scheme $SGN$ to *prevent truncation attacks* by computing signatures of counter values. Resilience against the traditional data forgery (without truncation) relies on EU-CMA property of *Schnorr* and target collision-freeness of $\mathcal{IH}$. In Theorem 1, we prove that a successful truncation attack against LogFAS is equivalent to breaking $SGN$, and a successful data modification (including re-ordering) against LogFAS is equivalent to breaking *Schnorr* or $\mathcal{IH}$.

## 4   LogFAS Schemes

In this section, we first present the intuition and detailed description of LogFAS, and then describe a LogFAS variation that has additional capabilities.

### 4.1   LogFAS Scheme

All existing FSA constructions [17–20, 29] rely on a direct combination of an aggregate signature (e.g., [8]) and a forward-secure signature (e.g., [1, 15]). Therefore, the resulting constructions simultaneously inherit all overheads of their base primitives: (i) Forward-secure signatures on individual data items, which are done separately from the append-only design, force verifiers to perform $O(l)$ ExpOps. (ii) These schemes either eliminate ExpOps from the logging phase with pre-computation but incur quadratic storage overhead to the verifiers (e.g., [29]), or require ExpOps in the logging phase for each log entry and incur linear storage overhead to the verifiers (e.g., [12, 17, 20]).

The above observations inspired us to design cryptographic mechanisms that can verify *the integrity of entire log entry set once directly* (preserving forward-security), instead of checking the integrity of each data item individually, though the signing operations have to be performed on individual data items. That is, instead of verifying each item one-by-one with the corresponding public key(s), verify all of them via a *single set of aggregated cryptographic components* (e.g., tokens as auxiliary signatures). These mechanisms also achieve constant storage overhead at the verifier side[3].

We achieve these goals with a provable security by using Schnorr signature and incremental hash $\mathcal{IH}$ as follows:

*a)* To compute a forward-secure and append-only Schnorr signature, we aggregate each individual signature $s_l$ on $D_l$ with the previous aggregate signature as $s_{0,l} \leftarrow s_{0,l-1} + s_l \bmod q$, $(0 < l \leq L - 1, s_{0,0} = s_0)$. This is done by using a distinct private key pair $(r_j, y_j)$ for $j = 0, \ldots, L - 1$ on each data item.

---

[3] In all existing forward-secure and/or aggregate (append-only) logging schemes (e.g., [7, 12, 17, 19, 20, 29]), the signer side storage overhead is dominated by the accumulated logs, which already incur a linear storage overhead.

*b)* Despite being forward-secure, the above construction still requires an ExpOp for each data item. To verify the signature on $D_0, \ldots, D_l$ with only a small-constant number of ExpOps, we introduce the notion of *token*.

In LogFAS, each Schnorr private $y_j$ is comprised of a random key pair $(a_j, d_j)$ for $j = 0, \ldots, L - 1$. Random key $a_j$ is mutually blinded with another random factor $x_j$ and also a long-term private key $b$ for $j = 0, \ldots, L - 1$. The result of these blinding operations is called *auxiliary signature* (token) $z_j$, which can be kept publicly without revealing information about $(a_j, x_j)$ and also can be authenticated with the long-term public key $B$ by all verifiers. Furthermore, these masked tokens $z = z_0, \ldots, z_l$ also serve as a one-time initialization key for the incremental hash as $\mathcal{IH}_z^{q,l}$ (Definition 4), which enable verifiers to reduce the integrity of each $D_j$ into the integrity of a final tag $z_{0,l}$. This operation preserves the integrity of each $D_j$ and verifiability of each $z_j$ (via public key $B$) without ExpOps.

*c)* To verify $(s_{0,l}, z_{0,l})$ via $B$ in an aggregate form, verifiers also aggregate tokens $R_j$ as $R_{0,l} \leftarrow \prod_{j=0}^{l} R_j \bmod p$, where $p$ a large prime on which the group was constructed. However, initially, $(s_{0,l}, R_{0,l}, z_{0,l})$ cannot be verified directly via $B$, since the reduction operations introduce some extra verification information. LogFAS handles this via *auxiliary signature* (token) $M'_{0,l}$ that bridges $(s_{0,l}, R_{0,l}, z_{0,l})$ to $B$. That is, the signer computes an aggregate token $M'_{0,l} \leftarrow M'_{0,l-1} M_l^{e_j} \bmod p$, where $0 < l \leq L - 1$ and $M_{0,0} = M_0$), along with $s_{0,l}$ in the signing process. During verification, this aggregate token eliminates the extra terms and bridges $(s_{0,l}, R_{0,l}, z_{0,l})$ with $B$.

This approach allows LogFAS to compute publicly verifiable signatures with only one ExpOp per-item, and this signature can be verified with only a small-constant number of ExpOps by storing only two public keys at the verifier side (regardless of the number of signers). This is much more efficient than all of its PKC-based counterparts, and also is as efficient as the symmetric schemes at the verifier side.

The detailed description of LogFAS algorithms is given below:

1) *LogFAS.Kg*$(1^\kappa, L)$: Given $1^\kappa$, generate primes $q$ and $p > q$ such that $q|(p-1)$, and then generate a generator $\alpha$ of the subgroup $G$ of order $q$ in $\mathbb{Z}_p^*$.

a) Generate $(b \overset{\$}{\leftarrow} \mathbb{Z}_q^*, B \leftarrow \alpha^{b^{-1}} \bmod p)$ and $(\widehat{sk}, \widehat{PK}) \leftarrow SGN.Kg(1^\kappa)$. *System-wide private key* of KGC is $\overline{sk} \leftarrow (b, \widehat{sk})$. This private key is used to compute the private key of all signers in the system. *System-wide public key* of all verifiers is $PK \leftarrow \{p, q, \alpha, B, \widehat{PK}, L\}$. This public key can verify any valid signature generated by a legitimate signer.

b) Generate $(r_j, a_j, d_j, x_j) \overset{\$}{\leftarrow} \mathbb{Z}_q^*$ for $j = 0, \ldots, L - 1$. The private key of signer $ID_i$ is $sk \leftarrow \{r_j, y_j, z_j, M_j, R_j, \beta_j\}_{j=0}^{L-1}$, where
   - Generate the Schnorr private key of each $ID_i$ as $y_j \leftarrow a_j - d_j \bmod q$. Generate the masked token of $ID_i$ as $z_j \leftarrow (a_j - x_j)b \bmod q$, which is used for integrity reduction at the verification phase.
   - $R_j \leftarrow \alpha^{r_j} \bmod p$, $M_j \leftarrow \alpha^{x_j - d_j} \bmod p$. Each $R_j$ serves as a part of Schnorr signature and it is aggregated by the verifier upon its receipt. $M_j$ is the aggregate token and is aggregated by the signer during the logging process.
   - $\beta_j \leftarrow SGN.Sig(\widehat{sk}, H(ID_i||j))$. Note that each $\beta_j$ is kept secret initially, and then released as a part of a signature publicly.

2) $LogFAS.FASig(\langle r_l, y_l, z_l, M_l, R_l, \beta_l \rangle, D_l, \sigma_{0,l-1})$: Given $\sigma_{0,l-1}$ on $D_0, \ldots, D_{l-1}$, compute $\sigma_{0,l}$ on $D_0, \ldots, D_l$ as follows,

a) $e_l \leftarrow H(D_l||l||z_l||R_l)$, $\quad M'_l \leftarrow M_l^{e_l} \bmod p$, $\quad s_l \leftarrow r_l - e_l y_l \bmod q$,

b) $s_{0,l} \leftarrow s_{0,l-1} + s_l \bmod q$, $\quad (0 < l \leq L - 1, \; s_{0,0} = s_0)$,

c) $M'_{0,l} \leftarrow M'_{0,l-1} M'_l \bmod p$, $\quad (0 < l \leq L - 1, \; M'_{0,0} = M_0)$,

d) $\sigma_{0,l} \leftarrow \{s_{0,l}, M'_{0,l}, \beta_l, R_j, e_j, z_j\}_{j=0}^l$ and erase $(r_l, y_l, s_{0,l-1}, s_l, \beta_{l-1})$.

3) $LogFAS.FAVer(PK, \langle D_0, \ldots, D_l \rangle, \sigma_{0,l})$:

a) If $SGN.Ver(\widehat{PK}, H(ID_i||l), \beta_l) = 0$ then return 0, else continue,

b) If $\prod_{j=0}^l R_j \bmod p = M'_{0,l} \cdot B^{z_{0,l}} \cdot \alpha^{s_{0,l}} \bmod p$ holds return 1, else return 0, where
$z_{0,l} = \mathcal{IH}_{z_0,\ldots,z_l}^{q,l}(D_0||w||z_0|| R_0, \ldots, D_l||w||z_l||R_l)$.

## 4.2   Selective Verification with LogFAS

All the previous FSA constructions (e.g., [17–19, 29, 30]) verify the set of log entries via only the final aggregate signature to prevent the truncation attack and save the storage. However, this approach causes performance drawbacks: (i) The verification of any subset of log entries requires the verification of the entire set of log entries (i.e., always $O(L)$ ExpOps for the subset verification). (ii) The failure of signature verification does not give any information about which log entries were corrupted.

Ma et al. proposed immutable-FssAgg (iFssAgg) schemes in [20] to allow fine-grained verification without being vulnerable to truncation attacks. However, iFssAgg schemes double the signing/verifying costs of their base schemes. In addition, even if the signature verification fails due to only a few corrupted log entries (i.e., accidentally damaged entry(ies)), detecting which log entry(ies) is (are) responsible for the failure requires verifying each individual signature.

LogFAS can address the above problems via a simple variation without incurring any additional costs: The signer keeps *all* signatures and tokens in their individual forms (including $s_j$ for $j = 0, \ldots, l$) without aggregation. The verifiers can aggregate them according to their needs by preserving the security and verifiability. This offers performance advantages over iFssAgg schemes [20]:

(i) LogFAS protects the number of log entries via pre-computed tokens $\beta_0, \ldots, \beta_l$, and therefore individual signatures can be kept without a truncation risk. This eliminates the necessity of costly immutability strategies used in iFssAgg schemes [20]. Furthermore, a verifier can selectively aggregate any subset of $l' < l$ log entries and verify them by performing only a small-constant number of ExpOps as in the original LogFAS. This is much more efficient than the iFssAgg schemes, which require $O(2l')$ ExpOps.

(ii) LogFAS can use a recursive subset search strategy to identify corrupted log entries causing the verification failure faster than linear search[4]. That is, the set of log en-

---

[4] Note that the previous PKC-based audit logging schemes *cannot* use such a recursive subset search strategy to identify corrupted log entries with a sub-linear number ExpOps, since they always require linear number of ExpOps to verify a given subset from the entire log entry set (in contrast to LogFAS that requires $O(1)$ExpOp to verify a given subset).

tries is divided into subsets along with their corresponding individual signatures. Each subset is then independently verified by *LogFAS.AVer* via its corresponding aggregate signature, which is efficiently computed from individual signatures. Subsets returning 1 are eliminated from the search, while each subset returning 0 is again divided into subsets and verified by *LogFAS.AVer* as described. This subset search continues recursively until all the corrupted log entries are identified.

The above strategy can quickly identify the corrupted entries when most log entries are intact. For instance, if only one entry is corrupted, it can identify the corrupted entry by performing $(2 \log_2 l)$ ExpOps + $O(l)$ hash operations. This is much faster than linear search used in the previous PKC-based schemes, which always requires $O(l)$ ExpOps + $O(l)$ hash operations.

Recursive subset strategy remains more efficient than linear search as long as the number of corrupted entries $c$ satisfies $c \leq \frac{l}{2 \log_2 l}$. When $c > \frac{l}{2 \log_2 l}$, depending on $c$ and the distribution of corrupted entries, recursive subset search might be more costly than linear search. To minimize the performance loss in such an inefficient case, the verifier can switch from recursive subset search to the linear search if the recursive division and search step continuously returns 0 for each verified subset. The verifier can ensure that the performance loss due to an inefficient case does not exceed the average gain of an efficient case by setting the maximum number of recursive steps to be executed to $l'/2 - \log_2 l'$ for each subset with $l'$ entries.

## 5   Security Analysis

We prove that LogFAS is a *FWEU-CMA* signature scheme in Theorem 1 below.

**Theorem 1.** $Adv_{LogFAS}^{FWEU\text{-}CMA}(t, L, \mu)$ is bounded as follows,

$$Adv_{LogFAS}^{FWEU\text{-}CMA}(t, L, \mu) \leq L \cdot Adv_{Schnorr}^{EU\text{-}CMA}(t', 1, \mu') +$$
$$Adv_{SGN}^{EU\text{-}CMA}(t'', L, \mu'') + Adv_{\mathcal{IH}_z^{q,L}}^{TCR}(t'''),$$

where $t' = O(t) + L \cdot O(\kappa^3)$ and $\mu' = \mu/L$.

The proof of the theorem can be found in our accompanying technical report [31].

**Remark 1.** Another security concern in audit logging is *delayed detection* identified in [19]. In delayed detection, log verifiers cannot detect whether the log entries are modified until an online TTP provides auxiliary keying information to them. LogFAS does not rely on an online TTP support or time factor to achieve the signature verification, and therefore it is not prone to delayed detection.

## 6   Performance Analysis and Comparison

In this section, we present the performance analysis of LogFAS and compare it with previous schemes.

**Computational Overhead:** From a verifier's perspective, LogFAS requires only a small-constant number of modular exponentiations regardless of the number of log entries to be verified. Therefore, it is much more efficient than all PKC-based schemes,

**Table 2.** Execution time (in ms) comparison of LogFAS and its counterparts

| Criteria | | LogFAS $(l = 10^4, l' < l)$ | FssAgg (l) / iFssAgg (l') | | | Logcrypt | BAF | Sym. |
|---|---|---|---|---|---|---|---|---|
| | | | BLS / i | BM / i | AR / i | | | |
| **Off.** | Kg, $L = 10^4$ | $5.06 \times 10^4$ | $3.3 \times 10^3$ | $8.8 \times 10^4$ | $1.7 \times 10^5$ | $2.6 \times 10^4$ | $4 \times 10^4$ | 20 |
| **Onl.** | Sig&Upd (1) | 1.2 | 1.8 / 3.6 | 13.1 / 26.2 | 28 / 56 | 2.05 | 0.007 | 0.004 |
| | Ver. $l' = 10^2$ | 72.87 | $4.8 \times 10^3$ | $1.8 \times 10^3$ | $1.6 \times 10^5$ | $1.4 \times 10^3$ | $0.2 \times 10^3$ | 0.2 |
| | Ver. $l' = 10^3$ | 75.2 | $4.8 \times 10^4$ | $1 \times 10^4$ | $1.8 \times 10^5$ | $1.5 \times 10^4$ | $2.05 \times 10^3$ | 2 |
| | Ver. $l = 10^4$ | 98.12 | $2.6 \times 10^5$ | $4.7 \times 10^4$ | $1.9 \times 10^5$ | $1.4 \times 10^5$ | $2.04 \times 10^4$ | 19.9 |

which require one modular exponentiation (or a pairing) per log entry. Besides, it does not double the verification cost to prevent the truncation attacks, providing further efficiency over iFssAgg schemes [20]. The verification of subsets from these entries with LogFAS is also much more efficient than all of its counterparts.

From a logger's perspective, LogFAS is also more efficient than its PKC-based counterparts with the exception of BAF.

We prototyped our schemes and their counterparts on a computer with an Intel(R) Xeon(R)-E5450 3GHz CPU and 4GB RAM running Ubuntu 9.04. We tested LogFAS, BAF [29], FssAgg-BLS [18], Logcrypt (with DSA), and the symmetric schemes (e.g., [7, 18, 25]) using the MIRACL library [27], and FssAgg-AR/BM using the NTL library [28] [5]. Table 2 compares the computational cost of LogFAS with its counterparts numerically in terms of their execution times (in ms). The execution time differences with LogFAS and its PKC-based counterparts grow linearly with respect to the number of log entries to be verified. Initially, the symmetric schemes are more efficient than all PKC-based schemes, including ours. However, since the verification operations of LogFAS are dominated by $H$, their efficiency become comparable with symmetric schemes as the number of log entries increases (e.g., $l = 10^4$)[6].

Figure 1 and Figure 2 further compare LogFAS and previous schemes that allow public verification in terms of signature generation and verification times as the number of log entries increases. These figures demonstrate that LogFAS is the most verifier computationally efficient scheme among all these choices. It is also more efficient than its counterparts for the signature generation with the exception of BAF.

All PKC-based schemes require $O(L)$ ExpOps in the key generation phase.

**Signature/Key/Data Storage and Transmission Overheads:** LogFAS is a verifier storage friendly scheme; it requires each verifier to store only two public keys and an index along with system-wide parameters (e.g., $|q| + |4p|$), regardless of the number of signers or the number of log entries to be verified.

---

[5] Suggested bit lengths to achieve 80-bit security for each compared schemes are as follows (based on the parameters suggested by Lenstra et al. in [16] and Ma et al. in [17, 18]): Large primes ($|p| = 2048, |q| = 1600$) for LogFAS and Logcrypt, primes ($|p'| = 512, |q'| = 160$) for BAF and FssAgg-BLS, ($|n'| = 1024, z = 160$) for FssAgg-AR and FssAgg-BM, where $n'$ is Blum-Williams integer [17].

[6] To achieve TCR property for $\mathcal{IH}$, LogFAS uses relatively larger modulo sizes than its counterparts. However, since LogFAS requires only a small-constant number of ExpOps for the signature verification and a single ExpOp for the signature generation, the effect of large modulo size over its performance is negligible.

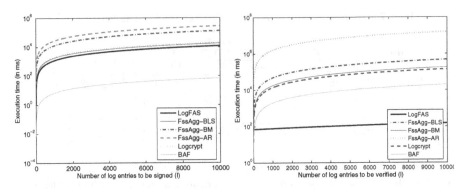

**Fig. 1.** Signing time comparison of LogFAS and its counterparts (in ms)

**Fig. 2.** Verification time comparison of LogFAS and its counterparts (in ms)

**Table 3.** Key size, signature size and storage overheads of LogFAS and previous schemes

| Criteria | | PKC-based | | | | | | Symmetric |
| --- | --- | --- | --- | --- | --- | --- | --- | --- |
| | | LogFAS | BAF | FssAgg Schemes [19,20] | | | Logcrypt [12] | Sym. [18,24,25] |
| | | | | BLS [18] | BM [17] | AR [17] | | |
| Sig. | Key size | $O(L)(|q|+|p|)$ | $3|q'|$ | $|q'|$ | $|n'|z$ | $3|n'|$ | $|q'|+|p'|$ | $|H|$ |
| | Sig. size | $O(l)(|q|+|p|)$ | $|q'|$ | $|p'|$ | $|n'|$ | $|n'|$ | $2|q'|$ | $|H|$ |
| | Storage | $O(L+l)(|q|+|p|)$ | $4|q'|$ | $2|q'|+3|p'|$ | $|n'|l$ | $4|n'|$ | $O(L)(|q'|+|p'|)$ | $O(V)|H|$ |
| Ver. | Key size | $|q|+4|p|$ | $2|p'|$ | $|q'|$ | $|n'|z$ | $3|n'|$ | $2|q'|+|p'|$ | $|H|$ |
| | Storage | $|q|+4|p|$ | $O(L\cdot S)(2|p'|)$ | $O(L\cdot S)|q'|$ | $O(S)|n'|z$ | $O(S)3n'$ | $O(L)(|q'|+|p'|)$ | $O(S)|H|$ |

The values in this table are simplified by omitting some constant/negligible terms. For instance, the overhead of data items to be transmitted are the same for all compared schemes and therefore are omitted.

In LogFAS, the append-only signature size is $|q|$. The key/token and data storage overheads on the logger side are linear as $O(L(5|q|+2|p|))+O(l|D|)$ (assuming $SGN$ is chosen as Schnorr [26]). LogFAS transmits a token set along with each data item requiring $O(l(|q|+|p|+|D|))$ transmission in total. The fine-grain verification introduces $O(l')$ extra storage/communication overhead due to the individual signatures.

From a verifier's perspective, LogFAS is much more storage efficient than all existing schemes, which require either $O(L\cdot S)$ storage (e.g., FssAgg-BLS [18] and BAF [29]), or $O(S)$ storage (e.g., [7, 12, 17, 20, 25]). From a logger's perspective, all the compared schemes both accumulate (store) and transmit linear number of data items (i.e., $O(l|D|)$ until their verifiers become available to them. This dominates the main storage and communication overhead for these schemes. In addition to this, LogFAS requires linear key storage overhead at the logger side, which is slightly less efficient than [17, 18, 29]. LogFAS with fine-grained verification and its counterpart iFssAgg schemes [20] both require linear key/signature/data storage/transmission overhead.

**Availability, Applicability and Security:** The symmetric schemes [7, 25] are not publicly verifiable and also require online server support to verify log entries. Furthermore, they are vulnerable to both truncation and delayed detection attacks [19, 20] with the exception of FssAgg-MAC [18]. In contrast, PKC-based schemes [12, 17–20] are publicly verifiable without requiring online server support, and they are secure against the truncation and delayed detection attacks, with the exception of Logcrypt [12].

## 7 Related Work

Most closely related are those forward-secure audit logging schemes [6,7,12,17–20,25, 29]. The comparison of these schemes with LogFAS has been presented in Section 6.

Apart from the above schemes, there is a set of works complementary to ours. Itkis [14] proposed cryptographic tamper resistance techniques that can detect tampering even if all the keying material is compromised. LogFAS can be combined with Itkis model as any forward-secure signature [14]. Yavuz et al. [30] proposed a Hash-based Forward-Secure and Aggregate Signature Scheme (HaSAFSS) for unattended wireless sensor networks, which uses timed-release encryption to achieve computational efficiency. Davis et al. proposed time-scoped search techniques on encrypted audit logs [10]. There are also authenticated data structures that can be used for audit logging in distributed systems [9,22]. LogFAS can serve as a digital signature primitive needed by these constructions.

## 8 Conclusion

In this paper, we proposed a new forward-secure and append-only audit logging scheme called LogFAS. LogFAS achieves public verifiability without requiring any online trusted server support, and is secure against truncation and delayed detection attacks. LogFAS is much more computationally efficient than all existing PKC-based alternatives, with a performance comparable to symmetric schemes at the verifier side. Log-FAS is also the most verifier storage efficient scheme among all existing alternatives. Last, a variation of LogFAS enables selective subset verification and efficient search of corrupted log entries. Overall, our comparison with the existing schemes shows that LogFAS is an ideal choice for secure audit logging by offering high efficiency, security, and public verifiability simultaneously for real-life applications.

## References

1. Abdalla, M., Reyzin, L.: A New Forward-Secure Digital Signature Scheme. In: Okamoto, T. (ed.) ASIACRYPT 2000. LNCS, vol. 1976, pp. 116–129. Springer, Heidelberg (2000)
2. Anderson, R.: Two remarks on public-key cryptology, invited lecture. In: Proceedings of the 4th ACM Conference on Computer and Communications Security (CCS 1997) (1997)
3. Bellare, M., Micciancio, D.: A New Paradigm for Collision-Free Hashing: Incrementality at Reduced Cost. In: Fumy, W. (ed.) EUROCRYPT 1997. LNCS, vol. 1233, pp. 163–192. Springer, Heidelberg (1997)
4. Bellare, M., Rogaway, P.: Random oracles are practical: A paradigm for designing efficient protocols. In: Proceedings of the 1st ACM Conference on Computer and Communications Security (CCS 1993), pp. 62–73. ACM, NY (1993)
5. Bellare, M., Rogaway, P.: Collision-Resistant Hashing: Towards Making UOWHFs Practical. In: Kaliski Jr., B.S. (ed.) CRYPTO 1997. LNCS, vol. 1294, pp. 470–484. Springer, Heidelberg (1997)

6. Bellare, M., Yee, B.S.: Forward integrity for secure audit logs. Technical report, San Diego, CA, USA (1997)
7. Bellare, M., Yee, B.S.: Forward-Security in Private-Key Cryptography. In: Joye, M. (ed.) CT-RSA 2003. LNCS, vol. 2612, pp. 1–18. Springer, Heidelberg (2003)
8. Boneh, D., Gentry, C., Lynn, B., Shacham, H.: Aggregate and Verifiably Encrypted Signatures from Bilinear Maps. In: Biham, E. (ed.) EUROCRYPT 2003. LNCS, vol. 2656, pp. 416–432. Springer, Heidelberg (2003)
9. Crosby, S., Wallach, D.S.: Efficient data structures for tamper evident logging. In: Proceedings of the 18th Conference on USENIX Security Symposium (August 2009)
10. Davis, D., Monrose, F., Reiter, M.: Time-Scoped Searching of Encrypted Audit Logs. In: López, J., Qing, S., Okamoto, E. (eds.) ICICS 2004. LNCS, vol. 3269, pp. 532–545. Springer, Heidelberg (2004)
11. Fall, K.: A delay-tolerant network architecture for challenged internets. In: Proceedings of the 9th Conference on Applications, Technologies, Architectures, and Protocols for Computer Communications (SIGCOMM 2003), pp. 27–34. ACM (2003)
12. Holt, J.E.: Logcrypt: Forward security and public verification for secure audit logs. In: Proc. of the 4th Australasian Workshops on Grid Computing and e-Research (ACSW 2006), pp. 203–211 (2006)
13. Impagliazzo, R., Naor, M.: Efficient cryptographic schemes provably as secure as subset sum. In: Proceedings of the 30th Annual Symposium on Foundations of Computer Science, pp. 236–241. IEEE Computer Society, Washington, DC (1989)
14. Itkis, G.: Cryptographic tamper evidence. In: Proc. of the 10th ACM Conference on Computer and Communications Security (CCS 2003), pp. 355–364. ACM, New York (2003)
15. Krawczyk, H.: Simple forward-secure signatures from any signature scheme. In: Proceedings of the 7th ACM Conference on Computer and Communications Security (CCS 2000), pp. 108–115. ACM (2000)
16. Lenstra, A.K., Verheul, E.R.: Selecting cryptographic key sizes. Journal of Cryptology 14(4), 255–293 (2001)
17. Ma, D.: Practical forward secure sequential aggregate signatures. In: Proceedings of the 3rd ACM Symposium on Information, Computer and Communications Security (ASIACCS 2008), pp. 341–352. ACM, NY (2008)
18. Ma, D., Tsudik, G.: Forward-secure sequential aggregate authentication. In: Proceedings of the 28th IEEE Symposium on Security and Privacy (S&P 2007), pp. 86–91 (May 2007)
19. Ma, D., Tsudik, G.: A new approach to secure logging. In: Proc. of the 22nd Annual IFIP WG 11.3 Working Conference on Data and Applications Security (DBSEC 2008), pp. 48–63 (2008)
20. Ma, D., Tsudik, G.: A new approach to secure logging. ACM Transaction on Storage (TOS) 5(1), 1–21 (2009)
21. Oprea, A., Bowers, K.D.: Authentic Time-Stamps for Archival Storage. In: Backes, M., Ning, P. (eds.) ESORICS 2009. LNCS, vol. 5789, pp. 136–151. Springer, Heidelberg (2009)
22. Papamanthou, C., Tamassia, R., Triandopoulos, N.: Authenticated hash tables. In: Proc. of the 15th ACM Conference on Computer and Communications Security (CCS 2008), pp. 437–448. ACM, New York (2008)
23. Pointcheval, D., Stern, J.: Security Proofs for Signature Schemes. In: Maurer, U.M. (ed.) EUROCRYPT 1996. LNCS, vol. 1070, pp. 387–398. Springer, Heidelberg (1996)
24. Schneier, B., Kelsey, J.: Cryptographic support for secure logs on untrusted machines. In: Proc. of the 7th Conference on USENIX Security Symposium. USENIX Association (1998)
25. Schneier, B., Kelsey, J.: Secure audit logs to support computer forensics. ACM Transaction on Information System Security 2(2), 159–176 (1999)
26. Schnorr, C.: Efficient signature generation by smart cards. Journal of Cryptology 4(3), 161–174 (1991)

27. Shamus. Multiprecision integer and rational arithmetic c/c++ library (MIRACL), http://www.shamus.ie/
28. Shoup, V.: NTL: A library for doing number theory, http://www.shoup.net/ntl/
29. Yavuz, A.A., Ning, P.: BAF: An efficient publicly verifiable secure audit logging scheme for distributed systems. In: Proceedings of 25th Annual Computer Security Applications Conference (ACSAC 2009), pp. 219–228 (2009)
30. Yavuz, A.A., Ning, P.: Hash-based sequential aggregate and forward secure signature for unattended wireless sensor networks. In: Proceedings of the 6th Annual International Conference on Mobile and Ubiquitous Systems (MobiQuitous 2009) (July 2009)
31. Yavuz, A.A., Ning, P., Reiter, M.K.: Efficient, compromise resilient and append-only cryptographic schemes for secure audit logging. Technical Report TR-2011-21, Raleigh, NC, USA (September 2011)

# On Secure Two-Party Integer Division

Morten Dahl[1], Chao Ning[2,3,*], and Tomas Toft[1]

[1] Aarhus University, Denmark[**,***,†]
{mdahl,ttoft}@cs.au.dk
[2] IIIS, Tsinghua University, Beijing, China
ncnfl@mail.tsinghua.edu.cn
[3] School of Computer Science and Technology, Shandong University, Jinan, China

**Abstract.** We consider the problem of *secure integer division*: given two Paillier encryptions of $\ell$-bit values $n$ and $d$, determine an encryption of $\lfloor \frac{n}{d} \rfloor$ without leaking any information about $n$ or $d$. We propose two new protocols solving this problem.

The first requires $\mathcal{O}(\ell)$ arithmetic operations on encrypted values (secure addition and multiplication) in $\mathcal{O}(1)$ rounds. This is the most efficient constant-rounds solution to date. The second protocol requires only $\mathcal{O}\left((\log^2 \ell)(\kappa + \log\log \ell)\right)$ arithmetic operations in $\mathcal{O}(\log^2 \ell)$ rounds, where $\kappa$ is a correctness parameter. Theoretically, this is the most efficient solution to date as all previous solutions have required $\Omega(\ell)$ operations. Indeed, the fact that an $o(\ell)$ solution is possible at all is highly surprising.

**Keywords:** Secure two-party computation, Secure integer division.

## 1 Introduction

Secure multiparty computation (MPC) allows two or more mutually mistrusting parties to evaluate a function on private data without revealing additional information. Classic results show that any function can be computed with polynomial overhead but specialised protocols are often used to improve efficiency: integer arithmetic can for instance be *simulated* using $\mathbb{Z}_M$ arithmetic. On the other hand, this makes non-arithmetic operations difficult, including determining which of two sums is the larger (as needed in the double auction of Bogetoft

* This work was supported in part by the National Basic Research Program of China Grant 2011CBA00300, 2011CBA00301, the National Natural Science Foundation of China Grant 61033001, 61061130540, 61073174 and 61173139.

** The authors acknowledge support from the Danish National Research Foundation and The National Science Foundation of China (under the grant 61061130540) for the Sino-Danish Center for the Theory of Interactive Computation, within which part of this work was performed.

*** The authors acknowledge support from the Center for research in the Foundations of Electronic Markets (CFEM), supported by the Danish Strategic Research Council.

† The authors acknowledge support from Confidential Benchmarking (COBE), supported by The Danish Research Council for Technology and Production.

A.D. Keromytis (Ed.): FC 2012, LNCS 7397, pp. 164–178, 2012.

et al. [BCD⁺09]), or performing an integer division of sums (essentially the *computation of the mean* problem of Kiltz et al. [KLM05]).

In this paper we consider the problem of secure integer division – computing $\lfloor n/d \rfloor$ given $n$ and $d$ – in the two-party setting. Immediate applications include statistics on data from companies in the same line of business, as well as data-mining tasks, e.g., the $k$-means clustering protocol of Jagannathan and Wright [JW05]. Further, since the problem of secure integer division is equivalent to that of secure modulo reduction – $n \bmod m = n - m \cdot \lfloor n/m \rfloor$ – any such protocol may be utilized in joint key-generation, e.g., as done by Algesheimer et al. [ACS02].

*Related Work.* Algesheimer et al. introduced the problem of secure integer division in the context of passively secure RSA-modulus generation with honest majority [ACS02]; active security is achievable using standard techinques. Their solution was based on Newton iteration and required $\mathcal{O}(\ell)$ work and communication (using the notation of this paper) in $\mathcal{O}(\log \ell)$ rounds, where $\ell$ is the bit-length of the inputs. The protocols were implemented by From and Jakobsen in the passively secure three-party setting [FJ05]. Recently, Catrina and Dragulin have used similar ideas to construct secure fixed-point arithmetic [CD09].

Regarding constant-rounds solutions, Kiltz et al. proposed specialised protocols based on Taylor series for the related, but simpler, problem of computing the means in a two-party setting [KLM05]. Damgård et al. [DFK⁺06] observed that combining the ideas of [ACS02, KLM05] and bit-decomposition (BD) implied constant-rounds modulo reduction and hence integer division. No details were presented, though naturally complexity was at least that of BD, $\mathcal{O}(\ell \log \ell)$.

The simpler problem where $d$ is known to all parties (a single party) has been studied by Guajardo et al. [GMS10] and Ning and Xu [NX10] (Veugen [Veu10]).

Finally, we remark that it is possible to "switch technique" mid-protocol and use homomorphic encryption for arithmetic and (small) Yao circuits for primitives such as integer division as done by Henecka et al. [HKS⁺10]. However, achieving active security in this setting typically requires the use of cut-and-choose techniques. Moreover, while it is possible to use generic non-interactive zero-knowledge proofs to demonstrate correct protocol execution to independent observers – e.g. clients which have supplied the inputs as in the Danish "sugar beet auction" [BCD⁺09] – this will be much more expensive than using non-generic zero-knowledge proofs as our solution allows.

*Contribution.* We present two two-party protocols for the problem of secure integer division: given Paillier encryptions of $\ell$-bit values $n$ and $d$, compute an encryption of $\lfloor n/d \rfloor$ without leaking any information. Both are based on Taylor series. The first protocol requires $\mathcal{O}(\ell)$ encryptions to be exchanged between the parties in a constant number of rounds; this is quite practical for small inputs, e.g., up to 40 bits. The second protocol communicates $\mathcal{O}\left((\log^2 \ell)(\kappa + \log\log \ell)\right)$ encryptions in $\mathcal{O}(\log^2 \ell)$ rounds. Moreover, we are able to avoid bit-decomposition; indeed, as the latter complexity is *sub-linear* in the bit-length, it precludes the use of bit-decomposition. That a sub-linear solution is possible at all is quite surprising, but the construction is of theoretical rather than practical interest.

Though our protocols are presented in the two-party Pailler-based setting, they are applicable in other settings providing secure arithetmic, e.g. the protocols of Ben-Or et al. [BGW88]. However, the sub-linear solution requires the presence of two mutually incorruptible parties, at least with current knowledge.

## 2   Preliminaries

After presenting Paillier encryption and secure two-party computations we introduce a set of protocols used in our constructions. All sub-protocols are secure against malicious (i.e., potentially deviating) attackers. Regarding complexity, we shall use $R_\pi$ and $C_\pi$ to denote respectively the number of rounds used and the number of ring elements communicated during a single run of protocol $\pi$.

*Paillier Encryption.* Paillier's encryption scheme [Pai99] is an additively homomorphic, sematically secure public key encryption scheme based on the decisional composite residuosity assumption of RSA-moduli. Suppressing the randomness used for encryption, we write $[m]$ to denote an encryption of $m$.

*Secure Computation.* Secure multi-party computation can be based on Paillier encryption with a threshold key using the protocols of Cramer et al. [CDN01]. The threshold sharing can be constructed using the ideas of Damgård and Jurik [DJ01]. Though not explicitly stated, apart from guaranteed termination, the protocols of [CDN01] are still valid even if all but a single party are corrupt. In particular this allows the two-party setting. We assume the following setting:

- Alice and Bob know a public Paillier key and share the decryption key.
- Inputs and intermediary values are held in encrypted form by *both* parties.

Paillier encryption is additively homomorphic, hence given $[m]$ and $[m']$ both parties may compute an encryption $[m + m']$. We will use infix operations in the plaintext space and write $[m + m'] \leftarrow [m] + [m']$ for this operation. To perform a multiplication, the parties need to run a protocol; see [CDN01] for details.

*Zero-Knowledge Proof of Boundedness.* In addition to secure arithmetic in $\mathbb{Z}_M$ we require a zero-knowledge proof of boundedness, i.e. that Alice and Bob may demonstrate to each other that the plaintext of an encryption $[m]$ sent to the other party (where the sender knows $m$) is smaller than some public bound $B$. For Paillier encryption this can be achieved with $\mathcal{O}(1)$ communication (of ring elements) using integer commitments and the fact that any non-negative integer can be written as a sum of four squares. See [Bou00, Lip03] for further discussion.

*Computing the greater-than relation.* Given encryptions $[m]$ and $[m']$ of $\ell$-bit values, obtain an encryption $[b]$ of a bit $b$ such that $b = 1$ iff $m > m'$. A constant-rounds protocol $\pi^c_{>?}$ for this can be based off of the comparison protocol of Nishide and Ohta [NO07]; communication complexity is $C_{\pi^c_{>?}} = \mathcal{O}(\ell)$ ring elements. We use $\pi^c_{\leq?}$ as syntactic sugar for running $\pi^c_{>?}$ with inputs swapped.

A sub-linear protocol, denoted $\pi^s_{>?}$ and $\pi^s_{\leq?}$, is possible due to Toft [Tof11]. Its complexity is $C_{\pi^s_{>?}} = \mathcal{O}\left((\log \ell)(\kappa + \log\log \bar{\ell})\right)$ ring elements in $R_{\pi^s_{>?}} = \mathcal{O}(\log \ell)$ rounds, where $\kappa$ is a correctness parameter.

*Computing the Inverse of an Element.* Given an encryption $[x]$ of $x \in \mathbb{Z}^*_M$, compute an encryption $\left[x^{-1}\right]$ of its inverse. We use the protocol from [BB89] which performs this task in a constant number of rounds and communicating a constant number of field elements. We shall use this protocol in both the constant-rounds and the sub-linear protocol and hence simply denote it by $\pi_{\text{inv}}$.

*Bit-Decompositon (BD).* Decomposing an encrypted $\ell$-bit value $[m]$ into binary form – i.e. computing bits $[m_{\ell-1}], \ldots, [m_0]$ such that $m = \sum_{i=0}^{\ell-1} 2^i \cdot m_i$ – is not strictly required (details appear in the full version) but we use it here for clarity. We denote by $\pi^c_{\text{BD}}$ the BD protocol of Reistad and Toft [RT10]; this uses $C_{\pi^c_{\text{BD}}} = \mathcal{O}(\ell)$ communication.

*Prefix-or of a Sequence of Bits.* Given encrypted bits $[x_{\ell-1}], \ldots, [x_0]$, compute encrypted bits $[y_{\ell-1}], \ldots, [y_0]$ such that $y_i = \bigvee_{j=i}^{\ell-1} x_j$. An $\mathcal{O}(1)$-rounds protocol communicating $C_{\pi^c_{\text{pre-V}}} = \mathcal{O}(\ell)$ elements, $\pi^c_{\text{pre-V}}$, is provided in [DFK+06].

*Powers of a number.* Given an encrypted number $[x]$ and public $\omega \in \mathbb{Z}$, compute $\left[x^1\right], \left[x^2\right], \ldots, \left[x^\omega\right]$. $\pi^c_{\text{pre-}\Pi}$ achieves this using $C_{\pi^c_{\text{pre-}\Pi}} = \mathcal{O}(\omega)$ communication in $\mathcal{O}(1)$ rounds using a prefix-product computation, [BB89, DFK+06].

## 3   The Intuition Behind the Constructions

In this section we take a high-level view and present the ideas behind the desired computation. The following sections then explain how to do this securely in the stated complexity. Assume in the following that $n$ and $d$ are $\ell$-bit integers, and let $k$ be a suitable large, public integer. Our solutions then consist of two steps:

I. Compute an encrypted approximation $[\tilde{a}]$ of $a = \lfloor 2^k/d \rfloor$
II. Compute $[\lfloor n/d \rfloor]$ as $\lfloor ([\tilde{a}] \cdot [n])/2^k \rfloor$

Step I is explained over the reals in Section 3.1. This is then converted to integer computation in Section 3.2 and finally realised using $\mathbb{Z}_M$ arithmetic in Section 3.3. Note that the integer division in step II is simpler as $2^k$ is public.

### 3.1   The Taylor Series

As in [KLM05] or the constant depth division circuit of Hesse et al. [HAB02], we start with a geometric series to compute a "$k$-shifted" approximation of $1/d$:

$$\frac{1}{\alpha} = \sum_{i=0}^{\infty}(1-\alpha)^i = \sum_{i=0}^{\omega}(1-\alpha)^i + \epsilon_\omega \tag{1}$$

where $\epsilon_\omega = \sum_{i=\omega+1}^{\infty}(1-\alpha)^i$. This is easily verified for any real $0 < \alpha < 1$. Further, approximating $1/\alpha$ by keeping only the first $\omega + 1$ terms of the summation introduces an additive error of $\epsilon_\omega$. If $0 < 1 - \alpha \leq 1/2$ then this error is at most

$$\epsilon_\omega = \sum_{i=\omega+1}^{\infty}(1-\alpha)^i = (1-\alpha)^{\omega+1} \cdot \sum_{i=0}^{\infty}(1-\alpha)^i \leq 2^{-\omega-1} \cdot \frac{1}{\alpha} \leq 2^{-\omega}. \quad (2)$$

By picking $\omega$ sufficiently large this ensures an appropriately small error below.

## 3.2   Converting the Taylor Series to an Integer Computation

Multiplying $1/\alpha$ by a power of two "shifts" the value; this ensures that each of the $\omega + 1$ terms of the finite sum of Eq. (1) are integer. The non-integer part of the shifted value is entirely contained in $\epsilon_\omega$, which will be discarded.

Let $\ell_d = \lfloor \log_2(d) + 1 \rfloor$ be the bit-length of $d$, i.e. $2^{\ell_d-1} \leq d < 2^{\ell_d}$; define $\ell_n$ similarly. Any $\omega \geq max\{\ell_n - \ell_d, 0\}$ provides sufficient accuracy, however, the public $\omega$ cannot depend on the secret $\ell_n$ and $\ell_d$. Thus, we let $\omega = \ell \geq \ell_n - \ell_d$. For $\alpha = d/2^{\ell_d}$ and $k = \ell^2 + \ell$ the following provides $1/d$ shifted up by $k$ bits:

$$\frac{2^k}{d} = 2^{k-\ell_d} \cdot \frac{1}{d/2^{\ell_d}} = \left(2^{k-\ell_d(\omega+1)} \sum_{i=0}^{\omega}\left(2^{\ell_d} - d\right)^i \cdot 2^{\ell_d(\omega-i)}\right) + 2^{k-\ell_d} \cdot \epsilon_\omega.$$

We define the desired approximation of $2^k/d$ as

$$\tilde{a} = 2^{k-\ell_d(\omega+1)} \cdot \sum_{i=0}^{\omega}\left(2^{\ell_d} - d\right)^i \cdot 2^{\ell_d(\omega-i)}. \quad (3)$$

Note that not only is this an integer since $k \geq \ell_d(\omega + 1)$ and $2^{\ell_d} > d$, it may also be computed as the product of $2^{k-\ell_d(\omega+1)}$ and the evaluation of the integer polynomial with coefficients $2^{\ell_d(\omega-i)}$ for $0 \leq i \leq \omega$ at point $2^{\ell_d} - d$. Furthermore, since $0 < 1 - d/2^{\ell_d} \leq 1/2$ we have a bound on the additive error by Eq. (2):

$$2^{k-\ell_d} \cdot \epsilon_\omega \leq 2^{k-\ell_d-\omega}.$$

This ensures that the result computed in step II is off by at most 1; we have:

$$\left\lfloor \frac{n}{d} \right\rfloor = \left\lfloor \frac{n \cdot (\tilde{a} + 2^{k-\ell_d} \cdot \epsilon_\omega)}{2^k} \right\rfloor = \left\lfloor \frac{n \cdot \tilde{a}}{2^k} + \frac{n \cdot 2^{k-\ell_d} \cdot \epsilon_\omega}{2^k} \right\rfloor \quad (4)$$

and see that the second summand is bound by

$$\frac{n \cdot 2^{k-\ell_d} \cdot \epsilon_\omega}{2^k} \leq \frac{n \cdot 2^{k-\ell_d-\omega}}{2^k} < \frac{2^k}{2^k} = 1$$

since $\ell_n \leq \omega$. $\lfloor \frac{n\cdot\tilde{a}}{2^k} \rfloor$ is the desired result *except* that the sum of the error, $n \cdot 2^{k-\ell_d} \cdot \epsilon_\omega$, and the discarded bits of the approximation, $n \cdot \tilde{a} \bmod 2^k$, may be greater than $2^k$; i.e. there may be an additive error of $-1$ due to a lost carry.

To recap: Given integers $2^{k-\ell_d(\omega+1)}$, $2^{\ell_d} - d$ and $2^{\ell_d(\omega-i)}$ for $0 \leq i \leq \ell$, performing step I yields an approximation $\tilde{a}$ of $2^k/d$ using Eq. (3). Down-shifting this almost gives the desired result, namely $\tilde{q} \in \{q, q-1\}$, where $q = \lfloor n/d \rfloor$.

## 3.3    Performing the Integer Computation Using $\mathbb{Z}_M$ Arithmetic

The underlying primitives provide secure $\mathbb{Z}_M$ arithmetic, with $M = p \cdot q$ being the Paillier key whose secret key is held jointly by the parties. We assume[1] that

$$M \gg 2^{\ell^2 + \ell + \kappa_s},$$

where $\kappa_s$ is a statistical security parameter, e.g. $\kappa_s = 100$. This implies that no "overflow" modulo $M$ occurs in Eq. (3), hence it can be seen as occurring in $\mathbb{Z}_M$. However, for efficiency reasons we rephrase the expression as

$$\tilde{a} = 2^{k - \ell_d(\omega+1)} \cdot \sum_{i=0}^{\omega} \left(2^{\ell_d} - d\right)^i \cdot 2^{\ell_d(\omega-i)} = 2^{k-\ell_d} \cdot \sum_{i=0}^{\omega} \left(\left(2^{\ell_d} - d\right) \cdot 2^{-\ell_d}\right)^i \quad (5)$$

where addition and multiplication occur in $\mathbb{Z}_M$. Although this should no longer be seen as an integer computation, the key observation is that it is irrelevant *how* the encryption $[\tilde{a}]$ is obtained; what matters is that the plaintext is correct. Essentially this altered calculation can be viewed as using the encoding of rational values suggested in [FSW02]. Note that this simplifies the desired calculation: we now only need the values $2^{k-\ell_d}$, $2^{\ell_d} - d$, and $2^{-\ell_d}$ as well as the evaluation of a $\mathbb{Z}_M$-polynomial with known coefficients (all equal to 1).

## 4    The Overall Division Protocol

Having presented the desired $\mathbb{Z}_M$-expression for computing the approximation $\tilde{a} \approx 2^k/d$ in Section 3.3 above, the goal now is to give a high-level view of the actual protocol. We first formalise the required sub-tasks, and then present the overall protocol based on assumed protocols for these. Instantiating these protocols with either the constant-rounds (Section 5) or the sub-linear (Section 6) versions of the sub-protocols we obtain our two division protocols.

### 4.1    Sub-tasks and Sub-protocols

In addition to the basic primitives of Section 2 we require the following sub-protocols:

- $\pi_{\mathrm{BL}}$: Given an encryption $[d]$ of an $\ell$-bit value $d$, determine an encryption $[2^{\ell_d}]$ for $\ell_d = \lfloor log_2(d) + 1 \rfloor$
- $\pi_{\mathrm{poly}}$: Given an encryption $[p]$ of $p \in \mathbb{Z}_M^*$, evaluate the known polynomial $A(x) = \sum_{i=0}^{\omega} x^i$ over $\mathbb{Z}_M$ securely at point $p$, i.e. compute encryption $[A(p)]$
- $\pi_{\mathrm{trunc}}$: Given an encryption $[\hat{q}]$ of an $(\ell + k)$-bit value $\hat{q} \in \mathbb{Z}_M$, compute an encryption $[\tilde{q}]$ of an approximation of $\lfloor \hat{q}/2^k \rfloor$ s.t. $\tilde{q} = \lfloor \hat{q}/2^k \rfloor + \epsilon$ for $\epsilon \in \{0, 1\}$.

---

[1] $M$ needs to be at least a thousand bits long to ensure security of the Paillier scheme and hence this assumption is not as bad as it may appear at first glance.

## 4.2   The High-Level View

The full division protocol is seen in Figure 1 and proceeds by the following steps:

I. Compute an encryption $[\tilde{a}]$ of the approximation
   (a) Determine $\left[2^{\ell_d}\right]$ and in turn compute $\left[2^{k-\ell_d}\right]$ and $[p] = \left[\left(2^{\ell_d} - d\right) \cdot 2^{-\ell_d}\right]$
   (b) Evaluate the polynomial of Eq. (5) in $[p]$ and securely multiply by $\left[2^{k-\ell_d}\right]$
II. Compute $[\lfloor n/d \rfloor]$
   (a) Obtain encryption $[\tilde{q}]$ of $\tilde{q} \approx \lfloor n/d \rfloor$ by computing and truncating $[n \cdot \tilde{a}]$
   (b) Eliminate errors introduced by approximations, i.e., compute $[q]$ from $[\tilde{q}]$

where the elimination of errors are performed by two secure comparions.

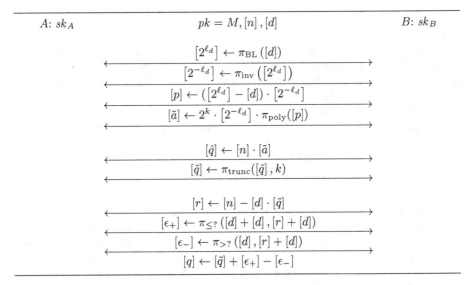

**Fig. 1.** The full division protocol, $\pi_{\text{div}}([n], [d]) \mapsto [\lfloor n/d \rfloor]$

*Correctness.* Correctness follows almost entirely from the previous section. For the plaintext of $[\hat{q}]$, the most significant bits are off by at most 1:

$$\lfloor \hat{q}/2^k \rfloor \in \{\lfloor n/d \rfloor, \lfloor n/d \rfloor - 1\}.$$

The execution of $\pi_{\text{trunc}}$ may introduce an additional additive error, i.e. we have

$$\tilde{q} \in \{\lfloor n/d \rfloor - 1, \lfloor n/d \rfloor, \lfloor n/d \rfloor + 1\}.$$

Using $r = n - d \cdot \tilde{q} \in [-d; 2d[$ we can securely determine which case we are in. Namely, $\tilde{q} + 1 = \lfloor n/d \rfloor$ when $d \leq r$ and $\tilde{q} - 1 = \lfloor n/d \rfloor$ when $0 > r$. In order to deal only with positive integers we scale these tests to respectively $2d \leq r + d$ and $d > r + d$. Letting $\epsilon_+$ and $\epsilon_-$ denote the Boolean outcome of these tests, it follows that $q = \tilde{q} + \epsilon_+ - \epsilon_- = \lfloor n/d \rfloor$.

*Privacy.* The protocol reveals no information about the inputs (other than the desired encryption of the result). This follows from the fact that no value is ever decrypted and that we only invoke secure sub-protocols which do not leak information. We note that $\pi_{\mathrm{inv}}$ and $\pi_{\mathrm{poly}}$ require the input to be invertible – this is indeed the case as $M$ is the product of two odd primes, $p, q \approx \sqrt{M}$, while $2^{\ell_d}, 2^{\ell_d} - d \leq 2^{\ell} \ll \sqrt{M}$. Further, the input $[n \cdot \tilde{a}]$ for the truncation is $\ell + k$-bit long as $n < 2^{\ell}$ and $\tilde{a} \leq 2^k/d \leq 2^k$, and hence the input is of the correct size.

A formal security proof using the real/ideal paradigm requires the construction of a simulator for each party. These are straightforward to construct from the simulators of the sub-protocols; as our protocol consists of the sequential evaluation of sub-protocols, the overall simulator simply consists of the sequential execution of the simulators of these.

*Complexity.* The complexity depends on the details of the sub-protocols $\pi_{\mathrm{BL}}$, $\pi_{\mathrm{poly}}$, $\pi_{\mathrm{trunc}}$, and $\pi_{>?}$. Formally we have

$$R_{\pi_{\mathrm{div}}} = R_{\pi_{\mathrm{BL}}} + R_{\pi_{\mathrm{inv}}} + R_{\pi_{\mathrm{poly}}} + R_{\pi_{\mathrm{trunc}}} + 2 \cdot R_{\pi_{>?}} + 3 \cdot R_{\pi_{\mathrm{mult}}}$$
$$= R_{\pi_{\mathrm{BL}}} + R_{\pi_{\mathrm{poly}}} + R_{\pi_{\mathrm{trunc}}} + \mathcal{O}(R_{\pi_{>?}}) + \mathcal{O}(1)$$

$$(6)$$

$$C_{\pi_{\mathrm{div}}} = C_{\pi_{\mathrm{BL}}} + C_{\pi_{\mathrm{inv}}} + C_{\pi_{\mathrm{poly}}} + C_{\pi_{\mathrm{trunc}}} + 2 \cdot C_{\pi_{>?}} + 3 \cdot C_{\pi_{\mathrm{mult}}}$$
$$= C_{\pi_{\mathrm{BL}}} + C_{\pi_{\mathrm{poly}}} + C_{\pi_{\mathrm{trunc}}} + \mathcal{O}(C_{\pi_{>?}}) + \mathcal{O}(1)$$

such that for the constant-rounds instantiation we get $R_{\pi_{\mathrm{div}}^c} = R_{\pi_{\mathrm{BL}}^c} + R_{\pi_{\mathrm{poly}}^c} + R_{\pi_{\mathrm{trunc}}^c} + \mathcal{O}(1)$ and $C_{\pi_{\mathrm{div}}^c} = C_{\pi_{\mathrm{BL}}^c} + C_{\pi_{\mathrm{poly}}^c} + C_{\pi_{\mathrm{trunc}}^c} + \mathcal{O}(\ell)$. Likewise, for the sublinear instantiation we get $R_{\pi_{\mathrm{div}}^s} = R_{\pi_{\mathrm{BL}}^s} + R_{\pi_{\mathrm{poly}}^s} + R_{\pi_{\mathrm{trunc}}^s} + \mathcal{O}(\log \ell)$ and $C_{\pi_{\mathrm{div}}^s} = C_{\pi_{\mathrm{BL}}^s} + C_{\pi_{\mathrm{poly}}^s} + C_{\pi_{\mathrm{trunc}}^s} + \mathcal{O}\left((\log \ell)(\kappa + \log\log \ell)\right)$. Finally, a slight optimisation regarding rounds is possible by invoking $\pi_{>?}$ and $\pi_{\leq?}$ in parallel.

*Active Security.* The protocol in Figure 1 is only passively secure. However, obtaining active security is straightforward by executing appropriate ZK proofs. This increases the communication complexity by a constant factor.

## 5    The Constant-Rounds Protocol

In this section we plug in protocols for the three sub-tasks. All protocols use a constant number of rounds and linear communication. Combined with the previous section this provides a constant-rounds protocol for division.

### 5.1    The Constant-Rounds $\pi_{\mathrm{BL}}^c$ Protocol

In the full version of this paper [DNT12] we give a $\pi_{\mathrm{BL}}^c$ protocol that, somewhat surprising, does not rely on bit-decomposition. However, for clarity the $\pi_{\mathrm{BL}}^c$ protocol presented here in Figure 2 is composed of two protocols introduced in Section 2: $\pi_{\mathrm{BD}}^c$ and $\pi_{\mathrm{pre-V}}^c$. To recap, given $[d]$ the former returns a vector of encrypted bits $[x_{\ell-1}], \ldots, [x_0]$ for which it holds that $\sum_{i=0}^{\ell-1} x_i \cdot 2^i = d$. The latter takes such a vector of encrypted bits and returns another such that $y_i = \bigvee_{j=i}^{\ell-1} x_j$.

| A: $sk_A$ | $pk = M, [d]$ | B: $sk_B$ |
|---|---|---|

$$[x_{\ell-1}], \ldots, [x_0] \leftarrow \pi^c_{\text{BD}}([d])$$

$$[y_{\ell-1}], \ldots, [y_0] \leftarrow \pi^c_{\text{pre-}\vee}([x_{\ell-1}], \ldots, [x_0])$$

$$[2^{\ell_d}] \leftarrow 1 + \sum_{i=0}^{\ell-1} [y_i] \cdot 2^i$$

**Fig. 2.** Constant-rounds bit-length protocol, $\pi^c_{\text{BL}}([d]) \mapsto [2^{\ell_d}]$

*Correctness.* By the correctness of the two sub-protocols we only have to argue the correctness of the final step. Note that the result of $\pi^c_{\text{pre-}\vee}$ is a set such that $y_i = 1$ if and only if $d \geq 2^i$. This means that $1 + \sum_{i=0}^{\ell-1} y_i \cdot 2^i$ is the desired $2^{\ell_d}$.

*Privacy and Active Security.* Follows immediately by the privacy and security guarantees of the two sub-protocols.

*Complexity.* Since the final step of $\pi^c_{\text{BL}}$ is a local computation we simply have that $R_{\pi^c_{\text{BL}}} = R_{\pi^c_{\text{BD}}} + R_{\pi^c_{\text{pre-}\vee}} = \mathcal{O}(1)$ and $C_{\pi^c_{\text{BL}}} = C_{\pi^c_{\text{BD}}} + C_{\pi^c_{\text{pre-}\vee}} = \mathcal{O}(\ell)$.

## 5.2 The Constant-Rounds $\pi_{\text{poly}}$ Protocol

As shown in the protocol in Figure 3, we simply evaluate polynomial $A(x) = \sum_{i=0}^{\omega} x^i$ in point $p = (2^{\ell_d} - d) \cdot 2^{-\ell_d}$ using the prefix-product protocol $\pi^c_{\text{pre-}\Pi}$. This gives encryptions of $p^1, p^2, \ldots, p^\omega$ – and knowing these, all there is left to do is to sum them together with $p^0 = 1$ to form $A(p)$.

| A: $sk_A$ | $pk = M, [x]$ | B: $sk_B$ |
|---|---|---|

$$[p^1], \ldots, [p^\omega] \leftarrow \pi^c_{\text{pre-}\Pi}([x], \ldots, [x])$$

$$[y] \leftarrow 1 + \sum_{i=1}^{\omega} [p_i]$$

**Fig. 3.** Constant-rounds polynomial evaluation protocol, $\pi^c_{\text{poly}}([x]) \mapsto [A(x)]$

*Correctness, Privacy, Complexity, and Active Security.* Noting that the second step of $\pi^c_{\text{poly}}$ is a local computation, all properties directly reflect those of the $\pi^c_{\text{pre-}\Pi}$ subprotocol. Formally, $R_{\pi^c_{\text{poly}}} = \mathcal{O}(1)$ and $C_{\pi^c_{\text{poly}}} = \mathcal{O}(\omega)$.

## 5.3 The Constant-Rounds $\pi_{\text{trunc}}$ Protocol

Our constant-rounds protocol for truncation (shown in Figure 4) takes encryption $[\hat{q}]$ and public $k$ as input and returns $[\tilde{q}]$ such that $\tilde{q} \approx \lfloor q/2^k \rfloor$. The result may have an additive error $c \leq 1$. It is possible to eliminate this error with a comparison $[c] \leftarrow ([\tilde{q}] \cdot 2^k >_? [\hat{q}])$, and computing the correct result as $[q] \leftarrow [\tilde{q}] - [c]$. However, instead of comparing two $\ell^2$-bit numbers here, we handle the error in the main protocol with a comparison of two $\ell$-bit numbers instead.

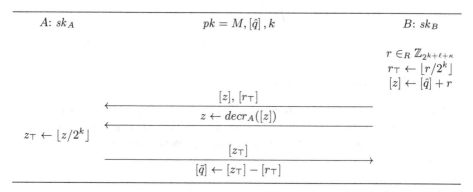

**Fig. 4.** Constant-rounds truncation protocol, $\pi_{\text{trunc}}^c([\hat{q}], k) \mapsto \left[\lfloor \hat{q}/2^k \rfloor + c\right]$

To perform the truncation, party $B$ first picks a random integer of a bit-length sufficient for using it as a mask for $\hat{q}$. He also stores the $\ell + \kappa$ most significant bits of $r$ as $r_{\top}$ and computes an encryption of it. Upon receiving $[z]$, the masked value of $\hat{q}$, $A$ and $B$ now decrypt $[z]$ for $A$ to see. After learning this value $z$, $A$ can locally perform the truncation to form $z_{\top}$. She sends an encryption of this value to $B$ and both can finally compute the output locally by $[z_{\top}] - [r_{\top}]$.

*Correctness.* When computing $z$ it may happen that $r$ causes a carry bit $c$ from the $k$ least significant bits to spill over into the $\ell + \kappa$ most significant bits. In this case the truncation of $z$ will maintain this carry bit, causing the result of $z_{\top} - r_{\top}$ to be $\lfloor \hat{q}/2^k \rfloor + 1$ instead of $\lfloor \hat{q}/2^k \rfloor$. For efficiency we allow this error.

*Privacy.* The only point where information could potentially be leaked is through $A$ seeing $z$. However, since $r$ is chosen uniformly at random and $\kappa$ bit longer than $\hat{q}$, $z$ leaks information about $\hat{q}$ with probability negligible in $\kappa$.

*Complexity.* We see that the complexity of $\pi_{\text{trunc}}^c$ is $R_{\pi_{\text{trunc}}^c} = 2 + R_{decr} = \mathcal{O}(1)$ where $R_{decr}$ is the round complexity of a decryption, assumed to be constant. Likewise the communication complexity is $C_{\pi_{\text{trunc}}^c} = 3 + C_{decr} = \mathcal{O}(1)$.

*Active Security.* To obtain active security $B$ must also send $\left[r_{\perp} = r \bmod 2^k\right]$ to $A$, who in turn must also send $\left[z_{\perp} = z \bmod 2^k\right]$. $B$ can now append a zero-knowledge proof that $z = (r_{\top} \cdot 2^k + r_{\perp}) + \hat{q}$ as well as proofs that both $r_{\top}$ and $r_{\perp}$ are within the correct bounds. Similary, $A$ also appends a proof of $z = z_{\top} \cdot 2^k + z_{\perp}$ and that $z_{\top}$ and $z_{\perp}$ are within bounds.

## 5.4   Combined Protocol and Analysis

By plugging the protocols introduced in this section into the $\pi_{\mathrm{div}}$ protocol of Section 4 we obtain our constant-rounds division protocol $\pi_{\mathrm{div}}^{c}$. Correctness, privacy, and active security follow from the discussions above. Using the complexity expressions in Eq. 6 from Section 4 and the fact that $\omega = \ell$ we get:

$$R_{\pi_{\mathrm{div}}^{c}} = R_{\pi_{\mathrm{BL}}^{c}} + R_{\pi_{\mathrm{poly}}^{c}} + R_{\pi_{\mathrm{trunc}}^{c}} + \mathcal{O}(1) = \mathcal{O}(1)$$

$$C_{\pi_{\mathrm{div}}^{c}} = C_{\pi_{\mathrm{BL}}^{c}} + C_{\pi_{\mathrm{poly}}^{c}} + C_{\pi_{\mathrm{trunc}}^{c}} + \mathcal{O}(\ell) = \mathcal{O}(\omega) + \mathcal{O}(\ell) = \mathcal{O}(\ell).$$

# 6   The Sub-linear Protocol

In this section we give the protocols needed for giving the division protocol of Section 3 a sub-linear communication complexity. We can reuse the truncation protocol $\pi_{\mathrm{trunc}}^{c}$ from Section 5 and hence only present two new $\pi_{\mathrm{BL}}$ and $\pi_{\mathrm{poly}}$ protocols.

## 6.1   The Sub-linear $\pi_{\mathrm{BL}}$ Protocol

To compute $[2^{\ell_d}]$ from $[d]$ in sub-linear communication complexity we take inspiration from [Tof11] and perform, in a sense, a binary search. Assuming we have a protocol $\pi_{\leq?}^{s}$ for performing comparison of two encrypted numbers, we give the protocol in Figure 5. For simplicity we assume that $\ell = 2^{\gamma}$ for some integer $\gamma$.

Intuitively, our construction recursively computes a pointer $p$ into the binary representation of $d$. Initially $p$ points to the first bit position ($p_0 = 2^0$). In the first round we then ask in which half of the binary representation of $d$ the most significant 1 occurs and store the result in bit $c_1$. Next we update $p$ to point to position $\ell/2^1$ if $c = 1$ (i.e. $p_1 = p_0 \cdot 2^{\ell/2^1}$) and to the same position as before if $c = 0$ (i.e. $p_1 = p_0 \cdot 1$). Iterating in this way $p$ will eventually point to the position of the most significant bit of $d$. Shifting the position by one will give us integer $2^{\ell_d}$.

*Correctness and Privacy.* Correctness follows from the above description of the protocol, and privacy follows immediately from the sub-protocols as we only compute on encrypted values.

*Complexity.* The protocol requires $\gamma = \log_2 \ell$ iterations, each requiring one comparison and one multiplication (not counting multiplication by public values). Hence we get round complexity $R_{\pi_{\mathrm{BL}}^{s}} = \gamma \cdot (R_{\pi_{\leq?}^{s}} + R_{\pi_{\mathrm{mult}}}) = \mathcal{O}(\log^2 \ell)$ and communication complexity $C_{\pi_{\mathrm{BL}}^{s}} = \gamma \cdot (C_{\pi_{\leq?}^{s}} + C_{\pi_{\mathrm{mult}}}) = \mathcal{O}\left((\log^2 \ell)(\kappa + \log\log \ell)\right)$.

*Active Security.* Since the sub-protocol is actively secure, we only have to append zero-knowledge proofs of correctness to every multiplication in order to make the protocol resistant against active attackers. This increases the number of messages communicated but only by a constant factor.

| A: $sk_A$ | $pk = M, [d]$ | B: $sk_B$ |
|---|---|---|

$$[p_0] \leftarrow 1$$

$$[c_1] \leftarrow \pi^s_{\leq?}\left(2^{\ell/2} \cdot [p_0], [d]\right)$$
$\longleftarrow\qquad\qquad\qquad\qquad\qquad\qquad\longrightarrow$

$$[p_1] \leftarrow [p_0] \cdot \left([c_1] \cdot (2^{\ell/2} - 1) + 1\right)$$
$\longleftarrow\qquad\qquad\qquad\qquad\qquad\qquad\longrightarrow$

$$\vdots$$

$$[c_\gamma] \leftarrow \pi^s_{\leq?}\left(2^{\ell/2^\gamma} \cdot [p_{\gamma-1}], [d]\right)$$
$\longleftarrow\qquad\qquad\qquad\qquad\qquad\qquad\longrightarrow$

$$[p_\gamma] \leftarrow [p_{\gamma-1}] \cdot \left([c_\gamma] \cdot (2^{\ell/2^\gamma} - 1) + 1\right)$$
$\longleftarrow\qquad\qquad\qquad\qquad\qquad\qquad\longrightarrow$

$$\left[2^{\ell_d}\right] \leftarrow 2 \cdot [p_\gamma]$$

**Fig. 5.** Sub-linear bit-length protocol, $\pi^s_{\mathrm{BL}}([d]) \mapsto \left[2^{\ell_d}\right]$

## 6.2 The Sub-linear $\pi_{\mathrm{poly}}$ Protocol

Evaluating the $A(x) = \sum_{i=0}^{\omega} x^i$ polynomial at a point $p$ can be done by a method similar to "square and multiply". We give the protocol in Figure 6 where for simplicity we have assumed that $\omega = 2^\gamma$ for some integer $\gamma$. The intuition behind the notation is that $\sigma_j = \sum_{i=1}^{2^j} x^i$ and $x_j = x^{2^j}$ – it is not hard to see that this is indeed the case. Specifically this gives us that $\sigma_\gamma = \sum_{i=1}^{2^\gamma} x^i$ and hence $\sigma_\gamma + 1 = \left(\sum_{i=1}^{\omega} x^i\right) + 1 = \sum_{i=0}^{\omega} x^i$ as required.

*Correctness, Privacy, and Complexity.* The first two follow respectively from the description above and from that fact that only arithmetical operations on encryptions are performed. For complexity we have that the protocol requires $\gamma = \log_2 \omega$ iterations with two multiplications in each. Hence the round complexity is $R_{\pi^s_{\mathrm{poly}}} = \gamma \cdot (2 \cdot R_{\pi_{\mathrm{mult}}}) = \mathcal{O}(\log \omega)$, and likewise for the communication complexity $C_{\pi^s_{\mathrm{poly}}} = \gamma \cdot (2 \cdot C_{\pi_{\mathrm{mult}}}) = \mathcal{O}(\log \omega)$.

*Active Security.* By appending zero-knowledge proofs of correctness to every multiplication we make the protocol resistant against active attackers. This increases the number of messages communicated but only by a constant factor.

## 6.3 The Sub-linear $\pi_{\mathrm{trunc}}$ Protocol

The truncation protocol $\pi^c_{\mathrm{trunc}}$ of Section 5 is efficient enought to be reused for the sub-linear protocol $\pi^s_{\mathrm{trunc}}$: only a single operation is performed, namely the decryption of $[z]$. The remaining operations can be carried out locally.

---

A: $sk_A$ $\qquad\qquad\qquad$ $pk = M, [x]$ $\qquad\qquad\qquad$ B: $sk_B$

$$[\sigma_0] \leftarrow [x]$$

$$[x_0] \leftarrow [x]$$
$$[\sigma_1] \leftarrow ([x_0] + 1) \cdot [\sigma_0]$$

$$\vdots$$

$$[x_{\gamma-1}] \leftarrow [x_{\gamma-2}] \cdot [x_{\gamma-2}]$$
$$[\sigma_\gamma] \leftarrow ([x_{\gamma-1}] + 1) \cdot [\sigma_{\gamma-1}]$$

$$\left[\textstyle\sum_{i=0}^{\omega} x^i\right] \leftarrow [\sigma_\gamma] + 1$$

---

**Fig. 6.** Sub-linear polynomial evaluation protocol, $\pi_{\text{poly}}^s([x]) \mapsto [A(x)]$

### 6.4   Combined Protocol and Analysis

Our sub-linear division protocol $\pi_{\text{div}}^s$ is obtained from the $\pi_{\text{div}}$ protocol of Section 4. Correctness, privacy, and active security follow from the discussions in the previous sections and in this section. As for complexity, since $\omega = \ell$, we get:

$$R_{\pi_{\text{div}}^s} = R_{\pi_{\text{BL}}^s} + \cdots + \mathcal{O}(\log \ell) = \mathcal{O}(\log^2 \ell) + \mathcal{O}(\log \omega) + \mathcal{O}(\log \ell) = \mathcal{O}(\log^2 \ell)$$

$$C_{\pi_{\text{div}}^s} = C_{\pi_{\text{BL}}^s} + \cdots + \mathcal{O}\left((\log \ell)(\kappa + \log\log \ell)\right) = \mathcal{O}\left((\log^2 \ell)(\kappa + \log\log \ell)\right).$$

## 7   Variations and Extensions

*The multiparty case.* Though we have presented our protocols in the two-party setting, the ideas are also applicable to the multiparty case, based e.g. on the protocols of [CDN01]. Arithmetic operations on encrypted values are immediate, hence we must only consider $\pi_{\text{BL}}$, $\pi_{\text{trunc}}$, and the sublinear comparison $\pi_{>?}$.

For the constant-rounds protocol we may use the arithmetic-based comparison of [NO07] while $\pi_{\text{BL}}$ is essentially the bit-decomposition of [RT10]. Thus, these immediately work in the multiparty setting. The $\pi_{\text{trunc}}$ protocol in Figure 4 can be jointly played by the parties. Part $A$ is played publicly and part $B$ is played using the protocols of [CDN01]. First each party $P_i$ ($1 \le i \le n$) supplies an encryption of a random value $[r^{(i)}]$ as well as $\left[r_T^{(i)}\right]$ with plaintext $\lfloor r^{(i)}/2^k \rfloor$. The parties then compute and decrypt $[z] \leftarrow [\hat{q}] + \sum_{i=1}^{n} \left[r^{(i)}\right]$ and in turn $[\hat{q}] \leftarrow \lfloor z/2^k \rfloor - \sum_{i=1}^{n} \left[r_T^{(i)}\right]$. This is the right result plus an additive error originating from a carry in the addition of $r$. Since $r$ is a sum itself, the possible error grows linearly in the number of parties. However, as in the main protocol (Figure 1) this may be corrected using a number of secure comparisons.

With the additional requirement of two named and mutually incorruptible parties, the sub-linear case follows analogously by the protocols of [Tof11]. Since

$\pi_{\mathrm{BL}}$ is based on comparison and arithmetic, and $\pi_{\mathrm{trunc}}$ is the same as the constant-rounds case, a sub-linear multiparty protocol is possible too.

*Unconditionally secure integer division.* Unconditionally secure variations of our protocols are possible, based e.g. on Shamir's secret sharing scheme and the protocols of Ben-Or et al. [Sha79, BGW88]. The construction is straightforward as all sub-protocols are applicable in this setting as well.

*Improving the complexity of the sub-linear protocol.* Using the other comparison protocol given in [Tof11] we may obtain slightly better bounds on our division protocol, namely $\mathcal{O}(\log \ell)$ rounds and $\mathcal{O}\left((\log \ell)\sqrt{\ell}(\kappa + \log \ell)\right)$ communications.

**Acknowledgements.** The authors would like to thank Troels Sørensen, Jesper Buus Nielsen, and the anonymous reviewers for their comments and suggestions.

# References

[ACS02]    Algesheimer, J., Camenisch, J., Shoup, V.: Efficient Computation Modulo a Shared Secret with Application to the Generation of Shared Safe-Prime Products. In: Yung, M. (ed.) CRYPTO 2002. LNCS, vol. 2442, pp. 417–432. Springer, Heidelberg (2002)

[BB89]    Bar-Ilan, J., Beaver, D.: Non-cryptographic fault-tolerant computing in a constant number of rounds of interaction. In: Rudnicki, P. (ed.) Proceedings of the Eighth Annual ACM Symposium on Principles of Distributed Computing, pp. 201–209. ACM Press, New York (1989)

[BCD+09]    Bogetoft, P., Christensen, D.L., Damgård, I., Geisler, M., Jakobsen, T., Krøigaard, M., Nielsen, J.D., Nielsen, J.B., Nielsen, K., Pagter, J., Schwartzbach, M., Toft, T.: Secure Multiparty Computation Goes Live. In: Dingledine, R., Golle, P. (eds.) FC 2009. LNCS, vol. 5628, pp. 325–343. Springer, Heidelberg (2009)

[BGW88]    Ben-Or, M., Goldwasser, S., Wigderson, A.: Completeness theorems for noncryptographic fault-tolerant distributed computations. In: 20th Annual ACM Symposium on Theory of Computing, pp. 1–10. ACM Press (1988)

[Bou00]    Boudot, F.: Efficient Proofs that a Committed Number Lies in an Interval. In: Preneel, B. (ed.) EUROCRYPT 2000. LNCS, vol. 1807, pp. 431–444. Springer, Heidelberg (2000)

[CD09]    Catrina, O., Dragulin, C.: Multiparty computation of fixed-point multiplication and reciprocal. In: International Workshop on Database and Expert Systems Applications, pp. 107–111 (2009)

[CDN01]    Cramer, R., Damgård, I., Nielsen, J.B.: Multiparty Computation from Threshold Homomorphic Encryption. In: Pfitzmann, B. (ed.) EUROCRYPT 2001. LNCS, vol. 2045, pp. 280–300. Springer, Heidelberg (2001)

[DFK+06]    Damgård, I.B., Fitzi, M., Kiltz, E., Nielsen, J.B., Toft, T.: Unconditionally Secure Constant-Rounds Multi-party Computation for Equality, Comparison, Bits and Exponentiation. In: Halevi, S., Rabin, T. (eds.) TCC 2006. LNCS, vol. 3876, pp. 285–304. Springer, Heidelberg (2006)

[DJ01]    Damgård, I., Jurik, M.: A Generalisation, a Simplification and Some Applications of Paillier's Probabilistic Public-Key System. In: Kim, K. (ed.) PKC 2001. LNCS, vol. 1992, pp. 119–136. Springer, Heidelberg (2001)

[DNT12]   Dahl, M., Ning, C., Toft, T.: On secure two-party integer division. Technical report (2012), http://eprint.iacr.org/2012/164

[FJ05]    From, S., Jakobsen, T.: Secure multi-party computation on integers. Master's thesis, Aarhus University (2005), http://users-cs.au.dk/tpj/uni/thesis/

[FSW02]   Fouque, P., Stern, J., Wackers, J.: Cryptocomputing with Rationals. In: Blaze, M. (ed.) FC 2002. LNCS, vol. 2357, pp. 136–146. Springer, Heidelberg (2003)

[GMS10]   Guajardo, J., Mennink, B., Schoenmakers, B.: Modulo Reduction for Paillier Encryptions and Application to Secure Statistical Analysis. In: Sion, R. (ed.) FC 2010. LNCS, vol. 6052, pp. 375–382. Springer, Heidelberg (2010)

[HAB02]   Hesse, W., Allender, E., Mix Barrington, D.A.: Uniform constant-depth threshold circuits for division and iterated multiplication. Journal of Computer and System Sciences 65(4), 695–716 (2002)

[HKS+10]  Henecka, W., Kögl, S., Sadeghi, A., Schneider, T., Wehrenberg, I.: TASTY: tool for automating secure two-party computations. In: CCS 2010: Proceedings of the 17th ACM Conference on Computer and Communications Security, pp. 451–462. ACM, New York (2010)

[JW05]    Jagannathan, G., Wright, R.N.: Privacy-preserving distributed k-means clustering over arbitrarily partitioned data. In: Grossman, R., Bayardo, R.J., Bennett, K.P. (eds.) KDD, pp. 593–599. ACM (2005)

[KLM05]   Kiltz, E., Leander, G., Malone-Lee, J.: Secure Computation of the Mean and Related Statistics. In: Kilian, J. (ed.) TCC 2005. LNCS, vol. 3378, pp. 283–302. Springer, Heidelberg (2005)

[Lip03]   Lipmaa, H.: On Diophantine Complexity and Statistical Zero-Knowledge Arguments. In: Laih, C.-S. (ed.) ASIACRYPT 2003. LNCS, vol. 2894, pp. 398–415. Springer, Heidelberg (2003)

[NO07]    Nishide, T., Ohta, K.: Multiparty Computation for Interval, Equality, and Comparison Without Bit-Decomposition Protocol. In: Okamoto, T., Wang, X. (eds.) PKC 2007. LNCS, vol. 4450, pp. 343–360. Springer, Heidelberg (2007)

[NX10]    Ning, C., Xu, Q.: Multiparty Computation for Modulo Reduction without Bit-Decomposition and a Generalization to Bit-Decomposition. In: Abe, M. (ed.) ASIACRYPT 2010. LNCS, vol. 6477, pp. 483–500. Springer, Heidelberg (2010)

[Pai99]   Paillier, P.: Public-Key Cryptosystems Based on Composite Degree Residuosity Classes. In: Stern, J. (ed.) EUROCRYPT 1999. LNCS, vol. 1592, pp. 223–238. Springer, Heidelberg (1999)

[RT10]    Reistad, T., Toft, T.: Linear, Constant-Rounds Bit-Decomposition. In: Lee, D., Hong, S. (eds.) ICISC 2009. LNCS, vol. 5984, pp. 245–257. Springer, Heidelberg (2010)

[Sha79]   Shamir, A.: How to share a secret. Communications of the ACM 22(11), 612–613 (1979)

[Tof11]   Toft, T.: Sub-linear, Secure Comparison with Two Non-colluding Parties. In: Catalano, D., Fazio, N., Gennaro, R., Nicolosi, A. (eds.) PKC 2011. LNCS, vol. 6571, pp. 174–191. Springer, Heidelberg (2011)

[Veu10]   Veugen, T.: Encrypted integer division. In: IEEE Workshop on Information Forensics and Security (WIFS 2010). IEEE, Seattle (2010)

# A Non-interactive Range Proof
# with Constant Communication

Rafik Chaabouni[1,2], Helger Lipmaa[1], and Bingsheng Zhang[1]

[1] Institute of Computer Science, University of Tartu, Estonia
[2] Security and Cryptography Laboratory, EPFL, Switzerland

**Abstract.** In a range proof, the prover convinces the verifier in zero-knowledge that he has encrypted or committed to a value $a \in [0, H]$ where $H$ is a public constant. Most of the previous non-interactive range proofs have been proven secure in the random oracle model. We show that one of the few previous non-interactive range proofs in the common reference string (CRS) model, proposed by Yuen et al. in COCOON 2009, is insecure. We then construct a secure non-interactive range proof that works in the CRS model. The new range proof can have (by different instantiations of the parameters) either very short communication (14 080 bits) and verifier's computation (81 pairings), short combined CRS length and communication ($\log^{1/2+o(1)} H$ group elements), or very efficient prover's computation ($\Theta(\log H)$ exponentiations).

**Keywords:** NIZK, pairings, progression-free sets, range proof.

## 1 Introduction

In a range proof, the prover convinces the verifier in zero-knowledge that he has encrypted or committed to a value $a \in [0, H]$, where $H$ is a public constant. Range proofs are needed in a wide variety of cryptographic protocols, like e-voting (to show that a ballot corresponds to a valid candidate), e-auctions, anonymous credentials, e-cash, or any other protocol that needs for its correctness that the inputs are from a valid range. Given the need for range proofs in a large variety of protocols, it is not surprising that there is a large amount of research on this topic.

Most of the existing efficient range proofs fall in one of the next two categories. The first category uses a classical result of Lagrange that every non-negative integer is a sum of four squares [13,7,21]. However, in this case the underlying group has to be of unknown order which seriously limits the available cryptographic techniques. In particular, all known *secure* Lagrange's theorem based range proofs are based on operations in $\mathbb{Z}_n^*$ for a hard-to-factor $n$. Since to achieve 128-bit security level, $n$ must be at least 3072 bits long, arithmetic in $\mathbb{Z}_n^*$ is relatively slow. One also has to compute the four squares of the Lagrange's theorem which is inefficient by itself. Furthermore, this means that it is not known how to instantiate such schemes with bilinear groups. (This is exemplified by the fact

A.D. Keromytis (Ed.): FC 2012, LNCS 7397, pp. 179–199, 2012.
© International Financial Cryptography Association 2012

that we break the range proof of [21] where the Lagrange theorem is used in the bilinear setting with known group order.)

Due to such considerations, one usually considers the second approach. There, one uses the fact that $a \in [0, H]$, if and only if for some well chosen coefficients $G_i$, there exist $b_i \in [0, u-1]$ such that $a = \sum_{i=1}^{n} G_i b_i$. Here, $u \ll H$ and $n$ is also small. One then proves separately for every $b_i$ that $b_i \in [0, u-1]$, and uses additively homomorphic properties of the used commitment scheme to verify that $a = \sum_{i=1}^{n} G_i b_i$. The goal is to minimize the communication (which is approximately $n$ times the cost of a more basic proof that $b_i \in [0, u-1]$) of that type of range proofs.

Clearly, $a \in [0, 2^d - 1]$ iff $a = \sum_{i=1}^{d} 2^{i-1} b_i$ and $b_i \in \{0, 1\}$. Then one can prove that $a \in [0, H]$ for arbitrary $H$ by showing that both $a$ and $H - a$ belong to $[0, 2^{\lfloor \log_2 H \rfloor + 1} - 1]$. Showing that $b_i \in \{0, 1\}$ is straightforward, e.g., by using an AND of two $\Sigma$-protocols. This means that one has to execute two basic range proofs for $[0, 2^d - 1]$. Lipmaa, Asokan and Niemi showed in [16] that by choosing the coefficients $G_i$ cleverly, one obtains a simpler result that $a \in [0, H]$, for any $H > 1$, iff $a = \sum_{i=1}^{\lfloor \log_2 H \rfloor + 1} G_i b_i$ and $b_i \in \{0, 1\}$.

In [3], the authors considered the general case $u \geq 2$, following the fact that $a \in [0, u^d - 1]$ iff $a = \sum_{i=1}^{d} u^i b_i$ and $b_i \in [0, u-1]$. They showed that $b_i \in [0, u-1]$ by letting the verifier to sign every integer in $[0, u-1]$, and then letting the prover to prove that he knows the signature on committed $b_i$. One can show that $a \in [0, H]$ for general $H$ by using an AND of two $\Sigma$-protocols. Nontrivially generalizing [16] (by using methods from additive combinatorics), Chaabouni, Lipmaa and shelat [4] showed that there exist (efficiently computable) coefficients $G_i$ such that $(u-1)a \in (u-1) \cdot [0, H]$ iff $a = \sum_{i=1}^{\lceil \log_u((u-1) \cdot H + 1) \rceil} G_i b_i$ for some $b_i \in [0, u-1]$. The range proof from [4] has the communication complexity of $\Theta(\log_u H + u)$ group elements, which obtains the minimal value $\Theta(\log H / \log \log H)$ if $u \approx \log H / \log \log H$. (See [9] for recent related work.)

Usually, it is desired that the range proof is non-interactive. For example, in the e-voting scenario, range proof is a part of the vote validity proof that is verified by various parties without any active participation of the voter. Most of the previous non-interactive range proofs first construct a $\Sigma$-protocol which is then made non-interactive in the random oracle model by using the Fiat-Shamir heuristic. While the random oracle model allows to construct efficient protocols, it is also known that there exist protocols that are secure in the random oracle models and insecure in the plain model.

Motivated by this, [5,21,18] have proposed non-interactive range proofs without random oracles. The range proof from [5] is of mainly theoretical value. The range proof from [21] uses Lagrange's theorem, but we will demonstrate an attack on it. The range proof from [18] combines the range proof of [3] with the Groth-Sahai non-interactive zero-knowledge (NIZK) proofs [11] and P-signatures. The range proof from [18] is not claimed to be zero-knowledge (only NIWI, that is, non-interactive witness-indistinguishable).

We first show that the protocol from [21] is insecure. Their protocol works in a group of known order. In this case, using Lagrange's theorem to prove that a non-negative number is the sum of four squares fails. We can only conclude that the sum of four squares is computed modulo the group order. Hence an attacker can prove that any number is "non-negative" and completely break the protocol in [21]. See Sect. 4 for more information.

We then construct a new NIZK range proof (for an encrypted $a$ — if one needs $a$ to be committed, one can use the same cryptosystem as a perfectly binding commitment) that works in the common-reference string model. We do this by using recent NIZK arguments by Groth and Lipmaa [8,15]. We also use the additive combinatorics results from [4], that is, we base a range proof $a \in [0, H]$ on the fact that $(u-1)a \in (u-1) \cdot [0, H]$ iff $a = \sum_{i=1}^{n} G_i b_i$ and $b_i \in [0, u-1]$, where $G_i$ are as defined in [4]. However, differently from [4], we prove that $b_i \in [0, u-1]$ by proving (by a recursive use of the method from [16,4]) that $b_i = \sum_{j=0}^{n_v} G'_j b'_{ji}$ with $b'_{ji} \in [0, 1]$. Here, $n_v := \lfloor \log_2(u-1) \rfloor$.

By using the commitment scheme of [8,15] that enables to succinctly commit to a vector $(b_1, \ldots, b_n)$, and the Hadamard product argument of [8,15], we can do all $n_v + 1$ small range proofs in parallel. In addition, in Sect. 5 we construct a new non-interactive argument that a knowledge-commited value is equal to a BBS-encrypted [2] value. (Due to the use of knowledge assumptions, this proof is computationally more efficient than the one constructed by using Groth-Sahai proofs [11].) The new range proof does not rely on the random oracle model or use any proofs of knowledge of signatures.

The conceptual novelty of the new range proof as compared to all previous range proofs of the "second approach" is that in all latter schemes, $a \in [0, H]$ is proven by executing in parallel $N \approx \log_u H$ smaller zero-knowledge proofs of type $b_i \in [0, u-1]$. In the new range proof, $N$ elements $b_i$ are arranged in an $n_v \times n$ matrix, where it takes only one zero-knowledge proof (the complexity of which depends on $n$) to prove that all elements in one row belong to the range $[0, u-1]$. By appropriately choosing the values $n_v$ and $n$ (and $u$), one can achieve different complexity trade-offs.

The complexity of the new range proof is described in Tbl. 1. Setting $u = 2$ results in a constant argument length (but CRS of $\Theta((\log H)^{1+o(1)})$ group elements). By using an efficient variation of Barreto-Naehrig curves (where the group elements are either 256 or 512 bits), the communication drops to 14 080 bits. The range proof of [18] does not allow for constant communication. Moreover, if $u = 2$ then the communication is even smaller than that of the known range proofs based on the Lagrange's theorem like [13]. We note that constant communication is achieved since the new range proof uses permutation arguments only for permutations that do not depend on the statement. On the other hand, setting $u = H$ results in summatory CRS and argument length of $\log^{1/2+o(1)} H$, and setting $u = 2^{\sqrt{\log H}}$ results in prover's computational complexity dominated by $\Theta(\log H)$ exponentiations. The previous non-interactive range proofs did not allow for such a flexibility.

One can obtain a zap (that is, a 2-message public-coin witness-indistinguishable proof) from the NIZK range proof by first letting the verifier create and send a CRS to the prover, and then letting the prover to send

**Table 1.** Comparison of NIZK arguments for range proof. Here, M/E/P means the number of multiplications, exponentiations and pairings. Communication is given in group elements. Here, $n_v = \lfloor \log(u-1) \rfloor$, $n \approx \log H / \log u$ and $\varepsilon = o(1)$, and the basis of all logarithms is 2. To fit in page margins, in this table only, we write $h = \log_2 H$.

| | CRS length | Argument length | Prover comp. | Verifier comp. |
|---|---|---|---|---|
| [18] | $\Theta(1)$ | $\Theta(h)$ | $\Theta(h)$ | $\Theta(h)$ |
| [18] | $\Theta(\frac{h}{\log h})$ | $\Theta(\frac{h}{\log h})$ | $\Theta(\frac{h}{\log h})$ | $\Theta(\frac{h}{\log h})$ |
| | | This paper | | |
| General | $n^{1+\varepsilon}$ | $5n_v + 40$ | $\Theta(n^2 n_v)\mathrm{M} + \Theta(n^{1+o(1)}n_v)\mathrm{E}$ | $(9n_v + 81)$ P |
| $u = 2$ | $h^{1+\varepsilon}$ | $40$ | $\Theta(h^2)\mathrm{M} + h^{1+\varepsilon}\mathrm{E}$ | $81$ P |
| $u = 2^{\sqrt{h}}$ | $h^{1/2+\varepsilon}$ | $\approx 5\sqrt{h} + 40$ | $\Theta(h^{3/2})\mathrm{M} + h^{1+\varepsilon}\mathrm{E}$ | $\approx (9\sqrt{h} + 81)$ P |
| $u = H$ | $\Theta(1)$ | $\approx 5h + 40$ | $\Theta(h)\mathrm{E}$ | $\approx (9h + 81)$ P |

the range proof to the verifier. This zap works in the standard model (without needing a CRS since it is generated on run) and has the total communication $\log^{1/2+o(1)} H$ in the case $u = H$.

# 2    Preliminaries

Let $[L, H] = \{L, L+1, \ldots, H-1, H\}$ and $[H] = [1, H]$. Let $S_n$ be the set of permutations from $[n]$ to $[n]$. By $\boldsymbol{a}$, we denote the vector $\boldsymbol{a} = (a_1, \ldots, a_n)$. If $A$ is a value, then $x \leftarrow A$ means that $x$ is set to $A$. If $A$ is a set, then $x \leftarrow A$ means that $x$ is picked uniformly and randomly from $A$. If $y = h^x$, then let $\log_h y := x$. Let $\kappa$ be the security parameter. We abbreviate probabilistic polynomial-time as PPT, and let $\mathrm{negl}(\kappa)$ be a negligible function. We say that $\Lambda = (\lambda_1, \ldots, \lambda_n) \subset \mathbb{Z}$ is an $(n, \kappa)$-*nice tuple*, if $0 < \lambda_1 < \cdots < \lambda_i < \cdots < \lambda_n = \mathrm{poly}(\kappa)$.

By using notation from additive combinatorics, if $\Lambda_1$ and $\Lambda_2$ are subsets of some additive group ($\mathbb{Z}$ or $\mathbb{Z}_p$ within this paper), then $\Lambda_1 + \Lambda_2 = \{\lambda_1 + \lambda_2 : \lambda_1 \in \Lambda_1 \wedge \lambda_2 \in \Lambda_2\}$ is their *sum set* and $\Lambda_1 - \Lambda_2 = \{\lambda_1 - \lambda_2 : \lambda_1 \in \Lambda_1 \wedge \lambda_2 \in \Lambda_2\}$ is their *difference set*. If $\Lambda$ is a set, then $k\Lambda = \{\lambda_1 + \cdots + \lambda_k : \lambda_i \in \Lambda\}$ is an *iterated sumset*, and $k \cdot \Lambda = \{k\lambda : \lambda \in \Lambda\}$ is a *dilation* of $\Lambda$. Let $2\hat{\ }\Lambda = \{\lambda_1 + \lambda_2 : \lambda_1 \in \Lambda \wedge \lambda_2 \in \Lambda \wedge \lambda_1 \neq \lambda_2\} \subseteq \Lambda + \Lambda$ denote a *restricted sumset* [20].

A set $\{\lambda_1, \ldots, \lambda_n\} \subset \mathbb{Z}^+$ is *progression-free*, if no three of the numbers are in arithmetic progression, so that $\lambda_i + \lambda_j = 2\lambda_k$ only if $i = j = k$. Let $r_3(N)$ denote the cardinality of the largest progression-free set that belongs to $[N]$. Recently, Elkin [6] showed that $r_3(N) = \Omega((N \cdot \log_2^{1/4} N)/2^{2\sqrt{2\log_2 N}})$. It is also known that $r_3(N) = O(N(\log \log N)^5 / \log N)$ [19]. Thus, the minimal $N$ such that $r_3(N) = n$ is $\omega(n)$, while according to Elkin, $N = n^{1+o(1)}$.

**Fact 1 (Lipmaa [15]).** *For any fixed $n > 0$, there exists $N = n^{1+o(1)}$, such that $[N]$ contains a progression-free subset $\Lambda$ of odd integers of cardinality $n$.*

**Bilinear Groups.** Let $\mathcal{G}_{bp}(1^\kappa)$ be a bilinear group generator that outputs a description of a bilinear group $\mathsf{gk} := (p, \mathbb{G}_1, \mathbb{G}_2, \mathbb{G}_T, \hat{e}) \leftarrow \mathcal{G}_{bp}(1^\kappa)$ such that $p$ is a $\kappa$-bit prime, $\mathbb{G}_1$, $\mathbb{G}_2$ and $\mathbb{G}_T$ are multiplicative cyclic groups of order $p$, $\hat{e} : \mathbb{G}_1 \times \mathbb{G}_2 \to \mathbb{G}_T$ is a bilinear map (pairing) such that $\forall a, b \in \mathbb{Z}$, $t \in \{1, 2\}$ and $g_t \in \mathbb{G}_t$, $\hat{e}(g_1^a, g_2^b) = \hat{e}(g_1, g_2)^{ab}$. If $g_t$ generates $\mathbb{G}_t$ for $t \in \{1, 2\}$, then $\hat{e}(g_1, g_2)$ generates $\mathbb{G}_T$. Moreover, it is efficient to decide the membership in $\mathbb{G}_1$, $\mathbb{G}_2$ and $\mathbb{G}_T$, group operations and the pairing $\hat{e}$ are efficiently computable, generators are efficiently sampleable, and the descriptions of the groups and group elements each are $O(\kappa)$ bit long. One can implement an optimal (asymmetric) Ate pairing [12] over a subclass of Barreto-Naehrig curves [1,17] very efficiently. In that case, at security level of 128-bits, an element of $\mathbb{G}_1/\mathbb{G}_2/\mathbb{G}_T$ can be represented in respectively $256/512/3072$ bits.

A bilinear group generator $\mathcal{G}_{bp}$ is DLIN (decisional linear) secure [2] in group $\mathbb{G}_t$, for $t \in \{1, 2\}$, if for all non-uniform PPT adversaries $\mathcal{A}$, the next probability is negligible in $\kappa$:

$$\left| \Pr \left[ \begin{array}{l} \mathsf{gk} \leftarrow \mathcal{G}_{bp}(1^\kappa), \\ (f, h) \leftarrow (\mathbb{G}_t^*)^2, (\sigma, \tau) \leftarrow \mathbb{Z}_p^2 : \\ \mathcal{A}(\mathsf{gk}; f, h, f^\sigma, h^\tau, g_t^{\sigma+\tau}) = 1 \end{array} \right] - \Pr \left[ \begin{array}{l} \mathsf{gk} \leftarrow \mathcal{G}_{bp}(1^\kappa), \\ (f, h) \leftarrow (\mathbb{G}_t^*)^2, (\sigma, \tau, z) \leftarrow \mathbb{Z}_p^3 : \\ \mathcal{A}(\mathsf{gk}; f, h, f^\sigma, h^\tau, g_t^z) = 1 \end{array} \right] \right| .$$

Let $\Lambda$ be an $(n, \kappa)$-nice tuple for some $n = \mathrm{poly}(\kappa)$. A bilinear group generator $\mathcal{G}_{bp}$ is $\Lambda$-PSDL secure, if for any non-uniform PPT adversary $\mathcal{A}$,

$$\Pr \left[ \begin{array}{l} \mathsf{gk} := (p, \mathbb{G}_1, \mathbb{G}_2, \mathbb{G}_T, \hat{e}) \leftarrow \mathcal{G}_{bp}(1^\kappa), g_1 \leftarrow \mathbb{G}_1 \setminus \{1\}, \\ g_2 \leftarrow \mathbb{G}_2 \setminus \{1\}, x \leftarrow \mathbb{Z}_p : \mathcal{A}(\mathsf{gk}; (g_1^{x^s}, g_2^{x^s})_{s \in \{0\} \cup \Lambda}) = x \end{array} \right] = \mathrm{negl}(\kappa) .$$

Let $\Lambda$ be an $(n, \kappa)$-nice tuple. According to [15], any successful generic adversary for $\Lambda$-PSDL requires time $\Omega(\sqrt{p/\lambda_n})$ where $p$ is the group order and $\lambda_n$ is the largest element of $\Lambda$.

The soundness of NIZK arguments (for example, an argument that a computationally binding commitment scheme commits to 0) seems to be an unfalsifiable assumption in general. We will use a weaker version of soundness in the case of subarguments, but in the case of the range proof, we will prove soundness. Similarly to [8,15], we will base the soundness of that argument on an explicit knowledge assumption.

For two algorithms $\mathcal{A}$ and $X_\mathcal{A}$, we write $(y; z) \leftarrow (\mathcal{A} \| X_\mathcal{A})(x)$ if $\mathcal{A}$ on input $x$ outputs $y$, and $X_\mathcal{A}$ on the same input (including the random tape of $\mathcal{A}$) outputs $z$. Let $\Lambda$ be an $(n, \kappa)$-nice tuple for some $n = \mathrm{poly}(\kappa)$. Consider $t \in \{1, 2\}$. The bilinear group generator $\mathcal{G}_{bp}$ is $\Lambda$-PKE secure in group $\mathbb{G}_t$ if for any non-uniform PPT adversary $\mathcal{A}$ there exists a non-uniform PPT extractor $X_\mathcal{A}$,

$$\Pr \left[ \begin{array}{l} \mathsf{gk} := (p, \mathbb{G}_1, \mathbb{G}_2, \mathbb{G}_T, \hat{e}) \leftarrow \mathcal{G}_{bp}(1^\kappa), g_t \leftarrow \mathbb{G}_t \setminus \{1\}, \\ (\hat{\alpha}, x) \leftarrow \mathbb{Z}_p^2, \mathsf{crs} \leftarrow (\mathsf{gk}; (g_t^{x^s}, g_t^{\hat{\alpha} x^s})_{s \in \{0\} \cup \Lambda}), \\ (c, \hat{c}; (a_s)_{s \in \{0\} \cup \Lambda}) \leftarrow (\mathcal{A} \| X_\mathcal{A})(\mathsf{crs}) : \hat{c} = c^{\hat{\alpha}} \wedge c \neq \prod_{s \in \{0\} \cup \Lambda} g_t^{a_s x^s} \end{array} \right] = \mathrm{negl}(\kappa).$$

Groth [8] proved that the $[n]$-PKE assumption holds in the generic group model; his proof can be modified to the general case.

In the case of both the PSDL and PKE assumptions, we will define straightforward generalizations in Sect. 5.

**BBS Cryptosystem.** A public-key cryptosystem $(\mathcal{G}_{pkc}, \mathcal{E}nc, \mathcal{D}ec)$ is a triple of efficient algorithms (key generation, encryption, and decryption), where for any $(sk, pk) \leftarrow \mathcal{G}_{pkc}(1^\kappa)$ and any valid $m$ and randomizer $r$, $\mathcal{D}ec_{sk}(\mathcal{E}nc_{pk}(m; r)) = m$. A cryptosystem is IND-CPA secure, if for any $(sk, pk) \leftarrow \mathcal{G}_{pkc}(1^\kappa)$ and any two messages $m_0$ and $m_1$, the distributions $\mathcal{E}nc_{pk}(m_0; \cdot)$ and $\mathcal{E}nc_{pk}(m_1; \cdot)$ are computationally indistinguishable. In the *lifted BBS cryptosystem* [2] (in group $\mathbb{G}_1$), the system parameters are equal to $(gk; g_1)$, where $gk \leftarrow \mathcal{G}_{bp}(1^\kappa)$ and $g_1 \leftarrow \mathbb{G}_1 \setminus \{1\}$. The secret key $sk$ is $(sk_1, sk_2) \leftarrow (\mathbb{Z}_p^*)^2$, the public key $pk$ is $(f, h) \leftarrow (g_1^{1/sk_1}, g_1^{1/sk_2})$. One encrypts $a \in \mathbb{Z}_p$ as $\mathcal{E}nc_{pk}(ck_1; a; r_f, r_h) \leftarrow (c_g, c_f, c_h) = (g_1^{r_f + r_h + a}, f^{r_f}, h^{r_h})$, where $(r_f, r_h) \leftarrow \mathbb{Z}_p^2$. One decrypts $(c_g, c_f, c_h)$ by returning the discrete logarithm of $c_g/(c_f^{sk_1} c_h^{sk_2})$. The BBS cryptosystem is IND-CPA secure under the DLIN assumption.

**Commitment Schemes in the CRS Model.** A (batch) commitment scheme $(\mathcal{G}_{com}, \mathcal{C}om)$ in a bilinear group consists of two PPT algorithms: a randomized CRS generation algorithm $\mathcal{G}_{com}$, and a randomized commitment algorithm $\mathcal{C}om$. Here, $\mathcal{G}_{com}^t(1^\kappa, n)$, $t \in \{1, 2\}$, produces a CRS $ck_t$, and $\mathcal{C}om^t(ck_t; \mathbf{a}; r)$, with $\mathbf{a} = (a_1, \ldots, a_n)$, outputs a commitment value $A$ in $\mathbb{G}_t^b$ for $b > 1$ (in our case, $b = 2$ or $b = 3$). A commitment $\mathcal{C}om^t(ck_t; \mathbf{a}; r)$ is opened by revealing $(\mathbf{a}, r)$.

A commitment scheme $(\mathcal{G}_{com}, \mathcal{C}om)$ is *computationally binding in group* $\mathbb{G}_t$, if for every non-uniform PPT adversary $\mathcal{A}$ and positive integer $n = \mathrm{poly}(\kappa)$,

$$\Pr\left[ \begin{array}{l} ck_t \leftarrow \mathcal{G}_{com}^t(1^\kappa, n), (\mathbf{a_1}, r_1, \mathbf{a_2}, r_2) \leftarrow \mathcal{A}(ck_t) : \\ (\mathbf{a_1}, r_1) \neq (\mathbf{a_2}, r_2) \wedge \mathcal{C}om^t(ck_t; \mathbf{a_1}; r_1) = \mathcal{C}om^t(ck_t; \mathbf{a_2}; r_2) \end{array} \right] = \mathrm{negl}(\kappa) \ .$$

A commitment scheme $(\mathcal{G}_{com}, \mathcal{C}om)$ is *perfectly hiding in group* $\mathbb{G}_t$, if for any positive integer $n = \mathrm{poly}(\kappa)$ and $ck_t \in \mathcal{G}_{com}^t(1^\kappa, n)$ and any two messages $\mathbf{a_1}, \mathbf{a_2}$, the distributions $\mathcal{C}om^t(ck_t; \mathbf{a_1}; \cdot)$ and $\mathcal{C}om^t(ck_t; \mathbf{a_2}; \cdot)$ are equal.

A trapdoor commitment scheme has 3 additional efficient algorithms: (a) A trapdoor CRS generation algorithm inputs $t$, $n$ and $1^\kappa$, and outputs a CRS $ck^*$ (that has the same distribution as $\mathcal{G}_{com}^t(1^\kappa, n)$) and a trapdoor $td$, (b) a randomized trapdoor commitment algorithm takes $ck^*$ and a randomizer $r$ as inputs, and outputs $\mathcal{C}om^t(ck^*; \mathbf{0}; r)$, and (c) a trapdoor opening algorithm takes $ck^*$, $td$, $\mathbf{a}$ and $r$ as inputs, and outputs an $r'$ such that $\mathcal{C}om^t(ck^*; \mathbf{0}; r) = \mathcal{C}om^t(ck^*; \mathbf{a}; r')$.

An *extractable commitment scheme* is a commitment scheme $(\mathcal{G}_{com}, \mathcal{C}om)$ with an additional extractor $(\mathsf{Extr}_1, \mathsf{Extr}_2)$ such that: $\mathsf{Extr}_1^t(1^\kappa)$ creates a CRS $ck^*$ (indistinguishable from the real CRS $ck$) and a trapdoor $td$, and $\mathsf{Extr}_2(ck^*, td; A)$ returns $(a; r)$ such that $A = \mathcal{C}om(ck; a; r)$, given that $A$ is a valid commitment. An extractable commitment scheme can only be computationally hiding.

We use the *knowledge commitment scheme*, defined in [15], as follows.

**CRS generation:** Let $\Lambda$ be a $(n, \kappa)$-nice tuple with $n = \text{poly}(\kappa)$. Let $\lambda_0 = 0$. Given a bilinear group generator $\mathcal{G}_{\mathsf{bp}}$, set $\mathsf{gk} := (p, \mathbb{G}_1, \mathbb{G}_2, \mathbb{G}_T, \hat{e}) \leftarrow \mathcal{G}_{\mathsf{bp}}(1^{\kappa})$. Let $g_1 \in \mathbb{G}_1$ and $g_2 \in \mathbb{G}_2$ be generators, and choose random $\hat{a}, x \leftarrow \mathbb{Z}_p$. Consider $t \in \{1, 2\}$. The CRS is $\mathsf{ck}_t \leftarrow (\mathsf{gk}; (g_{t,\lambda_i}, \hat{g}_{t,\lambda_i})_{i \in \{0,\ldots,n\}})$, where $g_{t,\lambda_i} = g_t^{x^{\lambda_i}}$, and $\hat{g}_{t,\lambda_i} = g_t^{\hat{a}x^{\lambda_i}}$.

**Commitment:** To commit to $\boldsymbol{a} = (a_1, \ldots, a_n) \in \mathbb{Z}_p^n$, one chooses a random $r \leftarrow \mathbb{Z}_p$, and computes $\mathcal{C}om^t(\mathsf{ck}_t; \boldsymbol{a}; r) := (g_t^r \cdot \prod_{i=1}^n g_{t,\lambda_i}^{a_i}, \hat{g}_t^r \cdot \prod_{i=1}^n \hat{g}_{t,\lambda_i}^{a_i})$.

Let $t = 1$. Fix a commitment key $\mathsf{ck}_1$ that in particular specifies $g_2, \hat{g}_2 \in \mathbb{G}_2$. A commitment $(A, \hat{A}) \in \mathbb{G}_1^2$ is *valid*, if $\hat{e}(A, \hat{g}_2) = \hat{e}(\hat{A}, g_2)$. The case $t = 2$ is dual.

According to [15], the knowledge commitment scheme is statistically hiding in group $\mathbb{G}_t$, and computationally binding in group $\mathbb{G}_t$ under the $\Lambda$-PSDL assumption in group $\mathbb{G}_t$. If the $\Lambda$-PKE assumption holds in group $\mathbb{G}_t$, then for any non-uniform PPT algorithm $\mathcal{A}$, that outputs some valid knowledge commitments, there exists a non-uniform PPT extractor $X_{\mathcal{A}}$ that, given as an input the input of $\mathcal{A}$ together with $\mathcal{A}$'s random coins, extracts the contents of these commitments. The knowledge commitment scheme is also trapdoor, with the trapdoor being $\mathsf{td} = x$: after trapdoor-committing $A \leftarrow \mathcal{C}om^t(\mathsf{ck}; \boldsymbol{0}; r) = g_t^r$ for $r \leftarrow \mathbb{Z}_p$, the committer can open it to $(\boldsymbol{a}; r - \sum_{i=1}^n a_i x^{\lambda_i})$ for any $\boldsymbol{a}$.

**Non-interactive Zero-Knowledge.** Let $\mathcal{R} = \{(C, w)\}$ be an efficiently computable binary relation such that $|w| = \text{poly}(|C|)$. Here, $C$ is a statement, and $w$ is a witness. Let $\mathcal{L} = \{C : \exists w, (C, w) \in \mathcal{R}\}$ be an **NP**-language. Let $n = |C|$ be a fixed input length. For fixed $n$, we have a relation $\mathcal{R}_n$ and a language $\mathcal{L}_n$. A *non-interactive argument* for $\mathcal{R}$ consists of the next PPT algorithms: a common reference string (CRS) generator $\mathcal{G}_{\mathsf{crs}}$, a prover $\mathcal{P}$, and a verifier $\mathcal{V}$. For $\mathsf{crs} \leftarrow \mathcal{G}_{\mathsf{crs}}(1^{\kappa}, n)$, $\mathcal{P}(\mathsf{crs}; C, w)$ produces an argument $\psi$. The verifier $\mathcal{V}(\mathsf{crs}; C, \psi)$ outputs either 1 (accept) or 0 (reject).

A non-interactive argument $(\mathcal{G}_{\mathsf{crs}}, \mathcal{P}, \mathcal{V})$ is *perfectly complete*, if for all values $n = \text{poly}(\kappa)$, all $\mathsf{crs} \leftarrow \mathcal{G}_{\mathsf{crs}}(1^{\kappa}, n)$ and all $(C, w) \in \mathcal{R}_n$, $\mathcal{V}(\mathsf{crs}; C, \mathcal{P}(\mathsf{crs}; C, w)) = 1$. A non-interactive argument $(\mathcal{G}_{\mathsf{crs}}, \mathcal{P}, \mathcal{V})$ is *computationally (adaptively) sound*, if for all non-uniform PPT adversaries $\mathcal{A}$ and all $n = \text{poly}(\kappa)$,

$$\Pr[\mathsf{crs} \leftarrow \mathcal{G}_{\mathsf{crs}}(1^{\kappa}, n), (C, \psi) \leftarrow \mathcal{A}(\mathsf{crs}) : C \notin \mathcal{L} \wedge \mathcal{V}(\mathsf{crs}; C, \psi) = 1] = \text{negl}(\kappa) \ .$$

A non-interactive argument $(\mathcal{G}_{\mathsf{crs}}, \mathcal{P}, \mathcal{V})$ is *perfectly witness-indistinguishable*, if (given that there are several possible witnesses) it is impossible to tell which witness the prover used. That is, for all $n = \text{poly}(\kappa)$, if $\mathsf{crs} \in \mathcal{G}_{\mathsf{crs}}(1^{\kappa}, n)$ and $((C, w_0), (C, w_1)) \in \mathcal{R}_n^2$, then the distributions $\mathcal{P}(\mathsf{crs}; C, w_0)$ and $\mathcal{P}(\mathsf{crs}; C, w_1)$ are equal. $(\mathcal{G}_{\mathsf{crs}}, \mathcal{P}, \mathcal{V})$ is *perfectly zero-knowledge*, if there exists a polynomial-time simulator $\mathcal{S} = (\mathcal{S}_1, \mathcal{S}_2)$, such that for all stateful interactive non-uniform PPT adversaries $\mathcal{A}$ and $n = \text{poly}(\kappa)$,

$$\Pr\begin{bmatrix} \mathsf{crs} \leftarrow \mathcal{G}_{\mathsf{crs}}(1^{\kappa}, n), \\ (C, w) \leftarrow \mathcal{A}(\mathsf{crs}), \\ \psi \leftarrow \mathcal{P}(\mathsf{crs}; C, w) : \\ (C, w) \in \mathcal{R}_n \wedge \mathcal{A}(\psi) = 1 \end{bmatrix} = \Pr\begin{bmatrix} (\mathsf{crs}, \mathsf{td}) \leftarrow \mathcal{S}_1(1^{\kappa}, n), \\ (C, w) \leftarrow \mathcal{A}(\mathsf{crs}), \\ \psi \leftarrow \mathcal{S}_2(\mathsf{crs}, C, \mathsf{td}) : \\ (C, w) \in \mathcal{R}_n \wedge \mathcal{A}(\psi) = 1 \end{bmatrix} \ .$$

---

**System parameters:** Let $n = \text{poly}(\kappa)$. Let $\Lambda = \{\lambda_i : i \in [n]\}$ be a progression-free set of odd integers, such that $\lambda_{i+1} > \lambda_i > 0$. Denote $\lambda_0 := 0$. Let $\hat{\Lambda} := \{0\} \cup \Lambda \cup 2\hat{}\Lambda$.

**CRS generation** $\mathcal{G}_{\text{crs}}(1^\kappa)$: Let $\text{gk} := (p, \mathbb{G}_1, \mathbb{G}_2, \mathbb{G}_T, \hat{e}) \leftarrow \mathcal{G}_{\text{bp}}(1^\kappa)$. Let $\hat{\alpha}, x \leftarrow \mathbb{Z}_p$. Let $g_1 \leftarrow \mathbb{G}_1 \setminus \{1\}$ and $g_2 \leftarrow \mathbb{G}_2 \setminus \{1\}$. Denote $g_{t\ell} \leftarrow g_t^{x^\ell}$ and $\hat{g}_{t\ell} \leftarrow g_t^{\hat{\alpha}x^\ell}$ for $t \in \{1, 2\}$ and $\ell \in \{0\} \cup \hat{\Lambda}$. Let $D \leftarrow \prod_{i=1}^n g_{2,\lambda_i}$. The CRS is $\text{crs} \leftarrow (\text{gk}; (g_{1\ell}, \hat{g}_{1\ell})_{\ell \in \{0\} \cup \Lambda}, (g_{2\ell}, \hat{g}_{2\ell})_{\ell \in \hat{\Lambda}}, D)$. Let $\widehat{\text{ck}}_1 \leftarrow (\text{gk}; (g_{1\ell}, \hat{g}_{1\ell})_{\ell \in \{0\} \cup \Lambda})$.

**Common inputs:** $(A, \hat{A}, B, \hat{B}, B_2, C, \hat{C})$, where $(A, \hat{A}) \leftarrow \mathcal{C}om^1(\widehat{\text{ck}}_1; \boldsymbol{a}; r_a)$, $(B, \hat{B}) \leftarrow \mathcal{C}om^1(\widehat{\text{ck}}_1; \boldsymbol{b}; r_b)$, $B_2 \leftarrow g_2^{r_b} \cdot \prod_{i=1}^n g_{2,\lambda_i}^{b_i}$, $(C, \hat{C}) \leftarrow \mathcal{C}om^1(\widehat{\text{ck}}_1; \boldsymbol{c}; r_c)$, s.t. $a_i b_i = c_i$ for $i \in [n]$.

**Argument generation** $\mathcal{P}_\times(\text{crs}; (A, \hat{A}, B, \hat{B}, B_2, C, \hat{C}), (\boldsymbol{a}, r_a, \boldsymbol{b}, r_b, \boldsymbol{c}, r_c))$: Let $I_1(\ell) := \{(i, j) : i, j \in [n] \wedge j \neq i \wedge \lambda_i + \lambda_j = \ell\}$. For $\ell \in 2\hat{}\Lambda$, the prover sets $\mu_\ell \leftarrow \sum_{(i,j) \in I_1(\ell)} (a_i b_j - c_i)$. He sets $\psi \leftarrow g_2^{r_a r_b} \cdot \prod_{i=1}^n g_{2,\lambda_i}^{r_a b_i + r_b a_i - r_c} \cdot \prod_{\ell \in 2\hat{}\Lambda} g_{2\ell}^{\mu_\ell}$, and $\hat{\psi} \leftarrow \hat{g}_2^{r_a r_b} \cdot \prod_{i=1}^n \hat{g}_{2,\lambda_i}^{r_a b_i + r_b a_i - r_c} \cdot \prod_{\ell \in 2\hat{}\Lambda} \hat{g}_{2\ell}^{\mu_\ell}$. He sends $\psi^\times \leftarrow (\psi, \hat{\psi}) \in \mathbb{G}_2^2$ to the verifier as the argument.

**Verification** $\mathcal{V}_\times(\text{crs}; (A, \hat{A}, B, \hat{B}, B_2, C, \hat{C}), \psi^\times)$: accept iff $\hat{e}(A, B_2)/\hat{e}(C, D) = \hat{e}(g_1, \psi)$ and $\hat{e}(g_1, \hat{\psi}) = \hat{e}(\hat{g}_1, \psi)$.

---

**Protocol 1.** Hadamard product argument $[\![(A, \hat{A})]\!] \circ [\![(B, \hat{B}, B_2)]\!] = [\![(C, \hat{C})]\!]$

Here, td is the *simulation trapdoor*. $(\mathcal{G}_{\text{crs}}, \mathcal{P}, \mathcal{V})$ is *computationally zero-knowledge* if these two probabilities are computationally indistinguishable.

## 3 Groth-Lipmaa Arguments

In this section, we describe two of our building-blocks, an Hadamard product argument and a (known) permutation argument. In both cases, Groth [8] proposed efficient (weakly) sound and non-interactive witness-indistinguishable (NIWI) arguments that were further refined by Lipmaa [15], who used the theory of progression-free sets to optimize Groth's arguments. Since [15] is very new, we will give here a full description of Lipmaa's NIWI arguments. We refer to [15] (and its full version, [14]) for details.

### 3.1 Hadamard Product Argument

Let $(\mathcal{G}_{\text{com}}, \mathcal{C}om)$ be the knowledge commitment scheme. An Hadamard product of two vectors $\boldsymbol{a}$ and $\boldsymbol{b}$ is equal to their entrywise product vector $\boldsymbol{c}$, that is, $c_j = a_j \cdot b_j$ for $j \in [n]$. In an *Hadamard product argument*, the prover aims to convince the verifier that for given three commitments $(A, \hat{A})$, $(B, \hat{B})$ and $(C, \hat{C})$, he knows how to open them as $(A, \hat{A}) = \mathcal{C}om^1(\text{ck}; \boldsymbol{a}; r_a)$, $(B, \hat{B}) = \mathcal{C}om^1(\text{ck}; \boldsymbol{b}; r_b)$, and $(C, \hat{C}) = \mathcal{C}om^1(\text{ck}; \boldsymbol{c}; r_c)$, such that $c_j = a_j \cdot b_j$ for $j \in [n]$. Prot. 1 has a full description of Lipmaa's Hadamard product argument $[\![(A, \hat{A})]\!] \circ [\![(B, \hat{B}, B_2)]\!] = [\![(C, \hat{C})]\!]$, where $B_2$ is the equivalent of $B$ in $\mathbb{G}_2$: $B_2 \leftarrow g_2^{r_b} \cdot \prod_{i=1}^n g_{2,\lambda_i}^{b_i}$.

**Fact 2 (Lipmaa [15]).** *The above Hadamard product argument is perfectly complete and perfectly witness-indistinguishable. If the bilinear group generator*

$\mathcal{G}_{bp}$ *is $\hat{\Lambda}$-PSDL secure, then a non-uniform PPT adversary has negligible chance of outputting $inp^{\times} \leftarrow (A, \hat{A}, B, \hat{B}, B_2, C, \hat{C})$ and an accepting argument $\psi^{\times} \leftarrow (\psi, \hat{\psi})$ together with an opening witness $w^{\times} \leftarrow (\boldsymbol{a}, r_a, \boldsymbol{b}, r_b, \boldsymbol{c}, r_c, (f'_s)_{s\in\hat{\Lambda}})$, such that $(A, \hat{A}) = \mathcal{C}om^1(\hat{ck}_1; \boldsymbol{a}; r_a)$, $(B, \hat{B}) = \mathcal{C}om^1(\hat{ck}_1; \boldsymbol{b}; r_b)$, $B_2 = g_2^{r_b} \cdot \prod_{i=1}^{n} g_{2i}^{b_i}$, $(C, \hat{C}) = \mathcal{C}om^1(\hat{ck}_1; \boldsymbol{c}; r_c)$, $(\psi, \hat{\psi}) = (g_2^{\sum_{s\in\hat{\Lambda}} f'_s x^s}, \hat{g}_2^{\sum_{s\in\hat{\Lambda}} f'_s x^s})$, and for some $i \in [n]$, $a_i b_i \neq c_i$.*

For the product argument to be useful in more complex arguments, we must also assume that the verifier there additionally verifies that $\hat{e}(A, \hat{g}_2) = \hat{e}(\hat{A}, g_2)$, $\hat{e}(B, \hat{g}_2) = \hat{e}(\hat{B}, g_2)$, $\hat{e}(g_1, B_2) = \hat{e}(B, g_2)$, and $\hat{e}(C, \hat{g}_2) = \hat{e}(\hat{C}, g_2)$. Note that $(f'_s)_{s\in\hat{\Lambda}}$ is the opening of $(\psi, \hat{\psi})$.

**Fact 3 (Lipmaa [15]).** *For any $n > 0$ and $y = n^{1+o(1)}$, let $\Lambda \subset [y]$ be a progression-free set of odd integers from Fact 1, such that $|\Lambda| = n$. The communication (argument size) of the Hadamard product argument is 2 elements from $\mathbb{G}_2$. The prover's computational complexity is $\Theta(n^2)$ scalar multiplications in $\mathbb{Z}_p$ and $n^{1+o(1)}$ exponentiations in $\mathbb{G}_2$. The verifier's computational complexity is dominated by 5 bilinear pairings. The CRS consists of $n^{1+o(1)}$ group elements.*

Finally, if $\boldsymbol{a}$, $\boldsymbol{b}$ and $\boldsymbol{c}$ are Boolean vectors then the prover's computational complexity is $\Theta(n^2)$ scalar additions in $\mathbb{Z}_p$ and $n^{1+o(1)}$ exponentiations in $\mathbb{G}$ [15].

### 3.2 Permutation Argument

In a *permutation argument*, the prover aims to convince the verifier that for given permutation $\varrho \in S_n$ and two commitments $(A, \tilde{A})$ and $(B, \tilde{B})$, he knows how to open them as $(A, \tilde{A}) = \mathcal{C}om^1(ck; \boldsymbol{a}; r_a)$ and $(B, \tilde{B}) = \mathcal{C}om^1(ck; \boldsymbol{b}; r_b)$, such that $b_j = a_{\varrho(j)}$ for $j \in [n]$. We denote this non-interactive argument by $\varrho([\![(A, \tilde{A})]\!]) = [\![(B, \tilde{B}, B_2)]\!]$, where $B_2$ is again the equivalent of $B$ in $\mathbb{G}_2$. As in the case of the Hadamard product argument, we describe a version of the argument due to [15]. See Prot. 2.

Let $T_\Lambda(i, \varrho) := |\{j \in [n] : 2\lambda_{\varrho(i)} + \lambda_j = 2\lambda_{\varrho(j)} + \lambda_i\}|$, clearly $T_\Lambda(i, \varrho) \geq 1$. One proves that $a_{\varrho(i)} = b_i$ for $i \in [n]$ by using a subargument that shows that for separately committed $a_i^*$, $a_{\varrho(i)}^* = T_\Lambda(i, \varrho) \cdot b_i$ for $i \in [n]$. Showing in addition that $a_i^* = T_\Lambda(\varrho^{-1}(i), \varrho) \cdot a_i$ (which is equivalent to $a_{\varrho(i)}^* = T_\Lambda(i, \varrho) \cdot a_{\varrho(i)}$), one obtains that $a_{\varrho(i)} = b_i$ for $i \in [n]$. We only consider the case where $\varrho$ is fixed and thus the element $E_\varrho$ can be put to the CRS. We also use the fact that $\hat{\Lambda} \cup \tilde{\Lambda} = \{0\} \cup \tilde{\Lambda}$, where $\tilde{\Lambda}$ is defined in Prot. 2.

We denote the full permutation argument by $\varrho([\![(A, \tilde{A})]\!]) = [\![(B, \hat{B}, \tilde{B})]\!]$.

**Fact 4 (Lipmaa [15]).** *The above permutation argument is perfectly complete and perfectly witness-indistinguishable. If the bilinear group generator $\mathcal{G}_{bp}$ is $\tilde{\Lambda}$-PSDL secure, then a non-uniform PPT adversary has negligible chance of outputting $inp^{perm} \leftarrow (A, \tilde{A}, B, \hat{B}, \tilde{B}, \varrho)$ and an accepting argument $\psi^{perm} \leftarrow (A^*, \hat{A}^*, \psi^{\times}, \hat{\psi}^{\times}, \psi^\varrho, \tilde{\psi}^\varrho)$ together with an opening witness*

$$w^{perm} \leftarrow (\boldsymbol{a}, r_a, \boldsymbol{b}, r_b, \boldsymbol{a}^*, r_{a^*}, (f'_{(\times,\ell)})_{\ell\in\hat{\Lambda}}, (f'_{(\varrho,\ell)})_{\ell\in\tilde{\Lambda}}) ,$$

---

**System parameters:** Same as in Prot. 1, but let $\tilde{\Lambda} := \Lambda \cup \{2\lambda_k - \lambda_j\}_{i,k\in[n]} \cup 2^\frown\Lambda \cup$
$(\{2\lambda_k + \lambda_i - \lambda_j\}_{i,j,k\in[n]\wedge i\neq j} \setminus 2 \cdot \Lambda)$.

**CRS generation** $\mathcal{G}_{\mathsf{crs}}(1^\kappa)$: Let $\mathsf{gk} := (p, \mathbb{G}_1, \mathbb{G}_2, \mathbb{G}_T, \hat{e}) \leftarrow \mathcal{G}_{\mathsf{bp}}(1^\kappa)$. Let $\hat{\alpha}, \tilde{\alpha}, x \leftarrow \mathbb{Z}_p$.
Let $g_1 \leftarrow \mathbb{G}_1 \setminus \{1\}$ and $g_2 \leftarrow \mathbb{G}_2 \setminus \{1\}$. Let $\hat{g}_t \leftarrow \hat{g}_t^{\hat{\alpha}}$ and $\tilde{g}_t \leftarrow \tilde{g}_t^{\tilde{\alpha}}$ for $t \in \{1,2\}$.
Denote $g_{t\ell} \leftarrow g_t^{x^\ell}$, $\hat{g}_{t\ell} \leftarrow \hat{g}_t^{x^\ell}$, and $\tilde{g}_{t\ell} \leftarrow \tilde{g}_t^{x^\ell}$ for $t \in \{1,2\}$ and $\ell \in \{0\} \cup \tilde{\Lambda}$. Let
$(D, \tilde{D}) \leftarrow (\prod_{i=1}^n g_{2,\lambda_i}, \prod_{i=1}^n \tilde{g}_{2,\lambda_i})$. The CRS is

$$\mathsf{crs} \leftarrow (\mathsf{gk}; (g_{1\ell}, \hat{g}_{1\ell}, \tilde{g}_{1\ell})_{\ell\in\{0\}\cup\Lambda}, (g_{2\ell})_{\ell\in\{0\}\cup\tilde{\Lambda}}, (\hat{g}_{2\ell})_{\ell\in\hat{\Lambda}}, (\tilde{g}_{2\ell})_{\ell\in\tilde{\Lambda}}, D, \tilde{D}) \; .$$

Let $\hat{\mathsf{ck}}_1 \leftarrow (\mathsf{gk}; (g_{1\ell}, \hat{g}_{1\ell})_{\ell\in\{0\}\cup\Lambda})$, $\tilde{\mathsf{ck}}_1 \leftarrow (\mathsf{gk}; (g_{1\ell}, \tilde{g}_{1\ell})_{\ell\in\{0\}\cup\Lambda})$.

**Common inputs:** $(A, \tilde{A}, B, \hat{B}, \tilde{B}, \varrho)$, where $\varrho \in S_n$, $(A, \tilde{A}) \leftarrow \mathcal{C}om^1(\tilde{\mathsf{ck}}_1; \mathbf{a}; r_a)$,
$(B, \hat{B}) \leftarrow \mathcal{C}om^1(\hat{\mathsf{ck}}_1; \mathbf{b}; r_b)$, and $(B, \tilde{B}) \leftarrow \mathcal{C}om^1(\tilde{\mathsf{ck}}_1; \mathbf{b}; r_b)$, s.t. $b_j = a_{\varrho(j)}$ for $j \in [n]$.

**Argument generation** $\mathcal{P}_{\mathsf{perm}}(\mathsf{crs}; (A, \tilde{A}, B, \hat{B}, \tilde{B}, \varrho), (\mathbf{a}, r_a, \mathbf{b}, r_b))$:

1. Let $(T^*, \hat{T}^*, T_2^*) \leftarrow (\prod_{i=1}^n g_{1,\lambda_i}^{T_\Lambda(\varrho^{-1}(i),\varrho)}, \prod_{i=1}^n \hat{g}_{1,\lambda_i}^{T_\Lambda(\varrho^{-1}(i),\varrho)}, \prod_{i=1}^n g_{2,\lambda_i}^{T_\Lambda(\varrho^{-1}(i),\varrho)})$.
2. Let $r_{a^*} \leftarrow \mathbb{Z}_p$, $(A^*, \hat{A}^*) \leftarrow \mathcal{C}om_1(\hat{\mathsf{ck}}_1; T_\Lambda(\varrho^{-1}(1), \varrho) \cdot a_1, \ldots, T_\Lambda(\varrho^{-1}(n), \varrho) \cdot a_n; r_{a^*})$. Create an argument $\psi^\times$ for $[\![(A, \hat{A})]\!] \circ [\![(T^*, \hat{T}^*, T_2^*)]\!] = [\![(A^*, \hat{A}^*)]\!]$.
3. Let $\tilde{\Lambda}'_\varrho := 2^\frown\Lambda \cup (\{2\lambda_{\varrho(j)}+\lambda_i-\lambda_j : i,j \in [n]\wedge i \neq j\}\backslash2\cdot\Lambda) \subset \{-\lambda_n+1, \ldots, 3\lambda_n\}$.
4. For $\ell \in \tilde{\Lambda}'_\varrho$, $I_1(\ell)$ as in Prot. 1, and $I_2(\ell) := \{(i,j) : i,j \in [n] \wedge j \neq i \wedge 2\lambda_{\varrho(i)} + \lambda_j \neq \lambda_i+2\lambda_{\varrho(j)}\wedge2\lambda_{\varrho(j)}+\lambda_i-\lambda_j = \ell\}$, set $\mu_{\varrho,\ell} \leftarrow \sum_{(i,j)\in I_1(\ell)} a_i^* - \sum_{(i,j)\in I_2(\ell)} b_i$.
5. Let $(E_\varrho, \tilde{E}_\varrho) \leftarrow (\prod_{i=1}^n g_{2,2\lambda_{\varrho(i)}-\lambda_i}, \prod_{i=1}^n \tilde{g}_{2,2\lambda_{\varrho(i)}-\lambda_i})$.
6. Let $\psi^\varrho \leftarrow D^{r_a^*} \cdot E_\varrho^{-r_b} \cdot \prod_{\ell\in\tilde{\Lambda}'_\varrho} g_{2\ell}^{\mu_{\varrho,\ell}}$, $\tilde{\psi}^\varrho \leftarrow \tilde{D}^{r_a^*} \cdot \tilde{E}_\varrho^{-r_b} \cdot \prod_{\ell\in\tilde{\Lambda}'_\varrho} \tilde{g}_{2\ell}^{\mu_{\varrho,\ell}}$,

   Send $\psi^{\mathsf{perm}} \leftarrow (A^*, \hat{A}^*, \psi^\times, \psi^\varrho, \tilde{\psi}^\varrho) \in \mathbb{G}_1^2 \times \mathbb{G}_2^4$ to the verifier as the argument.

**Verification** $\mathcal{V}_{\mathsf{perm}}(\mathsf{crs}; (A, \tilde{A}, B, \hat{B}, \tilde{B}, \varrho), \psi^{\mathsf{perm}})$: Let $E_\varrho$ and $(T^*, \hat{T}^*, T_2^*)$ be computed as in $\mathcal{P}_{\mathsf{perm}}$. If $\psi^\times$ verifies, $\hat{e}(A^*, D)/\hat{e}(B, E_\varrho) = \hat{e}(g_1, \psi^\varrho)$, $\hat{e}(A^*, \hat{g}_2) = \hat{e}(\hat{A}^*, g_2)$, and $\hat{e}(g_1, \tilde{\psi}^\varrho) = \hat{e}(\tilde{g}_1, \psi^\varrho)$, then $\mathcal{V}_{\mathsf{perm}}$ accepts. Otherwise, $\mathcal{V}_{\mathsf{perm}}$ rejects.

---

**Protocol 2.** Permutation argument $\varrho([\![(A, \tilde{A})]\!]) = [\![(B, \tilde{B})]\!]$ from [15]

such that $(A, \tilde{A}) = \mathcal{C}om^1(\tilde{\mathsf{ck}}_1; \mathbf{a}; r_a)$, $(B, \hat{B}) = \mathcal{C}om^1(\hat{\mathsf{ck}}_1; \mathbf{b}; r_b)$, $(B, \tilde{B}) = \mathcal{C}om^1(\tilde{\mathsf{ck}}_1; \mathbf{b}; r_b)$, $(A^*, \hat{A}^*) = \mathcal{C}om^1(\hat{\mathsf{ck}}_1; \mathbf{a}^*; r_{a^*})$, $(\psi^\times, \hat{\psi}^\times) = (g_2^{\sum_{\ell\in\hat{\Lambda}} f'(\times,\ell)}, \hat{g}_2^{\sum_{\ell\in\hat{\Lambda}} f'(\times,\ell)})$, $(\psi^\varrho, \hat{\psi}^\varrho) = (g_2^{\sum_{\ell\in\tilde{\Lambda}} f'(\varrho,\ell)}, \tilde{g}_2^{\sum_{\ell\in\tilde{\Lambda}} f'(\varrho,\ell)})$, $a_i^* = T_\Lambda(\varrho^{-1}(i), \varrho) \cdot a_i$ (for $i \in [n]$), and for some $i \in [n]$, $a_{\varrho(i)} \neq b_i$.

For the permutation argument to be useful in more complex arguments, we must also assume that the verifier there verifies that $\hat{e}(\tilde{A}, g_2) = \hat{e}(A, \tilde{g}_2)$, $\hat{e}(\hat{B}, g_2) = \hat{e}(B, \hat{g}_2)$, and $\hat{e}(\tilde{B}, g_2) = \hat{e}(B, \tilde{g}_2)$.

**Fact 5 (Lipmaa [15]).** *The permutation argument has a CRS of length $n^{1+o(1)}$ and communication of 4 group elements. The prover's computational complexity is $\Theta(n^2)$ scalar additions in $\mathbb{Z}_p$ and $n^{1+o(1)}$ exponentiations in $\mathbb{G}$. The verifier's computational complexity is dominated by 12 bilinear pairings.*

## 4    Breaking the COCOON 2009 Range Proof

In [21], the authors proposed a non-interactive range proof. In what follows, we show that their argument is not secure.

Their goal is to prove that a committed secret $w$ is in some range $[a, b]$. To do so they prove that both $w - a$ and $b - w$ are non-negative by making use of Lagrange theorem stating that any non-negative integer can be decomposed as the sum of four squares. Hence,

$$w - a = \sum_{j=1}^{4} w_{1j}^2 \quad \text{and} \quad b - w = \sum_{j=1}^{4} w_{2j}^2 \ , \tag{1}$$

for some $w_{ij}$. The range proof of [21] is based on (symmetric) bilinear groups of composite order, i.e., on bilinear groups $(n, \mathbb{G}, \mathbb{G}_T, \hat{e})$, where $n = pq$. To commit to a message $w$, the committer picks a random[1] $r \in \mathbb{Z}_q$ and computes $C = g^w u^r$, where $g$ is a random generator of $\mathbb{G}$ (of order $n$), and $u$ is a random generator of subgroup $\mathbb{G}_q$ (of order $q$). Given $C$, $w$ is uniquely determined in $\mathbb{Z}_p$ as $C^q = g^{wq}$.

In their range proof, the prover finds the witnesses $w_{ij}$ in Eq. (1) and outputs a proof $\psi = (\{C_{1j}, C_{2j}\}_{j \in [4]}, C_w, \varphi_1, \varphi_2)$, where $C_w \equiv g^w u^{r_w} \in \mathbb{G}$, $C_{ij} \equiv g^{w_{ij}} u^{r_{ij}} \in \mathbb{G}$ for $i \in [2]$ and $j \in [4]$, $\varphi_1 \equiv g^{-r_w + 2 \sum_{j=1}^{4} r_{1j} w_{1j}} \cdot u^{\sum_{j=1}^{4} r_{1j}^2} \in \mathbb{G}$, $\varphi_2 \equiv g^{r_w + 2 \sum_{j=1}^{4} r_{2j} w_{2j}} \cdot u^{\sum_{j=1}^{4} r_{2j}^2} \in \mathbb{G}$. The verifier checks whether $\hat{e}(g^a C_w^{-1}, g) \cdot \prod_{j=1}^{4} e(C_{1j}, C_{1j}) = \hat{e}(u, \varphi_1)$ and $\hat{e}(C_w g^{-b}, g) \cdot \prod_{j=1}^{4} \hat{e}(C_{2j}, C_{2j}) = \hat{e}(u, \varphi_2)$.

Now assume that a malicious prover $P^*$ picks an integer $w^* \in \{0, \ldots, p-1\} \setminus [a, b]$. We have that either $w^* - a$ or $b - w^*$ is negative as an integer. Suppose $b - w^* < 0$, then $P^*$ chooses $\{w_{2j}^*\}_{j \in [4]}$ such that $n + (b - w^*) = \sum_{j=1}^{4}(w_{2j}^*)^2$, sets $C_w \leftarrow g^{w^*} u^{r_w}$, $C_{2j} \leftarrow g^{w_{2j}^*} u^{r_{2j}}$, $\varphi_1$ as above, and $\varphi_2 \leftarrow g^{r_w + 2 \cdot \sum_{j=1}^{4} r_{2j} w_{2j}^*} \cdot u^{\sum_{j=1}^{4} r_{2j}^2}$. Let $u = g^\alpha$ for some $\alpha$. It is easy to see that the second verification equation still holds:

$$\hat{e}(C_w g^{-b}, g) \cdot \prod_{j=1}^{4} \hat{e}(C_{2j}, C_{2j}) = \hat{e}(g, g)^{(w^* - b) + \alpha r_w + \sum_{j=1}^{4}(w_{2j}^* + \alpha r_{2j})^2}$$

$$= \hat{e}(g, g)^{(w^* - b) + \alpha r_w + \sum_{j=1}^{4}(w_{2j}^*)^2 + \sum_{j=1}^{4} \alpha^2 r_{2j}^2 + 2 \sum_{j=1}^{4} \alpha r_{2j} w_{2j}^*}$$

$$= \hat{e}(g, g)^{\alpha \cdot (r_w + 2 \sum_{j=1}^{4} r_{2j} w_{2j}^* + \alpha \cdot \sum_{j=1}^{4} r_{2j}^2)} = \hat{e}(u, \varphi_2) \ .$$

We have successfully constructed a polynomial time adversary who can always break the scheme. Therefore, the NIZK range proof in [21] is not sound.

## 5   New Subargument for Correct Encryption

In the new range proof of Sect. 6, we need a subargument that if $(A_c, \bar{A}_c)$ is a knowledge-commitment of some $a$ (with $n = 1$ and some randomness $r$), and $(A_g, A_f, A_h)$ is a BBS ciphertext of some $a'$, then $a = a'$. That is, $A_c = g_1^r g_{1,\lambda_1}^a$ and $(A_g, A_f, A_h) = (g_1^{r_f + r_h + a}, f^{r_f}, h^{r_h})$ for randomness $(r_f, r_h)$ and public key $(f, h)$. (The generator $g_{1,\lambda_1}$ is required in Sect. 6.)

---

[1] In [21], the scheme uses $r \in \mathbb{Z}_n$ to facilitate their security proof (crs switching).

We will construct this argument in the current section, by combining ideas from [11] and [8,15]. Intuitively, for every multi-exponentiation $h_1^{a_1} \ldots h_m^{a_m} = t$ that we want to prove, we write down a verification equation $\hat{e}(h_1, \mathcal{C}om(a_1)) \cdot \cdots \cdot \hat{e}(h_m, \mathcal{C}om(a_m)) = \hat{e}(\psi, g_2)\hat{e}(t, \mathcal{C}om(1))$, where $\psi$ "compensates" for the fact that $\mathcal{C}om(a_m)$ are probabilistic commitments. In addition, we use knowledge commitments (though for small values 0 or 1 of $n$) so that one can extract all committed values. Since the argument uses three committed values ($a$, $r_f$ and $r_h$) and three equations, according to Fig. 6 of [10] (the full version of [11]), the corresponding pure Groth-Sahai argument will have length of 15 group elements. Our argument has the same length, but is computationally more efficient.

**System parameters:** An $(n, \kappa)$-nice tuple $\Lambda = (\lambda_1, \ldots, \lambda_n)$.
**Common reference string generation** $\mathcal{G}_{\mathsf{crs}}(1^\kappa)$: Set

$$\mathsf{gk} := (p, \mathbb{G}_1, \mathbb{G}_2, \mathbb{G}_t, \hat{e}) \leftarrow \mathcal{G}_{\mathsf{bp}}(1^\kappa) \ .$$

Generate random $\alpha_g, \alpha_f, \alpha_h, \bar{\alpha}, \alpha_{g/c}, x \leftarrow \mathbb{Z}_p$. Let $g_1 \leftarrow \mathbb{G}_1 \setminus \{1\}$ and $g_2 \leftarrow \mathbb{G}_2 \setminus \{1\}$. Denote $g_{1,\lambda_1} \leftarrow g_1^{x^{\lambda_1}}$, $g_{2,\lambda_1} \leftarrow g_2^{x^{\lambda_1}}$, $\mathring{g}_1 \leftarrow g_1^{\alpha_g}$, $\mathring{g}_2 \leftarrow g_2^{\alpha_g}$, $\bar{g}_1 \leftarrow g_1^{\bar{\alpha}}$, $\bar{g}_{1,\lambda_1} \leftarrow g_{1,\lambda_1}^{\bar{\alpha}}$, $\bar{g}_2 \leftarrow g_2^{\bar{\alpha}}$, $\bar{g}_{2,\lambda_1} \leftarrow g_{2,\lambda_1}^{\bar{\alpha}}$, $\mathring{g}_{1,g/c} \leftarrow g_1^{\alpha_{g/c}\cdot(1-x^{\lambda_1})}$, $\mathring{g}_{2,g/c} \leftarrow g_2^{\alpha_{g/c}\cdot(1-x^{\lambda_1})}$, $\mathring{g}_{1,f} \leftarrow g_1^{\alpha_f}$, $\mathring{g}_{2,f} \leftarrow g_2^{\alpha_f}$, $\mathring{g}_{1,h} \leftarrow g_1^{\alpha_h}$, and $\mathring{g}_{2,h} \leftarrow g_2^{\alpha_h}$. The common reference string is

$$\mathsf{crs} \leftarrow (\mathsf{gk}; g_1, g_{1,\lambda_1}, g_2, g_{2,\lambda_1}, \mathring{g}_1, \mathring{g}_2, \bar{g}_1, \bar{g}_{1,\lambda_1}, \bar{g}_2, \bar{g}_{2,\lambda_1}, \mathring{g}_{1,g/c}, \mathring{g}_{2,g/c}, \mathring{g}_{1,f}, \mathring{g}_{2,f},$$
$$\mathring{g}_{1,h}, \mathring{g}_{2,h}) \ .$$

A third party also creates $\mathsf{sk} := (\mathsf{sk}_1, \mathsf{sk}_2) \leftarrow (\mathbb{Z}_p^*)^2$, and sets $\mathsf{pk} := (f, h, \mathring{f}, \mathring{h}) \leftarrow (g_1^{1/\mathsf{sk}_1}, g_1^{1/\mathsf{sk}_2}, \mathring{g}_{1,f}^{1/\mathsf{sk}_1}, \mathring{g}_{1,h}^{1/\mathsf{sk}_2})$.
**Common inputs:** $(\mathsf{crs}; \mathsf{pk}, A_g, A_f, A_h, A_c)$, where $\mathsf{pk} = (f, h, \mathring{f}, \mathring{h})$, $(A_g, A_f, A_h) = (g_1^{r_f+r_h+a}, f^{r_f}, h^{r_h})$, and $A_c = g_1^{r_f+r_h} g_{1,\lambda_1}^a$.
**Argument** $\mathcal{P}(\mathsf{crs}; (\mathsf{pk}, A_g, A_f, A_h, A_c), (a, r_f, r_h))$: let $\bar{A}_c \leftarrow \bar{g}_1^{r_f+r_h} \bar{g}_{1,\lambda_1}^a$, $(\mathring{A}_g, \mathring{A}_f, \mathring{A}_h) \leftarrow (\mathring{g}_1^{r_f+r_h+a}, \mathring{f}^{r_f}, \mathring{h}^{r_h})$, $\mathring{A}_{g/c} \leftarrow \mathring{g}_{1,g/c}^a$. Let $R_f, R_h \leftarrow \mathbb{Z}_p$. Let $(C_f, \bar{C}_f) \leftarrow (g_2^{R_f} g_{2,\lambda_1}^{r_f}, \bar{g}_2^{R_f} \bar{g}_{2,\lambda_1}^{r_f})$, $(C_h, \bar{C}_h) \leftarrow (g_2^{R_h} g_{2,\lambda_1}^{r_h}, \bar{g}_2^{R_h} \bar{g}_{2,\lambda_1}^{r_h}) \in \mathbb{G}_2^2$. Let $(\psi_g, \mathring{\psi}_g) \leftarrow (g_1^{r+R_f+R_h}, \mathring{g}_1^{r+R_f+R_h}) \in \mathbb{G}_1^2$, $(\psi_f, \mathring{\psi}_f) \leftarrow (f^{R_f}, \mathring{f}^{R_f}) \in \mathbb{G}_1^2$, $(\psi_h, \mathring{\psi}_h) \leftarrow (h^{R_h}, \mathring{h}^{R_h}) \in \mathbb{G}_1^2$.
Send $\psi^{ce} \leftarrow (\mathring{A}_g, \mathring{A}_f, \mathring{A}_h, \mathring{A}_c, \psi_g, \mathring{\psi}_g, C_f, \bar{C}_f, \psi_f, \mathring{\psi}_f, C_h, \bar{C}_h, \psi_h, \mathring{\psi}_h, \mathring{A}_{g/c})$ to the verifier.
**Verification** $\mathcal{V}(\mathsf{crs}; (\mathsf{pk}, A_g, A_f, A_h, A_c), \psi^{ce})$: Verify that $\hat{e}(\mathring{f}, g_2) = \hat{e}(f, \mathring{g}_{2,f})$, $\hat{e}(\mathring{h}, g_2) = \hat{e}(h, \mathring{g}_{2,h})$, $\hat{e}(A_g, \mathring{g}_2) = \hat{e}(\mathring{A}_g, g_2)$, $\hat{e}(A_f, \mathring{g}_{2,f}) = \hat{e}(\mathring{A}_f, g_2)$, $\hat{e}(A_h, \mathring{g}_{2,h}) = \hat{e}(\mathring{A}_h, g_2)$, $\hat{e}(A_c, \bar{g}_2) = \hat{e}(\bar{A}_c, g_2)$, $\hat{e}(\psi_g, \mathring{g}_2) = \hat{e}(\mathring{\psi}_g, g_2)$, $\hat{e}(\psi_f, \mathring{g}_{2,f}) = \hat{e}(\mathring{\psi}_f, g_2)$, $\hat{e}(\psi_h, \mathring{g}_{2,h}) = \hat{e}(\mathring{\psi}_h, g_2)$, $\hat{e}(\bar{g}_1, C_f) = \hat{e}(g_1, \bar{C}_f)$, $\hat{e}(\bar{g}_1, C_h) = \hat{e}(g_1, \bar{C}_h)$, and $\hat{e}(A_g/A_c, \mathring{g}_{2,g/c}) = \hat{e}(\mathring{A}_{g/c}, g_2)$.
Verify that $\hat{e}(f, C_f) = \hat{e}(\psi_f, g_2) \cdot \hat{e}(A_f, g_{2,\lambda_1})$, $\hat{e}(h, C_h) = \hat{e}(\psi_h, g_2) \cdot \hat{e}(A_h, g_{2,\lambda_1})$, and $\hat{e}(g_1, C_f C_h) = \hat{e}(\psi_g A_c^{-1}, g_2) \cdot \hat{e}(A_g, g_{2,\lambda_1})$.

As mentioned in Sect. 2, to prove the security of this argument, we will need a generalization of the PSDL and PKE assumptions.

Let $\Phi \subset \mathbb{Z}[X]$, with $d := \max_{\varphi \in \Phi} \deg \varphi$, be a set of linearly independent polynomials, such that $|\Phi|$, all coefficients of all $\varphi \in \Phi$, and $d$ are polynomial in $\kappa$. Let 1 be the polynomial $\phi(x) = 1$. We say that a bilinear group generator $\mathcal{G}_{\mathsf{bp}}$ is $\Phi$-*PSDL secure*, if for any non-uniform PPT adversary $\mathcal{A}$,

$$\Pr\left[\begin{array}{l} \mathsf{gk} := (p, \mathbb{G}_1, \mathbb{G}_2, \mathbb{G}_T, \hat{e}) \leftarrow \mathcal{G}_{\mathsf{bp}}(1^\kappa), g_1 \leftarrow \mathbb{G}_1 \setminus \{1\}, g_2 \leftarrow \mathbb{G}_2 \setminus \{1\}, \\ x \leftarrow \mathbb{Z}_p : \mathcal{A}(\mathsf{gk}; (g_1^{\varphi(x)}, g_2^{\varphi(x)})_{\varphi \in \{1\} \cup \Phi}) = x \end{array}\right]$$

is negligible in $\kappa$. By a straightforward generalization of the proof from [15], any successful generic adversary for $\Phi$-PSDL requires time $\Omega(\sqrt{p/d})$, where $p$ is the group order.

Let $\Phi$ be as before. Consider $t \in \{1, 2\}$. The bilinear group generator $\mathcal{G}_{\mathsf{bp}}$ is $\Phi$-*PKE secure in group* $\mathbb{G}_t$ if for any non-uniform PPT adversary $\mathcal{A}$ there exists a non-uniform PPT extractor $X_{\mathcal{A}}$,

$$\Pr\left[\begin{array}{l} \mathsf{gk} := (p, \mathbb{G}_1, \mathbb{G}_2, \mathbb{G}_T, \hat{e}) \leftarrow \mathcal{G}_{\mathsf{bp}}(1^\kappa), g_t \leftarrow \mathbb{G}_t \setminus \{1\}, (\hat{\alpha}, x) \leftarrow \mathbb{Z}_p^2, \\ \mathsf{crs} \leftarrow (\mathsf{gk}; (g_t^{\varphi(x)}, g_t^{\hat{\alpha}\varphi(x)})_{\varphi \in \{1\} \cup \Phi}), (c, \hat{c}; (a_\varphi)_{\varphi \in \{0\} \cup \Phi}) \leftarrow (\mathcal{A} \| X_{\mathcal{A}})(\mathsf{crs}) : \\ \hat{c} = c^{\hat{\alpha}} \wedge c \neq \prod_{\varphi \in \{1\} \cup \Phi} g_t^{a_\varphi \varphi(x)} \end{array}\right]$$

is negligible in $\kappa$. Groth's proof [8] that the $[n]$-PKE assumption holds in the generic group model can be modified to the general case.

Note that $\mathcal{G}_{\mathsf{bp}}$ is $\Lambda$-PSDL secure (resp., $\Lambda$-PKE secure) iff it is $\{X^\lambda : \lambda \in \Lambda\}$-PSDL secure (resp., $\{X^\lambda : \lambda \in \Lambda\}$-PKE secure).

**Theorem 1.** *The argument of this subsection is a perfectly argument for the next claim: for some $a, r_f, r_h \in \mathbb{Z}_p$, $A_c = g_1^r g_{1,\lambda_1}^a$ and $(A_g, A_f, A_h) = (g^{r_f + r_h + a}, f^{r_f}, h^{r_h})$. If the $\{1 - X^{\lambda_1}\}$-PSDL assumption and the $\{1 - X^{\lambda_1}\}$-PKE assumption (in both $\mathbb{G}_1$ and $\mathbb{G}_2$) hold, then this argument is computationally sound. If the DLIN assumption holds in group $\mathbb{G}_1$, then this argument is computationally zero-knowledge.*

(The proof of this theorem is given in App. A.) Clearly, this argument has CRS of length $\Theta(1)$, its argument consists of 13 elements of $\mathbb{G}_1$ and 2 elements of $\mathbb{G}_2$. The prover's computational complexity is dominated by 20 exponentiations. The verifier's computational complexity is dominated by 33 pairings.

## 6    New Range Proof

In the next range proof, the prover has an encrypted $a \in \mathbb{Z}_p$, and he aims to convince the verifier that $a \in [0, H]$. We will use the lifted BBS cryptosystem $(\mathcal{G}_{\mathsf{pkc}}, \mathcal{E}\mathsf{nc}, \mathcal{D}\mathsf{ec})$ that can be thought of as a perfectly binding commitment scheme if decryption is not necessary. Since we are interested in obtaining a sublinear argument, we will also use the (computationally binding) knowledge commitment scheme $(\mathcal{G}_{com}, \mathcal{C}om)$. We use the following result that was stated for $u = 2$ in [16] and for general $u$ in [4].

**Fact 6.** *Let $H > 0$ and $u > 1$. Let $\ell(u, H) \leq \log_u(H + 1)$ be defined as in [4]. Then $a \in [0, H]$ if and only if for some $b_i \in [0, u - 1]$,*

$$(u - 1)a = \sum_{i=1}^{\ell(u,(u-1)H)} G_i b_i \; ,$$

*where $G_i \in \mathbb{Z}$ are values defined in [4]. That is, $(u-1) \cdot [0, H] = \sum_{i=1}^{\ell(u,(u-1)H)} G_i \cdot [0, u - 1]$. In particular, $[0, H] = \sum_{i=0}^{\lfloor \log_2 H \rfloor} \lfloor (H + 2^i)/2^{i+1} \rfloor \cdot [0, 1]$.*

The precise values of $\ell(u, H)$ and $G_i$ are not important in the next description. It suffices to know that they can be efficiently evaluated. We note that

$$G_i = \lfloor H/u^{i+1} \rfloor + \lfloor (H_i + (\sum_{j=0}^{i-1} H_j \mod (u - 1)) + 1)/u \rfloor \; ,$$

where $H = \sum 2^i H_i$ [4].

The basic idea of the next range proof is as follows. Choose a $u > 1$, and let $n = \ell(u, (u-1)H)$. According to Fact 6, $a \in [H]$ iff for $G_i$ computed as in Fact 6, one has $(u - 1)a = \sum_{i=1}^{n} G_i b_i$ for some $b_i \in [u - 1]$. The prover shows by using a parallel version of range proof from [16] that for $i \in [n]$, $b_i \in [0, u - 1]$. The latter is done by writing $b_i$ as $b_i = \sum_{j=0}^{\lfloor \log_2(u-1) \rfloor} G'_j b'_{ji}$ (by again using Fact 6) and then showing that $b'_{ji} \in [0, 1]$ by using an Hadamard product arguments from [15]. This will be achieved with commitments on $(b'_{j1}, \ldots, b'_{jn})$ for $j \in [\lfloor \log_2(u-1) \rfloor]$.

The prover then commits to the vector $(c_1, \ldots, c_n)$, where $c_j = \sum_{i=j}^{n} G_i b_i$, and shows that the values $c_j$ are correctly computed by using a small constant number of Hadamard product and permutation arguments. More precisely, he commits to $(G_1 b_1, \ldots, G_n b_n)$ (and shows this has been done correctly), then to $(c_2, \ldots, c_n, c_1)$ (and shows this was done correctly), then to $(c_2, \ldots, c_n, 0)$ (and shows this was done correctly), and then shows that $(c_1, \ldots, c_n) = (G_1 b_1, \ldots, G_n b_n) + (c_2, \ldots, c_n, 0)$. Thus, the verifier is convinced that $c_j = \sum_{i=j}^{n} G_i b_i$. Then, by Fact 6, $c_1 = \sum_{i=1}^{n} G_i b_i \in (u - 1) \cdot [H]$, and thus the prover has to show (by using a single product argument) that $(A_c^{u-1}, \hat{A}_c^{u-1})$ commits to $(c_1, 0, \ldots, 0)$, and that $(A_g, A_f, A_h)$ is a lifted BBS encryption of $A$ with randomizer $(r_f, r_h)$ where $r = r_f + r_h$.

As in [15], in a few cases, instead of computing two different commitments $\mathcal{C}om^t(\check{c}k_t; \boldsymbol{a}; r) = (g_t^r \cdot \prod g_{t,\lambda_i}^{a_i}, \hat{g}_t^r \cdot \prod \hat{g}_{t,\lambda_i}^{a_i})$ and $\mathcal{C}om^t(\check{c}k_t; \boldsymbol{a}; r) = (\tilde{g}_t^r \cdot \prod \tilde{g}_{t,\lambda_i}^{a_i}, \tilde{g}_t^r \cdot \prod \tilde{g}_{t,\lambda_i}^{a_i})$, we compute a composed commitment $\mathcal{C}om^t(ck_t; \boldsymbol{a}; r) = (g_t^r \cdot \prod g_{t,\lambda_i}^{a_i}, \hat{g}_t^r \prod \hat{g}_{t,\lambda_i}^{a_i}, \tilde{g}_t^r \cdot \prod \tilde{g}_{t,\lambda_i}^{a_i})$.

The common input to both parties is equal to a BBS encryption $(A_g, A_f, A_h)$ of $a$, accompanied by $(A_c, \hat{A}_c)$ such that $(A_c, \hat{A}_c)$ is a knowledge commitment to $a$.

**Theorem 2.** *Let $u > 1$. Let $H = \text{poly}(\kappa)$ and $n = \ell(u, (u - 1)H)$ where $\ell$ is defined as in Fact 6. Let $\Lambda = \{\lambda_i\}_{i \in [n]}$ be an $(n, \kappa)$-nice tuple. Denote $\lambda_0 := 0$.*

**System parameters:** $H, G_i, n, u, n_v := \lfloor \log_2(u-1) \rfloor$, and $G'_j := \lfloor (u+2^j)/2^{j+1} \rfloor$.

**Common reference string generation** $\mathcal{G}_{\mathsf{crs}}(1^\kappa)$: Set $\mathsf{gk} := (p, \mathbb{G}_1, \mathbb{G}_2, \mathbb{G}_T, \hat{e}) \leftarrow \mathcal{G}_{\mathsf{bp}}(1^\kappa)$. Generate random $\hat{\alpha}, \tilde{\alpha}, \alpha_g, \alpha_f, \alpha_h, \bar{\alpha}, \alpha_{g/c}, x \leftarrow \mathbb{Z}_p$. Let $g_1 \leftarrow \mathbb{G}_1 \backslash \{1\}$ and $g_2 \leftarrow \mathbb{G}_2 \backslash \{1\}$. Denote $g_{ts} \leftarrow g_t^{x^s}$, $\hat{g}_{ts} \leftarrow g_t^{\hat{\alpha} x^s}$, $\tilde{g}_{ts} \leftarrow g_t^{\tilde{\alpha} x^s}$, $\mathring{g}_1 \leftarrow g_1^{\alpha_g}$, $\mathring{g}_2 \leftarrow g_2^{\alpha_g}$, $\bar{g}_1 \leftarrow g_1^{\bar{\alpha}}$, $\bar{g}_{1,\lambda_1} \leftarrow g_{1,\lambda_1}^{\bar{\alpha}}$, $\bar{g}_2 \leftarrow g_2^{\bar{\alpha}}$, $\bar{g}_{2,\lambda_1} \leftarrow g_{2,\lambda_1}^{\bar{\alpha}}$, $\mathring{g}_{1,g/c} \leftarrow g_1^{\alpha_{g/c} \cdot (1-x^{\lambda_1})}$, $\mathring{g}_{2,g/c} \leftarrow g_2^{\alpha_{g/c} \cdot (1-x^{\lambda_1})}$, $\mathring{g}_{1,f} \leftarrow g_1^{\alpha_f}$, $\mathring{g}_{2,f} \leftarrow g_2^{\alpha_f}$, $\mathring{g}_{1,h} \leftarrow g_1^{\alpha_h}$, and $\mathring{g}_{2,h} \leftarrow g_2^{\alpha_h}$. Set $D \leftarrow \prod_{i=1}^n g_{1,\lambda_i}$, $E_{\mathsf{rot}} \leftarrow \prod_{i=1}^n g_{2,2\lambda_{\mathsf{rot}(i)} - \lambda_i}$, and $\tilde{E}_{\mathsf{rot}} \leftarrow E_{\mathsf{rot}}^{\tilde{\alpha}}$. The common reference string is $\mathsf{crs} \leftarrow (\mathsf{gk}; (g_{1,s}, \hat{g}_{1,s}, \tilde{g}_{1,s})_{s \in \{0\} \cup \Lambda}, g_2, (\hat{g}_{2,s})_{s \in \hat{\Lambda}}, (g_{2,s}, \tilde{g}_{2,s})_{s \in \tilde{\Lambda}}, D, E_{\mathsf{rot}}, \tilde{E}_{\mathsf{rot}})$.

Set $\mathsf{ck}_1 \leftarrow (\mathsf{gk}; (g_{1s}, \hat{g}_{1s}, \tilde{g}_{1s})_{s \in \{0\} \cup \Lambda})$, $\widehat{\mathsf{ck}}_1 \leftarrow (\mathsf{gk}; (g_{1s}, \hat{g}_{1s})_{s \in \{0\} \cup \Lambda})$ and $\tilde{\mathsf{ck}}_1 \leftarrow (\mathsf{gk}; (g_{1s}, \tilde{g}_{1s})_{s \in \{0\} \cup \Lambda})$. The prover creates a secret key $\mathsf{sk} := (\mathsf{sk}_1, \mathsf{sk}_2) \leftarrow \mathbb{Z}_p^2$, and sets $\mathsf{pk} \leftarrow (f, h, \mathring{f}, \mathring{h}) \leftarrow (g_1^{1/\mathsf{sk}_1}, g_1^{1/\mathsf{sk}_2} \mathring{g}_{1,f}^{1/\mathsf{sk}_1}, \mathring{g}_{1,h}^{1/\mathsf{sk}_2})$. Here, $\mathcal{E}\mathsf{nc}_{\mathsf{pk}}(m; (r_f, r_h)) := (g_1^{r_f + r_h + m}, f^{r_f}, h^{r_h})$.

**Common inputs:** $(\mathsf{pk}, A_g, A_f, A_h, A_c, \hat{A}_c)$, where $(A_g, A_f, A_h) = (g_1^{r+a}, f^{r_f}, h^{r_h})$ and $(A_c, \hat{A}_c) = g_1^r g_{1,\lambda_1}^a, \hat{g}_1^r \hat{g}_{1,\lambda_1}^a)$, for $r = r_f + r_h$.

**Argument** $\mathcal{P}(\mathsf{crs}; (\mathsf{pk}, A_g, A_f, A_h, A_c, \hat{A}_c), (a, r_f, r_h))$: The prover does the following:

1. Compute $(b_1, \ldots, b_n) \in \mathbb{Z}_u^n$ such that $(u-1)a = \sum_{i=1}^n G_i b_i$.
2. For $i \in [n]$ do: compute $(b'_{0i}, \ldots, b'_{n_v,i}) \in \mathbb{Z}_2^{n_v+1}$ such that $b_i = \sum_{j=0}^{n_v} G'_j \cdot b'_{ji}$.
3. For $j \in [0, n_v]$ do:
   - Let $r_j \leftarrow \mathbb{Z}_p$, $(B'_j, \hat{B}'_j) \leftarrow \mathcal{C}\mathsf{om}^1(\widehat{\mathsf{ck}}_1; b'_{j1}, \ldots, b'_{jn}; r_j)$, $B'_{j2} \leftarrow g_2^{r_j} \cdot \prod_{i=1}^n g_{2,\lambda_i}^{b'_{ji}}$.
   - Create an argument $(\psi'_j, \hat{\psi}'_j)$ for $[\![(B'_j, \hat{B}'_j)]\!] \circ [\![(B'_j, \hat{B}'_j, B'_{j2})]\!] = [\![(B'_j, \hat{B}'_j)]\!]$.
4. For $i \in [n]$, let $c_i \leftarrow \sum_{k=i}^n G_k b_k$.
5. Set $r'_0, r'_1, r'_2 \leftarrow \mathbb{Z}_p$, $(B^\dagger, \hat{B}^\dagger) \leftarrow \mathcal{C}\mathsf{om}^1(\widehat{\mathsf{ck}}_1; G_1 b_1, \ldots, G_n b_n; r'_0)$, $(C, \hat{C}, \tilde{C}) \leftarrow \mathcal{C}\mathsf{om}^1(\mathsf{ck}_1; c; r'_1)$, and $(C_{\mathsf{rot}}, \hat{C}_{\mathsf{rot}}, \tilde{C}_{\mathsf{rot}}) \leftarrow \mathcal{C}\mathsf{om}^1(\mathsf{ck}_1; c_2, \ldots, c_{n-1}, c_n, c_1; r'_2)$.
6. Create an argument $(\psi_1^\times, \hat{\psi}_1^\times)$ for $[\![(\prod_{j=0}^{n_v}(B'_j)^{G'_j}, \prod_{j=0}^{n_v}(\hat{B}'_j)^{G'_j})]\!] \circ [\![(\mathcal{C}\mathsf{om}^1(\widehat{\mathsf{ck}}_1; G_1, \ldots, G_n; 0), \prod_{i=1}^n g_{2,\lambda_i}^{G_i})]\!] = [\![(B^\dagger, \hat{B}^\dagger)]\!]$.
7. Create an argument $(A^*, \hat{A}^*, \psi_2^\times, \hat{\psi}_2^\times, \psi_2^{\mathsf{rot}}, \hat{\psi}_2^{\mathsf{rot}})$ for $\mathsf{rot}([\![(C, \tilde{C})]\!]) = [\![(C_{\mathsf{rot}}, \hat{C}_{\mathsf{rot}}, \tilde{C}_{\mathsf{rot}})]\!]$.
8. Create an argument $(\psi_3^\times, \hat{\psi}_3^\times)$ for $[\![(C_{\mathsf{rot}}, \hat{C}_{\mathsf{rot}})]\!] \circ [\![(\mathcal{C}\mathsf{om}^1(\widehat{\mathsf{ck}}_1; 1, 1, \ldots, 1, 0; 0), \prod_{i=1}^{n-1} g_{2,\lambda_i})]\!] = [\![(C/B^\dagger, \hat{C}/\hat{B}^\dagger)]\!]$.
9. Create an argument $(\psi_4^\times, \hat{\psi}_4^\times)$ for $[\![(C, \hat{C})]\!] \circ [\![(\mathcal{C}\mathsf{om}^1(\widehat{\mathsf{ck}}_1; 1, 0, \ldots, 0, 0; 0), g_{2,\lambda_1})]\!] = [\![(A_c^{u-1}, \hat{A}_c^{u-1})]\!]$.
10. Create an argument $\psi_5^{ce}$ that $A_c$ commits to the same value that $(A_g, A_f, A_h)$ encrypts.
11. Send $\psi \leftarrow ((B'_j, \hat{B}'_j, B'_{j2}, \psi'_j, \hat{\psi}'_j)_{j \in [0, n_v]}, (B^\dagger, \hat{B}^\dagger), (C, \hat{C}, \tilde{C}), (C_{\mathsf{rot}}, \hat{C}_{\mathsf{rot}}, \tilde{C}_{\mathsf{rot}}), (\psi_1^\times, \hat{\psi}_1^\times), (A^*, \hat{A}^*, \psi_2^\times, \hat{\psi}_2^\times, \psi_2^{\mathsf{rot}}, \hat{\psi}_2^{\mathsf{rot}}), (\psi_3^\times, \hat{\psi}_3^\times), (\psi_4^\times, \hat{\psi}_4^\times), \psi_5^{ce})$ to $\mathcal{V}$.

**Verification** $\mathcal{V}(\mathsf{crs}; (\mathsf{pk}, A_g, A_f, A_h, A_c, \hat{A}_c), \psi)$: $\mathcal{V}$ does the following:

1. For $j \in [0, n_v]$ do:
   (a) Check that $\hat{e}(B'_j, g_2) = \hat{e}(g_1, B'_{j2})$ and $\hat{e}(B'_j, \hat{g}_2) = \hat{e}(\hat{B}'_j, g_2)$.
   (b) Verify $(\psi'_j, \hat{\psi}'_j)$ for inputs as specified above.
2. For $K \in \{A_c, B^\dagger, C, C_{\mathsf{rot}}\}$: check that $\hat{e}(K, \hat{g}_2) = \hat{e}(\hat{K}, g_2)$.
3. For $K \in \{C, C_{\mathsf{rot}}\}$: check that $\hat{e}(K, \tilde{g}_2) = \hat{e}(\tilde{K}, g_2)$.
4. Verify the arguments $(\psi_1^\times, \hat{\psi}_1^\times), (A^*, \hat{A}^*, \psi_2^\times, \hat{\psi}_2^\times, \psi_2^{\mathsf{rot}}, \hat{\psi}_2^{\mathsf{rot}}), (\psi_3^\times, \hat{\psi}_3^\times), (\psi_4^\times, \hat{\psi}_4^\times), \psi_5^{ce}$ for inputs as specified above.

**Protocol 3.** The new range proof

Let $\widehat{\Lambda} := \{0\} \cup \Lambda \cup 2\hat{}\Lambda$, and $\tilde{\Lambda}$ be as in Sect. 3.2. Let $\mathsf{rot} \in S_n$ be such that $\mathsf{rot}(i) = i - 1$ if $i > 1$, and $\mathsf{rot}(1) = n$. Define $G_i$ as in Fact 6. The argument in Prot. 3 is perfectly complete. If $\mathcal{G}_{\mathsf{bp}}$ is $\{1 - X^{\lambda_1}\}$-PKE, $\Lambda$-PKE and DLIN secure in $\mathbb{G}_1$, then the argument in Prot. 3 is computationally zero-knowledge. If $\mathcal{G}_{\mathsf{bp}}$ is $(\{X^s\}_{s \in \tilde{\Lambda}} \cup \{1 - X^{\lambda_1}\})$-PSDL, $\Lambda$-PKE and $\{1 - X^{\lambda_1}\}$-PKE secure in both $\mathbb{G}_1$ and $\mathbb{G}_2$, then the argument in Prot. 3 is computationally sound.

This argument is computationally zero-knowledge because $(A_c, \hat{A}_c)$ was provided by a prover and not generated during the argument. To achieve perfect zero-knowledge, one must be able to open $(A_c, \hat{A}_c)$ given only the CRS trapdoor. That is, one has to use an extractable commitment scheme. It is easy to see that the knowledge commitment scheme is extractable, however, extractability is only achieved under the PKE assumption. The use of a cryptosystem also makes achieving perfect zero-knowledge impossible.

*Proof ([Of Thm. 2).* PERFECT COMPLETENESS: Recall that in the case of the product arguments, the inputs of $\mathcal{P}$ are $(A, \hat{A}, B, \hat{B}, B_2, C, \hat{C})$. Within this proof we say that $(B, \hat{B}, B_2)$ (assuming $B_2$ is correctly defined, that is, $\hat{e}(B, g_2) = \hat{e}(g_1, B_2)$) commits to the same values as $(B, \hat{B})$.

The pairing verifications (for example, that $\hat{e}(K, \hat{g}_2) = \hat{e}(\hat{K}, g_2)$) hold by construction of the protocol. Since $(B'_j, \hat{B}'_j)$ commits to $(b'_{j1}, \ldots, b'_{jn})$ for binary $b'_{ji}$ then the argument $(\psi'_j, \hat{\psi}'_j)$ verifies.

Note that $(\prod_{j=0}^{n_v} (B'_j)^{G'_j}, \prod_{j=0}^{n_v} (\hat{B}'_j)^{G'_j})$ commits to $(b_1, \ldots, b_n)$. Thus argument $(\psi_1^\times, \hat{\psi}_1^\times)$ verifies. Since $(C_{\mathsf{rot}}, \hat{C}_{\mathsf{rot}})$ commits to a rotation of $(C, \hat{C})$, then $(A^*, \hat{A}^*, \psi_2^\times, \hat{\psi}_2^\times, \psi_2^{\mathsf{rot}}, \hat{\psi}_2^{\mathsf{rot}})$ verifies. Since $(C_{\mathsf{rot}}, \hat{C}_{\mathsf{rot}})$ commits to $(0, c_1, \ldots, c_{n-1})$ and $(C/B^\dagger, \hat{C}/\hat{B}^\dagger)$ commits to $(c_1 - G_1 b_1, c_2 - G_2 b_2, \ldots, c_n - G_n b_n) = (0, c_1, \ldots, c_{n-1})$, then $(\psi_3^\times, \hat{\psi}_3^\times)$ verifies. Finally, since $(u - 1)a = \sum_{i=1}^n G_i b_i$ and $c_n = \sum_{i=1}^n G_i b_i$, then $(\psi_4^\times, \hat{\psi}_4^\times)$ verifies.

COMPUTATIONAL SOUNDNESS: let $\mathcal{A}$ be a non-uniform PPT adversary who creates a statement $(\mathsf{pk}, A_g, A_f, A_h, A_c, \hat{A}_c)$ and an accepting range proof $\psi$. By the DLIN assumption, the BBS cryptosystem is IND-CPA secure, and thus the adversary obtains no information from $(A_g, A_f, A_h)$. By the $\Lambda$-PKE and the $\{1 - X^{\lambda_1}\}$-PKE assumptions, there exists a non-uniform PPT extractor $X_{\mathcal{A}}$ that, running on the same inputs and seeing $\mathcal{A}$'s random tape, extracts the following openings:

- $(A_c, \hat{A}_c) = \mathcal{C}om^1(\widehat{\mathsf{ck}}_1; \boldsymbol{a}; r)$, $(B'_j, \hat{B}'_j) = \mathcal{C}om^1(\widehat{\mathsf{ck}}_1; \boldsymbol{b}'_j; r_j)$ for $j \in [0, n_v]$,
- $(B^\dagger, \hat{B}^\dagger) = \mathcal{C}om^1(\widehat{\mathsf{ck}}_1; \boldsymbol{b}^\dagger; r'_0)$,
- $(C, \hat{C}) = \mathcal{C}om^1(\widehat{\mathsf{ck}}_1; \boldsymbol{c}; r'_1)$ and $(C_{\mathsf{rot}}, \hat{C}_{\mathsf{rot}}) = \mathcal{C}om^1(\widehat{\mathsf{ck}}_1; \boldsymbol{c}_{\mathsf{rot}}; r'_2)$,
- $(\psi_1^\times, \hat{\psi}_1^\times) = (\prod_{s \in \hat{\Lambda}} g_{2s}^{f'_{(\times 1, s)}}, \prod_{s \in \hat{\Lambda}} \hat{g}_{2s}^{f'_{(\times 1, s)}})$,
- $(A^*, \hat{A}^*) = \mathcal{C}om^1(\widehat{\mathsf{ck}}_1; \boldsymbol{a}^*; r_{a^*})$,
- $(\psi_2^\times, \hat{\psi}_2^\times) = (\prod_{s \in \hat{\Lambda}} g_{2s}^{f'_{(\times 2, s)}}, \prod_{s \in \hat{\Lambda}} \hat{g}_{2s}^{f'_{(\times 2, s)}})$,
- $(\psi_2^{\mathsf{rot}}, \hat{\psi}_2^{\mathsf{rot}}) = (\prod_{s \in \tilde{\Lambda}} g_{2s}^{f'_{(\mathsf{rot} 2, s)}}, \prod_{s \in \tilde{\Lambda}} \hat{g}_{2s}^{f'_{(\mathsf{rot} 2, s)}})$,

- $(\psi_3^\times, \hat{\psi}_3^\times) = (\prod_{s \in \hat{A}} g_{2s}^{f'_{(\times 3, s)}}, \prod_{s \in \hat{A}} \hat{g}_{2s}^{f'_{(\times 3, s)}})$, and
- $(\psi_4^\times, \hat{\psi}_4^\times) = (\prod_{s \in \hat{A}} g_{2s}^{f'_{(\times 4, s)}}, \prod_{s \in \hat{A}} \hat{g}_{2s}^{f'_{(\times 4, s)}})$.

It will also create the openings that correspond to $\psi_5^{ce}$. If any of the openings fails, we are done. Since $\tilde{\Lambda}$-PSDL and $\{1 - X^{\lambda_1}\}$-PSDL assumptions are supposed to hold, all the following is true. (If it is not true, one can efficiently test it, and thus we have broken the PSDL assumption.)

Since $\hat{e}(B'_j, g_2) = \hat{e}(g_1, B'_{j2})$ for $j \in [0, n_v]$, then $(B_{j1}, \hat{B}_{j1}, B_{j2})$ commits to $b'_j$. Therefore, due to the $\hat{\Lambda}$-PSDL assumption, the fact that the adversary knows the openings of $(B'_j, \hat{B}'_j)$ and $(\psi'_j, \hat{\psi}'_j)$, and the last statement of Fact 2, since $(\psi'_j, \hat{\psi}'_j)$ verifies, then $b'_{ji} \in \{0, 1\}$ for all $j \in [0, n_v]$ and $i \in [1, n]$. Thus, by Fact 6, $\boldsymbol{b} = (b_1, \ldots, b_n) := (\sum_{j=0}^{n_v} G'_j b'_{j1}, \ldots, \sum_{j=0}^{n_v} G'_j b'_{jn}) \in [0, u - 1]^n$, and thus $(\prod_{j=0}^{n_v} (B'_j)^{G'_j}, \prod_{j=0}^{n_v} (\hat{B}'_j)^{G'_j})$ commits to $\boldsymbol{b}$ with $b_i \in [0, u - 1]$.

Due to the $\hat{\Lambda}$-PSDL assumption, the fact that the adversary knows the openings of $(B'_j, \hat{B}'_j)$, $(B^\dagger, \hat{B}^\dagger)$ and $(\psi_1^\times, \hat{\psi}_1^\times)$, and the last statement of Fact 2, since $(\psi_1^\times, \hat{\psi}_1^\times)$ verifies, then $b_i^\dagger = G_i b_i$. Due to the $\tilde{\Lambda}$-PSDL assumption, the fact that the adversary knows the openings of $(C, \tilde{C})$, $(C_{\mathsf{rot}}, \hat{C}_{\mathsf{rot}})$ and

$$(A^*, \hat{A}^*, \psi_2^\times, \hat{\psi}_2^\times, \psi_2^{\mathsf{rot}}, \hat{\psi}_2^{\mathsf{rot}}),$$

and the last statement of Fact 2, since $(A^*, \hat{A}^*, \psi_2^\times, \hat{\psi}_2^\times, \psi_2^{\mathsf{rot}}, \hat{\psi}_2^{\mathsf{rot}})$ verifies, then $c_{\mathsf{rot}, 1} = c_n$ and $c_{\mathsf{rot}, i+1} = c_i$ for $i \geq 1$.

Due to the $\hat{\Lambda}$-PSDL assumption, the fact that the adversary knows the openings of $(C_{\mathsf{rot}}, \tilde{C}_{\mathsf{rot}})$, $(C, \hat{C})$, $(B^\dagger, \hat{B}^\dagger)$, and $(\psi_3^\times, \hat{\psi}_3^\times)$, and the last statement of Fact 2, since $(\psi_3^\times, \hat{\psi}_3^\times)$ verifies, then $c_1 - G_1 b_1 = 0$ and $c_i - G_i b_i = c_{\mathsf{rot}, i} = c_{i-1}$ for $i > 1$. Therefore, $c_1 = G_1 b_1$, $c_2 = G_2 b_2 + G_1 b_1$, and by induction $c_i = \sum_{j=1}^n G_j b_j$ for $i \geq 1$. In particular, $c_n = \sum_{i=1}^n G_i b_i$ for $b_i \in [0, u - 1]$.

Due to the $\hat{\Lambda}$-PSDL assumption, the fact that the adversary knows the openings of $(C, \hat{C})$, $(A_c, \hat{A}_c)$, and $(\psi_4^\times, \hat{\psi}_4^\times)$, and the last statement of Fact 2, since $(\psi_4^\times, \hat{\psi}_4^\times)$ verifies, then $(A_c, \hat{A}_c) = (g_1^r g_{1,\lambda_1}^a, \hat{g}_1^r \hat{g}_{1,\lambda_1}^a)$ commits to $(a, 0, \ldots, 0)$ such that $(u - 1)a = \sum_{i=1}^n G_i b_i$ for $b_i \in [0, u - 1]$, and therefore by Fact 6, $a \in [0, H]$.

Due to the $\{1 - X^{\lambda_1}\}$-PSDL assumption and since $\psi_5^{ce}$ verifies, then $(A_g, A_f, A_h)$ encrypts $a \in [0, H]$.

COMPUTATIONAL ZERO-KNOWLEDGE: we construct the following simulator $\mathcal{S} = (\mathcal{S}_1, \mathcal{S}_2)$. First, $\mathcal{S}_1$ creates a correctly formed common reference string together with a simulation trapdoor $\mathsf{td} = (\hat{\alpha}, \tilde{\alpha}, \ldots, x)$. After that, the prover creates a statement $inp^r := (\mathsf{pk}, A_g, A_f, A_h, A_c, \hat{A}_c)$ and sends it to the simulator. Second, $\mathcal{S}_2(\mathsf{crs}; inp^r; \mathsf{td})$ uses a knowledge extractor to extract $(\boldsymbol{a}, r)$ from the prover's random coins and $(A_c, \hat{A}_c)$. Since we are only interested in the case of a honest prover, we have that $\boldsymbol{a} = (a, 0, \ldots, 0)$ with $a \in [0, H]$. Thus, using the fact that the knowledge commitment scheme is also trapdoor, the simulator computes $r'' \leftarrow a x^{\lambda_n} + r$; clearly $A = g_1^{r''}$. Since both $r$ and $r''$ are uniformly random, $r''$ does not leak any information on the prover's input. After that, the simulator creates all commitments $(B'_j, \hat{B}'_j, B'_{j2})_{j \in [0, n_v]}$, $(B^\dagger, \hat{B}^\dagger)$, $(C, \hat{C}, \tilde{C})$ and

$(C_{\mathsf{rot}}, \hat{C}_{\mathsf{rot}}, \tilde{C}_{\mathsf{rot}})$ as in the argument, but replacing $a$ with $0$ and $r$ with $r''$. (Note that all the mentioned commitments just commit to $\mathbf{0}$.) Thus, the simulator can simulate all product and permutation arguments and the argument of Sect. 5. Clearly, this simulated argument $\psi^{sim}$ is perfectly indistinguishable from the real argument $\psi$.                                                                □

**Theorem 3.** *Let $u > 1$. Let $\Lambda$ be as in Fact 1 and let $n = \ell(u, (u-1)H) \leq \lfloor \log_u((u-1)H+1)\rfloor \approx \log H/\log u + 1$, where $\ell(\cdot,\cdot)$ is defined as in Fact 6. Let $n_v = \lceil \log_2(u-1)\rceil$. Assume that we use the Hadamard product argument and the permutation argument from Sect. 3. The range proof in Prot. 3 has a length-$n^{1+o(1)}$ common reference string, communication of $2n_v + 25$ elements from $\mathbb{G}_1$ and $3n_v + 15$ elements from $\mathbb{G}_2$, the prover's computational complexity of $\Theta(n^2 n_v)$ scalar multiplications in $\mathbb{Z}_p$ and $n^{1+o(1)}n_v$ exponentiations in $\mathbb{G}_1$ or $\mathbb{G}_2$. The verifier's computational complexity is dominated by $9n_v + 81$ pairings.*

*Proof.* The communication complexity: $n_v + 1$ tuples $(B'_j, \hat{B}'_j, B'_{j2}, \psi_j)$ (each has 2 elements of $\mathbb{G}_1$ and 3 elements of $\mathbb{G}_2$), and then 8 extra elements from $\mathbb{G}_1$, 3 Hadamard product arguments (2 elements from $\mathbb{G}_2$ each), 1 permutation argument (2 elements from $\mathbb{G}_1$ and 4 elements from $\mathbb{G}_2$), and argument $\psi^{ce}$ (13 elements from $\mathbb{G}_1$ and 2 elements from $\mathbb{G}_2$). In total, thus $2(n_v+1)+8+2+13 = 2n_v + 25$ elements from $\mathbb{G}_1$ and $3(n_v+1)+3\cdot 2+4+2 = 3n_v + 15$ elements from $\mathbb{G}_2$.

The prover's computational complexity is dominated by $(n_v+1)+3 = n_v+4$ Hadamard product arguments and 1 permutation argument ($\Theta(n^2)$ scalar multiplications and bilinear-group $n^{1+o(1)}$ exponentiations each), that is in total $\Theta(n^2 \cdot n_v) = \Theta(n^2 \cdot \log u)$ scalar multiplications and $n^{1+o(1)}\log u$ exponentiations.

The verifier's computational complexity is dominated by verifying $n_v + 4$ Hadamard product arguments (5 pairings each), 1 permutation argument (12 pairings), and the argument $\psi^{ce}$ (33 pairings). In addition, the verifier performs $2 \cdot (2(n_v+1)+6) = 4n_v + 16$ pairings. The total number of pairings is thus $9n_v + 81$. The rest follows.                                                                □

The communication complexity is minimized when $n_v$ (and thus $u$) is as small as possible, that is, $u = 2$. Then $n_v = \lfloor \log_2 1\rfloor = 0$. In this case the communication consists of 12 elements from $\mathbb{G}_1$ and 13 elements from $\mathbb{G}_2$. The same choice $u = 2$ is also optimal for verifier's computational complexity (81 pairings). As noted before, at the security level of $2^{128}$, elements of $\mathbb{G}_1$ can be represented in 256 bits, and elements of $\mathbb{G}_2$ in 512 bits. Thus, at this security level, if $u = 2$ then the communication is $25 \cdot 256 + 25 \cdot 512 = 14\,080$ bits, that is, only about 4 to 5 times longer than the current recommended length of a $2^{128}$-secure RSA modulus. Therefore, the communication of the new range proof is even smaller than that of Lagrange theorem based arguments like [13].

The optimal prover's computational complexity is achieved when the number of exponentiations, $n^{1+o(1)} \cdot n_v = (\log H/\log u)^{1+o(1)} \cdot \lfloor \log_2(u-1)\rfloor$, is minimized. This happens if $u = H$, then the prover's computation is dominated by $\Theta(\log H)$ scalar multiplications and exponentiations. Moreover, in this case the CRS length

$n^{1+o(1)}$ is constant. Finally, we might want the summatory length of the CRS and the communication to be minimal, that is, $n^{1+o(1)} + \Theta(n_v)$. Considering $n \approx \log_u H$ and $n_v \approx \log_2 u$, we get that the sum is $(\log H / \log u)^{1+o(1)} + \Theta(\log u)$. One can approximately minimize the latter by choosing $u = e^{\sqrt{\ln H}}$. Then the summatory length is $\log^{1/2+o(1)} H$. (In this case, it would make sense to change the role of groups $\mathbb{G}_1$ and $\mathbb{G}_2$ to get better efficiency.) The efficiency of the new range proof in all three cases is given in Tbl. 1.

**Acknowledgments.** The authors were supported by Estonian Science Foundation, grant #9303, and European Union through the European Regional Development Fund. The first author was also supported by European Social Fund's Doctoral Studies and Internationalization Programme DoRa.

# References

1. Barreto, P.S.L.M., Naehrig, M.: Pairing-Friendly Elliptic Curves of Prime Order. In: Preneel, B., Tavares, S. (eds.) SAC 2005. LNCS, vol. 3897, pp. 319–331. Springer, Heidelberg (2006)
2. Boneh, D., Boyen, X., Shacham, H.: Short Group Signatures. In: Franklin, M. (ed.) CRYPTO 2004. LNCS, vol. 3152, pp. 41–55. Springer, Heidelberg (2004)
3. Camenisch, J., Chaabouni, R., Shelat, A.: Efficient Protocols for Set Membership and Range Proofs. In: Pieprzyk, J. (ed.) ASIACRYPT 2008. LNCS, vol. 5350, pp. 234–252. Springer, Heidelberg (2008)
4. Chaabouni, R., Lipmaa, H., Shelat, A.: Additive Combinatorics and Discrete Logarithm Based Range Protocols. In: Steinfeld, R., Hawkes, P. (eds.) ACISP 2010. LNCS, vol. 6168, pp. 336–351. Springer, Heidelberg (2010)
5. Di Crescenzo, G., Herranz, J., Sáez, G.: Reducing Server Trust in Private Proxy Auctions. In: Katsikas, S.K., López, J., Pernul, G. (eds.) TrustBus 2004. LNCS, vol. 3184, pp. 80–89. Springer, Heidelberg (2004)
6. Elkin, M.: An Improved Construction of Progression-Free Sets. Israeli Journal of Mathematics 184, 93–128 (2011)
7. Groth, J.: Honest Verifier Zero-Knowledge Arguments Applied. PhD thesis, University of Århus, Denmark (October 2004)
8. Groth, J.: Short Pairing-Based Non-interactive Zero-Knowledge Arguments. In: Abe, M. (ed.) ASIACRYPT 2010. LNCS, vol. 6477, pp. 321–340. Springer, Heidelberg (2010)
9. Groth, J.: Efficient Zero-Knowledge Arguments from Two-Tiered Homomorphic Commitments. In: Lee, D.H., Wang, X. (eds.) ASIACRYPT 2011. LNCS, vol. 7073, pp. 431–448. Springer, Heidelberg (2011)
10. Groth, J., Sahai, A.: Efficient Non-Interactive Proof Systems for Bilinear Groups. Technical Report 2007/155, International Association for Cryptologic Research (April 27, 2007), http://eprint.iacr.org/2007/155 (version 20100222:192509) (retrieved in December 2011)
11. Groth, J., Sahai, A.: Efficient Non-interactive Proof Systems for Bilinear Groups. In: Smart, N. (ed.) EUROCRYPT 2008. LNCS, vol. 4965, pp. 415–432. Springer, Heidelberg (2008)
12. Hess, F., Smart, N.P., Vercauteren, F.: The Eta Pairing Revisited. IEEE Transactions on Information Theory 52(10), 4595–4602 (2006)

13. Lipmaa, H.: On Diophantine Complexity and Statistical Zero-Knowledge Arguments. In: Laih, C.-S. (ed.) ASIACRYPT 2003. LNCS, vol. 2894, pp. 398–415. Springer, Heidelberg (2003)
14. Lipmaa, H.: Progression-Free Sets and Sublinear Pairing-Based Non-Interactive Zero-Knowledge Arguments. Technical Report 2011/009, International Association for Cryptologic Research (January 5, 2011), http://eprint.iacr.org/2011/009
15. Lipmaa, H.: Progression-Free Sets and Sublinear Pairing-Based Non-Interactive Zero-Knowledge Arguments. In: Cramer, R. (ed.) TCC 2012. LNCS, vol. 7194, pp. 169–189. Springer, Heidelberg (2012)
16. Lipmaa, H., Asokan, N., Niemi, V.: Secure Vickrey Auctions without Threshold Trust. In: Blaze, M. (ed.) FC 2002. LNCS, vol. 2357, pp. 87–101. Springer, Heidelberg (2003)
17. Pereira Geovandro, C.C.F., Simplício Jr., M.A., Naehrig, M., Barreto, P.S.L.M.: A Family of Implementation-Friendly BN Elliptic Curves. Journal of Systems and Software 84(8), 1319–1326 (2011)
18. Rial, A., Kohlweiss, M., Preneel, B.: Universally Composable Adaptive Priced Oblivious Transfer. In: Shacham, H., Waters, B. (eds.) Pairing 2009. LNCS, vol. 5671, pp. 231–247. Springer, Heidelberg (2009)
19. Sanders, T.: On Roth's Theorem on Progressions. Annals of Mathematics 174(1), 619–636 (2011)
20. Tao, T., Vu, V.: Additive Combinatorics. Cambridge Studies in Advanced Mathematics. Cambridge University Press (2006)
21. Yuen, T.H., Huang, Q., Mu, Y., Susilo, W., Wong, D.S., Yang, G.: Efficient Non-interactive Range Proof. In: Ngo, H.Q. (ed.) COCOON 2009. LNCS, vol. 5609, pp. 138–147. Springer, Heidelberg (2009)

# A    Proof of Thm. 1

*Proof.* PERFECT COMPLETENESS: correctness verifications are straightforward. Clearly,

$$\hat{e}(f, C_f) = \hat{e}(f, g_2^{R_f} g_{2,\lambda_1}^{r_f}) = \hat{e}(f, g_2^{R_f}) \cdot \hat{e}(f, g_{2,\lambda_1}^{r_f}) = \hat{e}(f^{R_f}, g_2) \cdot \hat{e}(f^{r_f}, g_{2,\lambda_1})$$
$$= \hat{e}(\psi_f, g_2) \cdot \hat{e}(A_f, g_{2,\lambda_1}) \ .$$

Analogously, $\hat{e}(h, C_h) = \hat{e}(\psi_h, g_2) \cdot \hat{e}(A_h, g_{2,\lambda_1})$. Finally, $\hat{e}(A_c \psi_g^{-1}, g_2) \cdot \hat{e}(g_1, C_f C_h) = \hat{e}(g_1^r g_{1,\lambda_1}^a \cdot g_1^{-r-R_f-R_h}, g_2) \cdot \hat{e}(g_1, g_2^{R_f+R_h}) \cdot \hat{e}(g_1, g_{2,\lambda_1}^{r_f+r_h}) = \hat{e}(g_{1,\lambda_1}^a \cdot g_1^{-R_f-R_h}, g_2) \cdot \hat{e}(g_1^{R_f+R_h}, g_2) \cdot \hat{e}(g_1^{r_f+r_h}, g_{2,\lambda_1}) = \hat{e}(g_1^a, g_{2,\lambda_1}) \cdot \hat{e}(g_1^{r_f+r_h}, g_{2,\lambda_1}) = \hat{e}(g_1^{r_f+r_h+a}, g_{2,\lambda_1})$.

COMPUTATIONAL SOUNDNESS: By the $\{1 - X^{\lambda_1}\}$-PKE assumption in $\mathbb{G}_1$ and $\mathbb{G}_2$, one can open the next values: $(A_c, \bar{A}_c) = (g_1^r g_{1,\lambda_1}^a, \bar{g}_1^r \bar{g}_{1,\lambda_1}^a)$, $(A_g/A_c, \mathring{A}_{g/c}) = ((g_1 g_{1,\lambda_1}^{-1})^{a'}, \mathring{g}_{1,g/c}^{a'})$, $(A_g, \mathring{A}_g) = (g_1^{a''}, \mathring{g}_1^{a''})$, $(A_f, \mathring{A}_f) = (f^{r_f}, \mathring{f}^{r_f})$, $(A_h, \mathring{A}_h) = (h^{r_h}, \mathring{h}^{r_h})$, $(C_f, \bar{C}_f) = (g_2^{R_f} g_{2,\lambda_1}^{r'_f}, \bar{g}_2^{R_f} \bar{g}_{2,\lambda_1}^{r'_f})$, $(C_h, \bar{C}_h) = (g_2^{R_h} g_{2,\lambda_1}^{r'_h}, \bar{g}_2^{R_h} \bar{g}_{2,\lambda_1}^{r'_h})$, $(\psi_g, \mathring{\psi}_g) = (g_1^{r''_a}, \mathring{g}_1^{r''_a})$, $(\psi_f, \mathring{\psi}_f) = (g_1^{r''_f}, \mathring{g}_{1,f}^{r''_f})$, and $(\psi_h, \mathring{\psi}_h) = (g_1^{r''_h}, \mathring{g}_{1,h}^{r''_h})$.

Since $A_c = g_1^r g_{1,\lambda_1}^a$, $A_g = g_1^{a''}$ and $A_g/A_c = (g_1 g_{1,\lambda_1}^{-1})^{a'}$, we have that $g_1^{a''} = g_1^{r+a'} g_{1,\lambda_1}^{a-a'}$. Thus, if $a \neq a'$, one can compute $x^{\lambda_1} \leftarrow (a'' - r - a')/(a - a')$, and from this compute $x$ and thus break the $\{1 - X^{\lambda_1}\}$-PSDL assumption. (To verify whether $x$ is the correct root, one can check whether $g_1^{x^{\lambda_1}} = g_{1,\lambda_1}$.) Thus $a = a'$, and thus also $a'' = r + a$ and $A_g = g_1^{r+a}$.

Due to $C_f = g_2^{R_f} g_{2,\lambda_1}^{r_f'}$, $\psi_f = g_1^{r_f''}$, $A_f = f^{r_f}$ and $\hat{e}(f, C_f) = \hat{e}(\psi_f, g_2) \cdot \hat{e}(A_f, g_{2,\lambda_1})$, we have $\hat{e}(f, g_2^{R_f} g_{2,\lambda_1}^{r_f'}) = \hat{e}(g_1^{r_f''}, g_2)\hat{e}(f^{r_f}, g_2^{x^{\lambda_1}})$ for unknown $x$. Taking the discrete logarithm of the both sides of the last equation, we get that $R_f/\mathsf{sk}_1 + r_f' x^{\lambda_1}/\mathsf{sk}_1 = r_f'' + r_f x^{\lambda_1}/\mathsf{sk}_1$, or $(r_f - r_f')x^{\lambda_1} = R_f - r_f'' \cdot \mathsf{sk}_1$. Thus, if $r_f \neq r_f'$, then we can compute $x^{\lambda_1}$, and find from this $x$, and thus break the $\{1 - X^{\lambda_1}\}$-PSDL assumption. Thus, $r_f = r_f'$ and therefore also $C_f = g_2^{R_f} g_{2,\lambda_1}^{r_f}$. Moreover, $\psi_f = g_1^{r_f''} = f^{R_f}$.

Analogously, we get that $r_h = r_h'$ and therefore $C_h = g_1^{R_h} g_{1,\lambda_1}^{r_h}$ and $\psi_h = h^{R_h}$.

Due to $C_f = g_2^{R_f} g_{2,\lambda_1}^{r_f}$, $C_h = g_1^{R_h} g_{1,\lambda_1}^{r_h}$, $\psi_g = g_1^{r_a''}$, $A_c = g_1^r g_{1,\lambda_1}^a$, $A_g = g_1^{r+a}$ and $\hat{e}(g_1, C_f C_h) = \hat{e}(\psi_g A_c^{-1}, g_2) \cdot \hat{e}(A_g, g_{2,\lambda_1})$, we have $\hat{e}(g_1, g_2^{r+R_f+R_h+(r_f+r_h)x^{\lambda_1}}) = \hat{e}(g_1^{r_a''} g_1^{-r} g_{1,\lambda_1}^{-a}, g_2) \cdot \hat{e}(g_1^{r+a}, g_{2,\lambda_1}) = \hat{e}(g_1^{r_a'' - r + rx^{\lambda_1}}, g_2)$ for unknown $x$. Taking the discrete logarithm of both sides of the last equation, we get $r + R_f + R_h + (r_f + r_h)x^{\lambda_1} = r_a'' - r + rx^{\lambda_1}$. Again, if $r_f + r_h \neq r$, then one can compute $x^{\lambda_1}$ and thus also $x$. Thus, $r = r_f + r_h$, and thus also $r_a'' = r + R_f + R_h$. This means that $A_c = g_1^{r_f + r_h} g_{1,\lambda_1}^a$ and $(A_g, A_f, A_h) = (g_1^{r_f+r_h+a}, f^{r_f}, h^{r_h})$.

COMPUTATIONAL ZERO-KNOWLEDGE: we construct the next simulator $(\mathcal{S}_1, \mathcal{S}_2)$. $\mathcal{S}_1$ creates a CRS according to the protocol together with a trapdoor $\mathsf{td} = (\alpha_g, \alpha_f, \alpha_h, \bar{\alpha}, \alpha_{g,c}, x)$. On input $\mathsf{td}$, $\mathcal{S}_2$ creates $z_f, z_h \leftarrow \mathbb{Z}_p$. He then sets $C_f \leftarrow g_2^{z_f}$, $\psi_f \leftarrow f^{z_f}/A_f^{x^{\lambda_1}}$, $C_h \leftarrow g_2^{z_h}$, $\psi_h \leftarrow h^{z_h}/A_h^{x^{\lambda_1}}$, and $\psi_g \leftarrow g_1^{z_f+z_h}/A_g^{x^{\lambda_1}}$. He creates the knowledge elements $(\mathring{A}_g, \mathring{A}_f, \mathring{A}_h, \mathring{A}_c, \mathring{\psi}_g, \bar{C}_f, \mathring{\psi}_f, \bar{C}_h, \mathring{\psi}_h, \mathring{A}_{g/c})$ by using the trapdoor. For example, $\mathring{A}_{g/c} \leftarrow (A_g/A_c)^{\alpha_{g/c}}$. One can now check that the verification succeeds. For example, $\hat{e}(\psi_f, g_2)\hat{e}(A_f, g_{2,\lambda_1}) = \hat{e}(f^{z_f}/A_f^{x^{\lambda_1}}, g_2) \cdot \hat{e}(A_f, g_{2,\lambda_1}) = \hat{e}(f^{z_f}, g_2)/\hat{e}(A_f^{x^{\lambda_1}}, g_2)\hat{e}(A_f, g_{2,\lambda_1}) = \hat{e}(f^{z_f}, g_2) = \hat{e}(f, C_f)$, and finally, $\hat{e}(A_c\psi_g^{-1}, g_2) \cdot \hat{e}(g_1, C_f C_h) = \hat{e}(g_1^{-z_f-z_h} A_g^{x^{\lambda_1}} A_c, g_2) \cdot \hat{e}(g_1, g_2^{z_f+z_h}) = \hat{e}(A_g, g_{2,\lambda_1})$. If the DLIN assumption is true, then $(A_g, A_f, A_h)$ is indistinguishable from an encryption of $0 \in [0, H]$, and thus the whole argument is computationally zero-knowledge. $\qquad\square$

# Privacy-Preserving Stream Aggregation
# with Fault Tolerance

T.-H. Hubert Chan[1], Elaine Shi[2], and Dawn Song[2]

[1] The University of Hong Kong
[2] UC Berkeley

**Abstract.** We consider applications where an *untrusted aggregator* would like to collect privacy sensitive data from users, and compute aggregate statistics periodically. For example, imagine a smart grid operator who wishes to aggregate the total power consumption of a neighborhood every ten minutes; or a market researcher who wishes to track the fraction of population watching ESPN on an hourly basis.

We design novel mechanisms that allow an aggregator to accurately estimate such statistics, while offering provable guarantees of user privacy against the untrusted aggregator. Our constructions are resilient to user failure and compromise, and can efficiently support dynamic joins and leaves. Our constructions also exemplify the clear advantage of combining applied cryptography and differential privacy techniques.

## 1 Introduction

Many real-world applications have benefitted tremendously from the ability to collect and mine data coming from multiple individuals and organizations. These applications have also spurred numerous concerns over the privacy of user data. In this paper, we study how an *untrusted aggregator* can gather information and learn aggregate statistics from a population without harming individual privacy. For example, consider a smart grid operator who wishes to track the total electricity consumption of a neighborhood every 15 minutes, for scheduling and optimization purposes. Since such power consumption data can reveal sensitive information about individual's presence and activities, we wish to perform such aggregation in a privacy-preserving manner.

More generally, we consider the *periodic distributed stream aggregation* model. Imagine a group of $n$ users. In every time period, each user has some data point within a certain range $(-\Delta, +\Delta)$. An untrusted aggregator wishes to compute the sum of all users' values in each time period. Each user considers her data as sensitive, and does not want to reveal the bit to the untrusted aggregator. How can we allow an untrusted aggregator to periodically learn aggregate information about a group of users, while preserving each individual's privacy?

The problem of privacy-preserving stream aggregation was first studied by Rastogi *et al.* [13] and Shi *et al.* [14]. These two works demonstrate how to combine cryptography with differential privacy and achieve $O(1)$ error, while using differential privacy techniques alone would result in at least $\Omega(\sqrt{N})$ error [3] in this setting[1].

---

[1] The lower bound holds when the aggregator sees all the messages in the protocol, for example, in the case where each user communicates only with the aggregator.

A.D. Keromytis (Ed.): FC 2012, LNCS 7397, pp. 200–214, 2012.

Specifically, these two works [13,14] both employ special encryption schemes which work as follows: in each aggregation period, each user encrypts its (perturbed) data value and sends the encrypted value to the aggregator. The aggregator has a cryptographic capability allowing it to decrypt the sum of all users' values, but learn nothing else. In constructing such encryptions schemes, both works [13,14] rely on the following key idea: each user would incorporate a random value into their ciphertext; and the aggregator's capability also incorporates a random value. All of these random values sum up to 0, and would cancel out in the decryption step, such that the aggregator can recover the sum of all users' values, but learn nothing else.

One major drawback of these earlier works [13, 14] is that these schemes are not tolerant of user failures. Even if a single user fails to respond in a certain aggregation round, the server would not be able to learn anything. This can be a big concern in real-world applications where failures may be unavoidable. For example, in a smart sensing applications, where data is collected from multiple distributed sensors, it is quite likely that some sensor might be malfunctioning at some point, and fails to respond. Failure tolerance is an important challenge left open by Shi *et al.* [14] and Rastogi *et al.* [13].

**Summary of Contributions.** Our main contribution is to introduce a novel technique to achieve *fault tolerance*, while incurring only a very small (logarithmic or polylogarithmic) penalty in terms of communication overhead and estimation error (see Table 1). In our construction, the aggregator is still able to estimate the sum over the remaining users when an arbitrary subset of users (unknown in advance) fail.

As a by-product of the fault tolerance technique, our scheme also supports *dynamic joins and leaves*, which is another problem left open by previous work [13,14]. Specifically, our scheme supports dynamic joins and leaves without having to perform costly rekeying operations with every join and leave.

Apart from failure tolerance and dynamic joins/leaves, our scheme has another desirable feature in that it requires only *a single round of client-to-server communication*. On a very high level, our construction works as follows: in every time period, each user uploads an encrypted and perturbed version of her data, and then the aggregator can compute the noisy sum by using a cryptographic capability obtained during an initial one-time setup phase.

**Techniques.** Our main technique for achieving failure tolerance may be of independent interest. Specifically, we build a *binary interval tree* over $n$ users, and allow the aggregator to estimate the sum of contiguous intervals of users as represented by nodes in the interval tree. In comparison with Shi et al. [14], the binary-tree technique allows us to handle user failures, joins and leaves, with a small logarithmic (or polylog) cost in terms of communication and estimation error.

**More Applications.** Apart from the smart grid example mentioned earlier, the distributed stream aggregation problem is also widely applicable in a variety of problem domains, such as distributed hot item identification, sensing and monitoring, as well as medical research. We elaborate more on these applications in the online full version [2].

**Table 1. Comparison between existing schemes and our contributions.** The asympototic bounds hide the privacy parameters $\epsilon$ and $\delta$. The parameter $\rho$ denotes any constant between 0 and 1. The $\tilde{O}(\cdot)$ notation hides a $\log \log n$ factor.

In our full online technical report [2], we also propose two variants of sampling-based constructions, in which a random subset of users respond by sending a perturbed version of their data. The sampling constructions can be useful in applications where bandwidth efficiency is a major concern. In particular, for arbitrarily small $\rho$ between 0 and 1, we can achieve error $O(\rho n)$ with $O(\frac{1}{\rho^2})$ words of total communication.

| Scheme | Total comm. | Avg comm. per user | Error | Fail-safe/Dynamic joins & leaves | Security Model | Comm. model |
|---|---|---|---|---|---|---|
| Naive | $O(n)$ | $O(1)$ | $O(\sqrt{n})$ | Yes | DP | C → S |
| Rastogi *et al.* [13] | $O(n)$ | $O(1)$ | $O(1)$ | No | CDP AO | C ⇔ S |
| Shi *et al.* [14] | $O(n)$ | $O(1)$ | $O(1)$ | No | CDP AO | C → S |
| **This paper:** | | | | | | |
| Sampling (Online TR) | $O(\frac{1}{\rho^2})$ | $O(\frac{1}{\rho^2 n})$ | $O(\rho n)$ | Yes | DP | C ⇔ S |
| Binary | $O(n \log n)$ | $O(\log n)$ | $\tilde{O}((\log n)^{\frac{3}{2}})$ | Yes | CDP | C → S |

DP: Differential Privacy     CDP: Computational Differential Privacy     AO: Aggregator Obliviousness (explanations in Section 1.1)     $C \to S$: client-to-server uni-directional $C \Leftrightarrow S$: interactive between client and server

## 1.1 Related Work

Differential privacy [1, 5, 6, 8] was traditionally studied in a setting where a trusted curator, with access to the entire database in the clear, wishes to release statistics in a way that preserves each individual's privacy. The trusted curator is responsible for introducing appropriate perturbations prior to releasing any statistic. This setting is particularly useful when a company or a government agency, in the possession of a dataset, would like to share it with the public.

In real-world applications, however, users may not trust the aggregator. A recent survey by Microsoft [15] found that "...58% of the public and 86% of business leaders are excited about the possibilities of cloud computing. But, more than 90% of them are worried about security, availability, and privacy of their data as it rests in the cloud."

Recently, the research community has started to consider how to guarantee differential privacy in the presence of an untrusted aggregator [13, 14]. Rastogi *et al.* [13] and Shi *et al.* [14] proposed novel algorithms that allow an untrusted aggregator to periodically estimate the sum of $n$ users' values, without harming each individual's privacy. In addition to (computational) differential privacy, these two schemes also provide *aggregator obliviousness*, meaning that the aggregator only learns the noisy sum, but no intermediate results.

Both of these schemes [13, 14], however, would suffer in the face of user failures, thereby leaving resilience to node failure as one of the most important open challenges in this area. Our Binary Protocol utilizes Shi *et al.*'s encryption scheme as a building block, and we successfully solve the node failure problem.

Dwork *et al.* [7] study distributed noise generation, however, their scheme requires interactions among all users.

The use of a binary tree in our construction may be reminiscent of Dwork *et al.* [9] and Chan *et al.* [4], where they use a binary-tree-like construction for a completely different purpose, i.e., to achieve high utility when releasing statistics continually in a trusted aggregator setting.

## 2    Problem Definition and Assumptions

For simplicity, consider a group of $n$ users each holding a private bit $x_i \in \{0,1\}$ – although our approach can be trivially adapted to the case where each user has a data point within a certain discrete range. We use the notation $\mathbf{x} := (x_1, x_2, \ldots, x_n) \in \{0,1\}^n$ to denote the vector of all users' bits, also referred to as an *input configuration*. An aggregator $\mathcal{A}$ wishes to estimate the count, denoted $\text{sum}(\mathbf{x}) := \sum_{i \in [n]} x_i$.

**Periodic Aggregation.** We are particularly interested in the case of periodic aggregation. For example, a market researcher may wish to track the fraction of the population watching ESPN during different hours of the day. In general, in each time period $t \in \mathbb{N}$, we have a vector $\mathbf{x}^{(t)} \in \{0,1\}^n$, e.g., indicating whether each of the surveyed users is currently watching ESPN. The aggregator wishes to evaluate $\text{sum}(\mathbf{x}^{(t)}) := \sum_{i \in [n]} x_i^{(t)}$ in every time period. For ease of exposition, we often focus our attention on the aggregation algorithm in one time step, and as a result, omit the superscript $t$.

**Failure Tolerance.** When a user fails, it stops participating in the protocol. A protocol is *failure tolerant*, if for any subset of failed users, the aggregator can still make an estimate on the sum of the bits from the remaining functioning users.

**Communication Model.** In real-world applications, peer-to-peer communication is undesirable as it requires all users to be online simultaneously and interact with each other. This paper will focus on schemes that requires no user-to-user communication, i.e., all communication takes place between an aggregator and a user.

### 2.1    Assumptions and Privacy Definitions

**Trust Model.** We consider the scenario when the aggregator is untrusted. We think of the aggregator as the adversary from whom we wish to protect the users' privacy. The aggregator does not have access to the users' bits directly, but may have arbitrary auxiliary information a priori. Such auxiliary information can be harvested in a variety of ways, e.g., from public datasets online, or through personal knowledge about a user. Our constructions ensure individual privacy even when the aggregator may have arbitrary auxiliary information.

**Compromise.** We assume a semi-honest model, where *compromised* users can collude with the aggregator by revealing their input bits or random noises to the aggregator. However, we assume that all users honestly use their inputs in the aggregation. The *data pollution* attack, where users inflate or deflate their input values, is out of the scope of this paper, and can be solved using orthogonal techniques such as [12]. In this paper, we assume a slightly relaxed model of compromise, where the compromised nodes are chosen independently from the randomness used in the algorithm (more details in Section 4).

**Key Distribution.** We assume that any cryptographic keys or privacy parameters required are already distributed to the aggregator and users in a separate setup phase ahead of time. The setup phase needs to be performed only once at system initialization, and need not be repeated during the periodic aggregation rounds.

We define a transcript $\pi$ to be the sequence of all messages sent by the users and the aggregator at the end of the protocol. As we consider protocols with no peer-to-peer communication, i.e., all communication takes place between the users and the aggregator, the view of the aggregator during the protocol is essentially the transcript $\pi$.

Users (and the aggregator) may contribute randomness to the protocol, for example, users will add noise to perturb their input bits. Therefore, we can define a distribution on the transcripts. Formally, we use the notation $\Pi$ to denote a randomized protocol, and use $\Pi(\mathbf{x})$ to denote the random transcript when the input configuration is $\mathbf{x}$.

In this paper, we consider the computational version of differential privacy, as in practice it suffices to secure the protocol against computationally-bounded adversaries. We now define computational differential privacy (CDP), similar to the CDP notion originally proposed by Mironov *et al.* [11].

In addition to the users' data $\mathbf{x}$, the protocol $\Pi$ also takes a security parameter $\lambda \in \mathbb{N}$. We use the notation $\Pi(\lambda, \mathbf{x})$ to denote the distribution of the transcript when the security parameter is $\lambda$ and the input configuration is $\mathbf{x}$.

**Definition 1 (Computational Differential Privacy Against Compromise).** *Suppose the users are compromised by some underlying randomized process $\mathcal{C}$, and we use $C$ to denote the information obtained by the adversary from the compromised users. Let $\epsilon, \delta > 0$. A (randomized) protocol $\Pi$ preserves computational $(\epsilon, \delta)$-differential privacy (against the compromise process $\mathcal{C}$) if there exists a negligible function $\eta : \mathbb{N} \to \mathbb{R}^+$ such that for all $\lambda \in \mathbb{N}$, for all $i \in [n]$, for all vectors $\mathbf{x}$ and $\mathbf{y}$ in $\{0, 1\}^n$ that differ only at position $i$, for all probabilistic polynomial-time Turing machines $\mathcal{A}$, for any output $b \in \{0, 1\}$,*
$$\mathrm{Pr}_{\mathcal{C}_i}[\mathcal{A}(\Pi(\lambda, \mathbf{x}), C) = b] \leq e^{\epsilon} \cdot \mathrm{Pr}_{\mathcal{C}_i}[\mathcal{A}(\Pi(\lambda, \mathbf{y}), C) = b] + \delta + \eta(\lambda),$$
*where the probability is taken over the randomness of $\mathcal{A}$, $\Pi$ and $\mathcal{C}_i$, which denotes the underlying compromise process conditioning on the event that user $i$ is uncompromised.*

*A protocol $\Pi$ preserves computational $\epsilon$-differential privacy if it preserves computational $(\epsilon, 0)$-differential privacy.*

## 3    Preliminaries

### 3.1    Tool: Geometric Distribution

Two noise distributions are commonly used to perturb the data and ensure differential privacy, the Laplace distribution [8], and the Geometric distribution [10]. The advantage of using the geometric distribution over the Laplace distribution is that we can keep working in the domain of integers. The geometric distribution is particularly useful when used in combination with a crypto-system, e.g., our Binary Protocol described in Section 4. Most crypto-systems work in discrete mathematical structures, and are not designed to work with (truly) real numbers.

We now define the *symmetric* geometric distribution.

**Definition 2 (Geometric Distribution).** *Let* $\alpha > 1$. *We denote by* Geom$(\alpha)$ *the symmetric geometric distribution that takes integer values such that the probability mass function at $k$ is* $\frac{\alpha-1}{\alpha+1} \cdot \alpha^{-|k|}$.

The following property of Geom distribution is useful for designing differentially private mechanisms that output integer values.

**Fact 1** *Let* $\epsilon > 0$. *Suppose $u$ and $v$ are two integers such that* $|u - v| \leq \Delta$. *Let $r$ be a random variable having distribution* Geom$(\exp(\frac{\epsilon}{\Delta}))$. *Then, for any integer $k$,* $Pr[u + r = k] \leq \exp(\epsilon) \cdot Pr[v + r = k]$.

In our setting, changing 1 bit can only affect the sum by at most 1. Hence, it suffices to consider Geom$(\alpha)$ with $\alpha = e^\epsilon$. Observe that Geom$(\alpha)$ has variance $\frac{2\alpha}{(\alpha-1)^2}$. Since $\frac{\sqrt{\alpha}}{\alpha-1} \leq \frac{1}{\ln\alpha} = \frac{1}{\epsilon}$, the magnitude of the error added is $O(\frac{1}{\epsilon})$. The following diluted geometric distributions is useful in the description of our protocols.

**Definition 3 (Diluted Geometric Distribution).** *Let* $0 < \beta \leq 1$, $\alpha > 1$. *A random variable has $\beta$-diluted Geometric distribution* Geom$^\beta(\alpha)$ *if with probability $\beta$ it is sampled from* Geom$(\alpha)$, *and with probability $1 - \beta$ is set to 0.*

### 3.2 Naive Scheme

We describe a simple scheme as a warm-up, and as a baseline of comparison. In the Naive Scheme, each user generates an independent Geom$(e^\epsilon)$ noise, which is added to her bit. Each user sends her perturbed bit to the aggregator, who computes the sum of all the noisy bits. As each user adds one copy of independent noise to her data, $n$ copies of noises would accumulate in the sum. As some positive and negative noises may cancel out, the accumulated noise is $O(\frac{\sqrt{n}}{\epsilon})$ with high probability. Notice that if we employs the information-theoretic (as opposed to computational) differential privacy notion, the naive scheme is in some sense the best one can do. Chan et al. [3] show in a recent work that in a setting with $n$ users and one aggregator, any (information theoretically) differential private summation protocol with no peer-to-peer interaction must result in an error of $\Omega(\sqrt{N})$.

## 4 Binary Protocol: Achieving Failure Tolerance

### 4.1 Intuition

Consider the periodic aggregation scheme proposed by Shi et al. [14], henceforth referred to as the Block Aggregation (BA) scheme. In the BA scheme, every time period,

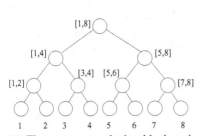
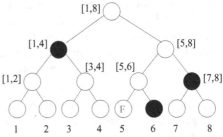

(a) The aggregator obtains block estimates corresponding to all nodes appearing in the binary interval tree.

(b) When user 5 fails, the aggregator sums up
the block estimates corresponding to the black
nodes.

**Fig. 1.** Intuition for the Binary Protocol

each user sends a perturbed and encrypted version of her data to the aggregator. The aggregator has a cryptographic capability to decrypt the sum of all encrypted values, but can learn nothing else. The BA scheme achieves $O(1)$ error. and guarantees all users' differential privacy against polynomial-time adversaries.

Unfortunately, the use of cryptography in the BA scheme introduces the all-or-nothing decryption model. Therefore, the aggregator learns nothing if a single user fails.

**The Challenge.** On one hand, we have the naive scheme which achieves $O(\sqrt{n})$ error, and is failure tolerant On the other hand, we have the BA Scheme which achieves $O(1)$ error (by combining cryptography with differential privacy), but is unfortunately not failure tolerant. Can we seek middle-ground between these approaches, such that we can obtain the best of both worlds, i.e., achieve both fault tolerance and small error?

**Binary Tree Idea.** One idea is to form user groups (henceforth referred to as *blocks*), and run the BA Scheme for each block. The aggregator is then able to estimate the sum for each block. If a subset of the users fail, we must be able to find a set of disjoint blocks to cover the functioning users. In this way, the aggregator can estimate the sum of the functioning users. The challenge is how to achieve this with only a small number of groups.

As depicted in Figure 1, our construction is based on a binary interval tree, hence the name Binary Protocol. For ease of exposition, assume for now that $n$ is a power of 2. Each leaf node is tagged with a number in $[n]$. Each internal node in the tree represents a contiguous interval covering all leaf nodes in its subtree. As a special case, we can think of the leaf nodes as representing intervals of size 1. For each node in the tree, we also use the term *block* to refer to the contiguous interval represented by the node.

Intuitively, the aggregator and users would simultaneously perform the BA Scheme for every interval (or block) appearing in the binary tree. Hence, the aggregator would obtain an estimated sum for each of these blocks. Normally, when $n$ is a power of 2, the aggregator could simply output the block estimate for the entire range $[1, n]$. However, imagine if a user $i$ fails to respond, the aggregator would then fail to obtain block estimates for any block containing $i$, including the block estimate for the entire range $[1, n]$.

Fortunately, observe that any contiguous interval within $[n]$ can be covered by $O(\log n)$ nodes in the binary interval tree. If $\kappa$ users have failed, the numbers 1 through $n$ would be divided into $\kappa + 1$ contiguous intervals, each of which can be covered by $O(\log n)$ nodes. This means that the aggregator can estimate the sum of the remaining users by summing up $O((\kappa + 1) \log n)$ block estimates.

**Example.** For convenience, we use the notation sum$[i..j]$ (where $1 \leq i \leq j \leq n$) to denote the estimated sum for the block $x_i, x_{i+1}, \ldots, x_j$ of user inputs. Figure 1 depicts a binary tree of size $n = 8$. When all users are active, the aggregator can obtain block estimates corresponding to all nodes in the tree. Therefore, the aggregator can simply output block estimate sum$[1..8]$. Figure 1 illustrates the case when user 5 has failed. When this happens, the aggregator fails to obtain the block estimates sum$[5..5]$, sum$[5..6]$, sum$[5..8]$, and sum$[1..8]$, since these blocks contain user 5. However, the aggregator can still estimate the sum of the remaining users by summing up the block estimates corresponding to the black nodes in the tree, namely, sum$[1..4]$, sum$[6..6]$, and sum$[7..8]$.

**Privacy-Utility Tradeoff.** We now give a quick and informal analysis of the privacy-utility tradeoff. It is not hard to see that each user is contained in at most $O(\log n)$ blocks. This means that if a user's bit is flipped, $O(\log n)$ blocks would be influenced. Roughly speaking, to satisfy $\epsilon$-differential privacy, it suffices to add noise proportional to $O(\frac{\log n}{\epsilon})$ to each block.

If $\kappa$ users fail, we would be left with $\kappa + 1$ intervals. Each interval can be covered by $O(\log n)$ nodes in the binary tree. Therefore, the final estimate would consist of $O((\kappa + 1) \log n)$ block estimates. Since each block estimate contains $O(\frac{\log n}{\epsilon})$ noise, the final estimate would contain $O((\kappa + 1) \log n)$ copies of such noises. As some positive and negative noises cancel out, the final estimate would contain noise of roughly $O(\frac{(\log n)^{1.5} \sqrt{\kappa+1}}{\epsilon})$ magnitude.

In the remainder of the section, we first give a formal description of the BA Scheme [14] used as a building block of the Binary Protocol. Then we formally describe the Binary Protocol and state the theorems on the privacy and utility tradeoff.

## 4.2   Background: Basic Block Construction

We will use the BA Scheme [14] as a building block to aggregate the sum for each block (or subset) $B \subseteq [n]$ of users. We now explain at a high level how the BA scheme works. Note that in place of the BA scheme by Shi *et al.* [14], the binary tree framework also readily applies on top of the scheme by Rastogi *et al.* [13]. The tradeoffs are discussed later in Section 5.

**Encryption Scheme.** The BA Scheme leverages an encryption scheme that *allows an aggregator to decrypt the sum of all users' encrypted values (with an appropriate cryptographic capability), but learn nothing more.* The encryption scheme has three (possibly randomized) algorithms.

- Setup$(m, \lambda)$: A one-time setup algorithm, run by a trusted dealer, takes the number of users $m$, and a security parameter $\lambda$ as inputs. It outputs the following:

$$(\mathsf{params}, \mathsf{cap}, \{\mathsf{sk}_i\}_{i \in [m]}),$$

where params are system parameters, e.g., a description of the selected algebraic group. Capability cap is distributed to the aggregator, and $\mathsf{sk}_i$ ($i \in [m]$) is a secret key distributed to user $i$. The users will later use their secret keys to encrypt, and the aggregator will use its capability to decrypt the sum, in each aggregation period. The setup algorithm is performed *only once at system initialization*, and need not be repeated for each periodic aggregation round.
- Encrypt$(\mathsf{sk}_i, x_i, t)$: During time step $t$, user $i$ uses $\mathsf{sk}_i$ to encrypt its (possibly perturbed) data $x_i$. The user uploads the outcome ciphertext $c_i$ to the aggregator.
- Decrypt$(\mathsf{cap}, \{c_i\}_{i \in [m]}, t)$: During time step $t$, after the aggregator collects all users' ciphertexts $\{c_i\}_{i \in [m]}$, it calls the decryption algorithm Decrypt to retrieve the sum $\sum_{i \in [m]} x_i$. Apart from this sum, the aggregator is unable to learn anything else.

The BA scheme relies on the following key idea. In the Setup phase, each user $i$ ($1 \leq i \leq m$) obtains a secret-key which incorporates a random value $r_i$. The aggregator obtains a capability which incorporates a random value $r$. Furthermore, the condition $r + \sum_{i=1}^{m} r_i = 0$ is satisfied. In every aggregation period, each user incorporates its random value $r_i$ into its ciphertext. After collecting all ciphertexts from users, the aggregator can homomorphically "sum up" all ciphertexts, such that the random values $r, r_1, \ldots, r_m$ cancel out, and the aggregator can thus decrypt the sum of all users' encrypted values. The above is a grossly simplified view of the BA scheme intended to capture the intuition. The full construction is more sophisticated, and requires additional techniques to allow the random values distributed in the Setup phase to be reusable in multiple aggregation phases, while still maintaining security.

**Input Perturbation.** Revealing the exact sum to the aggregator can still harm an individual's differential privacy. To guarantee differential privacy, each user adds some noise to her data before encrypting it.

Recall that in the naive scheme, each user must add one copy of geometric noise to guarantee its own differential privacy. In the BA Scheme, however, the aggregator can only decrypt the sum, and cannot learn each individual's perturbed values. Therefore, as long as the all users' noises sum up to roughly one copy of geometric noise, each user's differential privacy can be guaranteed. This is why the BA Scheme construction can guarantee $O(1)$ error.

Let $\epsilon, \delta$ denote the privacy parameters. In every time step $t$, each user $i$ generates an independent $r_i$ from the diluted geometric distribution $\mathsf{Geom}^\beta(\alpha)$ and computes $\widehat{x}_i := x_i + r_i$. In other words, with probability $\beta$, the noise $r_i$ is generated from the geometric distribution $\mathsf{Geom}(\alpha)$, and with probability $1 - \beta$, $r_i$ is set to 0. Specifically, we choose $\alpha := e^\epsilon$, and $\beta := \min\{\frac{1}{m} \ln \frac{1}{\delta}, 1\}$. This ensures that with high probability, at least one user has added $\mathsf{Geom}(e^\epsilon)$ noise. More generally, if $1 - \gamma$ fraction of the users are compromised, then we set $\beta := \min(\frac{1}{\gamma m} \ln \frac{1}{\delta}, 1)$.

The user then computes the ciphertext $c_i := \mathsf{Encrypt}(\mathsf{sk}_i, \widehat{x}_i, t)$, where $\widehat{x}_i$ is the purtubed data, and uploads the ciphertext to the aggregator.

| $\text{SETUP}(n, \lambda, \epsilon, \delta)$: # run by a trusted dealer |
|---|
| 1: $K \leftarrow \lfloor \log_2 n \rfloor + 1$ |
| 2: $\epsilon_0 \leftarrow \frac{\epsilon}{K}, \delta_0 \leftarrow \frac{\delta}{K}$ |
| 3: Give $\epsilon_0$ and $\delta_0$ to all users. |
| 4: for $B \in \mathcal{T}(n)$ do |
| 5: $\quad$ (params, $\text{cap}_B, \{\text{sk}_{i,B}\}_{i \in B}$) $\leftarrow$ BA.Setup$(|B|, \lambda)$ |
| 6: $\quad$ Give params to aggregator and all users. |
| 7: $\quad$ Give $\text{cap}_B$ to the aggregator. |
| 8: $\quad$ Give $\text{sk}_{i,B}$ and $|B|$ to each user $i \in B$. |
| 9: end for |

| $\text{ALGUSER}(x_i, t, \mathcal{B}(i), \{\text{sk}_{i,B}\}_{i \in \mathcal{B}(i)}, \epsilon_0, \delta_0)$: |
|---|
| # Periodic aggregation – user $i$'s algorithm |
| 1: for $B \in \mathcal{B}(i)$ do |
| 2: $\quad \beta \leftarrow \min(\frac{1}{|B|} \ln \frac{1}{\delta_0}, 1)$ |
| 3: $\quad r \leftarrow \text{Geom}^\beta(e^{\epsilon_0})$ |
| 4: $\quad \widehat{x}_{i,B} \leftarrow x_i + r$ |
| 5: $\quad c_{i,B} \leftarrow \text{BA.Encrypt}(\text{sk}_{i,B}, \widehat{x}_{i,B}, t)$ |
| 6: $\quad$ Send $c_{i,B}$ to aggregator. |
| 7: end for |

| $\text{ALGAGGR}(S, \{\text{cap}_B\}_{B \in \mathcal{T}(n)}, \{c_{i,B}\}_{i \in S, B \in \mathcal{B}(i)})$: |
|---|
| # Periodic aggregation – the aggregator's algorithm |
| 1: Find a set of blocks $\mathcal{B}$ to uniquely cover $S$. |
| 2: $s \leftarrow 0$ |
| 3: for $B \in \mathcal{B}$ do |
| 4: $\quad s_B \leftarrow \text{BA.Decrypt}(\text{cap}_B, \{c_{i,B}\}_{i \in B})$ |
| 5: $\quad s \leftarrow s + s_B$ |
| 6: end for |
| 7: return the estimated sum $s$ |

| | |
|---|---|
| $\lambda$ | security parameter |
| $n$ | total number of users |
| $t$ | current round |
| $x_i$ | user $i$'s data in current round |
| $\mathcal{T}(n)$ | set of all blocks corresponding to nodes in a binary tree of size $n$ |
| $\epsilon, \delta$ | privacy parameters |
| $\text{sk}_{i,B}$ | user $i$'s secret key for block $B$ where $i \in B$ |
| $\text{cap}_B$ | aggregator's capability for block $B$ |
| $S$ | set of functioning users in current round |
| $\mathcal{B}(i)$ | $\mathcal{B}(i) := \{B \mid B \in \mathcal{T}(n) \text{ and } i \in B\}$ set of blocks containing user $i$ |

**Fig. 2.** The Binary Protocol

**Theorem 1 (Computational Differential Privacy of BA).** *Let $\epsilon > 0$, $0 < \delta < 1$ and $\beta := \min\{\frac{1}{\gamma m} \ln \frac{1}{\delta}, 1\}$, where $\gamma$ is the probability that each user remains uncompromised. If each user adds diluted Geometric noise $\text{Geom}^\beta(\alpha)$ (where $\alpha = e^\epsilon$), then at each time step, the Block Aggregation Scheme is computationally $(\epsilon, \delta)$-differentially private against compromised users.*

### 4.3 Binary Protocol: Construction

The Binary Protocol consists of running the BA Scheme over a collection of blocks simultaneously. Specifically, if $n$ is a power of 2, then one can build a binary interval tree of the $n$ users such as in Figure 1(a). Each node in the tree represents a contiguous interval, which we call a block. The aggregator and users would run the BA Scheme for all blocks depicted in the interval tree. It is not hard to see that each user $i$ is contained in at most $K := \lfloor \log_2 n \rfloor + 1$ blocks, represented by nodes on the path from the $i$-th leaf node to the root of the tree.

We now state the above description more formally. Given integers $k \geq 0$ and $j \geq 1$, the $j$th block of rank $k$ is the subset $B_j^k := \{2^k(j-1) + l : 1 \leq l \leq 2^k\}$ of integers. If there are $n$ users, we only need to consider the blocks $B_j^k$ such that $B_j^k \subseteq [n]$. Define $\mathcal{T}(n)$ to be the set of all relevant blocks when there are $n$ users.

$$\mathcal{T}(n) := \{B_j^k | k \geq 0, j \geq 1, B_j^k \subseteq [n]\}$$

Specifically, when $n$ is a power of 2, $\mathcal{T}(n)$ basically corresponds to the collection of all nodes in the binary interval tree with $n$ leaf nodes. It is not hard to see that the total number of blocks is at most $2n$. The following observations will be important in the design of the Binary Protocol.

**Observation 1.** *Each user* $i \in [n]$ *is contained in at most* $K := \lfloor \log_2 n \rfloor + 1$ *blocks. In particular, each user is in at most one block of rank k.*

**Setup Phase.** Like in the BA Scheme, a one-time trusted setup is performed at system initialization. A trusted dealer distributes $O(\log n)$ secret keys to each user. In particular, each user $i \in [n]$ obtains one secret key corresponding to each block containing the user (i.e., the path from the $i$-th leaf node to the root). We use the notation $\mathsf{sk}_{i,B}$ to denote user $i$'s secret key corresponding to the block $B$.

For each block $B \in \mathcal{T}(n)$, the trusted dealer issues a capability $\mathsf{cap}_B$ to the aggregator. The aggregator thus receives $O(n)$ capabilities. The parties also agree on other system parameters including the privacy parameters $(\epsilon, \delta)$.

**Periodic Aggregation: User Algorithm.** In each time step $t \in [n]$, each user $i$ performs the following:

For each block $B$ containing the user $i$, the user generates a fresh random noise $r$ from the diluted geometric distribution $\mathsf{Geom}^\beta(e^{\epsilon_0})$, where the choice of parameters $\beta$ and $\epsilon_0$ will be explained later. The user adds the noise $r_{i,B}$ to her input bit $x_i$, and obtains $\widehat{x}_{i,B} := x_i + r_{i,B}$. The user then encrypts $\widehat{x}_{i,B}$ using $\mathsf{sk}_{i,B}$, i.e., her secret key corresponding to the block $B$. Specifically, user $i$ computes

$$c_{i,B} := \mathsf{BA.Encrypt}(\mathsf{sk}_{i,B}, \widehat{x}_{i,B}, t)$$

The final ciphertext $c_i$ uploaded to the aggregator is the collection of all ciphertexts, one corresponding to each block containing the user $i$.

$$c_i := \{c_{i,B} | B \in \mathcal{T}(n), i \in B\}$$

As each user is contained in $O(\log n)$ blocks, the ciphertext size is also $O(\log n)$.

**Parameter Choices.** Suppose we wish to guarantee computational $(\epsilon, \delta)$-differential privacy for the Binary Protocol, where $(\epsilon, \delta)$ are parameters agreed upon by all parties in the setup phase. Each user needs to determine the parameters $\epsilon_0$ and $\beta$ when generating a noise from the diluted geometric distribution $\mathsf{Geom}^\beta(e^{\epsilon_0})$. Specifically, each user chooses $\epsilon_0 := \frac{\epsilon}{K}$, where $K := \lfloor \log_2 n \rfloor + 1$. When selecting noise for a block $B$ of size $|B|$, the user selects an appropriate $\beta := \min\{\frac{1}{|B|} \ln \frac{1}{\delta_0}, 1\}$, where $\delta_0 = \frac{\delta}{K}$. Notice that due to Theorem 1, the above choice of $\epsilon_0$ and $\beta$ ensures that each separate copy of the BA Scheme satisfies computational $(\epsilon_0, \delta_0)$-differential privacy. This fact is used later to analyze the differential privacy of the entire Binary Protocol.

Intuitively, using the diluted geometric distribution, each user effectively adds a geometric noise with probability $\beta$, and adds 0 noise with probability $1 - \beta$. Notice that $\beta$ is smaller if the block size is bigger, since we wish to guarantee that at least one user added a real geometric noise.

More generally, if each user may be compromised with independent probability $1-\gamma$, then each (uncompromised) user would choose $\epsilon_0 := \frac{\epsilon}{K}$, and $\beta := \frac{1}{\gamma|B|} \ln \frac{1}{\delta_0}$ for a block $B$ whose size is $|B|$, where $\delta_0 := \frac{\delta}{K}$.

**Periodic Aggregation: Aggregator Algorithm.** Suppose $0 \leq \kappa < n$ users have failed to respond. Then the entire range $[n]$ would be divided up into $\kappa+1$ contiguous interval. The aggregator will recover the noisy sum for each of these intervals, and the sum of these will be the estimate of the total sum.

It suffices to describe how to recover the noisy sum for each of these contiguous intervals. An important observation is that each contiguous interval within $[n]$ can be covered uniquely by $O(\log_2 n)$ blocks. This is stated more formally in the following observation.

**Observation 2 (Unique cover for a contiguous interval).** *Let $[s,t]$ denote a contiguous interval of integers within $[n]$, where $1 \leq s \leq t \leq n$. We say that $[s,t]$ can be covered uniquely by a set of blocks $\mathcal{B} \subseteq \mathcal{T}(n)$, if every integer in $[s,t]$ appears in exactly one block in $\mathcal{B}$. For any interval $[s,t] \subseteq [n]$, it is computationally easy to find set of at most $2 \lceil \log_2 n \rceil + 1$ blocks that uniquely cover $[s,t]$.*

Therefore, to recover the noisy sum for an interval $[s,t] \subseteq [n]$, the aggregator first finds a set of blocks $\mathcal{B}$ to uniquely cover $[s,t]$. Then, the aggregator decrypts the noisy sum for each block $B \in \mathcal{B}$ by calling the decryption algorithm: BA.Decrypt($\mathrm{cap}_B, \{c_{i,B}\}_{i \in B}$). The sum of all these block estimates is an estimate of the total sum.

One possible optimization for decryption is to leverage the homomorphic property of the BA Scheme [14]. Instead of decrypting each individual block estimates, the aggregator can rely on the homomorphic property to compute an encryption of the sum of all block estimates. In this way, only one decryption operation is required to decrypt the estimated sum. As mentioned in Section 4.7 decryption takes $O(n)$ time using the brute-force approach, and $O(\sqrt{n})$ time using Pollard's Rho method.

This concludes the description of our Binary Protocol. Earlier in Section 4.1, we explained the intuition of the above Binary Protocol with a small-sized example. In the remainder of this section, we will focus on the privacy and utility analysis.

## 4.4 Theoretic Guarantees

Theorem 2 below states that our Binary Protocol satisfies computational $(\epsilon, \delta)$-differential privacy, and achieves an error bound of $\tilde{O}(\frac{(\log n)^{1.5}}{\epsilon} \sqrt{\frac{\kappa+1}{\gamma}})$ with high probability (hiding a $\log \log n$ factor and $\delta$, $\eta$ parameters). Here $\kappa$ is the number of failed users, and $\gamma$ is the fraction of users that remain uncompromised.

The intuition behind the proof was explained earlier in Section 4.1. Due to space constraint, we defer the full proof of this theorem to the online full version [2].

**Theorem 2 (Error Bound with $\kappa$-Failed Users).** *Let $\epsilon > 0$ and $0 < \delta < 1$. Suppose each of the $n$ users remains uncompromised independently with probability $\gamma$. Then, the Binary Protocol can be run such that it is computationally $(\epsilon, \delta)$-differentially private. Moreover, when there are $\kappa$ failed users, for $0 < \eta < 1$ subject to some technical condition[2], with probability at least $1 - \eta$, the aggregator can estimate the sum of the participating users' bits with additive error at most $O(\frac{(\log n)^{1.5}}{\epsilon} \cdot \sqrt{\frac{\kappa+1}{\gamma}} \cdot \sqrt{(\log \log n + \log \frac{1}{\delta}) \log \frac{1}{\eta}})$.*

### 4.5 Dynamic Joins

First, imagine that the system knows beforehand an upper-bound $n = 2^K$ on the total number of users – if $n$ is not a power of 2, assume we round it up to the nearest power of 2. We will later discuss the case when more than $n$ users actually join. In this case, when a new user $i$ joins, it needs to contact the trusted dealer and obtain a secret key $\mathsf{sk}_{i,B}$ for every block $B \in \mathcal{T}(n)$ that contains $i$. However, existing users need not be notified. In this case, the trusted dealer must be available to register newly joined users, but need not be online for the periodic aggregation phases. The trusted dealer may permanently erase a user's secret key (or the aggregator's capability) after its issuance.

What happens if more users join than the anticipated number $n = 2^K$? We propose 2 strategies below.

**Key Updates at Every Power of Two.** When the number of users exceeds the budget $n = 2^K$, the trusted dealer sets the new budget to be $n' := 2^{K+1}$, and issues new keys and capabilities to the users and aggregator as follows. For every new block $B$ that forms in $\mathcal{T}(n')$ but is not in $\mathcal{T}(n)$, a new secret key (or capaiblity) needs to be issued to every user contained in $B$ (and the aggregator). Notice that the secret keys for existing blocks in $\mathcal{T}(n)$ need not be updated. In this way, each existing user obtains one additional secret key, the newly joined user obtains $O(\log n)$ secret keys, and the aggregator obtains $O(n)$ capabilities. Notice that such key updates happen fairly infrequently, i.e., every time the number of users reach the next power of 2.

**Allocate a New Tree.** When the number of users reach the next power $2^K$ of two, the trusted dealer allocates a new tree of size $2^K$. For every block in the new tree, the trusted dealer issues a capability to the aggregator corresponding to that block. For the next $2^K$ users that join the system, each user is issued $O(K)$ secret keys corresponding to blocks in the new tree. Hence, the sizes of the trees are $1, 1, 2, 4, 8, \dots$ and so on.

When the aggregator estimates the sum, it will simply sum up the estimate corresponding to each tree. Suppose the number of current users is $n$. Then, there are $O(\log n)$ such trees. A straightforward calculation shows that the additive error made by the aggregator will be $\tilde{O}(\frac{(\log n)^3}{\epsilon})$ with high probability.

The advantage of this approach is that only the aggregator needs to be notified when the number of users changes. The existing users need not be notified. Therefore, this

---

[2] The following condition is satisfied certainly when $n$ is large enough: $\frac{(\kappa+1)\log_2 n}{\gamma} \ln \frac{\log_2 n}{\delta} \geq \exp(\frac{\epsilon}{\log_2 n}) \ln \frac{2}{\eta}$.

approach is particularly suited when making push notifications to users may be difficult (e.g., when users are frequently offline).

### 4.6 Dynamic Leaves

When a user leaves, that user can be treated as permanently failed. As mentioned in Theorem 2, the estimation error grows only sub-linearly in the number of absent users.

For reduced error and higher utility, sometimes we may consider repeating the setup phase when too many users have left. The application designer can make this choice to fit the characteristics and requirements of the specific application.

### 4.7 Practical Performance

Consider a scenario with $n \simeq 10,000$ users. The Binary Protocol leverages the BA Scheme scheme proposed by Shi *et al.* [14]. According to their performance estimates [14], each encryption takes about $0.6\ ms$ on a modern computer, when we use high-speed elliptic curves such as "curve25519". When $n \simeq 10,000$, each user needs to perform roughly $\lfloor \log_2 n \rfloor + 1 = 14$ encryptions. Therefore, a user's computation overhead is roughly $8 \sim 9\ ms$ on a modern computer.

Decryption of the underlying BA Scheme requires taking a discrete logarithm. The brute-force method involves enumerating the plaintext space. It takes one modular exponentiation, roughly $0.3\ ms$ to try each possible plaintext. With $n = 10,000$ users, our simulation shows that the additive error is under 500 with $> 99\%$ probability (when $\epsilon = 0.5$, $\delta = 0.05$, and in the absence of failures). Therefore, the brute-force method takes on average 1.5 seconds to decrypt the sum. We can speed up decryption significantly using one of the following methods: 1) Use Pollard's Rho method, which reduces the decryption overhead to about $\sqrt{n + o(n)}$. 2) Exploit parallelism. The brute-force method is trivially parallelizable, and particularly suited for modern clusters such as MapReduce or Hadoop.

## 5 Discussions

**Faster Decryption.** One limitation of the proposed scheme is that the decryption time is $O(\sqrt{n})$ using Pollard's Rho method. As a result, we need the plaintext space to be polynomially sized. While Sections 4.3 and 4.7 have proposed some methods to make decryption faster in practice, we also point out that another method would be to replace the encryption scheme entirely with the encryption scheme used by Rastogi *et al.* [13]. Basically, the binary tree method can be regarded as a generic approach which can be applied on top of both the works by Rastogi *et al.* [13] and Shi *et al.* [14]. If we use the scheme by Rastogi *et al.* [13] as a building block, we remove the constraint of polynomially-sized plaintext space, at the cost of introducing interactions between the users and the server (however, still, no peer-to-peer interaction would be needed).

**Operations in an Algebraic Group.** Due to the use of cryptography, integer additions are in fact performed in a discrete mathematical group of prime order $p$, which is needed by the encryption algorithm in the BA Scheme. Our error analysis also guarantees that with high probability, no integer overflow or underflow will happen.

## 6  Conclusion

We investigated how an untrusted aggregator can learn aggregate statistics about a group of users without harming each individual's privacy. Our construction addresses fault tolerance, a question left open by earlier works in this area [13,14]. Our construction is desirable in the sense that it requires no peer-to-peer communication (unlike the traditional approach of Secure Multi-Party Computation), and achieves high utility guarantees.

**Acknowledgments.** This work is partially supported by the National Science Foundation under Grants No. 0716230, 0448452 and CCF-0424422, and by the Office of Naval Research under MURI Grant No. N000140911081. Any opinions, findings, and conclusions or recommendations expressed in this material are those of the authors and do not necessarily reflect the views of the National Science Foundation, or the Office of Naval Research.

## References

1. Blum, A., Ligett, K., Roth, A.: A learning theory approach to non-interactive database privacy. In: STOC (2008)
2. Chan, H., Shi, E., Song, D.: Privacy-preserving stream aggregation with fault tolerance. Full online technical report (2011), http://eprint.iacr.org/2011/722.pdf
3. Chan, H., Shi, E., Song, D.: Tight lower bounds for distributed private data analysis (2011) (submission)
4. Hubert Chan, T.-H., Shi, E., Song, D.: Private and Continual Release of Statistics. In: Abramsky, S., Gavoille, C., Kirchner, C., Meyer auf der Heide, F., Spirakis, P.G. (eds.) ICALP 2010. LNCS, vol. 6199, pp. 405–417. Springer, Heidelberg (2010)
5. Dwork, C.: Differential Privacy. In: Bugliesi, M., Preneel, B., Sassone, V., Wegener, I. (eds.) ICALP 2006. LNCS, vol. 4052, pp. 1–12. Springer, Heidelberg (2006)
6. Dwork, C.: A firm foundation for private data analysis. Communications of the ACM (2010)
7. Dwork, C., Kenthapadi, K., McSherry, F., Mironov, I., Naor, M.: Our Data, Ourselves: Privacy Via Distributed Noise Generation. In: Vaudenay, S. (ed.) EUROCRYPT 2006. LNCS, vol. 4004, pp. 486–503. Springer, Heidelberg (2006)
8. Dwork, C., McSherry, F., Nissim, K., Smith, A.: Calibrating Noise to Sensitivity in Private Data Analysis. In: Halevi, S., Rabin, T. (eds.) TCC 2006. LNCS, vol. 3876, pp. 265–284. Springer, Heidelberg (2006)
9. Dwork, C., Naor, M., Pitassi, T., Rothblum, G.N.: Differential privacy under continual observation. In: STOC (2010)
10. Ghosh, A., Roughgarden, T., Sundararajan, M.: Universally utility-maximizing privacy mechanisms. In: STOC (2009)
11. Mironov, I., Pandey, O., Reingold, O., Vadhan, S.: Computational Differential Privacy. In: Halevi, S. (ed.) CRYPTO 2009. LNCS, vol. 5677, pp. 126–142. Springer, Heidelberg (2009)
12. Przydatek, B., Song, D., Perrig, A.: Sia: secure information aggregation in sensor networks. In: ACM Sensys (2003)
13. Rastogi, V., Nath, S.: Differentially private aggregation of distributed time-series with transformation and encryption. In: SIGMOD 2010, pp. 735–746 (2010)
14. Shi, E., Chan, H., Rieffel, E., Chow, R., Song, D.: Privacy-preserving aggregation of time-series data. In: NDSS (2011)
15. Whitney, L.: Microsoft urges laws to boost trust in the cloud, http://news.cnet.com/8301-1009_3-10437844-83.html

# Dynamic Accumulator Based Discretionary Access Control for Outsourced Storage with Unlinkable Access

## (Short Paper)

Daniel Slamanig

Department of Engineering and IT, Carinthia University of Applied Sciences,
Primoschgasse 10, 9020 Klagenfurt, Austria
d.slamanig@cuas.at

**Abstract.** In this paper we are interested in privacy preserving discretionary access control (DAC) for outsourced storage such as increasingly popular cloud storage services. Our main goal is to enable clients, who outsource data items, to delegate permissions (**read**, **write**, **delete**) to other clients such that clients are able to unlinkably and anonymously perform operations on outsourced data items when holding adequate permission. In contrast to recent approaches based on oblivious RAM, oblivious transfer combined with anonymous credentials or attribute based encryption, we propose a solution based on dynamic accumulators. In doing so, our approach naturally reflects the concept of access control lists (ACLs), which are a popular means to implement DAC.

## 1 Introduction

Ensuring confidentiality, integrity and authenticity when outsourcing organizational data(bases) to untrusted third parties has been a research topic for many years [7,10,12]. With the growing popularity of cloud computing, security in distributed access to data outsourced by "ordinary users" becomes also relevant. This is underpinned by the fact that so called cloud storage services increasingly gain in popularity. Besides confidentiality issues, i.e. for many types of data it may be valuable that the cloud provider (CP) solely has access to encrypted data but is still able to perform operations like searches on encrypted data [11], many recent works focus on more subtle privacy issues, i.e. unlinkable and potentially anonymous *access* to and *operations* on data stored in the cloud [3,4,9,13,14].

Some works [3,4,8] thereby focus on mandatory access control (MAC), i.e. access control policies for stored data are specified by the cloud provider, and others [9,14] on discretionary access control (DAC). In the latter scenario, clients can store data in the cloud and delegate access permissions to other clients - thereby specifying access control on their own - without the CP being able to determine who is sharing with whom, link operations (reads, writes) of clients together and to identify the users. Nevertheless, the CP can be sure that access control is enforced, i.e. clients need to have adequate permissions for the data.

A.D. Keromytis (Ed.): FC 2012, LNCS 7397, pp. 215–222, 2012.

**Our Contribution.** In the DAC setting, the access control in a system is enforced by a trusted reference monitor. A commonly used approach is to employ access control lists (ACLs), whereas every data item has its associated ACL representing a list of users with their corresponding permissions which can be modified dynamically. Thus, data owners can add or remove other users and their permissions to or from an ACL. A user who wants to perform an operation on a data item has to authenticate to the system and the reference monitor decides (using the corresponding ACL) whether he is allowed to perform the operation. It is straightforward to use pseudonyms in ACLs to hide the real identities of users in this setting. However, all operations of a user within the system can be linked to the user's pseudonym and achieving *unlinkability* is not that straightforward. We solve this problem and basically our approach is to stick with ACLs, but to "modify" ACLs in a way that the reference monitor 1) can still decide if a user is allowed to perform the operation, 2) users can delegate/revoke access rights to/from other users but 3) the reference monitor (CP) is *not able to identify users* as well as *link operations conducted by users together*.

We provide two solutions to this problem. The first solutions has the drawback that convincing the "reference monitor" of holding the respective permission has proof complexity $O(k)$, where $k$ is the number of authorized users. The key idea is to have one ACL for every type of permission and data item and the ACL contains commitments to "pseudonyms". A user essentially proves to the "reference monitor" that he possesses *one* valid pseudonym in the ACL without revealing which one. The second approach reduces the proof complexity to $O(1)$ and uses a similar idea, whereas ACLs are represented by cryptographic accumulators [1]. A cryptographic accumulator allows to represent a set by a single value (the accumulator) whose size is independent of the size of the set. For every accumulated value of this set one can compute a witness and having this witness one can prove in zero-knowledge that one holds a witness corresponding to one accumulated value without revealing which one. Dynamic accumulators [6] in addition allow an efficient update of an accumulator by adding elements to (and possibly deleting elements from) it along with efficient update of the remaining witnesses. In particular, our second construction relies on a dynamic accumulator with efficient updates proposed by Camenisch et al. in [5], whereas efficient updates mean that witnesses can be updated without the knowledge of accumulator-related secret information by any party.

## 2    Related Work and Background

In this section we briefly present three different approaches bearing some similarities with the one proposed in this paper, but employing entirely different building blocks. Then, we present the concept of dynamic accumulators.

**Anonymous Credentials.** Camenisch et al. [3,4] use anonymous credentials within oblivious transfer protocols to access items from a database at a server. Thereby, the server defines the access control policies but neither learns which items a user accesses nor which attributes or roles the user has. Still, he is able to enforce access control. An approach supporting complex access control policies such as the Brewer-Nash or the Bell-LaPadula model based on oblivious transfer and so called stateful anonymous credentials is proposed in [8].

**Oblivious RAM.** In [9], Franz et al. present an oblivious RAM (ORAM) based approach, which enables an owner of a database to outsource the database to an untrusted storage service. Thereby, the data owner can delegate read and write permissions to clients and clients can only perform operations on data items when they possess appropriate permissions. A key feature of their so called delegated ORAM solution is that the storage service does not learn how often data items are accessed by a user while access control is still enforced. Additionally, their approach employs symmetric encryption to provide data confidentiality. However, revocation of access rights is not explicitly realized. They propose to encrypt data items with a fresh key and to use broadcast encryption to distribute the key amongst all remaining authorized clients, which is rather involved.

**Attribute Based Encryption.** Very recently Zarandioon et al. [14] introduced K2C, an approach for hierarchical (file system like) cryptographic cloud storage, which can be implemented (like the approach presented here) on top of existing cloud services like Amazon S3[1]. Here, clients can organize their encrypted data items hierarchically at an untrusted storage provider and delegate `read` and `write` permissions to other clients. The approach is based on key-policy attribute based encryption (KP-ABE) and signatures from KP-ABE to provide anonymous access. Although quite elegant, the revocation of permissions in this approach, as above, requires re-encryption of data items w.r.t. updated policies and distribution of respective keys to all remaining authorized clients.

Re-encryption (even when using lazy revocation on write accesses) is a cumbersome task and we avoid this by guaranteeing that revoked clients will no longer be able to even read data items, since they will not be able to successfully pass the prove protocol with the "reference monitor" at the CP any longer.

**Dynamic Accumulator with Efficient Updates.** In our construction we make use of a dynamic accumulator with efficient updates introduced in [5]. Accumulatable values are in the set $\{1, \dots, n\}$, by $V$ we denote the set of values contained in the accumulator, $V_w$ represents status information about the accumulator, $state_U$ are state information containing some parameters for the accumulator and the set $U$ represents all elements that were ever accumulated. We provide an abstract definition below (see [5] for technical details):

AccGen($1^k, n$) generates an accumulator key pair $(sk, pk)$, an initially empty accumulator $acc_\emptyset$, which is capable of accumulating up to $n$ values, and an initial state $state_\emptyset$.

AccAdd($sk, i, acc_V, state_U$) adds value $i$ to the accumulator $acc_V$ and outputs a new accumulator $acc_{V \cup \{i\}}$, a state $state_{U \cup \{i\}}$ and a witness $wit_i$ for value $i$.

AccUpdate($pk, V, state_U$) outputs an accumulator $acc_V$ for values $V \subset U$.

---

[1] http://aws.amazon.com/s3/

AccWitUpdate($pk, wit_i, V_w, acc_V, V, state_U$) outputs a witness $wit_i'$ for $acc_V$ if $wit_i$ was a witness for $acc_{V_w}$ and $i \in V$.

AccVerify($pk, i, wit_i, acc_V$) verifies whether $i \in V$ using an actual witness $wit_i$ and accumulator $acc_V$. If this holds it outputs accept otherwise reject.

Note that the AccVerify algorithm among other parameters gets $(i, wit_i)$[2] and thus knows who "proves" that his corresponding value $i$ was indeed accumulated. Fortunately, dynamic accumulators are usually designed having in mind that they should come along with efficient proofs to prove in zero-knowledge that a value was accumulated without revealing the value itself.

**ZKP of Accumulated Value.** Camenisch et al. [5] provide an elegant and efficient ZKP for accumulated values. Therefore, instead of signing the values $i$ using an arbitrary signature scheme, one uses a variant of the weakly secure Boneh-Boyen signature scheme [2] (therefore the AccAdd algorithm has to be modified accordingly [5]). This in combination with a randomization technique allows a user to provide a proof of knowledge (PK) of a randomization value that allows to de-randomize a commitment to value $i$ such that $i$ was signed and $i$ is accumulated in $acc_V$. The PK can be made non-interactive using the Fiat-Shamir heuristic, whereas the corresponding signature of knowledge will be denoted as $spk$. Thus, we can modify the AccVerify algorithm to take input parameters $(pk, spk, acc_V)$ and this allows for verification without the necessity of revealing the value $i$ and the witness $wit_i$.

## 3    Implementing DAC with Unlinkable Access

In this section we present the model, a first (rather inefficient) construction and a detailed description of our main construction. Then, we comment on some aspects and briefly argue about the security.

**Model.** Let CP be a cloud provider who runs a cloud storage service, which allows clients $C = \{c_1, \ldots, c_n\}$ to store (outsource), retrieve and manipulate data items. Clients access data via a very simple interface as it is quite common in block oriented cloud storage services such as Amazon S3, i.e. storing key-value pairs and supporting the operations insert, read, write and delete. Now, the owner of a data item (the client who inserts the data into the cloud storage) should be able to delegate the permissions read, write and delete (r,w and d for short) for single data items to other clients and can also revoke all these permissions whenever necessary.

One main design goal is, that the CP "enforces" the access control, i.e. only allows an operation if the client is able to prove the possession of the respective permission, but at the same time is not able to link different operations of the clients together. Additionally, clients may also stay anonymous as we will discuss later on and will be clear from our construction. We assume that a client can establish a secure communication channel to an owner of data items and vice

---

[2] When instantiating the accumulator scheme of [5] the values $i$ are actually group elements $g_i$ and can either be made public or the values $g_i \| i$ are signed.

versa (for instance by sharing encrypted messages via Amazon's Simple Queue Service). Furthermore, we assume the CP to represent an honest but curious (passive) adversary and that the CP does not collude with clients.

**A First Approach.** To provide a better understanding, we begin with a first approach: Consider a data owner $c_m$, who wants to insert a data item $d_i$ at CP. He generates a key pair $(sk_{d_i}, pk_{d_i})$ of a signature scheme and chooses suitable random values $s_{m,i,r}, r_{m,i,r}$, $s_{m,i,w}, r_{m,i,w}$ and $s_{m,i,d}, r_{m,i,d}$ for an unconditionally hiding commitment scheme, i.e. Pedersen commitments. He computes the commitments $c_{m,i,r} = C(s_{m,i,r}, r_{m,i,r})$ as well as $c_{m,i,w}$ and $c_{m,i,d}$ and signs every single commitment using $sk_{d_i}$. Then he sends $d_i$, the verification key $pk_{d_i}$ along with the commitments and respective signatures to CP. CP checks whether the single signatures are valid and creates three empty ACLs, $ACL_{d_i,r}$, $ACL_{d_i,w}$ and $ACL_{d_i,d}$ for r, w and d permissions respectively and adds the commitments to the corresponding ACLs.

If $c_m$ wants to delegate a permission to another client $c_j$ for data item $d_i$, he simply chooses new random values $s_{j,i,x}, r_{j,i,x}$ for permission $x \in \{r, w, d\}$, computes and signs the commitments and requests CP to add the commitments to the respective ACLs (who accepts this if the signatures are valid). Then, he gives $(s_{j,i,x}, r_{j,i,x})$ as well as the parameters for the commitment scheme to $c_j$.

Assume a user wants to perform a r operation for data item $d_i$, then he has to retrieve the respective ACL $ACL_{d_i,r}$ (which we assume has $k$ entries) and perform an OR-composition of a ZKP of the opening of a commitment, i.e. $PK\{(\alpha, \beta) : \bigvee_{l=1}^{k}(c_{l,i,x} = C(\alpha, \beta))\}$. This proof is an efficient OR-composition of DL-representation proofs in case of Pedersen commitments, can easily be made non-interactive and succeeds if $c_j$ knows at least one opening for a commitment in $ACL_{d_i,r}$. If the verification of this proof succeeds, CP can allow the r operation for data item $d_i$, but is not able to identify $c_j$. Nor is CP able to link different operations of $c_j$ together due to employing zero-knowledge OR-proofs. Obviously, if there is only a single commitment in the ACL, then there will be no unlinkability. However, it is straightforward for the data owner to initially insert some dummy commitments into the ACLs, which will provide unlinkability - the CP cannot distinguish between such dummies and real users.

In order to revoke permission $x$ for $d_j$ for client $c_j$, the data owner simply provides the opening information of the commitment $(s_{j,i,x}, r_{j,i,x})$ along with the signature for the respective commitment to the CP. Then, the CP computes the commitment, checks the signature and if the verification holds removes the commitment from $ACL_{d_i,x}$.

**Our Main Construction.** The above presented approach is very simple, but has some drawbacks. Let $k$ be the number of clients in an ACL, then 1) the representation of every ACL has size $O(k)$, 2) clients have to retrieve $k$ commitments prior to every operation and most importantly 3) the proof complexity of client's OR-proofs is $O(k)$. In contrast, within the approach presented below all these complexities are $O(1)$ and thus independent of the number of clients. Before going into details, we provide an abstract description of the operations. The additional input $params_{\mathsf{Acc}}$ will be discussed subsequently.

Store($id_i, d_i$): The owner of data item $d_i$ identified by $id_i$ stores ($id_i, d_i$) at CP.

Delegate($c_j, id_i, per, params_{Acc}$): Delegate permission $per \in \{r, w, d\}$ for data item identified by $id_i$ to client $c_j$.

Revoke($c_j, id_i, per, params_{Acc}$): Revoke permission $per \in \{r, w, d\}$ for data item identified by $id_i$ for client $c_j$.

Read($id_i, params_{Acc}$): Read data item $d_i$ identified by $id_i$. If the client holds the corresponding permission, $d_i$ will be delivered, otherwise return $\bot$.

Write($id_i, d_i', params_{Acc}$): Modify data item $d_i$ identified by $id_i$ to $d_i'$. If the client has the corresponding permission, $d_i'$ will be written, otherwise return $\bot$.

Delete($id_i, params_{Acc}$): Delete data item $d_i$ identified by $id_i$. If the client has the corresponding permission, $d_i$ will be deleted, otherwise return $\bot$.

Below, we provide a more detailed description of the operations involved in our construction and the meaning of the parameters $params_{Acc}$:

**Store.** A data owner who wants to insert ($id_i, d_i$) at the CP needs to specify the maximum numbers of clients for every permission. Let us assume that he sets this number for $r$, $w$ and $d$ to $n$. Then he runs AccGen($1^k, n$) three times and obtains ($sk_{d_i,x}, pk_{d_i,x}, acc_{\emptyset,d_i,x}, state_{\emptyset,d_i,x}$) for $x \in \{r, w, d\}$ and adds himself (represented by value 1, the first accumulatable value) to all accumulators by running AccAdd($sk_{d_i,x}, 1, acc_{\emptyset,d_i,x}, state_{\emptyset,d_i,x}$) and sends ($id_i, d_i$) along with ($pk_{d_i,x}, acc_{\{1\},d_i,x}, state_{\{1\},d_i,x}$) and bookkeeping information $V_{d_i}, V_{w,d_i}$ to the CP. He stores $sk_{d_i,x}$, the witnesses $wit_{1,d_i,x}$ and $V_{d_i}, V_{w,d_i}$.

**Delegate.** A data owner who wants to delegate permission $x \in \{r, w, d\}$ for data item $d_i$ to client $c_j$ proceeds as follows: He parses $params_{Acc}$ (which can be retrieved from CP) as ($pk_{d_i,x}, acc_{V,d_i,x}, state_{U,d_i,x}$). Using $state_{U,d_i,x}$ he determines a value $z$ not already accumulated and obtains the updated accumulator $acc_{V \cup \{z\},d_i,x}$, updated state information $state_{U \cup \{z\},d_i,x}$ and a witness $wit_{z,d_i,x}$ by running AccAdd($sk_{d_i,x}, z, acc_{V,d_i,x}, state_{U,d_i,x}$). The data owner securely communicates ($z, wit_{z,d_i,x}$) to client $c_j$ and stores the signature part of $wit_{z,d_i,x}$ for revocation purposes. Then, he sends ($acc_{V,d_i,x}, state_{U,d_i,x}$) along with updated bookkeeping information to the CP.

**Revoke.** A data owner who wants to revoke permission $x \in \{r, w, d\}$ for data item $d_i$ and client $c_j$ proceeds as follows: The data owner parses $params_{Acc}$ as $z$, where $z$ represents the value accumulated for $c_j$ in $acc_{V,d_i,x}$. Then he sends $z$ along with the signature for the corresponding witness to CP, who checks the signature. If the verification holds, CP runs AccUpdate($pk_{d_i,x}, V \setminus \{z\}, state_{U,d_i,x}$) and stores the resulting accumulator $acc_{V \setminus \{z\},d_i,x}$, otherwise CP terminates.

**Read/Write/Delete.** A client who wants to perform operation $x \in \{r, w, d\}$ for data item $d_i$ first parses $params_{Acc}$ as ($pk_{d_i,x}, wit_{d_i,x}, V_w, acc_{V,d_i,x}, V, state_{U,d_i,x}$). Then he has to check whether the accumulator $acc_{V,d_i,x}$ has changed, i.e. a new client was added or a client was revoked. If this is the case, the user has to run AccWitUpdate($pk_{d_i,x}, wit_{d_i,x}, V_w, acc_{V,d_i,x}, V, state_{U,d_i,x}$) to compute the updated witness $wit_{d_i,x}'$. Then, he uses the actual witness to compute a signature of knowledge $spk$ to prove that the value corresponding to the witness was accumulated. He then sends $spk$ to CP and the CP runs AccVerify($pk_{d_i,x}, spk, acc_{V,d_i,x}$).

If it returns `accept`, then CP depending on the operation either delivers $d_i$ to the client (`read`), overwrites $d_i$ with $d_i'$ provided by the client (`write`) or deletes $d_i$ along with corresponding accumulators and bookkeeping information (`delete`) and terminates otherwise.

**Remark.** Delegate and Revoke operations need to be authorized, since otherwise "ACLs" could be maliciously manipulated. We have omitted this above, but this can be efficiently realized by signing the values sent to the CP at the end of the two above mentioned operations. For the sake of convenience and efficiency, the data owner can use the Boneh-Boyen signature scheme whose respective keys are part of the private and public key of the accumulator respectively.

**Confidentiality and Integrity of Stored Data.** When storing encrypted data, all that data owners have to do is to additionally send the respective encryption key along with the witness to the user. Note that we do not require re-encryption (as in [9,14]) since revoked users will no longer be able to access data items. To provide integrity verification, one can store signatures or HMACs along with data items and distribute the keys together with the witnesses to clients.

**Security Analysis.** First, we consider *security against malicious clients*: All clients other than the data owner do not know $sk_{d_i,x}$. Thus they will not succeed in producing new witnesses, i.e. authorizing unauthorized clients, or trigger unauthorized Delegate or Revoke operations to manipulate the accumulator. Consequently, clients can only perform operations on data objects with permissions they have been granted. Secondly, we consider *security against a curious CP*: The CP does not learn the identities of clients (when they obtain a permission, they are only identified by the value to be accumulated - which is unrelated to their identity). Furthermore, due to employing ZKPs in the AccVerify protocol to prove the possession of witnesses, the respective witnesses and corresponding values are not disclosed. Consequently, clients conduct operations in an unlinkable and anonymous fashion.

## 4   Extensions and Future Work

**Hierarchical Delegation.** It may be desirable to augment simple DAC in a way that clients who have obtained permissions for some data from a data owner are able to delegate the obtained permissions for this data to further clients on their own. But then, data owners very likely would like to recursively revoke granted permission. For instance, if the data owner has provided permission $x$ to client $c_i$ and $c_i$ has granted permission $x$ to $c_j$, then revoking permission $x$ for $c_i$ should immediately imply revoking permission $x$ for $c_j$. This can be realized as follows: If the data owner wants to allow further delegation for a specific data item, permission $x$ and client $c_i$, he simply gives $m$ witnesses to this client and remembers the corresponding values and signatures. Client $c_i$ can then delegate $m-1$ permissions $x$ to other clients (or give other clients more witnesses for further delegation). If the data owner revokes the permission $x$ for client $c_i$, then he simply "removes" all $m$ witnesses from the respective accumulator.

Discretionary access control is an admittedly simple but often sufficient access control model. Especially when outsourcing data to popular cloud storage services, such an access control model is reasonable and can be deployed quite easily. Due to increasing privacy demands, a mechanism - as the one proposed in this paper - can be valuable. We leave the gathering of practical experiences when deploying our construction in this scenario as important future work.

**Acknowledgements.** We thank the anonymous reviewers for their helpful feedback on the paper. This work has been supported by an internal grant (zentrale Forschungsförderung - ZFF) of the Carinthia University of Applied Sciences.

# References

1. Benaloh, J.C., de Mare, M.: One-Way Accumulators: A Decentralized Alternative to Digital Signatures (Extended Abstract). In: Helleseth, T. (ed.) EUROCRYPT 1993. LNCS, vol. 765, pp. 274–285. Springer, Heidelberg (1994)
2. Boneh, D., Boyen, X.: Short Signatures Without Random Oracles. In: Cachin, C., Camenisch, J. (eds.) EUROCRYPT 2004. LNCS, vol. 3027, pp. 56–73. Springer, Heidelberg (2004)
3. Camenisch, J., Dubovitskaya, M., Neven, G.: Oblivious Transfer with Access Control. In: ACM Conference on Computer and Communications Security, pp. 131–140. ACM (2009)
4. Camenisch, J., Dubovitskaya, M., Neven, G., Zaverucha, G.M.: Oblivious Transfer with Hidden Access Control Policies. In: Catalano, D., Fazio, N., Gennaro, R., Nicolosi, A. (eds.) PKC 2011. LNCS, vol. 6571, pp. 192–209. Springer, Heidelberg (2011)
5. Camenisch, J., Kohlweiss, M., Soriente, C.: An Accumulator Based on Bilinear Maps and Efficient Revocation for Anonymous Credentials. In: Jarecki, S., Tsudik, G. (eds.) PKC 2009. LNCS, vol. 5443, pp. 481–500. Springer, Heidelberg (2009)
6. Camenisch, J., Lysyanskaya, A.: Dynamic Accumulators and Application to Efficient Revocation of Anonymous Credentials. In: Yung, M. (ed.) CRYPTO 2002. LNCS, vol. 2442, pp. 61–76. Springer, Heidelberg (2002)
7. Ciriani, V., De Capitani di Vimercati, S., Foresti, S., Jajodia, S., Paraboschi, S., Samarati, P.: Fragmentation and Encryption to Enforce Privacy in Data Storage. In: Biskup, J., López, J. (eds.) ESORICS 2007. LNCS, vol. 4734, pp. 171–186. Springer, Heidelberg (2007)
8. Coull, S.E., Green, M., Hohenberger, S.: Access Controls for Oblivious and Anonymous Systems. ACM Trans. Inf. Syst. Secur. 14(1), 10 (2011)
9. Franz, M., Williams, P., Carbunar, B., Katzenbeisser, S., Peter, A., Sion, R., Sotakova, M.: Oblivious Outsourced Storage with Delegation. In: Danezis, G. (ed.) FC 2011. LNCS, vol. 7035, pp. 127–140. Springer, Heidelberg (2012)
10. Hacigümüs, H., Mehrotra, S., Iyer, B.R.: Providing Database as a Service. In: ICDE. IEEE (2002)
11. Kamara, S., Lauter, K.: Cryptographic Cloud Storage. In: Sion, R., Curtmola, R., Dietrich, S., Kiayias, A., Miret, J.M., Sako, K., Sebé, F. (eds.) FC 2010 Workshops. LNCS, vol. 6054, pp. 136–149. Springer, Heidelberg (2010)
12. Mykletun, E., Narasimha, M., Tsudik, G.: Authentication and Integrity in Outsourced Databases. In: NDSS. The Internet Society (2004)
13. Williams, P., Sion, R., Carbunar, B.: Building Castles out of Mud: Practical Access Pattern Privacy and Correctness on Untrusted Storage. In: ACM Conference on Computer and Communications Security, pp. 139–148. ACM (2008)
14. Zarandioon, S., Yao, D(D.), Ganapathy, V.: K2C: Cryptographic Cloud Storage with Lazy Revocation and Anonymous Access. In: Rajarajan, M., et al. (eds.) SecureComm 2011. LNICST, vol. 96, pp. 59–76. Springer, Heidelberg (2012)

# Privacy Enhanced Access Control
# for Outsourced Data Sharing

Mariana Raykova, Hang Zhao, and Steven M. Bellovin

Columbia University, Department of Computer Science,
New York, NY 10027-7003, USA
{mariana,zhao,smb}@cs.columbia.edu

**Abstract.** Traditional access control models often assume that the entity enforcing access control policies is also the owner of data and resources. This assumption no longer holds when data is outsourced to a third-party storage provider, such as the *cloud*. Existing access control solutions mainly focus on preserving confidentiality of stored data from unauthorized access and the storage provider. However, in this setting, access control policies as well as users' access patterns also become privacy sensitive information that should be protected from the cloud. We propose a two-level access control scheme that combines coarse-grained access control enforced at the cloud, which provides acceptable communication overhead and at the same time limits the information that the cloud learns from his partial view of the access rules and the access patterns, and fine-grained cryptographic access control enforced at the user's side, which provides the desired expressiveness of the access control policies. Our solution handles both *read* and *write* access control.

## 1 Introduction

The emerging trend of outsourcing of data storage at third parties – "cloud storage" – has recently attracted tremendous amount of attention from both research and industry communities. Outsourced storage makes shared data and resources much more accessible as users can retrieve them anywhere from personal computers to smart phones. This alleviates data owner from the burden of data management and leaves this task to service providers with dedicated resources and more advanced techniques. By adopting the cloud computing solution, government agencies will drastically save budget and increase productivity by utilizing low-cost and maintenance-free services available on the Internet rather than purchasing, designing and installing new IT infrastructure themselves. Similar benefits could be realized in financial services, health care, education, etc [10].

Security remains the critical issue that concerns potential clients, especially for the banks and government sectors. A major challenge for any comprehensive access control solution for outsourced data is the ability to handle requests for resources according to the specified security policies to achieve confidentiality, and at the same time protect the users' privacy. Several solutions have been proposed in the past [6,8,12,13,15], but none of them considers protecting privacy

A.D. Keromytis (Ed.): FC 2012, LNCS 7397, pp. 223–238, 2012.

of the policies and users' access patterns as an essential goal. In this paper we address these privacy requirements and propose a mechanism to achieve a flexible level of privacy guarantee for the client. We introduce a two-level access control model that combines *fine-grained access control*, which supports the precise granularity for access rules, and *coarse-grained access control*, which allows the storage provider to manage access requests while learning only limited information from its inputs. This is achieved by arranging outsourced resources into units called *access blocks* and enforcing access control at the cloud only at the granularity of blocks. The fine-grained access control within each access block is enforced at the user's site and remains oblivious to the cloud. The mapping between files and access blocks is transparent to the users in the sense that they can submit file requests without knowing in what blocks the files are contained. While most existing solutions [2,13,15] focus on read request, we present a solution that provides both *read and write access control*.

## 1.1 Motivation

Traditional access control models often make an implicit assumption that the entity enforcing access control policies is also the owner of data. However, in many cases of distributed computing, this assumption no longer holds, and access control policies are enforced at points which should not have direct access to the data content itself, such as data outsourced to an untrusted third party. Hence we need to store data in encrypted form and enforce access control over the encrypted data. The setting of cloud computing falls into this category. The cloud servers are considered to be *honest* but *curious*. They will follow our proposed protocol in general, but try to find out as much information as possible based on their inputs. Hence data confidentiality is not the only security concern. Privacy becomes one of the major reasons that drives big companies to build their own private cloud infrastructure rather than making use of the public cloud services.

First of all, access control policies defined by the data owner that govern who can have access to what data become private information with respect to the storage provider. For example, suppose that a business newspaper reports that a secretive company has just hired a new top-level executive who has specialized in a particular field. By watching what other organizations in the company – perhaps first research, then development, then procurement and manufacturing – share access groups with this executive, an observer can learn significant details about the company's strategy and progress. This is similar to what military intelligence agencies do when using traffic analysis to determine an enemy's order of battle [7]. In fact, protecting access rules against privacy leakage is a long-standing problem, and has been studied a lot in the past especially for enforcing access control in databases [3]. This problem is mitigated by the use of cryptography as an enforcement mechanism, which translates the access control problem into the question of key management for decryption keys.

A more challenging task, that cannot be solved by data encryption alone, is to protect data access patterns from careful observations on the inputs of the storage provider. Even if data is stored and transferred in an encrypted format, traffic analysis techniques can reveal privacy sensitive information. For example, analysis on the length of encrypted traffic could reveal certain properties of the enclosed data; access history could disclose a particular user's access habits and privileges; access to the same data object from multiple users could suggest a common interest or collaborative relationship; a ranking of data popularity can also be built upon access requests that the cloud receives. One trivial solution is to return all encrypted data upon any access request. However, this comes with prohibitive communication costs for data transfer as well as storage and computation costs for decryption at the user's side, which rules out this obvious solution. The question of hiding access pattern is challenging while avoiding work proportional to the total size of all stored files. There have been several cryptographic solutions that realize the notion of oblivious RAM and manage to achieve improved amortized complexity for queries while hiding access patterns [4,11,1,5]. However, such solutions are highly interactive and still require communication polylogarithmic in the size of the database, which in the setting of large storage cloud providers, weak client devices and expensive network communication will not be practical (e.g., wireless network communication with limited bandwidth). Furthermore, they assume that the user submitting the query is the owner of all data, which does not fit into our scenario where access control is enforced on data shared by multiple users, not limited to the data owner.

An equally important, but often overlooked, aspect of access control for outsourced data is to enforce the *write* access. Existing solutions often handle only read requests, which is obviously impractical in a more flexible data sharing scenario. For example, co-workers contribute to the same project document in a collaborative working environment. While data encryption naturally preserves authorization of the read access through key management, the procession of a decryption key implies authorized read access but not necessarily the write. Therefore, different cryptographic schemes are mandatory to manage read and write accesses separately. Further, a full-fledged access control solution should assume no relationship between read and write access rules (a user may have both types of access, only one of them or none).

Therefore we summarize that a privacy-aware access control solution for data sharing in outsourced storage needs to meet the following requirements:

1. it provides data confidentiality by implementing a fine-grained cryptographic access control mechanism;
2. it supports practical and flexible data sharing scheme by handling both read and write operations in the access control model;
3. it enhances data and user privacy by protecting access control rules and access patterns from the storage provider.

# 2 Two-Level Access Control Model – Solution Overview

We consider the following scenario: a set of users outsource their data to a remote storage (cloud) provider. These users further would like to be able to share selectively some of their data among themselves. This data sharing should be enabled directly at the cloud through appropriate access control rules that allow users to retrieve all data that they are authorized to access (i.e. not involving the actual data owner). Further, the access control rules governing the data sharing and the data that users access are private information of the users and our goal will be to protect this information from the cloud provider.

We distinguish the following three roles in this access control model: the *data owner* who creates data to be stored at the remote storage in an encrypted format and regulates who has what access to each part of the data; the *data user* who may have read and write access to the protected data; the *cloud provider* that stores the encrypted data and responds to access requests. While a solution that enforces access control solely through encryption of the data and appropriate decryption key distribution can achieve complete privacy for the access patterns and access control rules by allowing users to retrieve the whole encrypted database, such an approach will be completely impractical requiring an enormous amount of communication. We suggest a hybrid solution that offers a way to trade off privacy and efficiency guarantees. The basic idea behind it is to provide two levels of access control: *coarse-grained* and *fine-grained*. The coarse-grained level access control will be enforced explicitly by the cloud provider and it would also represent the granularity at which he will learn the access pattern of users. Even though the cloud provider will learn the access pattern over all user requests, he will not be able to distinguish requests from different users, which would come in the form of anonymous tokens. The fine-grained access control will be enforced obliviously to the cloud through encryption and would prevent him from differentiating requests that result in the same coarse-grained access control decision but have different fine-grained access pattern.

We realize the above two levels of access control by introducing division of the data resources of the same owner into units called *access blocks*, which would represent the coarse-level granularity in the system. Now the cloud provider would be able to map user requests to the respective access blocks containing the relevant data only if the user has access to the requested data and without learning which part of the block is accessed. The provider would also not learn the reason for no match: missing data or no access authorization. Our solution does not require users to know the exact access blocks that would contain the data they are searching for. Files might be moved between different blocks, and the only information that users would need in order to request them will be a unique file identifier rather than the id of the current block where the file is residing. We will enable this oblivious mapping of files to blocks using techniques from predicate encryption and some extensions to the scheme [9]. Once a user retrieves the content of the matching block, he would be able to decrypt only the part of the block, which he is authorized to access. We use the ideas of [13] to minimize the decryption keys that need to be distributed for fine-grained access control within access blocks.

While the above suffices for read access control, handling write access control is a little more subtle. The main issue there is that the cloud would need to allow users to submit updates for different parts of an access block without learning which part are updated, and at the same time prevent users authorized to write to one file in the block from writing to another file. In order to facilitate this functionality the cloud provider would accept write updates for blocks only from users that provide tokens granting them write access to some part of the block (not revealing which part). These updates will be appended to the content of the block but also the cloud would obliviously tag the updates with the id of the file for which the user has been authorized, but without learning which this file is. We achieve this functionality again through a modification of the searchable ciphertexts in a predicate encryption scheme.

# 3    Read Access Control

In this section, we present in detail the two-level access control scheme for read access only after describing the following techniques applied in our protocol.

## 3.1    Techniques

**Fine-Grained Access Control.** Fine-grained access control is applied to files inside each access block to explicitly enforce access control rules. While the cloud provider is able to determine whether a user submits a legitimate request for some file within a block, he should remain oblivious to the access control rules defined for that file. To guarantee this property the access control view presented to the cloud treats blocks as entities, and the cloud grants a read access by providing the content of an entire block. Fine-grained access control is enforced by encrypting files per block under different keys, and the access control problem is mitigated to appropriate key distribution. Even a user receives the encrypted content of a block, he is able to decrypt only the files that he has access to. Access revocation requires re-encryption of the resource and re-distribution of the new key to the remaining authorized users. Our goal is to minimize the amount of work and interaction between users and the system upon policy updates.

The work of [13] proposes an encryption-based access control solution for outsourced data. Their key distribution is facilitated by the construction of a public tree structure that allows each user to derive file decryption keys using a secret, which he establishes once in the beginning. The leaf nodes in the tree represent initial secrets distributed to users when they join the system, and the internal nodes denote the file decryption keys derivable from leaf nodes using public tokens along a directed path. Any update of the access control rules entails a change in the tree. Access revocation requires re-encryption of affected files.

In our scheme, each user generates a public-private key pair, and the public key is used by data owners as initial secret to construct trees. Hence each user only needs to maintain one key in the system and the distribution of leaf nodes is implicit through the asymmetric key scheme. If some resources are only accessible by a single user, instead of encrypting files using a leaf node (i.e., the public key), we generate a symmetric key for file encryption, which is further encrypted under that public key to avoid expensive computation of asymmetric scheme. In that case, the initial secret needs to be explicitly distributed to an authorized user. Unlike in [13], key derivation tokens have to be protected. First a user's initial secret is generally available to anyone in the system. More importantly, the tree structure itself can reveal certain sensitive information to the cloud. For example, a user having access to one file will have access to all the files along a directed path. So the ontent of each node, a pointer to next node and the token to derive next key are all protected under the current encryption key. Thus we can achieve efficient key distribution without requiring any direct interaction between data owners and users beyond some initial set-up assuming only the cloud will be online all the time. A list of algorithms for key distribution and management are summarized in Figure 1.

- **Publish**$(r, o, e_o, acl)$: adds a resource $r$ owned by $o$ with a secret $e_o$ and an access control list $acl = acl\_read(r)$ for read access.
- **Access_Read**$(u, r, o)$: returns the encryption key for a resource $r$ owned by $o$, if $u$ is an authorized user.
- **Find_Chain**$(u, r)$: finds the shortest chain of tokens from the secret key of user $u$ to derive the decryption key for resource $r$.
- **Compute_Key**$(u, chain)$: derives the secret key for a user $u$ given a chain of transition tokens.
- **Find_Resources**$(u, r)$: finds the set of nodes that lie on any path from the user $u$ to the node corresponding to resource $r$.
- **Update**$(r, acl)$: if there is another resource with the same access control list $acl$, i.e., there is a node in the tree accessable exactly by a subset of users in $acl$, then encrypt $r$ with the key contained in that node. Otherwise, encrypt $r$ with a new key, add a new node containing this key to the tree and add appropriate edges to connect the new node to the users who have access to $r$. (Note that certain subgroups of the users in $acl$ might already have a shared key through another node in tree, and in that case we connect to that node rather than all the users' nodes separately.)

**Fig. 1.** Algorithms for key distribution and management for fine-grained AC

**Coarse-Grained Access Control.** The main goal to achieve at the level of coarse-grained access control is to enable the cloud provider to obliviously match a user's request to an access block without learning which part of the block the user is authorized to access. In addition we provide *unlinkability* among multiple requests for the same resource even if coming from the same user, which further protects users' access patterns from the cloud provider. In order to achieve these goals we apply the predicate encryption scheme of [9]. Observing that in this scheme ciphertext can be re-randomized even without knowledge of the secret key, we define a re-randomization algorithm in Definition 1.

**Definition 1.** *A re-randomizable predicate encryption scheme consists of the following algorithms:*

- Setup($1^n$): *produces a master secret key SK and public parameters;*
- Enc$_{SK}(x)$: *encrypts an attribute x using key SK;*
- GenKey$_{SK}(f)$: *generate a decryption key $SK_f$ associated with a function f;*
- Dec$_{SK_f}(c)$: *outputs 1 if the attribute encrypted in $c = $ Enc$_{SK}(x)$ satisfies f, i.e. $f(x) = 1$, and output a random value, otherwise;*
- Rand($c$): *computes a new encryption $c'$ of the value encrypted in c but with different randomness* without the secret key.

We present the predicate encryption scheme of [9] and the instantiation of the function Rand($c$) for that scheme in Appendix A. This scheme handles a class of functions $f$, which includes polynomials of bounded degree. We use polynomial functions of the type $f(x) = (x - id_1) \cdots (x - id_n)$, to implement coarse-grained access control. Figure 2 present a list of algorithms to enforce access control on the block level granularity without revealing the exact files that are being accessed insider a block. The algorithm **File_Access_Check** grants access if the submitted access token matches any of the files in the block without revealing the file identity. The request token produced by **File_Access_Request** is an encryption that does not leak information about the file id it contains.

---

- **Block_Access_Setup:** data owner runs $Setup(1^n)$, publishes the public parameters and keeps the master secret key $SK$. For files $id_1, \ldots, id_n$ in each block, he computes $SK_f = $ GenKey$_{SK}(f)$ for $f(x) = (x-id_1)\cdots(x-id_n)$ and sends $SK_f$ to the cloud provider.
- **File_Access_Authorization:** data owner provides access to a file $id$ by sending $c_{id} = $ Enc$_{SK}(id)$ to an authorized user.
- **File_Access_Request:** user generates a token $t_{id} = $ Rand($c_{id}$) for file $id$.
- **File_Access_Check:** upon receiving a request token $t$, the cloud computes Dec$_{SK_f}(t)$ for each block, and returns those blocks that compute to 1.

---

**Fig. 2.** Algorithms for enforcing coarse-grained AC at the access block level

## 3.2 Read Access Control

We present a read access control solution consisting of the following algorithms. Unless explicitly stated, all the actions are performed by individual data owners.

- **System Setup:** At the *fine-grained level*, files are distributed into access blocks. Generate a tree graph per block by running **Publish**($r, o, e_o, acl$) for each resource $r$ owned by $o$ with initial ACLs, and encrypt resources using keys from the tree graph. At the *coarse-grained level*, each data owner computes parameters for a predicate encryption scheme. Then he constructs a separate tree graph over all resources he owns to distribute authorization tokens of the form $c_{id} = $ Enc$_{PK}(id)$ (i.e., now tree nodes contain authorizations tokens rather than file decryption keys). Finally, data owner computes a key $SK_f = $ GenKey$_{SK}(f)$ per block where $f$ is the polynomial derived from the ids of the files contained in that block as described above, and gives this key to the cloud provider, which will use it to obliviously check read access on authorization tokens.

– **Access Authorization:** At the *fine-grained level*, add a leaf node containing the new user's public key to the corresponding tree graph with encryption keys. Update the graph by adding new internal nodes and appropriate edges if necessary. Update file encryptions if new internal nodes were added previously. At the *coarse-grained level*, perform similar operations with respect to the tree graph containing read access tokens.

– **Access Request:** At the *fine-grained level*, an authorized user $u$ derives the decryption key from the tree graph for resource $r$ by calling **Find_Chain**$(u, r)$, **Find_Resources** $(u, r)$ and **Compute_Key**$(u, chain)$. At the *coarse-grained level*, he calls the same set of functions but to query the tree graph with access tokens and find token $c_{id} = \text{Enc}_{SK}(id)$ for the requested file $id$, and then submit a randomized token $t_{id} = \text{Rand}(c_{id})$ to the cloud.

– **Access Check:** At the *fine-grained level*, only authorized users can derive the correct decryption key for any file using the public tree structure. At the *coarse-grained level*, the cloud provider executes **File_Access_Check** to identify the block that contains the requested file.

– **Access Rule Update:** At the *fine-grained level*, changes are applied immediately upon policy updates. If the policy update involves access revocation, the data owner changes the encryption of corresponding files. The data owner identifies the blocks affected by those files and updates their tree graphs with decryption keys. The changes at the *coarse-grained level* happen at longer intervals of time, the length of which would depend on the resources of the data owner. They involve updating of the tree graph with access tokens.

## 4   Write Access Control

Enforcing write access control presents more challenges, mainly for the fact that access control through data encryption does not apply to cases when data can be modified. Without revealing fine-grained access control policies, it is not guaranteed that a user will modify only files that he is granted write access to. An unauthorized user can overwrite and destroy data without being detected by the cloud, regardless of whether he has the read privilege. A trivial solution is to rely on the cloud provider to restrict the memory regions to which users may submit changes, which however reveals to the cloud access rules and access patterns.

The approach that we adopt is to record modifications of files in new regions of memory without overwriting previous content. The coarse-grained access control enforced by the cloud allows users to submit changes for files only if they can demonstrate write permission for some resource in that block, without revealing the exact content to be changed. At the fine-grained level, a public encryption scheme is used to separate read and write privileges by providing a key pair for each file. The only information that the cloud tags to each file change obliviously contains implicit information on file identifier. However, using a submitted write authorization token directly as an update identifier will enable users with only read access to copy and reuse it later to obtain write privilege. To prevent this undesired situation, we take advantage of the predicate encryption ciphertexts constituting access tokens, which allows us to use part of the token as identifier. We generate predicate that allows users with read access to identify relevant updates, but this identifier on its own is not sufficient to grant write access.

### 4.1   Techniques

**File Encryption.** We apply an asymmetric encryption scheme to handle all possible combinations of read and write access to a file. Since such scheme is computationally expensive for large size of data, file content is still encrypted using a symmetric key (e.g., AES), which is further encrypted under the public key. Two trees are constructed for key distribution per block – one for the public (encryption) keys and the other for the private (decryption) keys. These two trees share the same set of internal nodes for an one to one correspondence between public and private key pair. Only files readable and writable by the same set of users can share the same public key pair.

**Access Authorization Tokens.** Two trees are constructed by each data owner for the distribution of read and write access tokens respectively.

**File Identifiers for Write Updates.** We observe that the write authorization token is a valid encryption for a predicate encryption that provides polynomials evaluation, and the structure of the encrypted plaintext for access to file $id$ is a vector of the form $(1, id, id^2, \ldots, id^n)$, where $n$ is the number of files placed in a block. The structure of the ciphertext allows it to be split into parts where one part is an encryption of the vector $(1, id, id^2, \ldots, id^k)$ ($k < n$, $n > 2$), which is no longer a valid write access token for that file, but can still be used identify file updates for users with read privilege. This can be achieved using a decryption predicate for a polynomial of degree $k$ that has $id$ as a zero point. (See Appendix A for details.)

### 4.2   Integrated Read and Write Access Control

We realize the above proposal for the write access control enforcement and describe an integrated solution for both read and write access. Because of space constraints we describe only the functionality associated with write access enforcement. The read access is the same as the construction in the previous section with the exception that once a client has retrieved a block he needs to identify both the original encryption of the file as well as all updates for that file. The latter will be achieved using an additional key (a new part in his authorization token) that will allow him to identify the valid updates submitted for that file.

– **Setup:** At the *fine-grained level*, construct a key distribution tree per block based on read access rules. For each node in the tree, generate a public-private key pair $(sk_n, pk_n)$, but only store the secret key $sk_n$. Construct another tree with the same set of nodes to store the public key $pk_n$, with edges determined by write access rule. For each file $id$ generate a AES key $sk_{id}^{aes}$ for encryption, and append to the ciphertext $\text{Enc}_{pk_n}(sk_{id}^{aes})$. At the *coarse-grained level*, each data owner generates two sets of parameters $(pk', sk')$ and $(pk'', sk'')$ for the predicate encryption. Then he constructs a tree graph, where each node contains read access token $\text{Enc}_{pk'_{ra}}(id)$ (used by the cloud provider to check the read access) and $SK_{x-id} = \text{GenKey}_{sk''_{ra}}(f)$ where $f(x) = x - id$ (used by the user to identify all updates to the file within the retrieved block). Similarly, construct another tree to distribute write access tokens $\text{Enc}_{pk_{wa}}(id)$.

– **Access Authorization:** At the *coarse-grained level*, extend the trees with read and write access tokens with new leaves for the new user and update the edges according to his read and write permissions. This may involve splitting of nodes and re-encrypting files with new keys if the user has read access only to a subset of files that have been encrypted with the same key.

– **Write Access Request:** At the *fine-grained level*, obtain the encryption key $pk_n$ for the file to be updated from the write tree. Encrypt the new content for that file with key $pk_n$. At the *coarse-grained level*, submit to the cloud a re-randomized copy of the write authorization token for that file.

– **Write Access Check:** At the *fine-grained level*, a user can modify a file only if he has the encryption key and the write authorization token. Upon read he will check at the end of a block a list of updates with valid write access tokens. At the *coarse-grained level*, the cloud finds if there is a block for which the authorization token grants write access. The write access token is of the form $(C_0, \{C_{1,i}, C_{2,i}\}_{i=1}^n)$, and the cloud uses the first components $(C_0, \{C_{1,i}, C_{2,i}\}_{i=1}^2)$ as an identifier for updates appended to a block.

– **Write Access Rule Update:** Update per-block trees for encryption keys and the tree for distributing write access tokens accordingly.

### 4.3   An Example

To facilitate our discussion, consider a system with five users $U = \{A, B, C, D, E\}$. Let $R_o$ denote the set of resources owner by user $o \in U$, and we have $R_A = \{r_1, r_2, r_3, r_4\}$, $R_B = \{r_5, r_6, r_7\}$ and $R_C = R_D = R_E = \emptyset$. Access control lists (ACLs) are used to represent fine-grained level access policies, and the owner of each resource automatically entails both read and write access privilege. At the coarse-grained level, user $A$ maintains two blocks $b_1 = \{r_1, r_2\}$ and $b_2 = \{r_3, r_4\}$, and user $B$ maintains a single block $b_3 = \{r_5, r_6, r_7\}$.

1. $acl\_read(r_1) = \{A, B, C\}$, $acl\_write(r_1) = \{A, B, C\}$;
2. $acl\_read(r_2) = \{A, B, C\}$, $acl\_write(r_2) = \{A, B, C\}$;
3. $acl\_read(r_3) = \{A, E\}$, $acl\_write(r_3) = \{A\}$;
4. $acl\_read(r_4) = \{A, B, C, E\}$, $acl\_write(r_4) = \{A, D\}$;

5. $acl\_read(r_5) = \{A, B\}$, $acl\_write(r_5) = \{A, B, C\}$;
6. $acl\_read(r_6) = \{B, C, D\}$, $acl\_write(r_6) = \{B, D, E\}$;
7. $acl\_read(r_7) = \{A, B, C, D, E\}$, $acl\_write(r_7) = \{A, B, C, D, E\}$.

Follow the above example, two trees are constructed per block for read and write access respectively at the fine-grained level in Figure 3. Each block stores files owned by a single user (shaded), and a public key pair is generated for each contained resource $r_i$, where $sk_{id}$ is stored in the read tree and $pk_{id}$ in the write tree. Leaf nodes $v_{1n}^{*j}$ store users' initial public keys, which are connected to internal nodes following key derivation paths (think links). Each row in the table states $r_i$ in block $b_j$ is associated with key $sk_{id}$ ($pk_{id}$) at vertex $v_{mn}^{Rj}$ ($v_{mn}^{Wj}$). Different ACLs on read and write for the same resource entail different labels of user list, e.g., $v_{31}^{R2}$ is labeled as $[ABCE]$ since $acl\_read(r4) = \{A, B, C, E\}$; whereas $v_{31}^{W2}$ is labeled as $[AD]$ given $acl\_write(r4) = \{A, D\}$. In Figure 3(a), both trees share the same set of vertexes and edges, as $acl\_read(r_1) = acl\_read(r_2) = acl\_write(r_1) = acl\_write(r_2) = \{A, B, C\}$. Figure 4 depicts tree graphs per data owner to distribute read and write access tokens respectively at the coarse-grained level. (Due to space limitation, coarse-grained graphs for resources owned by user $B$ are omitted.) Each row in the table states $r_i$ is associated with an unique read (write) access token $Enc_{pk'_{ra}}(id)$ ($Enc_{pk_{wa}}(id)$) encrypted on its $id$ and stored at vertex $v_{mn}^{RO}$ ($v_{mn}^{WO}$). For example, $r_1$ and $r_2$ are now given different access tokens at vertexes $v_{21}^{*A}$ and $v_{22}^{*A}$ respectively. Each authorized write operation requires an additional update token $SK_{x-id}$ distributed to authorized users the same way as read access tokens.

## 5  Analysis

### 5.1  Security Guarantees

Our two-leveled access control scheme provides the following privacy guarantees for data owners and users in the system:

**Read Access.** For the privacy of the data owners, the cloud provider does not learn any of the content of the files that he stores. The cloud learns the frequency of access to particular blocks but not the exact files that have been accessed within a block. For users' privacy, the cloud provider cannot relate access requests to particular users', neither can he infer which requests were submitted from the same user. However, he can observe the block access pattern from the requests of all users. The data owner does not learn anything about the access requests for the data.

**Write Access.** For privacy of the data owners, the cloud provider learns how often update requests are submitted for each block but without finding out which files have been written. Similarly to the read requests, write requests coming from the *users* are anonymous and unlinkable. Thus the cloud provider cannot learn anything about the access behavior of a particular user, but only a cumulative view over the requests from all users.

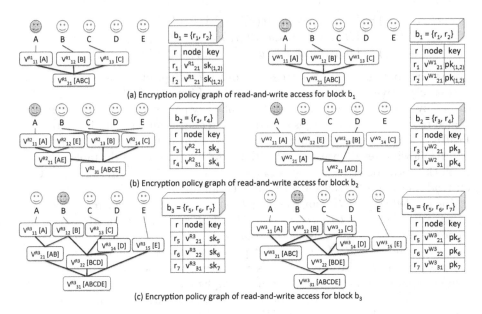

Fig. 3. Tree graphs per block for read and write access at the fine-grained level

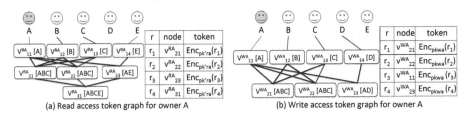

Fig. 4. Distribution of read and write access tokens at the coarse-grained level

## 5.2 Performance Analysis

**Read Access.** During setup, *data owners* compute of the authorization trees with decryption keys and access tokens. The work is proportional to the number of files in the database and the number of users. In order to authorize or to revoke file access to a user, data owner updates the tree with decryption keys and the tree with access tokens: in the worst case proportional to the depth of the trees. The updates for the tree with the access tokens can be executed at larger intervals of time to achieve better amortized efficiency for updates. For *users*, retrieving access tokens requires reading the coarse-level tree with access tokens for the data of a particular provider. Decryption keys retrieval can be proportional to the number of files that the user is authorized to access. For the *cloud provider*, in order to map an access request to a particular block the cloud provider will have to execute the **File_Access_Check** function for the submitted token and each block. We describe in the following optimization section how we can reduce the costs estimated here.

**Write Access.** From the perspective of a *data owner*, the enforcement of write access control requires duplication of the tree structures that were necessary for the read access control but this time with credentials necessary for the write access. This comes as an overhead in the setup phase when these structures are computed by the data owner and also each update of the access rules will necessitate update of both types of trees since the encryption and decryption (relevant for write and read access) need to be synchronized. Also periodically the data owner would need to process the blocks and compact the updates for each file back in its initial memory location. For a *user*, the size of the blocks that he receives, and hence the time he needs to locate the file and its updates at read access, will increase depending on the frequency of the updates for a block as well as the time period at which the data owner processes the blocks and brings the updates back in place. The *cloud provider* would need to transfer larger blocks including both the original files as well as the updates. He would need to compute the identification tag for each authorized write update, which requires constant time.

*Optimizations.* Some optimizations that help improve the performance of the scheme are as follows. If the user has enough memory, he can cache both authorization tokens and decryption keys for multiple accesses of the same files. This optimization applies to the read and the write access tokens as well as the decryption key for read. The only exception is the encryption key for write access — the user should always derive the current public encryption key for the file, which he wants to update since if the key has been changed, he will not be able to detect it and will submit an invalid update. Similarly the user can cache the identifier of the block in which a file is located and use it in repeated requests, which will save the search time at the cloud avoiding checks of all blocks. Further the user can trade-off the privacy guarantee for his request within its block for smaller communication overhead by revealing the exact memory address of the file after proving that he is authorized to access the block.

## 5.3    Discussion

Choosing the granularity for the access blocks in the read and write access control schemes affects the privacy guarantees for the scheme as well as its efficiency performance. The right granularity for each specific usage scenario will depend on the privacy and efficiency requirements for it, the expected patterns of access to the files and the expected frequency of access control rules' updates. The following points should be taken into consideration when choosing how to divide the files into access blocks: the size of a block should depend on the expected bandwidth of the clients and the acceptable delays for the system. Files that contain "complementary" information, i.e., a user is likely to access only one of a these files (e.g. a file to sell stocks, a file to buy stocks) should be located in the same block since their access pattern is highly sensitive. Data that requires frequent updates should be split into smaller blocks since the size of those blocks will grow faster. Accessing files with frequently changing access rules will require derivation of the corresponding decryption keys, which is proportional to the number of files in the block, such files should be located in blocks with fewer items (that can still be of big size). Since the view of the cloud provider of the access requests amounts to the frequency at which each access block is matched, files that are expected to have high access rates should be distributed across different blocks.

# 6   Related Work

Existing access control solution in outsourced storage usually apply crypto-graphic methods by disclosing data decryption keys only to authorized users. [8] proposed a cryptographic storage system, called Plutus, which arranges files with similar attributes into filegroups, applying two-level file encryption and distin-guishes read and write access. [6] designed a secure file system to be layered over insecure network and P2P file system, like NFS. Each file is attached a meta data containing the file's access control list. [15] defines and enforces fine-grained ac-cess control policies based on data attributes, and delegates most of computation tasks to untrusted cloud server without disclosing data content. [12] proposed a cloud storage system, called CloudProof, that enables meaningful security Service Level Agreements (SLAs) by providing a solution to detect violations of security properties, namely confidentiality, integrity, write-serializability, and read freshness. The problem presented in this paper shares some similarity with the proposals in [14,2]. [14] introduced a practical oblivious data access protocol using pyramid-shaped database layout and an enhanced reordering techniques to ensure access pattern confidentiality. [2] proposed a shuffle index structure, adapting traditional B-tree, to achieve content, access and pattern confidential-ity in the scenario of outsourced data. All those proposals focus on one or more aspects, such as scalability, efficiency, minimizing key distribution, etc., but none of them consider privacy issues as well as write access control.

# 7   Conclusion

We presented a two-level access control scheme enabling data sharing in out-sourced storage, like the cloud environment. The fine-grained and the coarse-grained access control schemes complement each other to achieve both data confidentiality and privacy protection on access patterns. To the best of our knowledge, we are the first to handle both read and write access rights entailing a more practical data sharing solution. As follow-on work, we will conduct ex-periments on a full implementation of our scheme. As a more ambitious goal, we would like to further extend our scheme for a complete solution that guarantees both security and privacy protection for a remote file storage system.

# References

1. Damgård, I., Meldgaard, S., Nielsen, J.B.: Perfectly Secure Oblivious RAM without Random Oracles. In: Ishai, Y. (ed.) TCC 2011. LNCS, vol. 6597, pp. 144–163. Springer, Heidelberg (2011)
2. De Capitani di Vimercati, S., Foresti, S., Paraboschi, S., Pelosi, G., Samarati, P.: Efficient and private access to outsourced data. In: Proc. of the 31st International Conference on Distributed Computing Systems (ICDCS 2011), Minneapolis, Minnesota, USA (June 2011)
3. De Capitani di Vimercati, S., Foresti, S., Samarati, P.: Recent advances in access control. In: Gertz, M., Jajodia, S. (eds.) Handbook of Database Security: Applications and Trends. Springer (2008)
4. Goldreich, O., Ostrovsky, R.: Software protection and simulation on oblivious RAMs. Journal of the ACM (JACM) 43(3), 473 (1996)
5. Goodrich, M.T., Mitzenmacher, M.: Privacy-Preserving Access of Outsourced Data via Oblivious RAM Simulation. In: Aceto, L., Henzinger, M., Sgall, J. (eds.) ICALP 2011, Part II. LNCS, vol. 6756, pp. 576–587. Springer, Heidelberg (2011)
6. Goh, E.J., Shacham, H., Modadugu, N., Boneh, D.: Sirius: Securing remote untrusted storage. In: Proc. Network and Distributed Systems Security (NDSS) Symposium 2003, pp. 131–145 (2003)
7. Kahn, D.: The Codebreakers. Macmillan, New York (1967)
8. Kallahalla, M., Riedel, E., Swaminathan, R., Wang, Q., Fu, K.: Plutus: Scalable secure file sharing on untrusted storage. In: USENIX Conference on File and Storage Technologies (2003)
9. Katz, J., Sahai, A., Waters, B.: Predicate Encryption Supporting Disjunctions, Polynomial Equations, and Inner Products. In: Smart, N.P. (ed.) EUROCRYPT 2008. LNCS, vol. 4965, pp. 146–162. Springer, Heidelberg (2008)
10. Kundra, V.: Tight budget? look to the 'Cloud'. The New York Times (2011), http://www.nytimes.com/2011/08/31/opinion/tight-budget-look-to-the-cloud.html?_r=1
11. Pinkas, B., Reinman, T.: Oblivious RAM Revisited. In: Rabin, T. (ed.) CRYPTO 2010. LNCS, vol. 6223, pp. 502–519. Springer, Heidelberg (2010)
12. Popa, R.A., Lorch, J.R., Molnar, D., Wang, H.J., Zhuang, L.: Enabling security in cloud storage slas with cloudproof. In: Proc. USENIX Annual Technical Conference, ATC 2011 (2011)
13. De Capitani di Vimercati, S., Foresti, S., Jajodia, S., Paraboschi, S., Pelosi, G., Samarati, P.: Encryption-based policy enforcement for cloud storage. In: Proceedings of the 2010 IEEE 30th International Conference on Distributed Computing Systems Workshops, ICDCSW 2010, pp. 42–51 (2010)
14. Williams, P., Sion, R., Carbunar, B.: Building castles out of mud: practical access pattern privacy and correctness on untrusted storage. In: Proceedings of the 15th ACM Conference on Computer and Communications Security, CCS 2008, pp. 139–148. ACM, New York (2008)
15. Yu, S., Wang, C., Ren, K., Lou, W.: Achieving secure, scalable, and fine-grained data access control in cloud computing. In: Proceedings of the 29th Conference on Information Communications, INFOCOM 2010, pp. 534–542. IEEE Press, Piscataway (2010)

# A    Predicate Encryption and Extensions

We present the construction of predicate encryption of [9] as follows:

- Setup($1^n$): Choose primes $p$, $q$ and $r$ and groups $\mathbf{G}_p$, $\mathbf{G}_q$ and $\mathbf{G}_r$ with generator $g_p, g_q$ and $g_r$ respectively. Let $\mathbf{G} = \mathbf{G}_p \times \mathbf{G}_q \times \mathbf{G}_r$. Choose $R_{1,i}, R_{2,i} \in \mathbf{G}_r$, $h_{1,i}, h_{2,i} \in \mathbf{G}_p$ uniformly at random for $1 \leq i \leq n$ and $R_0 \in \mathbf{G}_r$. The public parameters for the scheme are $(N = pqr, \mathbf{G}, \mathbf{G}_T, e)$. The public key $PK$ and master secret key $SK$ are defined as follows:
$$PK = (g_p, g_r, Q = g_q \cdot R_0, \{H_{1,i} = h_{1,i} \cdot R_{1,i}, H_{2,i} = h_{2,i} \cdot R_{2,i}\}_{i=1}^n),$$
$$SK = (p, q, r, g_q, \{h_{1,i}, h_{2,i}\}_{i=1}^n).$$

- $\text{Enc}_{SK}(x_1, \ldots, x_n)$: Choose randoms $s, \alpha, \beta \in \mathbf{Z}_N$, $R_{3,i}, R_{4,i} \in \mathbf{G}_r$ for $1 \leq i \leq n$, then output the following ciphertext:
$$C = \left(C_0 = g_p^s, \{C_{1,i} = H_{1,i}^s \cdot Q^{\alpha \cdot x_i} \cdot R_{3,i}, C_{2,i} = H_{2,i}^s \cdot Q^{\beta \cdot x_i} \cdot R_{4,i}\}_{i=1}^n\right).$$

- $\text{GenKey}_{SK}(v_1, \ldots, v_n)$: Choose randoms $r_{1,i}, r_{2,i} \in \mathbf{Z}_p$ for $1 \leq i \leq n$, $R_5 \in \mathbf{G}_r$, $f_1, f_2 \in \mathbf{Z}_q$ and $Q_6 \in \mathbf{G}_q$, then output $SK_{\mathbf{v}}$ that consists of
$$\left(K = R_5 \cdot Q_6 \cdot \prod_{i=1}^n h_{1,i}^{-r_{1,i}} \cdot h_{2,i}^{-r_{2,i}}, \ \{K_{1,i} = g_p^{r_{1,i}} \cdot g_q^{f_1 \cdot v_i}, K_{2,i} = g_p^{r_{2,i}} \cdot g_q^{f_2 \cdot v_i}\}_{i=1}^n\right)$$

- $\text{Dec}_{SK_f}(c)$: The decryption algorithm outputs 1 if and only if
$$e(C_0, K) \prod_{i=1}^n e(C_{1,i}, K_{1,i}) \cdot e(C_{2,i}, K_{2,i}) = 1.$$

We define an algorithm called Rand($C$) that re-randomizes any ciphertext produced by the predicate encryption. Given a ciphertext of form $(C_0, \{C_{1,i}, C_{2,i}\}_{i=1}^n)$, choose a random $s' \in \mathbf{Z}_N$ and output $C' = C_0 \cdot g_p^{s'}, \{C_{1,i} \cdot H_{1,i}^{s'}, C_{2,i} \cdot H_{2,i}^{s'}\}_{i=1}^n$. The resulting ciphertext is the same as freshly generated ciphertext for the encrypted value using random value $s + s'$, if $s$ was the value used in $C$.

Now we look closely at the instantiation of the predicate encryption scheme that handles polynomial evaluation as its predicate. In this case the predicate $(v_1, \ldots, v_n)$ consists of the coefficients of the polynomial that is being evaluated and the attribute vector that is used for an evaluation point $x$ is of the form $(1, x, x^2, \ldots, x^{n-1})$. The ciphertext for the encryption of $(1, x, x^2, \ldots, x^{n-1})$ has components $(C_0, \{C_{1,i}, C_{2,i}\}_{i=1}^n)$, where $C_{1,i}, C_{2,i}$ correspond to the vector point $x^{i-1}$. Thus we can view the first view components of the ciphertext $(C_0, \{C_{1,i}, C_{2,i}\}_{i=1}^2)$ as an encryption of the vector $(1, x)$ that can be used for evaluation of predicates that are linear functions.

We use the above observation in the instantiation of the tags that the cloud derives for each of the accepted write updates. He uses the token that the client has used to prove his write access to a particular block, which a predicate encryption ciphertext $(C_0, \{C_{1,i}, C_{2,i}\}_{i=1}^n)$, to derive identifier for the files with which the submitted update will be associated by taking the first part of the ciphertext $(C_0, \{C_{1,i}, C_{2,i}\}_{i=1}^2)$. This identifier cannot be used as a write access token since it is missing substantial part of the ciphertext, and no party without the master secret key can extend an identifier to a valid write token. Also any party that has read access to the file associated with the update will be given a key that would allow it to recognize the updates for that file. This key is the predicate corresponding to the linear function that evaluates to zero at the file id.

# Designing Privacy-Preserving Smart Meters with Low-Cost Microcontrollers

Andres Molina-Markham[1], George Danezis[2],
Kevin Fu[1], Prashant Shenoy[1], and David Irwin[1]

[1] University of Massachusetts Amherst
[2] Microsoft Research Cambridge

**Abstract.** Smart meters that track fine-grained electricity usage and implement sophisticated usage-based billing policies, e.g., based on time-of-use, are a key component of recent smart grid initiatives that aim to increase the electric grid's efficiency. A key impediment to widespread smart meter deployment is that fine-grained usage data indirectly reveals detailed information about consumer behavior, such as when occupants are home, when they have guests or their eating and sleeping patterns. Recent research proposes cryptographic solutions that enable sophisticated billing policies without leaking information. However, prior research does not measure the performance constraints of real-world smart meters, which use cheap ultra-low-power microcontrollers to lower deployment costs. In this paper, we explore the feasibility of designing privacy-preserving smart meters using low-cost microcontrollers and provide a general methodology for estimating design costs. We show that it is feasible to produce certified meter readings for use in billing protocols relying on Zero-Knowledge Proofs with microcontrollers such as those inside currently deployed smart meters. Our prototype meter is capable of producing these readings every 10 seconds using a $3.30USD MSP430 microcontroller, while less powerful microcontrollers deployed in today's smart meters are capable of producing readings every 28 seconds. In addition to our results, our goal is to provide smart meter designers with a general methodology for selecting an appropriate balance between platform performance, power consumption, and monetary cost that accommodates privacy-preserving billing protocols.

## 1 Introduction

The goal of recent smart grid initiatives is to increase the electric grid's efficiency by reducing both its monetary and environmental cost. One way to increase efficiency is to alter electricity demand by either shifting some of it to off-peak hours or better aligning it with intermittent renewable generation. Since directly controlling the grid's electricity consumption, e.g., by forcibly disconnecting loads, is infeasible, smart grids focus on incentivizing consumers to change their own consumption patterns by altering the price of electricity to accurately reflect generation costs and aggregate demand.

A.D. Keromytis (Ed.): FC 2012, LNCS 7397, pp. 239–253, 2012.
© International Financial Cryptography Association 2012

A variety of billing policies that properly incentivize consumers are available to utilities. For instance, time-of-use (TOU) pricing alters the price for electricity ($/kWh) based on the time of day, with peak daytime rates more expensive than off-peak nighttime rates. Utilities implicitly assume that TOU pricing requires them to know not only how much electricity consumers use each month, but also *when* they use it. Unfortunately, prior research demonstrates that fine-grained usage data indirectly reveals sensitive private information about a consumer's activity patterns, e.g., when they are home, when they have guests, their eating and sleeping patterns, etc. [21]. Vast collections of fine-grained electricity data for many buildings over long periods of time raise both legal and economic concerns. To address these issues, researchers have proposed a variety of privacy-preserving billing protocols that prevent utilities from linking fine-grained usage patterns to individual households, but still allow them to implement sophisticated billing policies. The solutions draw on common cryptographic techniques, including commitment schemes, digital signatures and Zero-Knowledge Proofs (ZKP).

A key impediment to the widespread adoption of privacy-preserving billing protocols is the computational and memory constraints of smart meters, which, due to cost, size, and power considerations, typically use embedded microcontrollers. Prior work does not measure these resource constraints, and, thus, implicitly assumes that meters are capable of executing protocols in a reasonable amount of time. In this paper, we explore the economic feasibility of implementing the cryptographic techniques required for privacy-preserving smart metering, and propose a general methodology for evaluating the cost of a solution. We take into account current smart meter deployments and look at the hardware technologies utilities are adopting over both the short- and long-term. Our focus is on implementing cryptographic techniques on smart meters such as those proposed by Rial et al. [25], Molina-Markham et al. [21], Kursawe et al. [18] and Jawurek et al. [17]. However, our methodology also applies to estimating the cost of similar metering systems that require privacy, including natural gas, water, and toll roads, such as the one proposed by Balasch et al. [2]. We summarize our contributions below:

**Implementation.** We implement a privacy-friendly smart meter using low-cost microcontrollers from both the MSP430 and ARM families. We present the first experimental results that actually measure the performance of a Camenisch-Lysyanskaya (CL) based scheme using elliptic curves in constrained environments. Previous work [25] discusses and estimates, but does not include implementation results. The most comparable realization of a CL based scheme uses a Java Card [5] and does not include an elliptic curve version.

**Cost Evaluation.** We outline a cost evaluation strategy for implementing privacy-preserving smart meters that accounts for the special characteristics of low-cost microcontrollers and industry trends. In particular, we list a set of system variables that designers may modify to balance security, privacy, and cost. We are the first to discuss the issues surrounding ultra-low-power implementations, which in some applications may make the difference between a meter that requires a battery replacement every few years versus every few days.

**Feasibility Analysis.** We present evidence to support the hypothesis that ZKP billing protocols are feasible on current deployments of smart meters and cost effective on deployments over both the short- and long-term. Because some smart meters can be remotely updated, it is plausible that a deployment may be implemented in one of these updates. In the long-term, our experimental results may help system designers to assess the performance and cost benefits of utilizing elliptic curve primitives. Our analysis takes into account the evolution of the storage and computational capabilities of low-cost microcontrollers and contrasts it to the evolution of personal computer processors.

## 2   Cryptographic Building Blocks

This work builds on protocols for privacy-preserving calculations of time-of-use based bills for smart electricity metering. In that setting a customer fitted with a smart meter proves to a utility provider the amount to be paid for their electricity consumption within a specific time period, without revealing any details about their fine-grained consumption. The bill is calculated on the basis of detailed readings, every half hour or fifteen minutes, that are each billed according to the dynamic price of electricity at that time, or a pre-defined but time variable tariff scheme. These protocols are applicable when consumers do not trust the utility with their detailed electricity usage information, and the utility does not rely on consumers to honestly report their usage. Our work focuses on efficient implementations of the meter components on different families of processors necessary to support those protocols.

### 2.1   Commitment Schemes and Zero-Knowledge Proofs

Commitment schemes are cryptographic primitives that enable a party to create the digital equivalent of an envelope for a secret. Commitments support two important properties: *hiding* protects the secrecy of the committed message, and *binding* ensures it can only be opened to the committed message.

Pedersen commitments [23] are information-theoretically hiding, and binding under the discrete logarithm assumption. They rely on a set of global parameters, namely a group $G$ of prime order $p$ with generators $g$ and $h$. Under that scheme a commitment $C$ to message $r \in \mathbb{Z}_p$ is computed as $C = g^r h^o$ where $o$ is an *opening* nonce chosen uniformly at random in $\mathbb{Z}_p$. Opening a commitment $C$ involves disclosing the values $r$ and $o$ to a verifier. In addition to opening the commitment, efficient protocols exist for a prover to convince a verifier that they know the committed value without disclosing it.

Fujisaki-Okamoto commitments [13] are similar to Pedersen commitments, except that they make use of a group of composite, hidden order instead of a group of prime order. They allow the committed value to be any integer, including negative integers. We can use Pedersen or Fujisaki-Okamoto commitments depending on whether the meter needs to encode negative values or not.

For the purposes of time-of-use billing, the meter periodically commits to meter readings. Those commitments are signed and the customer can use the signature to prove functions of the bill to a verifier. Different signature schemes may be used to achieve different security properties. A standard signature scheme, such as DSA, can be used to ensure the integrity of any further statement proved on the basis of the meter readings. On the downside, it is not possible to eliminate covert channels that may allow a dishonest meter to signal some information back to the utility verifier. When meters are not trusted for privacy, a signature scheme such as Camenisch-Lysyanskaya (CL) signatures [7] can be used to sign readings individually.

CL-signatures allow a requesting party to obtain a digital signature on a commitment from an authorized signer. In particular, Camenisch and Lysyanskaya [7] provide efficient protocols for computing a signature on a commitment message, as well as for constructing zero-knowledge proofs of knowledge of a signature on a committed or encrypted message. Note that there are two digital signature schemes attributed to Camenisch and Lysyanskaya; their earlier scheme [6] relies on the Strong RSA assumption, while the later scheme relies on a discrete-logarithm-based assumption (the LRSW assumption) [20]. CL-signatures [7] can be implemented using elliptic curve groups, as long as we have an efficient bilinear map that is non-degenerate. We describe the key generation function, the signing function and the signature verification function for CL-signatures using the notation in [26]:

1. $CLKeyGen(1^k)$. Given a security parameter $k$, and the number of block messages to sign $n$, the signer generates the first part of their public key: $(p, \mathbb{G}, \mathbb{H}, g, h, e)$, such that there is a mapping $e : \mathbb{G} \times \mathbb{G} \to \mathbb{H}$, which is bilinear, non-degenerate and efficient to compute. The signer then chooses the following parameters for their private key: $x, y, z_1, \ldots, z_n \in_R \mathbb{Z}_p$. Next, the signer uses these parameters to compute $X = g^x, Y = g^y$ and $Z_i = g^{z_i}$ for all $i \in [1, n]$. The public key is $pubkey = (p, \mathbb{G}, \mathbb{H}, g, h, e, X, Y, \{Z_i\}, \{W_i\})$, and the secret key is the public key concatenated with $(x, y, \{z_i\})$.

2. $CLSign((x, y, \{z_i\}), \{m_i\})$. To sign $n$ blocks $\{m_i\}$, the signer first chooses $a \in_R \mathbb{G}$, and computes $b = a^y$. The signer then computes $A_i = a^{z_i}$ and $B_i = (A_i)^y$ for all $i \in [2, n]$. Finally, the signer computes $\sigma = a^{x + xym_1} \prod_{i=2}^n A_i^{xym_i}$. The signature is $sig = (a, \{A_i\}, b, \{B_i\}, \sigma)$.

3. $CLVerifySign(pubkey, \{m_i\}, sig)$. The verifier performs the following computations and outputs $accept$ if the following equalities hold: $e(a, Y) = e(g, b)$; $e(a, Z_i) = e(g, A_i), \forall i \in [1, n]$; $e(A_i, Y) = e(g, B_i), \forall i \in [1, n]$; and $e(g, \sigma) = e(X, a) \cdot e(X, b)^{m_1} \cdot \prod_{i=2}^n e(X, B_i)^{m_i}$.

ZKPs make use of commitments and CL-signatures to prove to a third party an aggregate function of the committed readings without revealing the enclosed readings. The full billing protocol proposed by Rial et. al. [25] decomposes a bill's proof of correctness into a small set of ZKPs – effectively proving the correctness of a commitment to the price component of each period of consumption separately before aggregating them and disclosing the final bill. All proofs in their scheme are non-interactive by using the well known Fiat-Shamir heuristic [12].

## 2.2   A Smart Metering Billing Protocol

Our study focuses on the efficient implementation of the meter cryptographic components for the Rial and Danezis [25] privacy preserving smart metering protocols. Proposals by [17] can be adapted to use the same meter components.

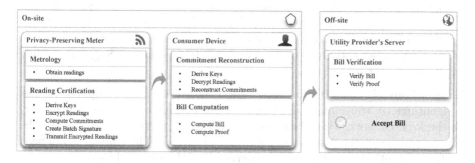

**Fig. 1.** Architecture of the privacy-preserving smart metering system. A smart meter, in addition to its metrologic unit, has a microcontroller capable of encrypting and certifying its readings. The meter also has a wireless transceiver used to send encrypted readings to the consumer's device. The consumer uses the information from the meter for consumption planning, and in the computation of bills and corresponding proofs.

We illustrate the protocol with an example that includes three principals, as depicted in Figure 1: the smart meter, the prover, and the verifier. The smart meter first measures and certifies consumer electricity readings, and then communicates them to the prover using a secure channel. The prover, a consumer-owned device, computes a bill along with a non-interactive ZKP that ensures the bill's validity. The prover sends the bill and the proof to the utility company, which verifies the bill's correctness before accepting it. Below, we describe in detail the computations the meter has to perform, and provide a brief outline of the protocols between the prover and the verifier.

**Smart Meter Computations.** To support privacy protocols, smart meters need to perform the following computations: sensing and measuring electricity usage, deriving session keys, certifying and encrypting readings, and finally transmitting readings to the consumer.

*Sensing and measuring electricity.* The meter's primary function is sensing and measuring electricity usage. Thus, other computations must not interfere with this fundamental task. We denote $\Delta t$ as the measurement interval, such that duration between meter readings $t_{i+1} - t_i = \Delta t$.

*Deriving session keys.* The protocol encrypts readings using a symmetric encryption algorithm before passing them to the user. To ensure the encrypted reading's secrecy, each reading is encrypted with a distinct session key. For every $t_i$ the meter encrypts reading $r_i$ using key $K_i = H_0(K, t_i)$, where $H_0$ is a secure hash function and $K$ is a master symmetric key known by the consumer.

Additionally, the meter derives from the master key an opening value for the commitment $o_i = H_1(K, t_i)$ where $H_1$ is a hash function.

*Certification and encryption.* After deriving $K_i$ and $o_i$, the meter both encrypts the reading $r_i$ using $K_i$ and computes a *commitment* $c_i$ for the reading. More formally, the meter generates an encrypted reading $Er_i = E(K_i, r_i)$ using a symmetric encryption algorithm, and a commitment $c_i = g^{r_i} \cdot h^{o_i}$ using globally known constants $g$, $h$, and their group. The protocol also requires the meter to generate cryptographic signatures for each commitment $c_i$. To reduce the necessary computations, the protocol computes batch signatures $Sig_j$ for multiple commitments $c_i, c_{i+1}, \ldots, c_{i+k}$.

*Network transmission.* After the meter encrypts readings and computes batches of signatures, it transmits the batches to the consumer's device (the prover) via the local network. More formally, for each batch $j$, the meter transmits the following tuples to the consumer: $\{\{t_i\}_j, \{Er_i\}_j, Sig_j\}$. The commitments need not be transmitted, which keeps the overheads of the protocol low.

**Consumer prover computations.** The prover computes the bill's payment and its corresponding proof of correctness. First, the prover derives the session keys $K_i = H_0(K, t_i)$ on the basis of times $t_i$ and the master key $K$; decrypts the readings $r_i$ from $Er_i = E(K_i, r_i)$, and derives the opening values from each commitment as $o_i = H_1(K, t_i)$. Then all commitments to readings can be reconstructed as $c_i = g^{r_i} \cdot h^{o_i}$ using the public parameters of the commitment scheme and the recovered readings and openings. Finally, a batch of commitments are accepted as authentic after checking the signature $Sig_j$. This ensures that the received encrypted readings have not been tampered with. After the readings and their signed commitments are available, an arbitrary billing function can be applied to each reading (or aggregates of readings) to establish the final bill. The prover calculates a ZKP of correctness and provides it to the verifier.

**Summary.** The details of those computations, and families of functions that can be practically proved and verified in zero-knowledge are provided in [25] along with the detailed security proofs for the protocol. To summarize, fine-grained meter readings are only available to the consumer, while simultaneously allowing the consumer to self-calculate their bill and ensuring the utility that the consumer has not manipulated or under-reported the payment. Thus, the utility has a guarantee over each bill's authenticity, and the consumer has a guarantee over their data's privacy. To resolve disputes, the meter may optionally store readings and decryption keys to permit audits by a trusted third party.

## 3   Implementation on Low-Cost Microcontrollers

In this section we describe a few different implementations of the cryptographic primitives discussed in Section 2 that would be required to run on a smart meter. We start by pointing out that the computational capabilities of low-cost and ultra-low-power microcontrollers have not developed at the same pace as high-performance microprocessors employed in servers and personal computers. System designers should, therefore, use different means to evaluate the economic feasibility of a cryptographic solution in the low-cost spectrum of embedded devices. We present the set of design variables that we control in our various implementations with the purpose of illustrating their effects on performances and costs in subsequent sections.

### 3.1   Computing Capabilities of Low-Cost Microcontrollers

Moore's law predicted that the number of transistors placed in an integrated circuit would double approximately every two years. This prediction, however, does not directly address two issues that are pertinent to microcontrollers. First, the production costs associated with maintaining this trend have not remained constant. Second, with the addition of more transistors, the problem of efficient power management has significantly increased [11]. As a consequence, microcontrollers that are often constrained by production costs and power budgets have not increased their computational capabilities at the same rate as microprocessors for servers and personal computers. In Figure 2 we illustrate this by showing the evolution in processing capabilities across different technologies.

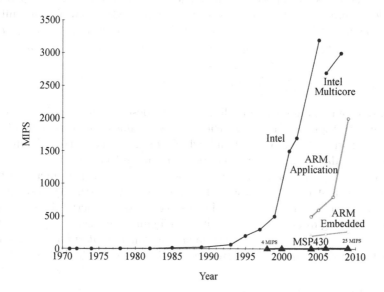

**Fig. 2.** While it is difficult to compare the performances of microprocessors using millions of instructions per second, this graph provides a visual representation of performance improvements as seen across a few popular architectures. The trends in microprocessors targeting desktop computers and servers, as well as the performance improvements observed in ARM application microprocessors have followed exponential curves. However, the performance improvements observed in embedded ARM microprocessors and MSP430 microcontrollers have followed linear curves [1,8,16].

## 3.2    Design Variables

In this section, we enumerate a set of design variables that we consider in our implementations with the purpose of illustrating their effect on various properties of the system. As we show, some of these design variables correspond to features, such as qualitative privacy or security guarantees, e.g. properties of a trust or security model. Other design variables correspond to quantitative properties, for example computation performance, storage and communication requirements. The design variables that we consider in our implementation are in one of two categories, system variables or crypto variables. **System variables** include the selection of an MCU platform and a multitasking approach. **Crypto variables** include the selection of a digital signature scheme, and the selection of cryptographic primitives that rely on large integer multiplicative groups or elliptic curve cryptography. We should note that a complete analysis of the economic feasibility of a metering solution should also include a variety of **economic variables**, for example, the costs of implementation, deployment, maintenance and customer support. These economic variables are not considered explicitly in this work. We assume that if a solution can be implemented using microcontrollers, such as those in currently deployed meters, and those meters support software updates, then the solution is economically feasible given that it does not require a complete change in infrastructure. For example, rather than forcing millions of deployments, utility companies could offer concerned customers the option to request a meter update that implements the privacy features mentioned here.

## 3.3    Anatomy of a Smart Meter

In order to provide context for our discussion, we describe the generic anatomy of a smart meter. Figure 3 shows the schematics of a smart meter. In general, they are equipped with an analog front end, which is part of the metrologic unit used to convert the data coming from the load sensors and preprocess the measurements before they are passed to the microcontroller unit. The microcontroller unit handles this stream of data as well as the general functionality of storing the data in flash memory, and driving an LCD screen. More modern microcontrollers replace the analog front end with an integrated embedded signal processor. Current deployments of smart meters use microcontrollers that run at clock speeds ranging from 8-25 MHz and have storage ranging from 32-256 KB [14].

## 3.4    Implementation Details

We implement the algorithms *Commit*, *CLSign* and *DSA*, using both large integer multiplicative groups and elliptic curve cryptography. We also implement the symmetric key derivation algorithm *DeriveAESKeys* to encrypt readings with AES for on-site wireless transmission. We integrate these algorithms to produce *certified readings*, as discussed in Section 2. In our experiments, we use the libraries bnlib [24] and Miracl [27] to perform integer or elliptic curve arithmetic, together with one of the following Real-Time Operating Systems: FreeRTOS [4],

SYS/BIOS [30] and MicroC/OS-III [19]. We write the rest of the implementation in C, with some minimal amount of assembly code. We describe the particular details of the ECC implementation in Section 3.5. We focus primarily on the MSP430 family of microcontrollers with a 16-bit RISC architecture. The motivation behind this focus is that current deployments already include microcontrollers in this family. We use the evaluation board MSP-EXP430F5438, in combination with the microcontrollers MSP430BT5190 and MSP430F5438A. The board includes an LCD screen and connectors for radio components. We also use the radio stack CC2567-PAN1327. Both microcontrollers are from the same family (MSP430x5xx). Shared characteristics include the availability of a hardware multiplier supporting 32-bit operations, size of flash (256 KB), frequency (25 MHz), and power consumption ($\sim$ 230 $\mu$A/MHz in active mode). The manufacturers designed the MSP430BT5190 for use with the radio stack; however, the MSP430F5438A has a larger RAM (16 KB). In our evaluation, we compare a few ARM microcontrollers and processors. For this we use readily available ARM ports for all the libraries mentioned above. We compile our code and the libraries using IAR Embedded Workbench for ARM version 6.30 [15]. The most significant difference is that the word size for the multi-precision arithmetic is 32 instead of 16, which we use in the MSP430 implementations. The other microcontroller board we use is the TI Stellaris Evaluation Board EKB-UCOS3-EVM. The ARM processors we measure are capable of running full Linux distributions; nevertheless, we perform the measurements using IAR Workbench as well.

### 3.5 Elliptic Curve Cryptography Details

The full ZKP based billing protocol requires the selection of various building blocks, such as commitment schemes and signatures. The security of these building blocks may depend on either the strong RSA (SRSA) assumption [6], or on the discrete logarithm (LRSW) assumption [7]. One important side-effect of the selection of these building blocks is that in order for the SRSA assumption to hold, the cryptographic operations need to be performed over multiplicative groups of integers with large moduli (1,024 to 2,048 bits in length). However, by leveraging modern Elliptic Curve Cryptography, the designer can

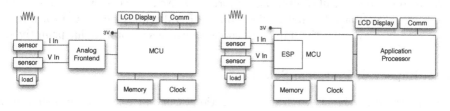

**Fig. 3.** Main components of a smart meter. On the left we illustrate a simple meter with a single microcontroller unit (MCU) that controls the metrologic unit, storage and communication interfaces. On the right we show a smart meter that replaces the analog front end with an embedded signal processor (ESP) and has an additional application processor that controls communication, OS, power monitoring, and analytics.

use building blocks that rely on the discrete logarithm assumption employing considerably smaller key sizes. Therefore, for the ECC based commitments and ECDSA implementations, we use the NIST curves P-192 and P-224 [9]. For the ECC versions of the CL Signatures, we use the pairing-friendly elliptic curves $E(\mathbb{F}_{2^{379}}) : y^2 + y = x^3 + x + 1$ and $E(\mathbb{F}_p) : y^2 = x^3 + Ax + B$ with a 512-bit prime $p$ as presented in [29].

The criteria for choosing curve parameters for ECDSA and the commitment scheme that we used are well known. However, choosing appropriate parameters for pairing-based cryptography is still an active area of research. That is, to use an elliptic curve implementation for CL-signatures, we require an appropriate bilinear map $e : \mathbb{G} \times \mathbb{G} \to \mathbb{H}$ that is non-degenerate and easy to compute. There is no unique way to obtain this map using elliptic curve groups $\mathbb{G}, \mathbb{H}$. While most protocols, such as signatures and identity based encryption protocols, are designed using a *type-1* pairing, it is often possible to use a *type-3* pairing. The latter are typically more efficient in practice. In other words, protocols often assume the existence of a pairing $e : \mathbb{G} \times \mathbb{G} \to \mathbb{H}$ (type-1). However, in some cases the designer can implement a protocol that assumes the existence of a pairing $e : \mathbb{G}_1 \times \mathbb{G}_2 \to \mathbb{H}$ with $\mathbb{G}_1 \neq \mathbb{G}_2$ such that there is no isomorphism $\psi : \mathbb{G}_2 \to \mathbb{G}_1$ (type-3). We choose to implement type-1 pairings on a supersingular curve defined over $GF(2^m)$ using the $\eta_T$ pairing [3] and on a supersingular curve defined over $GF(p)$ using a modified Tate pairing [28]. In order for the curves to provide an adequate security guarantee, the size of the key must be large enough so that the corresponding dilogarithm problem in $\mathbb{H}$ is hard. For the purposes of the particular billing protocol described in this paper, we note that a smart meter needs to compute signatures and not necessarily verify them. Therefore, we want to make operations on the curve as cheap as possible, even if that means computing more expensive parings on the consumer's device. For more details on pairings, we refer the reader to Devegili et al. [10].

## 4   Experimental Evaluation

In this section, we evaluate the impact of choosing each of the design variables overviewed in Section 3. We first describe the impact of choosing a family of microcontrollers on overall computing performance. Next, we discuss the impact of choosing an approach for multitasking on the RAM requirements and total cost size. Finally, we discuss the impact of choosing various cryptographic primitives.

### 4.1   Impact of Platform Selection

We implemented the cryptographic operations *Commit* and *CLSign* using microcontrollers from two of the most popular families, specifically, a microcontroller MSP430F5438A with 256 KB flash, 16 KB RAM and a microcontroller Stellaris LM3S9B92 (ARM Cortex M) with 256 KB flash, 96 KB SRAM; and two ARM application microprocessors OMAP3 (ARM Cortex A8) and OMAP4 (ARM Cortex A9) capable of running full Linux operating systems. These two microprocessors are commonly used in smart phones. The performances of these operations on these platforms are summarized in Table 1.

## 4.2    Impact of Multitasking Approach

Meters need to be able to interrupt cryptographic computations periodically to perform measurements, logging and communication. One way of handling multitasking is with the use of an RTOS. Another way is the modeling of an application using a finite state machine and the implementation of it using timers and interrupts. Generally, the footprint of an RTOS is larger than the footprint of a state machine approach. We explore the following three RTOS in our work: FreeRTOS, SYS\BIOS and $\mu$C-OSIII. Our configurations for each of the RTOS use 4 KB, 16 KB and 12 KB of code size respectively. The finite state machine requires approximately 2 KB of code. RTOS have the capability of managing memory; some by reserving particular regions of the stack for different applications, and some by allowing for the use of dynamic memory allocation even with multiple heaps, such as SYS\BIOS. It is typically not a trivial engineering exercise to fit each cryptographic algorithm in RAM. We should also note that the system designer should probably base the decision of whether or not to use an RTOS on the necessity of additional required functionality, such as occasional tasks like secure updates, secure audits, key exchange and key revocation, etc.

**Table 1.** Running time of commitments and signatures across multiple platforms. The tasks are run exclusively and uninterrupted on each of the platforms. The signatures are performed on 16 bytes of data. DSA uses a 1,024-bit prime $p$, a 160-bit prime $q$, and SHA-256. The timing does not include the generation of randomness, which depends on the source. Prices are in USD (Sept., 2011).

| | MSP430F5438A | LM3S9B92 | Cortex-A8 | Cortex-A9 |
|---|---|---|---|---|
| Operating Freq | 25 MHz | 80 MHz | 720 MHz | 1 GHz |
| Operating Power | 330 - 690 $\mu$W | 333 - 524 mW | 0.4 W | 1.9 W |
| Family Price Range | $0.25 - $9 | $1 - $8 | $41 - $46 | +$50 |
| **Commitments - Key Size 1,024 bits** | | | | |
| Avg. Running Time | 19.56 s | 0.82 s | 51 ms | 36 ms |
| **DSA Signatures - Key Size 1,024 bits** | | | | |
| Avg. Running Time | 2.71 s | 0.13 s | 8 ms | 6 ms |
| **CL Signatures - Key Size 1,024 bits** | | | | |
| Avg. Running Time | 43.1 s | 2.3 s | 150 ms | 81 ms |

## 4.3    Impact of ECC Utilization

In this subsection, we evaluate the impact of using elliptic curve cryptography instead of cryptography relying on large integer multiplicative groups. The code sizes of the bnlib [24] and Miracl [27] libraries and their RAM requirements depend on the features that are included. In our experimental setting using a microcontroller MSP430F5438A, the code size of Miracl was 23 KB and the code size of bnlib was 18 KB. The performance of bnlib and Miracl on non-ECC arithmetic is comparable. In our experiments, the running times of the same operation using either library differed by less than 5% of the total computation time of the operation. The RAM footprint for various functions is summarized in Table 2. As we can see, given a security level, ECC cryptographic primitives utilize RAM more efficiently. Similarly, Table 2 shows that given a microcontroller and a security level, an improvement in performance of about one order of magnitud can be achieved by using elliptic curve primitives.

### 4.4    Impact of Signature Scheme Selection

Table 2 shows running times for performing a CLSign algorithm with four readings. We highlight in particular the benefit of using an elliptic curve based library. If a designer uses elliptic curves, he or she can reduce a monthly batch signature with 1,440 readings (one reading every half hour) from 15.6 hours to 2.5 hours. If the designer assumes a different trust level in which zero-knowledge is not required, signatures are less expensive. On an MSP430F5438A at 25 MHz, signing a 16-byte message using regular DSA with a 1,024-bit prime $p$, a 160-bit prime $q$, and SHA-256 takes 2.71 seconds excluding the generation of randomness, which depends on the source. Signing a 16-byte message using ECDSA using a curve in $GF(p)$ for a 192-bit prime and SHA-256 takes 3.78 seconds excluding the generation of randomness. DSA signatures scale better than CL-signatures because the only overhead for a larger message would be the cost of the hash, which for the computations above is less than 0.01% of the computation.

**Table 2.** On the left we show the running time of commitments (single reading) and signatures (4 reading batches) on an MSP430F5438A at 25 MHz. These times are obtained when the algorithms are running exclusively and uninterrupted. We use Miracl for the elliptic curve versions as described in Section 3. The key sizes are in bits. On the right we show the RAM utilization for the various algorithms we implement on an MSP430F5438A all using the Miracl library. The measurements do not include RAM utilization by an RTOS, a radio stack or I/O.

| Algorithm | Key Size | Library | Time | Algorithm | Key Size | RAM |
|---|---|---|---|---|---|---|
| Commit | 1,024 | bnlib | 19.9 sec | Commit | 1,024 | 5.8 KB |
| Commit | 2,048 | bnlib | 303.0 sec | Commit | 2,048 | 10.2 KB |
| ECC Commit | 192 | miracl | 5.6 sec | CLSign | 1,024 | 6.3 KB |
| ECC Commit | 224 | miracl | 8.3 sec | CLSign | 2,048 | 11.3 KB |
| CLSign | 1,024 | bnlib | 41.2 sec | ECC Commit | 192 | 2.2 KB |
| CLSign | 2,048 | bnlib | 313.8 sec | ECC Commit | 224 | 2.5 KB |
| ECC CLSign | 379 | miracl | 6.7 sec | ECC CLSign | 379 | 3.1 KB |
| ECC CLSign | 512 | miracl | 35.6 sec | ECC CLSign | 512 | 3.6 KB |
| AES Key Gen | 128 | miracl | 0.1 sec | AES Key Gen | 128 | 2 KB |

## 5    Feasibility and Costs in Real-World Deployments

We now discuss a strategy for estimating the cost of deploying privacy preserving smart meters according to the system variables that we discussed in Section 3.

## 5.1   Cost Estimation Strategy

**Step 1: Determine the performance and power requirements.** The first step is to determine the acceptable levels of general computational performance and the power requirements of the meter. Depending on the specific application, meter readings may need to be certified with a frequency of seconds, minutes or hours. Also, the meter may need to operate on a battery. Thus, using an ultra-low-power microcontroller may be the difference between replacing the battery every few years or every few days. For example, the performance shown in Table 1 may make the LM3S9B92 MCU look very attractive for its ratio of cost/performance. However, the power consumption is roughly three orders of magnitude greater than the MSP430 MCU. Mobile processors are still far from being ultra-low power, although their computational and storage capabilities are increasing faster than those of the MCUs.

**Step 2: Determine the code and RAM requirements.** Once the performance and power requirements are met by a family of microcontrollers, it is then necessary for the designer to estimate the code size and RAM requirements for the implementation of the reading certification functions in a meter, taking into account whether multitasking needs to be supported.

## 5.2   Economic Feasibility

The results in Section 4 support the hypothesis that privacy-preserving billing protocols based on ZKP are economically feasible. We note that existing smart meters that have the ability to be remotely updated rely on microcontrollers similar to those we use in our implementation. Furthermore, if a microcontroller in the MSP430 family is used, it is possible to generate commitments and CL-signatures every 10 seconds when running at 25 MHz or every 28 seconds when running at a more conservative 8 MHz. Thus, a remote update that enables meters with privacy preserving functionality appears feasible.

Other metering applications may require that readings be certified at a finer granularity, for example every one or two seconds. This would require higher computational performance and larger storage than is currently available on low-cost ultra-low-power microcontrollers. For this reason, while obtaining certified readings at fine granularities is technologically feasible, it is to this date a feature that may incur a greater cost. Finally, in some circumstances, billing transactions may be required to take milliseconds. In that case, only high-end mobile processors could provide the required performance, and thus the cost of that application would be high based on current technological trends.

While in our analysis we did not cover all manufacturers of low cost MCUs, other leading manufacturers have similar offerings. For example *Atmel* also has AVR ultra low power microcontrollers, and various ARM based MCUs comparable to those discussed here. *Microchip* has the PIC microcontroller line with 8-, 16- and 32-bit MCUs. We did not consider 8-bit microcontrollers because they are perhaps too constrained for the kind of crypto application described here.

## 5.3   Best Utilization of Resources

The measurements in Section 4 show that the best security/cost ratio can be achieved by using ECC primitives. If current MCUs are targeted, maximizing the use of RAM can be achieved via ECC. Looking toward the future, performance will most likely regain importance due to the increasing economic feasibility of Ferroelectric RAM (FRAM), a kind of memory that enables high-performance on ultra-low power microcontrollers, with a unified memory model. Texas Instruments has started to ship MCUs with 16 KB of FRAM ($1.20 USD), and they are already producing chips with 4 MB of FRAM [22].

## 6   Conclusion

Our evidence supports the notion that ZKP-based billing protocols are economically feasible. We show that evaluating the cost of a cryptographic solution in an embedded system such as a smart meter depends first on the family of microcontrollers used, then on the storage and RAM requirements, and finally on additional features such as communication and user interface. Our empirical analyses show that with the use of Elliptic Curve Cryptography, it is possible to reduce the RAM requirements by about 50% and obtain performance improvements of one order of magnitude, thus obtaining a better performance/cost ratio.

**Acknowledgments.** This material is supported by a Sloan Research Fellowship, the NSF under CNS-0136228, CNS-136650, CNS-1143655, CNS-0916577, CNS-0855128 and a gift from Cisco. Any opinions, findings, and conclusions expressed in this material are those of the authors and do not necessarily reflect the views of the NSF.

## References

1. ARM: ARM Company Milestones (2011), http://www.arm.com/about/company-profile/milestones.php
2. Balasch, J., Rial, A., Troncoso, C., Geuens, C., Preneel, B., Verbauwhede, I.: PrETP: Privacy-Preserving Electronic Toll Pricing. In: USENIX Security (2010)
3. Barreto, P., Galbraith, S., Ó'hÉigeartaigh, C., Scott, M.: Efficient Pairing Computation on Supersingular Abelian Varieties. Designs, Codes and Cryptography (2007)
4. Barry, R.: FreeRTOS-a free RTOS for small embedded real time systems (2006)
5. Bichsel, P., Camenisch, J., Groß, T., Shoup, V.: Anonymous Credentials on a Standard Java Card. In: Proceedings of the 16th ACM Conference on Computer and Communications Security (2009)
6. Camenisch, J., Lysyanskaya, A.: A Signature Scheme with Efficient Protocols. In: Cimato, S., Galdi, C., Persiano, G. (eds.) SCN 2002. LNCS, vol. 2576, pp. 268–289. Springer, Heidelberg (2003)
7. Camenisch, J., Lysyanskaya, A.: Signature Schemes and Anonymous Credentials from Bilinear Maps. In: Franklin, M. (ed.) CRYPTO 2004. LNCS, vol. 3152, pp. 56–72. Springer, Heidelberg (2004)

8. Chen, J.: MSP430 Overview and Key Applications (2008)
9. Daley, W.: Digital Signature Standard (DSS). Tech. rep., DTIC (2000)
10. Devegili, A.J., Scott, M., Dahab, R.: Implementing Cryptographic Pairings over Barreto-Naehrig Curves. In: Takagi, T., Okamoto, T., Okamoto, E., Okamoto, T. (eds.) Pairing 2007. LNCS, vol. 4575, pp. 197–207. Springer, Heidelberg (2007)
11. Dreslinski, R., Wieckowski, M., Blaauw, D., Sylvester, D., Mudge, T.: Near-Threshold Computing: Reclaiming Moore's Law Through Energy Efficient Integrated Circuits. Proceedings of the IEEE (2010)
12. Fiat, A., Shamir, A.: How to Prove Yourself: Practical Solutions to Identification and Signature Problems. In: Odlyzko, A.M. (ed.) CRYPTO 1986. LNCS, vol. 263, pp. 186–194. Springer, Heidelberg (1987)
13. Fujisaki, E., Okamoto, T.: Statistical Zero Knowledge Protocols to Prove Modular Polynomial Relations. In: Kaliski Jr., B.S. (ed.) CRYPTO 1997. LNCS, vol. 1294, pp. 16–30. Springer, Heidelberg (1997)
14. Gas, P., Company, E.: PG & E: Full Installation Schedule
15. IAR Systems: IAR Embedded Workbench (2011), http://www.iar.com/ewarm
16. Intel: Corporate Timeline (2011), http://www.intel.com/about/companyinfo/mu-seum/archives/timeline.html
17. Jawurek, M., Johns, M., Kerschbaum, F.: Plug-In Privacy for Smart Metering Billing. In: Fischer-Hübner, S., Hopper, N. (eds.) PETS 2011. LNCS, vol. 6794, pp. 192–210. Springer, Heidelberg (2011)
18. Kursawe, K., Danezis, G., Kohlweiss, M.: Privacy-Friendly Aggregation for the Smart-Grid. In: Fischer-Hübner, S., Hopper, N. (eds.) PETS 2011. LNCS, vol. 6794, pp. 175–191. Springer, Heidelberg (2011)
19. Labrosse, J.: MicroC/OS-III: The Real-Time Kernel. Micri$\mu$m Press (2010)
20. Lysyanskaya, A., Rivest, R.L., Sahai, A., Wolf, S.: Pseudonym Systems (Extended Abstract). In: Heys, H.M., Adams, C.M. (eds.) SAC 1999. LNCS, vol. 1758, pp. 184–199. Springer, Heidelberg (2000)
21. Molina-Markham, A., Shenoy, P., Fu, K., Cecchet, E., Irwin, D.: Private Memoirs of a Smart Meter. In: Proceedings of the 2nd ACM Workshop on Embedded Sensing Systems for Energy-Efficiency in Building (2010)
22. Pearson, J., Moise, T.: The Advantages of FRAM-Based Smart ICs for Next Generation Government Electronic IDs (2007)
23. Pedersen, T.P.: Non-interactive and Information-Theoretic Secure Verifiable Secret Sharing. In: Feigenbaum, J. (ed.) CRYPTO 1991. LNCS, vol. 576, pp. 129–140. Springer, Heidelberg (1992)
24. Plumb, C., Zimmermann, P.: bnlib: Extended Precision Integer Math Library
25. Rial, A., Danezis, G.: Privacy-Preserving Smart Metering. In: Workshop on Privacy in the Electronic Society (2011)
26. Rosenberg, B.: Handbook of Financial Cryptography and Security. Chapman & Hall/CRC (2010)
27. Scott, M.: MIRACL - Multiprecision Integer and Rational Arithmetic C Library
28. Devegili, A.J., Scott, M., Dahab, R.: Implementing Cryptographic Pairings over Barreto-Naehrig Curves. In: Takagi, T., Okamoto, T., Okamoto, E., Okamoto, T. (eds.) Pairing 2007. LNCS, vol. 4575, pp. 197–207. Springer, Heidelberg (2007)
29. Scott, M., Costigan, N., Abdulwahab, W.: Implementing Cryptographic Pairings on Smartcards. In: Goubin, L., Matsui, M. (eds.) CHES 2006. LNCS, vol. 4249, pp. 134–147. Springer, Heidelberg (2006)
30. Texas Instruments: SYS/BIOS Real-Time Operating System (2011)

# Memory-Efficient Garbled Circuit Generation for Mobile Devices

Benjamin Mood, Lara Letaw, and Kevin Butler

Department of Compter & Information Science
University of Oregon, Eugene, OR 97405 USA
{bmood,zephron,butler}@cs.uoregon.edu

**Abstract.** Secure function evaluation (SFE) on mobile devices, such as smartphones, creates compelling new applications such as privacy-preserving bartering. Generating custom garbled circuits on smartphones, however, is infeasible for all but the most trivial problems due to the high memory overhead incurred. In this paper, we develop a new methodology of generating garbled circuits that is memory-efficient. Using the standard SFDL language for describing secure functions as input, we design a new pseudo-assembly language (PAL) and a template-driven compiler that generates circuits which can be evaluated with Fairplay. We deploy this compiler for Android devices and demonstrate that a large new set of circuits can now be generated on smartphones, with memory overhead for the set intersection problem reduced by 95.6% for the 2-set case. We develop a password vault application to show how runtime generation of circuits can be used in practice. We also show that our circuit generation techniques can be used in conjunction with other SFE optimizations. These results demonstrate the feasibility of generating garbled circuits on mobile devices while maintaining high-level function specification.

## 1 Introduction

Mobile phones are extraordinarily popular, with adoption rates unprecedented in the history of product adoption by consumers. Smartphones in particular have been embraced, with over 296 million of these devices shipped in 2010 [4]. The increasing importance of the mobile computing environment requires functionality tailored to the limited resources available on a phone. Concerns of portability and battery life necessitate design compromises for mobile devices compared to servers, desktops, and even laptops. In short, mobile devices will always be resource-constrained compared to their larger counterparts. However, through careful design and implementation, they can provide equivalent functionality while retaining the advantages of ubiquitous access.

Privacy-preserving computing is particularly well suited to deployment on mobile devices. For example, two parties bartering in a marketplace may wish to conveal the nature of their transaction from others, and share minimal information with each other. Such a transaction is ideally suited for *secure function evaluation*, or SFE. Recent work, such as by Chapman et al. [6], demonstrates the myriad applications of SFE on smartphones.

A.D. Keromytis (Ed.): FC 2012, LNCS 7397, pp. 254–268, 2012.

However, because of computational and memory requirements, performing many of these operations in the mobile environment is infeasible; often, the only hope is outsourcing computation to a cloud or other trusted third party, thus raising concerns about the privacy of the computation.

In this paper, we describe a memory-efficient technique for generating the garbled circuits needed to perform secure function evaluation on smartphones. While numerous research initiatives have considered how to *evaluate* these circuits more efficiently [16,7], little work has gone towards efficient *generation*. Our port of the canonical Fairplay [12] compiler for SFE to the Android mobile operating system revealed that because of intensive memory requirements, the majority of circuits could not be compiled in this environment. As a result, our main contribution is a novel design to compile the high-level Secure Function Definition Language (SFDL) used by Fairplay and other SFE environments into garbled circuits with minimal memory usage. We created Pseudo Assembly Language (PAL), a mid-level intermediate representation (IR) compiled from SFDL, where each instruction represents a pre-built circuit. We created a Pseudo Assembly Language Compiler (PALC), which takes in a PAL file and outputs the corresponding circuit in Fairplay's syntax. We then created a compiler to compile SFDL files into PAL and then, using PALC, to the Secure Hardware Definition Language (SHDL) used by Fairplay for circuit evaluation.

Using these compilation techniques, we are able to generate circuits that were previously infeasible to create in the mobile environment. For example, the set intersection problem with sets of size two requires 469 KB of memory with our techniques versus over 10667 KB using a direct port of Fairplay to Android, a reduction of 95.6%. We are able to evaluate results for the set intersection problem using four and eight sets, as well as other problems such as Levenshtein distance; none of these circuits could previously be generated at all on mobile devices due to their memory overhead. Combined with more efficient evaluation, our techniques provide a new arsenal for making privacy-preserving computation feasible in the mobile environment.

The rest of this paper is organized as follows. Section 2 provides background on secure function evaluation, garbled circuits, and the Fairplay SFE compiler. Section 3 describes the design of PAL, our pseudo assembly language, and our associated compilers. Section 4 describes our testing environment and methodology, and provides benchmarks on memory and execution time. Section 5 describes applications that demonstrate circuit generation in use, while Section 6 describes related work and Section 7 concludes.

## 2    Background

### 2.1    Secure Function Evaluation with Fairplay

The origins of SFE trace back to Yao's pioneering work on garbled circuits [18]. SFE enables two parties to compute a function without knowing each other's input and without the presence of a trusted third party. More formally, given participants Alice and Bob with input vectors $a = a_0, a_1, \cdots a_{n-1}$ and $b = b_0, b_1, \cdots b_{m-1}$ respectively, they wish to compute a function $f(a, b)$ without revealing any information about the inputs that cannot be gleaned from observing the function's output. Fundamentally, SFE is predicated on two cryptographic primitives. *Garbled circuits* allow for the evaluation of a function without any party gaining additional information about the participants. This is possible since one party creates a garbled circuit and the other party evaluates the circuit without knowing what the wires represent. Secondly, *oblivious transfer* allows the party executing the garbled circuit to obtain the correct wires for setting inputs from the other party without gaining additional information about the circuit; in particular, a 1-out-of-$n$ OT protocol allows Bob to learn about one piece of data without gaining any information on the remaining $n - 1$ pieces.

A garbled circuit is composed of many garbled gates, with inputs represented by two random fixed-length strings. Like a normal boolean gate, the garbled gate evaluates the inputs and gives a single output, but alterations are made to the garbled gate's truth table: aside from the randomly chosen input values, the output values are uniquely encrypted by the input wires and an initialization vector. The order of the entries in the table is then permuted to prevent the order from giving away the value. Consequently, the only values saved for the truth table are the four encrypted output values. A two-input gate is thus represented by the two inputs and four encrypted output values.

The garbled circuit protocol requires that both parties are able to provide inputs. If Bob creates the circuit and Alice receives it, Bob can determine which wires to set, and Alice performs an oblivious transfer to receive her input wires. Once she knows her input wires she runs the circuit by evaluating each gate in order. To evaluate a gate, she uses the input values as the key to decrypt the output value. To find the correct entry in the table, Alice uses a decryption step using the input wires as keys. To find her output, Alice acquires a translation table, a hash of the wires, from Bob for her possible output values. She then can perform the hash on her output wires to see which wires were set. Alice sends Bob's output in garbled form since she cannot interpret it.

Fairplay is the canonical tool for generating and evaluating garbled circuits for secure function evaluation. The Fairplay group is notable for creating the abstraction of a high-level language, known as SFDL. This language describes secure evaluation functions and is compiled SHDL, which is written in the style of a hardware description language such as VHDL and describes the garbled circuit. The circuit evaluation portion of Fairplay provides for the execution of the garbled circuit protocol and uses oblivious transfer (OT) to exchange information. Fairplay uses the 1-out-of-2 OT protocols of Bellare et al. [1] and Naor et al. [14] which allows for Alice to pick one of two items that Bob is offering and also prevents Bob from knowing which item she has picked.

Examining the compiler in more detail, Fairplay compiles each instruction written in SFDL into a so-called *multi-bit instruction*. These multi-bit (e.g. integer) instructions are transformed to *single-bit instructions* (e.g., the 32 separate bits to represent that integer). From these single-bit instructions, Fairplay then

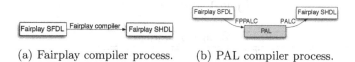

(a) Fairplay compiler process.    (b) PAL compiler process.

**Fig. 1.** Compilation with Fairplay versus PAL

unrolls variables, transforms the instructions into SHDL, and outputs the file, either immediately or after further circuit optimizations.

Fairplay's circuit generation process is very memory-intensive. We performed a port of Fairplay directly to the Android mobile platform (described further in Section 4) and found that a large number of circuits were completely unable to be compiled. We examined the results of circuit compilation on a PC to determine the scope of memory requirements. From tests we performed on a 64-bit Windows 7 machine, we observed that Fairplay needed at least 245 MB of memory to run the compilation of the keyed database program, a program that matches database keys with values and employs SFE for privacy preservation (described further in Section 4). In order to determine the cause of this memory usage, we began by analyzing Fairplay's compiler.

From our analysis, Fairplay uses the most memory during the mapping operation from multi-bit to single-bit instructions. During this phase, the memory requirements increased by 7 times when the keyed database program ran. We concluded that it would be easier to create a new system for generating the SHDL circuit file, rather than making extensive modifications to the existing Fairplay implementation. To accomplish this, we created an intermediate language that we called PAL, described in detail in section 3.

## 2.2 Threat Model

As with Fairplay, which is secure in the random oracle model implemented using the SHA-1 hash function, our threat model accounts for an honest-but-curious adversary. This means the participants will obey the given protocol but may look at any data the protocol produces. Note that this assumption is well-described by others considering secure function and secure multiparty computation, such as Kruger et al.'s OBDD protocol [10], Pinkas et al.'s SFE optimizations [16], the TASTY proposal for automating two-party communication [5], Jha et al.'s privacy-preserving genomics [8], Brickell et al.'s privacy-preserving classifiers [3] and Huang et al.'s recent improvements to evaluating SFE [6]. Similarly, we make the well-used assumption that parties enter correct input to the function.

## 3    Design

To overcome the intensive memory requirements of generating garbled circuits within Fairplay, we designed a *pseudo assembly language*, or PAL, and a *pseudo*

Table 1. PAL Operations

| Possible Operations | |
|---|---|
| Operation | Syntax |
| Addition | DEST + V1 V2 |
| Greater than or Equal to | DEST >= V1 V2 |
| Equal to | DEST == V1 V2 |
| Bitwise AND | DEST & V1 V2 |
| If Conditional | DEST IF COND V1 V2 |
| Input line | INPUT V1 a (or INPUT V1 b) |
| Output line | INPUT V1 a (or INPUT V1 b) |
| For loop | V1 FOR X (an integer) to Y (an integer) |
| Call a procedure | V1 PROC |
| Call a function | DEST,...,DEST = FunctionName(param, ... ,param) |
| Multiple Set Equals | DEST,...,DEST=V,...,V |

*assembly language compiler* called PALC. As noted in Figure 1, we change Fairplay's compilation model by first compiling SFDL files into PAL using our FP-PALC compiler, and generating the SHDL file which can then be run using Fairplay's circuit evaluator with our PALC compiler.

### 3.1 PAL

We first describe PAL, our memory-efficient language for garbled circuit creation. PAL resembles an assembly language where each instruction corresponds to a pre-optimized circuit. PAL is composed of at least two parts: variable declarations and instructions. PAL files may also contain functions and procedures. A full table showing all headings can be found in the full technical report [13] and is elided here because of space constraints.

Table 1 lists an abbreviated set of operations that are available in PAL along with their instruction signatures. The full set can be found in our technical report [13]. Each operation consists of a destination, an operator, and one to three operands. DEST, V1, V2, and COND are variables in our operation listing. PAL also has operations not found in Fairplay, such as shift and rotate.

Note that conditionals can be reduced to the IF conditional. Unlike in regular programs, all parts of an IF circuit must be executed on every run.

The first part of a PAL program is the set of variable declarations. These consist of a variable name and bit length, and the section is marked by a *Variables:* label. In this low-level language there are no structs or objects, only integer variables and arrays. Each variable in a PAL file must be declared before it can be used. Array indices may be declared at any point in the variable name.

Figure 2 shows an example of variables declared in PAL. `Alicekey` and `Bobkey` have a bit length of 6, `Bobin` and `Aliceout` have a bit length of 32, `COND` is a boolean like variable which has a bit length of 1, and `Array[7]` is an array of seven elements where each have a bit length of 5. All declared variables are

```
Variables:
Alicekey    6
Bobin      32
Bobkey      6
Aliceout   32
COND        1
Array[7]    5
```

```
Instructions:
Bobin IN b
Bobkey IN b
Alicekey IN a
COND == Alicekey Bobkey
Aliceout IF COND Bobin Aliceout
Aliceout OUT a
```

**Fig. 2.** Example of variable declarations in PAL

**Fig. 3.** Example of number comparison (for keyed database problem) in PAL

```
Variables:
i 6
in.a 6
in.b[16].data 24
in.b[16].key 6
out.a 24
$c0 1
$t0 1
DBsize 64

Procedure: $p0
$t0 == in.a in.b[i].key
```

```
$c0 = $t0
out.a IF $c0 in.b[i].data out.a

Instructions:
in.b[16].data IN b
in.b[16].key IN b
in.a IN a
DBsize = 16
i FOR 0 15
$p0 PROC
out.a OUT a
```

**Fig. 4.** Representation of keyed database program in PAL

initialized to 0. After variable declarations, a PAL program can have function and procedure definitions preceding the instructions, which is the main function.

Figure 3 shows the PAL instructions for comparing two keys as used in the keyed database problem, described more fully below. The first two statements are input retrieval for Bob, while the third retrieves input for Alice. A boolean like variable COND is set based on a comparison and the output is set accordingly. Note that constants are allowed in place of V1, V2, or COND in any instruction. PAL supports loops, functions, and procedures.

To illustrate a full program, Figure 4 shows the keyed database problem in PAL, where a user selects data from another user's database without any information given about the item selected. In this program, Bob enters 16 keys and 16 data entries and Alice enters her key. If Alice's key matches one of Bob's then Alice's output of the program is Bob's data entry that held the corresponding key. The PAL program shows how each key is checked against Alice's key. If one of those keys matches, then the output is set.

## 3.2 PALC

Circuits generated by our PALC compiler, which generates SHDL files from PAL, are created using a database of pre-generated circuits matching instructions to their circuit representations. These circuits, other than equality, were generated using simple Fairplay programs that represent equivalent functionality. Any operation that does not generate a gate is considered a *free* operation. Assignments, shifts, and rotates are free.

Variables in PALC have two possible states: they are either specified by a list of gate positions or they have a real numerical value. If an operation is performed on real value variables, the result is stored as a real value. These real value operations do not need a circuit to be created and are thus free.

When variables of two different sizes are used, the size of the operation is determined by the destination. If the destination is 24 bits and the operands are 32 bits, the operation will be performed 24-bit operands. This will not cause an error but may yield incorrect results if false assumptions are made.

There are currently a number of known optimizations, such as removing static gates, which are not implemented inside PALC; these optimization techniques are a subject of future work.

### 3.3   FPPALC

To demonstrate the feasibility of compileing non-trivial programs on a phone, we modified Fairplay's SFDL compiler to compile into PAL and then run PALC to compile to SHDL. This compiler is called FPPALC. Compiling in steps greatly reduces the amount of memory that is required for circuit generation.

We note our compiler will not yield the same result as Fairplay's compiler in two cases, which we believe demonstrate erroneous behavior in Fairplay. In these instances, Fairplay's circuit evaluator will crash or yield erroneous results. A more detailed explanation can be found in our technical report [13], To summarize, unoptimized constants in SFDL can cause the evaluator to crash, while programs consisting of a single if statement can produce inconsistent variable modifications. Apart from these differences, the generated circuits have equivalent functionality.

For our implementation of the SFDL to PAL compiler we took the original Fairplay compiler and modified it to produce the PAL output by removing all elements besides the parser. From the parser we built our own type system, support for basic expressions, assignment statements, and finally if statements and for loops. All variables are represented as unsigned variables in the output but input and other operations treat them as signed variables. Our implementation of FPPALC and PALC, which compile SFDL to PAL and PAL to SHDL respectively, comprises over 7500 lines of Java code.

### 3.4   Garbled Circuit Security

A major question posed about our work is the following: *Does using an intermediate metalanguage with precompiled circuit templates change the security guarantees compared to circuits generated completely within Fairplay?* The simple answer to this question is no: we believe that the security guarantees offered by the circuits that we compile with PAL are equivalent to those from Fairplay.

**Table 2.** FPPALC on Android: total memory application was using at end of stages and the time it took

| Program | Initial | Memory (KB) | | Time (ms) | | |
|---|---|---|---|---|---|---|
| | | SFDL→PAL | PAL→SHDL | SFDL→PAL | PAL→SHDL | Total |
| Millionaires | 4931 | 5200 | 5227 | 90 | 29 | 119 |
| Billionaires | 4924 | 5214 | 5365 | 152 | 54 | 206 |
| CoinFlip | 5042 | 5379 | 5426 | 139 | 122 | 261 |
| KeyedDB | 4971 | 5365 | 5659 | 142 | 220 | 362 |
| SetInter 2 | 5064 | 5393 | 5533 | 161 | 305 | 466 |
| SetInter 4 | 5078 | 5437 | 5600 | 135 | 1074 | 1209 |
| SetInter 8 | 5122 | 5542 | 5739 | 170 | 6659 | 6829 |
| Levenshtein Dist 2 | 5184 | 5431 | 5576 | 183 | 336 | 519 |
| Levenshtein Dist 4 | 5233 | 5436 | 5638 | 190 | 622 | 802 |
| Levenshtein Dist 8 | 5264 | 5473 | 5693 | 189 | 2987 | 3172 |

Because there are no preconditions about the design of the circuit in the description of our garbled circuit protocol, any circuit that generates a given result will work: there are often multiple ways of building a circuit with equivalent functionality. Additionally, the circuit construction is a composition of existing circuit templates that were themselves generated through Fairplay-like constructions. Note that the security of Fairplay does not rely on how the circuits are created but on the way garbled circuit constructs work. Therefore, our circuits will provide the same security guarantees since our circuits also rely on using the garbled circuit protocol.

# 4   Evaluation

In this section, we demonstrate the performance of our circuit generator to show its feasibility for use on mobile devices. We targeted the Android platform for our implementation, with HTC Thunderbolts as a deployment platform. These smartphones contain a 1 GHz Qualcomm Snapdragon processor and 768 MB of RAM, with each Android application limited to a 24 MB heap.

## 4.1   Testing Methodology

We benchmarked compile-time resource usage with and without intermediate compilation to the PAL language. We tested on the Thunderbolts; all results reported are from these devices. Memory usage on the phones was measured by looking at the PSS metric, which measures pages that have memory from multiple processes. The PSS metric is an approximation of the number of pages used combined with how many processes are using a specific page of memory.

Several SFDL programs, of varying complexity, were used for benchmarking. Each program is described below. We use the SFDL programs representing the

Millionaires, Billionaires, and Keyed Database problems as presented in Fairplay [11]. The other SFDL files that we have written can be found in the full technical report [13]. We describe these below in more detail.

The *Millionaire's* problem describes two users who want to determine which has more money without either revealing their inputs. We used a 4-bit integer input for this problem. The *Billionaire's* problem is identical in structure but uses 32-bit inputs instead. The *CoinFlip* problem models a trusted coin flip where neither party can determine the program's outcome deterministically. It takes two inputs of 24-bit inputs per party. In the *Keyed database* program, a user performs a lookup in another user's database and returns a value without the owner being aware of which part of the database is looked up – we use a database of size 16. The keys are 6-bits and the data members are 24-bits. The *Set intersection* problem determines elements two users have in common, e.g., friends in a social network. We measured with sets of size 2, 4, and 8 where 24-bit input was used. Finally, we examined *Levenshtein distance*, which measures edit distance between two strings. This program takes in 8-bit inputs.

## 4.2   Results

Below the results of the compile-time tests performed on the HTC Thunderbolts. We measured memory allocation and time required to compile, for both the Fairplay and PAL compilers. In the latter case, we have data for compiling to and from the PAL language. Our complete compiler is referred to FPPALC in this section.

**Memory Usage & Compilation Time.** Table 2 provides memory and execution benchmarks for circuit generation, taken over at least 10 trials per circuit. We measure the initial amount of memory used by the application as an SFDL file is loaded, the amount of memory consumed during the SFDL to PAL compilation, and memory consumed at the end of the PAL to SHDL compilation.

As an example of the advantages of our approach, we successfully compiled a set intersection of size 90 that had 33,000,000 gates on the phone. The output file was greater than 2.5 GB. Android has a limit of 4 GB per file and if this was not the case we believe we could have compiled a file of the size of the memory card (30 GB). This is because the operations are serialized and the circuit never has to fully remain in memory.

Although we did not focus on speed, Table 2 gives a clear indication of where the most time is used per compilation: the PAL to SHDL phase, where the circuit is output. The speed of this phase is directly related to the size of the program that is being output, while the speed of the SFDL to PAL compliation is related to the number of individual instructions.

**Comparison to Fairplay.** Table 3 compares the Fairplay compiler with FP-PALC. Where results are not present for Fairplay are situations where it was unable to compile these programs on the phone. For the set intersection problem

**Table 3.** Comparison of memory increase by Fairplay and FPPALC during circuit generation

| | Memory (KB) | |
|---|---|---|
| Program | Fairplay | FPPALC |
| Millionaires | 658 | 296 |
| Billionaires | 1188 | 441 |
| CoinFlip | 1488 | 384 |
| KeyedDB 16 | NA | 688 |
| SetInter 2 | 10667 | 469 |
| SetInter 4 | NA | 522 |
| SetInter 8 | NA | 617 |
| Levenshtein Dist 2 | NA | 392 |
| Levenshtein Dist 4 | NA | 405 |
| Levenshtein Dist 8 | NA | 429 |

**Table 4.** Evaluating FPPALC circuits on Fairplay's evaluator with both Nipane et al.'s OT and the suggested Fairplay OT

| | Memory (KB) | | | Time (ms) | | |
|---|---|---|---|---|---|---|
| Program | Initial | Open File | End | Open File | Fairplay | Nipane |
| Millionaires | 5466 | 5556 | 5952 | 197 | 533 | 406 |
| Billionaires | 5451 | 5894 | 6287 | 579 | 1291 | 981 |
| CoinFlip | 5461 | 5933 | 6426 | 789 | 1795 | 1320 |
| KeyedDB 16 | 5315 | 6197 | 7667 | 1600 | 1678 | 1593 |
| SetInter 2 | 5423 | 5993 | 6932 | 1511 | 2088 | 1719 |
| SetInter 4 | 5414 | 7435 | 11711 | 8619 | 7714 | 7146 |
| Levenshtein Dist 2 | 5617 | 6134 | 7162 | 1799 | 2220 | 2004 |
| Levenshtein Dist 4 | 5615 | 7215 | 10787 | 7448 | 6538 | 6150 |
| Levenshtein Dist 8 | 5537 | 12209 | 20162 | 29230 | 29373 | 27925 |

with set 2, FPPALC uses 469 KB of memory versus 10667 KB by Fairplay, a reduction of 95.6%. Testing showed that the largest version of the keyed database problem that Fairplay could handle is with a database of size 10, while we easily compiled the circuit with a database of size 16 using FPPALC.

**Circuit Evaluation.** Table 4 depicts the memory and time of the evaluator running the programs compiled by FPPALC. Consider again the two parties Bob and Alice, who create and receive the circuit respectively in the garbled circuit protocol. This table is from Bob's perspective, who has a slightly higher memory usage and a slightly lower run time than Alice. We present the time required to open the circuit file for evaluation and to perform the evaluation using two different oblivious transfer protocols. Described further below, we used both Fairplay's evaluator and an improved oblivious transfer (OT) protocol developed by Nipane et al. [15]. Note that Fairplay's evaluator was unable to evaluate

**Table 5.** Results from programs compiled with Fairplay on a PC evaluated with Nipane et al.'s OT

| Program | Memory (KB) | | | Time (ms) | |
|---|---|---|---|---|---|
| | Initial | After File Opening | End | File Opening | Evaluating |
| Millionaires | 5640 | 5733 | 5995 | 194 | 302 |
| Billionaires | 5536 | 5885 | 6303 | 631 | 958 |
| +CoinFlip | 5528 | 5796 | 6280 | 428 | 1062 |
| KeyedDB 16 | 5551 | 6255 | 7848 | 2252 | 1955 |
| SetInter 2 | 5439 | 6018 | 7047 | 1663 | 2131 |
| SetInter 4 | 5553 | 7708 | 13507 | 10540 | 9555 |
| +Levenshtein Dist 2 | 5568 | 5872 | 6316 | 529 | 781 |
| +Levenshtein Dist 4 | 5577 | 6088 | 7178 | 1704 | 2213 |
| Levenshtein Dist 8 | 5488 | 7670 | 13011 | 9745 | 8662 |

programs with around 20,000 mixed two and three input gates on the phone. This limit translates to 209 32-bit addition operations in our compiler.

While the circuits we generate are not optimized in the same manner as Fairplay's circuits, we wanted to ensure that their execution time would still be competitive against circuits generated by Fairplay. Because of the limits of generating Fairplay circuits on the phone, we compiled them using Fairplay on a PC, then used these circuits to compare evaluation times on the phone. Table 5 shows the results of this evaluation. Programs denoted with a + required edits to the SHDL to run in the evaluator, in order to prevent their crashing due to the issues described in Section 3.3. In many cases, evaluating the circuit generated by FPPALC resulted in faster evaluation. One anomaly to this trend was Levenshtein distance, which ran about three times slower using FPPALC. We speculate this is due to the optimization of constant addition operations and discuss further in Section 5. Note, however, that these circuits are unable to be generated on the phone using Fairplay and require pre-compilation.

### 4.3   Interoperability

To show that our circuit generation protocol can be easily used with other improved approaches to SFE, we used the faster oblivious transfer protocol of Nipane et al. [15], who replace the OT operation in Fairplay with 1-out-of-2 OT scheme based on a two-lock RSA cryptosystem. Shown in Table 5, these provide an over 24% speedup for the Billionaire's problem and 26% speedup for the Coin Flip protocol. On average, there was an 13% decrease in evaluation time across all problems. For the *Millionaires, Billionaires,* and *CoinFlip* programs we disabled Nagle's algorithm as described by Nipane et al., leading to better performance on these problems. The magnitude of improvement decreased as circuits increased in size, a situation we continue to investigate. Our main findings, however, are that our memory-efficient circuit generation is complementary to other approaches that focus on improving execution time and can be easily integrated.

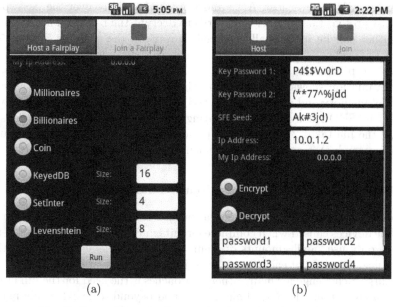

**Fig. 5.** Screenshots of editor and password wallet applications

# 5    Discussion

To demonstrate how our memory-efficient compiler can be used in practice, we developed Android apps capable of generating circuits at runtime. We describe these below.

## 5.1    GUI Based Editor

To allow compilation on a phone we have to address one large problem. Our experience porting Fairplay to Android showed the difficulty of writing a program on the phone. Figure 5 (a) shows an example of a GUI front-end for picking and compiling given programs based on parameters. A list of programs is given to the user who can then pick and choose which program they wish to run. For some of the programs there is a size variable that can also be changed.

## 5.2    Password Vault Application

We designed an Android application that introduces SFE as a mechanism to provide secure digital deposit boxes for passwords. In brief, this "password vault" can work in a decentralized fashion without reliance on the cloud or any third parties. If Alice fears that her phone may go missing and wants Bob to have a copy of her passwords, she and Bob can use their "master" passwords as inputs to a pseudorandom number generator. These passwords are not revealed to either party, nor is the output of the generators, which is used to encrypt the password.

If the passwords are ever lost, Alice and Bob can jointly recover the passwords; both must present their master passwords to decrypt the password file, ensuring that neither can be individually coerced to retrieve the contents. Figure 5(b) shows a screenshot of this application. which can encrypt passwords from the user or decrypt those in the database.

Our evaluation shows that compiling the password SFDL program requires 915 KB of memory and approximately 505 ms, with 60% of that time involving the PAL to SHDL conversion. Evaluating the circuit is more time intensive. Opening the file takes 2 seconds, and performing the OTs and gate evaluation takes 6.5 seconds. We are exploring efficiencies to reduce execution time.

### 5.3   Experiences with Garbled Circuit Generation

A major takeaway from our implementation was cognizance of the large burden on mobile devices caused when complete circuits must be kept in memory. Better solutions only use small amounts of memory to direct the actual computation, for instance, one copy of each circuit even if $n$ statements are required.

The largest challenge for many other approaches is the need for the full circuit to be created. Circuits for $O(n^2)$ algorithms and beyond scale extremely poorly. A different approach is needed for larger scalability. For instance, doubling the Levenshtien distance $n$ paremeter increased the circuit size by a factor of about 4.5 (decreasing the larger n grows), when n is 8 there are 11,268 gates, 16 is 51,348 gates, 32 is 218,676 gates, and 64 is 902,004 gates.

Our original version of PAL did not scale well due to its lack of loops, arrays, procedures, or functions. Once these structures were added, the length of PAL programs decreased dramatically. Instead of unrolling all programming control flow constructs we added them for smaller PAL programs, creating largely identical circuits with much fewer instructions.

## 6   Related Work

Other research has primarily focused on optimizing the actual evaluation for SFE, while we focus on generating circuits in a memory efficient manor. Kolesnikov et al. [9] demonstrated a "free XOR" evaluation technique to improve execution speed, while Pinkas et al. [16] implement techniques to reduce circuit size of the circuits and computation length. We plan to implement these enhancements in the next version of the circuit evaluator.

Huang et al. [7] have similarly focused on optimizing secure function evaluation, focusing on execution in resource-constrained environments. The approach differs considerably from ours in that users build their own functions directly at the circuit level rather than using high-level abstractions such as SFDL. While the resulting circuit may execute more quickly, there is a burden on the user to correctly generate these circuits, and because input files are generated at the circuit level in Java, compiling on the phone would require a full-scale Java compiler rather than the smaller-scale SFDL compiler that we use.

Another way to increase the speed of SFE has been to focus on leveraging the hardware of devices. Pu et al. [17] have considered leveraging Nvidia's CUDA-based GPU architecture to increase the speed of SFE. We have conducted preliminary investigations into leveraging vector processing capabilities on smartphones, specifically single-instruction multiple-data units available on the ARM Cortex processing cores found within many modern smartphones, as a means of providing better service for certain cryptographic functionality.

Kruger et al. [10] described a way to use ordered binary decision diagrams (OBDDs) to evaluate SFE, which can provide faster execution for certain problems. Our future work will involve determining whether the process of preparing OBDDs can benefit from our memory-efficient techniques. TASTY [5] also uses different methods of privacy-preserving computation, namely homomorphic encryption (HE) as well as garbled circuits, based on user choices. This approach requires the user to explicitly choose the computation style, but may also benefit from our generation techniques for both circuits and the homomorphic constructions. FairplayMP [2] showed a method of secure multiparty computation. We are examining how to extend our compiler to become multiparty capable.

## 7 Conclusion

We introduced a memory efficient technique for making SFE tractable on the mobile platform. We created PAL, an intermediate language, between SFDL and SHDL programs and showed that by using pre-generated circuit templates we could make previously intractable circuits compile on a smartphone, reducing memory requirements for the set intersection circuit by 95.6%. We demonstrate the use of this compiler with a GUI editor and a password vault application. Future work includes incorporating optimizations in the circuit evaluator and determining whether the pre-generated templates may work with other approaches to both SFE and other privacy-preserving computation primitives.

**Acknowledgements.** We would like to thank Patrick Traynor for his insights regarding the narrative of the paper, and Adam Bates and Hannah Pruse for their comments.

This work is supported by NSF grant CNS-1118046. Additionally, this material is based on research sponsored by DARPA under agreement number FA8750-11-2-0211. The U.S. Government is authorized to reproduce and distribute reprints for Governmental purposes notwithstanding any copyright notation thereon. The views and conclusions contained herein are those of the authors and should not be interpreted as necessarily representing the official policies or endorsements, either expressed or implied, of DARPA or the U.S. Government.

## References

1. Bellare, M., Micali, S.: Non-interactive oblivious transfer and applications. In: Brassard, G. (ed.) CRYPTO 1989. LNCS, vol. 435, pp. 547–557. Springer, Heidelberg (1990)

2. Ben-David, A., Nisan, N., Pinkas, B.: FairplayMP: a System for Secure Multi-Party Computation. In: 15th ACM Conference on Computer and Communications Security, CCS 2008, pp. 257–266. ACM, New York (2008)
3. Brickell, J., Shmatikov, V.: Privacy-Preserving Classifier Learning. In: Dingledine, R., Golle, P. (eds.) FC 2009. LNCS, vol. 5628, pp. 128–147. Springer, Heidelberg (2009)
4. Gartner: Gartner Says Worldwide Mobile Device Sales to End Users Reached 1.6 Billion Units in 2010; Smartphone Sales Grew 72 Percent in 2010 (2011), http://www.gartner.com/it/page.jsp?id=1543014
5. Henecka, W., Kögl, S., Sadeghi, A.-R., Schneider, T., Wehrenberg, I.: TASTY: Tool for Automating Secure Two-Party Computations. In: Proc. 17th ACM Symposium on Computer and Communications Security, CCS 2010, Chicago, IL (October 2010)
6. Huang, Y., Chapman, P., Evans, D.: Privacy-Preserving applications on smartphones: Challenges and opportunities. In: Proceedings of the 6th USENIX Workshop on Hot Topics in Security (HotSec 2011) (August 2011)
7. Huang, Y., Evans, D., Katz, J., Malka, L.: Faster Secure Two-Party Computation Using Garbled Circuits. In: Proceedings of the 20th USENIX Security Symposium, San Francisco, CA (August 2011)
8. Jha, S., Kruger, L., Shmatikov, V.: Towards Practical Privacy for Genomic Computation. In: Proceedings of the 2008 IEEE Symposium on Security and Privacy, Berkeley, CA, USA, pp. 216–230 (November 2008)
9. Kolesnikov, V., Schneider, T.: Improved Garbled Circuit: Free XOR Gates and Applications. In: Aceto, L., Damgård, I., Goldberg, L.A., Halldórsson, M.M., Ingólfsdóttir, A., Walukiewicz, I. (eds.) ICALP 2008, Part II. LNCS, vol. 5126, pp. 486–498. Springer, Heidelberg (2008)
10. Kruger, L., Jha, S., Goh, E.-J., Boneh, D.: Secure Function Evaluation with Ordered Binary Decision Diagrams. In: Proceedings of the 13th ACM conference on Computer and Communications Security (CCS 2006), Alexandria, VA (October 2006)
11. Malkhi, D., Nisan, N., Pinkas, B.: Fairplay Project, http://www.cs.huji.ac.il/project/Fairplay/
12. Malkhi, D., Nisan, N., Pinkas, B., Sella, Y.: Fairplay: a Secure Two-Party Computation System. In: Proceedings of the 13th USENIX Security Symposium, San Diego, CA (2004)
13. Mood, B., Letaw, L., Butler, K.: Memory-Efficient Garbled Circuit Generation for Mobile Devices. Technical Report CIS-TR-2011-04, Department of Computer and Information Science, University of Oregon, Eugene, OR, USA (September 2011)
14. Naor, M., Pinkas, B.: Efficient Oblivious Transfer Protocols. In: Proceedings of SODA 2001, Washington, DC (2001)
15. Nipane, N., Dacosta, I., Traynor, P.: "Mix-In-Place" Anonymous Networking Using Secure Function Evaluation. In: Proceedings of the Annual Computer Security Applications Conference (ACSAC) (December 2011)
16. Pinkas, B., Schneider, T., Smart, N.P., Williams, S.C.: Secure Two-Party Computation Is Practical. In: Matsui, M. (ed.) ASIACRYPT 2009. LNCS, vol. 5912, pp. 250–267. Springer, Heidelberg (2009)
17. Pu, S., Duan, P., Liu, J.-C.: Fastplay–A Parallelization Model and Implementation of SMC on CUDA based GPU Cluster Architecture. Cryptology ePrint Archive, Report 2011/097 (2011), http://eprint.iacr.org/
18. Yao, A.C.-C.: How to Generate and Exchange Secrets. In: Proceedings of the 27th IEEE Annual Symposium on Foundations of Computer Science (FOCS), pp. 162–167. IEEE Computer Society, Washington, DC (1986)

# Oblivious Decision Programs
# from Oblivious Transfer: Efficient Reductions

Payman Mohassel[1] and Salman Niksefat[2]

[1] University of Calgary
pmohasse@cpsc.ucalgary.ca
[2] Amirkabir University of Technology
niksefat@aut.ac.ir

**Abstract.** In this paper, we design efficient protocols for a number of *private database query* problems. Consider a general form of the problem where a client who holds a private input interacts with a server who holds a private decision program (e.g. a decision tree or a branching program) with the goal of evaluating his input on the decision program without learning any additional information. Many known private database queries such as Symmetric PIR, and Private Keyword Search can be formulated as special cases of this problem.

We design *computationally efficient* protocols for the above general problem, and a few of its special cases. In addition to being one-round and requiring a small amount of work by the client (in the RAM model), our protocols only require a small number of exponentiations (independent of the server's input) by both parties. Our constructions are, in essence, efficient and black-box reductions of the above problem to 1-out-of-2 oblivious transfer. We prove our protocols secure (private) against *malicious* adversaries in the standard ideal/real world simulation-based paradigm.

The majority of the existing work on the same problems focuses on optimizing communication. However, in some environments (supported by a few experimental studies), it is the computation and not the communication that may be the performance bottleneck. Our protocols are suitable alternatives for such scenarios.

## 1 Introduction

The *client/server paradigm* for computation and data retrieval is arguably the most common model for interaction over the internet. The majority of the services currently provided over the web are laid out in this framework wherein an often more resourceful entity (i.e. the server) provides its services to a large pool of clients. The need for the client/server model is even more justified given the widespread use of (small) mobile devices with varying computational and storage capacities.

Most client-server applications, in one way or another, deal with personal and/or sensitive data. Hence, it is not surprising that the protocols designed in this model have been the subject of extensive study by the cryptographic community. A few notable examples include private information retrieval and

A.D. Keromytis (Ed.): FC 2012, LNCS 7397, pp. 269–284, 2012.

its extensions [15,9,13], or the more recent effort on securely outsourcing computation [10,7].

*Communication vs. Computation.* Consider the problem of symmetric private information retrieval (SPIR) [15,5,16]. SPIR refers to a PIR scheme with the additional security requirement that the server's database also be kept private. The majority of the research on this problem is focused on improving the communication complexity, because communication between the client and the server is often considered to be the most expensive resource. Despite achieving this goal, other barriers continue to limit realistic deployment of SPIR schemes; the most limiting of which is computation. In particular, while servers often have higher computational resources, they also need to serve a large pool of clients; consequently, even a small increase in the computation of the server for a single run of the protocol, negatively affects its overall performance. Furthermore, a number of experimental studies [24,22] conclude that, in many network setups where private database queries are likely to be deployed, it is the computation (and not the communication) that might be the performance bottleneck.[1]

Unfortunately, given the security requirements for SPIR schemes (or even PIR), it is possible to show that the server's work has to be at least linear in the size of his database (e.g. see [3]). Hence, there is no hope of achieving better asymptotic efficiency. Nevertheless, the type of operations (e.g. asymmetric vs. symmetric-key) the server performs has a significant effect on the efficiency of the resulting scheme. This is particularly important in real applications since based on existing benchmarks (e.g. http://bench.cr.yp.to) asymmetric operations (e.g. exponentiation) require *several thousand* times more cpu cycles compared to their symmetric-key counterparts. In all the constructions we are aware of for SPIR, except for one, the number of *exponentiations* the server has to perform is at least linear in the size of his database. The exception is the construction of Naor and Pinkas [19,21], who studied the problem under the different name of 1-out-of-$N$ oblivious transfer ($OT_1^N$).

The situation, however, is not the same for most of the generalized variants of SPIR. A number of generalizations and extensions to SPIR have been studied in the literature. Examples include private keyword search [6,9], private element rank [8], and even more generally, the problem of oblivious decision tree, and branching program evaluation [13,4]. The existing solutions for these problems often require a number of public-key operations that is proportional to the server's input size and hence are not computationally efficient for use in practice. The only exception (with a small number of asymmetric operations) is Yao's garbled circuit protocol which is unsuitable for our applications due to its high computational cost for the client (see the related work section for a more detailed discussion).

*Why OT extension does not solve the problem.* OT extension techniques (e.g. [12]) are often used to reduce the number of asymmetric operations in crypto-

---

[1] The experimental studies we cite here, focus on PIR but the implications are even more valid for SPIR schemes.

graphic constructions. They allow one to reduce the computation needed for a large number ($n$) of 1-out-of-2 OTs, to $k$ such OTs, and $O(n)$ symmetric-key operations, where $k$ is the security parameter. This yields significant savings when $n$ is large. One may wonder whether similar techniques can be applied to the existing solutions for the problems we are studying in order to reduce their computation. Specifically, the constructions of [15,13] can be seen as evaluation of many OTs which makes them suitable candidates for OT extension. These constructions, however, require additional properties from the underlying OT such as (i) *short OT answers* since the OT protocol is applied in multiple layers and (ii) a *strongness property* which requires the OT answer not to reveal the corresponding OT query (see future sections for more detail). Unfortunately, the existing OT extension techniques do not preserve either one of these properties and hence cannot be used to improve the computational efficiency of these solutions. Designing new extension techniques that preserves the above two properties is, however, an interesting research question.

In this work, we propose new and efficient protocols for oblivious tree and branching program evaluation which possess the following four efficiency properties:

- The number of exponentiations by both the client and the server is independent of the size of the server's input.
- The client's total computation is independent of the size of the server's input.
- Our protocols are black-box constructions based on $OT_1^2$ and a PRG, and hence can be instantiated using a number of assumptions.
- The protocols are non-interactive (one round) if the underlying $OT_1^2$ is.

*RAM model of computation.* When measuring client's computation in our protocols, we work in the RAM model of computation where lookups can be performed in constant time. In particular, even though the server communicates a somewhat large (proportional to the size of the program) encrypted decision program to the client, client only needs to lookup a small number of values and perform computation only on those values.

Next, we review our protocols in more detail.

## 1.1 Overview of Protocols

*Oblivious evaluation of trees.* Our first protocol deals with secure evaluation of arbitrary decision trees that are publicly known by both the client and the server, but where the input to the decision tree is only known to the client and the labels of the terminal nodes are only known to the server. This problem has a number of interesting applications. For example, 1-out-of-$N$ oblivious transfer can be seen as an instance of this more general problem. In fact, our protocol yields a new and more efficient 1-out-of-$N$ OT, that reduces the number of symmetric-key operations needed by the scheme of [19] from $O(N \log N)$ to $O(N)$, while maintaining the same asymmetric ($O(\log N)$) and communication ($O(kN)$) complexities.

*Hiding the tree structure.* Our first protocol mentioned above hides the leaf labels but assumes that the decision tree itself is public. We apply a number of additional tricks to hide all the structural information about the decision tree (except for its size), without increasing the computational cost for the client or the server. Once again, the resulting protocol preserves the above-mentioned efficiency properties. Unlike our first protocol, for this construction we need a $OT_1^2$ protocol with the slightly *stronger security* property that, the OT answers are not correlated with their corresponding queries. This notion of security for OT and its instantiation based on standard assumptions has already been studied by Ishai and Paskin [13] (see section 2.3).

*Extension to branching programs.* Finally, at the cost of a slightly higher number of OTs (though still independent of the size of the program), we extend the protocol from decision trees to decision programs (branching programs). The difficulty is to make sure the number of occurrences of a single variable during the evaluation of an input by the program is not revealed to the client. For decision trees, this number is always one, but for decision programs, it can be an arbitrary value.

Our protocols all follow the common paradigm of having the server encrypt his database/decision tree/branching program using a set of random strings; sending it to the client; and then engaging in a small number of $OT_1^2$ protocols such that the client learns enough keys to evaluate his input on the encrypted program and learn the output but nothing else. The main challenge is to devise an encryption strategy that is secure and at the same time allows our protocols to have the efficiency properties we are after.

We prove our protocols secure in the ideal/real world simulation paradigm. We also discuss how our new protocols yield computationally efficient constructions for a number of well-studied problems in the literature such as 1-out-of-N OT and private keyword search.

## 1.2   Related Work

There are a number of works that study the problem of oblivious decision program evaluation. In [13], a one-round protocol for oblivious branching program (BP) evaluation is proposed. This protocol hides the size of the BP as well as its structure. Although the number of client exponentiations are $O(n)$ and hence proportional to the size of its input, the number of exponentiations by the server is linear in the size of the BP which makes the protocol computationally quite expensive. This protocol was slightly improved in [17], where a more communication efficient protocol but with the same computational complexity is designed.

In [4] Yao's garbled circuit protocol is used in conjunction with homomorphic encryption and oblivious transfer to solve the problem of oblivious BP evaluation (with the application of remote diagnostic programs). This protocol has $O(|V|)$ rounds and requires $O(|V| + n)$ exponentiations on the client side and $O(|V|)$ exponentiations at server side where $|V|$ is the size of the program and $n$ is the size of client's input. This protocol was later generalized and improved in

[2] but the number of server's exponentiation is still dependent on $|V|$. These constructions, however, consider a more general form of BP where the decision nodes contain an attribute index as well as a threshold value which is used to decide whether to go left or right n next.

*Using fully homomorphic encryption schemes.* The problem of oblivious tree/ branching program evaluation can also be solved using the recent fully homomorphic encryption schemes [11]. The problem with such a solution is its high computation cost as the number of times the corresponding public-key encryption scheme is invoked is at least linear in the tree/branching program size and its input.

*Using yao's garbled circuit protocol.* It is also possible to use Yao's garbled circuit protocol to implement oblivious tree and branching program evaluation. One party's input to the circuit is his input string while the other party's input is the tree/branching program itself. However, Yao's protocol is not well-suited for the client/server model of computation since both parties have to perform work that is proportional to the size of the circuit, and the circuit in this case is at least linear in size of the program, and its input. In particular, in Yao-based solutions, the client ends up doing work that is proportional to the size of the server's input which does not meet our efficiency criteria.

We give a more detailed comparison of efficiency between our protocol and the existing solutions including the one based on Yao's garbled circuit protocol in Table 1.

## 2   Preliminaries

In this section, we introduce the notations, decision program definitions and the primitives we use throughout the paper. Readers can refer to the full version [18] for the security definitions we work with.

### 2.1   Notations

We denote by $[n]$ the set of positive integers $\{1, \ldots, n\}$. We use $\xleftarrow{\$}$ to denote generation of uniformly random strings.

Throughout the paper, we use $k$ to denote the security parameter. We denote an element at row $i$ and column $j$ of a matrix by $M[i, j]$. Vectors are denoted by over-arrowed lower-case letters such as $v$. We use $a||b$ to denote the concatenation of the strings $a$ and $b$.

We denote a random permutation function by *Perm*. $v \leftarrow Perm(V)$ takes as input a set of integers $V = \{1, \ldots, |V|\}$, permutes the set uniformly at random and returns the permuted elements in a row vector $v$ of dimension $|V|$.

### 2.2   Decision Trees and Branching Programs

Below we define decision trees and branching programs, two common models for computation which are also the main focus of this paper. Note that we only give one definition below for both models under the name of *decision programs*. If the directed acyclic graph we mention below is a tree, then we have a decision tree and otherwise we have a branching program. The description and the notations are mostly borrowed from [13].

**Definition 1 (Decision Program (DP)).** *A (deterministic) decision program over the variables* $x = (x_1, \ldots, x_n)$ *with input domain* $I$ *and output domain* $O$ *is defined by a tuple* $(G = (V, E), v_1, T, \psi_V, \psi_T, \psi_E)$ *where:*

- $G$ *is a directed acyclic graph (e.g. a binary tree as a special case). Denote by* $\Gamma(v)$ *the children set of a node* $v$.
- $v_1$ *is an initial node of indegree 0 (the root in case of a tree). We assume without loss of generality that every* $u \in V - \{v_1\}$ *is reachable from* $v_1$.
- $T \subseteq V$ *is a set of terminal nodes of outdegree 0 (the leaves in case of a tree).*
- $\psi_V : V - T \to [n]$ *is a node labeling function assigning a variable index from* $[n]$ *to each nonterminal node in* $V - T$.
- $\psi_T : T \to O$ *is a node labeling function asigning an output value to each terminal node in* $T$.
- $\psi_E : E \to 2^I$ *is an edge labeling function, such that every edge is mapped to a non-empty set, and for every node* $v$ *the sets labeling the edges to nodes in* $\Gamma(v)$ *form a partition of* $I$.

In this paper, for simplicity, we describe our protocols for *binary decision programs*. But, it is easy to generalize our constructions to *t*-ary decision protocols for arbitrary positive integers $t$.

**Definition 2 (Binary DP).** *A binary decision program is simply formed by considering* $I = \{0, 1\}$. *Also for simplicity instead of the children set function* $\Gamma$, *we define* $\Gamma_L(v)$ *and* $\Gamma_R(v)$ *which output the variable indices of the left and right children of* $v$. *Since edge labeling are fairly obvious for binary decision programs, we often drop* $\psi_E$ *when discussing such programs.*

**Definition 3 (Layered DP).** *We say that* $P = (G = (V, E), v_1, T, \psi_V, \psi_T, \psi_E, \psi_\ell)$ *is a layered decision program of length* $\ell$ *if the node set* $V$ *can be partitioned into* $\ell + 1$ *disjoint levels* $V = \cup_{i=0}^{\ell} V_i$, *such that* $V_1 = \{v_1\}, V_{\ell+1} = T$, *and for every* $e = (u, v)$ *we have* $u \in V_i, v \in V_{i+1}$ *for some* $i$. *We refer to* $V_i$ *as the i-th level of* $P$. *Note that we also introduced the function* $\psi_\ell : V \to [\ell]$ *which takes a vertex as input and returns its level as output.*

*How to evaluate a DP.* The output $P(x)$ of a decision program $P$ on an input assignment $x \in I^n$ is naturally defined by following the path induced by $x$ from $v_1$ to a terminal node $v_\ell$, where the successor of node $v$ is the unique node $v'$ such that $x_{\psi_V(v)} \in \psi_E(v, v')$. The output is the value $\psi_T(v_\ell)$ labeling the terminal node (leaf node) reached by the path.

*Parameters of a DP.* Let $P = (G = (V, E), v_1, T, \psi_V, \psi_T, \psi_E)$ be a decision program. The size of $P$ is $|V|$. The *height* of a node $v \in V$, denoted $height(v)$, is the length (in edges) of the longest path from $v$ to a node in $T$. The *length* of $P$ is the height of $v_1$.

## 2.3   Oblivious Transfer

Our protocols use Oblivious Transfer (OT) as a building block. Since we focus on protocols that run in a single round, we describe an abstraction for one-round OT protocols here [13]. A one-round OT involves a server holding a list of $t$ secrets $(s_1, s_2, \ldots, s_t)$, and a client holding a selection index $i$. The client sends a query $q$ to the server who responds with an answer $a$. Using $a$ and its local secret, the client is able to recover $s_i$.

More formally, a one-round 1-out-of-t oblivious transfer $(OT_1^t)$ protocol is defined by a tuple of $PPT$ algorithms $OT_1^t = (\mathrm{G_{OT}}, \mathrm{Q_{OT}}, \mathrm{A_{OT}}, \mathrm{D_{OT}})$. The protocol involves two parties, a client and a server where the server's input is a t-tuple of strings $(s_1, \ldots, s_t)$ of length $\tau$ each, and the client's input is an index $i \in [t]$. The parameters $t$ and $\tau$ are given as inputs to both parties. The protocol proceeds as follows:

1. The client generates $(pk, sk) \leftarrow \mathrm{G_{OT}}(1^k)$, computes a query $q \leftarrow \mathrm{Q_{OT}}(pk, 1^t, 1^\tau, i)$, and sends $(pk, q)$ to the server.
2. The server computes $a \leftarrow \mathrm{A_{OT}}(pk, q, s_1, \ldots, s_t)$ and sends $a$ to the client.
3. The client computes and outputs $\mathrm{D_{OT}}(sk, a)$.

In the case of semi-honest adversaries many of OT protocols in the literature are one-round protocols [1,20,14]. In case of malicious adversaries (CRS model), one can use the one-round OT protocols of [23].

**Strong Oblivious Transfer.** When OT is invoked multiple times as a subprotocol, sometimes it is crucial for the security of the protocol that the receiver (i.e. client) be unable to correlate OT answers with their corresponding queries. In particular, when the client receives an OT answer, he should not determine which OT query the answer belongs to.

This property can be formalized by requiring the distribution of the answer $a$ conditioned on the output $s_i$ to be independent of the query $q$. More formally,

**Definition 4 (Strong OT Property [13]).** *An OT protocol is said to have the strong OT property if there exists an expected polynomial time simulator* $\mathrm{Sim_{OT}}$ *such that the following holds. For every* $k, t, \tau, i \in [t]$*, pair* $(pk, q)$ *that can be generated by* $\mathrm{G_{OT}}, \mathrm{Q_{OT}}$ *on inputs* $k, t, \tau, i$*, and strings* $s_0, \ldots, s_{t-1} \in \{0,1\}^\tau$*, the distributions* $\mathrm{A_{OT}}(pk, q, s_1, \ldots, s_t)$ *and* $\mathrm{Sim_{OT}}(pk, 1^t, s_i)$ *are identical.*

Some implementations of one-round OT based on homomorphic encryption schemes [15,13] satisfy this strongness property.

## 3   Secure Evaluation of Binary Decision Trees

In this section we propose a new protocol for secure evaluation of any publicly known decision tree with privately held terminal nodes on private inputs. This problem has a number of interesting applications such as an improved $OT_1^N$ protocol which is described in Section 6.

*Protocol Overview.* Our first protocol deals with secure evaluation of arbitrary decision trees $(P = ((V, E), v_1, T, \psi_V))$ that are publicly known by both the client and the server, but where the input to the decision tree $(X = x_1 x_2 \ldots x_n \in \{0, 1\}^n)$ is only known to the client and the labels of the terminal nodes $(\psi_T)$ are only known to the server.

---

**The Protocol 1**

**Shared Inputs:** The security parameter $k$, and a binary decision tree $P = ((V, E), v_1, T, \psi_V)$ with $O = \{0, 1\}^k$ (note the missing $\psi_T$). Parties also agree on a 1-out-of-2 OT protocol $(G_{OT}, Q_{OT}, A_{OT}, D_{OT})$ and a PRG $G : \{0, 1\}^k \rightarrow \{0, 1\}^{2k}$.

**Server's Input:** The terminal node labeling function $\psi_T$.

**Client's Input:** A bitstring $X = x_1 x_2 \ldots x_n \in \{0, 1\}^n$.

1. **The client encrypts his inputs using OT queries, and sends them to the server.**

    Client computes $(pk, sk) \leftarrow G_{OT}(1^k)$
    for $1 \leq i \leq n$ do
        Client computes $q_i \leftarrow Q_{OT}(pk, 1^2, 1^k, x_i)$
    end for
    Client sends $pk$ and $q = (q_1, q_2, \ldots, q_n)$ to Server.

2. **Server computes the OT answer vector $a$.**

    for $1 \leq i \leq n$ do
        $(K_i^0, K_i^1) \xleftarrow{\$} \{0, 1\}^k$
        $a_i \leftarrow A_{OT}(pk, q_i, K_i^0, K_i^1)$
    end for
    $a \leftarrow (a_1, a_2, \ldots, a_n)$

3. **Server prepares the Encrypted Vertex Vector $\overrightarrow{EVV}$.**

    - Server generates a random pad vector $PAD$ of length $|V|$:
        for $i = 1$ to $|V|$ do
            $PAD[i] \xleftarrow{\$} \{0, 1\}^k$
        end for

- Server encrypts the non-terminal nodes:

    for $i \in V - T$ do
        $Enc_L = K_{\psi_V(i)}^0 \oplus PAD[\Gamma_L(i)]$
        $Enc_R = K_{\psi_V(i)}^1 \oplus PAD[\Gamma_R(i)]$
        $EVV[i] \leftarrow G(PAD[i]) \oplus (Enc_L || Enc_R)$
    end for

- Server encrypts the labels of the terminal nodes:

    for $i \in T$ do
        $EVV[i] \leftarrow PAD[i] \oplus \psi_T(i)$
    end for

4. **Server sends $(a, PAD[1], \overrightarrow{EVV})$ to the client.**

5. **Client retrieves the keys and computes the final output.**

    $node \leftarrow 1$
    $pad \leftarrow PAD[1]$
    while $node \notin T$ do
        $Enc_L || Enc_R \xleftarrow{parse} EVV[node] \oplus G(pad)$

        $i \leftarrow \psi_V(node)$
        $K_i^{x_i} \leftarrow D_{OT}(sk, a_i)$
        if $(x_i = 0)$ then
            $newpad \leftarrow K_i^0 \oplus Enc_L$
            $newnode \leftarrow \Gamma_L(node)$
        else
            $newpad \leftarrow K_i^1 \oplus Enc_R$
            $newnode \leftarrow \Gamma_R(node)$
        end if
        $pad \leftarrow newpad$
        $node \leftarrow newnode$
    end while
    Client outputs $(pad \oplus EVV[node])$ as his final output.

---

In our protocol, a pair of random keys $(K_{x_i}^0, K_{x_i}^1)$ is generated for each $x_i$, and is used by the server as his input in the $n$ 1-out-of-2 OTs. The idea is then to generate a set of random pads, one for each node in the decision tree. Each node stores a pair of values, i.e. the two random pads corresponding to its left and right children. However, this pair of values is not stored in plaintext. Instead, the left (right) component of the pair is encrypted using a combined key formed by XORing the left-half (right-half) of the expanded pad (expanded using a PRG) for the current node with $K_{x_i}^0$ $(K_{x_i}^1)$ where $i$ is the label of the current node. The encryption scheme is a simple one-time pad encryption. The encrypted values are stored in a vector we call the Encrypted Vertex Vector $(\overrightarrow{EVV})$.

The client who receives one of each pair of random keys, can then use them to decrypt a single path on the tree corresponding to the evaluation path of his input $X$, and recover his output, i.e. the output label associated with the reached terminal node. As we show in the proof, the rest of the terminal node labels remain computationally hidden from the client. A detailed description of the protocol is depicted in the box for the protocol 1.

**Security.** In the full version of the paper [18] we show that as long as the oblivious transfer protocol used is secure even when executed in parallel, so is our construction given above. Particularly, if the OT is secure against malicious (semi-honest) adversaries (when run in parallel), protocol 1 described above is also secure against malicious (semi-honest) adversaries. The following Theorem formalizes this statement.

**Theorem 1.** *In the OT-hybrid model, the above protocol is fully-secure (i.e. simulation-based security: see the definition in Appendix B of the full version [18]) against malicious adversaries.*

**Complexity.** The proposed protocol runs in one round which consists of a message from the client to the server and vice versa.

The only asymmetric computation required in this protocol is for the OT invocations and since there are $n$ OT invocations and each OT requires a constant number of exponentiations, the number of exponentiations is $O(n)$ for both parties. Using the OT extension of [12] we can reduce the number of exponentiations to $O(k)$ for both parties.

The number of other (symmetric-key) operations such as PRG invocations, and XORing is $O(|V|)$ on the server side and $O(l)$ on the client side where $l$ refers to the depth of the tree ($l \leq n$).

The communication complexity of the protocol is dominated by the total size of the elements in $\overrightarrow{EVV}$ which is bounded by $O(|V|k)$ where $k$ is the security parameter. This is due to the fact that each element of $\overrightarrow{EVV}$ is of size $2k$ and there are $|V|$ such elements.

## 4 Hiding the Tree Structure

We will show how to securely formulate via decision programs, other protocols such as the *private keyword search* problem [6,9] and the *private element rank* problem [8] (see the full version for discussion on the latter). For some of these problems, privacy of the server's database critically relies on keeping the structure of the corresponding decision program private. The program structure includes all the information available about it except for its size (number of its nodes) and the number of variables (both of which are publicly known).

For simplicity, in this section we assume that the decision tree we work with is layered. Alternatively, we could allow for arbitrary tree structures[2] and then consider the length of the evaluation path as public information available to our

---

[2] In a non-layered decision tree, the length of the evaluation path for different inputs need not be the same.

simulators (our protocol reveals the length). However, since in most applications one wants to keep this information private (see Section 6), we chose to work with this assumption instead. Note that there are generic and efficient ways of transforming any decision program (tree) into a layered one. In section 6, we give a customized and more efficient transformation for the private keyword search application.

Next, we show how to enhance the protocol of previous section in order to hide the decision tree's structure without increasing the computational cost of the client or the server (in the next section we extend this to decision programs). Once again, our protocol reduces the problem to $n$ $OT_1^2$ protocols.

Here we require the $OT_1^2$ protocol to have a slightly stronger security property compared to the standard one. We refer to such OTs as *strong* OTs. At a high level, we require that the OT answers do not reveal anything about the corresponding query. This property helps us hide from the client, the order in which the input variables are evaluated which would in part reveal some information about the structure of the tree. A formal definition of security as well as some existing constructions for strong OT are discussed in section 2.3.

**An Overview.** The high level structure of the protocol of this section is similar to the previous one. In particular, we still perform $n$ OTs and use a set of key pairs and random pads in order to garble the tree. But since this time we are also interested in hiding the structure of the tree, a more involved encryption process is necessary. The main changes to the previous construction are as follows: first, instead of revealing the labels of the non-terminal nodes to the client, we use a pointer (index) to the corresponding item in the *randomly permuted list of OT answers* ($a'$). In order for the permuted list of answers not to reveal the permutation, we need to use a *strong* OT protocol. Second, in order to hide the arrangement of the nodes in the tree, instead of revealing the outgoing edges of each non-terminal node, we use two pointers to the corresponding nodes in a *randomly permuted list of the nodes* in the tree ($\overrightarrow{EVV}$).

The three pointers mentioned above (one pointing to $a'$ and two pointing to $\overrightarrow{EVV}$) stored at each node, is all that the client needs in order to evaluate the decision tree on his input. All of this information will be encrypted using a combination of the random pads and the key pairs similar to the construction of previous section and is stored in the $\overrightarrow{EVV}$ vector. However, several subtleties exist in order to make sure the construction works. First, only the random pads (not the random keys) are to be used in encrypting the pointers to the OT answers since the random keys themselves are retrieved from the OT answers. Also, in order to hide from the client which bit value the retrieved key corresponds to (note that this can reveal extra information about the node labels which are to be kept private), the two values encrypted using the keys ($Enc_L$ and $Enc_R$) are randomly permuted and a redundant padding of $0^k$ is appended to the values before encryption to help the client recognize when the correct value is decrypted. A detailed description of the protocol is depicted in the box for protocol 2.

In the description above, the size of EVV for terminal vs. non-terminal nodes is different which leaks the total number of terminal nodes. However, we only did so to make the description of the protocol simpler. In particular, it is easy to pad the size of terminal nodes to the appropriate size, and then embed an indicator bit in each EVV cell (before encryption) that helps the client determine if he has reached a terminal node.

---

**The Protocol 2**

**Shared Inputs:** The security parameter $k$, size of the set $V$, i.e. $|V|$. We also let $k' = 2k + \log(|V|)$. Parties also agree on a *strong* $OT_1^2$ protocol $OT = (G_{OT}, Q_{OT}, A_{OT}, D_{OT})$ and a PRG $G : \{0,1\}^k \to \{0,1\}^{2k' + \log n}$.

**Server's Input:** A layered binary decision tree $P = ((V, E), v_1, T, \psi_V, \psi_T)$ with $O = \{0,1\}^k$.

**Client's Input:** A bitstring $X = x_1 x_2 \ldots x_n \in \{0,1\}^n$.

1. **Client encrypts his inputs using OT queries, and sends the vector $q$ to Server.** The first step of computing the OT queries for the client is identical to protocol of Section 3 and hence is omitted here.

2. **Server computes a permuted OT answer vector $a'$.**
   - Server computes the OT answer vector $a$:
     
     for $1 \le i \le n$ do
       $(K_i^0, K_i^1) \xleftarrow{\$} \{0,1\}^{k'}$
       $a_i \leftarrow A_{OT}(pk, q_i, K_i^0, K_i^1)$
     end for
     $a \leftarrow (a_1, a_2, \ldots, a_n)$
   - Server Generates a random permutation vector $PER_n$:
     
     $PER_n \leftarrow Perm(\{1, \ldots, n\})$
   - Server Permutes $a$ using $PER_n$:
     
     for $1 \le i \le n$ do
       $a'[PER_n[i]] \leftarrow a[i]$
     end for

3. **Server computes an encrypted vertex vector $\overrightarrow{EVV}$.**
   - Server generates a random pad vector $PAD$ of length $|V|$:
     
     for $i = 1$ to $|V|$ do
       $PAD[i] \xleftarrow{\$} \{0,1\}^k$
     end for
   - Server Generates a random permutation vector $PER_V$:
     
     $PER_V \leftarrow Perm(\{1, \ldots, |V|\})$

   - Server encrypts non-terminal nodes and their outgoing edges:
     
     for $i \in V - T$ do
       $Enc_L \leftarrow K_{\psi_V(i)}^0 \oplus$
         $(PAD[\Gamma_L(i)] \| PER_V[\Gamma_L(i)] \| 0^k)$
       $Enc_R \leftarrow K_{\psi_V(i)}^1 \oplus$
         $(PAD[\Gamma_R(i)] \| PER_V[\Gamma_R(i)] \| 0^k)$
       $b \xleftarrow{\$} \{0,1\}$
       if $b = 0$ then
         $EVV[PER_V[i]] \leftarrow$
           $G(PAD[i]) \oplus$
             $(PER_n[\psi_V(i)] \| Enc_L \| Enc_R)$
       else
         $EVV[PER_V[i]] \leftarrow$
           $G(PAD[i]) \oplus$
             $(PER_n[\psi_V(i)] \| Enc_R \| Enc_L)$
       end if
     end for
   - Server encrypts the labels of the terminal nodes:
     
     for $i \in T$ do
       $EVV[PER_V[i]] \leftarrow PAD[i] \oplus \psi_T(i)$
     end for

4. **Server sends $(PER_V[1], PAD[1], a', \overrightarrow{EVV})$ to Client.**

5. **Client retrieves the keys and computes the final result.**
   
   $node \leftarrow PER_V[1]$
   $pad \leftarrow PAD[1]$
   while $node \notin T$ do
     $(j \| Enc_0 \| Enc_1) \xleftarrow{parse} EVV[node] \oplus pad$
     $K \leftarrow D_{OT}(sk, a'[j])$
     $Dec_0 \leftarrow K \oplus Enc_0$
     $Dec_1 \leftarrow K \oplus Enc_1$
     if $k$ least significant bits of $Dec_0$ are 0 then
       $pad \| node \| 0^k \xleftarrow{parse} Dec_0$
     else
       $pad \| node \| 0^k \xleftarrow{parse} Dec_1$
     end if
     $pad \leftarrow G(pad)$
   end while
   Client outputs $(pad \oplus EVV[node])$ as his final output.

---

**Security.** The simulation proof for protocol 2 follows the same line of argument as that of protocol 1. The main difference in the security claim for protocol 2 is that it is *private* against a malicious server (as opposed to being fully-secure). The intuition behind this weakening in the security guarantee is that the server can construct an $\overrightarrow{EVV}$ that does no correspond to a valid decision tree, and our protocol does not provide any mechanisms for detecting this type of behavior. However, the protocol is still private, since all that the server sees in the protocol are the OT queries. Also note that the client is always able to compute an output even if the $\overrightarrow{EVV}$ is not a valid tree (there is no possibility of failure conditioned on specific input values), and hence the server cannot take advantage of the pattern of aborts by the client in order to learn additional information. It is possible to augment the protocol with zero-knowledge proofs that yield full security against a malicious server, but all the obvious ways of doing so would diminish the efficiency properties we are after. In particular both the server and the client would have to do a number of exponentiations that is proportional to the size of the tree.

Next, we state our security theorem. Readers are referred to the full version of the paper [18] for the proof of Theorem 2.

**Theorem 2.** *In the strong-OT-hybrid model, and given a cryptographically secure PRG G, the above protocol is* fully-secure *against a malicious client and is* private *against a malicious server.*

**Complexity.** Similar to protocol 1, protocol 2 runs in one round. The asymptotic computational complexity for the client and the server remains the same too. In other words, the client and the server perform $O(n)$ exponentiations for the OTs. Server performs $O(|V|)$ PRG invocations and XOR operations while the client performs $O(l)$ PRG and XOR operations where $l$ is the length of the decision tree.

The communication cost of the protocol is dominated by size of $\overrightarrow{EVV}$ which consists of $|V|$ elements of size $4k + \log|V|$. This leads to a total communication of $O(|V|(\log|V| + k)$ bits.

# 5    Extension to Branching Programs (BP)

In this section we extend our proposed protocol of previous section to branching programs (BP). BPs are decision programs that are represented as directed acyclic graphs [25], and hence may contain various paths from the root to some nodes. Because of the structure of the BPs, a variable may be evaluated more than once in a single evaluation. In order to hide the number of times a variable is visited from a curious party, and to obliviously evaluate a BP, we generate a separate OT answer vector for each level of the BP. This can be done by computing a permuted OT answer matrix ($A'$) instead of an OT answer vector described in protocol 2, and using the indices to this matrix when $\overrightarrow{EVV}$ is computed. Similar to the previous protocol, we need a strong OT as a sub-protocol to prevent correlation between OT queries, and answers.

More formally, assume that $PER_{ln}$ is a permutation matrix of dimension $l \times n$ where $l$ is the length of the program. $A'$ is computed as follows:

**for** $i = 1$ to $l$ **do**

  **for** $j = 1$ to $n$ **do**

    $(K_{i,j}^0, K_{i,j}^1) \xleftarrow{\$} \{0,1\}^{k'}$

    $A'[i, PER_{ln}[i,j]] \leftarrow A_{OT}(pk, q_j, K_{i,j}^0, K_{i,j}^1)$

  **end for**

**end for**

Moreover, in the $\overrightarrow{EVV}$ computation step, $PER_{ln}[height(i), \psi_V(i)]$ is used to point to the elements in $A'$. To compute the final result, the client will also use the elements in the $A'$ matrix to retrieve the keys and evaluate the BP.

The argument for the security of this scheme is almost the same as protocol 2.

**Theorem 3.** *In the strong-OT-hybrid model, and given a cryptographically secure PRG G, the above-mentioned protocol is* fully-secure *against a malicious client and is* private *against a malicious server.*

**Complexity.** As before, the protocol runs in one round. The number of exponentiations performed by the client remains the same but the server has to perform slightly more exponentiations. In other words, the client performs $O(n)$ exponentiations and the server performs $O(ln)$ exponentiations for the OTs where $l$ is the length of the branching program. The number of PRG invocations and XOR operations remains the same as protocol 2 which is $O(|V|)$ for the server and $O(l)$ for the client. The asymptotic communication cost of the protocol remains the same as protocol 2 which is $O(|V|(\log|V| + k))$ bits.

Table 1 compares the complexities of the related work with our proposed protocol for oblivious evaluation of BPs. The main advantage of our proposed protocol over the previous schemes is that the server's asymmetric computation is independent of the size of the branching program. This feature makes our protocol truly efficient when $|V|$ is large. In case of Yao-based constructions, the size of the circuit required for evaluating a branching program of size $|V|$ and length $l$ on an input of size $n$ is $O(|V|l(\log|V| + \log n))$. Therefore, using Yao's protocol for oblivious branching program evaluation yields a protocol which needs $O(|V|l(\log|V| + \log n))$ symmetric-key operations for both the client and the server, and a communication complexity of $O(|V|lk(\log|V| + \log n))$.

**Table 1.** Comparison of protocols for oblivious branching program evaluation

| | Rounds | Client Computations | | Server Computations | | Communication Complexity |
|---|---|---|---|---|---|---|
| | | Asymmetric | Symmetric | Asymmetric | Symmetric | |
| Yao [26] | 1 | $O(n)$ | $O(\|V\|l(\log\|V\| + \log n))$ | $O(n)$ | $O(\|V\|l(\log\|V\| + \log n))$ | $O(\|V\|lk(\log\|V\| + \log n))$ |
| [13] | 1 | $O(n+l)$ | none | $O(\|V\|)$ | none | $O(knl)$ |
| [4,2] | $O(\|V\|)$ | $O(\|V\|+n)$ | $O(\|V\|)$ | $O(\|V\|)$ | $O(\|V\|)$ | $O(k(n+\|V\|))$ |
| Ours | 1 | $O(n)$ | $O(1)$ | $O(ln)$ | $O(\|V\|)$ | $O(\|V\|(\log\|V\| + k))$ |

## 6   Applications

**An Improved $OT_1^N$ Protocol.** We review the Naor-Pinkas $OT_1^N$ and its efficiency in Appendix C of [18]. It is easy to observe that looking up an index

$X = x_1 \cdots x_{\log N}$ in a database of size $N$ can be efficiently described as evaluation of a decision tree on $X$, where the node variables are $x_i$'s and the terminal (leaf) node values are the elements of the database. This way, an $OT_1^N$ can be represented as a special case of our proposed protocol 1. This yields a more efficient $OT_1^N$ protocol with only $O(N)$ instead of $O(N \log N)$ PRG invocations which is the case in the Naor-Pinkas protocol [19].

**Claim 1.** *Let $N$ be the size of the database. Given a one-round 1-out-of-2 OT protocol with security against malicious adversaries, there exists a one-round two-party protocol for 1-out-of-N OT, with full-security against malicious adversaries. The protocol only requires $O(\log N)$ exponentiations by both parties. The total work of the client is $O(\log N)$, while the server performs $O(N)$ PRG invocations.*

The security of the construction follows from our more general construction in Section 3. It is also easy to verify the claimed computational complexities.

**A Private Keyword Search Protocol.** We first recall the setup for the private keyword search (PKS) problem. A server and a client are involved in this problem. The server's input is a database $D$ of $N$ pairs $(k_i, p_i)$, where $k_i \in \{0,1\}^\ell$ is a keyword, and $p_i \in \{0,1\}^m$ is the corresponding payload. The client's input is an $\ell$ bit searchword $w = w_1 w_2 \cdots w_\ell$. If there is a pair $(k_i, p_i)$ in the database such that $k_i = w$, then the output is the corresponding payload $p_i$. Otherwise the output is a special symbol $\perp$.

Designing efficient PKS protocols has been the focus of several works in the literature [6,9]. However, these works have mostly focused on optimizing the communication complexity of the protocols. In particular, they require $O(N)$ exponentiations by the server, which is a significant computational burden for large $N$.

Using the techniques we developed in previous section, we can design an efficient PKS with properties mentioned in the claim below. The details of the construction are available in the full version of the paper [18].

**Claim 2.** *Let $\ell$ be the length of the keywords and $N$ be the size of the database. Given a one-round OT protocol with security against malicious adversaries, there exists a one-round two-party protocol for private keyword search, with full-security against a malicious client and privacy against a malicious server. The protocol only requires $O(\ell)$ exponentiations by both parties. The total work of the client is $O(\ell)$, while the server performs $O(N\ell)$ symmetric operations.*

# References

1. Aiello, B., Ishai, Y., Reingold, O.: Priced Oblivious Transfer: How to Sell Digital Goods. In: Pfitzmann, B. (ed.) EUROCRYPT 2001. LNCS, vol. 2045, pp. 119–135. Springer, Heidelberg (2001)
2. Barni, M., Failla, P., Kolesnikov, V., Lazzeretti, R., Sadeghi, A.-R., Schneider, T.: Secure Evaluation of Private Linear Branching Programs with Medical Applications. In: Backes, M., Ning, P. (eds.) ESORICS 2009. LNCS, vol. 5789, pp. 424–439. Springer, Heidelberg (2009)

3. Beimel, A., Ishai, Y., Malkin, T.: Reducing the Servers Computation in Private Information Retrieval: PIR with Preprocessing. In: Bellare, M. (ed.) CRYPTO 2000. LNCS, vol. 1880, pp. 55–73. Springer, Heidelberg (2000)
4. Brickell, J., Porter, D., Shmatikov, V., Witchel, E.: Privacy-preserving remote diagnostics. In: ACM CCS 2007, pp. 498–507 (2007)
5. Cachin, C., Micali, S., Stadler, M.: Computationally Private Information Retrieval with Polylogarithmic Communication. In: Stern, J. (ed.) EUROCRYPT 1999. LNCS, vol. 1592, pp. 402–414. Springer, Heidelberg (1999)
6. Chor, B., Gilboa, N., Naor, M.: Private information retrieval by keywords (1997) (manuscript)
7. Chung, K.-M., Kalai, Y., Vadhan, S.: Improved Delegation of Computation Using Fully Homomorphic Encryption. In: Rabin, T. (ed.) CRYPTO 2010. LNCS, vol. 6223, pp. 483–501. Springer, Heidelberg (2010)
8. Dedic, N., Mohassel, P.: Constant-Round Private Database Queries. In: Arge, L., Cachin, C., Jurdziński, T., Tarlecki, A. (eds.) ICALP 2007. LNCS, vol. 4596, pp. 255–266. Springer, Heidelberg (2007)
9. Freedman, M.J., Ishai, Y., Pinkas, B., Reingold, O.: Keyword Search and Oblivious Pseudorandom Functions. In: Kilian, J. (ed.) TCC 2005. LNCS, vol. 3378, pp. 303–324. Springer, Heidelberg (2005)
10. Gennaro, R., Gentry, C., Parno, B.: Non-interactive Verifiable Computing: Outsourcing Computation to Untrusted Workers. In: Rabin, T. (ed.) CRYPTO 2010. LNCS, vol. 6223, pp. 465–482. Springer, Heidelberg (2010)
11. Gentry, C.: Fully homomorphic encryption using ideal lattices. In: ACM STOC 2009, pp. 169–178 (2009)
12. Ishai, Y., Kilian, J., Nissim, K., Petrank, E.: Extending Oblivious Transfers Efficiently. In: Boneh, D. (ed.) CRYPTO 2003. LNCS, vol. 2729, pp. 145–161. Springer, Heidelberg (2003)
13. Ishai, Y., Paskin, A.: Evaluating Branching Programs on Encrypted Data. In: Vadhan, S.P. (ed.) TCC 2007. LNCS, vol. 4392, pp. 575–594. Springer, Heidelberg (2007)
14. Kalai, Y.T.: Smooth Projective Hashing and Two-Message Oblivious Transfer. In: Cramer, R. (ed.) EUROCRYPT 2005. LNCS, vol. 3494, pp. 78–95. Springer, Heidelberg (2005)
15. Kushilevitz, E., Ostrovsky, R.: Replication is not needed: Single database, computationally-private information retrieval. In: FOCS 1997, pp. 364–373 (1997)
16. Lipmaa, H.: An Oblivious Transfer Protocol with Log-Squared Communication. In: Zhou, J., López, J., Deng, R.H., Bao, F. (eds.) ISC 2005. LNCS, vol. 3650, pp. 314–328. Springer, Heidelberg (2005)
17. Lipmaa, H.: Private branching programs: On communication-efficient cryptocomputing. Tech. rep., Cryptology ePrint Archive, Report 2008/107 (2008)
18. Mohassel, P., Niksefat, S.: Oblivious decision programs from oblivious transfer: Efficient reductions (full version) (2011), http://pages.cpsc.ucalgary.ca/~pmohasse/odp.pdf
19. Naor, M., Pinkas, B.: Oblivious transfer and polynomial evaluation. In: ACM STOC 1999, pp. 245–254. ACM (1999)
20. Naor, M., Pinkas, B.: Efficient oblivious transfer protocols. In: ACM SIAM 2001, pp. 448–457 (2001)
21. Naor, M., Pinkas, B.: Computationally secure oblivious transfer. Journal of Cryptology 18(1), 1–35 (2005)

22. Olumofin, F., Goldberg, I.: Revisiting the Computational Practicality of Private Information Retrieval. In: Danezis, G. (ed.) FC 2011. LNCS, vol. 7035, pp. 158–172. Springer, Heidelberg (2012)
23. Peikert, C., Vaikuntanathan, V., Waters, B.: A Framework for Efficient and Composable Oblivious Transfer. In: Wagner, D. (ed.) CRYPTO 2008. LNCS, vol. 5157, pp. 554–571. Springer, Heidelberg (2008)
24. Sion, R., Carbunar, B.: On the computational practicality of private information retrieval. In: NDSS 2007, pp. 2006–06 (2007)
25. Sipser, M.: Introduction to the Theory of Computation. International Thomson Publishing (1996)
26. Yao, A.: Protocols for secure computations. In: FOCS 1982, pp. 160–164 (1982)

# UC-Secure Searchable Symmetric Encryption

Kaoru Kurosawa and Yasuhiro Ohtaki

Ibaraki University, Japan
{kurosawa,y.ohtaki}@mx.ibaraki.ac.jp

**Abstract.** For searchable symmetric encryption schemes (or symmetric-key encryption with keyword search), the security against passive adversaries (i.e. privacy) has been mainly considered so far. In this paper, we first define its security against active adversaries (i.e. reliability as well as privacy). We next formulate its UC-security. We then prove that the UC-security against non-adaptive adversaries is equivalent to our definition of privacy and reliability. We further present an efficient construction which satisfies our security definition (hence UC-security).

**Keywords:** searchable symmetric encryption, UC-security, symmetric-key encryption.

## 1 Introduction

We consider the following problem [8]: a client wants to store his files (or documents) in an encrypted form on a remote file server (in the store phase). Later (in the search phase), the client wants to efficiently retrieve some of the encrypted files containing (or indexed by) specific keywords, keeping the keywords themselves secret and not jeopardizing the security of the remotely stored files. For example, a client may want to store old email messages encrypted on a server managed by Google or another large vendor, and later retrieve certain messages while traveling with a mobile device. Such a scheme is called a searchable symmetric encryption (SSE) scheme because symmetric key encryption schemes are used.

For this problem, the security against passive adversaries (i.e. privacy) has been mainly considered so far. After a series of works [10, 9, 1, 8], Curtmola, Garay, Kamara and Ostrovsky [6, 7] showed a rigorous definition of security about the client's privacy against a passive server, and an efficient scheme which satisfies their definition.

However, an active adversary (i.e. a server) may forge the encrypted files and/or delete some of them. Even if the clients uses MAC to authenticate the encrypted files, a malicious server may replace $(C_i, \mathtt{MAC}(C_i))$ with some $(C_j, \mathtt{MAC}(C_j))$ in the search phase, where $C_i$ is an encrypted file which should be returned. Then the client cannot detect cheating.

In this paper, we first formulate the security of *verifiable* SSE schemes against active adversaries by using the notion of privacy and reliability. Our definition of privacy is slightly stronger than "adaptive semantic security" of Curtmola et al.

A.D. Keromytis (Ed.): FC 2012, LNCS 7397, pp. 285–298, 2012.

[7, Definition 4.11]. Our definition of reliability means that even if the server is malicious, the client can receive the corresponding files correctly, or he outputs *fail* in the search phase.

We next formulate its UC-security, where UC means universal composability. (In the UC framework [3–5], the security of a protocol $\Sigma = (P_1, \cdots, P_n)$ is maintained under a general protocol composition if $\Sigma$ is UC-secure.) We then prove that the UC-security against non-adaptive adversaries is equivalent to our definition of privacy and reliability.

We further present an efficient scheme which satisfies our definition (hence UC-security). The communication overhead of our search phase is proportional to $N$, where $N$ is the number of stored files. (It is independent of the size of each file.) It will be an open problem to construct a UC-secure scheme such that the communication overhead of the search phase is sublinear in $N$.

## 2    Verifiable Searchable Symmetric Encryption (SSE)

In this section, we define *verifiable* searchable symmetric encryption (verifiable SSE) scheme and its security.

- Let $\mathcal{D} = \{D_1, \cdots, D_N\}$ be a set of documents (or files).
- Let $\mathcal{W} = \{0, 1\}^\ell$ be a set of keywords.
  (Hence $\ell$ denotes the bit length of each keyword.)
- Let $\mathrm{D}(w)$ denote the set of documents which contain a keyword $w \in \mathcal{W}$.

If $X$ is a string, then $|X|$ denotes the bit length of $X$. If $X$ is a set, then $|X|$ denotes the cardinality of $X$. PPT means probabilistic polynomial time.

### 2.1    Verifiable SSE

A verifiable SSE scheme consists of six polynomial time algorithms

$$\mathrm{vSSE} = (\mathrm{Gen}, \mathrm{Enc}, \mathrm{Trpdr}, \mathrm{Search}, \mathrm{Dec}, \mathrm{Verify})$$

such that

- $K \leftarrow \mathrm{Gen}(1^k)$: is a probabilistic algorithm which generates a key $K$, where $k$ is a security parameter.
- $(\mathcal{I}, \mathcal{C}) \leftarrow \mathrm{Enc}(K, \mathcal{D}, \mathcal{W})$: is a probabilistic encryption algorithm which outputs an encrypted index $\mathcal{I}$ and $\mathcal{C} = \{C_1, \cdots, C_N\}$, where $C_i$ is a ciphertext of $D_i$.
- $t(w) \leftarrow \mathrm{Trpdr}(K, w)$: is a deterministic algorithm which outputs a trapdoor $t(w)$ for a keyword $w$.
- $(\mathrm{C}(w), Tag) \leftarrow \mathrm{Search}(\mathcal{I}, \mathcal{C}, t(w))$: is a deterministic search algorithm, where

$$\mathrm{C}(w) = \{C_i \mid C_i \text{ is a ciphertext of } D_i \in \mathrm{D}(w)\} \tag{1}$$

- $\mathrm{accept/reject} \leftarrow \mathrm{Verify}(K, t(w), \tilde{\mathrm{C}}(w), Tag)$: is a deterministic verification algorithm which checks the validity of $\tilde{\mathrm{C}}(w)$.

- $D \leftarrow \text{Dec}(K, C)$: is a deterministic decryption algorithm, where $D$ is a document and $C$ is a string.

For the set of documents $\mathcal{D} = \{D_1, \cdots, D_N\}$ and a keyword $w \in \mathcal{W}$, it must be that

- $D_i = \text{Dec}(K, C_i)$ if $C_i$ is a ciphertext of $D_i$.
- $\text{Verify}(K, t(w), \text{C}(w), Tag) = \text{accept}$ if $(\mathcal{I}, \mathcal{C})$ is output by $\text{Enc}(K, \mathcal{D}, \mathcal{W})$, $t(w)$ is output by $\text{Trpdr}(K, w)$ for $w \in \mathcal{W}$, and $(\text{C}(w), Tag)$ is output by $\text{Search}(\mathcal{I}, \mathcal{C}, t(w))$.

The definition of usual searchable symmetric encryption (SSE) schemes [6, 7] is obtained by deleting $Tag$ and $\text{Verify}$ from the verifiable SSE schemes.

We next translate a vSSE into a protocol $\Sigma_{vsse}$ which is a protocol between a client and a server. It consists of the store phase and the search phase as shown below, where the store phase is executed once, and the search phase is executed for polynomially many times.

---
**Store phase:**

1. The client generates a key $K \leftarrow \text{Gen}(1^k)$ and keeps it secret.
2. On input $(\mathcal{D}, \mathcal{W})$, the client computes $(\mathcal{I}, \mathcal{C}) \leftarrow \text{Enc}(K, \mathcal{D}, \mathcal{W})$ and store them to the server,
   where $\mathcal{D}$ is a set of documents, $\mathcal{W}$ is the set of keywords, $\mathcal{I}$ is an encrypted index and $\mathcal{C}$ is a ciphertext of $\mathcal{D}$.

---
**Search phase:**

1. On input a keyword $w \in \mathcal{W}$, the client computes a trapdoor $t(w) \leftarrow \text{Trpdr}(K, w)$ and sends it to the server.
2. The server computes $(\text{C}(w), Tag) \leftarrow \text{Search}(\mathcal{I}, \mathcal{C}, t(w))$ and sends them to the client (where $\text{C}(w)$ is defined by eq.(1)).
3. If the client received $(\tilde{\text{C}}(w), Tag)$ from the server,
   then the client computes $\text{Verify}(K, t(w), \tilde{\text{C}}(w), Tag)$.
   - If the result is accept, then the client decrypts each ciphertext $C_i$ in $\text{C}(w)$ to the document $D_i$ by using $\text{Dec}(K, \cdot)$, and outputs the set of such $D_i$ as $\text{D}(w)$.
   - Otherwise the client outputs *fail*.

---

## 2.2   Privacy

In the above protocol, the server learns $|D_i|$ from $C_i$ for each $i$, and $\ell$ from $\mathcal{I}$ in the store phase. In the search phase, she also knows

$$\text{List}(w) = \{i \mid D_i \text{ contains } w\}$$

for each queried keyword $w$. We require that the server should not be able to learn any more information.

Based on the work of Curtmola, Garay, Kamara and Ostrovsky [6, 7], this security notion is formulated as follows. We consider a real game $\mathtt{Game}_{real}$ and a simulation game $\mathtt{Game}_{sim}$ as shown below, where $\mathtt{Game}_{real}$ is played by a challenger and an adversary $\mathbf{A}$, and $\mathtt{Game}_{sim}$ is played by a simulator $\mathbf{Sim}$ as well.

---
**Real Game ($\mathtt{Game}_{real}$)**

- Adversary $\mathbf{A}$ chooses $(\mathcal{D}, \mathcal{W})$ and sends them to the challenger.
- The challenger generates $K \leftarrow \mathtt{Gen}(1^k)$,
  and then sends $(\mathcal{I}, \mathcal{C}) \leftarrow \mathtt{Enc}(K, \mathcal{D}, \mathcal{W})$ to $\mathbf{A}$.
- For $i = 1, \cdots, q$, do:
  1. $\mathbf{A}$ chooses a keyword $w_i \in \mathcal{W}$ and sends it to the challenger.
  2. The challenger sends a trapdoor $t(w_i) \leftarrow \mathtt{Trpdr}_K(w_i)$ to $\mathbf{A}$.
- $\mathbf{A}$ outputs a bit $b$.
---

---
**Simulation Game ($\mathtt{Game}_{sim}$)**

- $\mathbf{A}$ chooses $(\mathcal{D}, \mathcal{W})$ and sends them to the challenger.
- The challenger sends $|D_1|, \cdots, |D_N|$ and $\ell$ to simulator $\mathbf{Sim}$,
  where $\mathtt{D} = \{D_1, \cdots, D_N\}$ and $\ell$ is the length of a keyword.
- $\mathbf{Sim}$ computes $(\mathcal{I}', \mathtt{C}')$ from $|D_1|, \cdots, |D_N|$ and $\ell$,
  and sends them to the challenger.
- The challenger relays $(\mathcal{I}', \mathtt{C}')$ to $\mathbf{A}$.
- For $i = 1, \cdots, q$, do:
  1. $\mathbf{A}$ chooses $w_i \in \mathcal{W}$ and sends it to the challenger.
  2. The challenger sends $\mathtt{List}(w_i)$ to $\mathbf{Sim}$.
  3. $\mathbf{Sim}$ computes $t(w_i)'$ from $\mathtt{List}(w_i)$ and sends it to the challenger.
  4. The challenger relays $t(w_i)'$ to $\mathbf{A}$.
- $\mathbf{A}$ outputs a bit $b$.
---

**Definition 1.** *We say that a verifiable SSE satisfies privacy if there exists a PPT simulator* $\mathbf{Sim}$ *such that*

$$|\Pr(\mathbf{A} \text{ outputs } b = 1 \text{ in } \mathtt{Game}_{real}) - \Pr(\mathbf{A} \text{ outputs } b = 1 \text{ in } \mathtt{Game}_{sim})| \quad (2)$$

*is negligible for any PPT adversary* $\mathbf{A}$.

"Adaptive semantic security" of Curtmola et al. [7, Definition 4.11] requires that for any PPT adversary $\mathbf{A}$, there exists a PPT $\mathbf{Sim}$ such that eq.(2) is negligible. On the other hand, our definition requires that there exists a PPT $\mathbf{Sim}$ such that for any PPT adversary $\mathbf{A}$, eq.(2) is negligible. Hence our definition is slightly stronger. This small change is important when we prove the relationship with UC-security. (See Remark 1 in the proof of Theorem 2.)

## 2.3   Reliability

In addition to the privacy, the server (an adversary $\mathbf{A}$) should not be able to forge $(\mathtt{C}(w), Tag)$ in the search phase. We formulate this security notion as follows.

Fix $(\mathcal{D}, \mathcal{W})$ and search queries $w_1, \cdots, w_q \in \mathcal{W}$ arbitrarily. In the store phase, suppose that the client generated $K$ and then computed $(\mathcal{I}, \mathtt{C})$.

- We say that $\mathtt{C}(w)^*$ is invalid for $t(w)$ if $\mathtt{C}(w)^* \neq \mathtt{C}(w)$, where $(\mathtt{C}(w), Tag) \leftarrow \mathtt{Search}(\mathcal{I}, \mathtt{C}, t(w))$.
- We say that $\mathbf{A}$ wins if she can return $(\mathtt{C}(w_i)^*, Tag^*)$ for some query $t(w_i)$ such that $\mathtt{C}(w_i)^*$ is invalid for $t(w_i)$ and $\mathtt{Verify}(K, t(w_i), \mathtt{C}(w_i)^*, Tag) = \mathtt{accept}$.

**Definition 2.** *We say that a verifiable SSE satisfies reliability if for any PPT adversary $\mathbf{A}$, $\Pr(\mathbf{A}$ wins$)$ is negligible for any $(\mathcal{D}, \mathcal{W})$ and any search queries $w_1, \cdots, w_q$.*

## 3   UC-Secure SSE

### 3.1   UC Security

The security of a protocol $\Sigma = (P_1, \cdots, P_n)$ is maintained under a general protocol composition if $\Sigma$ is secure in the universally composable (UC) security framework [3–5].

In this framework, there exists an environment $\mathcal{Z}$ which generates the input to all parties, reads all outputs, and in addition interacts with an adversary $\mathbf{A}$ in an arbitrary way throughout the computation.

A protocol $\Sigma$ is said to securely realize a given functionality $\mathcal{F}$ if for any adversary $\mathbf{A}$, there exists an ideal-world adversary $\mathbf{S}$ such that no environment $\mathcal{Z}$ can tell whether it is interacting with $\mathbf{A}$ and parties running the protocol, or with $\mathbf{S}$ and parties that interact with $\mathcal{F}$ in the ideal world.

The following universal composition theorem is proven in [3, 4]. Consider a protocol $\Sigma$ that operates in a hybrid model of computation where parties can communicate as usual, and in addition have ideal access to (an unbounded number of copies of) some ideal functionality $\mathcal{F}$. Let $\rho$ be a protocol that securely realizes $\mathcal{F}$ as sketched above, and let $\Sigma^\rho$ be the composed protocol. That is, $\Sigma^\rho$ is identical to $\Sigma$ with the exception that each interaction with some copy of $\mathcal{F}$ is replaced with a call to (or an invocation of) an appropriate instance of $\rho$. Similarly, $\rho$-outputs are treated as values provided by the appropriate copy of $\mathcal{F}$. Then $\Sigma$ and $\Sigma^\rho$ have essentially the same input/output behavior. In particular, if $\Sigma$ securely realizes some ideal functionality $\mathcal{G}$ given ideal access to $\mathcal{F}$, then $\Sigma^\rho$ securely realizes $\mathcal{G}$ from scratch.

For more details, see [3, 4].

### 3.2   Ideal Functionality of Verifiable SSE

We define the ideal functionality $\mathcal{F}_{vSSE}$ of verifiable SSE protocols as follows.

```
──────────── Ideal Functionality F_vSSE ────────────
```

Running with a dummy client $P_1$, a dummy server $P_2$ and an ideal world adversary **S**.

**Store:** Upon receiving input (**store**, $sid, D_1, \cdots, D_N, \mathcal{W}$) from $P_1$, verify that this is the first input from $P_1$ with (**store**, $sid$).
If so, store $D_1, \cdots, D_N$, and send $|D_1|, \cdots, |D_N|$ and $\ell$ to **S**.
Otherwise ignore this input.
**Search:** Upon receiving (**search**, $sid, w$) from $P_1$, send List($w$) to **S**.
  1. If **S** returns OK, then send D($w$) to $P_1$.
  2. If **S** returns $\perp$, then send $\perp$ to $P_1$.

Our $\mathcal{F}_{vSSE}$ provides an ideal world because

- The dummy client receives D($w$) correctly or $\perp$.
- The ideal world adversary **S** learns only $|D_1|, \cdots, |D_N|$ and $\ell$ in the store phase, and only List($w$) in the search phase.

(See the first paragraph of Sec.2.2.)

We say that a verifiable SSE protocol $\Sigma_{vSSE}$ is UC-secure if it securely realizes the ideal functionality $\mathcal{F}_{vSSE}$.

## 4    Equivalence

In this section, we prove that the UC-security notion of SSE is equivalent to the definitions of privacy and reliability presented in Sec.2. In the UC framework, a non-adaptive adversary corrupts some parties at the beginning of the protocol execution.

**Theorem 1.** *A verifiable SSE scheme vSSE satisfies privacy and reliability if the corresponding protocol $\Sigma_{vsse}$ is UC-secure against non-adaptive adversaries.*

(Proof) Assume that vSSE does not satisfy (one of) privacy or reliability. We show that $\Sigma_{vsse}$ does not securely realize $\mathcal{F}_{vSSE}$.

This is done by constructing an environment $\mathcal{Z}$ and an adversary **A** such that for any ideal world adversary **S**, $\mathcal{Z}$ can tell whether it is interacting with **A** in $\Sigma_{vsse}$, or with **S** in the ideal world which interacts with $\mathcal{F}_{vSSE}$.

(I) Assume that vSSE does not satisfy the privacy property defined by Def.1. That is, for any simulator **Sim**, there exists an adversary **B** such that eq.(2) is non-negligible.

$\mathcal{Z}$ asks **A** or **S** to corrupt $P_2$ (server) so that $P_2$ relays each message which he received from $P_1$ (client) to $\mathcal{Z}$ (in the real world). Except for this, $P_2$ behaves honestly. $\mathcal{Z}$ then internally runs **B** as follows.

– If **B** sends $(\mathcal{D}, \mathcal{W})$ to the challenger, then
  1. $\mathcal{Z}$ activates $P_1$ (client) with input (**store**, $sid, \mathcal{D}, \mathcal{W}$).
  2. In the real world,
     $P_1$ sends $(\mathcal{I}, \mathtt{C})$ to $P_2(= \mathbf{A})$, and $P_2(= \mathbf{A})$ relays it to $\mathcal{Z}$.
     In the ideal world,
     $P_1$ sends (**store**, $sid, \mathcal{D}, \mathcal{W}$) to $\mathcal{F}_{vSSE}$.
     $\mathcal{F}_{vSSE}$ sends $|D_1|, \cdots, |D_N|$ and $\ell$ to $\mathbf{S}(= P_2)$.
     $\mathbf{S}(= P_2)$ computes $(\mathcal{I}', \mathtt{C}')$, and sends it to $\mathcal{Z}$.
  3. $\mathcal{Z}$ sends $(\mathcal{I}, \mathtt{C})$ or $(\mathcal{I}', \mathtt{C}')$ to **B**.
– If **B** sends $w_i$ to the challenger, then

  1. $\mathcal{Z}$ activates $P_1$ with input (**search**, $sid, w_i$).
  2. In the real world,
     $P_1$ sends $t(w_i)$ to $P_2$, and $P_2$ relays it to $\mathcal{Z}$.
     In the ideal world,
     $P_1$ sends (**search**, $sid, w_i$) to $\mathcal{F}_{vSSE}$.
     $\mathcal{F}_{vSSE}$ sends $\mathtt{List}(w_i)$ to $\mathbf{S}(= P_2)$.
     $\mathbf{S}(= P_2)$ computes $t(w_i)'$, and sends it to $\mathcal{Z}$.
  3. $\mathcal{Z}$ sends $t(w_i)$ or $t(w_i)'$ to **B**.

Finally $\mathcal{Z}$ outputs 1 if and only if **B** outputs 1.

If $\mathcal{Z}$ interacts with $\Sigma_{vsse}$ (i.e. the real world), then it is easy to see that $\mathsf{Game}_{real}$ is simulated for **B**. On the other hand, suppose that $\mathcal{Z}$ interacts with **S** in the ideal world. Then $\mathsf{Game}_{sim}$ is simulated for **B** because the ideal functionality $\mathcal{F}_{vSSE}$ plays the role of the challenger and the ideal world adversary **S** plays the role of **Sim**.

Now from our assumption, for any ideal world adversary **S**, there exists some **B** which can distinguish $\mathsf{Game}_{real}$ from $\mathsf{Game}_{sim}$. This means that for any ideal world adversary **S**, there exists some $\mathcal{Z}$ which can distinguish $\Sigma_{vsse}$ (the real world) from the ideal world.

(II) Assume that vSSE does not satisfy reliability, i.e. there exists an adversary **B** which breaks the reliability defined by Def.2. $\mathcal{Z}$ asks **A** to corrupt $P_2$ (server) so that $P_2$ behaves in the same way as **B**. $\mathcal{Z}$ finally outputs 1 if and only if $\mathcal{Z}$ receives some set of documents $\mathcal{D}'$ from $P_1$ such that $\mathcal{D}' \neq \mathtt{D}(w)$ for some $w$.

If $\mathcal{Z}$ interacts with $\Sigma_{vsse}$, then **B** wins with non-negligible probability from our assumption. Hence $\mathcal{Z}$ outputs 1 with non-negligible probability. On the other hand, if $\mathcal{Z}$ interacts with **S** in the ideal world, $\mathcal{Z}$ never receives such $\mathcal{D}'$ from $P_1$. Hence $\mathcal{Z}$ never outputs 1. This means that $\mathcal{Z}$ can distinguish $\Sigma_{vsse}$ from the ideal world for any ideal world adversary **S**.                                Q.E.D.

**Theorem 2.** $\Sigma_{vSSE}$ *is UC-secure against non-adaptive adversaries if the underlying vSSE satisfies privacy and reliability.*

(Proof) Assume that $\Sigma_{vSSE}$ does not securely realize $\mathcal{F}_{vSSE}$ against non-adaptive adversaries. That is, there exists some $\mathcal{Z}$ who can distinguish between the real world and the ideal world.

We show that vSSE does not satisfy (one of) privacy or reliability. Assume that vSSE satisfies privacy. (Otherwise the theorem is proven). Then there exists a simulator **Sim** which satisfies Def.1.

Suppose that the real world adversary **A** does not corrupt any party. Then it is easy to see that no $\mathcal{Z}$ can distinguish the real world from the ideal world. (Note that $\mathcal{Z}$ interacts only with $P_1$.)

Suppose that $\mathcal{Z}$ asks **A** to corrupt $P_1$ (client). Note that **A** can report the communication pattern of $P_1$ to $\mathcal{Z}$. Consider an ideal world adversary **S** who runs **A** internally by playing the role of $P_2$. Note that **S** can play the role of $P_2$ faithfully because $P_2$ has no interaction with $\mathcal{Z}$ and $\mathcal{F}_{vSSE}$. Hence it is easy to see that no $\mathcal{Z}$ can distinguish the real world from the ideal world in this case, too.

Suppose that $\mathcal{Z}$ asks **A** to corrupt $P_2$ (server), but $P_2$ can not break the *reliability* at all. That is, $\Pr(P_2 \text{ wins}) = 0$ in Def.2. **A** may report the communication pattern of $P_2$ to $\mathcal{Z}$. Then our ideal world adversary **S** behaves in the same way as the above mentioned **Sim**, where the ideal functionality $\mathcal{F}_{vSSE}$ plays the role of the challenger. In this case, no $\mathcal{Z}$ can distinguish between the real world and the ideal world from the definition of *privacy*.

*Remark 1.* Def.1 says that there exists a **Sim** such that for any interactive distinguisher ($\mathcal{Z}$ in the above case), eq.(2) is negligible. This is the point where the privacy definition of of Curtmola et al. [7, Definition 4.11] does not work.

Suppose that $\mathcal{Z}$ asks **A** to corrupt $P_2$ (server), and $P_2$ breaks the *reliability* with negligible probability. That is, $\Pr(P_2 \text{ wins})$ is negligible in Def.2. Then similarly to the above, no $\mathcal{Z}$ can distinguish between the real world and the ideal world.

Therefore it must be that $\mathcal{Z}$ asks **A** to corrupt $P_2$ (server), and $P_2$ breaks *reliability* with non-negligible probability. That is, $\Pr(P_2 \text{ wins})$ is non-negligible in Def.2. (Otherwise no $\mathcal{Z}$ can distinguish between the real world and the ideal world.) This means that vSSE does not satisfy *reliability*.                    Q.E.D.

## 5   Construction

In this section, we construct an efficient *verifiable* SSE scheme which satisfies Def.1 and Def.2. Our scheme is based on SSE-2 of Curtmola et al. [6, 7]. (Note that SSE-2 is not verifiable).

### 5.1   Overview

We first illustrate SSE-2 of Curtmola et al. [6, 7] by using an example.

(Store phase:) The client constructs an array $\mathcal{I}$ as follows. Let $\pi_K$ be a pseudorandom permutation, where $K$ is the secret key of the client. Suppose that $\mathsf{D}(Austin) = (D_3, D_6, D_{10})$. That is, $D_3, D_6$ and $D_{10}$ contains a keyword $Austin$. First the client computes

$$\mathtt{addr}_{Austin,i} = \pi_K(Austin, i)$$

for $i = 1, \cdots, N$. Next let

$$\mathcal{I}(\text{addr}_{Austin,1}) = 3, \ \mathcal{I}(\text{addr}_{Austin,2}) = 6, \ \mathcal{I}(\text{addr}_{Austin,3}) = 10 \qquad (3)$$

and

$$\mathcal{I}(\text{addr}_{Austin,i}) = \text{dummy} \qquad (4)$$

for $i = 4, \cdots, N$. Do the same thing for all the other keywords. Finally the client stores $\mathcal{I}$ and $\mathcal{C} = \{C_1, \cdots, C_N\}$ to the server, where $C_i$ is a ciphertext of $D_i$.

(Search phase:) Suppose that the client wants to retrieve the documents which contain $Austin$. Then the client sends

$$t(Austin) = (\text{addr}_{Austin,1}, \cdots, \text{addr}_{Austin,N})$$

to the server. From eq.(3) and eq.(4), the server sees that $\text{List}(Austin) = \{3, 6, 10\}$. The server then returns $(C_3, C_6, C_{10})$ to the client. The client finally decrypts them to obtain $(D_3, D_6, D_{10})$.

The above scheme satisfies privacy, but not reliability. To achieve reliability, a naive approach is to replace $C_i$ with $\hat{C}_i = (C_i, \text{MAC}(C_i))$. The client stores the set of such $\hat{C}_i$ to the server. For a query $t(Austin)$, an (honest) server returns $(\hat{C}_3, \hat{C}_6, \hat{C}_{10})$ to the client. However, a malicious server would return $(\hat{C}_3, \hat{C}_6, \hat{C}_{11})$ or just $(\hat{C}_3, \hat{C}_6)$. Then the client cannot detect any cheating.

To overcome this problem, we construct $\mathcal{I}$ as follows.

$$\mathcal{I}(\text{addr}_{Austin,1}) = (3, tag_1 = \text{MAC}(\text{addr}_{Austin,1}, C_3))$$
$$\mathcal{I}(\text{addr}_{Austin,2}) = (6, tag_2 = \text{MAC}(\text{addr}_{Austin,2}, C_6))$$
$$\mathcal{I}(\text{addr}_{Austin,3}) = (10, tag_3 = \text{MAC}(\text{addr}_{Austin,3}, C_{10}))$$

and

$$\mathcal{I}(\text{addr}_{Austin,i}) = (\text{dummy}, tag_i = \text{MAC}(\text{addr}_{Austin,i}, \text{dummy}))$$

for $i = 4, \cdots, N$. For a query $t(Austin)$, the server returns $(C_3, C_6, C_{10})$ and $(tag_1, \cdots, tag_N)$ to the client.

The client checks the validity of each $tag_i$. This approach works because MAC binds the (query, answer) pair.

Another subtle point is that the index of each $D_i$ should appear in $\mathcal{I}$ the same number of times, say $\text{max}$ times. (Otherwise the simulator **Sim** in the definition of privacy cannot construct $\mathcal{I}'$ which is indistinguishable from $\mathcal{I}$. Remember that **Sim** must be able to construct $\mathcal{I}'$ only from $|D_1|, \cdots, |D_N|$ and $\ell$.)

For this problem, Curtmola et al. described the following method in SSE-2 [7, Fig.2].

For each index $i$:

- let $c$ be the number of entries in $\mathcal{I}$ that already contain $i$.
- for $1 \le \ell \le \text{max} - c$, set $\mathcal{I}[\pi_K(0^\ell, n + \ell)] = i$.

The last line is strange because $\ell$ is used in two different meanings. (In [7], $\ell$ is also defined as the bit length of each keyword.) Hence it must be that

– for $1 \le k \le \mathtt{max} - c$, set $\mathcal{I}[\pi_K(0^\ell, n + k)] = i$.

Even so, the above line does not work as shown below. For simplicity, suppose that $c = \mathtt{max} - 1$ for $i = 1, \cdots, N$. Then we have $\mathcal{I}[\pi_K(0^\ell, n+1)] = N$ at the end because the entry of $\mathcal{I}[\pi_K(0^\ell, n+1)]$ is overwritten for $i = 1, \cdots, N$. This means that in $\mathcal{I}$, only $N$ appears $\mathtt{max}$ times and the other each $i$ appears $\mathtt{max} - 1$ times.

We will show how to fix this flaw, too.

## 5.2   Proposed Verifiable SSE

Let $\mathtt{SKE} = (G, E, E^{-1})$ be a symmetric-key encryption scheme, where $G$ is a key generation algorithm, $E$ is an encryption algorithm and $E^{-1}$ is a decryption algorithm.

Remember that the set of documents is $\mathcal{D} = \{D_1, \cdots, D_N\}$, and the set of keywords is $\mathcal{W} = \{0,1\}^\ell$. Let $\pi : \{0,1\}^k \times \{0,1\}^{\ell+1+\log N} \to \{0,1\}^{\ell+1+\log N}$ be a pseudo-random permutation. For simplicity, we will write $y = \pi(x)$ instead of $y = \pi(K, x)$, where $K$ is a key.

Let $MAC : \{0,1\}^k \times \{0,1\}^* \to \{0,1\}^n$ be a MAC (a tag generation algorithm). For simplicity, we write $tag = \mathtt{MAC}(m)$ instead of $tag = \mathtt{MAC}(K, m)$, where $K$ is a key and $m$ is a message.

Now the proposed verifiable SSE scheme is as follows.

$\mathtt{Gen}(1^k)$: Run $G$ to generate a key $K_0$ of SKE. Choose a key $K_1 \in \{0,1\}^k$ of $\pi$ and a key $K_2 \in \{0,1\}^k$ of MAC randomly. Let $K = (K_0, K_1, K_2)$.

$\mathtt{Enc}(K, \mathcal{D}, \mathcal{W})$: First compute $C_i = E(K_0, D_i)$ for each $D_i \in \mathcal{D}$ and let $\mathcal{C} = \{C_1, \cdots, C_N\}$. Next let $\mathcal{I}$ be an array of size $2 \times 2^\ell N$ as follows.

1. First let

$$\mathcal{I}(i) \leftarrow (\mathtt{dummy}, \mathtt{MAC}(i, \mathtt{dummy}))$$

   for all $i = 1, \cdots, 2 \cdot 2^\ell N$.

2. Next for each $w \in \{0,1\}^\ell$, suppose that $\mathtt{D}(w) = (D_{s_1}, \cdots, D_{s_m})$. Define $(s_{m+1}, \cdots, s_N)$ as

$$\{s_{m+1}, \cdots, s_N\} = \{1, \cdots, N\} \setminus \{s_1, \cdots, s_m\}$$

   For $j = 1, \cdots, N$, do

$$\mathtt{addr}_j \leftarrow \begin{cases} \pi(0, w, j) \ if \ 1 \le j \le m \\ \pi(1, w, j) \ if \ m + 1 \le j \le N \end{cases}$$
$$tag_j \leftarrow \mathtt{MAC}(\mathtt{addr}_j, C_{s_j})$$
$$\mathcal{I}(\mathtt{addr}_j) \leftarrow (s_j, tag_j).$$

It is now easy to see that each index $i$ appears $2^\ell$ times in $\mathcal{I}$.

*Example 1.* Suppose that $N = 5$ and $\mathsf{D}(Austin) = (D_1, D_3, D_5)$. Then

$$\mathcal{I}(\pi(0, Austin, 1)) = (1, tag_1)$$
$$\mathcal{I}(\pi(0, Austin, 2)) = (3, tag_2)$$
$$\mathcal{I}(\pi(0, Austin, 3)) = (5, tag_3)$$
$$\mathcal{I}(\pi(1, Austin, 4)) = (2, tag_4)$$
$$\mathcal{I}(\pi(1, Austin, 5)) = (4, tag_5)$$

$\mathtt{Trpdr}(K, w)$: Output

$$t(w) = (\pi(0, w, 1), \cdots, \pi(0, w, N)).$$

$\mathtt{Search}(\mathcal{I}, \mathcal{C}, t(w))$: Parse $t(w)$ as $t(w) = (\mathtt{addr}_1, \cdots, \mathtt{addr}_N)$. Suppose that

$$\mathcal{I}(\mathtt{addr}_i) = (s_i, tag_i)$$

for $i = 1, \cdots, N$. First let $\mathsf{C}(w) \leftarrow empty$. Next for $i = 1, \cdots, N$, add $C_{s_i}$ to $\mathsf{C}(w)$ if $s_i \neq \mathsf{dummy}$. Finally let

$$Tag = (tag_1, \cdots, tag_N)$$

Output $(\mathsf{C}(w), Tag)$.

$\mathtt{Verify}(K, t(w), \tilde{\mathsf{C}}(w), Tag)$: Parse $t(w), \tilde{\mathsf{C}}(w)$ and $Tag$ as

$$t(w) = (\mathtt{addr}_1, \cdots, \mathtt{addr}_N)$$
$$\tilde{\mathsf{C}}(w) = (\tilde{C}_1, \cdots, \tilde{C}_m)$$
$$Tag = (tag_1, \cdots, tag_N)$$

First let $X_i \leftarrow \tilde{C}_i$ for $i = 1, \cdots, m$. Next let $X_i \leftarrow \mathsf{dummy}$ for $i = m+1, \cdots, N$. Finally if $tag_i = \mathtt{MAC}(\mathtt{addr}_i, X_i)$ for $i = 1, \cdots, N$, then output $\mathtt{accept}$. Otherwise output $\mathtt{reject}$.

$\mathtt{Dec}(K, C)$: Output a document $D = E^{-1}(K_0, C)$ for a ciphertext $C$.

## 5.3   Security

We assume that the symmetric-key encryption scheme $\mathtt{SKE} = (G, E, E^{-1})$ is left-or-right (LOR) CPA secure as defined by [2]. The common counter mode with AES satisfies this condition, where AES is assumed to be a pseudo-random permutation. We also assume that $\mathtt{MAC}$ is unforgeable against chosen message attack.

**Theorem 3.** *The above scheme satisfies privacy (see Def.1).*

(Proof) We construct a simulator **Sim** as follows. In the store phase, **Sim** is given $|D_1|, \cdots, |D_N|$ and $\ell$.

1. **Sim** runs $\mathtt{Gen}(1^k)$ to generate $K = (K_0, K_1, K_2)$.

2. Let $C_i' = E(K_0, 0^{|D_i|})$ for $i = 1, \cdots, N$, and let $C' = \{C_1', \cdots, C_N'\}$.
3. Construct $\mathcal{I}'$ as if $D(w) = (D_1, \cdots, D_N)$ for all $w \in \{0,1\}^\ell$. This means that for each $w \in \{0,1\}^\ell$,

$$\mathcal{I}'(\pi(0, w, i)) = (i, tag_i) \text{ for } i = 1, \cdots, N \tag{5}$$
$$\mathcal{I}'(\pi(1, w, i)) = (\texttt{dummy}, tag_i') \text{ for } i = 1, \cdots, N \tag{6}$$

where $tag_i = \texttt{MAC}(\pi(0, w, i), C_i')$ and $tag_i' = \texttt{MAC}(\pi(1, w, i), \texttt{dummy})$.
That is,

$$\mathcal{I}'(\pi(0, w, 1)) = (1, tag_1), \qquad \mathcal{I}'(\pi(1, w, 1)) = (\texttt{dummy}, tag_1')$$

$$\vdots \qquad\qquad\qquad\qquad \vdots$$

$$\mathcal{I}'(\pi(0, w, N)) = (N, tag_N), \qquad \mathcal{I}'(\pi(1, w, N)) = (\texttt{dummy}, tag_N')$$

4. Return $(\mathcal{I}', C')$.

In the search phase, for $i = 1, \cdots, q$, **Sim** is given

$$\texttt{List}(w_i) = \{s_1, \cdots, s_m\}$$

(but not $w_i$). Then **Sim** returns

$$t(w_i)' = (\pi(0, i, s_1), \cdots, \pi(0, i, s_m), \pi(1, i, m+1), \cdots, \pi(1, i, N)). \tag{7}$$

We will prove that any **A** cannot distinguish between $\textsf{Game}_{real}$ and $\textsf{Game}_{sim}$ by using a series of games $\textsf{Game}_0, \cdots, \textsf{Game}_2$, where $\textsf{Game}_0 = \textsf{Game}_{real}$. Let

$$p_i = \Pr(\textbf{A} \text{ outputs } b = 1 \text{ in } \textsf{Game}_i).$$

- $\textsf{Game}_1$ is the same as $\textsf{Game}_0$ except for that $C_i$ is replaced with $C_i'$ of the above for $i = 1, \cdots, N$. Then $|p_0 - p_1|$ is negligible from our assumption on SKE.
- $\textsf{Game}_2$ is the same as $\textsf{Game}_1$ except for that $\mathcal{I}$ is replaced with $\mathcal{I}'$ of the above, and $t(w_i)$ is replaced with $t(w_i)'$ of the above.
  Note that the index $i$ of each $D_i$ appears $2^\ell$ times in both $\mathcal{I}$ and $\mathcal{I}'$.
  Next on $t(w_i)'$, let

$$\texttt{addr}_1 = \pi(0, i, s_1), \cdots, \texttt{addr}_m = \pi(0, i, s_m),$$

$$\texttt{addr}_{m+1} = \pi(1, i, m+1), \cdots, \texttt{addr}_N = \pi(1, i, N).$$

Then from eq.(5) and eq.(6), it is easy to see that

$$\mathcal{I}'(\texttt{addr}_1) = (s_1, tag_1), \cdots, \mathcal{I}'(\texttt{addr}_m) = (s_m, tag_m),$$

$$\mathcal{I}'(\texttt{addr}_{m+1}) = (\texttt{dummy}, tag_{m+1}'), \cdots, \mathcal{I}'(\texttt{addr}_N) = (\texttt{dummy}, tag_N')$$

The value of such $\mathcal{I}'(\texttt{addr}_i)$ is the same as the real one. Further $\pi$ is a pseudo-random permutation. Hence $|p_1 - p_2|$ is negligible.

Consequently $|p_0 - p_2|$ is negligible. Further it is clear that $\mathtt{Game}_2 = \mathtt{Game}_{sim}$. This means that $\mathtt{Game}_{real}$ and $\mathtt{Game}_{sim}$ are indistinguishable for any $\mathbf{A}$. Q.E.D.

**Theorem 4.** *The above scheme satisfies reliability (see Def.2).*

(Proof) Suppose that there exists an adversary $\mathbf{A}$ who breaks the reliability for some $(\mathcal{D}, \mathcal{W})$ and some search queries $w_1, \cdots, w_q$. We will show a forger $\mathbf{B}$ for the underlying $\mathtt{MAC}$.

$\mathbf{B}$ runs $\mathbf{A}$ by playing the role of a client, where the input to the client is $(\mathcal{D}, \mathcal{W})$ in the store phase, and $w_1, \cdots, w_q$ in the search phase. In the search phase, $\mathbf{B}$ uses his $\mathtt{MAC}$ oracle to compute $\mathcal{I}$.

From our assumption, $\mathbf{A}$ returns $(\mathtt{C}(w)^*, Tag^*)$ for some query $t(w)$ such that $\mathtt{C}(w)^*$ is invalid for $t(w)$ and

$$\mathtt{Verify}(K, t(w), \mathtt{C}(w)^*, Tag^*) = \mathtt{accept} \tag{8}$$

with non-negligible probability, where $w \in \{w_1, \cdots, w_q\}$. Let

$$(\mathtt{C}(w), Tag) \leftarrow \mathtt{Search}(\mathcal{I}, \mathcal{C}, t(w)). \tag{9}$$

Then $\mathtt{C}(w)^* \neq \mathtt{C}(w)$ because $\mathtt{C}(w)^*$ is invalid for $t(w)$. Suppose that

$$t(w) = (\mathtt{addr}_1, \cdots, \mathtt{addr}_N)$$
$$\mathtt{C}(w) = (C_1, \cdots, C_k)$$
$$\mathtt{C}(w)^* = (C_1^*, \cdots, C_m^*)$$
$$Tag^* = (tag_1^*, \cdots, tag_N^*)$$

Since $\mathtt{C}(w)^* \neq \mathtt{C}(w)$, there are three cases.

**Case 1:** $m = k$ and there exists some $C_i^*$ such that $C_i^* \neq C_i$.
**Case 2:** $m < k$.
**Case 3:** $m > k$.

If (Case 1) occurs, then $\mathbf{B}$ outputs $(\mathtt{addr}_i, C_i^*)$ and $tag_i^*$ as a forgery. We will show that this is a valid forgery on $\mathtt{MAC}$. That is, $tag_i^* = \mathtt{MAC}(\mathtt{addr}_i, C_i^*)$ and $\mathbf{B}$ never queried $(\mathtt{addr}_i, C_i^*)$ to the $\mathtt{MAC}$ oracle.

First it is clear that $tag_i^* = \mathtt{MAC}(\mathtt{addr}_i, C_i^*)$ from eq.(8).

Next it is easy to see that $\mathbf{B}$ queried $(\mathtt{addr}_i, C_i)$ to his $\mathtt{MAC}$ oracle when computing $\mathcal{I}$ from eq.(9). It means that $\mathbf{B}$ did not query $(\mathtt{addr}_i, C_i^*)$ to the $\mathtt{MAC}$ oracle because $\mathbf{B}$ does not query $\mathtt{addr}_i$ to the $\mathtt{MAC}$ oracle more than once when computing $\mathcal{I}$. This means that $\mathbf{B}$ succeeds in forgery.

If (Case 2) occurs, then $B$ outputs $(\mathtt{addr}_{m+1}, \mathtt{dummy})$ and $tag_{m+1}^*$ as a forgery. If (Case 3) occurs, then $B$ outputs $(\mathtt{addr}_m, C_m^*)$ and $tag_m^*$ as a forgery. We can show that these are valid forgeries on $\mathtt{MAC}$ similarly.

This is against our assumption on $\mathtt{MAC}$. Hence our scheme satisfies reliability.                                                                    Q.E.D.

**Corollary 1.** *The corresponding protocol $\Sigma_{vSSE}$ is UC-secure against non-adaptive adversaries.*

(Proof) From Theorem 2.                                                        Q.E.D.

# References

1. Bellovin, S., Cheswick, W.: Privacy-Enhanced Searches Using Encrypted Bloom Filters, Cryptology ePrint Archive, Report 2006/210 (2006), http://eprint.iacr.org/
2. Bellare, M., Desai, A., Jokipii, E., Rogaway, P.: A Concrete Security Treatment of Symmetric Encryption. In: FOCS 1997, pp. 394–403 (1997)
3. Canetti, R.: Universally Composable Security: A New Paradigm for Cryptographic Protocols, Revision 1 of ECCC Report TR01-016 (2001)
4. Canetti, R.: Universally Composable Signatures, Certification and Authentication, Cryptology ePrint Archive, Report 2003/239 (2003), http://eprint.iacr.org/
5. Canetti, R.: Universally Composable Security: A New Paradigm for Cryptographic Protocols, Cryptology ePrint Archive, Report 2000/067 (2005), http://eprint.iacr.org/
6. Curtmola, R., Garay, J.A., Kamara, S., Ostrovsky, R.: Searchable symmetric encryption: improved definitions and efficient constructions. In: ACM Conference on Computer and Communications Security 2006, pp. 79–88 (2006)
7. Full version of the above: Cryptology ePrint Archive, Report 2006/210 (2006), http://eprint.iacr.org/
8. Chang, Y.-C., Mitzenmacher, M.: Privacy Preserving Keyword Searches on Remote Encrypted Data. In: Ioannidis, J., Keromytis, A.D., Yung, M. (eds.) ACNS 2005. LNCS, vol. 3531, pp. 442–455. Springer, Heidelberg (2005)
9. Goh, E.-J.: Secure Indexes. Cryptology ePrint Archive, Report 2003/216 (2003), http://eprint.iacr.org/
10. Song, D., Wagner, D., Perrig, A.: Practical Techniques for Searches on Encrypted Data. In: IEEE Symposium on Security and Privacy 2000, pp. 44–55 (2000)

# CTL: A Platform-Independent Crypto Tools Library Based on Dataflow Programming Paradigm*

Junaid Jameel Ahmad[1,**], Shujun Li[1,2], Ahmad-Reza Sadeghi[3,4], and Thomas Schneider[3]

[1] University of Konstanz, Germany
[2] University of Surrey, UK
[3] TU Darmstadt, Germany
[4] Fraunhofer SIT, Germany

**Abstract.** The diversity of computing platforms is increasing rapidly. In order to allow security applications to run on such diverse platforms, implementing and optimizing the same cryptographic primitives for multiple target platforms and heterogeneous systems can result in high costs. In this paper, we report our efforts in developing and benchmarking a platform-independent Crypto Tools Library (CTL). CTL is based on a dataflow programming framework called Reconfigurable Video Coding (RVC), which was recently standardized by ISO/IEC for building complicated reconfigurable video codecs. CTL benefits from various properties of the RVC framework including tools to 1) simulate the platform-independent designs, 2) automatically generate implementations in different target programming languages (e.g., C/C++, Java, LLVM, and Verilog/VHDL) for deployment on different platforms as software and/or hardware modules, and 3) design space exploitation such as automatic parallelization for multi- and many-core systems. We benchmarked the performance of the SHA-256 implementation in CTL on single-core target platforms and demonstrated that implementations automatically generated from platform-independent RVC applications can achieve a run-time performance comparable to reference implementations manually written in C and Java. For a quad-core target platform, we benchmarked a 4-adic hash tree application based on SHA-256 that achieves a performance gain of up to 300% for hashing messages of size 8 MB.

**Keywords:** Crypto Tools Library (CTL), Reconfigurable Video Coding (RVC), dataflow programming, reconfigurability, platform independence, multi-core.

---

* Extended edition of this paper is available at http://eprint.iacr.org/2011/679.

** Junaid Jameel Ahmad and Shujun Li were partially supported by the Zukunftskolleg of the University of Konstanz, Germany, which is part of the "Excellence Initiative" program of the DFG (German Research Foundation). The first author would like to thank International Financial Cryptography Association (IFCA) and Google Research for awarding him the "Google Student Award", which covered his registration fees to FC 2012 and associated workshops.

A.D. Keromytis (Ed.): FC 2012, LNCS 7397, pp. 299–313, 2012.

# 1  Introduction

Nowadays we are living in a fully digitized and networked world. The ubiq-uitous transmission of data over the open network has made security one of the most important concerns in almost all modern digital systems, being pri-vacy another. Both security and privacy concerns call for support from applied cryptography. However, the great diversity of today's computing hardware and software platforms is creating a big challenge for applied cryptography since we need building blocks that should ideally be reused at various platforms without reprogramming. For instance, a large-scale video surveillance system (like those we have already been seeing in many big cities) involves many different kinds of hardware and software platforms: scalar sensors, video sensors, audio sensors, mobile sensors (e.g. mobile phones), sensor motor controller, storage hub, data sink, cloud storage servers, etc. [11]. Supporting so many different devices in a single system or cross the boundary of multiple systems is a very challeng-ing task. Many cryptographic libraries have been built over the years to partly meet this challenge, but most of them are written in a particular programming language (e.g. C, C++, Java and VHDL) thus their applications are limited in nature. While it is always possible to port a library written in one language to the other, the process requires significant human involvement on reprogram-ming and/or re-optimization, which may not be less easier than designing a new library from scratch.

In this paper, we propose to meet the above-mentioned technical challenges by building a platform-independent[1] library based on a recently-established ISO / IEC standard called RVC (Reconfigurable Video Coding) [33, 34]. Unlike its name suggests, the RVC standard offers a general development framework for all data-driven systems including cryptosystems, which is not surprising because video codecs are among the most complicated data-driven systems we can have. The RVC framework follows the dataflow paradigm, and enjoys the following nice features at the level of programming language: *modularity, reusability, re-configuration, code analyzability* and *parallelism exploitability*. Modularity and reusability help to simplify the design of complicated programs by having func-tionally separated and reusable computational blocks; reconfigurability makes reconfiguration of complicated programs easier by offering an interface to con-figure and replace computational blocks; code analyzability allows automatic analysis of both the source code and the functional behavior of each compu-tational block so that code conversion and program optimization can be done in a more systematic manner. The automated code analysis enables to conduct a fully-/semi-automated design-space exploitation to find critical paths and/or parallel data-flows, which suggests different optimization refactorings (merging or splitting) of different computational blocks [43], and/or to achieve concurrency

---

[1] In the context of MPEG RVC framework, the word "platform" has a broader mean-ing. Basically, it denotes any computing environment that can execute/interpret code or compile code to produce executable programs, which includes both hardware and software platforms and also hybrid hardware-software systems.

by mapping different computational blocks to different computing resources [20]. In contrast to the traditional sequential programming paradigm, the dataflow programming paradigm is ideally suited for such optimizations thanks to its data-driven nature as described next.

The dataflow programming paradigm, invented in the 1960s [61], allows programs to be defined as a directed graph in which the nodes correspond to computational units and edges represent the direction of the data flowing among nodes [25,40]. The modularity, reusability and reconfigurability are achieved by making each computational unit's functional behavior independent of other computational units. In other words, the only interface between two computational units is the data exchanged. The separation of functionality and interface allows different computational units to run in parallel, thus easing parallelism exploitation. The dataflow programming paradigm is suited ideally for applications with a data-driven nature like signal processing systems, multimedia applications, and as we show in this paper also for cryptosystems.

**Our Contributions:** In this paper, we present the Crypto Tools Library (CTL) as the first (to the best of our knowledge) open and platform-independent cryptographic library based on a dataflow programming framework (in our case the RVC framework). In particular, the CTL achieves the following goals:

– **Fast development/prototyping:** By adapting the dataflow programming paradigm the CTL components are inherently *modular, reusable,* and easily *reconfigurable.* These properties do not only help to quickly develop/prototype security algorithms but also make their maintenance easier.
– **Multiple target languages:** The CTL cryptosystems are programmed only once, but can be used to automatically generate source code for multiple programming languages (C, C++, Java, LLVM, Verilog, VHDL, XLIM, and PROMELA at the time for this writing[2]).
– **Automatic code analyzability and optimization:** An automated design-space exploitation process can be performed at the algorithmic level, which can help to optimize the algorithmic structure by refactoring (merging or splitting) selected computational blocks, and by exploiting multi-/many-core computing resources to run different computational blocks in parallel.
– **Hardware/Software co-design:** Heterogenous systems involving software, hardware, and various I/O devices/channels can be developed in the RVC framework [62].
– **Adequate run-time performance:** Although CTL cryptosystems are highly abstract programs, the run-time performance of automatically synthesized implementations is still adequate compared to non-RVC reference implementations.

In this paper, along with the development of the CTL itself, we report some performance benchmarking results of CTL that confirm that the highly abstract

---

[2] More code generation backends are to be developed in the future, especially OpenCL for GPUs.

nature of the RVC code does not compromise the run-time performance. In addition, we also briefly discuss how different key attributes of the RVC framework can be used to develop different cryptographic algorithms and security applications.

**Outline:** The rest of the paper is organized as follows. In Sec. 2 we will give a brief overview of related work, focusing on a comparison between RVC and other existing dataflow solutions. Sec. 3 gives an overview of the building blocks of the RVC framework and Sec. 4 describes the design principles of CTL and the cryptosystems that are already implemented. In Sec. 5, we benchmark the performance of SHA-256 implemented in CTL on a single-core machine and a quad-core one. In Sec. 6, we conclude the paper by giving directions for future works.

## 2   Related Work

Many cryptographic libraries have been developed over the years (e.g., [16,24,30, 41,46,56,57,63,64]), but very few can support multiple programming languages. Some libraries do support more than one programming language, but often in the form of separate sets of source code and separate programming interfaces/APIs [63], or available as commercial software only [8,41]. There is also a large body of optimized implementations of cryptosystems in the literature [17,18,21,44,45, 55,67], which normally depend even more on the platforms (e.g., the processor architecture and/or special instruction sets [28,45,66,67]).

Despite being a rather new standard, the RVC framework has been successfully used to develop different kinds of data-driven systems especially multimedia (video, audio, image and graphics) codecs [12–14,19,35] and multimedia security applications [10]. In [10], we highlighted some challenges being faced by developers while building multimedia security applications in imperative languages and discussed how those challenges can be addressed by developing multimedia security applications in the RVC framework. In addition, we presented three multimedia security applications (joint H.264/MPEG-4 video encoding and decoding, joint JPEG image encoding and decoding and compressed domain JPEG image watermark embedding and detecting) developed using the CTL cryptosystems and the RVC implementations of H.264/MPEG-4 and JPEG codecs. Considering the focus of that paper, we only used and briefly summarized CTL. In this paper, we give a detailed discussion on CTL, its design principles, features and benefits, and performance benchmarking results.

The wide usage of RVC for developing multimedia applications is not the only reason why we chose it for developing CTL. A summary of advantages of RVC over other solutions is given in Table 1 (this is an extension of the table in [10]). We emphasize that this comparison focuses on the features relevant to achieve the goals of CTL, so it should not be considered as an exhaustive overview of all pros and cons of the solutions compared.

**Table 1.** Comparison of RVC framework with other candidate solutions. Candidates with similar characteristics are grouped together. These categories include 1) high-level specification languages for hardware programming languages, 2) frameworks for hardware/software co-design, 3) commercial products, and 4) other cryptographic libraries. The columns in the table represent the following features: A) high-level (abstract) modeling and simulation; B) platform independence; C) code analyzability (i.e., semi-automated design-space exploitation); D) hardware code generation; E) software code generation; F) hardware/software co-design; G) supported target languages; H) open-source or free implementations; I) international standard.

| Cat. | Candidate | A | B | C | D | E | F | G | H | I |
|---|---|---|---|---|---|---|---|---|---|---|
| | **RVC** | ✓ | ✓ | ✓ | ✓ | ✓ | ✓ | C, C++, Java, LLVM, Verilog, VHDL, XLIM, PROMELA | ✓ | ✓ |
| 1 | Handel-C [39] | ✗ | ✗ | ✗ | ✓ | ✗ | ✗ | VHDL | ✗ | ✗ |
| | ImpulseC [15] | ✗ | ✗ | ✗ | ✓ | ✗ | ✓ | VHDL | ✗ | ✗ |
| | Spark [29] | ✗ | ✗ | ✗ | ✓ | ✗ | ✓ | VHDL | ✗ | ✗ |
| 2 | BlueSpec [49] | ✓ | ✗ | ✓ | ✓ | ✓ | ✗ | C, Verilog | ✗ | ✗ |
| | Daedalus [65] | ✓ | ✓ | ✓ | ✓ | ✓ | ✓ | C, C++, VHDL | ✓ | ✗ |
| | Koski [38] | ✓ | ✓ | ✓ | ✓ | ✓ | ✓ | C, XML, VHDL | ✗ | ✗ |
| | PeaCE [31] | ✓ | ✓ | ✓ | ✓ | ✓ | ✓ | C, C++, VHDL | ✓ | ✗ |
| 3 | CoWare [58] | ✓ | ✓ | ✗ | ✓ | ✓ | ✓ | C, VHDL | ✗ | ✗ |
| | Esterel [1] | ✗ | ✓ | ✗ | ✓ | ✓ | ✗ | C, VHDL | ✓ | ✗ |
| | LabVIEW [3] | ✓ | ✓ | ✓ | ✗ | ✗ | ✗ | - | ✗ | ✗ |
| | Simulink [4] | ✓ | ✓ | ✓ | ✓ | ✓ | ✗ | C, C++, Verilog, VHDL | ✗ | ✗ |
| | Synopsys System Studio [7] | ✓ | ✓ | ✓ | ✓ | ✓ | ✓ | C++, SystemC, SystemVerilog | ✗ | ✗ |
| 4 | CAO [9,47] | ✓ | ✓ | ✗ | ✗ | ✓ | ✗ | C, x86-64 assembly, ARM | ✗ | ✗ |
| | Cryptol [8,41] | ✓ | ✓ | ✓ | ✓ | ✓ | ✗ | C, C++, Haskell, VHDL, Verilog | ✗ | ✗ |

## 3 Reconfigurable Video Coding (RVC)

The RVC framework was standardized by the ISO/IEC (via its working group JTC1 / SG29 / WG11, better known as MPEG – Motion Picture Experts Group [48]) to meet the technical challenges of developing more and more complicated video codecs [33,34]. One main concern of the MPEG is how to make video codecs more reconfigurable, meaning that codecs with different configurations (e.g., different video coding standards, different profiles and/or levels, different system requirements) can be built on the basis of a single set of platform-independent building blocks. To achieve this goal, the RVC standard defines a framework that covers different steps of the whole life cycle of video codec development. The RVC community has developed supporting tools [2,5,6] to make the RVC framework not only a standard, but also a real development environment.

While the RVC framework is developed in the context of video coding, it is actually a general-purpose framework that can model any data-driven applications such as cryptosystems. It allows developers to work with a single platform-independent design at a higher level of abstraction while still being able to generate multiple editions of the same design that target different platforms like embedded systems, general-purpose PCs, and FPGAs. In principle, the RVC framework also supports hardware-software co-design by converting parts of a design into software and other parts into hardware. Additionally, the RVC framework is based on two languages that allow automatic code analysis to facilitate large-scale design-space exploitation like enhancing parallelism of implementations running on multi-core and many-core systems [14, 20, 43].

The RVC standard is composed of two parts: MPEG-B Part 4 [34] and MPEG-C Part 4 [33]. MPEG-B Part 4 specifies the dataflow framework for designing and/or reconfiguring video codecs, and MPEG-C Part 4 defines a video tool library that contains a number of Functional Units (FUs) as platform-independent building blocks of MPEG standard compliant video codecs [33]. To support the RVC dataflow framework, MPEG-B Part 4 specifies three different languages: a dataflow programming language called RVC-CAL for describing platform-independent FUs, an XML dialect called FNL (FU Network Language) for describing connections between FUs, and another XML dialect called RVC-BSDL for describing the syntax format of video bitstreams. RVC-BSDL is not involved in this work, so we will not discuss it further.

The real core of the RVC framework is RVC-CAL, a general-purpose dataflow programming language for specifying platform-independent FUs. RVC-CAL is a subset of an existing dataflow programming language CAL (Caltrop Actor Language) [26]. In RVC-CAL, FUs are implemented as actors containing a number of fireable actions and internal states. In the RVC-CAL's term, the data exchanged among actors are called tokens. Each actor can contain both input and output port(s) that receive input token(s) and produce output token(s), respectively. Each action may fire depending on four different conditions: 1) input token availability; 2) guard conditions; 3) finite-state machine based action scheduling; 4) action priorities. In RVC-CAL, actors are the basic functional entities that can run in parallel, but actions in an actor are atomic, meaning that only one action can fire at one time. This structure gives a balance between modularity and parallelism, and makes automatic analysis of actor merging/splitting possible.

Figure 1 illustrates how an application can be modeled and how target implementations can be generated with the RVC framework. At the design stage, different FUs (if not implemented in any standard library) are first written in RVC-CAL to describe their I/O behavior, and then an FU network is built to represent the functionality of a whole application. The FU network can be built by simply connecting all FUs involved graphically via a supporting tool called Graphiti Editor [2], which translates the graphical FU network description into a textual description written in FU Network Language (FNL). The FUs and the FU network are instantiated to form an abstract model. This abstract model can be simulated to test its functionality without going to any specific platform.

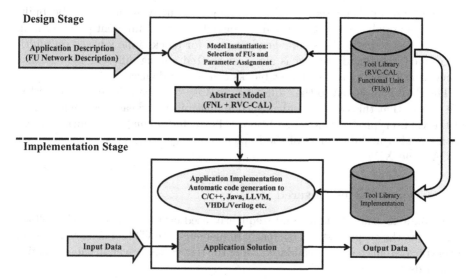

**Fig. 1.** Process of application implementation generation in the RVC framework

Two available supporting tools allowing the simulation are OpenDF [5] and ORCC [6]. At the implementation stage, the source code written in other target programming languages can be generated from the abstract application description *automatically*. OpenDF includes a Verilog HDL code generation backend, and ORCC contains a number of code generation backends for C, C++, Java, LLVM, VHDL, XLIM, and PROMELA. ORCC is currently more widely used in the RVC community and it is also the choice of our work reported in this paper.

## 4   Crypto Tools Library (CTL)

Crypto Tools Library (CTL) is a collection of RVC-CAL actors and XDF networks for cryptographic primitives such as block ciphers, stream ciphers, cryptographic hash functions and PRNGs (see Sec. 4.2 for a list of currently implemented algorithms). Being an open project, the source code and documentation of CTL is available at http://www.hooklee.com/default.asp?t=CTL.

As mentioned in Sec. 1, most existing cryptographic libraries are developed based on a single programming language (mostly C/C++ or Java) that can hardly be converted to other languages. In contrast, CTL is a platform-independent solution whose source code is written in RVC-CAL and FNL that can be automatically translated into multiple programming languages (C, C++, Java, LLVM, Verilog, VHDL, XLIM, PROMELA). More programming languages can be supported by developing new code generation tools for RVC applications.

### 4.1   Design Principles

The CTL is developed by strictly following the specifications/standards defining the implemented cryptosystems. For block ciphers, both enciphers and deciphers are implemented so that a complete security solution can be built. When it is possible, the CTL FUs are designed to exploit inherent parallelism in the implemented cryptosystems. For instance, for block ciphers based on multiple rounds, the round number is also transmitted among different FUs so that encryption/decryption of different blocks can be parallelized.

The CTL is designed so that different cryptosystems can share common FUs. We believe that this can help enhance code reusability and ease reconfigurability of the CTL cryptosystems. In addition, CTL includes *complete* solutions (e.g., both encipher and decipher) of the implemented cryptosystems, normally a set of CAL and XDF files.

## 4.2  Cryptosystems Covered

CTL contains some standard and frequently used cryptosystems. In the following, we list the cryptosystems currently implemented in CTL. The correctness of all cryptosystems has been validated using the test vectors given in the respective standards.

- Block Ciphers:
  - AES-128/192/256 [51],
  - DES [50] and Triple DES [50, 52],
  - Blowfish [59],
  - Modes of operations: CBC, CFB, OFB, CTR.
- Stream Ciphers: ARC4 [60] and Rabbit [23].
- Cryptographic hash functions: SHA-1, SHA-2 (SHA-224, SHA-256) [53].
- PSNRs: 32-bit and 64-bit LCG [60] and LFSR-based PRNG [60].

CTL also includes some common utility FUs (e.g., multiplexing/demultiplexing of dataflows, conversion of bytes to bits and vice versa etc.) that are shared among different cryptosystems and can also find applications in non-cryptography systems. Due to the space limitation, we refer the reader to the extended edition of this paper for a list of the utility FUs and more discussions of the cryptosystems implemented in CTL.

## 5  Performance Benchmarking of CTL

Previous work has demonstrated that the RVC framework can outperform other sequential programming languages in terms of implementing highly complex and highly parallelizable systems like video codecs [19]. However, there are still doubts about if the high-level abstraction of RVC-CAL and the automated code generation process may compromise the overall performance to some extent at the platform level. In this section, we clarify those doubts by showing that the automatically generated implementations from a typical RVC-based application can usually achieve a performance comparable to manually-written implementations in the target programming language. This was verified on AES and SHA-256 applications in CTL. In this section, we take SHA-256 as an example

**Table 2.** Configuration of the test machine

| Machine | Hardware and Operating System Details |
|---|---|
| Desktop PC: | – Model: HP Centurion<br>– CPU: Intel(R) Core(TM)2 Quad CPU Q9550 2.83GHz<br>– Memory: 8GB RAM<br>– OS1: Windows Vista Business with Service Pack 2 (64-bit Edition)<br>– OS2: Ubuntu Linux (Kernel version: 2.6.27.11) |

to show how we did the benchmarking on a single-core machine and a quad-core one. The main purpose of getting the quad-core machine involved is to show how easy one can divide an FU network and map different parts to different cores to make a better use of the computing resources. In the given example, the partitioning and mapping were both done manually, but they can be automated for large applications thanks to the code analyzability of RVC-CAL.

**Run-Time Performance Metric.** We ran our experiments on both Microsoft Windows and Linux OSs (see Table 2 for details). Both operating systems support high-resolution timers to measure time in nanoseconds. More specifically, we used the `QueryPerformanceCounter()` and `QueryPerformanceFrequency()` functions (available from Windows API) on Windows, and the `clock_gettime()` and `clock_getres()` functions with `CLOCK_MONOTONIC` clock (available from the Higher Resolution Timer [22] package) on Linux. In addition, to circumvent the caching problem, we conducted 100 independent runs (with random input data) of each configuration and used the average value as the final performance metric.

The concrete specifications of our test machine can be found in Table 2. Due to the multi-tasking nature of Windows and Linux operating systems, the benchmarking result can be influenced by other tasks running in parallel. In order to minimize this effect, we conducted all our experiments under the safe mode of both OSs. We used Microsoft Visual Studio 2008 and GCC 4.3.2 as C compilers for the Windows and the Linux operating systems, respectively. Both compilers were configured to maximize the speed of generated executables. For Java programs, we used Eclipse SDK 3.6.1 and Java(TM) SE Runtime Environment (build 1.6.0_12-b04).

**Benchmarking of SHA-256 on Single-Core Platform.** In this subsection, we present the results of benchmarking a single SHA-256 FU against some non-RVC reference implementations in C (OpenSSL [64], OGay [27], and sphlib [56]) and Java (Java Cryptography Architecture (JCA) [54]). Figure 2 shows the results of our benchmarking under Windows operating system while our test machine was configured to run only one CPU core. One can see that the run-time performance of CTL implementation is better than OpenSSL but inferior to carefully optimized implementations (OGay and sphlib). In addition, the CTL's Java implementation of SHA-256 does not outperform the JCA implementation.

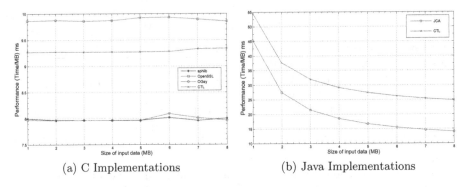

(a) C Implementations          (b) Java Implementations

**Fig. 2.** Benchmarking of CTL's SHA-256 implementation

This can probably be explained by the fact that the current edition of the ORCC Java backend does not generate very efficient code. These results indicate that the CTL's SHA-256 implementation can achieve a performance similar to reference implementations. We also did similar benchmarking experiments on the AES block cipher in CTL (included in the extended edition of the paper) and came to a similar conclusion.

**Benchmarking of SHA-256 on Multi-core Platform.** On a platform with multiple CPU cores, one can map different parts of an FU network to different CPU cores so that the overall run-time performance of the application can be improved. The C backend of the RVC supporting tool ORCC [6] supports multi-core mapping, so one can easily allocate different FUs or FU sub-networks to different CPU cores. To see how much benefit we can get from a multi-core platform, we devised a very simple RVC application called HashTree that implements the following functionality using five hash $H$ operations: given an input signal $x = x_1 \parallel x_2 \parallel x_3 \parallel x_4$ consisting of four blocks $x_i$, hash each block $h_i = H(x_i)$ and then output $H(h_1 \parallel h_2 \parallel h_3 \parallel h_4)$. In our implementation of HashTree, we instantiated $H$ with SHA-256. By comparing this application with the simple single-core SHA-256 application computing $H$ on the same input (i.e., $H(x_1 \parallel x_2 \parallel x_3 \parallel x_4)$), we can roughly estimate the performance gain.

In the benchmarking process, we considered three different configurations:

- **Single SHA-256:** This configuration represents a single SHA-256 FU running on a single-core, which processes an input $x$ and produces the hash. We used this configuration as the reference point to evaluate the performance gain of the following two configurations, which implement HashTree using five SHA-256 instances.
- **5-thread with manual mapping:** In this configuration, each SHA-256 instance is programmatically mapped to run as a separate thread on a specific CPU core of our quad core machine. At the start of the hashing process, we manually mapped the four threads (processing $h_i = H(x_i)$) to four CPU cores. The fifth thread performing the final hashing operation is created and mapped after the preceding four threads are finished with their execution.

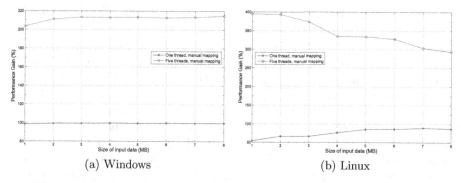

Fig. 3. The performance gain we got from the benchmarked configurations

- **1-thread with manual mapping:** Similar to the above configuration, this configuration also implements HashTree. However, all five SHA-256 instances are bounded to run in a single thread on a specific CPU core of our quad core machine.

It should be noted that thread creation and mapping also consume some CPU time, which is the cost one has to pay to achieve concurrency. Therefore, in order to make the study judicial, we also count the times spent on thread creation and thread mapping. The benchmarking results are shown in Fig. 3. One can see that the performance gain is between 200% to 300% when five threads are used.

## 6   Future Work

In order to allow researchers from different fields to extend CTL and use it for more applications, we have published CTL as an open-source project at `http://www.hooklee.com/default.asp?t=CTL`. In our future work, we plan to continue our research on the following possible directions.

*Cryptographic Primitives.* The CTL can be enriched by including more cryptographic primitives (especially public-key cryptography), which will allow creation of more multimedia security applications and security protocols. Another direction is to develop optimized versions of CTL cryptosystems. For instance, bit slicing can be used to optimize parallelism in many block ciphers [28, 45].

*Security Protocols.* Another direction is to use the RVC framework for the design and development of security protocols and systems with heterogenous components and interfaces. While RVC itself is platform independent, "wrappers" [62] can be developed to bridge the platform-independent FUs with physical I/O devices/channels (e.g., a device attached to USB port, a host connected via LAN/WLAN, a website URL, etc.). Although there are many candidate protocols that can be considered, as a first step we plan to implement the hPIN/hTAN e-banking security protocol [42], which is a typical (but small-scale) heterogeneous system involving a hardware token, a web browser plugin on the user's computer, and a web service running on the remote e-banking server. We have already implemented an hPIN/hTAN prototype system without using RVC, so the new RVC-based implementation can be benchmarked against the existing system.

*Cryptographic Protocols.* Many cryptographic protocols require a high amount of computations. One example are garbled circuit protocols [68] that allow secure evaluation of an arbitrary function on sensitive data. These protocols can be used as basis for various privacy-preserving applications. At a high level, the protocol works by one party first generating an encrypted form of the function to be evaluated (called garbled circuit) which is then sent to the other party who finally decrypts the function using the encrypted input data of both parties and finally obtains the correct result. Recent implementation results show that such garbled circuit based protocols can be implemented in a highly efficient way in software [32]. However, until now, there exist no software implementations that exploit multi-core architectures. It was shown that such protocols can be optimized when using both software and hardware together: For generation of the garbled circuit, a trusted hardware token can generate the garbled circuit locally and hence remove the need to transfer it over the Internet [36]. Here, the encrypted versions of the gates which require four invocations of a cryptographic hash function can be computed in parallel similar to the 4-adic hash tree we have shown in Sec. 5. Furthermore, the evaluation of garbled circuits can be improved when using hardware accelerations as shown in [37]. We believe that the RVC framework can serve as an ideal basis for hardware-software co-designed systems with parallelized and/or hardware-assisted garbled circuit-based protocols.

# References

1. Esterel Synchronous Language, http://www-sop.inria.fr/esterel.org/files/
2. Graphiti, http://graphiti-editor.sf.net
3. LabVIEW, http://www.ni.com/labview/whatis/
4. Mathworks Simulink: Simulation and Model-Based Design, http://www.mathworks.com/products/simulink/
5. Open Data Flow (OpenDF), http://sourceforge.net/projects/opendf
6. Open RVC-CAL Compiler (ORCC), http://sourceforge.net/projects/orcc
7. Synopsys Studio, http://www.synopsys.com/SYSTEMS/BLOCKDESIGN/DIGITALSIGNALPROCESSING/Pages/SystemStudio.aspx
8. Cryptol: The Language of Cryptography. Case Study (2008), http://corp.galois.com/downloads/cryptography/Cryptol_Casestudy.pdf
9. CAO and qhasm compiler tools. EU Project CACE deliverable D1.3, Revision 1.1 (2011), http://www.cace-project.eu/downloads/deliverables-y3/32_CACE_D1.3_CAO_and_qhasm_compiler_tools_Jan11.pdf
10. Ahmad, J.J., Li, S., Amer, I., Mattavelli, M.: Building multimedia security applications in the MPEG Reconfigurable Video Coding (RVC) framework. In: Proc. 2011 ACM SIGMM Multimedia and Security Workshop, MM&Sec 2011 (2011)
11. Akyildiz, I.F., Melodia, T., Chowdhury, K.R.: Wireless multimedia sensor networks: Applications and testbeds. Proc. IEEE 96(10), 1588–1605 (2008)
12. Ali, H.I.A.A., Patoary, M.N.I.: Design and Implementation of an Audio Codec (AMR-WB) using Dataflow Programming Language CAL in the OpenDF Environment. TR: IDE1009, Halmstad University, Sweden (2010)

13. Aman-Allah, H., Maarouf, K., Hanna, E., Amer, I., Mattavelli, M.: CAL dataflow components for an MPEG RVC AVC baseline encoder. J. Signal Processing Systems 63(2), 227–239 (2011)
14. Amer, I., Lucarz, C., Roquier, G., Mattavelli, M., Raulet, M., Nezan, J., Déforges, O.: Reconfigurable Video Coding on multicore: An overview of its main objectives. IEEE Signal Processing Magazine 26(6), 113–123 (2009)
15. Antola, A., Fracassi, M., Gotti, P., Sandionigi, C., Santambrogio, M.: A novel hardware/software codesign methodology based on dynamic reconfiguration with Impulse C and CoDeveloper. In: Proc. 2007 3rd Southern Conference on Programmable Logic, SPL 2007, pp. 221–224 (2007)
16. Barbosa, M., Noad, R., Page, D., Smart, N.P.: First steps toward a cryptography-aware language and compiler. Cryptology ePrint Archive: Report 2005/160 (2005), http://eprint.iacr.org/2005/160.pdf
17. Bernstein, D.J., Schwabe, P.: New AES Software Speed Records. In: Chowdhury, D.R., Rijmen, V., Das, A. (eds.) INDOCRYPT 2008. LNCS, vol. 5365, pp. 322–336. Springer, Heidelberg (2008)
18. Bertoni, G., Breveglieri, L., Fragneto, P., Macchetti, M., Marchesin, S.: Efficient Software Implementation of AES on 32-Bit Platforms. In: Kaliski Jr., B.S., Koç, Ç.K., Paar, C. (eds.) CHES 2002. LNCS, vol. 2523, pp. 159–171. Springer, Heidelberg (2003)
19. Bhattacharyya, S., Eker, J., Janneck, J.W., Lucarz, C., Mattavelli, M., Raulet, M.: Overview of the MPEG Reconfigurable Video Coding framework. J. Signal Processing Systems 63(2), 251–263 (2011)
20. Boutellier, J., Gomez, V.M., Silvén, O., Lucarz, C., Mattavelli, M.: Multiprocessor scheduling of dataflow models within the Reconfigurable Video Coding framework. In: Proc. 2009 Conference on Design and Architectures for Signal and Image Processing, DASIP 2009 (2009)
21. Canright, D., Osvik, D.A.: A More Compact AES. In: Jacobson Jr., M.J., Rijmen, V., Safavi-Naini, R. (eds.) SAC 2009. LNCS, vol. 5867, pp. 157–169. Springer, Heidelberg (2009)
22. Corbet, J.: The high-resolution timer (API) (2006), http://lwn.net/Articles/167897
23. Cryptico A/S: Rabbit stream cipher, performance evaluation. White Paper, Version 1.4 (2005), http://www.cryptico.com/DWSDownload.asp?File=Files%2FFiler%2FWP%5FRabbit%5FPerformance%2Epdf
24. Dai, W.: Crypto++ library, http://www.cryptopp.com
25. Dennis, J.: First Version of a Data Flow Procedure Language. In: Robinet, B. (ed.) Programming Symposium. LNCS, vol. 19, pp. 362–376. Springer, Heidelberg (1974)
26. Eker, J., Janneck, J.W.: CAL language report: Specification of the CAL actor language. Technical Memo UCB/ERL M03/48, Electronics Research Laboratory, UC Berkeley (2003)
27. Gay, O.: SHA-2: Fast Software Implementation, http://www.ouah.org/ogay/sha2
28. Grabher, P., Großschädl, J., Page, D.: Light-Weight Instruction Set Extensions for Bit-Sliced Cryptography. In: Oswald, E., Rohatgi, P. (eds.) CHES 2008. LNCS, vol. 5154, pp. 331–345. Springer, Heidelberg (2008)
29. Gupta, S., Dutt, N., Gupta, R., Nicolau, A.: SPARK: A high-level synthesis framework for applying parallelizing compiler transformations. In: Proc. 2003 16th International Conference on VLSI Design, VLSI Design 2003 (2003)
30. Gutmann, P.: Cryptlib, http://www.cs.auckland.ac.nz/~pgut001/cryptlib

312    J.J. Ahmad et al.

31. Ha, S., Kim, S., Lee, C., Yi, Y., Kwon, S., Joo, Y.P.: PeaCE: A hardware-software codesign environment for multimedia embedded systems. ACM Trans. on Design Automation of Electronic Syststems 12(3), Article 24 (2007)
32. Huang, Y., Evans, D., Katz, J., Malka, L.: Faster secure two-party computation using garbled circuits. In: Proc. 20th USENIX Security Symposium (2011)
33. ISO/IEC: Information technology – MPEG video technologies – Part 4: Video tool library. ISO/IEC 23002-4 (2009)
34. ISO/IEC: Information technology - MPEG systems technologies - Part 4: Codec configuration representation. ISO/IEC 23001-4 (2009)
35. Janneck, J., Miller, I., Parlour, D., Roquier, G., Wipliez, M., Raulet, M.: Synthesizing hardware from dataflow programs: An MPEG-4 Simple Profile decoder case study. J. Signal Processing Systems 63(2), 241–249 (2011)
36. Järvinen, K., Kolesnikov, V., Sadeghi, A.-R., Schneider, T.: Embedded SFE: Offloading Server and Network Using Hardware Tokens. In: Sion, R. (ed.) FC 2010. LNCS, vol. 6052, pp. 207–221. Springer, Heidelberg (2010)
37. Järvinen, K., Kolesnikov, V., Sadeghi, A.-R., Schneider, T.: Garbled Circuits for Leakage-Resilience: Hardware Implementation and Evaluation of One-Time Programs. In: Mangard, S., Standaert, F.-X. (eds.) CHES 2010. LNCS, vol. 6225, pp. 383–397. Springer, Heidelberg (2010)
38. Kangas, T., Kukkala, P., Orsila, H., Salminen, E., Hännikäinen, M., Hämäläinen, T.D., Riihimäki, J., Kuusilinna, K.: UML-based multiprocessor SoC design framework. ACM Trans. on Embedded Compututer Systems 5, 281–320 (2006)
39. Khan, E., El-Kharashi, M.W., Gebali, F., Abd-El-Barr, M.: Applying the Handel-C design flow in designing an HMAC-hash unit on FPGAs. Computers and Digital Techniques 153(5), 323–334 (2006)
40. Lee, E.A., Messerschmitt, D.G.: Synchronous data flow. Proc. IEEE 75(9), 1235–1245 (1987)
41. Lewis, J.R., Martin, B.: Cryptol: High assurance, retargetable crypto development and validation. In: Proc. 2003 IEEE Military Communication Conference, MILCOM 2003, pp. 820–825 (2003)
42. Li, S., Sadeghi, A.-R., Heisrath, S., Schmitz, R., Ahmad, J.J.: hPIN/hTAN: A Lightweight and Low-Cost E-Banking Solution against Untrusted Computers. In: Danezis, G. (ed.) FC 2011. LNCS, vol. 7035, pp. 235–249. Springer, Heidelberg (2012)
43. Lucarz, C., Mattavelli, M., Dubois, J.: A co-design platform for algorithm/architecture design exploration. In: Proc. 2008 IEEE International Conference on Multimedia and Expo., ICME 2008, pp. 1069–1072 (2008)
44. Manley, R., Gregg, D.: A Program Generator for Intel AES-NI Instructions. In: Gong, G., Gupta, K.C. (eds.) INDOCRYPT 2010. LNCS, vol. 6498, pp. 311–327. Springer, Heidelberg (2010)
45. Matsui, M., Nakajima, J.: On the Power of Bitslice Implementation on Intel Core2 Processor. In: Paillier, P., Verbauwhede, I. (eds.) CHES 2007. LNCS, vol. 4727, pp. 121–134. Springer, Heidelberg (2007)
46. Moran, T.: The Qilin Crypto SDK: An open-source Java SDK for rapid prototyping of cryptographic protocols, http://qilin.seas.harvard.edu/
47. Moss, A., Page, D.: Bridging the gap between symbolic and efficient AES implementations. In: Proc. 2010 ACM SIGPLAN Workshop on Partial Evaluation and Program Manipulation, PEPM 2010, pp. 101–110 (2010)
48. Moving Picture Experts Group (MPEG): Who we are, http://mpeg.chiariglione.org/who_we_are.htm

49. Nikhil, R.: Tutorial – BlueSpec SystemVerilog: Efficient, correct RTL from high-level specifications. In: Proc. 2nd ACM/IEEE International Conference on Formal Methods and Models for Co-Design, MEMOCODE 2004, pp. 69–70 (2004)

50. NIST: Data Encryption Standard (DES). FIPS PUB 46-3 (1999)

51. NIST: Specification for the Advanced Encryption Standard (AES). FIPS PUB 197 (2001)

52. NIST: Recommendation for the Triple Data Encryption Algorithm (TDEA) block cipher. Special Publication 800-67, Version 1.1 (2008)

53. NIST: Secure Hash Standard (SHS). FIPS PUB 180-3 (2008)

54. Oracle®: Java™ Cryptography Architecture (JCA) Reference Guide. http://download.oracle.com/javase/6/docs/technotes/guides/security/crypto/CryptoSpec.html

55. Osvik, D.A., Bos, J.W., Stefan, D., Canright, D.: Fast Software AES Encryption. In: Hong, S., Iwata, T. (eds.) FSE 2010. LNCS, vol. 6147, pp. 75–93. Springer, Heidelberg (2010)

56. Pornin, T.: sphlib 3.0, http://www.saphir2.com/sphlib

57. PureNoise Ltd Vaduz: PureNoise CryptoLib, http://cryptolib.com/crypto

58. Rompaey, K.V., Verkest, D., Bolsens, I., Man, H.D.: CoWare – a design environment for heterogeneous hardware/software systems. Design Automation for Embedded Systems 1(4), 357–386 (1996)

59. Schneier, B.: Description of a New Variable-Length Key, 64-bit Block Cipher (Blowfish). In: Anderson, R. (ed.) FSE 1993. LNCS, vol. 809, pp. 191–204. Springer, Heidelberg (1994)

60. Schneier, B.: Applied Cryptography: Protocols, algorithms, and source code in C, 2nd edn. John Wiley & Sons, Inc., New York (1996)

61. Sutherland, W.R.: The On-Line Graphical Specification of Computer Procedures. Ph.D. thesis. MIT (1966)

62. Thavot, R., Mosqueron, R., Dubois, J., Mattavelli, M.: Hardware synthesis of complex standard interfaces using CAL dataflow descriptions. In: Proc. 2009 Conference on Design and Architectures for Signal and Image Processing, DASIP 2009 (2009)

63. The Legion of the Bouncy Castle: Bouncy Castle Crypto APIs, http://www.bouncycastle.org

64. The OpenSSL Project: OpenSSL cryptographic library, http://www.openssl.org/docs/crypto/crypto.html

65. Thompson, M., Nikolov, H., Stefanov, T., Pimentel, A.D., Erbas, C., Polstra, S., Deprettere, E.F.: A framework for rapid system-level exploration, synthesis, and programming of multimedia MP-SoCs. In: Proc. 5th IEEE/ACM International Conference on Hardware/Software Codesign and System Synthesis, CODES+ISSS 2007, pp. 9–14 (2007)

66. Tillich, S., Großschädl, J.: Instruction Set Extensions for Efficient AES Implementation on 32-bit Processors. In: Goubin, L., Matsui, M. (eds.) CHES 2006. LNCS, vol. 4249, pp. 270–284. Springer, Heidelberg (2006)

67. Tillich, S., Herbst, C.: Boosting AES Performance on a Tiny Processor Core. In: Malkin, T. (ed.) CT-RSA 2008. LNCS, vol. 4964, pp. 170–186. Springer, Heidelberg (2008)

68. Yao, A.C.: How to generate and exchange secrets. In: Proc. 27th Annual Symposium on Foundations of Computer Science, FOCS 1986, pp. 162–167 (1986)

# A Cache Timing Attack on AES
# in Virtualization Environments

Michael Weiß*, Benedikt Heinz*, and Frederic Stumpf*

Fraunhofer Research Institution AISEC, Garching (Near Munich), Germany
{michael.weiss,benedikt.heinz,frederic.stumpf}@aisec.fraunhofer.de

**Abstract.** We show in this paper that the isolation characteristic of
system virtualization can be bypassed by the use of a cache timing attack. Using Bernstein's correlation in this attack, an adversary is able to
extract sensitive keying material from an isolated trusted execution domain. We demonstrate this cache timing attack on an embedded ARM-
based platform running an L4 microkernel as virtualization layer. An
attacker who gained access to the untrusted domain can extract the key
of an AES-based authentication protocol used for a financial transaction.
We provide measurements for different public domain AES implementations. Our results indicate that cache timing attacks are highly relevant
in virtualization-based security architectures, such as trusted execution
environments.

**Keywords:** Virtualization, Trusted Execution Environment, L4, Microkernel, AES, Cache, Timing, Embedded.

## 1 Introduction

Virtualization technologies provide a means to establish isolated execution environments. Using virtualization, a system can for example be split into two
security domains, one trusted domain and one untrusted domain. Security critical applications which perform financial transactions can then be executed in
the trusted domain while the general purpose operating system, also referred to
as rich OS, is executed in the untrusted domain. In addition, other untrusted
applications can be restricted to the untrusted domain.

It is generally believed that virtualization characteristics provide an isolated
execution environment where sensitive code can be executed isolated from un-
trustworthy applications. However, we will show in this paper that this isolation
characteristic can be bypassed by the use of cache timing attacks. Even though
it has already been stated that cache timing attacks may circumvent the virtualization barriers [14], we provide additional practical evidence to that matter.
Especially, we show how this side channel can also be exploited on embedded
ARM-based architectures for mobile devices, such as smartphones.

---

* The authors and their work presented in this contribution were supported by the
German Federal Ministry of Education and Research in the project *RESIST* through
grant number 01IS10027A.

A.D. Keromytis (Ed.): FC 2012, LNCS 7397, pp. 314–328, 2012.

A cache timing attack exploits the cache architecture of modern CPUs. The cache architecture has influence on the timing behavior of each memory access. The timing depends on whether the addressed data is already loaded into the cache (cache-hit) or it is accessed for the first time (cache-miss). In case of a cache-miss, the CPU has to fetch the data from the main memory which causes a higher delay compared to a cache-hit where the data can be used directly from the much faster cache. Based on the granularity of information an attacker uses for the attack, cache timing attacks can be divided into three classes: time-driven [7,17,2,16], trace-driven [1,9] and access-driven [17,15]. Time-driven attacks depend only on coarse timing observations of whole encryptions including certain computations. In this paper, we use a time-driven attack which is the most general attack of the three. To perform a trace-driven attack, an attacker has to be able to profile the cache activity during a single encryption. In addition, he has to know which memory access of the encryption algorithm causes a cache-hit. More fine grained information about the cache behaviour is needed to perform an access-driven attack. This attack additionally requires knowledge about the particular cache sets accessed during the encryption. That means that those attacks are highly platform dependent while time-driven attacks are portable to different platforms as we will show.

Although trace- and access-driven cache attacks would be feasible in a virtualized system, it would require much more effort to setup a spy-process. For an access-driven attack, the adversary needs the physical address of the lookup tables to know where they are stored in memory and thus the information to which cache lines they are mapped. This cannot be accomplished by a spy-process during runtime in the untrusted domain, as there is no shared library. By a time-driven attack, it is sufficient to see the attacked system as a black box.

Bernstein [7] for instance used this characteristic for a known plaintext attack to recover the secret key of an AES encryption on a remote server. However, Bernstein had to measure the timing on the attacked system to get rid of the noisy network channel between the attacked server and the attacking client. While this is a rather unrealistic scenario since the server needs to be modified, it is very relevant in the context of virtualization. In the context of virtualization, the noise is negligible since local communication channels are used for controlled inter-domain data exchange. These communication channels are based on shared memory mechanisms which introduce only a small and almost constant timing overhead.

This paper is organized as follows. In the next section we state related works. We analyze the general characteristics of a virtualization-based system and present a generic system architecture that provides strong isolation of execution environments in Section 3. We believe that this system architecture is representative for related architectures based on virtualization that establish secure execution environments. Based on this architecture, we show the feasibility to adapt Bernstein's attack. Further, in Section 4, we show that standard mutual authentication schemes based on AES are vulnerable to cache timing attacks executed as man-in-the-middle in the untrusted domain. We provide practical measurements on an ARM Cortex-A8 based SoC running the Fiasco.OC micro-kernel [23] and its corresponding runtime environment L4Re as virtualization layer to confirm our proposition in Section 5. Finally, we conclude with a discussion about the results and possible countermeasures in Section 6.

## 2     Related Work

Bernstein provides in [7] a practical cache-timing attack on the OpenSSL implementation of AES on a Pentium III processor. He describes a known plaintext attack to a remote server which provides some kind of authentication token. However, Bernstein does not provide an analysis of his methodology and an explanation why the attack is successful. This is revisited by Neve et al. [16]. They present a full analysis of Bernstein's attack technique and state the correlation model. Later Aciiçmez et al. [2] proposed a similar attack extended to use second round information of the AES encryption. However, they also provide only local interprocess measurements in a rather unrealistic attack setup similar to Bernstein's client-server scenario. Independently from Bernstein, Osvik et al. [17] also describe a similar time-driven attack with their *Evict+Time* method. Further, they depict an access-driven attack *Prime+Probe* with which they are able to extract the disk encryption key used by the operating system's kernel. However, they need access to the file system which is transparently encrypted with that key.

Gueron et al. [14] discussed several security aspects of current x86/x86-64 PC architectures including potential timing side channels which are caused by performance optimizations of the hardware architecture. They discussed that for example the cache may compromise the isolation of virtualization environments. Ristenpart et al. [20] consider side-channel leakage in virtualization environments on the example of the Amazon EC2 cloud service. They show that there is cross VM side-channel leakage. They used the *Prime+Probe* technique from [17] for analyzing the timing side-channel. However, Ristenpart et al. are not able to extract a secret encryption key from one VM.

There are also more sophisticated cache attacks which can recover the AES key without any knowledge of the plaintext nor the ciphertext. Lately, Gullasch et al. [15] describe an access-driven cache attack. They introduce a spy-process which is able to recover the secret key after several observed encryptions. However, this spy-process needs access to a shared crypto library which is used in the attacked process. Further, a DoS attack on the Linux' scheduler is used to monitor a single encryption. Recently, Bogdanov et al. [8] introduced an advanced time-driven attack and analyzed it on an ARM-based embedded system. It is a chosen plaintext attack which is using pairs of plaintexts. Those plaintexts are chosen in a way that they exploit the maximum distance separable code. This is a feature of AES used during `MixColumns` operation to provide a linear transformation with a maximum of possible branch number. For 128-bit key length, they have to perform exactly two full 16-byte encryptions for each plaintext pair where the timing of the second encryption has to be measured.

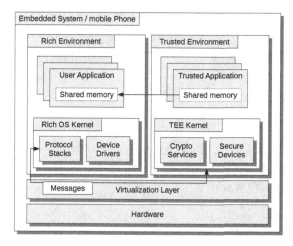

**Fig. 1.** High level security architecture of an embedded device based on virtualization

Even though these attacks could be demonstrated in a virtualization-based system, it would require strong adaptations of the system which may result in an unrealistic attacker model. In contrast, the approach by Bernstein is more flexible and provides a more realistic attacker model for a trusted execution environment.

## 3 System Architecture

We present in this section the system architecture of a generic virtualization-based system. This system architecture is representative for other systems based on virtualization and is later used to demonstrate our cache timing attack. The system architecture consists of a high level virtualization-based security architecture including the operating system and an authentication protocol used to authenticate a security sensitive application executed in the trusted domain.

### 3.1 Virtualization-Based Security Architecture

Virtualization techniques can be used to provide strong isolation of execution environments and thus enables the construction of compartments. One compartment can then be used to execute sensitive transactions while the other compartment is used for transactions with a lower trust level. This design process is already partly employed by smartphone architectures. The Dalvik VM on Android provides some sort of process virtualization [21, p. 83], however, without providing the same level of isolation achieved by system virtualization [21, p. 369]. Due to the insecurity of current smartphones' and other embedded systems' architectures, it is expected that virtualization solutions will be used in the near future to increase security and reliability. This assumption is supported by current developments in the embedded hardware architectures (ARM TZ [3],

**Table 1.** Mutual authentication protocol using symmetric AES encryption

| Verifier B | | Prover A |
|---|---|---|
| shared key: $k$ | | shared key: $k$ |
| $r_B := rnd()$ | | $r_A := rnd()$ |
| | $\xleftarrow{\quad connect() \quad}$ | |
| | $\xrightarrow{\quad ID_B, r_B \quad}$ | |
| | | $m_A := h(r_B\|r_A\|ID_A)$ |
| | $\xleftarrow{\quad ID_A, r_A, c_A \quad}$ $\quad c_A = E(m_A, k)$ | |
| $m'_A := h(r_B\|r_A\|ID_A)$ | | |
| $c_A \overset{?}{=} E(m'_A, k)$ | | |
| | | |
| $m_B := h(r_A\|ID_B)$ | | |
| $c_B := E(m_B, k)$ | $\xrightarrow{\quad c_B \quad}$ | |
| | | $m'_B := h(r_A\|ID_B)$ |
| | | $c_B \overset{?}{=} E(m'_B, k)$ |

Intel Atom VT-x [11]). GlobalPlatform is currently in the process of specifying
a high level system architecture of a trusted execution environment (TEE) [4].
The security architecture is mainly adapted from the TEE Client API Specification [13]. At the time of this writing, this is the publicly available part of the
complete specification. It is shown in Figure 1. The system architecture consists
of two execution domains, the trusted execution environment for the trusted
applications and the rich environment for the user controlled rich operating system[1]. It is much more likely that the rich environment is infected by malware due
to the greater software complexity. The trusted applications are either executed
in their own virtual machine or are separated in different address spaces and do
not share any memory to allow the deployment of trusted application by different vendors which may not trust each other. However, each trusted application
depends on the security of the underlying isolation layer.

## 3.2  Authentication Scheme

To keep the trusted computing base (TCB) small and to reduce implementation
complexity, the drivers and communication stacks are implemented in the rich
operating system executed in the untrusted domain. Thus, to achieve for example authenticity of a transaction in an online banking application, a protocol
resistant to man-in-the-middle attacks has to be used. The protocol's end point
has to be in the trusted domain and not in the rich OS since the rich OS could
be compromised. When the trusted application wants to communicate with its
backend system, it has to prove its authenticity against the backend and vice

---

[1] A rich operation system is a full operating system with drivers, userland and user
interfaces, e. g., Android.

Table 2. Timing attack on a trusted application

| Untrusted VM | | |
|---|---|---|
| To/From remote | | To/From trusted |
| $\xleftarrow{\text{connect()}}$ | | $\xleftarrow{\text{connect()}}$ |
| $\xrightarrow{ID_B, r_B}$ | startClk() | $\xrightarrow{ID_B, r_B}$ |
| $\xleftarrow{ID_A, r_A, c_A}$ | stopClk() | $\xleftarrow{ID_A, r_A, c_A}$ |
| | $m_A := h(r_B \| r_A \| ID_A)$ | |
| | $\vdots$ | |

versa. For this purpose, a mutual authentication protocol as shown in Table 1 between both parties needs to be employed. Note that this is only a simple example authentication scheme and also more sophisticated authentication schemes could be used. We assume that both parties have negotiated a secret symmetric key. The protocol uses random nonces as challenges and AES with the shared secret key $k$ to generate the responses. Also an identifier of the particular sender is included in the encrypted response. Before the execution of the encryption, this ID is concatenated with the challenges. Further, this concatenation is hashed to prevent concatenation attacks.

Both verifier and prover execute the mutual authentication protocol depicted in Table 1. The prover in this case is the trusted application whereas the verifier is a remote backend system. The untrusted domain is not taking part in the protocol and just acts as transparent relay. After execution of this scheme, the prover A has proven to the verifier B the knowledge of the secret $k$ and vice versa. Further, the freshness of the communication is provided by this scheme. This simple mutual authentication is used to demonstrate the vulnerability of virtualization-based trusted execution domains against the timing attack depicted in the next section.

## 4   Attack Setup

For our attack setup, we focus on a virtualization-based system architecture of an embedded mobile device as stated above. In the following, we show that an attacker who has overtaken the rich OS in the untrusted domain, e. g., by the use of malware, can circumvent the isolation mechanism with a cache timing side-channel.

Our introduced authentication scheme is secure against man-in-the-middle attacks on protocol level. However, due to the fact that the untrusted domain is relaying the messages between the client application and the remote server, malware can use a time-driven cache attack to at least partially recover the AES-encryption key $k$. To this end, we use a template attack derived from the attack in [7] which is conducted in two phases, first the profiling phase (offline and online) and second the correlation phase. We assume that an attacker has gained access to the rich operating system. The attacker is then able to execute a small attack process which is used to generate the timing profile.

## 4.1 Profiling Phase

The profiling phase is run twice, one time offline with a known key $k$ and a second time online on the real target with an unknown key $k'$. However, the malware program which is running on the attacked system only has to generate the online profile. The profiling phase in this context looks as follows. The attacker process has to hook into the messaging system between rich OS and the trusted execution environment as depicted in Table 2. Since the protocol stack is implemented in the rich OS, this could be done in the rich OS kernel. Thus, the attacker is able to capture the server's challenge $r_B$ and measure the time between relaying this challenge to the client and receiving the client's response message. This provides him the timing of the AES encryption of the known plaintext $m_A = h(r_B||r_A||ID_A)$, of course with the noise introduced by the hashing and other operations executed in addition to the actual encryption.

To recover the key in the later correlation phase, many challenge-response observations are needed to deal with the noise by averaging over all samples. Therefore, the attacker has to increase the number of challenge-response pairs to be collected. For that, he has several options depending on the used implementation of the virtualization layer and the client application. In upcoming TEE implementations, like the GlobalPlatform TEE, an untrusted user application may be used to initiate the trusted application. Thus, malware could initiate the trusted application as well and some kind of trigger application could be used to initiate the authentication process of the trusted application. The following connection request to the remote server can be blocked by the attacker as he has full control over the untrusted rich operating system and thus can intercept any communication. Instead of relaying the connection request to the remote server, the attacker establishes a local fake connection and sends an own generated nonce to the trusted application. After receiving the answer with the ciphertext, the attacker can send a connection reset and depending on how the trusted application is implemented, the protocol will just restart and a new challenge can be sent.

## 4.2 Correlation Phase

After receiving sufficient challenge-response pairs for the online timing profile, the attacker can correlate the profiles to recover at least partially the key $k'$. We provide detailed measurement results in Section 5. We use a correlation based on timing information during the first round of AES. It would be possible to also use information from the second round to reduce the amount of samples needed. However, to show that time-driven cache attacks are a threat to virtualization-based systems, it is sufficient to use the easier first round attack.

At first we define the function $timing()$ which computes the timing difference between the start and end of an operation. During the first run of the profiling phase, for each plaintext $p$, the overall encryption time is stored accumulated in a matrix $\mathbf{t}$ which is indexed by the byte number $0 \leq j < 16$ and the byte value $0 \leq b < 256$.

$$\mathbf{t}_{j,b} = \mathbf{t}_{j,b} + timing(enc\_AES(p,k)) \tag{1}$$

Further, the total amount of captured samples for each plaintext byte value is traced in a matrix **tnum** as shown in Equation 2.

$$\mathbf{tnum}_{j,b} = \mathbf{tnum}_{j,b} + 1 \tag{2}$$

After several samples the matrix **v** which is computed as depicted in Equation 3 is stored in the profile.

$$\mathbf{v}_{j,b} = \frac{t_{j,b}}{\mathbf{tnum}_{j,b}} - t_{\text{avg}} \tag{3}$$

$t_{\text{avg}}$ shown in Equation 4 is the accumulated timing measurements of all plaintexts $p_m$ divided by the total number of encryptions $l$.

$$t_{\text{avg}} = \frac{\sum_{m=0}^{l} timing(enc\_AES(p_m, k))}{l} \tag{4}$$

During the online part of the profiling phase, the matrices $\mathbf{t}'$ and $\mathbf{tnum}'$ are generated and the output $\mathbf{v}'$ is generated for the unknown key $k'$.

Finally, for every key byte $j$ the correlation $\mathbf{c}$ for each possible value $0 \le u < 256$ is computed as shown in Equation 5.

$$\mathbf{c}_{j,u} = \sum_{w=0}^{255} \mathbf{v}_{j,w} \cdot \mathbf{v}'_{j,(u \oplus w)} \tag{5}$$

According to the probability which is derived from the variance also stored in the profile, the values of $\mathbf{c}$ are sorted. Further, the key values with the lowest probability below a threshold as defined in [7] are sorted out.

## 5    Empirical Results

For practical analyses of the above described use-case, we built a testbed based on an embedded ARM SoC with an L4 microkernel as virtualization layer. As hardware platform, we decided to use the beagleboard in revision c4 because it is widely spread community driven open source board and also comparable to the hardware of currently available smartphones, for instance the Apple iPhone as well as Android smartphones. It is based on Texas Instruments' OMAP3530 SoC which includes a 32-bit Cortex-A8 core with 720MHz as central processing unit. The Cortex-A8 implements a cache hierarchy consisting of a 4-way set associative level 1 and an 8-way set associative level 2 cache. The L1-cache is split into instruction and data cache. The cache line size of both is 64 byte. For precise timing measurement, we used the ARM CCNT register, which provides the current clockcycles, the CPU spent since last reset. This is a standard feature of the Cortex-A8 and thus also available in current smartphones. However, it needs system privileges by default.

We implemented the scenario shown in Figure 1 and employed the mutual authentication scheme from Table 1 in a trusted environment. For the virtualization environment, we used the Fiasco.OC microkernel and the L4Re runtime

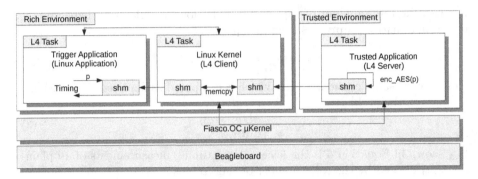

**Fig. 2.** Linux trigger application (simulating malware) connecting through L4Linux kernel services to trusted application executed as L4Server

environment from TUD's Operating Systems group. Fiasco.OC is a capability-based microkernel. In cooperation with the L4Re, it provides the functionality of a hypervisor for paravirtualized Linux machines. Further, it enables real time application and security applications to run directly on top of the microkernel in separated address spaces (L4Tasks) besides the Linux VMs. In fact, the L4Re virtualization runs Linux in user mode also in an L4Task. Further, each Linux application is executed in its own L4Task, however, with a special restriction that the L4Linux machine where the application belongs to is the registered pager of that task.

The rich OS is simulated by an L4Linux system. In L4Re an IPC mechanism in form of a C++ client server framework exists. This provides a synchronous control channel. The trusted application is implemented as an L4Server while the client part is implemented in the L4Linux kernel. A user level application is implemented on top of the L4Linux kernel to trigger the authentication of the trusted application. Instead of real challenges of a remote server, we also used this trigger application to generate random nonces as server challenges. This approach makes no difference to the timing measurement. The actual plaintext data (the remote server's nonce $r_B$) is written to a shared memory page by the client. The client, in our case the L4Linux kernel, requests this shared page in advance from the trusted application. The trusted application L4Server registers the page in the microkernel and transfers the capability for the page through the established IPC control channel to the Linux kernel. A detailed view of the software architecture of this attack is provided in Figure 2. As the rich OS is running in user mode, it is necessary to enable the access to the CCNT register beforehand in system mode. We used the boot loader $u$-boot to set this instruction before the hypervisor is executed. However, if the TEE would be realized for example with ARM TrustZone [3], the rich OS is executed in the so called NormalWorld. The SecureWorld of the processor is used for the trusted execution domain. An attacker could then access the CCNT register directly from the rich OS kernel since access rights of the NormalWorld's system mode are sufficient.

## 5.1   Measurement Setup

The side-channel leakage depend on the used AES implementation. Thus, we analyzed different AES implementations using our authentication protocol shown in Table 1. During the profiling phase, we used the null key for the offline part and for the online part we generated the randomly chosen key $k'$:

$$k' = \text{0x  2153  fc73  d4f3  4a98  1733  bb3f  1892  008b}$$

Further, we encrypt the plaintext generated by the trigger application directly and do not perform the hashing operation as described in the protocol. The reason for this is that the hashing generates more noise and makes the comparison between the different AES implementations less clear. Nevertheless, we provide the measurement result with the full protocol implementation exemplary for the AES implementation of Bernstein [6]. However, noise is not really considered in our work but clearly has an impact on the measurements.

We generate a profile every time when additionally 100K samples for each possible plaintext byte value are observed until 2M of each such samples were reached. To generate $N$ samples for each possible value of all plaintext bytes, approximately $N \cdot 256$ messages with 16-byte random plaintexts have to be observed.

## 5.2   Results

We evaluated a broad range of different AES implementations as shown in Table 3. The implementations of Bernstein [6], Barreto [5] and OpenSSL [22] are optimized for 32-bit architectures like the Cortex-A8 whereas Gladman's [12] is optimized for 8-bit micro controllers. Niyaz' [19] implementation is totally unoptimized. Table 3 visualizes the online and offline profile of each implementation. The first column shows the minimum and maximum of the overall timing in CPU cycles which is used for the correlation. The second column shows information about the variation of this timing computed over all measurements. To make propositions over

**Table 3.** Timing profile comparison between the different implementations

| Implemenation | | time (in cycles) | | variation | | | | time aes |
|---|---|---|---|---|---|---|---|---|
| | | min | max | min | max | median | interval | (in cycles) |
| Barreto [5] | offline 0 | 33745.96 | 33772.29 | -9.57 | 16.77 | -0.47 | 26.34 | ≈ 4231 |
| | online $k'$ | 33745.71 | 33772.31 | -9.87 | 16.73 | -0.49 | 26.59 | ≈ 4230 |
| OpenSSL [22] | offline 0 | 33584.26 | 33605.61 | -8.04 | 13.31 | -0.16 | 21.35 | ≈ 4222 |
| | online $k'$ | 33585.64 | 33607.81 | -8.99 | 13.18 | -0.14 | 22.17 | ≈ 4221 |
| Bernstein [6] | offline 0 | 33731.61 | 33778.54 | -11.44 | 35.49 | -0.94 | 46.93 | ≈ 4546 |
| | online $k'$ | 33745.04 | 33781.29 | -5.24 | 31.00 | -0.78 | 36.24 | ≈ 4573 |
| Gladman [12] | offline 0 | 35139.63 | 35158.00 | -6.26 | 12.10 | -0.16 | 18.37 | ≈ 5689 |
| | online $k'$ | 35139.48 | 35157.03 | -5.72 | 11.82 | -0.16 | 17.55 | ≈ 5689 |
| Niyaz [19] | offline 0 | 59266.99 | 59280.43 | -8.39 | 5.05 | 0.03 | 13.44 | ≈ 24840 |
| | online $k'$ | 59265.01 | 59278.61 | -8.88 | 4.72 | 0.01 | 13.60 | ≈ 24834 |

the signal to noise ratio, we also provide the average time spent in the AES encryption method. In Figure 3, the result of the correlation is shown. The plots depict the decreasing possibilities for each key byte by increasing samples. For each implementation, a subfigure is provided which plots the left choices $m$ with $m \in ]0; 256]$ in $z$-direction for each key byte $k_i$ with $i \in [0; 15]$ from left to right, while the amount of samples $N$ for the online profile with $N \in [100K; 2M]$ is plotted in $y$-direction from behind to front. For this result, a constant sample amount of 2M was used for the offline profile with the null key.

**Barreto.** Barreto's implementation which is part of many crypto libraries is showing a high vulnerability against this time-driven attack. Barreto uses four lookup tables, each of 1 KByte in size. Thus, the lookup tables do not fit into one cache line. Additionally for the last round, a fifth lookup table is used. This type of implementation is also called T-Tables implementation. After 100K samples, only key byte 3 and 7 have more than 200 possibilities left and for key byte 9, the choices are above 50. The other 13 key bytes are all below 50. After 800K almost any key is pinpointed to 4 choices except key byte 9. However, this seems to be the limit for this implementation. That means, using additional samples do not improve the results any further. After 1.6M samples also for key byte 9 the limit is reached and only 4 choices are left. Nothing changes afterwards until 2M samples are reached. See Figure 3(a).

**OpenSSL.** The OpenSSL implementation is almost the same as Baretto's implementation. However, the results of both implementations differ. For the OpenSSL implementation, the limit is reached at 16 choices per key byte. Furthermore, the attack was not able to reduce the key space for key byte 4 at all. One could believe that the results of Barreto's implementation and the results of OpenSSL have to be the same as the encryption function is exactly performing the same operations. However, as listed in Table 3, the overall time which is measured during the attack is about 200 cycles higher for Barreto's implementation because of the encryption function definition. Barreto passes parameters by value which are passed by reference in the OpenSSL encryption function header. Also the performed operations outside the measurement in the trigger application influences the cache evictions. In total, this causes more cache evictions and thus a higher variation of the AES signal, resulting in better correlation behaviour.

**Gladman.** The same holds for the implementation of Gladman which we compiled with tables and 32-bit data types enabled. Here, also the choices for several key bytes are reduced to 16 possibilities. However, Gladman uses only one 256-byte lookup table which means the signal to noise ratio is even worse than in the other implementations. Further, as the cache is 4-way associative with a cache line size of 64 byte, the lookup table fits into one cache block at once. This makes evictions by AES itself nearly impossible. However, other variables used during the computation can compete with the same lines in cache. This reduces the amount of cache evictions a lot in comparison to the 4 KByte tables implementations. So, there is no reduction of the key space for four key bytes at 2M samples.

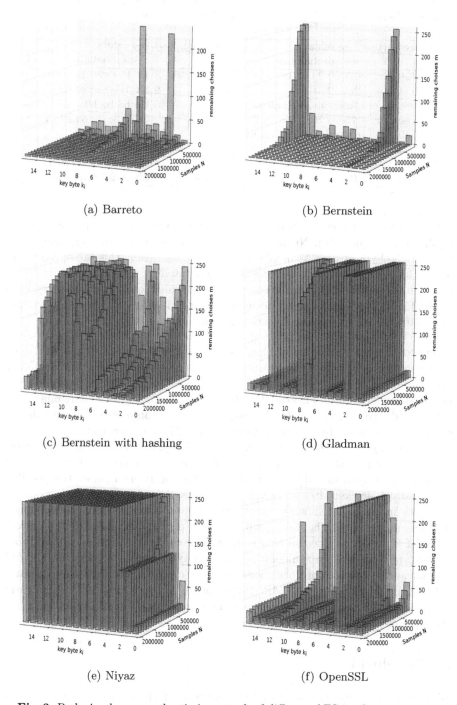

(a) Barreto

(b) Bernstein

(c) Bernstein with hashing

(d) Gladman

(e) Niyaz

(f) OpenSSL

**Fig. 3.** Reducing key space by timing attack of different AES implementations

**Table 4.** Correlation results after 100K samples of online profile received with the C version of Bernstein's AES implementation; offline profile with 2M samples

| choices | byte# | key values ← probability | choices | byte# | key values ← probability |
|---|---|---|---|---|---|
| 20 | 0 | **21** 20 23 22 fc 25 26 .. | 23 | 8 | **17** 15 ce c9 13 12 ca .. |
| 4 | 1 | **53** 52 51 50 | 27 | 9 | **33** 31 32 ec ea 30 ed .. |
| 256 | 2 | **fc** cb 9b a1 fd a6 a4 .. | 4 | 10 | **bb** b8 ba b9 |
| 80 | 3 | **73** 70 76 71 75 74 72 .. | 27 | 11 | **3f** 3e 3c 3b 3a e2 e5 .. |
| 10 | 4 | **d4** d6 d5 d7 d3 0a df .. | 4 | 12 | **18** 1b 19 1a |
| 4 | 5 | **f3** f1 f0 f2 | 11 | 13 | **92** 90 91 93 97 96 9a .. |
| 6 | 6 | **4a** 49 4b 48 4f 4d | 51 | 14 | **00** c0 01 02 20 e9 21 .. |
| 3 | 7 | **98** 9a 99 | 256 | 15 | **8b** 06 93 8f 33 b3 0f .. |

**Niyaz.** The implementation of Niyaz seems almost secure against this attack as shown in Figure 3(e). Niyaz also implements the AES with only one S-Box table of 256 byte in size. As in Gladman's implementation, this table also fits in one cache block. Thus, the timing leakage generated by the S-Box lookups is reduced. Further, the unoptimized code beside the table lookups in the encryption method will decrease the signal-to-noise ratio to make it even harder to extract information from the measurements using the correlation.

**Bernstein.** Our results show that Bernstein's AES implementation is most vulnerable to our cache timing attack. However, we used the C compatibility version which is part of his Poly1305-AES [6] message authentication code since no ARM implementation is available. This implementation is the only one which totally leaks the secret key $k'$. Already after 400K samples, the key is almost completely recovered by the correlation and only 2 key bytes need to be computed using brute-force. Further, during the correlation phase, the possible key bytes are sorted by probability, thus, already after 100K, the correct key $k'$ can be extracted as shown in Table 4. The first column of Table 4 shows the possible choices which are left after correlation. In the second column, the corresponding key byte index is listed while the third column shows the key values sorted by their probability. The values with highest probability are also the correct bytes of $k'$ we introduced in this section. The correct values are printed bold in the table. For this implementation, we also executed the attack with the full mutual authentication protocol, with hashing enabled. We used the reference SHA1 implementation of the L4Re crypto package. In Figure 3(c), it can clearly be seen that the additional noise generated by the hashing function increases the amount of samples needed for the attack.

# 6   Conclusion

We have shown that the isolation characteristic of virtualization environments can be circumvented using a cache timing attack. Even if authentication schemes with hashing are used, the side-channel leakage of the cache can be used to significantly reduce the key space. Nevertheless, our attack requires many measurement samples and noise also makes our attack more difficult. As there are doubts about practicability of this kind of attacks, further research has to examine proper workloads and real noise. Indeed, cache timing attacks remain a threat and have to be considered during design of virtualization-based security architectures. Switching the algorithm for authentication would not be a solution to this problem. For instance, there exist cache-based timing attacks against asymmetric algorithms like RSA by Percival [18] and ECDSA by Brumley and Hakala [10] as well.

The first step to mitigate those attacks is to not use a T-Tables implementation. However, also the implementations of Gladman and Niyaz with the 256-byte S-Box tables leak timing information which reduces the key space. An additional option for implementations with a 256-byte S-Box would be to use the preload engine in cooperation with the cache locking mechanism of the Cortex-A8 processor, as the whole S-Box fits in a cache-set. On a higher abstraction layer, the communication stack and all relevant protocol stacks and drivers could be implemented in the trusted domain. However, this would increase the TCB significantly and thus also the probability to be vulnerable to buffer-overflow attacks. Another solution would be to use a crypto co-processor implemented in hardware. This could be either a simple micro controller which does not use caching, or a sophisticated hardware security module (HSM) with a hardened cache-architecture that provides constant encryption timing.

# References

1. Acıiçmez, O., Koç, Ç.K.: Trace-Driven Cache Attacks on AES (Short Paper). In: Ning, P., Qing, S., Li, N. (eds.) ICICS 2006. LNCS, vol. 4307, pp. 112–121. Springer, Heidelberg (2006)
2. Acıiçmez, O., Schindler, W., Koç, Ç.K.: Cache Based Remote Timing Attack on the AES. In: Abe, M. (ed.) CT-RSA 2007. LNCS, vol. 4377, pp. 271–286. Springer, Heidelberg (2006)
3. ARM Limited. ARM Security Technology - Building a Secure System using Trust-Zone Technology, prd29-genc-009492c edition (April 2009)
4. Bailey, S.A., Felton, D., Galindo, V., Hauswirth, F., Hirvimies, J., Fokle, M., Morenius, F., Colas, C., Galvan, J.-P.: The trusted execution environment: Delivering enhanced security at a lower cost to the mobile market. Technical report. Global Platform Inc. (2011)
5. Barreto, P., Bosselaers, A., Rijmen, V.: Optimised ANSI C code for the Rijndael cipher, now AES (2000), http://fastcrypto.org/front/misc/rijndael-alg-fst.c
6. Bernstein, D.J.: Poly1305-AES for generic computers with IEEE floating point (February 2005), http://cr.yp.to/mac/53.html
7. Bernstein, D.J.: Cache-timing attacks on AES. Technical report (2005)
8. Bogdanov, A., Eisenbarth, T., Paar, C., Wienecke, M.: Differential cache-collision timing attacks on aes with applications to embedded cpus. In: The Cryptographer's Track at RSA Conference, pp. 235–251 (2010)

9. Bonneau, J., Mironov, I.: Cache-Collision Timing Attacks Against AES. In: Goubin, L., Matsui, M. (eds.) CHES 2006. LNCS, vol. 4249, pp. 201–215. Springer, Heidelberg (2006)

10. Brumley, B.B., Hakala, R.M.: Cache-Timing Template Attacks. In: Matsui, M. (ed.) ASIACRYPT 2009. LNCS, vol. 5912, pp. 667–684. Springer, Heidelberg (2009)

11. Intel Corporation. Intel® virtualization technology list (accessed September 15 (2011), http://ark.intel.com/VTList.aspx

12. Brian Gladman (2008), http://gladman.plushost.co.uk/oldsite/AES/aes-byte-29-08-08.zip

13. GlobalPlatform Inc. TEE Client API Specification Version 1.0 (July 2010)

14. Gueron, S., Stronqin, G., Seifert, J.-P., Chiou, D., Sendag, R., Yi, J.J.: Where does security stand? new vulnerabilities vs. trusted computing. IEEE Micro 27(6), 25–35 (2007)

15. Gullasch, D., Bangerter, E., Krenn, S.: Cache Games – Bringing access-based cache attacks on AES to practice. In: IEEE Symposium on Security and Privacy, S&P 2011. IEEE Computer Society (2011)

16. Neve, M., Seifert, J.-P., Wang, Z.: A refined look at bernstein's aes side-channel analysis. In: ASIACCS, p. 369 (2006)

17. Osvik, D.A., Shamir, A., Tromer, E.: Cache Attacks and Countermeasures: The Case of AES. In: Pointcheval, D. (ed.) CT-RSA 2006. LNCS, vol. 3860, pp. 1–20. Springer, Heidelberg (2006)

18. Percival, C.: Cache missing for fun and profit. In: Proc. of BSDCan 2005 (2005)

19. Niyaz, P.K.: Advanced Encryption Standard implementation in C

20. Ristenpart, T., Tromer, E., Shacham, H., Savage, S.: Hey, you, get off of my cloud: exploring information leakage in third-party compute clouds. In: Proceedings of the 16th ACM Conference on Computer and Communications Security, CCS 2009, pp. 199–212. ACM, New York (2009)

21. Smith, J., Nair, R.: Virtual Machines: Versatile Platforms for Systems and Processes. The Morgan Kaufmann Series in Computer Architecture and Design. Morgan Kaufmann Publishers Inc., San Francisco (2005)

22. The OpenSSL Project. OpenSSL: The Open Source toolkit for SSL/TLS (February 2011), http://www.openssl.org

23. TU Dresden Operating Systems Group. The Fiasco microkernel, http://os.inf.tu-dresden.de/fiasco/ (accessed April 6, 2011)

# Softer Smartcards
## Usable Cryptographic Tokens with Secure Execution

Franz Ferdinand Brasser[1], Sven Bugiel[1], Atanas Filyanov[2],
Ahmad-Reza Sadeghi[1,2,3], and Steffen Schulz[1,2,4]

[1] System Security Lab, Technische Universität Darmstadt
[2] System Security Lab, Ruhr-University Bochum
[3] Fraunhofer SIT, Darmstadt
[4] Information and Network System Security, Macquarie University

**Abstract.** Cryptographic smartcards provide a standardized, interoperable way for multi-factor authentication. They bridge the gap between strong asymmetric authentication and short, user-friendly passwords (PINs) and protect long-term authentication secrets against malware and phishing attacks. However, to prevent malware from capturing entered PINs such cryptographic tokens must provide secure means for user input and output. This often makes their usage inconvenient, as dedicated input key pads and displays are expensive and do not integrate with mobile applications or public Internet terminals. The lack of user acceptance is perhaps best documented by the large variety of non-standard multi-factor authentication methods used in online banking.

In this paper, we explore a novel compromise between tokens with dedicated card reader and USB or software-based solutions. We design and implement a cryptographic token using modern secure execution technology, resulting in a flexible, cost-efficient solution that is suitable for mobile use yet secure against common malware and phishing attacks.

**Keywords:** trusted computing, security tokens, secure execution.

# 1 Introduction

Although available for over a decade, cryptographic security tokens with asymmetric multi-factor authentication are still not in common use for many daily authentication procedures. Despite their significant advantages, service providers and users still prefer more usable but weak password-based authentication protocols that are highly vulnerable to simple malware and phishing attacks. Moreover, the lack of scalability in password-based authentication resulted in the widespread deployment of password managers and federal ID systems, creating single points of failures that pose a serious threat to a user's online identity, personal data and business relationships.

In contrast, cryptographic tokens allow strong user authentication and secure storage of authentication secrets. The PKCS#11 cryptographic token interface specification [26] is widely accepted and, when combined with a card reader

A.D. Keromytis (Ed.): FC 2012, LNCS 7397, pp. 329–343, 2012.

with dedicated user input/output pad, enables the secure authentication and authorization of transactions even on untrusted systems. However, while a clear return of investment can be identified for well-defined environments like large enterprises and organizations [10], end users face significantly higher costs for the deployment and maintenance of cryptographic token solutions. Moreover, currently available solutions still fail to meet the flexibility and security required in mobile usage scenarios. For example, the secure encryption of files and emails with smartcards is easily implemented at the work place but it is inconvenient to use a dedicated keypad in addition to a laptop or smartphone, only to secure the PIN entry process against malware attacks.

USB tokens were proposed to address the mobile usage scenario by integrating card reader and smartcard into a single USB stick [20]. However, in this case the critical PIN entry and transaction confirmation to the user is done in software on the PC and thus again vulnerable to malware and interface spoofing attacks. Alternatively, one-time password systems are sometimes deployed as a compromise between usability and security. However, such systems essentially use a symmetric authentication mechanism and do not easily scale to authenticate a user towards multiple service providers. Moreover, as demonstrated in the recent security breach at RSA Security[1], the employed centralized server-side storage of master secrets and lack of scalable revocation mechanisms represents a severe security risk. Similarly, the several proposed authentication and transaction confirmation methods for online banking (e.g., [11]) are often special-purpose solutions: Approaches that use dedicated security hardware are not easily extendible for use with multiple service providers, while software-based solutions, such as using a mobile phone to transmit a transaction confirmation number out of band (mobileTAN), are again vulnerable to malware attacks. In contrast, a secure general-purpose solution using smartcards, like "Secoder/HBCI-3"[2], again requires dedicated secure hardware, making it inconvenient for mobile use.

In recent years, consumer hardware was extended with the ability to execute programs independently from previously loaded software, including the main operating system [16,1]. These so-called Secure Execution Environment (SEE) allow the secure re-initialization of the complete software state at runtime and can be used to launch a new OS or simply execute a small security-sensitive program while the main OS is suspended. Sophisticated systems have been proposed to use these capabilities for securing online transactions, however, they require substantial modification of existing authentication procedures and software stacks. In contrast, this work presents a conservative approach that uses secure execution to implement a standards-compliant cryptographic token, thus simplifying deployment and interoperability with existing software infrastructures.

---

[1] A security breach of the RSA Security servers resulted in a compromise of the widely deployed SecurID tokens, incurring an estimated $66 million in replacement costs: www.theregister.co.uk/2011/07/27/rsa_security_breach/

[2] http://www-ti.informatik.uni-tuebingen.de/~borchert/Troja/ Online-Banking.shtml#HBCI-3

*Contribution.* In this paper, we present the design and integration of a software security token that uses secure execution technology available in commodity PCs. Our solution achieves comparable security features to hardware tokens in face of software attacks and basic protection against common hardware attacks such as device theft and offline brute-force attacks. In contrast to previously proposed secure transaction systems using trusted computing, our solution aims for interoperability and deployment, supporting the widely accepted PKCS#11 standard. Hence, our prototype is directly usable with many existing applications, such as enterprise single sign-on solutions, authentication in VPN, e-Mail and WiFi clients and password managers. By implementing secure facilities for user input/output, we can also provide secure and convenient mechanisms for deployment, backup and migration of our software token. We implement a prototype using Flicker and OpenCryptoki, providing an easily deployable solution that can be used on many standard Laptops and PCs today.

## 2    Background and Related Work

*Cryptographic Smartcards and Tokens.* Smartcards and cryptographic tokens are used in many large organizations today. The Cryptographic Token Information Format Standard PKCS#15 [25] was developed to provide interoperability between cryptographic smartcards and is today maintained as ISO 7816-15. On a higher layer, the Cryptographic Token Interface Standard PKCS#11 specifies a logical API for accessing cryptographic tokens, such as PKCS#15-compatible smartcards or Hardware Security Modules (HSMs). Alternative standards and APIs exist to access security tokens but are outside the scope of this work.

Apart from smartcards with external card readers, security tokens are also available in form of USB tokens or microSD cards[3]. The TrouSerS [15] TCG software stack also provides a PKCS#11 interface, using the TCG TPM [31] to prevent password guessing attacks against a purely software-based security token implementation. Similar to our work, these solutions offer different kinds of compromises between security and usability. However, in contrast to the aforementioned systems our solution provides secure facilities for user input/output (trusted user I/O) and is therefore resilient against common malware attacks.

*TCG Trusted Computing.* The Trusted Computing Group (TCG) [30] published a number of specifications to extend computing systems with trusted computing. Their core component is the Trusted Platform Module (TPM), a processor designed to securely record system state changes and bind critical functions, such as decryption, to pre-defined system states [31]. For this purpose, the TPM introduces Platform Configuration Registers (PCRs) to record of state change measurements in form of SHA-1 digests. By resetting the PCRs only at system reboot and otherwise always only *extending* the current PCR value with the newly recorded state change, a chain of measurements is built. This chain

---

[3] E.g., Aladdin eToken Pro, Marx CrypToken or Certgate SmartCard microSD.

can be used to securely verify the system state. The TPM then supports basic mechanisms to bind cryptographic keys or data to specific system states. Most significantly for our design, keys can be *sealed* to a given system state by encrypting them together with the desired target PCR values under a storage root key (SRK)[4]. Since the SRK is only known to the TPM, it can check upon *unsealing* if the current system state recorded by the PCRs matches the desired state stored together with the sealed key, and otherwise reject the request.

A major problem of this approach is dealing with the huge amount and complexity of software in today's systems, resulting in a very large chain of measurements. Moreover, the problem of runtime compromise is currently unsolved, i.e., the TPM is only informed of explicit program startups but cannot assure that already running software was not manipulated.

*Secure Execution and Flicker.* A recent extension in many hardware platforms is the SEE, a mechanism that executes code independently from previously executed software. Essentially, the CPU is reset at runtime, so that the subsequently executed program (the payload) is not affected by previously executed, potentially malicious, software.

A major advantage of this technology is that the aforementioned chain of measurements can be reset, since previously executed software does not influence the security of the current software state anymore. For this purpose, the TPM was extended with a set of PCRs that can be reset by the CPU when entering the SEE. The CPU then measures the SEE payload and stores the measurements in the previously reset PCRs. This allows the use of shorter, more manageable measurement chains that are easier to verify. Several implementations of SEEs are available, most notably Secure Virtual Machines (SVM) [1], Trusted Execution Technology (TXT) [16] and M-Shield [4].

A flexible framework for using the SEE provided by Intel TXT and AMD SVM is Flicker [22,23]. Flicker implements a framework for executing a security critical Piece of Application Logic (PAL) by temporarily suspending the main OS and diverting execution to the SEE. In this work we use and extend Flicker to implement the security-critical cryptographic operations and secure user I/O inside the SEE.

*Secure Transaction Schemes.* Several previous proposals aim to protect user credentials, typically using either a persistent security kernel that protects the credentials [14,17,6] or relying on external trusted hardware [18]. We know of only one system that uses Flicker, aiming to provide a uni-directional trusted path [13] as an instrument for transaction confirmation. It uses Flicker to take control of devices for user I/O and then asks the user to confirm a specific transaction. Using remote attestation, a remote system can then verify that the transaction was securely confirmed by a human user. All of these approaches require substantial modification of individual applications or even the addition

---

[4] It is also possible to use a hierarchy of keys, however, for the purpose of this work we simply assume all sealed data to be encrypted using the SRK.

of a hypervisor. In contrast, our solution uses the widely established PKCS#11 interface [26] and works seamlessly with existing applications and operating systems that make use of this interface.

The On-board Credentials (ObC) framework was introduced for mobile embedded devices [21]. ObC uses device-specific secrets of M-Shield to provide an open provisioning protocol for credentials (code and data), that are securely executed/used inside the SEE. TruWalletM [8] implements a secure user authentication for web-services based on ObC. ObC is complementary to our solution and may be used to provide a similar solution for mobile embedded devices. However, in its current state ObC supports only very limited applications due to high memory constraints.

## 3    A Softer Smartcard with Secure Execution

In the following we present the security requirements, architecture and protocols of our solution. We identify the following security requirements for a secure cryptographic token:

**Secure Token Interface:** The interface used for interaction between the (trusted) token and the (untrusted) outside world must prevent the leakage or manipulation of any secret information contained in the token, such as keys or key properties.

**Secure User I/O:** The user interface of the token solution must provide a secure mechanism for the user to (1) judge the current security status of the token, (2) infer the details of a pending transaction to be authorized and (3) input the authorization secret (Personal Identification Number, PIN).

Moreover we can identify the following functional requirements:

**Interoperability:** The token should use a standards-compliant interface to provide interoperability with existing applications, such as the PKCS#11 or Cryptographic Service Provider (CSP).

**Usability:** The token should be usable in the sense that it's use should not impose a significant burden on the user. In particular, the user should not be required to buy additional hardware and the token should be usable in mobile scenarios.

**Migration and Backup:** The token should provide facilities for secure migration between different hardware platforms or implementations, and for the creation of secure data backups.

*Adversary Model.* We assume an adversary that can compromise the user's operating system and applications (malware, trojan horse attacks) or tries to lure the user into revealing authentication secrets by imitating local applications and web services (phishing, spoofing). However, the adversary has no physical control over the user's cryptographic token and is thus restricted to the application interface of the token. The goal of the adversary is to compromise long-term secret keys, to authorize transactions or decrypt confidential data of the user.

## 3.1  System Architecture

We aim to protect the user's sensitive information by implementing the functionality of a cryptographic token in a Secure Execution Environment (SEE). The SEE manages and protects the credentials even if the underlying operating system is untrusted and potentially compromised. Hence, the secure execution environment must also establish a trusted input/output path between user and token and must be able to authenticate itself towards the user. We combine the SEE with the data sealing mechanism of the TPM to let only the locally authenticated user access the secret token state, and to assure that only a trusted token implementation running in the SEE can access the sensitive token state.

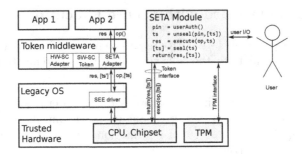

**Fig. 1.** Integration of an SEE-based cryptographic token

The overall architecture of our SEE-based token is depicted in Figure 1. It consists of a "legacy" software stack with operating system, token middleware, and the secure execution environment on the left-hand side, which runs our Secure Execution Token Application (SETA) in parallel to the legacy operating system.

Applications must be compatible with the middleware interface to make use of cryptographic tokens. Multiple tokens can be supported by the token middleware, and in our design we add another type of token beside hardware and software tokens that calls the SEE with appropriate parameters. The call into the SEE is implemented using an SEE driver provided by the legacy OS, such as Flicker. Finally, the SETA is started as the main component of this architecture, implementing the semantics of the cryptographic token and enforcing the security-critical interfaces based on (1) isolated execution using the SEE and (2) state-specific data encryption using the TPM sealing operation (cf. Section 2). The SETA component running in the SEE supports three major interfaces, as shown in Figure 1. The user interface (*user I/O*) implements interaction with the platform peripherals for user input and output using keyboard and graphics card. The TPM interface is used for basic interaction with the TPM, specifically for the sealing, unsealing and interaction with the TPM's monotonic counters. Finally, the input and output of the SETA module, upon entering and leaving the SEE, is used to implement the cryptographic token interface. The token interface operation *op()* that is to be executed is provided together with the encrypted token state [*ts*]. SETA must then request authorization for executing *op()* by requesting the PIN *pin* via user I/O, decrypt the token state $ts = \mathsf{unseal}(pin, [ts])$ using the TPM interface and compute the result $res = \mathsf{execute}(op(), ts)$ to be returned as the output of SETA.

### 3.2 Component Interaction and Protocols

Usability and flexibility are among the main concerns when using cryptographic tokens today. In the following, we present more detailed protocol flows for the main smartcard operation and caching of the user's PIN, and discuss the problems of deployment, migration and backup.

### 3.3 Deployment

Before using the software token for the first time, the user must initialize it in a trusted enrollment environment and choose an individual picture *img* and PIN number *pin*, as illustrated in Figure 2(a). The picture is used later on to authenticate Secure Execution Token Application (SETA) towards the user, while the PIN is used to authenticate the user towards the token. After initialization, the token state is sealed to the expected TPM PCR values of SETA, which are also supplied as input, so that only SETA can open and modify the token.

Note that if the initialization and enrollment system is different from the user's target platform, the SEE-based token can be created centrally and deployed to the user's target platform using the token migration procedure described in Section 3.4. This is particularly interesting for enterprises, which often require central enrollment and backup of authentication and encryption secrets. Hence, the overall procedure remains identical to the deployment of regular smartcards, except that the user is not required to (but could) use a physical device to transport the token state from enrollment platform to the target platform.

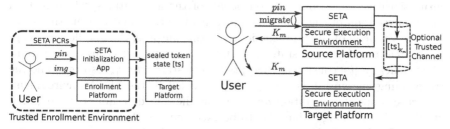

(a) Initialization of SEE-token state.   (b) Secure migration of token state [ts] under passphrase $K_m$ and/or trusted channel.

**Fig. 2.** Procedures for the secure deployment and migration/backup of SETA

### 3.4  Migration and Backup

Secure backup and migration of credentials is essential for both enterprise and personal use. Note that backup and migration are very similar, since backup can be regarded as a "migration into the future", using either a dedicated backup platform as intermediate migration target or a direct migration to a target platform of yet unknown configuration.

For best usability in personal usage scenarios, we propose to realize secure migration simply based on trusted user I/O and a user passphrase $K_m$ as illustrated in Figure 2: To migrate the token, the user must first launch SETA and enter the correct PIN $pin$ to access the protected token state $ts$. Upon issuing the $migrate()$ command, SETA encrypts $ts$ using a symmetric randomly chosen passphrase $K_m$ and returns the encrypted token state $[ts]_{K_m}$ to the untrusted environment of the source platform. The passphrase $K_m$ is disclosed to the user via trusted I/O, enabling the owner of the token (authorized by the entered PIN) to import the encrypted token state $[ts]_{K_m}$ at the target platform.

Additionally, the migration procedure can be wrapped in a trusted channel if the target platform is known in advance and is equipped with a TPM: As proposed in [3,9], the encrypted token state $[ts]_{K_m}$ can be bound to a specific target platform's TPM and platform state before disclosing it to the source platform's untrusted environment. As a result, the protected token state can only be imported by the designated target platform, and only from within the trusted SETA environment. Token migration using trusted channels can thus effectively mitigate brute-force attacks on $K_m$ and, based on the authentication image $img$ sealed to SETA, also prevent impersonation of the importing application at the target platform. Note that if the backup system is equipped with a TPM, this extended migration protocol can also be used for secure backups.

### 3.5  Token Operation

The protocol for the regular operation of our SEE-based token is illustrated in Figure 3. As outlined in previous Section 3.1, the token middleware executes security-sensitive operations $op()$ on behalf of the applications, which in turn delegates execution of the required algorithms to SETA and returns the result $res$ at the very end of the protocol flow. For this purpose, the middleware keeps track of one or more token states $[ts]$ and their supported types of operations $op()$. Specifically, $[ts]$ consists of encrypted token state $cstate_{tk}, cstate_{pal}$ and the corresponding encryption keys $[K_{tk}], [K_{pal}]$ sealed to the SETA environment. To execute a specific operation $op()$, the middleware determines the required cryptographic token algorithm $algo$ to be executed and then asks the operating system's SEE driver to launch an instance of the SETA module, supplying the algorithm identifier $algo$, the token identifier $id$ and the respective protected token state $[ts]$ as shown in step 2.

Once launched, SETA unseals $K_{pal}$ in step 3 to decrypt the PAL meta-data state $state_{pal}$ to retrieve the master key $K_{ctr}$ of the counter list $clist$ and the secret authentication picture $img$. $K_{ctr}$ is used to decrypt $ctrs$, a list of counters

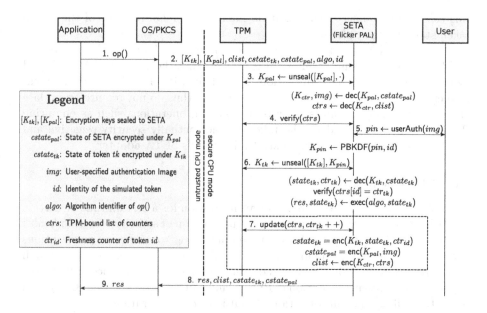

**Fig. 3.** System component interaction during normal operation

that is shared by all trusted applications on the platform. In correspondence with previous work on secure virtual counters [27], the sum of the elements in $ctrs$ is compared with a predefined secure monotonic counter in the TPM in step 4. If the sum matches, $ctrs$ and thus also $cstate_{pal}$ and the individual token's counter $ctrs[id]$ and $img$ are fresh. In step 5, the picture $img$ is used to authenticate SETA to the user and retrieve the authentication PIN $pin$. The PIN and token identifier $id$ are fed into the password-based key derivation function (PBKDF2 [19]) to generate the user authentication key $K_{pin}$. This secret is in turn used in step 6 to unseal $K_{tk}$, so that $cstate_{tk}$ can be decrypted to retrieve the secret token state $state_{tk}$ and the verification counter $cntr_{tk}$. To assure the freshness of $cstate_{tk}$, SETA checks if known fresh $cntr_{id}$ is equal to $cntr_{tk}$. If successful, the actual token algorithm $algo$ can finally be executed in the context of $state_{tk}$, yielding the return value $res$. If the state $state_{tk}$ was updated during the execution of $algo$, we must increment the freshness counters $cntr_{tk}$ and $ctrs[id]$ (step 7), update the TPM hardware counter accordingly and then re-encrypt the token state $cstate_{tk}, cstate_{pal}$ (dashed box). If updated, the new states $cstate_{tk}, cstate_{pal}$ are returned together with the result $res$ in step 8. Finally, the result of the operation $op()$ can be returned to the application in step 9.

Note that even if verification of the virtual counter vector $ctrs$, which is shared together with $K_{ctr}$ among all trusted applications that require secure TPM-bound counters, is *unsuccessful*, the application can still recover the desired secret states and also determine the number of version rollbacks that have occurred as $num = cntr_{ID} - cntr_{tk}$. Hence, in case of system crashes or misbehavior of other software components SETA can inform the user and offer recovery. However, in this case the user must assure that no malicious version rollback of the sealed token state [$ts$] took place.

While the TPM specification imposes a frequency limit on the use of the TPM's secure monotonic counters, it is unlikely that the use of SETA is affected by this limit: Most common operations carried out with the token, such as signature creation, do not modify the token state and thus do not require an update of the TPM secure counters. Moreover, common operations such as enquiring the algorithms supported by the token are not actually security sensitive and can be implemented within the token middleware's SETA adapter.

### 3.6   PIN Caching

It is often useful to cache a given user authorization for a certain time or certain number of uses. For example, in the current adoption of security tokens in health care systems it is often simply too time consuming to authorize prescriptions and other documents of minor sensitivity individually. Hence, so-called "batch signatures" were introduced that sign multiple documents at once [12]. In the following, we present an optional PIN caching mechanism for our SEE-based token that allows the authorization of multiple token operations.

Instead of requiring the PIN for each transaction, our system is able to securely cache the PIN for multiple uses. For this purpose, we seal the cached authorization secret $K_{pin}$ to the trusted system state of SETA and add a usage counter $uses$ to be maintained by the (untrusted) token middleware. We verify the value of $uses$ based on the non-invertible status of a PCR register $p$, so that the usage count can be tracked independently from the token state $cstate_{tk}, cstate_{pal}$. Another advantage of this construction is that an unexpected reset of the platform or update of the PCR $p$ does not invalidate the token state but only the cached PIN.

Figure 4 shows a modified version of the main protocol in Figure 3 to support PIN caching. When the PIN is provided for the first time and should be cached, the maximum desired number of PIN uses $uses_{max}$, the user authorization secret $K_{pin} \leftarrow \text{PBKDF}(pin, id)$ and a randomly chosen secret $s$ are added to the token state $cstate_{pal}$. For subsequent SETA executions with cached $K_{pin}$, the respective values are recovered from $cstate_{pal}$ as shown in Figure 4 after step 2.

In step 4, the current value $reg'$ of PCR $p$ is read in addition to the verification of $ctrs$. Due to the non-invertibility of the PCR states, this allows to verify the value of $uses$ based on the purported PCR pre-image $reg$ and the secret $s$. If this verification succeeds and $uses < uses_{max}$, the cached PIN can be used and the PCR $p$ is updated for the incremented $uses$ counter in step 5a. Otherwise, the user is asked for authorization in step 5b. After successful execution of the following steps 6 and 7, the result $res$ is returned together with the current usage counter $uses$ and possibly updated state [$ts$] in step 8 and 9.

If step 6 executes successfully following step 5b, the caching state can be reset as $reg = reg', uses = 0$. Otherwise, if the PIN was (repeatedly) entered incorrectly, $K_{pin}$ should be purged from $cstate_{pal}$. As a result of this construction, the PIN caching works mostly independent from the more expensive token state

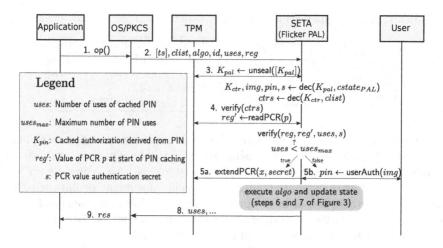

**Fig. 4.** Protocol extension for PIN-caching

updates: The values of $uses_{max}$ and $s$ can be considered relatively static and remain in $cstate_{pal}$ even if PIN caching is not used. Moreover, an unexpected modification of PCR $p$, including platform reset, only invalidates the PIN caching status, requiring only a regular user authentication to continue operation.

# 4    Implementation and Results

We implemented a proof of concept prototype of our SEE-based token based on the software token of the OpenCryptoki middleware [5]. OpenCryptoki implements the PKCS#11 interface [26], a well-known standard supported by many applications, including major web browsers, eMail clients, several VPN clients and other authentication solutions.

To build SETA, we separated the security-sensitive functions implemented by the OpenCryptoki software token into a separate software module that is then executed using the Flicker SEE driver. Additionally, we implemented basic drivers for accessing keyboard and graphics hardware from within SETA, to provide a secure user input/output interface while the untrusted OS and applications are suspended by the SEE. In this respect, we extend the work of [13] that could only provide a basic text output from within the SEE.

## 4.1    Performance Evaluation

While the processors in many hardware tokens are optimized for low cost and resistance against physical attacks, our solution benefits from the high performance of today's CPUs. The main delay for executing operations with SETA is caused by the switch into the SEE itself using Flicker, and the interaction with the (often rather slow) TPM for unsealing and counter update.

**Table 1.** Speed comparison for a PKCS#11-compliant 1024 bit RSA signature

| Existing Tokens | Time |
|---|---|
| CrypToken MX2048 | 2.9s |
| eToken Pro 32k | 4.3s |
| opencryptoKi SW-Token | 0.05s |

| Our SETA Solution | Time |
|---|---|
| Switch to SEE | +1.20s |
| TPM interaction | +1.50s |
| Signing in SEE | +0.05s |
| Overall Signing in SETA | =2.75s |

We compared the time required for a PKCS#11 signing operation using hardware and software tokens versus using our SETA. The signature operation is perhaps the most common operation for security tokens, as it is used for authentication as well as document signing. The specific document or data length is insignificant in this case, as most applications simply hash the document themselves and only sign the hash digest, to reduce the amount of data that would otherwise have to be transferred and handled by the token.

Specifically, we compared an older Aladdin eToken Pro 32k and a newer MARX CrypToken MX2048 as hardware tokens against the opencryptoKi software token and our SEE-based solution on a standard Dell Optiplex 980 PC with an Intel 3.2 GHz Core i5 CPU. For the signature operation we use the PKCS#11 *C_Sign* command using RSA-1024 as the signature mechanism. As can be seen in Table 1, SETA is almost twice as fast as the older eToken Pro and still faster than the modern MX2048. As can be seen in the explicitly listed time overheads for switching to Flicker and interacting with the TPM, significant performance improvements can be expected for more complex token operations. We also expect improvements in the SEE switching and TPM interaction times once these components are relevant for daily use.

## 5   Security Considerations

The security of our overall scheme depends on the enforcement of information flow control to maintain the confidentiality and integrity of the internal token state. Specifically, our token must meet the two security requirements formulated in Section 3, (1) preventing unauthorized leakage or manipulation of the token state and (2) providing a user interface that is secure against spoofing or eavesdropping attacks by a compromised legacy operating system and that detects attempts to tamper with the SETA token implementation.

*Secure Token Interface.* Requirement (1) holds based on the assumption that the user and TPM are trusted and the PKCS#11 token interface is secure and securely implemented. The first two assumptions are standard assumptions and differ from the security of regular hardware-based cryptographic tokens mainly in that the TPM is not designed to be secure against hardware attacks.

Considering the limited security of hardware tokens against hardware attacks [2,29,24] and the prevalence of remote software attacks it is reasonable that we exclude hardware attacks in our adversary model. While some attacks on PKCS#11 implementations have been shown [7], the specification itself is considered highly mature and implementation flaws are independent from the token type.

*Secure User I/O.* Requirement (2) is met by our combination of SEE and TPM, which results in isolated execution of trusted code with full control over the local platform. The SEE suspends the legacy OS, preventing any potentially loaded malware from manipulating the execution of SETA payload and giving it full hardware access. By implementing appropriate keyboard and graphics drivers in SETA we can thus provide secure I/O on standard computing platforms. Additionally, to prevent the replacement of SETA by malicious applications, we use the TCG TPM's sealing capability to bind data to designated system states, such that a malicious SETA' $\neq$ SETA is unable to access the protected token state $[ts]$ and user authentication image $img$. Specifically, since only the pristine SETA program can access and display the secret authentication image $img$, the user can always recognize if the currently running application is the untampered SETA. A well-known open problem, in this context is that users often disregard such security indicators, allowing an adversary to spoof the user interface and intercept the secret PIN [28]. However, in our solution, an attacker that has gained knowledge of the user's PIN also requires the untampered SETA program to which the user's sealing key is bound and to which he thus has to enter the PIN (physical presence). Hence, although our solution cannot fully prevent interface spoofing against attacks against unmindful users, the attack surface is notably reduced by restricting the TPM unseal operation to pre-defined physical platforms and requiring physical presence. We suggest that enterprises monitor the migration and authorization of SETA modules for such events.

Some recent works also manage to break the rather novel SEE implementations through security bugs in BIOS and PC firmware [32,33]. The works show that PC-based SEE environments currently still require secure BIOS implementations, which can be verified using the respective TPM PCRs. Again, these vulnerabilities in the execution environment are not specific to our solution, as illustrated by recent attacks on dedicated smartcard readers [5]. However, similar to bugs in the PKCS#11 implementations such vulnerabilities are rare and usually very hard to exploit in comparison with common trojan horse or phishing attacks. Overall, SETA thus significantly improves the security of user authentication and transaction authorization by preventing the vast majority of malware attacks and significantly reducing the applicability of social engineering.

## 6    Conclusion and Future Work

We introduced an SEE-based PKCS#11 token that combines the flexibility of a software-based PKCS#11 token with the security of modern trusted computing

---

[5] E.g., a smartcard reader by Kobil allowed unauthorized firmware manipulation: http://h-online.com/-1014651

technology. While our solution does achieve the same resilience against hardware attacks as some hardware cryptographic tokens, it presents a significant improvement over software-based solutions or cryptographic tokens used without dedicated keypad and display for secure PIN entry and transaction confirmation. By integrating secure user I/O with increasingly deployed SEE technology and leveraging standard cryptographic token interfaces, we can provide a secure plug-in solution that is especially attractive for today's mobile computing environments.

For future work, we aim to further reduce time delay when accessing SETA by parallelizing TPM interactions with software computations. Moreover, we aim to port our prototype to other platforms such as ObC or the Windows OS and include additional PKCS#11 functionality such as elliptic curve cryptography.

# References

1. Advanced Micro Devices (AMD): AMD64 Virtualization Codenamed "Pacifica" Technology - Secure Virtual Machine Architecture Reference Manual (2005)
2. Anderson, R.J., Kuhn, M.: Tamper resistance – a cautionary note. In: USENIX Workshop on Electronic Commerce, pp. 1–11. USENIX (1996)
3. Asokan, N., Ekberg, J.E., Sadeghi, A.R., Stüble, C., Wolf, M.: Enabling Fairer Digital Rights Management with Trusted Computing. Research Report HGI-TR-2007-002, Horst-Görtz-Institute for IT-Security (2007)
4. Azema, J., Fayad, G.: M-Shield$^{TM}$ mobile security technology: making wireless secure. Tech. rep., Texas Instruments (2008)
5. Bade, S., Thomas, K., Rabinovitz, D.: PKCS#11 openCryptoki for Linux, IBM developerWorks (2001)
6. Balfe, S., Paterson, K.G.: e-EMV: emulating EMV for internet payments with trusted computing technologies. In: Workshop on Scalable Trusted Computing (STC), pp. 81–92. ACM (2008)
7. Bortolozzo, M., Centenaro, M., Focardi, R., Steel, G.: Attacking and fixing PKCS#11 security tokens. In: Computer and Communications Security (CCS), pp. 260–269. ACM (2010)
8. Bugiel, S., Dmitrienko, A., Kostiainen, K., Sadeghi, A.-R., Winandy, M.: TruWalletM: Secure Web Authentication on Mobile Platforms. In: Chen, L., Yung, M. (eds.) INTRUST 2010. LNCS, vol. 6802, pp. 219–236. Springer, Heidelberg (2011)
9. Catuogno, L., Dmitrienko, A., Eriksson, K., Kuhlmann, D., Ramunno, G., Sadeghi, A.-R., Schulz, S., Schunter, M., Winandy, M., Zhan, J.: Trusted Virtual Domains – Design, Implementation and Lessons Learned. In: Chen, L., Yung, M. (eds.) INTRUST 2009. LNCS, vol. 6163, pp. 156–179. Springer, Heidelberg (2010)
10. Datamonitor Group: The ROI case for smart cards in the enterprise (2004)
11. Dimitriadis, C.K.: Analyzing the security of Internet banking authentication mechanisms. Information Systems Control 3 (2007)
12. Federal Office for Information Security: Batch signature with the Health Professional Card (Stapelsignatur mit dem Heilberufsausweis) (2007)
13. Filyanov, A., McCune, J.M., Sadeghi, A.R., Winandy, M.: Uni-directional trusted path: Transaction confirmation on just one device. In: Dependable Systems and Networks (DSN), pp. 1–12. IEEE (2011)

14. Gajek, S., Sadeghi, A.R., Stüble, C., Winandy, M.: Compartmented security for browsers - or how to thwart a phisher with trusted computing. In: Availability, Reliability and Security (ARES). IEEE (2007)
15. IBM: TrouSerS trusted software stack (2011), trousers.sourceforge.net/
16. Intel Corp.: Intel Trusted Execution Technology MLE Developer's Guide (2009)
17. Jackson, C., Boneh, D., Mitchell, J.C.: Spyware resistant web authentication using virtual machines (2007)
18. Jammalamadaka, R.C., van der Horst, T.W., Mehrotra, S., Seamons, K.E., Venkatasubramanian, N.: Delegate: A proxy based architecture for secure website access from an untrusted machine. In: Annual Computer Security Applications Conference (ACSAC). IEEE (2006)
19. Kaliski, B.: PKCS #5: Password-Based Cryptography Specification Version 2.0. RFC 2898 (2000)
20. Kolodgy, C.: Identity management in a virtual world (2003)
21. Kostiainen, K., Ekberg, J.E., Asokan, N., Rantala, A.: On-board credentials with open provisioning. In: ACM Symposium on Information, Computer, and Communications Security (AsiaCCS), pp. 104–115. ACM (2009)
22. McCune, J.M., Parno, B., Perrig, A., Reiter, M.K., Seshadri, A.: Minimal TCB code execution. In: Research in Security and Privacy (S&P). IEEE (2007)
23. McCune, J.M., Parno, B.J., Perrig, A., Reiter, M.K., Isozaki, H.: Flicker: An execution infrastructure for TCB minimization. In: European Conference on Computer Systems (EuroSys), pp. 315–328. ACM (2008)
24. Nohl, K.: Reviving smart card analysis. Black Hat, Las Vegas (2011)
25. Nyström, M.: PKCS #15 - a cryptographic token information format standard. In: Workshop on Smartcard Technology, p. 5. USENIX (1999)
26. RSA: PKCS #11: Cryptographic token interface standard. Public-key cryptography standards (PKCS), RSA Laboratories, version 2.30 (2009)
27. Sarmenta, L.F.G., van Dijk, M., O'Donnell, C.W., Rhodes, J., Devadas, S.: Virtual monotonic counters and count-limited objects using a TPM without a trusted OS. In: Workshop on Scalable Trusted Computing (STC), pp. 27–42. ACM (2006)
28. Schechter, S.E., Dhamija, R., Ozment, A., Fischer, I.: The emperor's new security indicators – an evaluation of website authentication and the effect of role playing on usability studies. In: Research in Security and Privacy (S&P). IEEE (2007)
29. Tarnovsky, C.: Hacking the smartcard chip. Black Hat, DC (2010)
30. Trusted Computing Group (TCG) (2009), http://www.trustedcomputinggroup.org
31. Trusted Computing Group (TCG): TPM Main Specification, Version 1.2 (2011)
32. Wojtczuk, R., Rutkowska, J.: Attacking Intel Trusted Execution Technology. Black Hat, DC (2009)
33. Wojtczuk, R., Rutkowska, J., Tereshkin, A.: Another way to circumvent Intel Trusted Execution Technology (2009)

# The PACE|AA Protocol for Machine Readable Travel Documents, and Its Security

Jens Bender[1], Özgür Dagdelen[2], Marc Fischlin[2], and Dennis Kügler[1]

[1] Bundesamt für Sicherheit in der Informationstechnik (BSI), Germany
[2] Darmstadt University of Technology, Germany

**Abstract.** We discuss an efficient combination of the cryptographic protocols adopted by the International Civil Aviation Organization (ICAO) for securing the communication of machine readable travel documents and readers. Roughly, in the original protocol the parties first run the Password-Authenticated Connection Establishment (PACE) protocol to establish a shared key and then the reader (optionally) invokes the Active Authentication (AA) protocol to verify the passport's validity. Here we show that by carefully re-using some of the secret data of the PACE protocol for the AA protocol one can save one exponentiation on the passports's side. We call this the PACE|AA protocol. We then formally prove that this more efficient combination not only preserves the desirable security properties of the two individual protocols but also increases privacy by preventing misuse of the challenge in the Active Authentication protocol. We finally discuss a solution which allows deniable authentication in the sense that the interaction cannot be used as a proof towards third parties.

## 1 Introduction

Through ISO/IEC JTC1 SC17 WG3/TF5 [ICA10] the International Civil Aviation Organization (ICAO) has adopted the Password Authenticated Connection Establishment (PACE) protocol [BSI10] to secure the contactless communication between machine-readable travel documents (including identity cards), and a reader. Roughly, the protocol generates a secure Diffie-Hellman key out of a low-entropy password which the owner of the passport has to enter at the reader, or which is transmitted through a read-out of the machine-readable zone. The Diffie-Hellman key is subsequently used to secure the communication. In [BFK09] it has been shown that the PACE protocol achieves the widely accepted security notion of password-based authenticated key agreement of Bellare-Pointcheval-Rogaway [BPR00], in its strong form of Abdalla et al. [AFP05]. This holds under a variant of the Diffie-Hellman assumption, assuming secure cryptographic building blocks, and idealizing the underlying block cipher and the hash function.

According to European endeavors, the PACE protocol should be followed by the extended access control (EAC) authentication steps, called Chip Authentication (CA) and Terminal Authentication (TA), with high-entropic certified keys. This should ensure that access for either party is granted based on strong

A.D. Keromytis (Ed.): FC 2012, LNCS 7397, pp. 344–358, 2012.
© International Financial Cryptography Association 2012

cryptographic keys (i.e., not relying on low-entropy passwords only). The security of the EAC protocols and of the composition with PACE has been discussed in [DF10].

In the specifications of the ICAO 9303 standard [ICA06] for the border control scenario, the normative document about machine-readable travel documents, however, only passive authentication of the passport is mandatory, where the passport essentially merely sends its (authenticated) data. Active Authentication (AA) of the passport, implemented through a signature-based challenge-response protocol, is only optional. If AA is not enforced this potentially allows to bypass authentication through cloning of passports. Even if AA is used, then the (plain) challenge-response protocol introduces a potential threat to privacy, as discussed in [BSI10] (see also [BPSV08b, BPSV08a, MVV07]). Namely, if the terminal can encode a time stamp or the location into the challenge, then the signature on that challenge can be used as a proof towards third parties about the location or time of the border check. In this sense, the passport cannot deny this interaction. This problem has been explicitly addressed in the European Chip Authentication protocol (where a message authentication code for a shared key is used for the challenge-response step instead).

*Combining PACE and AA.* We discuss that, on the chip's side, we can re-use some of the (secret) data in the PACE step for the AA step to save the exponentiation for the signature in AA on the chip's side, giving Active Authentication (almost) for free.

To understand our technique, we need to take a closer look at the PACE protocol. The PACE protocol first maps the short password to a random group element through an interactive sub protocol Map2Point, followed by a Diffie-Hellman key exchange step for this group element, and concludes with an authentication step. While the latter steps are somewhat canonical, the Map2Point step can be instantiated by different means and allows a modular design. The most common instantiations are based on another Diffie-Hellman step (used within the German identity card), or on hashing into elliptic curves as proposed by Icart [Ica09] and Brier et al. [BCI+10]. The security proof for PACE [BFK09] holds for general Map2Point protocols satisfying some basic security properties.

Our improvement works for the Diffie-Hellman based Map2Point protocol as implemented on the German identity cards, for example, since the chip can re-use its secret exponent from the Diffie-Hellman step of the Map2Point protocol. We discuss two alternatives how to carry out the AA step with this exponent more efficiently, one based on DSA signatures and the other one using Schnorr signatures. We note that the idea applies more generally to other discrete-log based signature schemes. The challenge in the new AA step is now the authentication data sent by the terminal in the PACE step.

*Security of the Combined Protocol.* Whenever secret data is used throughout several sub protocols great care must be taken in cryptography not to spoil the security of the overall protocol. We thus show that sharing the data between the PACE protocol and the new AA sub protocol preserves the desirable security properties. More precisely, we show that:

- In the combined PACE|AA protocol we still achieve the security of a password-based authenticated key exchange protocol (thus showing that the deployment of the randomness in the extra AA step does not violate the security of the PACE protocol), and
- the overall protocol still authenticates the chip securely (in a high-entropy sense), even when many executions of PACE|AA take place. To this end, we define a strong security model for authentication, essentially only excluding trivial attacks, e.g., if the adversary gets possession of the secret key, or simply relays information in executions.

It follows that the PACE|AA protocol achieves the previous security standards of the individual protocols but comes with a clear efficiency improvement. We note that the underlying assumptions are essentially the same as for PACE and AA, i.e., besides the common assumptions about secure encryption, signature, and MAC algorithms, we reduce the security of the combined protocol to the security of PACE (as an authenticated key-exchange protocol) and to a variant of the security of Schnorr signatures resp. DSA signatures (where the adversary now also gets access to a decisional Diffie-Hellman oracle and can decide upon the message to be signed after seeing the first half of the signature).

*A Deniable Schnorr Version.* As explained before, for privacy reasons it may be important that the terminal cannot derive a proof for others from the interaction with the passport or identity card *that* an interaction took place. Put differently, the protocol should provide *deniable authentication* [DDN00]. This roughly means that the terminal could have generated its view in the protocol itself from the public data, without communicating with the passport. This implies that the passport holder can deny any actual interaction and claim the terminal to have made up this conversation.

We note that the previously discussed signature based protocols do not support deniability. The reason is that the terminal could not have created the signature under the passport's key without the signing key —or without communicating with the actual chip. For the (ordinary) AA variant the terminal is even allowed to encode *any* information in the challenge, in our improved combinations the challenge is "only" a MAC computed over data provided by the passport and the shared Diffie-Hellman key. If this allows to encode information depends on the MAC.

In contrast, our proposed deniable variant does not rely on Schnorr signatures, but in some sense rather on the interactive Schnorr identification scheme for honestly chosen challenges. This identification scheme is deniable because one can simulate the interaction via the well-known zero-knowledge simulator.[1]

---

[1] It is this property which is not known to work for the DSA case and why we restrict ourself to the Schnorr scheme. Note also that Schnorr signatures are also somewhat simulatable but only if one programs the random oracle hash function; this, however, is not admissible for the notion of deniability. We nonetheless still use a hash function in the solution but use programmability only to show the unforgeablity/impersonation resistance property, not the deniability proof.

Interestingly, our variant is essentially as efficient as the signature based one, but comes with the advantage of deniability.

## 2 Security Model

We use the real-or-random security model of Abdalla et al. [AFP05] which extends the model of Bellare et al. [BPR00] for password-based key exchange protocols. Due to space limitations, we refer the reader to [BFK09] for the description of the attack model and security notion. Some changes are necessary, though, because we now incorporate a long-term signing key of the chip. These minor modifications follow next.

*Attack Model.* We consider security against active attacks where the adversary has full control over the network, and the adversary's goal is to distinguish genuine keys from random keys in executions, which are picked independently of the actual protocol run. This corresponds to the so-called real-or-random setting [AFP05], a stronger model than the original find-then-guess model of [BPR00], where the adversary can see several test keys (instead of a single one only).

In the attack, each user instance is given as an oracle to which an adversary has access, basically providing the interface of the protocol instance (via the usual Send, Execute, Reveal, and Test commands to send messages to parties, to observe executions between honest parties, to reveal the session key, and to be challenged for a test key). In addition, there exists a Corrupt oracle in the model from [AFP05]. The adversary can gain control over a user during the execution by issuing a Corrupt query with which the adversary obtains the secrets of an honest party. For sake of convenience, here we split these queries into Corrupt.pw and Corrupt.key queries, where the former reveals the password only and the latter discloses the long-term key only (in case of a chip); in both cases, the other secret remains private. Note that we now can model Corrupt queries by both queries (since we work in the weak corruption model where the parties' internal states are not revealed upon corruption). An honest party gets adversarially controlled if it does not have any secrets left (i.e., if the adversary issues both Corrupt query types for a chip, or the Corrupt.pw query for the terminal).

The adversary can make the following queries to the interface oracles other than these from [AFP05]:

**Corrupt.pw**($U$) The adversary obtains the party's password $\pi$.
**Corrupt.key**($U$) The adversary obtains the party's cryptographic key $sk$ (if it exists).

In addition, since the original PACE protocol was cast in the random oracle and ideal cipher model where oracles providing a random hash function oracle and an encryption/decryption oracle are available, the attacker may also query these oracles here. (We note that we only use the ideal cipher implicitly through the reduction to the security to PACE.)

*Partners, Correctness and Freshness.* Upon successful termination, we assume that an instance $U_i$ outputs a session key $k$, the session ID *sid*, and a user ID *pid* identifying the intended partner (assumed to be empty in PACE for anonymity reasons but containing the chip's certificate in the combined PACE|AA protocol). We note that the session ID usually contains the entire transcript of the communication but, for efficiency reasons, in PACE it only contains a part thereof. This is inherited here. We say that instances $A_i$ and $B_j$ are *partnered* if both instances have terminated in accepting state with the same output. In this case, the instance $A_i$ is called a partner to $B_j$ and vice versa. Any untampered execution between honest users should be partnered and, in particular, the users should end up with the same key (this correctness requirement ensures the minimal functional requirement of a key agreement protocol).

Neglecting forward security for a moment, an instance $(U, i)$ is called *fresh* at the end of the execution if there has been no Reveal$(U, i)$ query at any point, neither has there been a Reveal$(B, j)$ query where $B_j$ is a partner to $U_i$, nor has somebody been corrupted (i.e., neither kind of Corrupt query has been issued). Else, the instance is called *unfresh*. In other words, fresh executions require that the session key has not been leaked (by neither partner) and that no Corruptquery took place.

To capture forward security we refine the notion of freshness and further demand from a fresh instance $(U, i)$ as before that the session key has not been leaked through a Reveal-query, and that for each Corrupt.pw$(U)$- or Corrupt.key$(U)$-query there has been no subsequent Test$(U, i)$-query involving $U$, or, if so, then there has been no Send$(U, i, m)$-query for this instance at any point.[2] In this case we call the instance *fs-fresh*, else *fs-unfresh*. This notion means that it should not help if the adversary corrupts some party after the test query, and that even if corruptions take place before test queries, then executions between honest users are still protected (before or after a Test-query).

*AKE Security.* The adversary eventually outputs a bit $b'$, trying to predict the bit $b$ of the Test oracle. We say that the adversary wins if $b = b'$ and instances $(U, i)$ in the test queries are fresh (resp. fs-fresh). Ideally, this probability should be close to $1/2$, implying that the adversary cannot significantly distinguish random keys from session keys.

To measure the resources of the adversary we denote by $t$ the number of steps of the adversary, i.e., its running time, (counting also all the steps required by honest parties); $q_e$ the maximal number of initiated executions (bounded by the number of Send- and Execute-queries); $q_h$ the number of queries to the hash oracle, and $q_c$ the number of queries to the cipher oracle. We often write $Q = (q_e, q_h, q_c)$ and say that $\mathcal{A}$ is $(t, Q)$-bounded.

Define now the AKE advantage of an adversary $\mathcal{A}$ for a key agreement protocol $P$ by

---

[2] In a stronger notion the adversary may even issue a Corrupt.key command for the user before the testing; Due to the entanglement of the PACE and the AA protocol here our protocol does not achieve this, though.

$$\mathbf{Adv}_P^{ake}(\mathcal{A}) := 2 \cdot \mathrm{Prob}[\mathcal{A}\ \mathrm{wins}] - 1$$

$$\mathbf{Adv}_P^{ake}(t, Q) := \max\left\{ \mathbf{Adv}_P^{ake}(\mathcal{A})\ \Big|\ \mathcal{A}\ \text{is}\ (t, Q)\text{-bounded} \right\}$$

The forward secure version is defined analogously and denoted by $\mathbf{Adv}_P^{ake-fs}$ $(t, Q)$.

*Impersonation Resistance.* This security property says that the adversary, in the above attack, *successfully impersonates* if an honest reader in some session accepts with partner identity *pid* and session id *sid*, but such that (a) the intended partner $U$ in *pid* is not adversarially controlled or the public key in *pid* has not been registered, and (b) no Corrupt.key command to $U$ has been issued before the reader has accepted, and (c) the session id *sid* has not appeared in another accepting session. This roughly means that the adversary managed to impersonate an honest chip or to make the reader accept a fake certificate, without knowing the long-term secret or relaying the data in a trivial man-in-the-middle kind of attack.

Define now the IKE advantage (I for impersonation) of an adversary $\mathcal{A}$ for a key agreement protocol $P$ by

$$\mathbf{Adv}_P^{ike}(\mathcal{A}) := \mathrm{Prob}[\mathcal{A}\ \text{successfully impersonates}]$$

$$\mathbf{Adv}_P^{ike}(t, Q) := \max\left\{ \mathbf{Adv}_P^{ike}(\mathcal{A})\ \Big|\ \mathcal{A}\ \text{is}\ (t, Q)\text{-bounded} \right\}$$

Note that we do not need to define a forward secure version here.

## 3   The PACE|AA Protocol

In this section, we describe the PACE|AA protocol and both options for authentication in the last message, i.e., active authentication (AA) via Schnorr and via DSA. The deniable Schnorr variant and its security is addressed in Section 6.

### 3.1   Protocol Description

Figure 1 illustrates the PACE|AA protocol with both options of authentication at the end. The scheme itself uses a block cipher $\mathcal{C}(K_\pi, \cdot) : \{0,1\}^\ell \rightarrow \{0,1\}^\ell$ and a hash function $\mathcal{H}$, with values $1, 2, \dots$ in fixed-length encoding prepended to make evaluations somewhat independent.

The chip already holds a certificate *cert$_C$* for its public key $X_A$ under the authorities' public key $pk_{CA}$, and (authenticated) group parameters $\mathcal{G} = (a, b, p, q, g, k)$ describing a subgroup of order $q$, generated by $g$, of an elliptic curve for parameters $a, b, p$ for security parameter $k$. We also note that, throughout the paper, we use the multiplicative notation for group operations. It is understood that, if working with elliptic curves, multiplications correspond to additions and exponentiations to multiplications. Then the parties run the PACE protocol,

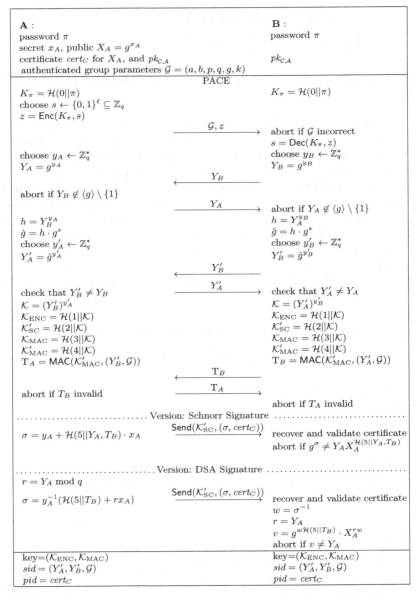

**Fig. 1.** The PACE|AA protocol (all operations are modulo $q$)

with the chip sending a nonce encrypted under the password, running the Diffie-Hellman based Map2Point protocol to derive another generator $\hat{g}$ on which another Diffie-Hellman key exchange is then performed. In this Map2Point step the chip uses some secret exponent $y_A$ to send $Y_A = g^{y_A}$. The parties in the PACE protocol finally exchange message authentication codes $T_A, T_B$.

The idea is now roughly to re-use the secret exponent $y_A$ in the Map2Point sub protocol on the chip's side for the signature generation, and use the authentication value $T_B$ of the terminal as the challenge on which the signature is computed. The chip then sends its certificate (along with the missing signature part) over the secure channel, via a Send command for the key $\mathcal{K}'_{SC}$ derived from the Diffie-Hellman exchange. The reader may think for now of the secure channel as an authenticated encryption, but other channel instantiations work as well.

## 3.2    Instantiations

There are essentially two possible instantiations. One is based on the Schnorr signature scheme [Sch90] where the chip uses the values $y_A$ and $Y_A$ as the (private resp. public) randomness and $T_B$ as the challenge for creating the signature under its long-term signature key $X_A$. We call this option *Active Authentication via Schnorr signatures*. Alternatively, the chip card might prove its authenticity by providing a DSA signature where again $y_A$ and $Y_A$ are used as the randomness for the signature generation [Kra95]. This version is called *Active Authentication via DSA signatures*. We note that the computation of the final signatures requires only modular multiplications (and, in case of DSA, an inversion) instead of exponentiations.

# 4    Security Assumptions

As remarked above we carry out our security analysis assuming an ideal hash function (random oracle model). Basically, this assumption says that $\mathcal{H}$ acts like a random function to which all parties have access. We do not make any explicit assumption about the cipher $\mathcal{C}$ here, but note that the security proof for PACE in [BFK09] (to which we reduce AKE security to) relies on an ideal cipher.

## 4.1    Cryptographic Primitives

For space reasons, we omit the standard definitions of the cryptographic primitives for message authentication, signatures, certificates, and for secure channels. In the theorems' statements, we denote by $\mathbf{Adv}_{\mathcal{S}}^{attack}(t, Q)$ an upper bound on an adversary running in time $t$ (and making $Q$ queries of the corresponding type) and breaking the scheme $\mathcal{S}$ in an attack of type *attack*. For secure channels we consider a simultaneous attack in which the adversary either tries to distinguish messages sent through the channel or to successfully inject or modify transmissions. We denote the adversary's advantage in this case by $\mathbf{Adv}_{\mathcal{SC}}^{lor}(t, Q)$.

## 4.2    Number-Theoretic Assumptions

Our proof for the AKE security of the PACE|AA protocol follows by reduction to the security of the original PACE protocol (and from the security of cryptographic primitives for the channel). For the IKE security against impersonators, we nonetheless need two number-theoretic assumptions related to the Diffie-Hellman resp. discrete-log problems. The first one is the gap Diffie-Hellman problem [BLS01]. For a group $\mathcal{G}$ generated by $g$ let $DH(X, Y)$ be the Diffie-Hellman value $X^y$ for $y = \log_g Y$ (with $g$ being an implicit parameter for the function). Then the gap Diffie-Hellman assumption says that solving the computational DH problem for $(g^a, g^b)$, i.e., computing $DH(g^a, g^b)$ given only the random elements $(g^a, g^b)$ and $\mathcal{G}, g$, is still hard, even when one has access to a decisional oracle $DDH(X, Y, Z)$ which returns 1 iff $DH(X, Y) = Z$, and 0 otherwise. We let $\mathbf{Adv}^{GDH}(t, q_{DDH})$ denote (a bound on) the value $\epsilon$ for which the GDH problem is $(t, q_{DDH}, \epsilon)$-hard.

Furthermore, for the Schnorr signature based solution we rely on the following version which (a) allows access to a decisional DH oracle for the forger, and (b) considers access to a signer in an online/offline fashion in the sense that the adversary may ask to see the public randomness part first before deciding on a message to be signed. Still, the goal is to create a signature on a new message for which the signing has not been completed. We note that the proof in [PS00] for Schnorr signatures still holds, assuming that computing discrete-logarithms relative to a DDH-oracle is hard. In particular, the hardness of this "gap discrete-log problem" is implied by the GDH hardness. We call this security notion *robust* unforgeability as it should still hold in presence of the DDH oracle and the delayed message choice.

**Definition 1 (Robust Unforgeability of Schnorr Signatures).** *The Schnorr signature scheme is $(t, Q, \epsilon)$-robustly-unforgeable with $Q = (q_R, q_{DDH})$ if for any adversary $\mathcal{A}$ running in total time $t$, making at most $q_{DDH}$ DDH oracle queries and at most $q_R$ init-queries to oracle $\mathcal{O}$ the probability that the following experiment returns 1 is most $\epsilon$:*

> *pick $\mathcal{G}$ (including a generator $g$ of prime order $q$)*
> *pick $sk \leftarrow \mathbb{Z}_q$ and let $pk = g^{sk}$*
> *let $(m^*, \sigma^*) \leftarrow \mathcal{A}^{\mathcal{O}(sk, \cdot), DDH(\cdot, \cdot, \cdot)}(\mathcal{G}, g, pk)$ for $\sigma^* = (c^*, s^*)$*
> > *where stateful oracle $\mathcal{O}$ upon input init picks $r \leftarrow \mathbb{Z}_q$ and returns $R = g^r$;*
> > *and upon input (complete, $R, m$) checks if it has returned $R = g^r$ to a request init before, and if so, returns $r + \mathcal{H}(R, m)sk \bmod q$;*
> *output 1 iff $c^* = \mathcal{H}(g^{s^*} pk^{c^*}, m^*)$ and $m^*$ was no input to a complete-query*

We let $\mathbf{Adv}^{r-forge}_{Schnorr}(t, Q)$ be the maximal advantage for any adversary running in time $t$, making in total $Q = (q_R, q_{DDH})$ queries.

As it turns out to be useful for our deniable version, we remark that the proof of Pointcheval and Stern [PS00] holds as long as the input to the hash oracle in the forgery is new, i.e., one can extract the discrete-logarithm of the public key even if the hash function in signature requests is evaluated on quasi unique inputs, and the forgery, too, uses a previously unqueried hash function input. For the notion of signature unforgeability this holds because each signature request uses a high-entropic random group element and the message $m^*$ in the forgery cannot have been signed before. We take advantage of this fact for our deniable version where we insert $(Y'_A, \mathcal{G})$ instead of $(R, m)$ into the hash function for the random group element $Y'_A$ chosen by the chip respectively, signer. We also show that for the proof of impersonation resistance the adversary cannot re-use one of these values $(Y'_A, \mathcal{G})$ but needs to pick a new value $Y'_A$, thus showing the second property.

For the DSA based solution, we require an analogous assumption which is omitted here for space reasons and refer to the full version of this paper.

# 5  Security Analysis of PACE|AA

In this section, we discuss the security of the PACE|AA protocol when active authentication is done via Schnorr signatures; the case of DSA signatures follows, too, because we do not use any specific properties of the underlying signature scheme (except for the robust unforgeability). That is, we assume that the chip, holding public key $X_A = g^{x_A}$ with certificate $cert_C$, signs the message $Y_B$ with key $x_A$ and randomness $Y_A$. The signature is given by $\sigma = y_A + c x_A \bmod q$ for $c = \mathcal{H}(5||Y_A, T_B)$. After the final authentication step of PACE, the chip sends (using already a secure channel) the values $\sigma$ and $cert_C$ to the reader who verifies the signatures and the certificate (and aborts in case one of the verification fails).

As noted in [BFK09] using the derived keys already in the key agreement step does not allow for a proof in the Bellare-Pointcheval-Rogaway model. We hence also use the variant that the keys $\mathcal{K}'_{SC}$ and $\mathcal{K}'_{MAC}$ are independent from the keys output as the result of the key agreement.

## 5.1  Security as a Key Exchange Protocol

**Theorem 1.** *The protocol PACE|AA (with Schnorr or DSA signatures) satisfies:*

$$\mathbf{Adv}^{ake}_{PACE|AA}(t, Q) \leq \frac{q_e^2}{2q} + \mathbf{Adv}^{lor}_{SC}(t^*, q_e, q_e) + \mathbf{Adv}^{ake}_{PACE}(t^*, Q)$$

*where $t^* = t + O(kq_e^2 + kq_h^2 + kq_c^2 + k^2)$ and $Q = (q_e, q_c, q_h)$.*

We remark that the time $t^*$ covers the additional time to maintain lists and perform look-ups. Since PACE is secure (under cryptographic assumptions) it follows together with the security of the underlying encryption scheme that the PACE|AA scheme is secure as well.

The idea of the proof is roughly that the additional Schnorr signature does not violate the security of the underlying PACE protocol as it is encrypted. This is shown through a reduction to the security of the original PACE protocol, mildly exploiting the structure of the original proof in [BFK09] and the properties of the Schnorr signature scheme. We roughly show that, in the PACE|AA protocol, we can simulate the final transmission of the signature token by sending dummy values through the channel, because the keys used to secure this transmission are "as secure as" the PACE keys. That is, even though the strength of the keys is only password-protected (i.e., one can try to guess the low-entropy password), this is sufficient for our purpose, as we do not plan to be more secure than that.

*Proof.* The proof uses the common game-hopping technique, gradually taking away adversarial success strategies and discussing that each modification cannot contribute significantly to the overall success probability. Note that the original proof of PACE in [BFK09] actually shows something stronger than indistinguishability of keys (from random). The proof rather shows that computing the Diffie-Hellman key $\mathcal{K}$ in an execution is hard (unless one knows or has guessed the password); key indistinguishability then follows from this. We will use this more fine-grained view on the proof below and also consider the adversary on the PACE|AA protocol in this regard, i.e., we measure its success probability according to the probability of making a hash query about $\mathcal{K}$ in a Test session (called target hash query).

**Game 0:** Corresponds to an AKE attack on the PACE|AA protocol (with the more fine-grained success notion).

**Game 1:** Abort Game 0 if an honest chip would compute the same Diffie-Hellman key in two executions.

Note that, since the honest chip always goes second for the Diffie-Hellman key exchange step, sending $Y_A'$, the keys in such executions are random elements and the probability that such a collision occurs is thus at most $\frac{1}{2}q_e^2/q$.

**Game 2:** Change the previous game slightly such that, an honest chip when sending the encrypted signature, instead picks and uses random and independent (independent of the hash function output) keys $\mathcal{K}_{SC}'$.

Note that the only difference between the two cases can occur if the adversary makes a target hash query since Reveal and Test sessions never output these keys and Diffie-Hellman keys are distinct by the previous game. It follows that the adversarial success can only decrease by the probability of making a target hash query in this new game.

**Game 3:** Change the game once more and replace channeled transmissions of the signatures sent by an honest chip by encryptions of 0-bits of the same length and, at the same time, let any honest terminal reject any final message unless it has really been sent by the honest chip in the same session.

Note that the length (of the signature part and the certificate) is known in advance. Note also that the probability of making a target hash query in Game 3 cannot be significantly larger, by the distinguishing advantage of genuine transmissions from all-zero transmissions. To make this claim more formally, assume that we mount an attack on the left-or-right security of the (multi-user) encryption scheme by simulating the entire Game 2 with two exceptions: (1) If an honest chip is supposed to send the signature and certificate, then we simply call the next transmission challenge oracle about the signature part and the certificate and about an all-zero message of the same length. Then the challenge bit of the left-or-right oracle corresponds exactly to the difference between the two games. (2) If the adversary successfully modifies the final transmission of an honest chip and the honest terminal would accept the message, then this would also constitute a security breach of the channel protocol. Hence, if the success probabilities of the adversary dropped significantly, we would get a successful attacker against the secure channel scheme.

The final game can now be easily cast as an attack on the original PACE protocol. That is, if there was a successful attacker in Game 3 (making a target hash query), then there was a straightforward attacker with the same probability in the original PACE protocol: this attacker would run the Game 3-adversary and simulate the additional signature steps itself (i.e., creating keys and certificates), inject the values from the PACE protocol (i.e., relay the communication), but send dummy values $0\ldots0$ through the channel on behalf of honest chips under independent random keys. It follows that the probability of making a target hash query in Game 3 is also bounded by the PACE security.

Given that no target hash query is made, the advantage in the final game is now bounded from above by the advantage against PACE. Note that the advantage of breaking PACE simultaneously covers both the case of target hash queries and of breaks otherwise (such that we do not need to account for the advantage of target hash queries and then of other breaks, resulting in a factor 2). □

*On Forward Security.* Note that the PACE|AA protocol inherits the forward security of PACE (when used as authenticated key exchange protocol). That is, even if the adversary knows the password, then executions between honest parties remain protected. Since the security of PACE|AA essentially reduces to the security of PACE any successful attack against the forward security of PACE|AA would yield a successful attack against PACE; the other protocol steps do not violate this property.

## 5.2  Security against Impersonation

It remains to show that the protocol is IKE-secure. Here, we only rely on the unforgeability of certificates and MACs and the robust unforgeability of the Schnorr/DSA signature scheme.

**Theorem 2.** *For the PACE|AA protocol (with Schnorr or DSA signatures) it holds:*

$$Adv^{ike}_{PACE|AA}(t,Q)$$
$$\leq \frac{q_e^2 + q_e q_h}{q} + Adv^{forge}_{CA}(t^*,q_e) + 2q_e \cdot Adv^{forge}_{M}(t^*,2q_e,2q_e)$$
$$+ Adv^{r-forge}_{\{Schnorr|DSA\}}(t^*,q_e)$$

*where $t^* = t + O(kq_e^2 + kq_h^2 + k^2)$ and $Q = (q_e, q_h)$.*

The idea is to show first that the adversary cannot inject its own unregistered key (unless it breaks the unforgeability of the certification authority). Since any successful attack must be then for an uncorrupt party whose secret signing key was not revealed, it follows that the adversary must produce a signature under the (registered) public key of an honest user. Because the session id must be new and is somewhat signed via $T_B$, it follows that the adversary must forge Schnorr respectively DSA signatures in order to break the IKE property.

The formal proof appears in the full version of the paper.

## 6   A Deniable Schnorr Variant

Deniability basically demands that for any (possibly malicious) party on either side, there exists a simulator $S$ which produces the same output distribution as the malicious party but without communicating with the honest party (but only receiving the honest party's public input and the malicious party's secrets). This implies that the malicious party could have generated these data itself, without the help of the other party, and cannot use it as a proof towards a third party.

Since we work in the random oracle model, there is a peculiarity due to the (non-)programmability of the hash function [Pas03]. Roughly, it is important that the distinguisher (receiving either the view of the malicious party or the simulated view) cannot distinguish these two random variables, even if it gets access to the same random oracle as the parties and the simulator. The distinguisher's access to the same hash function prevents the simulator from programming the hash values (as in the case for a real-world hash function).

We omit a formal definition of deniability (in the random oracle model) and refer to [Pas03]. We note that there are even stronger versions, called *online* deniability [DKSW09] where the distinguisher can communicate with the malicious party resp. the simulator while the protocol is executed. This notion, however, is much harder to achieve and not known to work here.

*Deniability of Our Protocol.* Our deniable version of the Schnorr schemes works as before, only that this time we hash $(Y'_A, \mathcal{G})$ instead of $T_B$. We call this protocol the *deniable Schnorr-based PACE|AA protocol*. Roughly, the idea is now that the chip itself determines the challenge! Hence, given that the challenge can be determined beforehand, and that it is created independently of the first signature step one can simulate the final signature part as in the interactive Schnorr identification protocol [Sch91]. We only need to take care that the other security properties are not violated through this.

Note that security as an AKE protocol follows as in the Schnorr signature based version (with the very same bounds), even for such challenges, as discussed after Definition 1. It suffices to show impersonation resistance —which follows similar to the case of signatures, using the fact that the chip in the PACE protocol already provides some form of authentication through the token $T_A$— and to show deniability. We note that our deniability simulator will actually need some assistance in form of a decisional Diffie-Hellman oracle (which, for sake of fairness, we then also give the adversary and the distinguisher). We comment that this does not trivialize the task as such a decision oracle is not known to help compute discrete logarithms, such that the simulator cannot simply derive the chip's secret key from the public key and use this key to show deniability.

We omit a formal treatment of these two properties but merely sketch how the deniability simulator $S^{\mathcal{H}}$ works for this case. More insights can be found in the full version of this paper. The simulator only has access to the chip's public key $X_A$, the group data, and the password since it is considered a secret input to the terminal (but not the chip's secret key). The simulator now proceeds as follows, running a black-box simulation of the adversarial terminal (playing the honest chip). In each execution, the simulator initially picks values $y_A, y_A' \leftarrow \mathbb{Z}_q$ and computes $Y_A' = g^{y_A'}$ as well as $c = \mathcal{H}(Y_A', \mathcal{G})$ and $Y_A = X_A^{-c} g^{y_A}$. Note that both values are not computed according to the protocol description but still have the same distribution. In particular, even though the simulator may not be able to compute the shared Diffie-Hellman key $\mathcal{K}$ in the execution, it can later complete the signature generation by setting $s = y_A$ (such that $g^s = Y_A X^{\mathcal{H}(Y_A', \mathcal{G})}$). For the other steps the simulator proceeds as the chip would, using knowledge of the password. Only when the simulator receives $T_B$ from the malicious token, it searches (with the decisional Diffie-Hellman oracle) in the list of hash queries of the malicious terminal for queries about a key $DH(Y_A', Y_B')$. If no key is found, then abort this execution (this means that the adversary must have forged a MAC for an unknown key); else use the found key $\mathcal{K}$ to finish the execution (using the signature tokens as computed above). If the adversary stops, then let the simulator output the same value.

**Acknowledgments.** We thank the anonymous reviewers of FC'12 for helpful comments. This work was supported by CASED (http://www.cased.de).

# References

[AFP05]   Abdalla, M., Fouque, P.-A., Pointcheval, D.: Password-Based Authenticated Key Exchange in the Three-Party Setting. In: Vaudenay, S. (ed.) PKC 2005. LNCS, vol. 3386, pp. 65–84. Springer, Heidelberg (2005)

[BCI+10]  Brier, E., Coron, J.-S., Icart, T., Madore, D., Randriam, H., Tibouchi, M.: Efficient Indifferentiable Hashing into Ordinary Elliptic Curves. In: Rabin, T. (ed.) CRYPTO 2010. LNCS, vol. 6223, pp. 237–254. Springer, Heidelberg (2010)

[BFK09]   Bender, J., Fischlin, M., Kügler, D.: Security Analysis of the PACE Key-Agreement Protocol. In: Samarati, P., Yung, M., Martinelli, F., Ardagna, C.A. (eds.) ISC 2009. LNCS, vol. 5735, pp. 33–48. Springer, Heidelberg (2009)

[BLS01]   Boneh, D., Lynn, B., Shacham, H.: Short Signatures from the Weil Pairing. In: Boyd, C. (ed.) ASIACRYPT 2001. LNCS, vol. 2248, pp. 514–532. Springer, Heidelberg (2001)

[BPR00]   Bellare, M., Pointcheval, D., Rogaway, P.: Authenticated Key Exchange Secure against Dictionary Attacks. In: Preneel, B. (ed.) EUROCRYPT 2000. LNCS, vol. 1807, pp. 139–155. Springer, Heidelberg (2000)

[BPSV08a] Blundo, C., Persiano, G., Sadeghi, A.-R., Visconti, I.: Improved Security Notions and Protocols for Non-transferable Identification. In: Jajodia, S., Lopez, J. (eds.) ESORICS 2008. LNCS, vol. 5283, pp. 364–378. Springer, Heidelberg (2008)

[BPSV08b] Blundo, C., Persiano, G., Sadeghi, A.-R., Visconti, I.: Resettable and non-transferable chip authentication for e-passports. In: RFIDSec 2008 (2008)

[BSI10]   Advanced security mechanism for machine readable travel documents extended access control (eac). Technical Report (BSI-TR-03110) Version 2.05 Release Candidate, Bundesamt fuer Sicherheit in der Informationstechnik, BSI (2010)

358    J. Bender et al.

[DDN00]    Dolev, D., Dwork, C., Naor, M.: Nonmalleable cryptography. SIAM Jour-
           nal on Computing 30(2), 391–437 (2000)
[DF10]     Dagdelen, Ö., Fischlin, M.: Security Analysis of the Extended Access Con-
           trol Protocol for Machine Readable Travel Documents. In: Burmester, M.,
           Tsudik, G., Magliveras, S., Ilić, I. (eds.) ISC 2010. LNCS, vol. 6531, pp.
           54–68. Springer, Heidelberg (2011)
[DKSW09]   Dodis, Y., Katz, J., Smith, A., Walfish, S.: Composability and On-Line
           Deniability of Authentication. In: Reingold, O. (ed.) TCC 2009. LNCS,
           vol. 5444, pp. 146–162. Springer, Heidelberg (2009)
[ICA06]    Machine readable travel documents. Technical Report Doc 9303, Part 1
           Machine Readable Passports, 6th edn., International Civil Aviation Orga-
           nization, ICAO (2006)
[Ica09]    Icart, T.: How to Hash into Elliptic Curves. In: Halevi, S. (ed.) CRYPTO
           2009. LNCS, vol. 5677, pp. 303–316. Springer, Heidelberg (2009)
[ICA10]    ICAO. Supplemental access control for machine readable travel documents
           (2010), http://www2.icao.int/en/MRTD/Pages/Downloads.aspx
[Kra95]    Kravitz, D.W.: Digital signature algorithm. Computer Engineering 44(5),
           6–17 (1995)
[MVV07]    Monnerat, J., Vaudenay, S., Vuagnoux, M.: About machine-readable travel
           documents – privacy enhancement using (weakly) non-transferable data
           authentication. In: RFIDSEC 2007 (2007)
[Pas03]    Pass, R.: On Deniability in the Common Reference String and Random
           Oracle Model. In: Boneh, D. (ed.) CRYPTO 2003. LNCS, vol. 2729, pp.
           316–337. Springer, Heidelberg (2003)
[PS00]     Pointcheval, D., Stern, J.: Security arguments for digital signatures and
           blind signatures. Journal of Cryptology 13(3), 361–396 (2000)
[Sch90]    Schnorr, C.-P.: Efficient Identification and Signatures for Smart Cards. In:
           Brassard, G. (ed.) CRYPTO 1989. LNCS, vol. 435, pp. 239–252. Springer,
           Heidelberg (1990)
[Sch91]    Schnorr, C.-P.: Efficient signature generation by smart cards. Journal of
           Cryptology 4(3), 161–174 (1991)

# Oblivious Printing of Secret Messages in a Multi-party Setting

Aleksander Essex and Urs Hengartner

Cheriton School of Computer Science
University of Waterloo
Waterloo, ON, Canada N2L 2G1
{aessex,uhengart}@cs.uwaterloo.ca

**Abstract.** We propose oblivious printing, a novel approach to document printing in which a set of printers can cooperate to print a secret message—in human or machine readable form—without learning the message. We present multi-party protocols for obliviously printing a secret in three settings: obliviously printing the contents of a ciphertext, obliviously printing a randomized message, and generating and obliviously printing a DSA/Elgamal keypair. We propose an approach to improving the legibility of messages in the presence of numerous participants. Finally we propose some potential applications of oblivious printing in the context of electronic voting and digital cash.

## 1 Introduction

Since the days of Gutenberg the privacy model for document printing has been the same: a printer must learn the content of a message in order to print it. In this paper we take a fundamentally new approach to printing, one in which a human- or machine-readable message can be printed *without* the printers learning its content.

We believe oblivious printing can useful in a variety of real-world situations where it may advantageous to receive a secret in printed form. As an example, consider a scenario in which a user needs to receive a secret, but lacks access to the appropriate software, hardware or network infrastructure, such as in certain mobile or financial settings. Another potential scenario might be one in which a user needs to create a secret but does not understand how, or is otherwise unmotivated to take the proper steps to so securely, such as in the creation of strong passwords. Oblivious printing might even be useful when a user's computer cannot be trusted to handle a sensitive computation, such as in the case of internet voting. We describe several concrete applications later in the paper.

**The Oblivious Printing Model.** Oblivious printing is a protocol in which a group of printers cooperate to print a secret message. This message can be revealed and read by the intended recipient, but remains unknown to the printers. Oblivious printing is accomplished through a combination of cryptographic and document security techniques. The high level procedure is sketched as follows:

A.D. Keromytis (Ed.): FC 2012, LNCS 7397, pp. 359–373, 2012.
© International Financial Cryptography Association 2012

1. MESSAGE SELECTION: Printers execute a secure multi-party protocol to select a message (under encryption) from an alphabet of valid messages.
2. GRAPHICAL SECRET SHARING: Printers convert the message (under encryption) into a graphical image. Using a dealerless protocol they secret share the pixels between themselves.
3. INVISIBLE INK OVERPRINTING: Pixel shares are converted into a visual crypto pattern. Using invisible ink each printer successively prints their share on the same sheet of paper and in a known location/orientation.
4. MESSAGE RECOVERY: The recipient of the completed document activates the invisible ink of the combined shares (e.g., using a special activation pen), thereby revealing the message.

We presented a preliminary two-party protocol for oblivious printing of randomized messages based on oblivious transfers [10]. The techniques presented in this paper generalize the model to a fully multi-party setting. Additionally this approach allows for the secret message to be simultaneously output as an obliviously printed document and as an associated ciphertext allowing greater possibilities for integration into broader protocols.

**Contributions and Organization.** In this paper we present the oblivious printing paradigm and give three novel multi-party protocols: in Section 3 we present a protocol for obliviously printing the contents of an encrypted message, in Section 4 we present a protocol for obliviously printing a randomized message with improved contrast over the first protocol. We then present an extension to the second protocol for generating and obliviously printing an Elgamal/DSA keypair. In Section 5 we suggest a possible method for mitigating contrast drop-off as the number of printers increases based on the existence of AND-ing invisible inks. Finally in Section 6 we suggest some possible applications of oblivious printing for trustworthy electronic voting and electronic cash.

## 2   Preliminaries

### 2.1   Physical Security

Printing is ultimately a physical process, which means that any oblivious printing scheme will have a physical security component to it. In this paper we assume ideal security properties although we acknowledge in practice they can be challenging and costly to implement and difficult to guarantee.

**Invisible Ink.** Invisible ink is an ink that, as its name implies, is initially invisible when printed. The ink becomes visible (i.e., pigmented) after it is activated. Ideal invisible ink has two security properties,

- INVISIBILITY: Messages printed in invisible ink should be unreadable prior to activation,
- ACTIVATION-EVIDENT: Activated ink should always be plainly evident to anyone viewing the document.

Work has been done in developing invisible inks in the context of trustworthy optical-scan voting as part of the Scantegrity II system [5]. Ballots with confirmation codes printed in invisible ink were recently fielded in a live municipal election in the United States [4]. For the sake of our description we assume that there exists an ink printing process with the above properties.

**Document Authentication.** Techniques for determining a document's authenticity are an important component of oblivious printing. Ideally document authentication can efficiently and definitively distinguish between authentic and non-authentic (counterfeit) documents.

Anti-counterfeiting methods (e.g., watermarks, holographic foil, embedded magnetic strips, etc) exist but can be cost-prohibitive. It was shown by Buchanan et al. [3] that fiber patterns can be used to uniquely identify paper documents. Clarkson et al. [8] later developed a paper fiber identification method using commercial-grade scanners. Sharma et al. [24] implement a paper fingerprinting scheme based on texture speckles using a USB microscope costing under \$100.

For the sake of our description we assume that there exists an efficient scheme for determining a physical document's authenticity.

## 2.2  Visual Cryptography

A visual cryptography scheme (VCS) is a visual secret sharing scheme in which a (secret) message or graphical image is split into a number of shares. An early example of visual secret sharing is due to Kafri and Keren [16] (what they call "random grids"), although Shamir and Naor [18] are generally credited with the paradigm in the security literature. The latter outline a collection of visual crypto schemes for which the shares of some threshold $k > 2$ out of $n$ printers are necessary to recover the image and is denoted as $(k, n)$-VCS. Ateniese et al. [2] generalize this notion to access structures for which the message is recoverable under arbitrarily defined subsets of participants. A survey of a number of variations of visual cryptography is presented in [28].

**Optimal Contrast of an $(n, n)$-VCS.** An image is secret shared by a trusted dealer on a pixel-by-pixel basis. To share a pixel, the dealer issues each printer a unique and randomly assigned pattern of sub-pixels chosen to enforce the desired access structure. Shamir and Naor [18] prove the optimal number of sub-pixels for an $(n, n)$-VCS is $2^{n-1}$. In this scenario if the dealer wishes to share a black pixel, the shares are constructed such that when an authorized set of printers combine their shares, each of the resulting $2^{n-1}$ sub-pixels will be black. Similarly if the dealer wishes to share a white pixel, one of the resulting sub-pixels will be white (the other $2^{n-1}-1$ will be black). This is used to define a measure of contrast, $\alpha$, as being the relative difference in intensity between the combined shares resulting from a white pixel and a black pixel in the original image. The optimal contrast for an $(n, n)$-VCS is thus $\alpha = \frac{1}{2^{n-1}}$.

**Visual Crypto as Used for Oblivious Printing.** We make use of some aspects of visual cryptography for the purposes of oblivious printing; however there are several important differences with how it is typically presented in the literature:

1. INVISIBLE INK SHARES: Printers successively overprint their shares in invisible ink on a **single sheet of paper**. Activation of the combined invisible ink shares recovers the message.
2. DEARLERLESS SHARE CREATION: The message is distributed to shares by a multi-party computation.
3. FIXED SUB-PIXEL PATTERNS: Each printer has a fixed pair of sub-pixel patterns. Which of the two patterns the printer ends up printing is secret, but the patterns themselves are a public input to the protocol.

We will make use of a set of sub-pixel patterns that implement an XOR operation. Work has been done into visual cryptography in a variety of physically XOR-ing media including interferometers [17], light polarization [25], and even image reversal using modern photocopy machines [27]. In our approach, however, the XOR is approximated in an underlying physical medium (i.e., over-printed shares of invisible ink) that implements an OR.

**Definition 1.** *An n-input visual XOR, n-VCX, describes a set of sub-pixel patterns that visually implement an XOR of the input bits in a physically OR-ing medium.*

Let $S$ be an $n \times 2^{n-1}$ binary matrix for which each column is unique and has an even Hamming weight. Let $\overline{S}$ be the element-wise complement of $S$. Let sub-pixel pattern matrix $\Phi$ be as follows: $\Phi(l, 0) = S(l, :)$ and $\Phi(l, 1) = \overline{S(l, :)}$.

For a set of Boolean values $a_1 \ldots a_n \in \{0, 1\}$ and their associated logical exclusive-or $a' = \bigoplus_{i=1}^{n} a_i$, we say the sub-pixel pattern matrix $\Phi$ implements an n-input visual crypto exclusive-or, if the sub-pixel pattern produced by overlaying shares $\Phi(1, a_1) \ldots \Phi(n, a_n)$ has the following outcome: the total number of black sub-pixels is $2^{n-1} - 1$ if $a' = 0$, and respectively $2^{n-1}$ when $a' = 1$. If the $a_i$'s contain an even number of ones (i.e., the XOR is zero), then exactly one of the columns will end up with all 0's (i.e., a white sub-pixel) due to the way the matrix was designed and the pixel will be visually interpreted as white. If the $a_i$'s contain an odd number of ones (i.e., their XOR is one), all columns will contain a non-zero number of 1's due to the way the matrix was designed and the pixel will be visually interpreted as black. $\Phi$ implements an n-VCX.

*Example 1.* A 4-VCX: Let inputs $[a_1, a_2, a_3, a_4] = [1, 0, 0, 1]$ and,

$$
S = \begin{bmatrix}
0 & 0 & 0 & 1 & 0 & 1 & 1 & 1 \\
0 & 0 & 1 & 0 & 1 & 0 & 1 & 1 \\
0 & 1 & 0 & 0 & 1 & 1 & 0 & 1 \\
0 & 1 & 1 & 1 & 0 & 0 & 0 & 1
\end{bmatrix}.
$$

We have $\Phi(1, 1) = [1, 1, 1, 0, 1, 0, 0, 0]$, $\Phi(2, 0) = [0, 0, 1, 0, 1, 0, 1, 1]$, $\Phi(3, 0) = [0, 1, 0, 0, 1, 1, 0, 1]$, and $\Phi(4, 1) = [1, 0, 0, 0, 1, 1, 1, 0]$. When the vectors are OR-ed, it produces the sub-pixel pattern $[1, 1, 1, 1, 0, 1, 1, 1]$. Such a pattern is visually interpreted as intended, i.e., a white pixel with contrast $\alpha = \frac{1}{8}$.

# 3    Obliviously Printing an Encrypted Message

In this section we present a protocol for obliviously printing the contents of a ciphertext for which the associated plaintext is within a known, bounded, alphabet of $m$ possible valid messages. Given an encrypted plaintext $[\![p]\!]$, a set of $n$ printers $\mathcal{P}_1 \ldots \mathcal{P}_n$, each with a share of the decryption key, will jointly print $p$ as a $(u \times v)$-pixel image $I_p$ depicting $p$ in a human- or machine-readable form such that no printer learns $p$. We leave the origin of $[\![p]\!]$ generic although we envision it as being the output of some other (previous) multi-party computation.

## 3.1    Translation Table

A translation table is defined in which each element is a valid possible message that can be printed and for which each message consists of an association between a plaintext value and a bitmap that depicts it. The translation table is taken as input to the protocol and is used to facilitate the translation of a message—under encryption—from its plaintext form to its bitmap depiction.

Let translation table $T$ consist of $m$ message pairs representing the set of valid messages that can be printed. Each message pair $\langle t, I_t \rangle \in T$ consists of a plaintext value $t$ in the plaintext domain, and a $(u \times v)$-pixel monochrome bitmap $I_t$ depicting $t$ as a human- or machine-readable image. Each value $I_t(i, j) \in \{0, 1\}$ corresponds respectively to a white or black pixel.[1] We use the notation $[\![T]\!]$ to denote the element-wise encryption of $T$. Each message pair $\langle t, I_t \rangle \in T$, can be regarded as a vector of $uv + 1$ elements, $[t, I_t(0, 0), \ldots, I_t(u-1, v-1)]$ where each element is encrypted separately. The initial encryption of each element is taken with a known random factor (e.g., 0). Mixing $[\![T]\!]$ involves re-randomizing each element and shuffling by the message pair vectors.

In order to facilitate mixing and searching for elements in $[\![T]\!]$ under encryption, $|T|$ in practice will be small relative to the plaintext domain. Because $I_t$ will be encrypted at the pixel-level we note that for practical purposes the image size should be kept small. Using a technique described by Essex et al. [10], however, text can be optimized using segment-based display logic. A single alphanumeric character (or digit) can be fully described in 16 (respectively 7) encryptions regardless of the resolution of the visual crypto sub-pixel pattern used.

## 3.2    Setup

Let $\langle \mathsf{DKG}, \mathsf{Enc}, \mathsf{DDec} \rangle$ be an encryption scheme with distributed decryption. Distributed key generation $\mathsf{DKG(n)}$ generates a public key, $e$, and a private key share, $d_i$ associated with printer $\mathcal{P}_i$. Encryption $[\![m]\!] = \mathsf{Enc}_e(m, r)$ is semantically secure and homomorphic in one operation. Distributed decryption $\mathsf{DDec}_{d_i}(c)$ of a ciphertext $c$ is possible with all $n$ printers applying their shares $d_i$. Without loss of generality we use Elgamal [20].

---

[1] Printing uses a *subtractive* color model and thus the plaintext values assigned to color intensities are the reverse of that found in the computer graphics literature.

### 3.3 The Protocol

The protocol for obliviously printing a $p \in T$ given $[\![p]\!]$ is described in Protocol 1 and consists of Sub-protocols 1.1 and 1.2. Briefly, Sub-protocol 1.1 encrypts and mixes $T$ and searches it (under encryption) for the entry corresponding to $p$, outputting the associated encrypted bitmap. The process of searching the encrypted translation table for a value and outputting the associated encrypted image as described in Step 2 of Sub-protocol 1.1 is closely related to the Mix and Match system [13]. In Step 1 of Sub-protocol 1.2 the printers secret share a pixel by homomorphically XOR-ing it with random bits in a manner similar to the technique used by Cramer et al. [9].

**Finalization Layer.** Given $n$ printers note that Protocol 1 uses an $(n{+}1)$-VCX. An additional "finalization" layer allows the printers to verify the correctness of printing without ever revealing the message. For each pixel, each printer will generate a random bit, and using the sub-pixel pattern matrix, print it in invisible ink. A cut-and-choose proof is performed in Step 2 to demonstrate the printers correctly printed their random bits. Then an $(n{+}1)$-th finalization layer is computed by homomorphically XOR-ing the message bit with each of the random bits. Since the finalization layer is essentially a one-time pad, it can be decrypted without revealing the message. Finally, the finalization layer is printed using black ink, the correctness of which can be verified visually by inspection.

### 3.4 Obliviously Printing an Arbitrary Plaintext

In Protocol 1 we showed how to obliviously print a plaintext $p \in T$ given its encryption. As was previously mentioned, in order to make mixing and searching $[\![T]\!]$ feasible, $|T|$ will typically be quite small relative to the plaintext space.

We briefly sketch how any message from the plaintext space might be accommodated. To print an arbitrary $p$, first the printers would define an alphabet $\Sigma$ (e.g., the Latin alphabet) for which $p$ could be represented as a string $\Sigma^l$. The printers would execute a multi-party pre-protocol to convert $[\![p]\!]$ into a collection

---

**PROTOCOL 1 (Obliviously Print $p$ given $[\![p]\!]$)**

**Input:** Translation table $T$, encrypted plaintext $[\![p]\!]$, sub-pixel matrix $\Phi$ implementing an $(n{+}1)$-VCX, soundness parameter $\rho$.

**Output:** A document with a $(u \times v)$-pixel image depicting $p$, printed in invisible ink and with contrast $\alpha = \frac{1}{2^n}$.

**The protocol:**

1. TRANSLATE ENCRYPTED PLAINTEXT INTO ASSOCIATED PIXEL-WISE EN-CRYPTED IMAGE: Run Sub-protocol 1.1.
2. OBLIVIOUSLY PRINT ENCRYPTED IMAGE: Run Sub-protocol 1.2.

---

**SUB-PROTOCOL 1.1 (Translate $[\![p]\!]$ into $[\![I_p]\!]$)**

**Input:** Translation table $T$, encrypted plaintext $[\![p]\!]$.

**Output:** A $(u \times v)$ pixel-wise encrypted image of $p$ (i.e., $[\![I_p]\!]$).

**The protocol:**

1. ENCRYPT AND VERIFIABLY MIX TRANSLATION TABLE $T$: Each printer participates in a verifiable mix network, which encrypts and shuffles the message
   pairs $\langle t_i, I_{t_i} \rangle \in T$. The result is denoted $[\![T']\!]$.
2. FIND $[\![p]\!]$ IN $[\![T']\!]$: printers search $[\![T']\!]$ attempting to locate a $[\![t_i]\!]$ for which
   $t_i = p$:
   (a) For each message pair $\langle [\![t_i]\!], [\![I_{t_i}]\!] \rangle \in [\![T']\!]$, the printers perform a test of
       plaintext-equality between $[\![p]\!]$ and $[\![t_i]\!]$.
   (b) If a match is found, output the corresponding pixel-wise encrypted bitmap
       $[\![I_{t_i}]\!]$. If no match is found the protocol terminates and an error message
       is output.

*Remark: Various protocols exist for verifiable mix networks. One efficient and
statistically sound technique for multi-column mixing is due to Sako and Kilian
[23]. The plaintext equality test (PET) is due to Juels and Jakobsson [13].*

---

of ciphertexts $[\![p_1]\!] \ldots [\![p_l]\!]$ for which $p = p_1 || \ldots || p_l$ (a multi-party protocol for
extracting bit-fields under encryption is left to future work). The printers would
then run Protocol 1 for each $p_i$, printing the result on the same sheet of paper.

# 4   Obliviously Printing a Randomized Message

In this section we present a contrast optimization in the special case where the
printers are printing a randomized message $r \in_r T$. Although Protocol 1 can also
be used for this purpose the protocol presented in this section has a contrast of
$\alpha = \frac{1}{2^{n-1}}$ (as opposed to $\alpha = \frac{1}{2^n}$). Protocol 1 allows the printers to engage in
a cut-and-choose proof of correct printing without revealing $p$ directly. This is
done at the expense of contrast: the use of the finalization layer introduces an
additional layer forcing the $n$ printers use an $(n+1)$-VCX, which has half the
contrast relative to an $n$-VCX.

If the message is randomized, then revealing it as part of a cut-and-choose
process does not reveal information about the remaining (unactivated) messages.
So instead of partially printing $\rho$ copies of a single message $p$, auditing $\rho - 1$
copies and finalizing the remaining copy, the printers instead obliviously print $\rho$
complete and independently random messages, of which they audit $\rho - 1$. The
protocol is described in Protocol 2.

Arbitrary-length random messages can be built by repeated (independent)
executions of Protocol 2 on the same sheet of paper, which may be useful in the

**SUB-PROTOCOL 1.2 (Obliviously Print $[\![I_t]\!]$)**

**Input:** A $(u \times v)$ pixel-wise encrypted image $[\![I_t]\!]$, sub-pixel matrix $\Phi$ implementing an $(n+1)$-VCX, soundness parameter $\rho$.

**Output:** A document with $I_t$ printed in invisible ink with contrast $\alpha = \frac{1}{2^n}$.

**The protocol:**

1. OBLIVIOUSLY PRINT $\rho$ INSTANCES OF $I_t$: For each $1 \leq i \leq \rho$ :
   (a) PRINT A NEW INSTANCE (SHEET): For each pixel $[\![I_t(j,k)]\!]$:
      i. POST COMMITMENTS TO RANDOM BITS: Each printer $\mathcal{P}_{l \leq n}$ draws a random bit $b_{i,j,k,l} \in_R \{0,1\}$ and broadcasts a non-malleable commitment to it.
      ii. SECRET SHARE PIXEL: The $n$ printers jointly compute an encrypted finalization pixel $[\![f_{i,j,k}]\!] = [\![t(j,k) \oplus b_{i,j,k,1} \oplus \ldots \oplus b_{i,j,k,n}]\!]$ using a partially homomorphic XOR.
      iii. PRINT SUB-PIXEL PATTERN IN INVISIBLE INK: Each printer $\mathcal{P}_{l \leq n}$ records the unique physical characteristics of the paper sheet and overprints the sub-pixel pattern $\Phi(l, b_{i,j,k,l})$ in invisible ink on the $i$-th document instance at the position associated with pixel $(j,k)$.
2. PERFORM CUT-AND-CHOOSE PROOF OF CORRECT PRINTING: The printers select $\rho-1$ documents at random to audit (see remark). For each chosen sheet:
   (a) PROVE:
      i. UNVEIL COMMITMENTS: Each printer unveils their $uv$ commitments generated in Step 1a-i).
      ii. PROVE XOR: Each printer broadcasts their random factor used in computing the partially homomorphic XOR in Step 1a-ii).
      iii. ACTIVATE INVISIBLE INK: The printers collectively activate the invisible ink revealing the result of Step 1a-iii).
   (b) VERIFY: Each printer performs the following steps. If any of them do not hold, the protocol is terminated and an error message output:
      i. CHECK COMMITMENTS: Verify commitments produced in Step 2a-i).
      ii. CHECK XOR: Recompute the homomorphic XOR using $[\![t(j,k)]\!]$ and the random factors revealed in Step 2a-ii) and confirm the result equals the finalization pixel generated in Step 1a-ii).
      iii. CHECK PRINTING: For each pixel ensure the combined VC sub-pixel pattern created by the bits revealed in 2a-i corresponds to the printed version.
      iv. CHECK PAPER: Authenticate the sheet against those in Step 1a-iii.
3. FINALIZE THE REMAINING SHEET:
   (a) DECRYPT FINALIZATION LAYER: The printers decrypt the finalization pixels $[\![f_{i,j,k}]\!]$.
   (b) PRINT FINALIZATION LAYER: The printers authenticate authenticate the sheet. If the sheet is not recognized, the protocol terminates and an error message is output. Without loss of generality $\mathcal{P}_1$ prints the finalization layer: each pixel $\Phi(n+1, f_{i,j,k})$ is printed in black ink at the associated position. The other printers check the finalization layer is printed correctly. The resulting document is securely delivered to its intended recipient.

*Remark: A partially homomorphic XOR using exponential Elgamal is due to Neff [19]. The heuristic due to Fiat and Shamir [12] can be used to fairly select documents to audit.*

---

**PROTOCOL 2 (Obliviously Print a Random $r \in_r T$)**

**Input:** Translation table $T$, sub-pixel matrix $\Phi$ implementing an $n$-VCX, soundness parameter $\rho$

**Output:** A document with a $(u \times v)$-pixel image depicting a random $r \in_r T$, printed in invisible ink and with contrast $\alpha = \frac{1}{2^n - 1}$. Encrypted plaintext $[\![r]\!]$.

**The protocol:**

1. OBLIVIOUSLY PRINT $\rho$ INDEPENDENT RAND. MSGS.: For each $1 \leq i \leq \rho$:
   (a) SELECT RANDOM MESSAGE PAIR FROM $T$: Run Step 1) from Subprotocol 1.1 to generate $[\![T_i']\!]$. Without loss of generality the printers select encrypted message pair $[\![T_i'(0)]\!] = \langle [\![r_i]\!], [\![I_{r_i}]\!] \rangle$.
   (b) OBLIVIOUSLY PRINT $[\![I_{r_i}]\!]$: Run Step 1a) from Sub-protocol 1.2 with the following modifications:
      - Without loss of generality, the first $(n-1)$ printers $\mathcal{P}_{l < n-1}$ partially decrypt the secret shared pixel $[\![f_{i,j,k}]\!]$ created in Step 1a-ii) by applying their respective shares of the private key.
      - Similar to Step 1a-iii) each printer $\mathcal{P}_{l < n-1}$ overprints their VC subpixel pattern $\Phi(l, b_{i,j,k,l})$. Printer $\mathcal{P}_n$ decrypts the partial decryption of $[\![f_{i,j,k}]\!]$ and prints $\Phi(n, (b_{i,j,k,n} \oplus f_{i,j,k}))$ in invisible ink.
   (c) PERFORM CUT-AND-CHOOSE PROOF OF CORRECT PRINTING: The printers select and audit $\rho - 1$ documents as in Step 2) of Sub-protocol 1.1.
   (d) OUTPUT REMAINING SHEET: The remaining document $I_{r'}$ is securely delivered to its intended recipient. The associated ciphertext $[\![r']\!]$ is output.

---

creation of strong passwords, cryptographic keys or random tokens. Note in this setting the bit-field extraction step outlined in Section 3.4 would be unnecessary.

## 4.1 Generating and Obliviously Printing a DSA Keypair

One interesting variation of Protocol 2 might be generating and obliviously printing an DSA/Elgamal keypair for which the printers do not know the private key. This could potentially be an interesting approach to building a PKI in which a group of printers acting as a distributed CA issues keypairs in physical form.

Our initial work [10] allowed for the oblivious printing of random strings, but could not construct the associated ciphertext. In this paper we can obviously print random strings for which we have the associated ciphertext from which we can compute the associated public key.

The keypair can be rendered in a convenient encoding such as alphanumeric (e.g., Base64) or 2-D barcode (e.g., a QR-code). We note that 2-D barcodes often contain additional error correction information. Creating a valid error-correction codes under encryption is something we leave to future work. We present a protocol for generating and obliviously printing a DSA/Elgamal keypair in Protocol 3.

---

**PROTOCOL 3 (Generate and Obliviously Print an Elgamal Keypair)**

**Input:** A large prime $p = 2\alpha q + 1$ (for a small integer $\alpha$), a generator $g \in \mathbb{G}_q$, an encoding alphabet $\Sigma$ (e.g., Base64) for which $|\Sigma|$ is a power of 2.

**Output:** A document with public key $y = g^{sk}$ printed in black ink, and secret key $sk$ printed in invisible ink.

**The protocol:**

1. For $0 \leq i < \left\lfloor \dfrac{\log_2(q)}{|\Sigma|} \right\rfloor$:

   (a) INITIALIZE $T_i$: For $0 \leq j < |\Sigma|$: Add message pair $\langle g^{j+|\Sigma|i}, I_{\Sigma(j)} \rangle$ to $T_i$.
   (b) OBLIVIOUSLY PRINT PRIVATE KEY SEGMENT: Printing on the same sheet each time so as to build a string of characters, run Protocol 2 with $T_i$ as input, receiving an (encrypted) segment of the private key $c_i = [\![ g^{sk_i} ]\!]$.

2. RECOVER PUBLIC KEY: Printers decrypt $[\![ y ]\!] = [\![ g^{\sum_i r_i} ]\!] = \prod_i c_i$. Without loss of generality $\mathcal{P}_1$ prints the result in black ink and other printers confirm the value is correctly printed. The result is securely delivered to the intended recipient.

*Remark: If the secret key's bit-length does not evenly divide the encoding alphabet, the above loop is run one final time with a reduced alphabet $\Sigma' \subset \Sigma$ where $|\Sigma'| = \log_2(q) \bmod |\Sigma|$.*

---

## 5   Mitigating Contrast Drop-Off with AND-ing Inks

Using the basic invisible ink described above we note that contrast declines exponentially in the number of printers. In practice this greatly limits the number of printers that can participate and still produce a legible message. Other factors like image size, resolution and font play a role in legibility but in general we would not expect an obliviously printed document to be legible with more than about half a dozen printers.

We have discussed invisible ink in the context of a physical disjunction (i.e., an OR). In that setting a pixel will darken on activation if any of the shares contain invisible ink. However it seems invisible ink printing could offer other possibilities if the pigmentation reaction could be customized to realize a different logical construction. We briefly examine the properties that can be achieved if it were possible to formulate invisible inks that implement a physical conjunction (i.e., an AND). Chemically it seems possible such inks could be formulated; the basic ink process as described throughout this paper (cf. [4]) already forms a type of chemically-based conjunction between the invisible ink itself and the activating substance. Granted it would likely be a challenge to formulate conjunctive inks that were invisible for more than a small $k$. We are not aware of the existence of such inks. It is worth noting, however, that if such inks *could* be formulated, they have the potential, at least in theory, to achieve optimal contrast (i.e., $\alpha = 1$) in the presence of arbitrarily many printers.

**Definition 2.** *A set of $k$ inks are $k$-way conjunctive if, upon activation, a pixel darkens iff all $k$ inks are physically present.*

We denote an $n$-VCX implemented with $k$ such "AND-ing" inks as a $(k, n)$-VCXA. To create sub-pixel share matrix $\Phi$ in this setting we begin by constructing the $(n \times 2^{n-1})$ matrix $S$ (refer to Definition 1) and then evenly segmenting it into $\frac{2^{n-1}}{k}$ sub-matrices of size $(n \times k)$. Each sub-matrix represents a sub-pixel, and each element in the sub-matrix instructs the printer whether to print the associated ink in that sub-pixel or not. Using this approach a $(k, n)$-VCXA has a contrast $\alpha = \frac{k}{2^{n-1}}$ ($k$ is a power of 2 and the optimal contrast ratio remains $\alpha = 1$).

*Example 2.* A $(4,4)$-VCXA: Let inputs $[a_1, a_2, a_3, a_4]$ and $S$ be the same as in Example 1. The 4-way conjunctive inks are labeled $A, B, C,$ and $D$. Each share instructs the printer which of the four inks to print in each of the two-subpixels. The shares are: $\Phi(1,1) = [\{A, B, C\}, \{A\}]$, $\Phi(2,0) = [\{C\}, \{A, C, D\}]$, $\Phi(3,0) = [\{B\}\{A, B, D\}]$, and $\Phi(4,1) = [\{A\}, \{A, B, C\}]$. The conjunction of the shares produces $[\{A, B, C\}, \{A, B, C, D\}]$. Since the first sub-pixel will not contain the ink $D$ when the shares are printed, it will never activate. The second sub-pixel will contain all four inks when printed and therefore will darken when activated. The pixel therefore will contain one white and one black sub-pixel which is visually interpreted as intended, i.e., a white pixel with contrast $\alpha = \frac{1}{2}$. By comparison with Example 1 the contrast is 4x greater.

# 6    Example Applications

**Electronic Voting.** Cryptographically verifiable electronic voting is a natural application for oblivious printing. In this setting voters receive a receipt of their ballot that allows them to confirm their vote was correctly counted, yet without revealing it to anyone. A vital requirement of any secret ballot election employing the receipt paradigm is that no single party, *including* the ballot printer(s), may gain an advantage in deducing how a voter voted.

*Printing Verifiable Optical-scan Ballots.* Voting by paper optical-scan ballot is a common method used in the United States [26] today. However work into cryptographically verifiable optical-scan voting (cf. [5, 6, 21]) has continued to entrust ballot printers with secret and identifying information. Recently in [11] we presented a two-party approach to obliviously printing ballots based on the preliminary techniques in [10]. Through this work, we can extend it to a fully multi-party setting—a feature long realized in fully-electronic proposals.

*Multi-factor ballots for Internet Voting.* Internet voting has been a recent and popular topic of interest. One successful open-source and cryptographically-verifiable internet voting platform is Helios.[2] Helios accepts encrypted votes (along with zero-knowledge proofs of validity), which are then homomorphically tallied [1]. One fundamental and well-known limitation of this approach is that the voter's computer must be trusted to construct the encrypted ballot and is vulnerable to virus/malware. Using Protocol 3, encrypted Helios votes could be prepared on a voter's behalf and mailed to them on an obliviously printed ballot form. The voter would cast their vote by submitting the ciphertext corresponding to their candidate. Similarly, a verifiable internet voting scheme due to Ryan and Teague [22] proposes a multi-factor solution based on acknowledgment codes cards, which are mailed to the voter. The acknowledgment code cards contain secret information and so oblivious printing may of use here also.

*Coercion-resistant internet voting.* Beginning with Juels et al. [15], work into coercion-resistant internet voting has attempted to extend privacy protection to voters, even when casting their ballots in an unsupervised environment. Clark and Hengartner [7] propose a coercion-resistant scheme based in part on an in-person registration protocol requiring voters to select secret passphrases and be able to (privately) compute randomized encryptions of them. Such passphrases and their encryptions could instead be pre-computed and obliviously printed by a distributed election authority, potentially simplifying the in-person registration phase and simultaneously enforcing higher-entropy passphrases.

**Electronic Cash.** Bitcoin[3] is an interesting recent proposal for digital currency. Transactions are timestamped and inserted into a common transaction history (known as a "block chain") using a proof-of-work model. An account consists of a DSA keypair: a private signing key is used for sending funds and a public key is used for receiving them. A transaction consists of two components. The first component points to an earlier transaction in the block chain in which funds were sent to the account corresponding with the user's public key (and for which the funds have not already been spent). The second component involves the user signing the transaction (which includes the destination account) using the private signing key. Typically these keys are stored on a user's machine in a "wallet" file. One interesting alternative is Bitbills,[4] a service which issues Bitcoins in physical form. A Bitbill consists of a plastic card (similar to a credit card) corresponding to a set amount of Bitcoins. The associated private signing key is printed on the card as a 2-D barcode and hidden under a tamper-evident/holographic covering. The funds can be redeemed in by scanning the card with a smartphone.

Importantly, knowledge of the private signing key is necessary and sufficient to transfer funds and recent criminal activity has focused on stealing such keys from users' computersas well as online Bitcoin bank accounts[5]. Therefore any currency issuing service like Bitbills would have to be trusted never to redeem

---

[2] http://heliosvoting.org
[3] http://bitcoin.org
[4] http://bitbills.com
[5] http://mybitcoin.com/archives/20110804.txt

the cards it issues, and to prevent any private keys to fall into the hands of hackers. Oblivious printing could be used to create a *distributed* currency issuing service. With Protocol 3 adapted to an elliptic curve setting, keypairs could be generated and printed without any individual issuer knowing the private key thereby enforcing that only the cardholder can redeem the funds.

# 7   Security Analysis

We briefly sketch some of the security properties of our system. For space reasons we limit our discussion to Protocol 1 (i.e., Subprotocols 1.1 and 1.2).

**Cryptographic Security.** Informally there are two security properties we seek for the cryptographic component of the protocol. One is *integrity*: a printer should be convinced that the combined shares depict an image of the (encrypted) input. The other property is *secrecy*: an adversary in collusion with a subset of printers should not be able to determine the input.

We assume the commitment function is non-malleable, hiding and binding. The assumptions regarding encryption are stated in Section 3.2. The completeness, soundness and secrecy of Sub-protocol 1.1 follow directly from [14] [13]. If the printers follow Sub-protocol 1.2 they will always produce a finalization layer that, when XOR-ed with the individual shares, recovers the input. Secrecy of the commitments and encryptions follow from the assumptions. Secrecy of the decrypted finalization layer follows if one or more printers select random bits. Soundness is probabilistic and follows from the cut-and-choose proof. The independence of the random bits is enforced by the non-malleable commitment function. Correct computing of the homomorphic XOR is established by the cut-and-choose proof when printers reveal their commitments and the random factors used to compute the XOR.

**Physical Security.** For simplicity we proceed with our discussion of physical security in a setting in which the printers receive their shares from a trusted dealer through a private and authenticated channel. In the physical setting we seek two security properties. One is *integrity*: a printer should be convinced that the combined printed shares match the combined received shares. The other property is *tamper evidence* which is closely related to secrecy: an adversary should not be able to determine the output of the protocol without corrupting all printers or tampering with the document, which will then be evident.

We assume the invisible ink can only be read in its activated state and that activated ink is plainly evident. We assume that a sheet of paper can be authenticated. Completeness of Sub-protocol 1.2 is self-evident. Secrecy of the shares follows from the properties of an $n$-VCX. If a printer attempts to read the document by activating the ink it will be evident following from the assumptions of the invisible ink. If a printer attempts to replace a valid document with a fake it will be evident following the assumptions regarding document authentication. Soundness is probabilistic and follows the cut-and-choose proof. If a printer prints nothing in a sub-pixel where it was to print invisible ink, it will either be covered by invisible ink from another share, and does not alter the intended outcome, or, it will not be covered by another share in which case it will be detectable by the cut-and-choose and attributable by examining the electronic shares. If a printer prints invisible ink in a sub-pixel where it was to print nothing, it will be detected similarly but is not attributable.

It is important to note that nothing fundamentally prevents an adversary in physical possession a document from activating the ink and reading its contents. The severity of this threat will depend greatly on the use-case. For example if the document contains a *unique secret*, additional physical security measures are necessary to protect document secrecy. Alternatively if the document contains an *arbitrary secret* (e.g., a new password), it may suffice for the recipient of a tampered document to simply request it be invalidated and a new one be issued.

**Conclusion.** In this paper we introduced oblivious printing. We presented three protocols: a generic protocol for obliviously printing an encrypted plaintext, a protocol with improved contrast for obliviously printing a random message, and third protocol to generate and obliviously print a DSA/Elgamal keypair. We then proposed a contrast optimization based on the AND-ing invisible inks and provided some example applications for electronic voting and digital cash.

**Acknowledgements.** We thank Jeremy Clark, Ian Goldberg, and Doug Stinson for helpful feedback. The authors are supported in part by NSERC; the first through a Canada Graduate Scholarship, the second through a Discovery Grant.

# References

1. Adida, B., de Marneffe, O., Pereira, O., Quisquater, J.-J.: Electing a university president using open-audit voting: Analysis of real-world use of Helios. In: EVT/-WOTE (2009)
2. Ateniese, G., Blundo, C., Santis, A.D., Stinson, D.R.: Visual cryptography for general access structures. Information and Computation 129, 86–106 (1996)
3. Buchanan, J.D.R., Cowburn, R.P., Jausovec, A.-V., Petit, D., Seem, P., Xiong, G., Atkinson, D., Fenton, K., Allwood, D.A., Bryan, M.T.: Fingerprinting documents and packaging. Nature 436, 475 (2005)
4. Carback, R.T., Chaum, D., Clark, J., Conway, J., Essex, A., Hernson, P.S., Mayberry, T., Popoveniuc, S., Rivest, R.L., Shen, E., Sherman, A.T., Vora, P.L.: Scantegrity II municipal election at Takoma Park: the first E2E binding governmental election with ballot privacy. In: USENIX Security Symposium (2010)
5. Chaum, D., Carback, R., Clark, J., Essex, A., Popoveniuc, S., Rivest, R.L., Ryan, P.Y.A., Shen, E., Sherman, A.T.: Scantegrity II: end-to-end verifiability for optical scan election systems using invisible ink confirmation codes. In: EVT (2008)
6. Chaum, D., Ryan, P.Y.A., Schneider, S.: A Practical Voter-Verifiable Election Scheme. In: De Capitani di Vimercati, S., Syverson, P.F., Gollmann, D. (eds.) ESORICS 2005. LNCS, vol. 3679, pp. 118–139. Springer, Heidelberg (2005)
7. Clark, J., Hengartner, U.: Selections: Internet Voting with Over-the-Shoulder Coercion-Resistance. In: Danezis, G. (ed.) FC 2011. LNCS, vol. 7035, pp. 47–61. Springer, Heidelberg (2012)

8. Clarkson, W., Weyrich, T., Finkelstein, A., Heninger, N., Halderman, J.A., Felten, E.W.: Fingerprinting blank paper using commodity scanners. In: IEEE Symposium on Security and Privacy (2009)
9. Cramer, R., Damgård, I., Nielsen, J.B.: Multiparty Computation from Threshold Homomorphic Encryption. In: Pfitzmann, B. (ed.) EUROCRYPT 2001. LNCS, vol. 2045, pp. 280–300. Springer, Heidelberg (2001)
10. Essex, A., Clark, J., Hengartner, U., Adams, C.: How to print a secret. In: HotSec (2009)
11. Essex, A., Henrich, C., Hengartner, U.: Single layer optical-scan voting with fully distributed trust. In: VOTE-ID (2011)
12. Fiat, A., Shamir, A.: How to Prove Yourself: Practical Solutions to Identification and Signature Problems. In: Odlyzko, A.M. (ed.) CRYPTO 1986. LNCS, vol. 263, pp. 186–194. Springer, Heidelberg (1987)
13. Jakobsson, M., Juels, A.: Mix and Match: Secure Function Evaluation via Ciphertexts. In: Okamoto, T. (ed.) ASIACRYPT 2000. LNCS, vol. 1976, pp. 162–177. Springer, Heidelberg (2000)
14. Jakobsson, M., Juels, A., Rivest, R.L.: Making mix nets robust for electronic voting by randomized partial checking. In: USENIX Security Symposium, pp. 339–353 (2002)
15. Juels, A., Catalano, D., Jakobsson, M.: Coercion-resistant electronic elections. In: ACM WPES (2005)
16. Kafri, O., Keren, E.: Encryption of pictures and shapes by random grids. Optics Letters 12(6), 377–379 (1987)
17. Lee, S.-S., Na, J.-C., Sohn, S.-W., Park, C., Seo, D.-H., Kim, S.-J.: Visual cryptography based on an interferometric encryption technique. ETRI 24(5), 373–380 (2002)
18. Naor, M., Shamir, A.: Visual Cryptography. In: De Santis, A. (ed.) EUROCRYPT 1994. LNCS, vol. 950, pp. 1–12. Springer, Heidelberg (1995)
19. Neff, C.A.: Practical high certainty intent verification for encrypted votes. Technical report, VoteHere Whitepaper (2004)
20. Pedersen, T.P.: A Threshold Cryptosystem without a Trusted Party. In: Davies, D.W. (ed.) EUROCRYPT 1991. LNCS, vol. 547, pp. 522–526. Springer, Heidelberg (1991)
21. Popoveniuc, S., Hosp, B.: An introduction to punchscan. In: WOTE (2006)
22. Ryan, P.Y.A., Teague, V.: Pretty good democracy. In: Workshop on Security Protocols (2009)
23. Sako, K., Kilian, J.: Receipt-Free Mix-Type Voting Scheme- a Practical Solution to the Implementation of a Voting Booth. In: Guillou, L.C., Quisquater, J.-J. (eds.) EUROCRYPT 1995. LNCS, vol. 921, pp. 393–403. Springer, Heidelberg (1995)
24. Sharma, A., Subramanian, L., Brewer, E.: Paperspeckle: Microscopic fingerprinting of paper. In: CCS (2011)
25. Tuyls, P., Hollmann, H.D.L., van Lint, J.H., Tolhuizen, L.: Xor-based visual cryptography schemes. Designs Codes and Cryptography 37, 169–186 (2005)
26. United States Election Assistance Commission. 2008 election administration & voting survey report (2008)
27. Viet, D.Q., Kurosawa, K.: Almost Ideal Contrast Visual Cryptography with Reversing. In: Okamoto, T. (ed.) CT-RSA 2004. LNCS, vol. 2964, pp. 353–365. Springer, Heidelberg (2004)
28. Yang, C.-N. (ed.): Visual Cryptography and Secret Image Sharing. CRC Press (2011)

# Reverse Fuzzy Extractors: Enabling Lightweight Mutual Authentication for PUF-Enabled RFIDs

Anthony Van Herrewege[1], Stefan Katzenbeisser[2], Roel Maes[1], Roel Peeters[1], Ahmad-Reza Sadeghi[3], Ingrid Verbauwhede[1], and Christian Wachsmann[2]

[1] K.U. Leuven, ESAT/COSIC, Leuven, Belgium
{anthony.vanherrewege,roel.maes,roel.peeters,
ingrid.verbauwhede}@esat.kuleuven.be
[2] Technische Universität Darmstadt (CASED), Germany
katzenbeisser@seceng.informatik.tu-darmstadt.de
christian.wachsmann@trust.cased.de
[3] Technische Universität Darmstadt & Fraunhofer SIT Darmstadt, Germany
ahmad.sadeghi@trust.cased.de

**Abstract.** RFID-based tokens are increasingly used in electronic payment and ticketing systems for mutual authentication of tickets and terminals. These systems typically use cost-effective tokens without expensive hardware protection mechanisms and are exposed to hardware attacks that copy and maliciously modify tokens. Physically Unclonable Functions (PUFs) are a promising technology to protect against such attacks by binding security critical data to the physical characteristics of the underlying hardware. However, existing PUF-based authentication schemes for RFID do not support mutual authentication, are often vulnerable to emulation and denial-of service attacks, and allow only for a limited number of authentications.

In this paper, we present a new PUF-based authentication scheme that overcomes these drawbacks: it supports PUF-based mutual authentication between tokens and readers, is resistant to emulation attacks, and supports an unlimited number of authentications without requiring the reader to store a large number of PUF challenge/response pairs. In this context, we introduce reverse fuzzy extractors, a new approach to correct noise in PUF responses that allows for extremely lightweight implementations on the token. Our proof-of-concept implementation shows that our scheme is suitable for resource-constrained devices.

## 1 Introduction

Electronic payment and ticketing systems have been gradually introduced in many countries over the past few years. Typically, these systems use a large number of RFID-enabled tokens with constrained computing and memory capabilities (see, e.g., [35]). A fundamental security requirement in electronic payment and ticketing systems is *mutual authentication*: Only genuine tokens should be accepted by readers and only eligible readers should be able to modify the debit of a user's token. The widespread use of these systems makes them attractive

A.D. Keromytis (Ed.): FC 2012, LNCS 7397, pp. 374–389, 2012.

targets for different kinds of attacks. The most prominent example are attacks on widely used MiFare Classic tokens by NXP Semiconductors [35] that allow copying (cloning) and maliciously changing the debit of tokens [13]. Other MiFare products are claimed not to be affected. Existing solutions typically use cost-efficient tokens without expensive hardware protection mechanisms [35]. Hence, the authentication secrets of these tokens can often be recovered by basic side channel and invasive attacks, and used to emulate the token in software, which allows forging the information of the token (e.g., the debit of the ticket). To prevent such attacks, the secrets and information of the token should be cryptographically bound to the underlying RFID chip such that any attempt to extract or change them permanently deactivates the token.

In this context, Physically Unclonable Functions (PUFs) [31,27,2] promise to provide an effective and cost-efficient security mechanism. PUFs are physical systems embedded into a host device, that, when challenged with a stimulus, generate a noisy response. This means that, depending on environmental variations (e.g., temperature or voltage variations), a PUF will always return slightly different responses when challenged with the same stimulus. Further, due to manufacturing variations, responses to the same challenge vary across different PUFs and are typically hard to predict [27,2].

The common approach to authenticate a PUF-enabled token is querying its PUF with a challenge from a pre-recorded database of PUF challenges and responses. The token is accepted only if its response matches a PUF response in the database (such as in [32,6,10]). An alternative approach is using the PUF to generate the authentication secret of the token for use in a classical authentication protocol (such as in [38,34]). However, both approaches have serious drawbacks in practice: PUF-based key storage requires the token to reliably recover the (bit-exact) cryptographic secret from the noisy PUF response using some kind of error correction mechanism, which is expensive in terms of number of gates [12,7]. Further, existing PUF-based authentication schemes for RFID suffer from the following deficiencies: (1) there is no support for mutual authentication between token and reader; (2) most PUF types are vulnerable to emulation attacks [33] and would allow emulating the token in software; (3) some schemes are subject to denial-of-service attacks that permanently prevent tokens from authenticating to the reader [6]; and (4) all existing PUF-based authentication schemes are not scalable and allow only for a limited number of authentication protocol-runs since they rely on a database containing a large number of challenge/response pairs of the PUF of each token. It seems that emulation attacks could be mitigated by controlled PUFs [14]. However, controlled PUFs typically apply a cryptographic operation (such as a hash function) to the PUF response, which requires an expensive error correction mechanism on the token to maintain verifiability of the PUF.

*Our Contribution.* In this paper, we present the design and implementation of a new lightweight PUF-based authentication scheme for *mutual authentication* of

RFID tokens and readers. Our scheme supports an unlimited number of authentication protocol-runs, is resistant to emulation attacks, and does not require the reader to store a large number of PUF challenge/response pairs.

Furthermore, we introduce the concept of *reverse fuzzy extractors*, a novel approach to eliminate noise in PUF responses that moves the computationally expensive error correction process from the resource-constrained PUF-enabled token to the more powerful RFID reader. The resources required to implement our authentication scheme on the token are minimal since it is based on a reverse fuzzy extractor that requires significantly less hardware resources than the error correcting mechanisms used in existing PUF-based authentication schemes or PUF-based key storage.

*Outline.* In Section 2, we provide background information on Physically Unclonable Functions (PUFs). We propose reverse fuzzy extractors in Section 3 and present our PUF-based mutual authentication scheme in Section 4. We describe the implementation and evaluate the performance of our scheme in Section 5, and analyze its security in Section 6. Finally, we survey on related work in Section 7 and conclude in Section 8.

## 2    Background on Physically Unclonable Functions (PUFs)

A PUF is a noisy function that is embedded into a physical object, e.g., an integrated circuit [31,27,2]. When queried with a *challenge* $c$, a PUF generates a *response* $r \leftarrow \mathsf{PUF}(c)$ that depends on both $c$ and the unique device-specific intrinsic physical properties of the object containing the PUF. Since PUFs are subject to noise (e.g., environmental variations), they return slightly different responses when queried with the same challenge multiple times.

In literature, PUFs are typically assumed to be *robust, physically unclonable, unpredictable* and *tamper-evident*, and several approaches to heuristically quantify and formally define their properties have been proposed (see [2] for an overview). Robustness means that, when queried with the same challenge multiple times, the same PUF will return a similar response with high probability. Physical unclonability means that it is infeasible to produce two PUFs that cannot be distinguished based on their challenge/response behavior. Unpredictability requires that it is infeasible to predict the PUF response to an unknown challenge, even responses to other challenges can be obtained adaptively. Tamper-evidence means that any attempt to physically access the PUF irreversibly changes its challenge/response behavior.

There is a variety of PUF implementations (see [27] for an overview). The most appealing ones for integration into electronic circuits are electronic PUFs. The most prominent examples of this type are delay-based PUFs that exploit race conditions (arbiter PUFs [22,30]) and frequency variations (ring oscillator PUFs [15,37,28]) in integrated circuits; memory-based PUFs are based on the instability of volatile memory cells, like SRAM [16,18], flip-flops [26,23] and latches [36,21]; and coating PUFs [39] use capacitances of a dielectric coating applied to the chip housing the PUF.

| PUF Device | Verifier $\mathcal{V}$ |
|---|---|
| | DB |
| $r' \leftarrow \text{PUF}(c)$  $\xleftarrow{\;c,h\;}$  $(c,r,h) \in_R$ DB | |
| $r \leftarrow \text{Rep}(r',h)$ | |

| PUF Device | Verifier $\mathcal{V}$ |
|---|---|
| | DB |
| $r' \leftarrow \text{PUF}(c)$  $\xleftarrow{\;c\;}$  $(c,r) \in_R$ DB | |
| $h \leftarrow \text{Gen}(r')$  $\xrightarrow{\;h\;}$  $r' \leftarrow \text{Rep}(r,h)$ | |

(a) Typical use of fuzzy extractors    (b) Reverse fuzzy extractor concept

**Fig. 1.** Concept of fuzzy extractors and reverse fuzzy extractors

Note that the number of responses of a memory-based PUF is limited by the number of its memory cells. Further, most delay-based PUFs are subject to model building attacks [22,30,25,33] that allow emulating the PUF in software. To counter this problem, additional primitives must be used: Controlled PUFs [14] use cryptography in hardware to hide the responses of the underlying PUF to mitigate model building attacks. This requires correcting the noise of PUF responses before they are processed by the cryptographic operation to maintain verifiability of the PUF. The cryptographic and error correcting components as well as the link between them and the PUF must be protected against invasive and side channel attacks.

Many PUF-based applications, including PUF-based identification and key storage, require PUF responses to be reliably reproducible while at the same time being unpredictable [3,27,2]. However, since PUFs are inherently noisy and their responses are not uniformly random, they are typically combined with *fuzzy extractors* [12] (Figure 1(a)). Fuzzy extractors consist of a *secure sketch*, which maps similar PUF responses to the same value, and a randomness extractor, which extracts full-entropy bit-strings from a partially random source.

Secure sketches generally work in two phases: in the *generation phase* some *helper data* $h = \text{Gen}(r)$ is computed from PUF response $r$, which is used later in the *reproduction phase* to recover $r = \text{Rep}(r',h)$ from a distorted PUF response $r' = r + e$, where $e$ is the error caused by noise. An important property of secure sketches is that, after observing *one single* $h$, there is still some min-entropy left in $r$, which means that $h$ can be stored and transferred publicly without disclosing the full PUF response [12].

## 3   Reverse Fuzzy Extractors

Fuzzy extractors and secure sketches [12] are commonly used to correct noisy PUF responses on the PUF-enabled device, which is required when the PUF response is used in a cryptographic algorithm or protocol (such as in [14,11,38,3]). However, the underlying error decoding algorithms are typically complex and require a large number of gates and/or long execution times when multiple bit errors must to be corrected [12,7]. Hence, implementing the decoding algorithm on the PUF-enabled device is a huge disadvantage in many applications.

To overcome this problem, we propose *reverse fuzzy extractors* that allow for very compact and fast implementations of secure sketches and fuzzy extractors.

Instead of implementing the computationally intensive reproduction phase Rep(), we implement the much more efficient helper data generation phase Gen() on the PUF-enabled device and move Rep() to the typically more powerful verifier (Figure 1(b)). As a consequence, new helper data $h$ is generated each time the PUF is queried and the verifier corrects the reference value $r$ of its database to the noisy PUF response $r'$, which is different each time the PUF is evaluated.

There is one major pitfall that must be considered: Each execution of the helper data generator Gen() on a different noisy version of the same PUF response reveals new helper data. However, secure sketches give no guarantee about the min-entropy of the PUF response in case *multiple* helper data for different noisy variants of the same response is known [8]. Hence, reverse fuzzy extractors may leak the full PUF response, when Gen() and Rep() are based on a conventional fuzzy extractor. This is problematic in most PUF-based applications, such as controlled PUFs and PUF-based key storage (Section 2) that require at least some bits of the PUF response to be secret, and must be carefully considered when designing reverse fuzzy extractors.

We present an implementation of a reverse fuzzy extractor based on the syndrome construction [12], which is a secure sketch with a highly efficient helper data generation phase and that has been shown to ensure a certain amount of min-entropy in the PUF response even if multiple helper data for noisy variants of a response is known [8]. The syndrome construction implements the helper data generator $\mathsf{Gen}(r)$ as $h \leftarrow r \cdot H^T$, where $H$ is the parity check matrix of a binary linear block code and $h$ corresponds to the syndrome of $r$. The reproduction algorithm $\mathsf{Rep}(r', h)$ of the syndrome construction computes $r \leftarrow r' - e$, where $e$ is determined by decoding the syndrome $s = h - r' \cdot H^T$ using the decoding algorithm of the underlying error correcting code. Note that Gen() corresponds to computing a matrix product of the PUF response with the parity-check matrix $H$ of the underlying cyclic linear block code. Due to the special form of parity check matrices of these codes, this product can be computed very efficiently, as we show later when describing our prototype implementation in Section 5.

## 4    Our PUF-Based Mutual Authentication Scheme

A naive approach to authenticate a PUF-enabled RFID token is the following: The verifier sends a random PUF challenge from a reference database to the token and accepts the token only when its response is similar to the one in the database. However, since the token always responds to the same PUF challenge with a similar PUF response, replay attacks are possible. Moreover, for most PUF implementations, sending the PUF response in clear allows cloning the token by model building attacks [33]. Further, it is not trivial to authenticate the reader to the token following this approach.

Our scheme solves these problems by merging the idea of controlled PUFs [14] and logically reconfigurable PUFs [20]: We amend a PUF with a control logic that (1) hides the plain PUF response from the adversary and (2) allows dynamically changing the challenge/response behavior of the PUF in a random manner. Using reverse fuzzy extractors allows for a very compact implementation of our scheme that requires only minimal resources on the token.

## 4.1 System Model

The players in our scheme are (at least) a token issuer $\mathcal{I}$, a verifier $\mathcal{V}$ and a token $\mathcal{T}$. We denote the adversary with $\mathcal{A}$. Our scheme enables *mutual authentication* between $\mathcal{V}$ and $\mathcal{T}$. $\mathcal{V}$ has access to a database DB containing detailed information on all tokens $\mathcal{T}$ in the system. DB is initialized and maintained by $\mathcal{I}$.

## 4.2 Trust Model and Assumptions

*Issuer $\mathcal{I}$ and verifier $\mathcal{V}$.* We assume $\mathcal{I}$ and $\mathcal{V}$ to be trusted, which is a typical assumption in most RFID systems.[1] Further, $\mathcal{I}$ initializes $\mathcal{T}$ and $\mathcal{V}$ in a secure environment.

*Token $\mathcal{T}$.* We consider $\mathcal{T}$ to be a passive device that cannot initiate communication, has a narrow communication range (a few centimeters to meters) and erases its temporary state (all session-specific information and randomness) after it gets out of the electromagnetic field of $\mathcal{V}$. Further, we assume $\mathcal{T}$ to be equipped with a robust and unpredictable PUF (Section 2), a reverse fuzzy extractor (Section 3) and a lightweight hash function.

*Adversary $\mathcal{A}$.* As in most RFID security models, we assume $\mathcal{A}$ to control the wireless communication channel between $\mathcal{V}$ and $\mathcal{T}$. This means that $\mathcal{A}$ can eavesdrop, manipulate, delete and reroute all protocol messages sent by $\mathcal{V}$ and $\mathcal{T}$. Moreover, $\mathcal{A}$ can obtain useful information (e.g., by visual observation) on whether $\mathcal{V}$ accepted $\mathcal{T}$ as a legitimate token. Following the typical assumptions on PUF-based key storage (such as in [40,24,38]), we assume that $\mathcal{A}$ can read any information that is stored in the non-volatile memory of $\mathcal{T}$. However, $\mathcal{A}$ cannot access the responses of the PUF of $\mathcal{T}$ and cannot obtain temporary data stored in volatile memory (such as intermediate results of the computations) of $\mathcal{T}$ while it is participating in an authentication protocol. This can be achieved by using side-channel aware designs for the implementation of the underlying algorithms.

## 4.3 Protocol Specification

*System Initialization.* Token issuer $\mathcal{I}$ stores a random token identifier ID in the non-volatile memory of token $\mathcal{T}$. Moreover, $\mathcal{I}$ extracts $q > 0$ challenge/response pairs $(c_1, r_1'), \ldots, (c_q, r_q')$ from the PUF of $\mathcal{T}$ and stores them together with ID in database DB, which is later used by verifier $\mathcal{V}$ in the authentication protocol.

*Authentication Protocol.* The authentication protocol (Figure 2) works as follows: Verifier $\mathcal{V}$ starts by sending an authentication request auth to token $\mathcal{T}$,

---

[1] Note that there are papers considering revocation of malicious verifiers (such as in [4,29]). A simple approach to enable verifier revocation in our scheme is moving all computations of $\mathcal{V}$ to DB s.t. $\mathcal{V}$ has no access to the PUF challenge/response pairs.

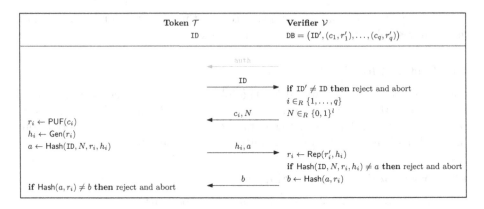

**Fig. 2.** Lightweight PUF-based mutual authentication protocol

which responds with its identifier ID. $\mathcal{V}$ chooses a random nonce $N$ and a random challenge/response pair $(c_i, r'_i)$ from database DB and sends $(c_i, N)$ to $\mathcal{T}$. Then, $\mathcal{T}$ evaluates $r_i \leftarrow \mathsf{PUF}(c_i)$, generates $h_i \leftarrow \mathsf{Gen}(r_i)$ using the reverse fuzzy extractor, computes $a \leftarrow \mathsf{Hash}(\mathtt{ID}, N, r_i, h_i)$ and sends $(h_i, a)$ to $\mathcal{V}$. Next, $\mathcal{V}$ reproduces $r_i \leftarrow \mathsf{Rep}(r'_i, h_i)$ using $r'_i$ from DB and checks whether $\mathsf{Hash}(\mathtt{ID}, N, r_i, h_i) = a$. If this is not the case, $\mathcal{V}$ aborts and rejects. Otherwise, $\mathcal{V}$ sends $b \leftarrow \mathsf{Hash}(a, r_i)$ to $\mathcal{T}$ and accepts. Eventually, $\mathcal{T}$ accepts if $\mathsf{Hash}(a, r_i) = b$ and rejects otherwise.

*Discussion.* Note that the case $q = 1$ is equivalent to PUF-based key storage, where $r_1$ represents the authentication secret of $\mathcal{T}$. In this case, $c_1$ can be stored in the non-volatile memory of $\mathcal{T}$ and needs not to be sent from $\mathcal{V}$ to $\mathcal{T}$. Hence, two protocol messages can be saved: $N$ can be sent with `auth` and ID can be sent with $(h_i, a)$. Using multiple challenge/response pairs corresponds to storing multiple (session) keys in the PUF, which limits the impact of side channel attacks that may recover only a subset of these keys.

## 5    Implementation and Performance Evaluation

We demonstrate the feasibility of reverse fuzzy extractors by presenting a prototype implementation of the protocol depicted in Figure 2. The prototype comprises three main primitives (Figure 3): A challenge expander, a syndrome generator and a hash function. A controller orchestrates these primitives to execute the protocol in the correct order.

The prototype is designed to be used with an arbiter PUF but can be easily modified to work with most existing intrinsic PUFs. The used arbiter PUF implementation accepts 64-bit challenges and generates 1-bit responses. Since our protocol requires multiple response bits, we use a linear feedback shift register (LFSR) to expand a single challenge $c$ into many consecutive 64-bit challenges $c'$, which are fed one after the other into the PUF. This allows generating PUF responses of arbitrary length for a single challenge. The expansion can be omitted for other PUF types that generate responses that have a sufficient length.

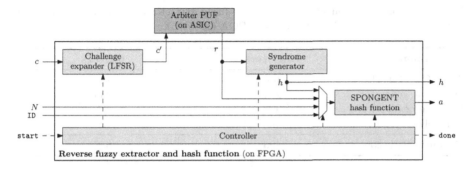

**Fig. 3.** Architecture of the reverse fuzzy extractor core

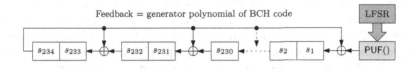

**Fig. 4.** Implementation of the syndrome generator

As described in Section 3, the syndrome generation consists of the matrix multiplication of an $n$-bit PUF response $r$ with the $n \times (n - k)$ parity check matrix $H^T$ of an error correcting linear block code. This $(n - k)$-bit result is called helper data $h$ for $r$ and can be used to correct a noisy version of $r$ if the number of bit errors is small enough. For our implementation, we use the parity-check matrix of a $[n = 255, k = 21, t = 55]$ BCH block code that can correct up to $t = 55$ erroneous bits in a $n = 255$ bit PUF response, using a $(n - k) = 234$-bit helper data vector. In case the probability of a single bit error is 10%, then the probability of observing more than 55 errors in 255 response bits (resulting in a decoding failure) will only happen with probability $10^{-7.82}$. Due to the special structure of parity-check matrices of BCH codes, the matrix multiplication can be efficiently implemented as an LFSR where the feedback polynomial is determined by the BCH code and the feedback bit is added to the next bit of the PUF response (Figure 4). The helper data must be sent from the token to the verifier, which causes an entropy loss of the actual PUF response of up to $n - k$ bits. Assuming the PUF response has full entropy, there will be only $k = 21$ bits of uncertainty left after observing the helper data. In order to obtain a security level equivalent to a 128-bit key, we need at least $\lceil 128/21 \rceil = 7$ responses, each 255 bits in length, and 7 corresponding helper data vectors. This leads to an overall PUF response length of $7 \cdot 255 = 1,785$ bits and an overall helper data length of $7 \cdot 234 = 1,638$ bits. The probability of an authentication failure due to a decoding failure in one of the 7 blocks is $1 - (1 - 10^{-7.82})^7 = 10^{-6.97}$. This means that this prototype implementation of the protocol achieves a false rejection rate of only one in approximately 10 million authentications. The final building block of our prototype is the lightweight hash function SPONGENT [5], which seems to be perfectly suited for resource-constrained tokens.

**Table 1.** Implementation size of the reverse fuzzy extractor core and its components when implemented on a Xilinx Virtex-5 FPGA (XC5VLX50)

| Component | Registers | 6-LUTs |
|---|---|---|
| SPONGENT hash | 146 | 160 |
| Syndrome generator | 234 | 235 |
| Challenge expander | 65 | 67 |
| Controller | 51 | 196 |
| Complete RFE core | 496 | 658 |

Table 1 provides the implementation size results when synthesizing our prototype design for a field-programmable gate array (FPGA). The target device is a Xilinx Virtex-5. The complete core (Figure 3) can be implemented using 496 one-bit flip-flops and 658 6-input lookup-tables (LUTs). We note that these results can be further optimized by designing specifically for implementation on FPGA. The HDL description of our design is platform independent.

# 6    Security Analysis

We now prove the security properties of our reverse fuzzy extractor construction and mutual authentication scheme. In this context, we formalize all necessary aspects and set up formal security definitions.

## 6.1    Security of the Reverse Fuzzy Extractor

*Secure sketch.* Let $M$ be a metric space with $n$ elements and distance metric dist. Moreover, let $C = \{w_1, \ldots, w_k\} \subseteq M$ be an error correcting code with codewords $w_i$ for $1 \leq i \leq k$. Let $d$ be the minimum distance and $t$ be the error correcting distance of $C$, which means that $C$ can detect up to $d$, and correct up to $t$ errors. In this paper, we only consider linear binary block codes, where $M = \mathbb{F}_2^n$ and dist corresponds to the Hamming distance. These codes are commonly denoted as $[n, k, d]$ codes and it holds $t = \lfloor (d-1)/2 \rfloor$. Following [12], we formally define a secure sketch as follows:

**Definition 1.** *A* $(M, m, m', t)$-*secure sketch is a pair of probabilistic polynomial time algorithms* Gen() *and* Rep() *with the following properties:* Gen() *takes input* $w \in M$, *which is chosen according to a distribution* $W$ *on* $M$, *and returns a bit-string* $h \in \{0, 1\}^*$. Rep() *takes inputs* $w' \in M$ *and* $h$, *and returns* $w'' \in M$. *Correctness ensures that* $w'' = w$ *if* $h = $ Gen$(w)$ *and* dist$(w, w') \leq t$. *The security property guarantees that for any distribution* $W$ *over* $M$ *with min-entropy* $m$, $w$ *can be recovered from (a single)* $h = $ Gen$(w)$ *with at most probability* $2^{-m'}$.

Next, we specify the syndrome construction that has been informally discussed in Section 3 and that has been shown to implement a secure sketch [12]:

**Definition 2.** *The syndrome construction is a* $(\mathbb{F}_2^n, n, k, t)$*-secure sketch (Definition1) that is based on a linear binary* $[n, k, d]$ *error correcting block code.* $\mathsf{Gen}(w)$ *computes* $h \leftarrow w \cdot H^T$, *where* $H$ *is the parity check matrix of the underlying code.* $\mathsf{Rep}(w', h)$ *computes* $w \leftarrow w' - e$, *where* $e$ *is determined by decoding the syndrome* $s = h - w' \cdot H^T$ *using the decoding algorithm of the underlying code.*

Note that helper data $h = w \cdot H^T$ corresponds to the syndrome of $w$. However, since the syndrome construction does not require $w$ to be a codeword, decoding $h$ may most likely fail. To overcome this problem, the reproduction algorithm $\mathsf{Rep}()$ of the syndrome construction decodes the syndrome $s = h - w' \cdot H^T = e \cdot H^T$.

*Security definition of reverse fuzzy extractors.* Similar to conventional fuzzy extractors, reverse fuzzy extractors should ensure that helper data does not leak the full PUF response. However, for reverse fuzzy extractors this must hold even when *multiple* different helper data for noisy variants of the *same* PUF response are known. This has been formalized by Boyen [8] as *outsider chosen perturbation security*, which is defined based on a security experiment between an unbounded adversary $\mathcal{A}$ and a challenger $\mathcal{C}_{\mathrm{PS}}$. In this experiment, $\mathcal{A}$ interacts with the helper data generator $\mathsf{Gen}()$ of a secure sketch (Definition 1) and obtains helper data for different $w_i = w + e_i$ for a fixed but secret $w$ and different noise vectors (perturbations) $e_i$ that can be adaptively chosen by $\mathcal{A}$. This allows $\mathcal{A}$ to influence the noise, which in case of PUFs can be done by changing the operating conditions such as ambient temperature or supply voltage. The outsider chosen perturbation security experiment is defined as follows: $\mathcal{A}$ sends a description of distribution $W$ over $\mathsf{M}$ to $\mathcal{C}_{\mathrm{PS}}$, which then samples $w \in \mathsf{M}$ according to $W$. Next, $\mathcal{A}$ interacts with $\mathsf{Gen}()$ and obtains an arbitrary number of helper data $h_i = \mathsf{Gen}(w_i)$ for different $w_i = w + e_i$, where $e_i \in \mathsf{M}$ can be adaptively chosen by $\mathcal{A}$ with the only restriction that the Hamming weight of $e_i$ is less or equal to $t$. Eventually, $\mathcal{A}$ returns a guess $w^*$ for $w$. $\mathcal{A}$ wins if $w^* = w$. Based on this security experiment, Boyen [8] sets up the following security definition:

**Definition 3.** *A* $(\mathsf{M}, m, m', t)$*-secure sketch (Definition 1) is unconditionally secure against adaptive outsider chosen perturbation attacks, if no unbounded adversary* $\mathcal{A}$ *can win the outsider chosen perturbation security experiment with probability greater than* $2^{-m'}$ *for any distribution* $W$ *over* $\mathsf{M}$ *with min-entropy* $m$.

Moreover, Boyen [8] shows that the at the syndrome construction achieves outsider chosen perturbation security:

**Theorem 1.** *The syndrome construction (Definition 2) is unconditionally secure against adaptive outsider chosen perturbation attacks (Definition 3).*

We now state the security of our reverse fuzzy extractor construction:

**Theorem 2.** *The reverse fuzzy extractor (Section 3) based on the syndrome construction (Definition 2) is a* $(\mathbb{F}_2^n, n, k, t)$*-secure sketch (Definition1) that achieves outsider perturbation security (Definition 3).*

*Proof (Sketch, Theorem 2).* Note that $\mathsf{Gen}()$ and $\mathsf{Rep}()$ of the syndrome construction and the the reverse fuzzy extractor based on the syndrome construction are identical. In fact, only the entities that execute Gen() and Rep() have been switched. Hence, it is easy to see that the syndrome construction and the reverse fuzzy extractor based on the syndrome construction are equivalent. Thus, since the syndrome construction is a $(\mathbb{F}_2^n, n, k, t)$-secure sketch, the reverse fuzzy extractor based on the syndrome construction is also a $(\mathbb{F}_2^n, n, k, t)$-secure sketch. Consequently, it follows from Theorem 1 that the reverse fuzzy extractor based on the syndrome construction achieves outsider perturbation security.    □

### 6.2   Security of the Authentication Protocol

*Correctness.* Correctness means that, in case token $\mathcal{T}$ and verifier $\mathcal{V}$ are honest, mutual authentication should be successful.

**Definition 4.** *A mutual authentication scheme is correct, if an honest $\mathcal{T}$ always makes an honest $\mathcal{V}$ accept, and an honest $\mathcal{V}$ always makes an honest $\mathcal{T}$ accept.*

**Theorem 3.** *The authentication scheme in Section 4.3 is correct, when based on a PUF that generates responses of length $n$ bits with at most $t$ bit errors, and a $(\mathbb{F}_2^n, n, k, t)$-secure sketch (Definition 1).*

*Proof (Sketch, Theorem 3).* It is easy to see that the protocol in Section 4.3 is correct if $\mathsf{Rep}(r_i', \mathsf{Gen}(r_i)) = r_i$ for all $(r_i, r_i')$. The correctness property of the $(\mathbb{F}_2^n, n, k, t)$-secure sketch (Definition 1) ensures that $\mathsf{Rep}(r_i', \mathsf{Gen}(r_i)) = r_i$ if $\mathsf{dist}(r_i, r_i') \leq t$. If the PUF generates responses of length $n$ bits with a bit error rate of at most $\rho$, then the probability of $\mathsf{dist}(r, r') \leq t$ can be expressed as the cumulative binomial distribution in $t$ with parameters $\rho$ and $n$. Note that $t$ is chosen such that this probability, which is an upper bound for the false rejection rate of the authentication, becomes very small. Hence, a $(\mathbb{F}_2^n, n, k, t)$-secure sketch can then recover $r$ from $r'$ with overwhelming probability.    □

Note that the implementation in Section 5 can handle PUFs with $\rho \leq 10\%$. When both verifier and token are trusted, it achieves an authentication failure rate of less than $10^{-6.97}$, which is acceptable for most commercial applications.

*Token Authentication.* Token authentication means that adversary $\mathcal{A}$ should not be able to make a legitimate verifier $\mathcal{V}$ to accept $\mathcal{A}$ as a legitimate token $\mathcal{T}$. Following [34,1], we formalize token authentication based on a security experiment, where $\mathcal{A}$ must make an honest $\mathcal{V}$ to authenticate $\mathcal{A}$ as $\mathcal{T}$. Hereby, $\mathcal{A}$ can arbitrarily interact with $\mathcal{T}$ and $\mathcal{V}$, which both are simulated by a challenger $\mathcal{C}_{\mathrm{TA}}$. However, since in general it is not possible to prevent simple relay attacks, $\mathcal{A}$ is not allowed to just forward all messages from $\mathcal{T}$ to $\mathcal{V}$.[2] This means that at least some of the protocol messages that made $\mathcal{V}$ accept must have been computed by $\mathcal{A}$. More specifically, the token authentication experiment is as follows: $\mathcal{C}_{\mathrm{TA}}$ initializes $\mathcal{T}$ and $\mathcal{V}$. Then, $\mathcal{C}_{\mathrm{TA}}$ initializes $\mathcal{A}$ with the public system parameters.

---

[2] Note that simple relay attacks can be mitigated by distance bounding techniques. However, for simplicity we excluded relay attacks because the main focus of the protocol is demonstrating the use of reverse fuzzy extractors.

Next, $\mathcal{A}$ can arbitrarily interact with $\mathcal{T}$ and $\mathcal{V}$ that are simulated by $\mathcal{C}_{\mathrm{TA}}$. Hereby, $\mathcal{A}$ can eavesdrop on authentication protocol-runs between an honest $\mathcal{T}$ and an honest $\mathcal{V}$, and manipulate protocol messages exchanged between $\mathcal{V}$ and $\mathcal{T}$. Further, $\mathcal{A}$ can start authentication protocol-runs as $\mathcal{V}$ or $\mathcal{T}$ with $\mathcal{C}_{\mathrm{TA}}$. $\mathcal{A}$ wins, if it makes $\mathcal{V}$ accept after a polynomial (in $l$) number of queries to $\mathcal{C}_{\mathrm{TA}}$.

**Definition 5.** *An authentication scheme achieves $\mu$-token authentication, if no probabilistic polynomial time adversary $\mathcal{A}$ wins the token authentication experiment with probability greater than $2^{-\mu}$.*

**Theorem 4.** *The authentication scheme in Section 4.3 achieves $k$-token authentication (Definition 5) in the random oracle model, when using the reverse fuzzy extractor (Section 3) based on the syndrome construction (Definition 2).*

In the following, we focus on the variant of our authentication scheme that uses only one single challenge/response pair, i.e., where $q = 1$ (Section 4.3). The proof can be easily extended for $q > 1$. Due to space restrictions we give only proof sketches and provide detailed proofs in the full version of the paper [17].

*Proof (Sketch, Theorem 4).* We show that, if there is an adversary $\mathcal{A}$ that violates token authentication (Definition 5) with probability greater than $2^{-k}$, then $\mathcal{A}$ can be transformed into an adversary $\mathcal{B}$ that violates outsider chosen perturbation security of the reverse fuzzy extractor (Theorem 2). Note that, in the chosen perturbation security experiment (Definition 3), $\mathcal{B}$ interacts with a helper data generator oracle $\mathsf{Gen}()$ that, when queried with $e_j$, returns $h_j = \mathsf{Gen}(r + e_j)$ for a fixed but unknown $r \in \mathbb{F}_2^n$. Based on this $\mathsf{Gen}()$-oracle, $\mathcal{B}$ simulates challenger $\mathcal{C}_{\mathrm{TA}}$ of the token authentication security experiment (Definition 5) such that $\mathcal{A}$ cannot distinguish between $\mathcal{B}$ and $\mathcal{C}_{\mathrm{TA}}$. Hereby, $\mathcal{A}$ and $\mathcal{B}$ have access to the same random oracle $\mathsf{Hash}()$, and $\mathcal{B}$ records all queries $x$ made by $\mathcal{A}$ to $\mathsf{Hash}()$ and the corresponding responses $\mathsf{Hash}(x)$ in a list $L$. Since, $\mathcal{A}$ cannot distinguish $\mathcal{B}$ from $\mathcal{C}_{\mathrm{TA}}$, by assumption $\mathcal{A}$ violates token authentication (Definition 5) with probability greater than $2^{-k}$. $\mathcal{B}$ uses $L$ to extract $r^* = r$ from the protocol message $(h, a)$ generated by $\mathcal{A}$ that finally makes $\mathcal{V}$ accept. Note that, the random oracle ensures that $(x, a) \in L$. Hence, $\mathcal{B}$ can extract $r$ with probability greater than $2^{-k}$, which contradicts outsider chosen perturbation security of the reverse fuzzy extractor (Theorem 2). $\qquad\square$

Note that in practice, the success probability $2^{-\mu}$ (Definition 5) of $\mathcal{A}$ may depend on the output length $t$ of the hash function implementing the random oracle: In case $t < k$ $\mathcal{A}$ could simply guess the correct hash digest $a$ with probability $2^{-t}$. For the implementation of the syndrome construction based reverse fuzzy extractor (Section 5), we have $t = 128 < k = 147$, and thus $\mu = 128$.

*Verifier Authentication.* Verifier authentication means that adversary $\mathcal{A}$ should not be able to make an honest token $\mathcal{T}$ to accept $\mathcal{A}$ as a legitimate verifier $\mathcal{V}$. This is formalized by a verifier authentication security experiment between $\mathcal{A}$ and a challenger $\mathcal{C}_{\mathrm{VA}}$ that is identical to the token authentication experiment with the only difference that $\mathcal{A}$ wins, if $\mathcal{A}$ makes $\mathcal{T}$ accept after a polynomial (in $t$ and the bit length of PUF responses) number of queries.

**Definition 6.** *An authentication scheme achieves $\mu$-verifier authentication, if no probabilistic polynomial time adversary $\mathcal{A}$ wins the verifier authentication experiment with probability greater than $2^{-\mu}$.*

**Theorem 5.** *The authentication scheme in Section 4.3 achieves $k$-verifier authentication (Definition 6) in the random oracle model, when using the reverse fuzzy extractor (Section 3) based on the syndrome construction (Definition 2), when the underlying PUF generates at least $\rho$ bit errors each time it is evaluated.*

*Proof (Sketch, Theorem 5).* We show that, if there is an adversary $\mathcal{A}$ that violates verifier authentication (Definition 6) with probability greater than $2^{-k}$, then $\mathcal{A}$ can be transformed into an adversary $\mathcal{B}$ that violates outsider chosen perturbation security of the reverse fuzzy extractor (Theorem 2). $\mathcal{B}$ simulates challenger $\mathcal{C}_{VA}$ of the verifier authentication security experiment (Definition 5) based on the Gen()-oracle such that $\mathcal{A}$ cannot distinguish between $\mathcal{B}$ and $\mathcal{C}_{VA}$ in a similar way as in the proof of Theorem 4. Hereby, $\mathcal{A}$ and $\mathcal{B}$ have access to the same random oracle, and $\mathcal{B}$ records all queries $x$ made by $\mathcal{A}$ to Hash() and the corresponding responses Hash($x$) in a list $L$. Since, $\mathcal{A}$ cannot distinguish between $\mathcal{B}$ and $\mathcal{C}_{VA}$, by assumption $\mathcal{A}$ violates verifier authentication (Definition 6) with probability greater than $2^{-k}$. $\mathcal{B}$ uses $L$ to extract $r^* = r$ from the protocol message $b$ generated by $\mathcal{A}$ that finally makes $\mathcal{T}$ accept. Note that, the random oracle assumption ensures that $(x, b) \in L$, while the bit errors in the PUF responses ensure that $\mathcal{A}$ cannot just replay an old $b$. Hence, $\mathcal{B}$ can extract $r$ with probability greater than $2^{-k}$, which contradicts outsider chosen perturbation security of the reverse fuzzy extractor (Theorem 2). ☐

# 7    Related Work

One of the first proposals of using PUFs in RFID systems is by Ranasinghe et al. [32], who propose storing a set of PUF challenge/response pairs (CRPs) in a database that can later be used by RFID readers to identify a token. The idea is that the reader queries the PUF of the token with a random challenge from the database and verifies whether the response of the token is similar to the database entry. One problem of this approach is that CRPs cannot be re-used since this enables replay attacks. Hence, the number of token authentications is limited by the number of CRPs in the database. This scheme has been implemented and analyzed by Devadas et al. [10]. Holcomb et al. [18] present a similar scheme based on an SRAM-PUF on RFID chips. Another approach to PUF-based authentication by Bolotnyy and Robins [6] aims to prevent unauthorized tracking of tokens. A major drawback of their scheme is that tokens can only be authenticated a limited number of times without being re-initialized, which enables denial-of-service attacks.

Tuyls and Batina [38] propose using a PUF to reconstruct the authentication secret of a token whenever it is needed instead of storing it in secure non-volatile memory. Since the key is inherently hidden in the PUF, obtaining the key by hardware-related attacks is supposed to be intractable. However, the scheme proposed by Tuyls and Batina [38] relies on public-key cryptography, which is still much too expensive for low-cost RFID tokens. Several other authentication schemes for RFID exist that use PUF-based key storage to protect against unauthorized tracking of tokens [9,34] and relay attacks [19]. However, these schemes require the expensive decoding operation of a fuzzy extractor to be implemented on the token, which is too expensive for low-cost RFIDs.

## 8    Conclusion

We presented a new lightweight PUF-based authentication scheme providing mutual authentication of RFID tokens and readers. Our scheme is resistant to emulation attacks, supports an unlimited number of token authentications, and does not require the reader to store a large number of PUF challenge/response pairs. Furthermore, we introduce the concept of *reverse fuzzy extractors*, a novel approach to correct noise in PUF responses moving the computationally expensive error correction process from the resource-constrained PUF-enabled token to the more powerful RFID reader. Reverse fuzzy extractors are applicable to device authentication and PUF-based key storage (where the key is used to communicate with an external entity) and can significantly reduce the area costs of secure PUF implementations. Future work includes a highly optimized implementation of our scheme and developing lightweight privacy-preserving authentication protocols based on PUFs and reverse fuzzy extractors.

**Acknowledgement.** This work has been supported in part by the European Commission under grant agreement ICT-2007-238811 UNIQUE.

## References

1. Armknecht, F., Chen, L., Sadeghi, A.R., Wachsmann, C.: Anonymous Authentication for RFID Systems. In: Ors Yalcin, S.B. (ed.) RFIDSec 2010. LNCS, vol. 6370, pp. 158–175. Springer, Heidelberg (2010)
2. Armknecht, F., Maes, R., Sadeghi, A.R., Standaert, F.X., Wachsmann, C.: A formal foundation for the security features of physical functions. In: IEEE Symposium on Security and Privacy, pp. 397–412. IEEE (May 2011)
3. Armknecht, F., Maes, R., Sadeghi, A.R., Sunar, B., Tuyls, P.: Memory Leakage-Resilient Encryption Based on Physically Unclonable Functions. In: Matsui, M. (ed.) ASIACRYPT 2009. LNCS, vol. 5912, pp. 685–702. Springer, Heidelberg (2009)
4. Avoine, G., Lauradoux, C., Martin, T.: When compromised readers meet RFID. In: The 5th Workshop on RFID Security, RFIDSec (2009)
5. Bogdanov, A., Knežević, M., Leander, G., Toz, D., Varıcı, K., Verbauwhede, I.: SPONGENT: A Lightweight Hash Function. In: Preneel, B., Takagi, T. (eds.) CHES 2011. LNCS, vol. 6917, pp. 312–325. Springer, Heidelberg (2011)
6. Bolotnyy, L., Robins, G.: Physically unclonable Function-Based security and privacy in RFID systems. In: IEEE International Conference on Pervasive Computing and Communications (PerCom), pp. 211–220. IEEE (2007)

7. Bösch, C., Guajardo, J., Sadeghi, A.-R., Shokrollahi, J., Tuyls, P.: Efficient Helper Data Key Extractor on FPGAs. In: Oswald, E., Rohatgi, P. (eds.) CHES 2008. LNCS, vol. 5154, pp. 181–197. Springer, Heidelberg (2008)

8. Boyen, X.: Reusable cryptographic fuzzy extractors. In: ACM Conference on Computer and Communications Security (ACM CCS), pp. 82–91. ACM (2004)

9. Bringer, J., Chabanne, H., Icart, T.: Improved Privacy of the Tree-Based Hash Protocols Using Physically Unclonable Function. In: Ostrovsky, R., De Prisco, R., Visconti, I. (eds.) SCN 2008. LNCS, vol. 5229, pp. 77–91. Springer, Heidelberg (2008)

10. Devadas, S., Suh, E., Paral, S., Sowell, R., Ziola, T., Khandelwal, V.: Design and implementation of PUF-based unclonable RFID ICs for Anti-Counterfeiting and security applications. In: International Conference on RFID, pp. 58–64. IEEE (2008)

11. Dodis, Y., Katz, J., Reyzin, L., Smith, A.: Robust Fuzzy Extractors and Authenticated Key Agreement from Close Secrets. In: Dwork, C. (ed.) CRYPTO 2006. LNCS, vol. 4117, pp. 232–250. Springer, Heidelberg (2006)

12. Dodis, Y., Reyzin, L., Smith, A.: Fuzzy Extractors: How to Generate Strong Keys from Biometrics and Other Noisy Data. In: Cachin, C., Camenisch, J.L. (eds.) EUROCRYPT 2004. LNCS, vol. 3027, pp. 523–540. Springer, Heidelberg (2004)

13. Garcia, F.D., de Koning Gans, G., Muijrers, R., van Rossum, P., Verdult, R., Schreur, R.W., Jacobs, B.: Dismantling MIFARE Classic. In: Jajodia, S., Lopez, J. (eds.) ESORICS 2008. LNCS, vol. 5283, pp. 97–114. Springer, Heidelberg (2008)

14. Gassend, B., Clarke, D., van Dijk, M., Devadas, S.: Controlled physical random functions. In: Computer Security Applications Conference, pp. 149–160. IEEE (2002)

15. Gassend, B., Clarke, D., van Dijk, M., Devadas, S.: Silicon physical random functions. In: ACM Conference on Computer and Communications Security (ACM CCS), pp. 148–160 (2002)

16. Guajardo, J., Kumar, S.S., Schrijen, G.J., Tuyls, P.: FPGA Intrinsic PUFs and Their Use for IP Protection. In: Paillier, P., Verbauwhede, I. (eds.) CHES 2007. LNCS, vol. 4727, pp. 63–80. Springer, Heidelberg (2007)

17. van Herrewege, A., Katzenbeisser, S., Maes, R., Peeters, R., Sadeghi, A.R., Verbauwhede, I., Wachsmann, C.: Reverse fuzzy extractors: Enabling lightweight mutual authentication for PUF-enabled RFIDs. Cryptology ePrint Archive (to appear)

18. Holcomb, D.E., Burleson, W.P., Fu, K.: Initial SRAM state as a fingerprint and source of true random numbers for RFID tags. In: Conference on RFID Security, RFIDSec (2007)

19. Kardas, S., Kiraz, M.S., Bingol, M.A., Demirci, H.: A novel RFID distance bounding protocol based on physically unclonable functions. Cryptology ePrint Archive, Report 2011/075 (2011)

20. Katzenbeisser, S., Koçabas, Ü., van der Leest, V., Sadeghi, A.-R., Schrijen, G.-J., Schröder, H., Wachsmann, C.: Recyclable PUFs: Logically Reconfigurable PUFs. In: Preneel, B., Takagi, T. (eds.) CHES 2011. LNCS, vol. 6917, pp. 374–389. Springer, Heidelberg (2011)

21. Kumar, S., Guajardo, J., Maes, R., Schrijen, G.J., Tuyls, P.: Extended abstract: The butterfly PUF protecting IP on every FPGA. In: IEEE Workshop on Hardware-Oriented Security and Trust (HOST), pp. 67–70 (2008)

22. Lee, J.W., Lim, D., Gassend, B., Suh, G.E., van Dijk, M., Devadas, S.: A technique to build a secret key in integrated circuits for identification and authentication application. In: Symposium on VLSI Circuits, pp. 176–159 (2004)

23. van der Leest, V., Schrijen, G.J., Handschuh, H., Tuyls, P.: Hardware intrinsic security from D flip-flops. In: ACM Workshop on Scalable Trusted Computing (ACM STC), pp. 53–62 (2010)
24. Lim, D., Lee, J.W., Gassend, B., Suh, G.E., van Dijk, M., Devadas, S.: Extracting secret keys from integrated circuits. IEEE Transactions on VLSI Systems 13(10), 1200–1205 (2005)
25. Lin, L., Holcomb, D., Krishnappa, D.K., Shabadi, P., Burleson, W.: Low-power sub-threshold design of secure physical unclonable functions. In: International Symposium on Low Power Electronics and Design (ISLPED), pp. 43–48 (2010)
26. Maes, R., Tuyls, P., Verbauwhede, I.: Intrinsic PUFs from flip-flops on reconfigurable devices. In: Workshop on Information and System Security (WISSec), p. 17 (2008)
27. Maes, R., Verbauwhede, I.: Physically unclonable functions: A study on the state of the art and future research directions. In: Towards Hardware-Intrinsic Security, pp. 3–37. Springer (2010)
28. Maiti, A., Casarona, J., McHale, L., Schaumont, P.: A large scale characterization of RO-PUF. In: IEEE Symposium on Hardware-Oriented Security and Trust (HOST), pp. 94–99 (2010)
29. Nithyanand, R., Tsudik, G., Uzun, E.: Readers behaving badly: Reader revocation in PKI-based RFID systems. Cryptology ePrint Archive, Report 2009/465 (2009)
30. Öztürk, E., Hammouri, G., Sunar, B.: Towards robust low cost authentication for pervasive devices. In: International Conference on Pervasive Computing and Communications (PerCom), pp. 170–178. IEEE (2008)
31. Pappu, R.S., Recht, B., Taylor, J., Gershenfeld, N.: Physical one-way functions. Science 297, 2026–2030 (2002)
32. Ranasinghe, D.C., Engels, D.W., Cole, P.H.: Security and privacy: Modest proposals for low-cost RFID systems. In: Auto-ID Labs Research Workshop (2004)
33. Rührmair, U., Sehnke, F., Sölter, J., Dror, G., Devadas, S., Schmidhuber, J.: Modeling attacks on physical unclonable functions. In: ACM Conference on Computer and Communications Security (ACM CCS), pp. 237–249 (2010)
34. Sadeghi, A.R., Visconti, I., Wachsmann, C.: Enhancing RFID Security and Privacy by Physically Unclonable Functions. In: Towards Hardware-Intrinsic Security, pp. 281–305. Springer (2010)
35. NXP Semiconductors: Web site of MiFare (December 2011), http://mifare.net/
36. Su, Y., Holleman, J., Otis, B.: A 1.6pJ/bit 96% stable chip-ID generating circuit using process variations. In: IEEE International Solid-State Circuits Conference (ISSCC), pp. 406–611 (2007)
37. Suh, G.E., Devadas, S.: Physical unclonable functions for device authentication and secret key generation. In: Design Automation Conference, pp. 9–14 (2007)
38. Tuyls, P., Batina, L.: RFID-Tags for Anti-counterfeiting. In: Pointcheval, D. (ed.) CT-RSA 2006. LNCS, vol. 3860, pp. 115–131. Springer, Heidelberg (2006)
39. Tuyls, P., Schrijen, G.J., Škorić, B., van Geloven, J., Verhaegh, N., Wolters, R.: Read-Proof Hardware from Protective Coatings. In: Goubin, L., Matsui, M. (eds.) CHES 2006. LNCS, vol. 4249, pp. 369–383. Springer, Heidelberg (2006)
40. Škorić, B., Tuyls, P., Ophey, W.: Robust Key Extraction from Physical Uncloneable Functions. In: Ioannidis, J., Keromytis, A.D., Yung, M. (eds.) ACNS 2005. LNCS, vol. 3531, pp. 407–422. Springer, Heidelberg (2005)

# CommitCoin: Carbon Dating Commitments with Bitcoin[*]
## (Short Paper)

Jeremy Clark[1] and Aleksander Essex[2]

[1] Carleton University
clark@scs.carleton.ca
[2] University of Waterloo
aessex@cs.uwaterloo.ca

**Abstract.** In the standard definition of a commitment scheme, the sender commits to a message and immediately sends the commitment to the recipient interested in it. However the sender may not always know at the time of commitment who will become interested in it. Further, when the interested party does emerge, it could be critical to establish when the commitment was made. Employing a proof of work protocol at commitment time will later allow anyone to "carbon date" when the commitment was made, approximately, without trusting any external parties. We present CommitCoin, an instantiation of this approach that harnesses the existing computational power of the Bitcoin peer-to-peer network; a network used to mint and trade digital cash.

## 1  Introductory Remarks

Consider the scenario where Alice makes a discovery. It is important to her that she receives recognition for her breakthrough, however she would also like to keep it a secret until she can establish a suitable infrastructure for monetizing it. By forgoing publication of her discovery, she risks Bob independently making the same discovery and publicizing it as his own.

Folklore suggests that Alice might mail herself a copy of her discovery and leave the letter sealed, with the postal service's timestamp intact, for a later resolution time. If Bob later claims the same discovery, the envelope can be produced and opened. In reality, this approach does not work as (among other shortcomings) most postal services are pleased to timestamp and deliver unsealed empty envelopes that can be retroactively stuffed with "discoveries."

In our approach, Alice will use a commitment scheme to put the discovery in a "digital envelope" which can be opened at some later time, but only by Alice. Alice can safely disclose the commitment value to anyone, but she does not know ahead of time that Bob will rediscover her breakthrough. Alice might attempt to reach Bob by broadcasting the commitment value to as many people as possible or she might have a trusted/distributed third party timestamp it, however she is neither guaranteed to reach Bob, nor choose a party that Bob will trust.

---

[*] Full version available: http://eprint.iacr.org/2011/677

A.D. Keromytis (Ed.): FC 2012, LNCS 7397, pp. 390–398, 2012.

Instead we show that Alice can produce a commitment and later convince Bob that the commitment was made at roughly the correct time, premised on the assumption that she does not have unusual computational power. We call this "carbon dating." We show a general approach to carbon dating using moderately hard puzzles and then propose a specific instantiation. CommitCoin harnesses the existing processing power of the Bitcoin network without trusting it, and is designed to leave the commitment value evident in the public Bitcoin transcript in a way that does not destroy currency. We use CommitCoin to augment the verifiability of a real-world election.

## 2    Preliminaries and Related Work

*Commitment Schemes.* Briefly, $\mathsf{Comm}(m, r)$ takes message $m$ and randomness $r$ and produces commitment $c$. $\mathsf{Open}(c, m, r)$ takes the commitment and purported message and returns accept iff $c$ is a valid commitment to $m$. Commitments should be binding and hiding. Respectively, it should be hard to find any $\langle m_1, m_2, r \rangle$ where $m_1 \neq m_2$ such that $\mathsf{Open}(\mathsf{Comm}(m_1, r), m_2, r)$ accepts, and it should be hard to find any $\langle m, r \rangle$ given $c$ such that $\mathsf{Open}(c, m, r)$ accepts.

*Secure Time-Stamping.* Secure time-stamping [18] is a protocol for preserving the chronological order of events. Generally, messages are inserted into a hash chain to ensure their relative temporal ordering is preserved under knowledge of any subsequent value in the chain. The chain is constructed by a distributed time-stamping service (TSS) and values are broadcast to interested participants. Messages are typically batched into a group, using a hash tree [4,3,7,27] or an accumulator [5], before insertion in the chain. Time-stamping is a mature field with standardization[1] and commercial implementations.

A secure timeline is a "tamper-evident, temporally-ordered, append-only sequence" of events [24]. If an event $E_{t_i}$ occurs at time $t_i$, a secure timeline can only establish that it was inserted after $E_{t_{i-1}}$ was inserted and before $E_{t_{i+1}}$ was. To determine $t_i$ by consulting the chain, one must either trust the TSS to vouch for the correct time, or, to partially decide, trust a recipient of a subsequent value in the chain to vouch for when that value was received (if at $t_j$, we can establish $t_i < t_j$). However should conflicting values emerge, implying different hash chains, there is no inherent way to resolve which chain is correct beyond consensus.

*Non-Interactive Time-Stamping.* An approach closely related to carbon dating is non-interactive time-stamping [25]. In such a scheme, stampers are not required to send any message at stamping time. The proposed scheme is in the bounded storage model. At each time interval, a long random bitstring is broadcast to all parties. Stampers store a subset that is functionally dependent on the message they are time-stamping. Verifiers also captured their own subset, called a sketch, at every time interval. This allows verification of the timestamp by anyone who

---

[1] ISO IEC 18014-3; IETF RFC 3161; ANSI ASC X9.95.

is participating in the protocol, but not by a party external to the protocol. By contrast, our notion of carbon dating allows verification by anyone but is not necessarily non-interactive.

*Proof of Work.* The literature considers applications of moderately hard functions or puzzles that take a certain amount of computational resources to solve. These are variably called pricing [14], timing [15], delaying [17], or cost [16,2] functions; and time-lock [29,6,22] or client [20,1,12,32,33,13,31,10,30] puzzles. Proof of work is sometimes used as an umbrella term [19]. Among other applications, proof of work can be used to deter junk email [14,16] and denial of service attacks [20,12,2,32,33], construct time-release encryption and commitments [29,6], and mint coins in digital currencies [28,2,26].

We consider proof of work as three functions: $\langle \mathsf{Gen}, \mathsf{Solve}, \mathsf{Verify} \rangle$. The generate function $p = \mathsf{Gen}(d, r)$ takes difficulty parameter $d$ and randomness $r$ and generates puzzle $p$. The solve function $s = \mathsf{Solve}(p)$ generates solution $s$ from $p$. Solve is a moderately hard function to compute, where $d$ provides an expectation on the number of CPU instructions or memory accesses needed to evaluate Solve. Finally, verification $\mathsf{Verify}(p, s)$ accepts iff $s$ is a correct solution to $p$.

*Time-Stamping & Proof of Work.* Bitcoin is a peer-to-peer digital currency that uses secure time-stamping to maintain a public transcript of every transaction [26]. However new events (groups of transactions) are appended to the hash chain only if they include the solution to a moderately hard puzzle generated non-interactively from the previous addition. Peers compete to solve each puzzle and the solver is awarded newly minted coins. A secure timeline with proof of work provides a mechanism to both limit the creation of new currency and to make it computationally difficult to change a past event and then catch up to the length of the original chain (peers accept the longest chain as canonical).

## 3   Commitments with Carbon Dating

A protocol for carbon dating commitments is provided in Protocol 1. It is a natural application of proof of work protocols but one that does not seem to have been specifically noted in the literature before.[2] Alice commits to a message $m$ and instantiates a puzzle $p$ based on the commitment value $c$ that will take, on expectation, $\Delta t$ units of time to solve. Alice begins solving $p$. Should a new party, Bob, become interested in when $c$ was committed to, Alice will later produce the solution $s$. When given $s$, Bob concludes that $p$, and thus $c$, were created $\Delta t$ time units before the present time. Since $p$ will not take exactly $\Delta t$ to solve, there is some variance in the implied instantiation time. We consider the case where Bob is only interested in whether the commitment was made well before a specific time of interest, which we call the pivot time.

If useful, a few extensions to Protocol 1 are possible. It should be apparent that carbon dating can be used for any type of sufficiently random message

---

[2] Concurrent to the review of this work, it is independently proposed and studied [23].

---

**PROTOCOL 1 (Commitments with Carbon Dating)**

**Input:** Alice has message $m$ at $t_1$.

**Output:** Bob decides if $m$ was known by Alice prior to pivot time $t_2$.

**The protocol:**

1. PRE-INSTANTIATION: At $t_0$, Alice commits to $m$ with randomness $r$ by computing $c = \mathsf{Comm}(m, r)$. She then generates puzzle based on $c$ with difficulty $d$ (such that the time to solve it is approximately $\Delta t$) by computing $p = \mathsf{Gen}(d, c)$. She outputs $\langle c, p \rangle$.
2. INSTANTIATION: At $t_1$, Alice begins computing $s = \mathsf{Solve}(p)$.
3. RESOLUTION: At $t_3 = t_1 + \Delta t$, Alice completes $s = \mathsf{Solve}(p)$ and outputs $\langle s, m, r \rangle$. Bob checks that both $\mathsf{Verify}(s, \mathsf{Gen}(d, c))$ and $\mathsf{Open}(c, m, r)$ accept. If so, Bob decides if $t_3 - \Delta t \overset{?}{\ll} t_2$

---

(e.g., plaintexts, ciphertexts, signatures, etc.) by replacing $c$ in $\mathsf{Gen}(d, c)$ with the message. Second, the commitment can be guaranteed to have been made *after* a given time by, e.g., including recent financial data in the puzzle instantiation [11]. Finally, the resolution period can be extended by instantiating a new puzzle with the solution to the current puzzle (assuming the puzzles are entropy-preserving; see [17] for a definition of this property).[3]

## 3.1   Puzzle Properties

For carbon dating, we require the proof of work puzzle to have specific properties. Consider two representative proof of work puzzles from the literature (and recall $c$ is the commitment value and $d$ is a difficulty parameter). The first puzzle ($\mathsf{P_{rs}}$), based on repeated squaring, is to compute $\mathsf{Solve}(d, c, N) = c^{2^d} \bmod N$ where $N = q_1 q_2$ for *unknown* large primes $q_1$ and $q_2$, and $2^d \gg N$ [29,6,21]. The second puzzle ($\mathsf{P_h}$), based on hash preimages, is to find an $x$ such that $y = \mathcal{H}(c, x)$ has $d$ leading zeros (where $\mathcal{H}$ is a cryptographic hash function)[4] [16,1,2,26]. We contrast the properties of $\mathsf{P_{rs}}$ and $\mathsf{P_h}$ with the properties of an ideal puzzle scheme for carbon dating ($\mathsf{P_{cd}}$).

$\mathsf{P_{cd}}$ should be moderately hard given a sufficiently random $c$ as a parameter. $\mathsf{P_{rs}}$ requires $d$ modular multiplications and $\mathsf{P_h}$ requires $2^{d-1}$ hashes on average. Neither precomputation, amortizing the cost of solving many puzzles, or parallelization should be useful for solving $\mathsf{P_{cd}}$. Parallelization is useful in solving $\mathsf{P_h}$, while $\mathsf{P_{rs}}$ is by design inherently sequential. $\mathsf{Verify}$ in $\mathsf{P_{cd}}$ should be efficient for

---

[3] It may be preferable to solve a chain of short puzzles, rather than a single long puzzle, to allow (by the law of large numbers) the average solution time to converge and to reduce the amount of time Bob must wait for the solution.

[4] Let $\mathcal{H} : \{0,1\}^* \rightarrow \{0,1\}^m$. Then for $d \leq m$, find any $x$ such that $y \in (\{0\}^d \| \{0,1\}^{m-d})$.

anyone. This is the case in $P_h$ but not $P_{rs}$, where efficient verification requires knowing the factorization of $N$,[5] making $P_{rs}$ useful only when the puzzle creator and solver are *different* parties.[6] When surveying the literature, we found that like $P_{rs}$ and $P_h$, each type of puzzle is either parallelizable or only verifiable by the puzzle creator. Designing a non-interactive, non-parallelizable puzzle appears to be an open problem.

Finally, we require a few properties specific to our scheme. It should be hard to choose $c$ such that the puzzle is not moderately hard. Given $s = \text{Solve}(\text{Gen}(d, c))$ and $s' = \text{Solve}(\text{Gen}(d, c'))$, it should be hard to find any pair of puzzles such that $s = s'$. Further, it should not be efficient to convert $\langle s, c \rangle$ into $\langle s', c' \rangle$.

### 3.2  Limitations

Aside from a good candidate for $P_{cd}$, the primary limitation to Protocol 1 is that the implied instantiation time is fuzzy. Carbon dating is best when the ratio between instantiation-to-pivot and pivot-to-resolution is maximized but the timing of the pivot is often unknowable. Another limitation is that Alice could commit to many different messages but only claim one. This excludes carbon dating (and non-interactive time-stamping) from, *e.g.*, predicting election results or game outcomes. Generally, the scheme only works for accepting a committed message from an exponentially large set. A final limitation is that Alice must devote a CPU to solely solving the problem for a long period of time. We address this last limitation with CommitCoin, and then latter provide an example where the first two limitations are not as applicable.

## 4  Carbon Dating with Bitcoin

Bitcoin is a peer-to-peer digital currency. A simplification of the scheme is as follows. Participants are identified by a public signing key. A transaction includes a sender, receiver, and amount to be transferred (units of bitcoins are denoted BTC), and it is digitally signed by the sender and broadcast to the network. Transactions are batched together (into a "block") and then appended to a hash chain ("block chain") by solving the $P_h$ hash puzzle on the block ($d = 53$ bits currently). The first node to broadcast a solution is awarded newly minted coins (currently 50 BTC) plus any transaction fees (currently optional). At the time of writing, one large Bitcoin mining pool, *Deepbit*, reports being able to compute $2^{42}$ hashes/second, while the network solves a puzzle on average every 10 minutes.[7]

---

[5] The totient of $N$ serves as a trapdoor: compute $\delta = 2^d \mod \phi(N)$ and then $s = c^\delta \mod N$.

[6] Alice could use $P_h$ with the smallest unfactored $N$ from the RSA challenges. Assuming continued interest in factoring these numbers, Alice's solution will eventually be verifiable. However she risks (a) it being factored before she solves the puzzle or (b) it never being factored at all. It also assumes non-collusion between Alice and RSA (assuming they know the factors).

[7] http://deepbit.net; http://blockexplorer.com/q/interval

---

**PROTOCOL 2 (CommitCoin)**

**Input:** Alice has message $m$, key pair $\langle sk, pk \rangle$ associated with a Bitcoin account. Without loss of generality the account has a balance of $>2$ BTC.

**Output:** The Bitcoin block chain visibly containing the commitment to $m$.

**The protocol:**

1. PRE-INSTANTIATION: At $t_0$, Alice does the following:
   (a) Alice commits to $m$ with randomness $r$ by computing $c = \mathsf{Comm}(m, r)$.
   (b) Alice generates new temporary key pair $\langle sk', pk' \rangle$ with $sk' = c$.
2. INSTANTIATION: At $t_1$, Alice does the following:
   (a) Alice generates transaction $\tau_1 = \langle pk \to pk', 2 \rangle$ to send 2 BTC from $pk$ to $pk'$ and signs it with randomness $\rho$: $\sigma_1 = \mathsf{Sign}_{sk}(\tau_1, \rho)$. She outputs $\langle \tau_1, \sigma_1 \rangle$ to the Bitcoin network.
   (b) Alice generates transaction $\tau_2 = \langle pk' \to pk, 1 \rangle$ to send 1 BTC from $pk'$ back to $pk$ and signs it with randomness $\rho'$: $\sigma_2 = \mathsf{Sign}_{sk'}(\tau_2, \rho')$. She outputs $\langle \tau_2, \sigma_2 \rangle$ to the Bitcoin network.
3. TAG & OPEN: At $t_2$, after $\tau_1$ and $\tau_2$ have been finalized, Alice generates transaction $\tau_3 = \langle pk' \to pk, 1 \rangle$ to send the remaining 1 BTC from $pk'$ back to $pk$ and signs it with *the same* randomness $\rho'$: $\sigma_3 = \mathsf{Sign}_{sk'}(\tau_3, \rho')$. She outputs $\langle \tau_3, \sigma_3 \rangle$ to the Bitcoin network.
4. EXTRACTION: At $t_3$, Bob can recover $c$ by extracting $sk'$ from $\sigma_2$ and $\sigma_3$.

*Remark: For simplicity we do not consider transaction fees.*

---

## 4.1 CommitCoin Protocol

If Alice can put her commitment value into a Bitcoin transaction, it will be included in the chain of puzzles and the network will provide carbon dating without Alice having to perform the computation herself. Bob only has to trust that Alice cannot produce a fraudulent block chain, longer than the canonical one and in less time. This idea has been considered on the Bitcointalk message board[8] in the context of the distributed network vouching for the timestamp. Our observation is that even if you do not trust the timestamp or any node in the network, the proof of work itself can be used to carbon date the transaction (and thus commitment value).

In a Bitcoin transaction, Alice has control over several parameters including her private key(s), her public key(s), and the randomness used in the signature algorithm which, importantly, is ECDSA. If she sets the receiver's public key[9] to be her commitment value $c$ and sends 1 BTC to it, the 1 BTC will be unrecoverable (akin to burning money). We consider this undesirable for two reasons: (a) it is financially wasteful for Alice and (b) it is not being a good citizen of the Bitcoin community.

---

[8] http://goo.gl/fBNnA
[9] Technically, it is a fingerprint of the public key.

By setting $c$ equal to a private key or the signature randomness and following the protocol, $c$ itself will never directly appear in the transcript. To get around this, Alice sets $c$ to the private key of a new account and then purposely leaks the value of the private key by signing two different transactions with the same randomness. The CommitCoin protocol is given in Protocol 2. Since $c$ is randomized, it has sufficient entropy to function (temporarily) as a secret key. A few bits of the secret key could be used as a pointer (*e.g.*, URL) to a place to post the opening of the commitment.

## 4.2    Implementation and Use with Scantegrity

An interesting application of carbon dating is in end-to-end verifiable (E2E) elections. Scantegrity is an election system where the correctness of the tally can proven unconditionally [9], however this soundness relies, in part, on commitments made prior to the election. If a corrupt election authority changed the pre-election commitments after the election without being noticed, an incorrect tally could be made to verify. It is natural to assume that many people may only become interested in verifying an election after it is complete. Since the pivot (election day) is known, the commitments can be made well in advance, reducing the uncertainty of the carbon dating protocol. Moreover, owing to the design of Scantegrity, invalid commitments will only validate negligibly, ruling out precommitting to many possible values as an attack. Scantegrity was used in the 2011 municipal election in Takoma Park, MD (for a second time [8]) and CommitCoin was used to provide carbon dating of the pre-election commitments.[10]

# References

1. Aura, T., Nikander, P., Leiwo, J.: DOS-Resistant Authentication with Client Puzzles. In: Christianson, B., Crispo, B., Malcolm, J.A., Roe, M. (eds.) Security Protocols 2000. LNCS, vol. 2133, pp. 170–177. Springer, Heidelberg (2001)
2. Back, A.: Hashcash: a denial of service counter-measure (2002)
3. Bayer, D., Haber, S.A., Stornetta, W.S.: Improving the efficiency and reliability of digital time-stamping. In: Sequences (1991)
4. Benaloh, J., de Mare, M.: Efficient broadcast time-stamping. Technical Report TR-MCS-91-1, Clarkson University (1991)
5. Benaloh, J.C., de Mare, M.: One-Way Accumulators: A Decentralized Alternative to Digital Signatures. In: Helleseth, T. (ed.) EUROCRYPT 1993. LNCS, vol. 765, pp. 274–285. Springer, Heidelberg (1994)
6. Boneh, D., Naor, M.: Timed Commitments. In: Bellare, M. (ed.) CRYPTO 2000. LNCS, vol. 1880, p. 236. Springer, Heidelberg (2000)
7. Buldas, A., Laud, P., Lipmaa, H., Villemson, J.: Time-Stamping with Binary Linking Schemes. In: Krawczyk, H. (ed.) CRYPTO 1998. LNCS, vol. 1462, p. 486. Springer, Heidelberg (1998)

---

[10] For full details, see http://eprint.iacr.org/2011/677

8. Carback, R.T., Chaum, D., Clark, J., Conway, J., Essex, A., Hernson, P.S., Mayberry, T., Popoveniuc, S., Rivest, R.L., Shen, E., Sherman, A.T., Vora, P.L.: Scantegrity II municipal election at Takoma Park: the first E2E binding governmental election with ballot privacy. In: USENIX Security Symposium (2010)

9. Chaum, D., Carback, R., Clark, J., Essex, A., Popoveniuc, S., Rivest, R.L., Ryan, P.Y.A., Shen, E., Sherman, A.T.: Scantegrity II: end-to-end verifiability for optical scan election systems using invisible ink confirmation codes. In: EVT (2008)

10. Chen, L., Morrissey, P., Smart, N.P., Warinschi, B.: Security Notions and Generic Constructions for Client Puzzles. In: Matsui, M. (ed.) ASIACRYPT 2009. LNCS, vol. 5912, pp. 505–523. Springer, Heidelberg (2009)

11. Clark, J., Hengartner, U.: On the use of financial data as a random beacon. In: EVT/WOTE (2010)

12. Dean, D., Subblefield, A.: Using client puzzles to protect TLS. In: USENIX Security (2001)

13. Doshi, S., Monrose, F., Rubin, A.D.: Efficient Memory Bound Puzzles Using Pattern Databases. In: Zhou, J., Yung, M., Bao, F. (eds.) ACNS 2006. LNCS, vol. 3989, pp. 98–113. Springer, Heidelberg (2006)

14. Dwork, C., Naor, M.: Pricing via Processing or Combatting Junk Mail. In: Brickell, E.F. (ed.) CRYPTO 1992. LNCS, vol. 740, pp. 139–147. Springer, Heidelberg (1993)

15. Franklin, M.K., Malkhi, D.: Auditable Metering with Lightweight Security. In: Luby, M., Rolim, J.D.P., Serna, M. (eds.) FC 1997. LNCS, vol. 1318, pp. 151–160. Springer, Heidelberg (1997)

16. Gabber, E., Jakobsson, M., Matias, Y., Mayer, A.: Curbing Junk E-Mail via Secure Classification. In: Hirschfeld, R. (ed.) FC 1998. LNCS, vol. 1465, pp. 198–213. Springer, Heidelberg (1998)

17. Goldschlag, D.M., Stubblebine, S.G.: Publicly Verifiable Lotteries: Applications of Delaying Functions. In: Hirschfeld, R. (ed.) FC 1998. LNCS, vol. 1465, pp. 214–226. Springer, Heidelberg (1998)

18. Haber, S., Stornetta, W.S.: How to Time-Stamp a Digital Document. In: Menezes, A., Vanstone, S.A. (eds.) CRYPTO 1990. LNCS, vol. 537, pp. 437–455. Springer, Heidelberg (1991)

19. Jakobsson, M., Juels, A.: Proofs of work and bread pudding protocols. In: Communications and Multimedia Security (1999)

20. Juels, A., Brainard, J.: Client puzzles: A cryptographic defense against con- nection depletion attacks. In: NDSS (1999)

21. Karame, G.O., Čapkun, S.: Low-Cost Client Puzzles Based on Modular Exponentiation. In: Gritzalis, D., Preneel, B., Theoharidou, M. (eds.) ESORICS 2010. LNCS, vol. 6345, pp. 679–697. Springer, Heidelberg (2010)

22. Mahmoody, M., Moran, T., Vadhan, S.: Time-Lock Puzzles in the Random Oracle Model. In: Rogaway, P. (ed.) CRYPTO 2011. LNCS, vol. 6841, pp. 39–50. Springer, Heidelberg (2011)

23. Mahmoody, M., Vadhan, S.P., Moran, T.: Non-interactive time-stamping and proofs of work in the random oracle model. IACR ePrint 553 (2011)

24. Maniatis, P., Baker, M.: Enabling the long-term archival of signed documents through time stamping. In: FAST (2002)

25. Moran, T., Shaltiel, R., Ta-Shma, A.: Non-interactive Timestamping in the Bounded Storage Model. In: Franklin, M. (ed.) CRYPTO 2004. LNCS, vol. 3152, pp. 460–476. Springer, Heidelberg (2004)

26. Nakamoto, S.: Bitcoin: A peer-to-peer electionic cash system (2008) (unpublished)

27. Preneel, B., Rompay, B.V., Quisquater, J.J., Massias, H., Avila, J.S.: Design of a timestamping system. Technical Report WP3, TIMESEC Project (1998)
28. Rivest, R.L., Shamir, A.: PayWord and MicroMint: Two Simple Micropayment Schemes. In: Lomas, M. (ed.) Security Protocols 1996. LNCS, vol. 1189, pp. 69–87. Springer, Heidelberg (1997)
29. Rivest, R.L., Shamir, A., Wagner, D.A.: Time-lock puzzles and timed-release crypto. Technical Report TR-684. MIT (1996)
30. Stebila, D., Kuppusamy, L., Rangasamy, J., Boyd, C., Gonzalez Nieto, J.: Stronger Difficulty Notions for Client Puzzles and Denial-of-Service-Resistant Protocols. In: Kiayias, A. (ed.) CT-RSA 2011. LNCS, vol. 6558, pp. 284–301. Springer, Heidelberg (2011)
31. Tritilanunt, S., Boyd, C., Foo, E., González Nieto, J.M.: Toward Non-parallelizable Client Puzzles. In: Bao, F., Ling, S., Okamoto, T., Wang, H., Xing, C. (eds.) CANS 2007. LNCS, vol. 4856, pp. 247–264. Springer, Heidelberg (2007)
32. Wang, X., Reiter, M.K.: Defending against denial-of-service attacks with puzzle auctions. In: IEEE Symposium on Security and Privacy (2003)
33. Waters, B., Juels, A., Halderman, J.A., Felten, E.W.: New client puzzle outsourcing techniques for DoS resistance. In: CCS (2004)

# Bitter to Better — How to Make Bitcoin
a Better Currency

Simon Barber [1], Xavier Boyen [1], Elaine Shi [2,*], and Ersin Uzun [1]

[1] Palo Alto Research Center
[2] University of California, Berkeley

**Abstract.** Bitcoin is a distributed digital currency which has attracted a substantial number of users. We perform an in-depth investigation to understand what made Bitcoin so successful, while decades of research on cryptographic e-cash has not lead to a large-scale deployment. We ask also how Bitcoin could become a good candidate for a long-lived stable currency. In doing so, we identify several issues and attacks of Bitcoin, and propose suitable techniques to address them.

## 1 Introduction

Bitcoin is a decentralized electronic cash system initially designed and developed by Satoshi Nakamoto (whose name is conjectured to be fake by some, and who has not been heard from since April 2011). The design of Bitcoin was first described in a self-published paper by Nakamoto [14] in October 2008, after which an open-source project was registered on sourceforge. The genesis block was established on January 3rd 2009, and the project was announced on the Cryptography mailing list on January 11th 2009.

Since its invention, Bitcoin has gained amazing popularity and much attention from the press. At the time of the writing, approximately 7M Bitcoins are in circulation; approximately USD $2M to $5M worth of transactions take place each day in Bitcoin; and about eighteen Bitcoin exchanges exist offering exchange services with many real world currencies, (e.g., EUR, USD, CAD, GBP, PLN, JPY, HKD, SEK, AUD, CHF, and so on). Bitcoin's exchange rate has varied widely, reaching as high as USD $30 per Bitcoin although at the time of writing is around USD $5 per Bitcoin.

Despite some pessimists' critiques and disbelief, Bitcoin has admittedly witnessed enormous success since its invention. To the security and cryptographic community, the idea of digital currency or electronic cash is by no means new. As early as 1982, Chaum has outlined his blueprint of an anonymous e-cash scheme in his pioneering paper [10]. Ever since then, hundreds of academic papers have been published to improve the efficiency and security of e-cash constructions — to name a few, see [15,8,9].

Naturally, an interesting question arises: *Despite three decades' research on e-cash, why have e-cash schemes not taken off, while Bitcoin — a system designed and initially implemented possibly single-handedly by someone previously unknown, a system that uses no fancy cryptography, and is by no means perfect — has enjoyed a swift rise to success?* Looking forward, one also wonders: *Does Bitcoin have what it takes to become a serious candidate for a long-lived stable currency, or is it yet another transient fad?*

---

* Work done while author was affiliated with PARC.

A.D. Keromytis (Ed.): FC 2012, LNCS 7397, pp. 399–414, 2012.

Intrigued by these questions, we investigated Bitcoin's design and history, and came to many interesting realizations. We therefore present this paper to the (financial) cryptography research community, with the following goals and expectations:

1. To investigate the Bitcoin phenomenon, and achieve a deeper understanding of the crucial factors underlying its success, especially compared to other e-cash schemes.
2. To scrutinize the design of Bitcoin and analyze its strengths and weakness, in order to expose and anticipate potential attacks, and focus investigation on key issues;
3. To suggest redesigns, improvements, or extensions, such as, e.g., our fail-safe mixer protocol that requires no third-party and no system modification (Section 7).
4. To pose open research problems stemming from our broad reflections on Bitcoin;
5. Last but not least, to bring Bitcoin to the attention of the cryptography research community, to encourage it to reflect on its success, and draw lessons therein.

## 2   The Intriguing Success of Bitcoin: A Comparative Study

As mentioned earlier, despite three decades' research on e-cash by the cryptographic community [10,15,8,9], all these efforts seem to have been dwindled by the swift success of Bitcoin. Has Nakamoto, a single individual whose name previously unheard of, outsmarted the ingenuity of all the cryptographers combined? Bitcoin is by no means perfect and some well-known problems are discussed later on. So what is it in Bitcoin that has ensured its success?

After an in-depth investigation of Bitcoin, we found that although Bitcoin uses no fancy cryptography, its design actually reflects a suprising amount of ingenuity and sophistication. Most importantly, it addresses the *incentive* problems most expeditiously.

**No Central Point of Trust.** Bitcoin has a completely distributed architecture, without any single trusted entity. Bitcoin assumes that the majority of nodes in its network are honest, and resorts to a majority vote mechanism for double spending avoidance, and dispute resolution. In contrast, most e-cash schemes require a centralized bank who is trusted for purposes of e-cash issuance, and double-spending detection. This greatly appeals to individuals who wish for a freely-traded currency not in control by any governments, banks, or authorities — from libertarians to drug-dealers and other underground economy proponents (note that apart from the aforementioned illegal usages, there are numerous legitimate uses as well, which will be mentioned later). In a spirit similar to the original motivation for a distributed Internet, such a purely decentralized system guarantees that no single entity, no matter how initially benevolent, can succumb to the temptation or be coerced by a government into subverting it for its own benefit.

**Incentives and Economic System.** Bitcoin's *eco-system* is ingeniously designed, and ensures that users have economic incentives to participate. First, the generation of new bitcoins happens in a distributed fashion at a predictable rate: "bitcoin *miners*" solve computational puzzles to generate new bitcoins, and this process is closely coupled with the verification of previous transactions. At the same time, miners also get to collect optional transaction fees for their effort of vetting said transactions. This gives users clear economic incentives to invest spare computing cycles in the verification of Bitcoin transactions and the generation of new Bitcoins. At the time of writing the investment of a GPU to accelerate Bitcoin puzzle solution can pay for itself in ∼6 months.

**Predictable Money Supply.** Bitcoin makes sure that new coins will be minted at a fixed rate, that is, the larger the Bitcoin community and the total computational resource devoted to coin generation, the more difficult the computational puzzle becomes. This provides strong incentives for early adopters — the earlier in the game, the cheaper the coins minted. (In a later section we discuss negative consequences that the adopted money supply schedule will have, in the long term, on value, incentives, and security.)

**Divisibility and Fungibility.** One practical appeal of Bitcoin is the ease with which coins can be both divided and recombined to create essentially any denomination possible. This is an Achilles' heel of (strongly anonymous) e-cash systems, because denominations had to be standardized to be unlinkable, which incidentally makes the computational cost of e-cash transactions linear in the amount. In Bitcoin, linkage is inherent, as it is what prevents double spending; but it is the identities that are "anonymous".

**Versatility, Openness, and Vibrancy.** Bitcoin is remarkably flexible partly due to its completely distributed design. The open-source nature of the project entices the creation of new applications and spurs new businesses. Because of its flexibility and openness, a rich extended ecosystem surrounding Bitcoin is flourishing. For example, *mixer* services have spawned to cater to users who need better anonymity guarantees (see Section 7 for details). There are payment processor services that offer gadgets venders can embed in their webpages to receive Bitcoin payments alongside regular currency.

**Scripting.** Another salient and very innovative feature is allowing users (payers and payees) to embed scripts in their Bitcoin transactions. Although today's reference implementations have not fully utilized the power of this feature, in theory, one can realize rich transactional semantics and contracts through scripts [2], such as deposits, escrow and dispute mediation, assurance contracts, including the use of external states, and so on. It is conceivable that in the future, richer forms of financial contracts and mechanisms are going to be built around Bitcoin using this feature.

**Transaction Irreversibility.** Bitcoin transactions quickly become irreversible. This attracts a niche market where vendors are concerned about credit-card fraud and charge-backs. Through personal communication with a vendor selling specialty magazines, he mentioned that before, he could not conduct business with customers in certain countries where credit-card fraud prevails. With Bitcoin, he is able to extend his business to these countries due to the protection he obtains from the irreversibility of transactions.

**Low Fees and Friction.** The Bitcoin verifiers' market currently bears very low transaction fees (which are optional and chosen by the payer); this can be attractive in micropayments where fees can dominate. Bitcoin is also appealing for its lack of additional costs traditionally tacked upon international money transfers, due to disintermediation.

**Readily Available Implementations.** Last but not the least, in comparison with other e-cash schemes, Bitcoin has provided readily available implementations, not only for the desktop computer, but also for mobile phones. The open-source project is maintained by a vibrant community, and has had healthy developments.

# 3    Under the Hood of the Bitcoin System

Bitcoin is based on a peer-to-peer network layer that broadcasts data to all nodes on the network. There are two types of object that are broadcast: transactions and blocks. Both object types are addressed by a hash of the object data, and are broadcast through the network to all nodes. Transactions are the operations whereby money is combined, divided, and remitted. Blocks record the transactions vetted as valid.

**Spending.** Suppose that Alice wishes to remit 1 bitcoin to Bob and 2 to Carol. Alice's coins "reside" in prior transactions that designate her public key as beneficiary. To spend coins, Alice creates a new transaction that endorses any such coins she has not spent yet, e.g., she can endorse, using a digital signature, 4 coins each received from Diane and Edgar as the *inputs* of her new transaction. As *outputs* she specifies 1 coin for Bob, 2 for Carol, and 4.99 of "change" back to herself. In this example, Alice chose to leave a residual of 0.01 coin, which can be claimed as a *fee* by whoever vets it first.

**Vetting.** In order for a transaction to be confirmed, its various components must be validated and checked against double spending. Once verified, transactions are incorporated in frequently issued official records called *blocks*. Anyone is allowed to create such blocks, and indeed two sorts of incentives are offered to attract verifiers to compete for block creation: (1) the collection of fees; and (2) the minting of new coins.

**Minting.** The bitcoin money supply expands as each block created may contain a special *generation transaction* (with no explicit input) that pays the block creator a time-dependent amount for the effort (50 coins today, rapidly decreasing). The rate of block, hence money, creation is limited by a *proof of work* of adaptive difficulty, that strives to maintain a creation rate of one block every 10 minutes across the whole network. Bitcoin transaction verification is thus a lucrative race open to all, but a computationally expensive one. Note: "bad" blocks will be rejected by peers, invalidating their rewards.

## 3.1    Transactions and Scripting: The Tools for Spending

One of the main powers of the Bitcoin system is that the input and output of transactions need not have a fixed format, but rather are constructed using a Forth-like stack-based flexible scripting language. We remark that transaction principals are not named users but anonymous public keys, which users may freely create in any number they wish.

**Transactions.** Transaction encapsulate the movement of bitcoins by transfering the value received from its *inputs* to its *outputs* (exception: *generation transactions* have no explicit input at all). An input identifies a previous transaction output (as the hash of the earlier transaction and an index to an output within it), and claims its full value. An output specifies an amount; the outputs' total must not exceed the inputs'. Both also contain fragments of executable script, on the input side for redeeming inflows, and on the output side for designating payees.

**Script Fragments.** The scripting language is a Forth-like stack-based language. Operators include cryptographic operations like SHA1 (which replaces the top item on the stack with its hash), and CHECKSIG (which pops an ECDSA public key and signature from the stack, verifies the signature for a "message" implicitly defined from the transaction data, and leaves the result as a true or false on the stack). For a transaction to be valid, its outputs must not exceed its inputs, and its issuer must show title to each input claimed. Title is tested by evaluating the input script fragment concatenated with the script fragment from the output (of an earlier transaction) that the input references.

**Standard Transfer.** To illustrate how the stack-based scripting language can be used, among other things, to designate and enforce the recipient of a transfer, we study the example of the standard Bitcoin transaction used for transfer. To send coins to an address stated as the hash of a public key, the payer, Alice, creates a transaction output with the following associated script fragment (recall that since the amount is specified in a special record associated with the output; the script only needs to enforce the recipient):

```
DUP HASH160 <recipient-address> EQUALVERIFY CHECKSIG       (*)
```

The recipient, Bob, will notice the remittance (since it is broadcast to all), and mark it for spending. Later on, to spend those received coins, he creates a transaction with an input that redeems them, and an output that spends them. The redeeming input script is:

```
<signature> <public-key>                                  (**)
```

Bob will have managed to spend coins received from Alice if his redemption is valid. This is checked by executing the concatenated script $(*, **)$: the input fragment $(*)$ pushes a signature and a key on the stack; the output fragment $(**)$ checks that the key hash matches the recipient, and checks the signature against transaction and key.

### 3.2   Blocks and Coin Creation: The Process of Verifying

Transactions become effective after they have been referenced in a *block*, which serve as the official record of executed transactions. Transactions may only be listed in a block if they satisfy such conditions as valid timestamping and absence of double spending.

**Blocks.** A block consists of one *"coinbase"* minting transaction, zero or more regular spending transactions, a computational proof of work, and a reference to the chronologically prior block. Thus the blocks form a singly linked *blockchain*, rooted in Nakamoto's genesis block whose hash is hardcoded in the software. The regular creation of new blocks serves the dual purpose of ensuring the timely vetting of new transactions, and the creation of new coins, all in a decentralized process driven by economic incentives (the minting of new coins and the collection of fees) balanced by computational costs. The *difficulty* of the required proof of work is adjusted by a feedback mechanism that ensures an average block creation interval of 10 minutes across the entire network.

**Coinbase.** Currently, each new block may contain a coinbase transaction with an implicit input value of 50 coins, with about $7M$ already minted as of this writing. The minting rate is slated to decrease shortly, eventually to reach zero when the total supply reaches about $21M$ bitcoins. The coinbase transaction also serves to claim all the *fees* in the transactions collected in the block. Both minting and fees motivate people to create blocks and hence keep the system alive.

### 3.3   Forking and Conflict Resolution

If two blocks are published nearly simultaneously, a fork in the chain can occur. Nodes are programmed to follow the blockchain whose total proof-of-work *difficulty* is the largest and discard blocks from other forks. Transactions on the discarded branch will eventually be collected into blocks on the prevailing branch. This mechanism ensures that one single ordering of transactions becomes apparent and accepted by all (although it may take a few blocks' time to become clear), and hence this solves the double-spending problem.

# 4    Structural Problems and Potential Solutions

Whether by accident or by design, the Bitcoin system as presently parameterized defines a currency with *extreme deflationary* characteristics built into it. Currently coins are minted by verifiers (i.e., block creators, or *"miners"*) as an incentive to keep the Bitcoin ecosystem running, but minting is poised to expire gradually, and rather soon, resulting in a hard cap on the coins total. Moreover, coins whose private key has been forgotten or destroyed — let us call them *zombie coins* — can never be replaced, resulting in further shrinkage of the money base. For perspective, of the 21M coins maximum, 7M have already been minted; and of those, tens of thousands have reportedly become zombies.

Aside from economic considerations that have been discussed at length [4], The potential deflationary spiral in a decentralized system like Bitcoin has security implications that should not be neglected.

## 4.1    Deflationary Spiral

In capped supply, bitcoins have no alternative but to appreciate tremendously should the system ever gain more than marginal acceptance. Even in a "mature market" scenario with, say, a stable 1% of the US GDP transacted in BitCoins and 99% in dollars, the real purchasing power of coins would still increase over time, as each coin would capture a correspondingly constant fraction of the country's growing wealth. Put in another way, while the Federal Reserve can increase the number of dollars in circulation to accommodate economic growth, in a Bitcoin economy the only outlet for growth would be appreciation of the currency. While it has been observed that the money supply cap could lead to a severe deflationary spiral [4], it is quite a paradox that the intrinsic strength of the Bitcoin currency could be its greatest weakness, causing an even more catastrophic unraveling than through "mere" deflation.

**Hoarding: A Moral Hazard?** Bitcoins much more than any other currency in existence derive their value from the presence of a live, dynamic infrastructure loosely constituted by the network of verifiers participating in block creation. Because of their appreciation potential, bitcoins will tend to be saved rather than spent. As hoarded bitcoins vanish from circulation, transaction volume will dwindle and block creation will become less profitable (fewer fees to collect). If circulation drops too much, it can precipitate a loss of interest in the system, resulting in "bit rot" and verifier dearth, until such point that the system has become too weak to heal and defend itself. Of particular concern is an unavoidable large-scale fraud that we describe in the next section, and whose aftermath includes sudden loss of confidence, collapse of value, and repudiation.

**Towards Decentralized Organic Inflation.** An antidote to the preceding predicament could take the form of a Bitcoin-like electronic currency with a decentralized inflationary feedback built-in, that could control the global minting rate based, e.g., on transaction volume statistics. While we leave the devising of monetary parameters for such an "organically inflationary" currency as an open problem, we show next how deflationary expectations negatively impact the long-term structural security of the Bitcoin system.

## 4.2   Doomsday, or the "History-Revision" Attack

In the Bitcoin world, transactions are irrevocably valid once they are incorporated into the ever growing Block Chain, *insofar as they do not end up in the discarded branch of a fork*. As previously described, short-lived forks may arise, but tend to be quickly resolved per the rule that the chain whose "total difficulty" is the greatest, prevails. Most forks are benign, causing the few transactions on the wrong side of the fork to be delayed — merely a temporary rejection, unless double spending was attempted.

This approach works well, under the crucial assumption that no attacker should ever be able to muster so much computational power that it is able to fake and publish an "alternative history", created *ex post facto*, that has greater total difficulty and hence is more authoritative than the actual history. In such event, the forking rules would cause the actual history to be discarded in favor of the alternative history, from the forking point onwards. We designate this as the *history-revision* attack. In the extreme case where the fork is made near time zero, a history-revision attacker would cause the entire coin base ever created to be replaced with a figment of its forgery.

One may take solace in the ludicrous amount of computing power that, one might hope, such a history-revision attack would require. Alas, the threat is very real — owing both to technical and monetary characteristics of Bitcoin.

**Technical Vulnerability.** The attack's feasibility stems from Moore's law, which empirically posits that computation power per unit cost is doubling every year or so. Assuming a stable population of verifiers, the *block difficulty* parameter (set by the system to maintain a block creation mean interval of 10 minutes) is thus an exponential function of time, $f(t) = \alpha\, e^{t/\tau}$. The *total difficulty* of the block chain at any point in time is thus approximated by the integral $F(t) = \int_{t_0}^{t} f(t')dt' \propto f(t)$. It follows that, regardless of the block chain's length, an attacker that can muster a small multiple (say $2\times$) of the computation power of the legitimate verifiers together, and starting an attack at time $t = t_1$, will be able to create an entire alternative history *forked at the origin time* $t_0$, whose total difficulty $F'(t)$ overtakes $F(t)$ at some future time $t = t_2$, where the attack length $\Delta t = t_2 - t_1$ is bounded by a constant (about 1–2 years for a $2\times$ multiple). [1]

**Economic Motivation.** The strong deflationary characteristic of Bitcoin further compounds the problem. On the one hand, Bitcoins are a currency poised to explode in value, *ceteris paribus*, as already discussed; and hence so will the incentive for theft. On the other hand, the way deflation comes into play, driven by a hard cap on the money supply, will all but eliminate the money-minting incentive that currently draws in the many verifiers that by their competition contribute to make block creation a difficult

---

[1] To underscore the seriousness of the threat, we note that it is common nowadays for *miners* to pool their resources and, by some estimates, one such *mining pool*, deepbit, contributes 40% of the total computation power devoted to mining in the entire system. Merely doubling its "market share" would make it able to revise the entire Bitcoin history in a year's time, owing to Moore's law. Botnets and governments may be there already.

problem. With this incentive dwindling, laws of economics dictate that the competitive effort devoted to verifying transactions and creating blocks will diminish. In other words, while block difficulty may continue to increase for some time into the future, it will eventually start to *decrease* relatively to the power of the day's typical PC. History revision attacks will thence become *easier* not harder.

### 4.3    Countering "Revisionism" by Checkpointing the Past

We outline a distributed strategy to tackle the history-revision attack threat in a simple and elegant way. Its principle is rooted in the commonsense notion that one ought to be suspicious of tales that conflict with one's own first-hand recollection of events. Translated in the Bitcoin world, we propose that a Verifier that has been running without interruption for a long time, should be "highly skeptical" of any long-range fork resolution that would drastically change its own private view of the transaction history acquired from *first-hand* data collection and block creation.

**Private Checkpointing.** Verifiers should thus timestamp published transactions as they see them, and privately take regular snapshots of their own view of the transaction history (such snapshots should be made tamper-proof, e.g., with a cryptographic forward-secure signature). If in the future a drastic fork is put forth that is inconsistent with many of the various snapshots taken, the verifier should demand an increasingly high burden of proof before accepting the "new" branch as correct. E.g., the verifier should not merely accept an alternative branch whose total difficulty exceeds that of the privately checkpointed history, but demand an increasingly high margin of excess, the longer and the more improbable the alternative branch is deemed w.r.t. the verifier's private knowledge.

**Implicit Voting and Phase Transition.** Verifiers ought to make such determination independently, based on *their own* remembered history. That is to say that "young" verifiers that recently came online, and acquired their history by downloading the transaction log *ex post facto*, would have little first-hand checkpointing to rely upon, and would thus behave as in the current system (merely favoring the most difficult branch in a fork). "Seasoned" verifiers that have seen and checkpointed ancient transactions first-hand, would on the contrary oppose a resisting force of skepticism against what they perceive could be an attempt to revise history. As a result, the network would partition into two camps, but only briefly, as certain verifiers that are on the fence "flip" one way or the other based on observing their peers' endorsement of either branch of the fork. Eventually, as more and more verifiers endorse one position over the other, and the corresponding branch of the fork grows faster, the whole network will "phase-transition" back to a single unified view.

**Comparative Behavior.** Our strategy is a strict improvement over the current Bitcoin handling of history-revision attacks, for in all cases where a history-revision attack would *fail* in the current system, our system would behave identically (and exhibit no partition, and no subsequent phase transition). It is only in cases where a history-revision attack would have *succeeded* in the current system, that a partition could occur in the new system. A partition could remain meta-stable for a certain time, but eventually ought to resolve itself by taking the bulk of the network to one side or the other.

**Checkpointing Today.** We remark that the current protocol already does what we would call "fiat checkpointing", where authoritative checkpoints (in the form of hard-coded hashes of certain blocks) are pushed out with software updates [12]. Alas, there is no reason to trust a download of the software any more than one of the transaction history itself. This is unlke our private checkpointing proposal which emphatically prescribes first-hand checkpoints, independently made by each verifier in a privately tamper-proof decentralized way.

We leave as an open problem the formal design and analysis of "anti-revisionism profiles" that offer marked security against vastly powerful history-revision attacks, while guaranteeing that partitions caused by accidental forks get quickly resolved.

## 5   Theft or Loss of Bitcoins

As all bitcoins are public knowledge (in the form of unredeemed transaction outputs), what enables a user to spend a coin is possession of the associated private key. Theft or loss of private keys, or signature forgeries, thus equate to loss of money in this world.

### 5.1   Malware Attacks

Reported malware attacks on Bitcoin are on the rise [16,1], resulting in the theft of private keys. The online wallet service mybitcoin.com recently lost $1.3 million worth of users' coins due to malware [1]. Several solutions can be envisaged; we mention:

**Threshold Cryptography.** A natural countermeasure to malware is to split private keys into random shares, using standard threshold cryptography techniques [11,13], and distribute them onto multiple locations, e.g., a user's desktop computer, her smart phone, and an online service provider. In this way, only when a threshold number of these devices collaborate, can a user spend her coins. Of course, doing so can harm the usability of the system, since coins can no longer be spent without operating multiple devices (even though not all the devices but only a chosen number of them are needed at once).

**Super-Wallets.** To address the usability concern, we propose the simple idea of *super-wallet*, i.e., a user's "personal bank" where most of her coins are stored. The super-wallet is split across multiple computing devices, using threshold techniques as above. In addition, the user carries a small *sub-wallet* with her on her smartphone. Pre-approved transactions are setup so that the user can withdraw money from her super-wallet onto her sub-wallet, periodically in small amounts (similar to how real banks let people withdraw cash from ATMs today). The user now only needs her smartphone to spend money in her wallet, and in case her smartphone is captured by an adversary, the user only loses the small amount of money that she has in her wallet, but not that in her personal bank. Large amounts can always be spent from the super-wallet using a threshold of devices.

Both approaches can be implemented as backward-compatible and incrementally deployable wrappers, requiring changes in the signature generation but not verification.

### 5.2   Accidental Loss of Bitcoins

Apart from malware, system failures or human errors can cause the accidental loss of the wallet file (which stores the private keys needed to spend coins), which in turn leads to the loss of coins (turning them into *zombies*). For example, bitomat, the third largest bitcoin exchange, recently lost about $200K$ worth of bitcoins (at the exchange rate at the time) due to the loss of its private wallet file — the cause was later identified to be human error, as the developer hosted the wallet on non-persistent cloud storage [3].

**Backups.** Naturally, the universal answer against accidental loss or adversarial destruction of data, is to follow best-practice backup procedures. For backup purposes, the wallet file should be treated like any other private cryptographic asset — meaning that backups are a non-trivial proposition, not because of volume, but because of secrecy. With Bitcoin, things are complicated by the incessant creation of keys.

**Pseudo-random Keys.** To avoid having to back up a constantly growing wallet file, a trivial solution is to generate all of one's private keys not at random, but pseudo-randomly from a master secret that never changes, using a standard PRG. The problem then reduces to that of backing up the short and static PRG seed, e.g., in a bank vault.

**Encryption.** A natural idea is to encrypt the wallet using a password sufficiently strong that the resulting ciphertext can be widely replicated without fear of cryptanalysis. This approach is especially useful in conjunction with pseudo-random keys, as then coins can be spent and received without requiring the ciphertext to be updated. The main problem, of course, is that strong passwords are prone to memory loss and palimpsest.

**Offline (Single-)Password-Based Encryption.** One solution relies on the "optimal" password-based encryption system of [7], which offers optimal trade-offs between password strength (how tough it is to guess) and "snappiness" (how quickly it can be used, which is also kept a secret). Users can even set multiple passwords with varying trade-offs for a common security goal: e.g., an everyday password, complex but snappy; and a backup password, simple but just as secure by virtue of being made "sluggish". A pseudo-random wallet seed, encrypted à la [7], would combine static portability with usable protection against both loss and theft, and is probably the best approach for an isolated user who trusts his mental possessions more than his physical ones.

**Online (Multi-)Password-Based Encryption.** Another approach is to combine the power of several memorable secrets into a single high-security "vault", using the protocols of [5]. Each member in some circle of friends holds a short totally private and long-term memorable phrase. One member is a distinguished *leader*. Without revealing their secrets, the members can perform private operations such as signing or decrypting a message on behalf of the leader. With this protocol, a group of users can cooperate to let the leader spend the coins from his wallet (kept as a public, static, accessible, encrypted file), by issuing signatures on messages created by the leader. This approach provides strong safety against loss, plus security against compromise of a subset of the group.

**Trusted Paths.** Any of the above approaches can be combined with *trusted-path* devices, which are dedicated hardware devices that let humans input and read out (tiny amounts of) cryptographic data out of the reach of any malware. European banks use the DigiPass, for example. Alas, while trusted-path protocols are well known and very safe when it can be assumed that the remote server is uncorrupted (e.g., when talking to a bank), in the Bitcoin case the server is the user's own PC, possibly infected. It is an interesting open problem to devise trusted-path protocols that are secure in this model, *when the trusted-path data is too tiny* to provide cryptographic strength by itself.

## 6   Scalability

Bitcoin suffers from several scalability issues, among which we note the following.

### 6.1   Data Retention and Communication Failures

The smooth operation of Bitcoin relies on the timely broadcast of transactions and blocks. A preprint [6] suggests that verifiers competing for the same reward have an incentive to withhold the information needed to do so. However, since *transactors* have an incentive to disseminate their data as quickly and widely as possible, not only is retention futile, but economic forces will counter it by fostering circumvention services.

### 6.2   Linear Transaction History

As discussed, the Bitcoin *wallet* software fetches the entire Bitcoin blockchain at installation, and all new transactions and blocks are (supposedly) broadcast to all nodes.

The Bitcoin nodes cryptographically verify the authenticity of all blocks and transactions as they receive them. Clearly, this approach introduces a scalability issue in the longer term, in terms of both network bandwidth, and computational overhead associated with cryptographic transaction verification. The scalability issue can be worrying for smart phones with limited bandwidth, computational power, and battery supply.

The scalability issue can be addressed with a subscription-based filtering service. Recall that Bitcoin nodes can be divided into broadly two classes, *verifiers* and *clients*. Verifiers create new blocks and hence mint new coins. Verifiers are mostly nodes with ample computational and bandwidth resources, typically desktop computers. By contrast, clients are Bitcoin nodes that are not actively minting new coins, such as smart phones. While verifiers have incentives to receive all transactions (to earn transaction fees), clients may not care. In particular, all that is needed for clients to spend their coins is that they receive transactions payable to their public key(s).

**Bitcoin Filtering Service.** Our filtering service is a third-party cloud service provider which filters Bitcoin transactions, and sends only relevant transactions to nodes that have registered for the service. A Bitcoin client (e.g., a user's smartphone) can send a cryptographic capability to the filtering service, which allows the filtering service to determine whether a transaction is payable to one or more of its public keys.

We identify the following desirable security and usability requirements.

- *Unlinkability without the capability.* While a user may allow the filtering service to determine which transactions are payable to itself, no other party should be able to link a user's multiple public keys better than they can today (i.e., without the filtering service).
- *Forward security.* The filtering service should be able to update its capability periodically, such that in the case of compromise or a subpoena, the revealed capability can allow one to identify new transactions targeted to a specific user, but cannot be used to link the users' transactions in the past.

– *Reasonable false positives and low false negatives.* A false positive is when the filtering service mistakenly sends a user a non-relevant transaction. False positives wastes a user's bandwidth and computational power, but a user can locally detect such false positives after receiving the transactions. A false negative is when the filtering service fails to send a user a relevant transaction. The false negative rate should ideally be 0.

**Constructing a Filtering Service.** We now propose a potential approach to build such a filtering service, in a way that is backward compatible with today's Bitcoin. Assume that the user and the filtering service are weakly time synchronized. A user can generate a random Message Authentication Code (MAC) key $K$ and share it with the filtering service. This MAC key $K$ will be used as the initial MAC key. For forward security, in every time epoch (e.g., every day), both the user and the filtering service will update their MAC key by applying a Pseudo-Random Generator (PRG): $K \leftarrow \mathsf{PRG}(K)$. The MAC key $K$ will then be used as below. When the user needs to pick a public key to receive money, it will pick a public key $\mathsf{PK}$ whose hash $H(\mathsf{PK})$ satisfies the following condition: $\mathsf{MAC}_K(H(\mathsf{PK})) \bmod 2^\ell = 0$. In particular, when $\ell$ is not too large, the user can find such a public key by randomly generating public-private key pairs until a public-key satisfying the above condition is found. $\ell$ is a parameter used to engineer the tradeoff between the false positive rate and the computation cost needed to generate public keys. Since a transaction payable to user $A$ includes user $A$'s public key hashes in one or more outputs, the filtering service can now identify transactions possibly targeted for user $A$ by checking the above condition.

### 6.3 Delayed Transaction Confirmation

Another related scalability issue is delayed transaction confirmation. In the current implementation, a new block is generated about every 10 minutes, so it takes at least 10 minutes or so to get a transaction confirmed. This can be problematic in certain application scenarios, e.g., on-demand video playback Worse still, after a single confirmation it is still possible the transaction is a double spend, and the blockchain has forked.

One approach, already seen in the Bitcoin ecosystem, uses intermediate "semi-trusted" third parties acting as short-term banks, issuing the Bitcoin equivalents to cashiers' checks (essentially, a transaction signed by the bank's key). Banks would have no incentive to double-spend, as their fraud would immediately become apparent to all.

Another approach is to fundamentally reduce the transaction confirmation delay by re-parameterizing the computational puzzles to reduce the average block creation interval from 10 minutes to 10 seconds. However, this would increase the forking propensity on slow communication networks, which could become a concern.

### 6.4 Dynamically Growing Private Key Storage

To achieve better anonymity, users are urged to use a different public key for each transaction. However, this means that the user has to store the corresponding private keys for all previously generated public keys — a private key should only be deleted if one is certain that no payment to its public key will ever be made (lest zombie coins result). Aside from size, the dynamic nature of the private key storage is another difficulty.

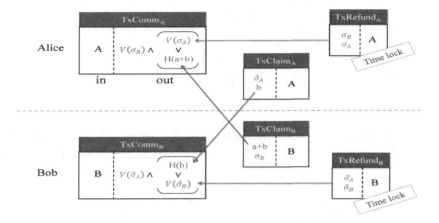

**Fig. 1.** A fair exchange protocol: mixing Bitcoins with an untrusted mixer

**Pseudo-random Generation of Private Keys.** An easy answer to both concerns, already mentioned, is to generate all of one's private keys pseudo-randomly from a static secret.

**Explicit Expiration of Public Keys.** Another way to address this problem is to introduce explicit expiration dates for public keys, and ensure that no money can be sent to expired keys, or that such money can be reclaimed somehow. In any case, it is good practice that keys be made to expire, and this should be encouraged. In view of this, it seems desirable to give the scripting language facilities for reading and comparing timestamps.

## 7  Improving Anonymity with Reduced Trust

Bitcoin partially addresses the anonymity and unlinkability issue, by allowing users to use different addresses and public keys in every transaction. However, Bitcoin still exposes their users to a weak form of linkability. Specifically, multiple public keys of the same user can potentially be linked when the user pays change to herself, in which case two or more of a single user's public keys will appear in the same transaction [17].

To improve users' anonymity, third-party services called *mixers* have emerged, that take multiple users' coins, mix them, and issue back coins in equal denominations. Today, the mixers are trusted entities, in the sense that users send money to the mixer, trusting that it will issue back the money later. As a malicious mixer can cheat and not pay the money back, a cautious user could send the money to the mixer in small amounts, and only continue sending when the mixer has paid back. However, this approach is unscalable, especially as each transaction can take 10 minutes to confirm.

An alternative and better approach is to implement a *fair exchange* protocol. One contribution of this paper is to demonstrate how to implement such a fair exchange protocol in Bitcoin in a backward compatible manner.

```
1. A:        Select random key pairs (PK_A1, SK_A1) and (PK_A2, SK_A2)
   B:        Select random key pairs (PK_B1, SK_B1) and (PK_B2, SK_B2)
   A ⇔ B :   Exchange public keys
2. A:        Select random secrets Ω_A = {a_1, a_2, ..., a_n}
   B:        Select random secrets Ω_B = {b_1, b_2, ..., b_n}
   A → B :   Ω_A
   B → A :   {H(a_i + b_i), H(b_i) : ∀i ∈ [n]}
3. A → B :   random index set I ⊆ [n], s.t. |I| = n − k
   B → A :   {b_i | i ∈ I}
   A:        ∀i ∈ I: verify correctness of previously received H(a_i + b_i), H(b_i)
```

**Fig. 2.** Secrets setup phase. A and B exchange keys then engage in cut-and-choose. At the end of the protocol, the remaining set of size $k$ indexed by $[n]\backslash I$ will later be used in the fair exchange.

```
<PK A2> CHECKSIGVERIFY
IF          // refund case
  <PK B2> CHECKSIG
ELSE        // claim case
  HASH
  DUP <H(b1)> EQUAL SWAP
  DUP <H(b2)> EQUAL SWAP
  <H(b3)> EQUAL
  BOOLOR BOOLOR
ENDIF
```

```
<PK B1> CHECKSIGVERIFY
IF          // refund case
  <PK A1> CHECKSIG
ELSE        // claim case
  HASH <H(a1 + b1)> EQUALVERIFY
  HASH <H(a2 + b2)> EQUALVERIFY
  HASH <H(a3 + b3)> EQUAL
ENDIF
```

**Fig. 3.** *On left:* Output script of TxComm_B. *On right:* Output script of TxComm_A.

### 7.1   A Fair Exchange Protocol

A fair exchange protocol consists of three types of transactions:

- A *commitment transaction*, denoted TxComm_A or TxComm_B, commits a party to the money exchange;
- A *refund transaction*, denoted TxRefund_A or TxRefund_B, refunds a party's committed money at a future date, in case the exchange protocol aborts.
- A *claim transaction* denoted TxClaim_A or TxClaim_B, allows a party to claim the other party's committed money. To ensure fairness one party conducts the first claim transaction in which it must publish a secret which enables the second claim.

**Secrets Setup Phase.** As depicted in Figure 2, Alice and Bob perform key generation, and exchange public keys. The reasons for each party to generate two key pairs is to later use different keys for different transactions to ensure unlinkability. Alice and Bob then engage in a cut-and-choose protocol. At the end of the protocol, the remaining set indexed by $\overline{I} := [n]\backslash I$ will later be used in the fair exchange. Specifically, the hash values $\{H(a_i + b_i) : \forall i \in \overline{I}\}$ will later be included in the output script of TxComm_A, and the hash values $\{H(b_i) : \forall i \in \overline{I}\}$ will be later included in the output script of TxComm_B. For Bob to claim Alice's committed money TxComm_A, it has to reveal all of the correct $\{a_i + b_i : i \in \overline{I}\}$, such that their hash values match those in TxComm_A. For Alice to later claim Bob's committed money TxComm_B, it only has to reveal one $b_i$ for some $i \in \overline{I}$, such that it matches one hash value in TxComm_B. The key to ensuring fairness is that when Bob claims TxComm_A, it has to reveal the secrets $\{a_i + b_i : i \in \overline{I}\}$, allowing Alice to learn the values of $\{b_i : i \in \overline{I}\}$, enabling Alice to claim TxComm_B.

A cheating Bob can potentially supply Alice with the wrong $H(b_i)$ values, in an attempt to prevent Alice from claiming $\mathsf{TxComm}_B$, while retaining its own ability to claim $\mathsf{TxComm}_A$. Suppose that $\overline{I}$ has size $k$. Through elementary probability analysis, we can show that a cheating $B$ can succeed only with very small probability: $\Pr[B$ succeeds in cheating$] = 1/\binom{n}{k} \simeq 1/n^k$.

**Transaction Setup Phase — Bob.** Bob generates $\mathsf{TxComm}_B$, using an output script that will allow 2 forms of redemption. The redemption can either be the refund transaction (dated in the future), with an input script signed by $\mathsf{SK}_{A2}$ and $\mathsf{SK}_{B2}$, or the claim transaction with an input script signed by $\mathsf{SK}_{A2}$ and supplying any one of Bob's secrets from the set $\{b_i : i \in \overline{I}\}$. Figure 3 shows an example of $\mathsf{TxComm}_B$'s output script for set $\overline{I}$ of size $k = 3$.

Bob then generates a partial $\mathsf{TxRefund}_B$ releasing his money, with the locktime set to t+3 (timing in units of 'certain transaction confirmation time', an agreed number of block times, plus a buffer), with this incomplete input script: <sig B2> 1. Bob sends the partial $\mathsf{TxRefund}_B$ to party A, who verifies the locktime, and adds his signature to the input script <sig B2> 1 <sig A2>, and returns the completed refund transaction to Bob. Bob verifies the signed $\mathsf{TxRefund}_B$ and publishes $\mathsf{TxComm}_B$ and $\mathsf{TxRefund}_B$, and is now committed to the exchange.

**Transaction Setup Phase — Alice.** Alice waits until $\mathsf{TxComm}_B$ confirms, verifies $\mathsf{TxRefund}_B$ and checks the value. Alice generates $\mathsf{TxComm}_A$, again using an output script that allows 2 forms of redemption. The first form enables the refund transaction, requiring signature by $\mathsf{SK}_{B1}$ and $\mathsf{SK}_{A1}$. The second form allows the claim transaction requiring signature by $\mathsf{SK}_{B1}$ and all of $\{a_i + b_i : i \in \overline{I}\}$. Figure 3 shows an example output script of $\mathsf{TxComm}_A$, for a set $\overline{I}$ of size $k = 3$.

Then, Alice generates $\mathsf{TxRefund}_A$, with the locktime set to t+1, with the incomplete input script <sig A1> 1 and with a standard output addressed to $\mathsf{PK}_{A1}$ (returning the money to herself). Alice sends this incomplete $\mathsf{TxRefund}_A$ to Bob. Bob verifies the locktime and adds his signature to the input script: <sig A1> 1 <sig B1>, and returns the now complete transaction to Alice. Alice verifies the returned $\mathsf{TxRefund}_A$ is unmodified and correctly signed. Alice now broadcasts $\mathsf{TxComm}_A$ and $\mathsf{TxRefund}_A$, and is now committed to the exchange.

**Money Claim Phase.** Bob waits for $\mathsf{TxComm}_A$ to confirm, and checks the amount is sufficient. Bob also needs to ensure he has enough time for his claim of Alice's money to confirm before $\mathsf{TxRefund}_A$'s time lock (hence the requirements on time locks). Now Bob claims Alice's money; he does this by taking $\mathsf{TxRefund}_A$ and modifying the time lock to "now" and the output to $\mathsf{PK}_{B1}$. He also updates the input script to become (modified to include $\{a_i + b_i : i \in \overline{I}\}$), <a3+b3> <a2+b2> <a1+b1> 0 <sig B1>, thus creating $\mathsf{TxClaim}_B$. Bob now publishes $\mathsf{TxClaim}_B$. This claims Alice's money, while also revealing Alice's $b_i$s for $i \in \overline{I}$. Now Alice can claim Bob's money by taking $\mathsf{TxRefund}_B$, removing the locktime, changing the output to $\mathsf{PK}_{A2}$, and updating the input script to this form (modified to include one $b_i$ from $\overline{I}$): <b> 0 <sig A2>. Alice earlier made sure that the locktime on $\mathsf{TxRefund}_B$ would give her sufficient time for this claim to confirm before the Bob's refund.

# 8   Conclusion

We have provided a preliminary but broad study of the crypto-monetary phenomenon Bitcoin, whose popularity has far overtaken the e-cash systems based on decades of research. Bitcoin's appeal lies in its simplicity, flexibility, and decentralization, making it easy to grasp but hard to subvert. We studied this curious contraption with a critical eye, trying to gauge its strengths and expose its flaws, suggesting solutions and research directions. Our conclusion is nuanced: while the instantiation is impaired by its poor parameters, the core design could support a robust decentralized currency if done right.

## References

1. Bitcoin ewallet vanishes from internet, http://www.tribbleagency.com/?p=8133
2. Bitcoin wiki: Contracts, http://en.bitcoin.it/wiki/Contracts
3. Bitomat loses data and mybitcoin shuts down, http://www.launch.is/blog
4. Deflationary spiral, http://en.bitcoin.it/wiki/Deflationary_spiral
5. Abdalla, M., Boyen, X., Chevalier, C., Pointcheval, D.: Distributed Public-Key Cryptography from Weak Secrets. In: Jarecki, S., Tsudik, G. (eds.) PKC 2009. LNCS, vol. 5443, pp. 139–159. Springer, Heidelberg (2009)
6. Babaioff, M., Dobzinski, S., Oren, S., Zohar, A.: On bitcoin and red balloons (2011), http://research.microsoft.com/pubs/156072/bitcoin.pdf
7. Boyen, X.: Halting password puzzles. In: Proc. Usenix Security (2007)
8. Camenisch, J.L., Hohenberger, S., Lysyanskaya, A.: Compact E-Cash. In: Cramer, R. (ed.) EUROCRYPT 2005. LNCS, vol. 3494, pp. 302–321. Springer, Heidelberg (2005)
9. Canard, S., Gouget, A.: Divisible E-Cash Systems Can Be Truly Anonymous. In: Naor, M. (ed.) EUROCRYPT 2007. LNCS, vol. 4515, pp. 482–497. Springer, Heidelberg (2007)
10. Chaum, D.: Blind signatures for untraceable payments. In: Proc. Crypto. (1982)
11. Gennaro, R., Jarecki, S., Krawczyk, H., Rabin, T.: Secure distributed key generation for discrete-log based cryptosystems. J. Cryptology (2007)
12. Laurie, B.: Decentralised currencies are probably impossible but let's at least make them efficient, http://www.links.org/files/decentralised-currencies.pdf
13. MacKenzie, P.D., Reiter, M.K.: Two-Party Generation of DSA Signatures. In: Kilian, J. (ed.) CRYPTO 2001. LNCS, vol. 2139, pp. 137–154. Springer, Heidelberg (2001)
14. Nakamoto, S.: Bitcoin: A peer-to-peer electronic cash system, http://www.bitcoin.org
15. Okamoto, T.: An Efficient Divisible Electronic Cash Scheme. In: Coppersmith, D. (ed.) CRYPTO 1995. LNCS, vol. 963, pp. 438–451. Springer, Heidelberg (1995)
16. Poulsen, K.: New malware steals your bitcoin, http://wired.com/threatlevel/2011/06
17. Reid, F., Harrigan, M.: An analysis of anonymity in the bitcoin system. Arxiv:1107.4524

# Author Index